The
Contemplated
Spouse

The Contemplated Spouse

The Letters of Wallace Stevens to Elsie

Edited by J. Donald Blount

University of South Carolina Press

© 2006 University of South Carolina

Published in Columbia, South Carolina,
by the University of South Carolina Press

Manufactured in the United States of America

10 09 08 07 06   5 4 3 2 1

Library of Congress Cataloging-in-Publication Data

Stevens, Wallace, 1879–1955.
    The contemplated spouse : the letters of Wallace Stevens to Elsie / edited by J. Donald
Blount.
        p. cm.
    Includes bibliographical references and index.
    ISBN 1-57003-248-3 (alk. paper)
1. Stevens, Wallace, 1879–1955—Correspondence. 2. Poets, American—20th century—
Correspondence. 3. Stevens, Elsie Viola Kachel Moll, 1886–1963—Correspondence.
4. Stevens, Wallace, 1879–1955—Marriage. I. Stevens, Elsie Viola Kachel Moll, 1886–
1963. II. Blount, J. Donald, 1941– III. Title.
    PS3537.T4753Z485 2006
    811'.52—dc22

                                                              2005020248

All letters published by permission of the Huntington Library

To the memory of my father, A. J. Blount (1916–2005), and for Liz

Contents

Acknowledgments

Many people have helped me in this project on which I have worked for more than a decade. I thank Vice-Chancellor for Academic Affairs at the University of South Carolina–Aiken, Blanche-Premo Hopkins, for financial support to make my initial visit to the Huntington Library in San Marino, California, in 1990 to read Stevens's letters of 1909 and for later sabbatical support that made it possible to annotate the letters and bring this project to completion. On my first visit to the Huntington, the mother lode of Stevens material, Sue Hodson, curator of the library's Wallace Stevens Papers, responded, when I asked her if anyone was editing these letters, "No. Why don't you do it?" I give heartfelt thanks to her for that suggestion and for her subsequent help in navigating the complex papers of the Stevens archives there. Warren Slesinger, former acquisitions editor of the University of South Carolina Press, gave his enthusiastic support from the beginning. Don Greiner and Matthew J. Bruccoli supported the project before the publications committee of the University of South Carolina Press. Helen Vendler gave me crucial support on this project at its very beginning in 1990 and several times since then, including a tour of Memorial Hall at Harvard, which she got a security guard to open so that she could show the "Pax" written on the windowpane on one of the windows in that important building Stevens certainly knew (see "Puella Parvula," *CP* 456). I am grateful to Barry Blose, acquisitions editor at USC Press, who played a crucial role in restarting this project after a hiatus of several years.

In the early stages, as I worked to read and digitize the letters, I had the help of a number of dedicated students: Loretta Austin, Tami Conner, Larry Bagwell, Tammy Mitchum, Greg Miller, and Joe Schneider. The Historical Society of Berks County in Reading, Pennsylvania, in the person of Barbara Gill, Librarian, and the willing volunteers, helped me to identify people and places in Reading that were connected with Stevens in several visits I made there in the 1990s. Edward Byers, Director of Libraries, Reading Public Library, arranged for me to get the *Catalogue of the Reading High Schools: 1856 to 1905* on interlibrary loan in 1994. Georgiann Babin, the owner and restorer of the Ephrata Hotel of Stevens's past, graciously gave me a tour of that place so important in Stevens's imagination, on May 22, 1996.

For a week in June 1996, I was given a cubicle in the office tower of the Hartford Insurance Group and given access to a closet in which material from a corporate display on Stevens's life at the Hartford was stored. I thank Kevin Marton of corporate relations for the Hartford for this opportunity and the employees there who showed such interest in my work as I read the bits of news and the names of officers from Stevens's time in the *Hartford Agent*.

The readers of versions of my text have made invaluable suggestions and provided encouragement: Alan Filreis, Milton J. Bates, and my colleague Dan Miller.

In my efforts to see places and to read letters tangentially related to this project, an endless occupation, I have had the comforting cooperation of a number of archives, those remarkable places of peace and quiet in a busy world. Blanche T. Ebeling-Koning, curator of rare books and manuscripts at the University of Maryland, showed me Stevens's letters to Ferdinand Reyher and Rodker and then sent me photocopies of them in 1992. At the University of Massachusetts–Amherst, Linda Seidman, acting head of special collections, and Ute Bargman, special collections assistant, helped me consult their Stevens material, including the 1927 telegram Elsie sent to Stevens, for two hours after normal closing hours in October 1992. In May 1993, I consulted the Stevens-Latimer material, the Stevens–Hi Simons material, and the Stevens–Harriet Monroe material at the Joseph Regenstein Memorial Library at the University of Chicago.

On several occasions in the early 1990s, I surveyed the Judge Arthur Gray Powell Papers at the Robert W. Woodruff Library of Emory University, with the expert help of Steve Enniss, manuscript librarian. For three days in 1996, the Chadwick-Healey database of British and American poetry was graciously made available to me by Michael Fitzgerald, electronic texts librarian at the Weidner Library at Harvard. For a week in 1996, I was granted the privilege of reading the Stevens material, especially that involving Renato Poggioli, at the Houghton Library at Harvard. Dawn Hughes and Becky Smith of the Historical Museum of South Florida in June 1997 helped me find material on the McCrary Construction Company and other Florida connections to Stevens.

Wallace Stevens wrote to Elsie Viola Moll[1] the following 272 handwritten letters, the originals of which are in the Huntington Library in San Marino, California.[2] Almost all of the letters written before their marriage are of four or eight pages, depending on whether Stevens used one sheet of paper (approximately

---

1. Stevens always addressed his letters thus, although Elsie, born Kachel, was never adopted by Lyman Moll, who married her mother when Elsie was eight.

2. The story of how these letters came to be sold to the Huntington Library by Holly Stevens, the poet's daughter, in 1974 is told by Daniel Woodward in *Wallace Stevens Journal* 16, no. 2 (Fall 1992): 227. The official announcement of this sale was made on April 12, 1975, in a ceremony at the Huntington. For a description of the overall collection of the Stevens manuscripts at the Huntington, see *Wallace Stevens Journal* 1, no. 1 (Spring 1977): 40–48.

eight-by-ten inches) or two; he folded each sheet in half to make four sides, and he made a final fold to fit the letters into small envelopes (four-by-five inches). (A few pieces of this correspondence are simply postcards, and two are night letters.) In the ten months of their official engagement, December 1908–September 1909, Stevens wrote to Elsie almost ever other day, a pace that hints at the hundreds of other letters from the four previous years that do not survive. What we still have of this correspondence is far less than what was originally written. (None of Elsie's letters to Stevens survive, although five of her postcards to him, one of 1908, three of 1912,[3] and one of 1915, and one telegram of 1927 are still extant.) Concerning the eight-page letter he wrote on December 2, 1908, Stevens reported that he worked on it for six and a half hours. Thus the entire project of letter writing during this period was of extraordinary proportions.

The earliest extant letter is dated March 7, 1907, and is part of a brief series that ends on April 22, 1907; the next letter (after a nineteen-month gap) is dated December 2, 1908, and is part of a series that runs through September 16, 1909, the period most completely represented by far. The letters written between the time of the wedding on September 21, 1909, and the publication of *Harmonium* in 1923 fall into two different categories: those of 1910 to early 1916 written by Stevens in New York to Elsie in Reading or at various rest resorts in the summer and those from March 1916 to 1923 written by Stevens from the road as he traveled for the Hartford. After 1923, there are only five more letters, from 1931 to 1935, written from Stevens's trips to Florida to Elsie in Hartford. This is a very small portion of the letters Stevens undoubtedly wrote from his many trips to Florida until 1936.

In addition to these letters (mostly complete, though a few have one of their two sheets missing), there are sixty-eight pages of excerpts Elsie made from Stevens' letters of 1904 to 1911. These excerpts are all that remains from the first three years of their correspondence, 1904 to 1907, and a comparison of these excerpts to existing letters indicates that she was careful and accurate but did introduce small changes. That she took excerpts from forty of the letters of 1909 that still exist intact, letters she was obviously preparing to destroy, makes it possible to speculate on her principles of selection and thus learn something more about her. Most of these excerpts have been published before.

Of the 272 letters in this collection, sixty-eight have been published in their entirety (or nearly so) in *The Letters of Wallace Stevens* or *Souvenirs and Prophecies,* both edited by Stevens's daughter Holly Stevens. Eight additional letters were published complete (or nearly so) in Joan Richardson's biography, *Wallace Stevens: The Early Years, 1879–1923.* In addition to these seventy-six completely

3. The texts of all three of these cards are given in a note to Stevens's letter of August 11, 1912.

or largely published letters, there are an additional fifteen letters of which somewhat less than 50 percent has been published. Thus some 180 letters have been published only fractionally or not at all. Of course, there are many references to and quotations of these otherwise unpublished letters in the literature on Stevens written in the years since Holly Stevens sold the letters to the Huntington in 1975, notably in Milton J. Bates's *Wallace Stevens: A Mythology of Self* (1985) and George Lensing's *Wallace Stevens: A Poet's Growth* (1986) and *Wallace Stevens and the Seasons* (2001).

My goal was to present the text of Stevens's letters as accurately and as unobtrusively as possible; these two goals come into conflict when Stevens is following a somewhat different convention of spelling and punctuation from that of the present. I regularized those features of his convention that seemed the least revealing of something important about him: his spelling of "don't" without the apostrophe, his omission of the apostrophe in other situations, his positioning of the comma relative to quotation marks, his use of dashes of various lengths. I have not indicated all of his departures from American spelling conventions as opposed to British, except in those cases in which he comments on such matters. I have kept his hyphen in "New York," "tonight," and "tomorrow."

Stevens's letters are remarkably neat with very few corrections, very few blotches of ink; most of those he himself comments upon. I point out the few additional cases.

Abbreviations

Brazeau	Peter Brazeau. *Parts of a World: Wallace Stevens Remembered.* New York: Random House, 1983.
CP	*Collected Poems of Wallace Stevens.* New York: Knopf, 1955.
Elsie's Book	Excerpts from Stevens's letters, 1904–11. Compiled by Elsie Stevens. WAS 1772, HEH.
HEH	Henry E. Huntington Library. San Marino, California.
LWS	*Letters of Wallace Stevens.* Edited by Holly Stevens. New York: Knopf, 1966.
OP	*Opus Posthumous.* Edited by Milton J. Bates. New York: Knopf, 1989.
Richardson	Joan Richardson. *Wallace Stevens: The Early Years, 1879–1923.* New York: Beech Tree Books (Morrow), 1986. Also the second volume, *Wallace Stevens: The Later Years, 1923–1955.* New York: Beech Tree Books (Morrow), 1988.
SP	*Souvenirs and Prophecies: The Young Wallace Stevens.* Edited by Holly Stevens. New York: Knopf, 1977
WAS	Letters that precede Huntington Library's accession number for its Stevens material. (The A was added arbitrarily between the initials of Stevens's name, because he had no middle initial.)

The
Contemplated
Spouse

Introduction

Wallace Stevens and Elsie

The second of a quick succession of three sons, Stevens was born on October 2, 1879, to a self-educated lawyer father and a mother who had briefly been a schoolteacher. His two sisters, Elizabeth and Catherine, were born in 1885 and 1889. The family seems to have been happy but not demonstrative in their affection, according to Stevens's niece, Jane MacFarland Wilson (see Brazeau, 267–68). In a letter of 1943 to this same niece, Stevens presented a portrait of his father that certainly applied to Stevens himself: "He needed what all of us need, and what most of us don't get: that is to say, discreet affection. So much depends on ourselves in that respect. I think that he loved to be at the house with us, but he was incapable of lifting a hand to attract any of us, so that, while we loved him as it was natural to do, we also were afraid of him, at least to the extent of holding off. The result was that he lived alone" (*LWS*, 454). Stevens's daughter Holly comments on this passage: "If that was true of my grandfather, and I can easily imagine it was since I have heard that he would not even talk on the telephone at home, it certainly was true of my father and of our house as I grew up; we held off from each other—one might say that my father lived alone" (*SP*, 4). Stevens was raised respecting his father's solitude, and he himself lived in similar isolation.

Though he had to repeat a grade in high school because of absences due to illness (a doctor's report of 1926 mentions "a history of malaria as a boy"; WAS 897 October 15, 1926), Stevens graduated with merit and distinguished himself in a public oration he delivered, "The Greatest Need of the Age," reported in the *Reading Eagle* (December 23, 1896), which on the following evening gave a drawing of Stevens and the caption: "Wallace Stevens who won the gold medal for oratory on 'Alumni Night' at the academy." For a man who, throughout his life, felt a need to belong,[1] the most gratifying aspect of the event had to be the description of the audience's reaction to his winning: "The judges were unani-

---

1. Stevens tells Elsie on January 24, 1909: "The Low-Germans, too, are very common at home. True-heartedness surely describes them. I love them, my dear. You must not think that I do nothing but poke fun at them—in spite of Theresa Powdermaker or Antoinette Himmelberger. —I felt my kinship, my race. To study them is to realize one's own identity." When he was seventy, he wrote that "one is always desperately in need of the fellowship of one's own kind. I don't mean intellectual fellowship, but the

mous. Then the boys in the audience broke loose, clapped their hands and applauded. The winner is a son of Garrett B. Stevens and a favorite in the school, as was proven by the send-off his classmates gave him. When he received his medal he bowed his thanks. Then the boys gave him the school yell and a cheer." In his letter of January 21, 1909, to Elsie (his most self-consciously auto-biographical letter), Stevens has this episode in mind as he says, with a certain amount of hyperbole, "You know I took all the prizes at school!"

Stevens went to Harvard as a special student, originally intending to stay for two years. His letter of application to Harvard was mailed on July 20, and he was admitted July 29, 1897. In his application, he indicated that he had not been examined for admission to any college but had a reason for wanting to study as a special student: "I only desire a college education in journalism. Time required in course is more satisfactory than a 4 year college course. Agrees with my plans." His planned course of study, he noted, would include "First year—English A. French A, History I, government I. Economics I Philosophy Second year—The same line of studies in higher courses, and in Fine Arts." He proposed to study these courses "because adapted to the study of journalism. Because as a course they are broad and catholic benefiting the student in any event. Because they are an attractive group of general educational value. Because they are just what I want, lacking nothing nor superfluous in anything."[2] After his first two years at Harvard, Stevens applied for and received an extension for a third year.

While at Harvard, Stevens joined the Cygnet Society and the *Harvard Advocate,* of which he was the president in his final year and for which he demonstrated in his writings the industriousness that would later make it possible for him to create some of his most important poems with amazing speed. For the *Advocate,* he wrote many poems, editorials, and a few short stories, and while on its staff, he developed a network of friends (for example, Pitts Sanborn and Walter Arensberg) and teachers (for example, Barrett Wendell and George Santayana) that would be of considerable importance to him in his New York and later years as he gained employment, began publishing poetry, and matured philosophically.

Directly after Harvard and during his first year in New York, 1900–1901, Stevens was an active journalist writing for the *New York Tribune,* one unsigned article on the dismal funeral of Stephen Crane being the only work identified as his from this time by Edelstein in his *Wallace Stevens: A Descriptive Bibliography.* Stevens's journals for that important year contain references to a number of

---

fellowship of one's province: membership in a clique, the fellowship of the landsman and compatriot" (*LWS,* 644).

2. This application is at the Harvard University Archives, Pusey Library.

other articles he wrote, such as "A Happy-Go-Lucky Irishman" and "Wharves and the Sea" (*SP,* 74); however, because the job did not provide the stability of income he profoundly desired, Stevens, after some debate with his father on the subject, decided to become a lawyer rather than a vagabond poet or writer:

> March 11. 1901. I had a good long talk with the old man in which he did most of the talking. One's ideas don't get much of a chance under such conditions. However he's a wise man. We talked about the law which he has been urging me to take up. I hesitated—because this literary life, as it is called, is the one I always had as an ideal & I am not quite ready to give it up because it has not been all that I wanted it to be. The other day, after returning to New York, I called on John Phillips of McClure; Phillips and I had a talk about the publishing business. . . . He told me that the business was chiefly clerical—unpleasant fact—& that I could hardly expect to live on my wages—etc. etc. I was considerably jarred by the time he got through. The mirage I had fancied disappeared in the desert—where I invariably land. (*SP,* 100–101)

Stevens once summarized this period of his life for a young interviewer: "When I got to New York I was not yet serious about poetry. I got a job on the *Herald Tribune* through letters of recommendation, but soon discovered that I was no reporter."[3] Another factor in Stevens's decision to seek a stable income rather than literary achievement at this period could have been his father's nervous breakdown in 1901, caused by the economic reversals he had encountered in several of his business ventures.

Stevens began New York Law School on October 1, 1901, graduated on June 10, 1903, and applied for the bar on May 11, 1904. During those years, he began his clerkship in the offices of W. G. Peckham, with whom he had perhaps the most adventuresome episode of his life, one that made him quite clearly one of the boys for a while: Stevens, in the company of Peckham and others, traveled to the Canadian Rockies for a camping and hunting trip of several weeks from August 2 to the middle of September 1903. Holly Stevens, in her edition of Stevens's journals, provides her unique insight into the importance of this experience to Stevens:

> The trip to British Columbia that my father made with W. G. Peckham left a great impression on him; not only did he keep his journal religiously, but in the last few weeks before his death he spoke of the trip frequently to me, the first time I recall his mentioning it. The names and places meant little to me then, and only with the discovery of his

---

3. Jerald E. Hatfield, "More About Legend," *Trinity Review* 8, no. 3 (May 1954): 30.

notebooks detailing the adventure did I discover its importance. It was
his last vacation before being admitted to the bar in the spring of 1904,
after completing his clerkship with Peckham. It took place high in unfamiliar mountains, and, primitive as conditions were, it was preparation
for and prelude to his struggle to become a successful attorney—a
struggle which he was not to win until he joined the insurance world; as
a practicing lawyer he would not be much better off than he had been as
a reporter. (*SP*, 117)

The summer after this trip, Stevens met the woman, Elsie (Viola née Kachel, raised
Moll, married Stevens), who would be the most important person or reality in his
life for the next fifty-one years. The best account of the meeting is that provided
by Elsie herself, an account in which she interestingly explains why Stevens was
socializing with younger people, something that was to be a lifelong penchant:

On July 7th 1903 ?,[4] Mr. John Repplier (then a slight acquaintance of the
writer, and a neighbor of the Stevens family) brought Mr. Wallace Stevens
to her parents home, and at this time introduced Mr. Stevens to her, and to
the three friends who were spending the evening with her; the sisters
Misses Alice and Clare Tragle, and Miss Harriet Heller.[5] Mr. Stevens had
been away from home a number of years, and was in his 25th year of age
when he came to Reading to spend the summer with his parents. On
returning to Reading, he found that his friends were either married, or had
left Reading, so he made friends with their younger brothers, and Johnny
Repplier was one of them. That evening, the six of us had a pleasant time
on the front porch, and singing Gilbert and Sullivan songs at the piano.
During the remaining summer Mr. Stevens spent many evenings and Sunday afternoons with the Tragle sisters, as well as with the writer, until September, when he returned to New York City to begin the practice of law.[6]

4. "One June evening" is struck through, and this beginning is handwritten above
the line. The actual year of this meeting was 1904.
5. The following two people from Reading High School's class of 1877 are probably
Miss Harriet Heller's parents:
HARRIET ELIZABETH BUXTON, 113 Windsor St., Reading, Pa.
CHARLES FRANCIS HELLER, d.
C. F. Heller Bindery, 610 Washington St. page 76 of the Reading High Alumni
    Bulletin.
Harriet Heller herself is listed in the class of 1902:
HARRIET BUXTON HELLER, 113 Windsor St., Reading, Pa.
Assistant, Free Library of Reading, Fifth and Franklin Sts.
6. This material, identified as "A Branch of the Bright Family," a typescript, is from
Box 75, Folder 2, HEH. It dates from the early 1940s.

When Elsie, born June 5, 1886, first met Wallace Stevens, she had just passed her eighteenth birthday, and according to the belief of her daughter, she was suffering, as she did throughout her life, from a sense of being from the wrong side of the tracks, partly because her parents had married only a few months before her birth: "All her life, at least during the time I knew her, she suffered from a persecution complex which undoubtedly originated during her childhood" (*SP,* 137).

Holly also reports that Elsie "left high school during her first year, owing to financial pressures on the family and, as she told me, because her eyes were so bad she couldn't see the blackboard" (137–38). Holly thought it likely that her family could not afford glasses for her, and one of Stevens's comments to Elsie indicates that as late as 1909 she was not wearing glasses: "The hard [pieces of music as opposed to the ones he is sending to her] are made for women with glasses and men with long hair" (WAS 1807 January 19, 1909).

When she met Stevens, however, she already had a circle of friends that were important to her, as indicated in her account above. In some of Stevens's letters to her, these friends are an important topic. She and Stevens had a different approach to the subject of friends: he felt that he wanted a friend who would be the only one for whom he lived and she did not feel that a person could live for just one other person.[7] It became important to Stevens to become the one friend for whom she lived and to replace the circle of friends on whom she had relied before she met him. It seems that he was ultimately more successful in this desire than was for his (or her) own good.

Another important part of Elsie's life before her marriage to Stevens was her work. The *Reading Directory* lists her occupations for 1903–9 as a saleslady for two years, a milliner for two years, and a stenographer for three years. After their marriage, her only work was that of a housewife.

When she met Stevens in 1904, Elsie was living at a relatively new address, 231 South Thirteenth Street in Reading. Somewhere in the numerous changes of address before that time, Elsie had learned to play the piano, though her daughter never learned whether her mother had studied with someone or taught herself. This ability at the piano was one thing she had in common with Stevens's mother. She was playing the piano and demonstrating music in a department store when Stevens first came to know her, and in his letters to her, he often mentions her playing and the sheet music he is buying for her. The

---

7. Elsie excerpted this passage from a Stevens letter of the end of 1904 or the beginning of 1905: "You said sometime ago that you did not believe that one lived for a single friend alone. But I do not think so. There is a part of one's self that only one other can share; and one lives most for that other, cherishing him, and desiring for him all good things and all pure things. That desire is nothing more than loving."

purchase of a used baby grand piano will be one of the main events of the letters of 1913, and undated clippings from the Hartford newspapers indicate that Elsie's piano playing continued for some years after the marriage, one clipping indicating that at a gathering of the Hartford Musical Club the program would include "Andante, Third Sonata, Opus 57, by MacDowell, piano solo, by Mrs. Stevens." Another undated clipping indicates that Elsie also gave a talk to this club: "'A Sketch of the New Italian Composers and Their Works,' by Mrs. Wallace Stevens."[8]

In the early 1940s, Elsie began investigating the story of her life before Stevens, and her considerably extensive genealogical work led to a typescript, "A Branch of the Bright Family."[9] Elsie traced the distinguished social and religious past of her mother's family as well as that of her father, Howard Kachel (1865–87), who was descended from "a family that had been Lutherans in Berks County for five preceding generations," a family founded by "one of the early Swiss pioneers of Berks County," and a family of "leading agriculturalists" and "foremost men in educational movements in Berks County." But most important for the letters presented here, she described herself and Wallace Stevens:

> (7) ELSIE VIOLA KACHEL (1886–) was born in Reading, Pa., on June 5th, 1886.[10] A few weeks before her eighth birthday, her mother was married to Mr. Lehman W. Moll. With her mother, she removed from her grandmother's home, to the new home that her mother and Mr. Moll had made ready to occupy immediately after their marriage. Elsie V. Kachel became a member of Grace Lutheran Sunday School, and attended Sunday School until about 1900. She became a member of Grace Lutheran church, and was confirmed by the pastor Rev. William H. Myers, on March 24th, 1907. Before entering the Girls High School at 4th and Washington streets, in Reading, she was a pupil in the Perkiomen Avenue public school, located between 14th and 15th streets. . . .

8. Box 80, Folder 18, the ephemera in the Wallace Stevens Papers, HEH. Mac-Dowell is one of the composers whose music Stevens mentions sending to Elsie in WAS 1810 January 26, 1909.

9. WAS 4033 [1940]. A letter from her mother in 1940 (quoted in this typescript) is obviously in answer to a pressing question Elsie had posed: "Rev Frank K Hunzering Pastor of St Luke's Lutheran Church Read[ing] Christened you at your Father's funeral. Your father died June 3rd 1887, just two days before you were one year old." The question that Elsie did not ask at this time, perhaps because she was all too aware of the answer, is when her parents were married, in February 1886, only four months before her birth.

10. She died on February 18, 1963.

WALLACE STEVENS (1879–) was born in Reading, Pa, on October 2nd., 1879, Son of GARRET [*sic,* for Garrett] BARCALOW STEVENS (born in Feasterville, Bucks county, Pa), and his wife, Mary Catherine (Zeller) STEVENS (born in Reading.)

Wallace Stevens was a member of the First Presbyterian Sunday School, and of the First Presbyterian church. He attended the pubic schools and graduated from the Reading Boys High School in 1897. Not having been prepared in High School for a college entrance, he became a special student at Harvard College,[11] and in three years at Harvard, completed sixteen and one-half courses, and then left college. (Only sixteen courses were required in four years.) . . .

During the following years, he worked as a writer for the New York Herald Tribune in New York City. Then he attended the New York Law School and was admitted to the bar in New York in 1904. He spent the summer of that year in Reading, before beginning a law practice in September, in New York City, with a partner under the name of Ward and Stevens.

A touching reminder of the importance to Elsie of her family's distinguished past is given in the account by Elizabeth Green and Joyce Horner of a meeting they had with Elsie in 1951,[12] as they had come to the Stevens house to pick him up and take him to Mount Holyoke to present his essay "Two or Three Ideas":

> We had a very curious conversation. She said, "What do you teach? My ancestors were concerned with education." Here there was an interruption from Wallace Stevens, who had come in. "Need we go into that?" She went on. She said, "I never went to college, but I made good marks in composition and art, and I got an A in composition."
>
> Then Elizabeth said, "I'd like to hear about your ancestors." She said they were Swiss schoolmasters, the first schoolmasters in Berks County.

11. This explanation for Stevens's status as a special student at Harvard varies somewhat from Stevens's explanation when he applied for admission. Perhaps, considering the lateness of his application and the fact that he had not taken any sort of placement exam, there is some truth in Elsie's version.

12. Elsie was still much concerned with these questions six years after Stevens's death. In a letter to Frank Pechin Law on August 4, 1961, she says, "I have never heard of a relative who was interested in the Bright lineage, excepting Albert Gallatin Green and my grandmother who was Catherine Bright before marriage. It was she who impressed it upon me. Before I was a year old, my father died of consumption, so then my mother and I lived with her until mother's second marriage eight years afterwards, when I took my stepfather's name in school. Because there was no adoption, however, I was married with my real father's name." Box 78, Folder 4, Wallace Stevens Papers, HEH.

Well, at this point Wallace Stevens got up, impatiently. "He doesn't like me to talk about myself," she said, "but I do like people to know that I am interested in something besides cooking and cleaning. Oh, dear, you haven't finished your cocoa!" He certainly gave the impression of being dominant. What I surmised, probably most unjustly, was that she had been different earlier, that maybe after childbirth she had changed. She gave such an impression of naivete, beyond any normal adult, in the language, in the sentences she spoke. (Brazeau, 187)

From Stevens's point of view in 1904, Elsie's family was not particularly relevant, perhaps something to overlook. What attracted him to Elsie was more likely her beauty and innocence. He once told someone that "she was the most beautiful girl in Reading"[13] (Brazeau, 286). According to the evidence of the letters, Stevens was attracted to her by a quality of innocence, simplicity, and honesty that he associated with an important part of his own personality and with the countryside around Reading. As their relationship developed, Stevens mentions her loyalty, gentleness, quietness, goodness, and, ultimately, the fact that she showed him affection: "That . . . is why my world centers around you—because you show me affection" (Elsie's Book, 47). This affection was obviously the "simple thing" he declared he needed in his journal entry of February 14, just a few months before meeting Elsie for the first time: "I'm in the Black Hole again, without knowing any of my neighbors. The very animal in me cries out for a lair. I want to see somebody, hear somebody speak to me, look at somebody, speak to somebody in turn. I want companions. I want more than my work, than the nods of acquaintances, than this little room. I do not want my dreams— my castles, my haunts, my nuits blanches, my companies of good friends. Yet I dare not say what I do want. It is such a simple thing" (*SP*, 128).

It may have been the desperation of this need that led Stevens to misread Elsie as seriously as he did; he repeatedly said, before their marriage, that he and Elsie were the same person, the same personality: "It is as if we were the same person" (Elsie's Book, 42). Though he made references to her "occasional defiances" (WAS 1780 March 18, 1907) and to her being "more or less unmanageable" (*SP*, 174, April 1, 1907), he continued to believe that they would indeed be one after their marriage. He had the highest expectations of their happiness: "It will exceed all Faery" (WAS 1801 January 5, 1909).

About Elsie's physical appearance Stevens makes few references in the surviving letters. He does mention her cheeks and her hair, or some article of her

---

13. This is the testimony of Elias Mengel, who reported what Holly had told him. The term "Elsie's Book" is often used to describe Elsie's excerpts from Stevens's letter to her, and will so be used throughout this volume.

clothing, such as slippers, ribbons, and dresses, and in his journals he mentions, without describing in any detail, her "golden head," her "blue eyes," and her "odor of sachet" (*SP,* 138, 140). In a letter of 1907, he writes that he has discussed Elsie with a friend from Reading: "I ought to tell you what Arthur said on Sunday. After we had been walking, he said, 'Why don't you ask me what I think of Elsie?' Well, he said that you went beyond his expectations! Remember that his expectations were high. He liked your voice and your manner. So he said! I shall not tell you what more he liked, because little girls should not hear such things about themselves" (WAS 1790 April 16, 1907). That Elsie was a beautiful young woman is apparent from photographs of her (see the first volume of Richardson's biography for several), and this beauty obviously played a role in Stevens's choice of a wife.[14] A widely known fact about Elsie, that she served Adolph Weinman as the model for the Mercury dime and the Liberty half-dollar, which were in circulation most of the time the Stevenses were married, is a strong indication of her physical attractiveness. However, along with this trait went another that would manifest itself in ways that would eventually surprise Stevens: an inflexibility that contrasted sharply with his willingness to display so many different personalities. According to Holly, "stiff" was the word one of her contemporaries used to describe her: "Claire Tragle Bauer told me in an interview that when she had first seen my mother, she noticed her walking down the street, 'very stiff, straight and stiff, like a gendarme almost.' She was very beautiful, but shy and uncomfortable if she became the center of attention; she was very self-conscious" (*SP,* 138). This stiffness became an inflexibility, a desire to resist the changes that life in New York with her increasingly sophisticated husband would require; it was a no-nonsense quality that contrasted strikingly with the many self-consciously whimsical and even foppish personalities Stevens assumed in his letters and, later, in his plays and poems.

This contrast between their personalities comes out clearest in the belated account Carl Van Vechten gave of a social evening in 1914. The Stevenses had come to a party at the apartment of Walter Arensberg, a Harvard acquaintance in whose New York circle Stevens experienced firsthand many of the revolutionary aesthetic attitudes of the day:

> Mrs. Stevens, upon arriving, ensconced herself on the couch and remained there. She was a pretty thing, prettier than I had expected, with wavy blond hair and violet eyes. But determination appeared in the corner of her mouth, as did her timidity and naïvety, and her teeth were an unredeeming feature. It is not difficult to find a picturesque way of

14. Brazeau (ibid., 260n14) cites a "Conversation with Holly Stevens" as support for this interpretation.

describing her: she was the model for the head of Liberty which preceded that of Roosevelt on the American dime.

Walter [Arensberg] and I had smoked our cigarettes in another room
before their arrival to avoid polluting the salon, but Stevens at once asked
why the cigarettes were not at hand, and they were produced. Soon he
brought out his poems, rather diffidently, and his wife, whose contributions to the conversation were accented by a painful nervous gulping laugh which came from her throat, gave a hint of her lack of
appreciation.

"She doesn't like them," he began. "Perhaps you will."

"I like Mr. Stevens's things," she said, "when they are not affected;
but he writes so much that is affected." And she settled down to the attitude of an unwilling listener.[15]

One of the poems Stevens read on this occasion was the sacrilegious and
highly mannered "Cy Est Pourtraicte, Madame Ste Ursule, et Les Unze Mille
Vierges," a favorite for everyone at this gathering but Elsie, for whom this poem
surely qualified as one of the "affected" ones.

Stevens's years of struggle as a practicing lawyer, years that included the
entire pre-marriage period of his relationship with Elsie, are not very well docu-
mented yet, but soon after being admitted to the bar, Stevens formed a law partnership with Lyman Ward, who had been at Harvard with him (for Stevens's
affectionate tribute to Ward after his death in an automobile accident in Florida
in 1937, see *LWS,* 17). This partnership soon failed, and Stevens subsequently
worked for a number of law firms from 1905 to 1907: Eugene A. Philbin, Eaton
and Lewis, and Eustis and Foster (see Brazeau, xii, 5). On several occasions during these years, he was out of work for months at a time. Interestingly, his journal shows that by July of 1905, he was traveling extensively on business that
took him to "Chicago—cheap; Kansas City—a mere imitation of civilization;
Kansas—glorious" (*SP,* 147) and later to Raton and Clayton, New Mexico,
Pueblo and Colorado Springs, Colorado, and through Nebraska and Iowa to
Niagara Falls, New York (*SP,* 148). In August 1905, he was traveling in the
South for the first time: Tennessee, Alabama, Mississippi, and Louisiana. It
could be that on this trip he met some of the people who would play a role in his
insurance life later, but it is not clear what sort of work he was doing. After
spending Christmas 1905 in Reading, most of the time with Elsie, he wrote in
his journal for December 31, conveying a sense of uncertainty that would last

15. Carl Van Vechten, "Rogue Elephant in Porcelain," originally published in the
Yale University Library Gazette 38 (October 1963): 41–50. This selection from Irvin
Ehrenpreis, ed., *Wallace Stevens: A Critical Anthology* (Middlesex, England: Penguin
Books, 1972), 32.

for two more years: "A weighty day, of course. Walked to Montclair and back, in the morning, rather meditatively. Very mild air. My head full of strange pictures—terra-cotta figurines of the Romans, ivory figurines of the Japanese, winter birds on winter branches, summer birds on summer branches, green mountains, etc. Reflections (sic) on Japanese life, on specificness, on minute knowledge as disclosing minute pleasures, on what I should wish my wife to be, on my future" (*SP,* 156).

In January 1908, however, he finally found his lifelong vocation and began to work in the insurance industry. He became the resident assistant secretary of the New York office of the American Bonding Company, a firm that served as a seed bed for the insurance industry for a generation to come and thus provided many contacts that would be helpful to Stevens in the future. The resident vice president and manager of the New York office, James L. D. Kearney, would play, until the time of his death on April 5, 1939, an especially prominent role in Stevens's success in the insurance industry. Stevens's new position gave him the economic security to propose marriage to Elsie, and their official engagement lasted ten months before the marriage on a Tuesday morning, September 21, 1909.

There is very little evidence of what sort of work Stevens did in these early years in the insurance industry, though it is clear that from the beginning he was gaining experience in surety bonds. One case on which he worked for the American Bonding Company in 1910 and 1911 has been analyzed in some detail by Steven Richman in "Ships in the Night: Stevens and the Mt. Desert."[16] Richman's conclusions about Stevens's handling of this case clash with "the readily accepted viewpoint of Stevens as a supreme technician and researcher" (55). In essence, after lengthy litigation, Stevens lost in his efforts to keep his company from paying minor court costs. Richman criticizes Stevens's handling of this surety bond case as being sloppy in presentation, indifferent to or unaware of "case precedents advantageous to him," and somewhat arbitrary in contesting a matter of only $121.98, about which the language in the bond in question was "on its face" "clear at least to the court" (64–68). Obviously, this work was that of a young man still finding his way in this complex field that he would eventually master well enough to be known for many years as "the dean of surety claims men in the United States."[17] He developed this respected reputation by virtue of his incredible doggedness and tenacity, qualities he exhibited in many different situations, including the writing of long poems in a short time, throughout his life.

16. Steven Richman, "Ships in the Night: Stevens and the Mt. Desert," *Wallace Stevens Journal* 21, no. 1 (Spring 1997): 55–70.

17. Judgment of Manning Heard, who worked for Stevens and then became president of the Hartford Accident and Indemnity Company after Stevens's death, in Brazeau, *Parts of a World,* 67.

After a series of company mergers and changes between 1914 and early 1916, Stevens was finally out of work when the company for which he was working dropped surety claims from its business. At this time, Stevens's old friend Kearney, who had been called to Hartford in August 1913, when the Hartford Fire Insurance Company was setting up a subsidiary, the Hartford Accident and Indemnity Company (Hartford A&I), offered Stevens a job. The following move to Hartford, surely rather traumatic for Elsie, took place over a period of several months, during which Stevens was away on long business trips for the Hartford, trips to the South and to the Midwest.

This move to Hartford could be seen as one of the four most important structural changes in Stevens's entire life, ranking in importance with his going off to Harvard, his moving to New York on leaving Harvard, and his marrying Elsie. It was certainly the presence of Kearney, someone he had known and trusted for eight years, that made the move acceptable to Stevens—that and the encouragement of one Heber Stryker, another American Bonding Company alumnus who had moved to Hartford in 1913 and had already introduced Stevens to some of the leading citizens of Hartford on a visit Stevens made there in that year.[18]

Stevens's new appointment at the Hartford Accident and Indemnity Insurance Company[19] was announced in an article in the *Hartford Agent* titled "Fidelity and Surety Expansion":

> Mr. Stevens will have charge of claim and legal matters in the Department. As a member of the New York Bar he specialized for a number of years in the Law of Suretyship, and in 1908 was induced by the American Bonding Company of Baltimore to devote himself exclusively to its legal matters in New York. On the merger of the American Bonding Company with the Fidelity and Deposit Company of Maryland, he went with the latter company as its law officer in New York. In these capacities he had unusual opportunities to gain the experience necessary for the efficient handling of claims arising out of suretyship, which in its beginnings as a business in this country may almost be said to have been a phase of the lawyer's profession.
>
> The Company considers it of the greatest importance that its surety claims be handled in the usual broad and open-minded "Hartford" way,

18. For more about Stryker, see a note to the letter of June 24, 1909.

19. This company had been created by Richard Mervin Bissell (1862–1941), the newly appointed president of the Hartford Fire Company, in 1913; for many years thereafter, the two companies were known as "the two Hartfords," with the Fire Company clearly in the leading role of father or older brother. In this new company, the emphasis on fidelity and surety bonds, relatively new forms of insurance, grew considerably under the guidance of Kearney and the dedicated road work of Stevens.

without technicalities and without offense, in both of which particulars, however, surety claims present many pitfalls for the inexperienced. The Company believes that in Mr. Stevens "Hartford" agents will find a man peculiarly fitted to maintain the traditions and practices of the Company in this respect.[20]

Immediately upon taking his new position in Hartford, Stevens began traveling for the company to Florida and other places in the South as well as the Midwest. As Stevens continued these travels (and the writing of his poetry and a prize-winning play, *Three Travelers Watch a Sunrise*), he was writing the legal documents to establish the Hartford Live Stock Insurance Company, a paper company established to circumvent the laws of some states against fire insurance companies' insuring live stock. Stevens served on the board of directors of this company for the rest of his life, taking a trip to New York for meetings once or twice a year. This was, however, a minor part of his business life.

From the very beginning of his employment by the Hartford A&I, he traveled to distant sites to handle complex fidelity and surety claims. Stevens continued his business trips to Florida for about twenty years, and though he worked on a number of other cases, such as one involving a bank in Palm Beach, the social side trips to the Florida Keys seem to have been the primary motivation. Stevens's travels to other parts of the country were far less frequent, after the hiring of an assistant, Ralph Mullen, in 1921. His last business trip to Florida was in 1936, when he unfortunately tried to punch out Ernest Hemingway, a vastly superior boxer.[21] Until his death in 1951, Mullen remained one of Stevens's closest associates, the one who helped him, after years of trying to achieve one of his social goals, to become a member of the Canoe Club of East Hartford in 1948.

After publishing *Harmonium* in 1923, Stevens took Elsie on a two-month trip, October 18–December 10, to San Francisco by way of the Panama Canal and back across the United States, including a stop in New Mexico to see an old Harvard friend, Witter Bynner. Nine months later, on August 10, 1924, their daughter Holly was born, and Stevens went into what is sometimes called his period of "second silence" during which he wrote almost no poetry, the first silent period being the years after leaving Harvard until he finally began publishing poems in 1914. This second period did not end until he began writing the poems that Alcestis Press would publish as *Ideas of Order* in 1935; thus for about a decade, Stevens produced almost no new poetry.[22] There are only

---

20. *Hartford Agent* 7, no. 9 (March 1916): 347
21. For an account of this episode, see the introduction to chapter 5.
22. This assertion should be qualified; it is possible, as Samuel French Morse has suggested, that Stevens was engaged on an extended poem during this period, one from which he took later fragments and published them separately: "The Woman Who

five extant letters to Elsie during this period, and very little evidence of any kind of Stevens's activities at home or at the office.[23] In a letter of January 1, 1925, to Louis Untermeyer, Stevens suggests three reasons for his silence: "There is a baby and a radio, and I am expecting to go to Florida in a week or so, etc." (*LWS*, 244). Later that year, on October 14, 1925, Stevens gives William Carlos Williams a similar set of reasons:

> I have seen very few littérateurs during the last year or two. Moreover I have read very little and written not at all. The baby has kept us both incredibly busy. True she is not under my jurisdiction and has been as well-behaved as a south-wind yet the fact remains that she dominates the house and that her requirements have to a large extent become our own. I have been moved to the attic, so as to be out of the way, where it ought to be possible for me to smoke and loaf and read and write and sometimes I feel like doing all of these things but, so far, I have always elected to go to bed instead. There-fore, I fear that I must be dropped for the present. . . . There's a poet from Paris visiting in Hartford at the moment. . . . But oh la-la: my job is not now with poets from Paris. It is to keep the fire-place burning and the music-box churning and the wheels of the baby's chariot turning and that sort of thing. Perhaps if I am fortunate, I shall be able to drop down into Florida for a few weeks bye and bye. (*LWS*, 245–46)

Blamed Life on a Spaniard," "Good Man, Bad Woman" (for *Poetry*'s twentieth anniversary issue). "The Woman Who Blamed Life on a Spaniard," "Good Man, Bad Woman," and the earlier "Red Loves Kit" (1924) were "all improvisations on a single theme, cut from the same fifteen-line stanza pattern he had used in "Sunday Morning" but reflecting the attitude of a man even older and more disillusioned than the protagonist of "Le Monocle de Mon Oncle," who had been "fairly well along in life, looking back and talking in a more or less personal way about life" (*LWS*, 251). "The sardonic, even abrasive irony of these seven stanzas on love, very different from the ambiguity of 'Peter Quince at the Clavier' and 'Le Monocle de Mon Oncle,' suggests the possibility that they may originally have been intended as parts of an unfinished whole; but because their bitterness was 'personal' in precisely the way he thought poetry ought not to be, he never republished them." Morse, *Wallace Stevens: Poetry as Life* (New York: Pegasus, 1970), 142–43. A. Walton Litz agrees with Morse and suggests that the style of this abortive long poem "on the elemental relations between man and woman," was "embarrassingly personal." Litz, *Introspective Voyager: The Poetic Development of Wallace Stevens* (New York: Oxford University Press, 1972), 142, 170.

23. However, a note by Holly Stevens in *LWS* (258) mentions a case in 1926 in which Stevens was acting as the attorney for the Hartford in some sort of action against J. C. Penney, represented by Jim Powers, who would become one of Stevens's assistants for two years and later one of the most important friends and correspondents for the rest of Stevens's life.

All of these distractions no doubt played their role, but a medical drama was also being played out in Stevens's life at this time, one revealed in a letter from Dr. W. W. Herrick to Dr. A. D. Mittendorf:[24]

> Mr. Wallace Stevens reported here October 11th because of disturbance of vision. History was given of former smoking and of the occasional use of alcohol. Mr. Stevens has traveled much and exercised little. He has become particularly sluggish with the last two or three years, and has not restrained himself, especially at the table. He has eaten much salt. There is a history of malaria as a boy and of a chronic discharge from the left ear. Early in September blurring of vision was noticed. There had been recent gain in weight. He also suffers from nycturia.
>
> Physical examination shows weight 229 lbs., a large frame carrying too much weight. There is the impression of a somewhat acromegalic type of individual.
>
> In my opinion Mr. Stevens has the following conditions: (1) Overweight; (2) Essential hypertension; (3) Moderate arterio-capillary fibrosis; (4) a vascular lesion in the right retina; (5) a possible pituitary disturbance; (6) mild diabetes mellitus.

Stevens fought against this formidable list of symptoms and conditions for the next several years (indeed, in 1946 he will still be seeing Dr. Mittendorf and will report that he has been taking three medicines for his eyes "for the last twenty years" [*LWS,* 542]), but in 1931, he was turned down for life insurance coverage because his blood pressure was too erratic. Though he eventually received on February 9, 1934, an optimistic report from Dr. Herrick ("It is apparent that the disorder for which you first consulted me in 1926 is not advancing materially"),[25] Stevens never qualified for life insurance, and after this period he decided to insure himself through his own savings.

During this period of poetic silence, Stevens continued his career in the Hartford Accident and Indemnity Company, slowly building up his department by hiring people who would often become executives, including company president, of the Hartford A&I. And though his business/pleasure trips to Florida during the winter season, usually including two or more weeks in February at the luxury resort Casa Marina in Key West, were without his wife or his new daughter, he also took less elaborate summer vacations with his family, as reported by Holly Stevens.[26] In 1929, the family went to Atlantic City together, Stevens staying

24. WAS 897 October 15, 1926, HEH.
25. WAS 894 February 9, 1934.
26. See Holly Stevens, "Holidays in Reality," in *Wallace Stevens: A Celebration,* ed. Frank Doggett and Robert Buttell (Princeton: Princeton University Press, 1980), 105–13.

"long corridors away" from Elsie's and Holly's room. The next year they all went to Pocono Manor, Pennsylvania, where Elsie had spent the summer of 1913. In the summer of 1931, Holly and Elsie attended the Institute of Euthenics at Vassar College, the school Stevens would later try, unsuccessfully, to get Holly to remain enrolled in during the early years of World War II. In 1931, they took the last vacation they would take together until the summer of 1939, when they all went to the Holly Inn in Christmas Cove, Maine, a resort managed by the same man, Peter Schutt, who managed the Casa Marina in Key West.

In September 1932, Stevens and his family moved to 118 Westerly Terrace in Hartford into the only home he ever owned, one for which he paid twenty thousand dollars in cash.[27] It was from this eleven-room house (in a neighborhood of houses somewhat more elaborate than his) near Elizabeth Park, that Stevens often walked the two or three miles to his office. Holly has described this house in some detail:

> The house was set on a half-acre lot, or larger. . . . The house itself was a white Colonial with dark green shutters. One entered a spacious front hall with a graceful staircase to the second floor. To the right was a living room that ran the depth of the house, with windows facing the front and back (west and east), and one to the south, so that the room was light all day.
> . . . Beyond the living room was an enclosed sunroom where my father often sat—here was the phonograph, a large table with many of his books and foreign periodicals, a couple of extremely comfortable easy chairs, and house plants on the radiator below the east windows that faced the garden. The dining room was off the other side of the living room, behind the front hall and also facing the garden. . . . The kitchen was beyond, through a butler's pantry, with stairs down to the garden. In front of it was the back hall section, with stairs to the second and third floors. . . . My father's bedroom and private bath were at the top of the front stairs facing the garden. . . . The piano was in the upstairs living room, over the one downstairs. Beyond that was a sleeping porch, where my mother and I moved from our separate rooms at the north end of the house during the summer months.
> The third floor had two maid's rooms, which gradually filled with books and records after the last maid we had, Josephine, left us in the late thirties to marry. And a large attic, also filled with books and complete runs of magazines from all over the world. After Dad died I discovered

27. Brazeau, *Parts of a World,* 231; on this page, Brazeau also lists Stevens's income for almost each year between 1916 and 1935 (from three thousand to twenty thousand dollars) and then for 1948 (twenty-four thousand dollars). In "The Man with the Blue Guitar," Stevens takes a patrician jab at subdivisions such as "Oxidia, banal suburb, / One-half of all its installments paid" (*CP,* 182).

that he had been using the closet in the maid's room that had been my playroom to store wine glasses and a few odd bottles of wine and spirits.[28]

Not long after acquiring this comfortable house, the biggest event in Stevens's business life (one that has been seen to play a role in his return to writing poetry) came in early 1934, when he loyally stood by James L. D. Kearney, the man who had brought him to the Hartford A&I in 1916. In 1934, Kearney was resisting being fired by the head of the Hartford Fire Insurance Company for not firing another employee (who eventually was found to have been embezzling money on a vast scale). For standing by Kearney (as did all of the other men who worked directly for him), Stevens was promoted to vice president, some eighteen years after he had begun working there, a length of time much longer than that taken by his original cohort of executives to become officers.[29]

After this, his last promotion in the company, Stevens began writing poetry regularly again, something he attributed to the influence of J. Ronald Lane Latimer, who, according to Alan J. Filreis, "might have provided the most important literary friendship Stevens ever had."[30] Stevens himself, writing to Hi Simons[31] on August 8, 1940, gave great importance to the role Latimer played: "I cannot tell you anything about Latimer. I have heard various unpleasant things said about him, but, for my own part, made up my mind long ago to speak nothing but good of him, since my own relations with him would not justify me in doing anything else. In fact, I should be justified, I think, in going far beyond speaking good of him, because I owe a very great deal to him. I don't mean to say because he published some of my things, but because he started me up[32] to doing

28. Holly Stevens, "Bits of Remembered Time," *Southern Review* 7 (1971): 651–57.

29. This exciting story was one of the great discoveries Brazeau made for his oral history, *Parts of a World*. See "Officer of the Hartford," 59–61.

30. "Stevens, 'J. Ronald Latimer,' and the Alcestis Press," *Wallace Stevens Journal* 17, no. 2 (Fall 1993): 180.

31. Stevens corresponded with Simons, a most dedicated nonprofessional, who was a very important student of Stevens's poetry from 1937 until he died in April 1945. Simons elicited from Steven some of his most detailed commentary on his poetry. In writing a bibliography of Stevens's poetry, Simons got Stevens to send him copies of periodicals that included his poetry, and for these publications he sent Stevens the following note that reveals the growing importance of Holly as someone, already at age fourteen, with responsibilities that might logically have been Elsie's: "I have received from Mr. Wallace Stevens the following publications . . . with the understanding that they are to be returned to him or to Miss Holly Stevens if either of them should ask for them during my lifetime" (WAS 83 October 2, 1938).

32. Conrad Aiken said that Stevens gave him similar credit: "In 1933 or 1934 I suggested to J. M. Dent, via Richard Church, that they should bring out HARMONIUM in their poetry series, and I was asked to write Stevens about this, or rather, to ask him for a new book—in their perverse way, they didn't want a book ten years old. Stevens in

them" (*LWS*, 359). Thus Stevens begins a new phase of his life as a home owner, an executive, and a poet. He began responding to the many requests for explication of his old poems and to the many requests for new poems.

This new poetry provides the most important evidence of the nature of Stevens's relations with Elsie in the mid- to late 1930s. The picture in these poems is not a pleasant one. Many of the poems of *Parts of a World,* published in periodicals from 1937 to 1940 and beyond, contain material that is personal, unhappy, and related to Elsie, including "Arrival at the Waldorf" and all six of the poems published as a group under the title "Illustrations of the Poetic as a Sense." Of those six poems, "Arcades of Philadelphia the Past" and "The Common Life" are the most particular in their revelations. It is as if during this period Stevens is reliving the pain and frustration that led to the series of poems about an unhappy relationship in the twenties, but this time he will publish his poems not only in scattered magazines but also in a major volume of his poetry.

In early 1940, Stevens finally delivered on the promises he had made to Elsie as early as 1917 to take her to Florida: "I wished sincerely that you might be here. I shall surely take you to Florida when we can afford it."[33] The actual trip was difficult for Elsie, according to Holly Stevens: "When we all flew to Florida in 1940 she was airsick. Rarely could she ride in a car for more that half an hour before being sick."[34] In another place, Holly has added details about this trip: "We flew from Hartford to Jacksonville, making several stops on the way; Eleanor Roosevelt was a fellow passenger between Washington, D.C., and Atlanta, and was much more attractive than any of us had imagined from her photographs. Even my mother commented on this, although she was airsick throughout the trip and didn't notice much else."[35] Other friends and acquaintances who were in Key West while the Stevenses were there that year were Robert Frost, Judge Powell and his wife, and an old friend from Reading, Edwin deTurck Bechtel, and his wife. Holly reports that this was the last vacation that the whole Stevens family took together.

Soon Stevens was to face a crisis that almost equaled the importance of the crisis of his marriage to Elsie: his daughter's rebellion against his wishes that she

---

due course replied that he didn't have anything, he hadn't been writing. End of correspondence. In 1936 I first met him at Ted Spencer's, after he had given a reading in Sanders Theatre. When we were introduced, he at once said that he regarded me as the godfather of all his recent work, and that it was my request for a book for Dent that had started him off again." *Selected Lettters of Conrad Aiken,* ed. Joseph Killorin (New Haven: Yale University Press, 1978), 305, letter of 1960.

33. WAS 2018 November 16[?], 1917[?], from Tampa, Florida.
34. Stevens, "Bits of Remembered Time," 657.
35. Stevens, "Holidays in Reality," 110.

continue to attend Vassar, a rebellion that drew from him one of the most direct statements of emotion he ever made, his letter of Oct. 7, 1942, to Holly:

> That your parents—or anyone's parents—have their imperfections is nothing to brood on. They also have their perfections. Yr mother has them to an exquisite degree, tough as she is. The blow-ups that we have are nothing more than blow-ups of the nerves—when they are over they are over. And I think and hope that you will look back some day and be happy about the whole thing. My own stubbornnesses and taciturn eras are straight out of Holland and I cannot change them any more than I can take off my skin. But I never hesitate to seek to undo any damage I may have done. (*LWS*, 422)

When Holly announced her decision to drop out of Vassar nineteen days later, Stevens wrote her a letter in which he amazingly contradicts one of the large claims he made for the centrality of his own professional life as an insurance executive in his career as a poet:

> Please don't allow yourself to come to a final decision about college and I beg you not to do this. It is difficult for me to write. But you cannot possibly know what you are doing, without any experience of life, however sure you may be otherwise. The uncertainty you feel should be dismissed from your mind. Everyone feels this when first confronted by himself and by the enormous complication of the world; and, if this is so in ordinary times, it is all the more so in the very centre of the huge struggle for survival that is now going on. But you don't find yourself or your way through life by getting a job, except for a very brief period of time. I think that you may have been influenced by the friends you have here, even unconsciously. We have not tried to influence you respecting your friends. But take my word for it that making your living is a waste of time. None of the great things in life have anything to do with making your living; and I had hoped that little by little, without now being able to say how, you would find the true field for your intelligence and imagination in something that was at least a part of one of the great things of life. Study at a college, a period of leisure and study and reflection at a sensitive period, is the readiest instrument by which to find yourself and your work. (*LWS*, 425)

When Holly dropped out of college and shortly afterward married John Hanchak, a blue-collar worker for Aetna, Stevens's relations with her were sharply curtailed for a number of years, during which he seems to have become closer to Elsie. One indication of the nature of his improving relationship to Elsie comes in his letter of August 27, 1943, to Henry Church, one of his primary correspondents in the 1940s, a man of great wealth whose life was one Stevens said that he him-self would most have liked to live.[36] Stevens is defending himself, somewhat humorously, from a charge made by Church that he is "a terrible tyrant":

> I am not really a tyrant; after all, it took me till after one o'clock the night you were with us to get things straightened out, so that I still think that such things are impossible. It is precisely the care with which she does things that makes Mrs. Stevens unwilling to let anyone else do them for her. Of course, it has its advantages: vegetables appear on the table in their own vivid colors, etc., and moderately high living of that sort goes well with an effort to think plainly and is incomparably better than the old plain living and high thinking. (*LWS*, 453)

This glimpse into his domestic life shows something of Stevens's potentially heavy-handed coping techniques and something of his ability to put the best face on a situation that to an outsider might seem troubled. Church's letter of August 24, 1943, the one that led to the letter above, had praised Elsie's cooking— "Anyone who can cook a duck like Mrs. Stevens is a poet"—and Church had defended Elsie's "preoccupation about her preacher ancestors."[37] It was Church who had perceptively observed to Stevens, after meeting Elsie in 1943, "I am convinced . . . that Mrs. Stevens has had an important part in the poetry of Wal-lace Stevens."[38] This observation, perhaps somewhat casual and meant to be flattering to Elsie, came from one of the sources Stevens most respected in his life and doubtless reflected the improved relations between them as they spent their last decade or so together.

These closer relations may have developed partly from their common inter-est in genealogy throughout the 1940s and until the end of Stevens's life. His diligent application to the study of genealogy in the 1940s may actually have begun with Elsie's attempts to find out more about her background, a concern that also lasted in her case until her death (in 1963). Stevens's extensive efforts in this matter tell us a lot about him: his first casual letter to the Holland Society of New York on January 16, 1942,[39] his letter of application to the society of November 21, 1944, the disappointed letter of May 5, 1945, retracting his application, which had been found lacking in a single generation some two hundred years earlier, and his last letter to this organization, which he was still

36. See *LWS*, 401, letter of January 28, 1942, to Henry Church.
37. Unpublished letter at Princeton University Library.
38. Letter of March 27, 1943. Quoted in Milton J. Bates, *Wallace Stevens: A Mythol-ogy of Self* (Berkeley and Los Angeles: University of California Press, 1985), 49.
39. See Box 73, Folder 10, HEH, for the forty-nine pieces of correspondence between Stevens and this society, especially letters to Florence McAleer, the society's secretary.

interested in joining not long before his death. The Stevens who was reintro-duced to his family in Reading at the time he attended his brother John Bergen Stevens's funeral in July 1940 knew almost nothing about either his immediate family or his ancestors, near or distant. However, something about the youth and vigor of the next generation interested him, and he became close to his sole surviving sibling, his sister Elizabeth (whom he had addressed as the "giantess" in a letter he had written back in 1912), and especially to her daughter Jane, whose birth in 1919 he had learned of almost by accident. He also got to know the children of his brother John, to one of whom he confided in 1944 that Elsie was a good cook: "That's why I've got this obese look about me. . . . She's a damn good cook and a faithful wife" (Brazeau, 276).

The rapid growth in Stevens's knowledge of his family, immediate and dis-tant, as well as his quick mastery of the manners and customs of genealogists and their art, reveals a man driven by more than disinterested curiosity. Stevens wanted very much to be accepted by the Holland Society of New York, and his disappointment was considerable when he failed. However, the search itself was rewarding, and the trip he and Elsie took to Hershey, Pennsylvania, in the first three weeks of September 1946 was, he reported, "one of the happiest holidays we have ever had," a rare phrase indeed for Stevens and one that returns in this letter as "one of the happiest times of our lives" (*LWS*, 535).

This growing closeness between Stevens and his wife is indicated by the increasing frequency in his last decade of letters of the phrase "my wife" or, as he more often referred to her, "Mrs. Stevens."[40] In a conversation with Louis Martz at the time he was writing "An Ordinary Evening in New Haven" (1949), Stevens made a statement that revealed a lot about his relationship to Elsie: "Now, I read every section as is my custom to my wife as I wrote it. She put her hands over her eyes and said, 'They're not going to understand this.' I was very careful to pick out the sections I thought would go over with an audience. But even so, my wife was terribly concerned about it" (Brazeau, 175). This sense of camaraderie with Elsie is a common note in the letters Stevens wrote in the final decade or so of his life; he uses the rare word "happy" to apply not only to the vacation they took for three weeks to Hershey in 1946 but also to his few weeks home with Elsie in January 1950 after he fell on the ice: "If it was an opportunity to write a little, it was an opportunity that I was glad to ignore. It was impossible even to think. It takes a squalid interval like this to realize the opportunities of low spirits and the ravages they make on one's pride and ambition. Fortunately, I

40. In his published letters, he refers to "Elsie" only in those of the late 1940s until his death, and then only in letters to Barbara Church, to his cousin Emma Stevens Jobbins, and to his niece Eleanor Stevens Sauer (daughter of his younger brother), especially the latter.

was not alone. Mrs. Stevens was a true angel and from the point of view of being at home with her it was a happy time" (*LWS,* 663).

This tone reaches its highest pitch in a letter of February 18, 1955, when he is still unaware of his own growing stomach cancer but is busy taking care of Elsie after her stroke on January 14:

> Mrs. Stevens had a thrombosis about a month ago. It is enough to say that we hope she will completely recover as time passes. She has made rapid progress, comes down stairs every day and stays down. Like many people who have gone through this she tries to grow well by main force. It is difficult to make her take it easy. She likes the nurse to brush her hair and to help her on the stairs. She yields nothing. She is cheerful and courageous, as women so often are in the face of illness. I feel certain that within a few months she will be fully or almost fully as she was before. For one thing, she would not want me to talk about all this and, in general, tries to exorcise the devil by not recognizing him or, rather, to expel him by turning her back on it. We don't want her to work in the garden next summer, where she is accustomed to spend her summer days. Will that be possible? . . . All this has made a great difference at home. The need of keeping the house quiet at night alone makes a difference. But it doesn't matter. One regime is as good as another. (*LWS,* 874)

That Stevens was dedicated to Elsie is indirectly and eloquently revealed in Holly's comment about her own troubled relations with her mother that did not improve until after her father's death: "Part of his legacy to me was to carry on the devotion he had for her; and as I began to understand, I also 'grew up'" (*SP,* 137).

Nota

These letters, the fossil remains of a part of the life of one of America's most important poets, are a partial record of some of his most productive years. Only one of these years, 1909, is represented completely enough to show the articulation of the bones, but other years, notably 1913, 1916, and 1923, are represented by "half a shoulder and half a head / To recognize him in after time" (*CP,* 513). These letters are a record that Stevens went to great lengths to create, and he took some steps to preserve them; they were an organized attempt to win a wife and reveal a history of himself and his education, both sentimental and intellectual. They provide us a way of understanding Stevens's poetry, a way that emphasizes the poet's personality and life more than his learning or philosophy, though importance evidence of Stevens's reading and approach to learning are also revealed here. For example, "Arcades of Philadelphia the Past" has been read as a statement about the Philadelphias of the past, as an allusion to Milton's Valombrosa and to myths of eye sharing, all quite sound readings. But these letters show that another possible meaning for Stevens is the highly personal event of meeting his fiancée in Philadelphia, unaccompanied, psychically at "the edge of a field," in 1909, an event that is possibly alluded to in some of his later poetry. Harold Bloom senses this possibility and relates this meeting to the "rendezvous" mentioned in "The Auroras of Autumn" in the winter of 1948 and "The meeting at noon at the edge of a field" in "The Rock" of 1950.[41] This possibility of personal background should be seen as an enrichment of more abstract reading of these poems, not as a competing interpretation. If the real is the base, as Stevens asserts in one of his most-often-quoted adagias, attention to this base, this soil as he puts it in another famous metaphor, should bring enlightenment or clarification to some of his most tenebrous lines.

However, the real is only the base, and in order to read these letters as Stevens wrote them (and read them—one could adduce considerable evidence that he did reread them over the years),[42] one has to read Stevens's poetry. Just as the letters cast light on the poems, so the poems reveal what was important in the letters to Stevens. By themselves the letters are so emotionally restrained that they often seem to be what Stevens several times calls them— history—though excisions and lacunae doubtless eliminated some of their original emotional charge. Stevens is so cautious in these letters that almost no one would read them in their entirety without having first developed a sense of the importance of his poetry, poetry that often suggests the troubled and powerful presence of an actual second person, what he calls a "second voice" in "Song" in the "Book of Verses" he wrote for Elsie in 1908. It is easy to see why an early reviewer of *The Letters of Wallace Stevens* could see the letters to Elsie as being "curiously pointless."[43] That reviewer had perhaps not read very much of Stevens's poetry,

41. See Harold Bloom, *Wallace Stevens: The Poems of Our Climate* (Ithaca: Cornell University Press, 1976), 278.

42. Joan Richardson repeats this point several times in the first volume of her biography of Stevens, most emphatically in the following passage: "From periodic perusals of his journals and early letters Stevens gathered many of the images and perceptions he worked into poems (a number of these examples have already been presented). Stevens went back to these sources again and again, not randomly picking or searching out a particular reference but reading through the entire sequence as it unfolded past stages of his life, and the poetry that emerged after each rereading represented, in part, a revisionary cycle. Each reworking of the primary material included the previous reworking and additional experiences of the poet between the completing of one cycle and the beginning of the next." Joan Richardson, *Wallace Stevens: A Biography: The Early Years*, 2 vols. (New York: Morrow, 1986, 1988), 1:297.

43. In an anonymous review of *Letters of Wallace Stevens*, edited by Holly Stevens, in the *London Times Literary Supplement* for March 30, 1967, the reviewer, perhaps Roy Fuller, says, "Following Stevens's death she [Elsie] destroyed a number of his letters to

certainly not enough to sense the presence of the second person or voice in it and to realize that those "pointless" letters were revealing crucial information about how important she was to him. As we come to see that Elsie is often that second person in his poetry, we read the letters to her differently. We see through the calm surface of these letters into rather deeper, more personal meanings. When he says the following, we begin to realize that he is trying to tell a truth that will remain a truth: "I will never love anybody but you—bad as you are—why it would be impossible, dear. I simply couldn't—wouldn't know how" (see WAS 1795 December, 8–9, 1908, below). When we see him say the following, we sense a personal, as opposed to traditional, source of the imagery of cold that will inform his poetry throughout his life: "Did you avoid writing just to punish me for the 'liberty' I took? But do not punish me when I am at home. Why should you ever? Let us keep such things for mid-winter" (see WAS 1786 March 29, 1907, below). Another use of this meaning for the word "winter" is in WAS 1787 April 1–2 1907, as he tells about an earlier cooling period in their relationship: "We must say that there has been a little winter in us." Also, in WAS 1952 September 2, 1913: "Well, I suppose you think I'm a hyena in human form. I know just how you are thinking of winter things. It was simply a piece of bad luck to have this unseasonable cold snap right now."

Thus Stevens's weather reporting is a matter of the greatest personal significance. There is for him an epic battle going on. For him, her letters were as powerful as the most powerful literature, and he refers to Elsie's letters to him in his most emotional language. Indeed, for the first five years of their relationship, Elsie is primarily a verbal reality for him, a reality he knows mainly in her letters. It may seem a shame that none of these letters remain, but it is doubtful that we would be able to read them as he did, though one can easily imagine that they were less restrained than Stevens's letters. For Stevens, letters were an act of love, both the writing and the reading of them, and the actual visits to Reading were often less satisfying than the reading of Elsie's letters.[44] When they were married, her letters to him stopped, and the reality of her actual presence did not fill that epistolary void. It took him many years to

---

her of this period [1904–9] (after first copying extracts she thought might be of interest), but this is probably no great loss. The letters of the long courtship are curiously pointless, a parallel to Stevens's career as a lawyer—and, indeed, as a writer—during the same epoch." Reprinted in Charles Doyle, ed., *Wallace Stevens: The Critical Heritage* (London: Routledge and Kegan Paul, 1985), 472. Joan Richardson has an opposite estimation of the value of the letters Stevens wrote to Elsie: "Apart from their human element, the most striking feature of these letters is that they contain in raw form, and in nearly exact chronological sequence, the germs of the major poems of *Harmonium*." Richardson, *Wallace Stevens* 1:296.

44. See WAS 1777 and WAS 1787 for two letters in which this point is intimated.

establish the optimum distance from the actual, as opposed to the paper, Elsie, one that would make possible both their personal relationship and his poetry. Without Elsie, the poetry of Wallace Stevens as we have it would have never been written. She was his genius, as he directly says in one of his letters to her. She was his poetic oxygen, absolutely necessary in the right amount and absolutely deadly in excessive doses.

∽ 1 ∽

Courtship

July 1904–November 1908

With the exception of the seventeen letters of 1907, the correspondence of this period of more than four years is represented only by Elsie's excerpts (sometimes referred to by Stevens scholars as "Elsie's Book"). The twenty poems he wrote for her twenty-second birthday on June 5, 1908, is also a part of their correspondence, since it appears that some of them were sent in letters before they were collected. These excerpts and letters, read in conjunction with Stevens's journal entries in *Souvenirs and Prophecies,* teach us things about Stevens that we need to know in order to read his poetry.

Elsie's excerpts, listed at the Huntington Library as WAS 1772, are all that remain of his letters to Elsie from 1904, 1905, and 1906. From 1907, there are seventeen extant letters, from six of which Elsie took excerpts. The only extant letters of 1908 are eight from the month of December, and they are thus treated as a part of the period of their engagement. Of the 107 extant letters of 1909 (2 of them coming after their marriage), Elsie made excerpts from thirty-nine. Of the eleven extant letters of 1910, she made excerpts from three, and, finally, she made excerpts from two of the eight extant letters of 1911. All of these excerpts will be given here in a single chapter; they reveal much about the woman making them, especially since many of the excerpts of 1907 and almost all of them of 1909 are from extant letters against which her selected passages can be read for context. What she chose to save would have been all we now have if she had carried her project to its conclusion.

Her method of selection seems to have involved arranging the letters in packets, probably twenty-eight of them, with about twenty-eight letters in each packet.[1] The next step seems to have been to type on three-by-five note

---

1. There are fifteen small cards, not note cards, of differing provenance, that seem to have served as indexes or markers for the twenty-eight packets of letters. Numbered from 14 to 28, four of them contain the following comments about the letters in their respective packets:

cards the packet number and the date of the letter from which she was making her selection. On several of the ten surviving cards, the date for letters of 1909 is given as 1959, an error that suggests that she was doing this project in 1959. After the packet number and date, she then typed a paragraph or two. The final step was the handwritten transcription of passages from these selections into her stenographer's notepad, which is Elsie's Book, or WAS 1772 at the Huntington. Quite likely, this "book" eventually would have been typed.

On the ten surviving note cards, there is material that did not make it to Elsie's Book. The final step seems to have been the destruction of the letters and the note cards. Obviously, Elsie did not finish this project, which was huge and undoubtedly emotionally demanding. We know that she had had her first stroke in early 1955, and that she had a series of other strokes in 1957, ultimately dying of this cause on February 18, 1963. It is probable that she was simply unable to finish her project.

Though there are minor exceptions, we can tell from the excerpts that come from extant letters that Elsie's selections are arranged in chronological order. Accepting that generalization and relying on internal indications made by Elsie, I have dated the page numbers provided by Elsie, so that one can see that the excerpts she has on the pages she numbered 1 to 6 are from 1904, those on her pages 7 and 8 are from 1905; those on pages 9 to 19 are from 1906, those on

---

16. Feb 29th is a good letter [There is no extant letter to Elsie dated February 29, though there is one for February 28, 1909 (WAS 1821), which is probably the one she has in mind, since she tended to date these excerpts from the date on the envelope, usually one day later than Stevens's indicated date of writing.]

20. July 23rd [WAS 1877 July 23, 1909]
    August 3rd [WAS 1880 August 3, 1909, the following comment refers to this letter.]
    A fairy tale ["This is the story of how golden hair and blue eyes came to be."]

21. W. in high spirits
    September 2nd [WAS 1897 September 2, 1909]
    1709 [*sic;* for 1909]
    September 8nd [WAS 1898 September 8, 1909]
    Wise letters June 6th [No extant letter of this date.]
    June 10th [WAS 1853 June 9, 1909]
    1909

25. Aug 30. [WAS 1965 August 29, 1915]
    Discouraged about
    writing poetry after
    working hours at office.

pages 19 to 33 are from 1907; those on pages 33 to 52 are from 1908, and those from pages 53 to 65 are from 1909. The excerpts from 1910 are also on her page 65, and those from 1911 are on her pages 65 and 66.[2] These dry statistics reveal that she made few excerpts from the letters of 1904 and 1905, perhaps the years in which the correspondence was least prolific.

Though it is not possible to say with any certainty how many letters Stevens wrote to Elsie in those four early years, mid-1904 to the beginning of December 1908, the number had to be in the hundreds. In those now represented only by Elsie's excerpts and the seventeen letters of 1907, we can see their importance to Stevens. This importance is also revealed in his references to them in his journals. Though he makes obvious reference to Elsie as early as August 6, 1904, in his journal (see *SP,* 138, for reference to "Dear me, that warm mouth counts too; and that ravishing hand; and that golden head trying to hide in my waistcoat somewhere; and those blue eyes looking at me sweetly though with intent"; also see *SP,* 140, for "the odor of sachet that she exhaled, of the spirituality she suggested"), it is not until September 13, 1904, that he writes, "Another letter from Elsie. I could write to her every night—but she will answer only once a week, and then four pages are all I get. Lord! how I study them— those four pages—& turn them into a volume" (*SP,* 141). On November 7, 1904, he makes a notation that reveals the influence of Elsie's writing on his emotions: "Last week was the first since Elsie and I began writing to one another that I have not had a letter from her. Everything hangs in suspense as a result. I say to myself that I am sure to hear from her in the morning

2. The Huntington also has two of Elsie's typed note cards from later letters that did not provide quotations for her "Book" of excerpts:

[1.] Packet No. 25. August 30th, 1915 [see WAS 1965 August 29, 1915]:
Saturday evening I spent at home, writing a little. I am quite blue about the flimsy little things I have done in the month or so you have been away. They seem so slight and unimportant, considering the time I have spent on them. Yet I am more interested than ever. I wish that I could give all my time to the thing, instead of a few hours each evening when I am often physically and mentally dull. It takes me so long to get the day out of my mind and to focus myself on what I am eager to do. It takes a great deal of thought to come to the points that concern me—and I am, at best, an erratic and inconsequential thinker. Wallace Stevens.

[2.] Packet No. 28. April 4th, 1926 [actually WAS 2047 February 28–March 1, 1931]:
Spring is an end of darkness and of ugliness and much more, it is a feeling of new life or of the activity of life returned, immense and fecund. In south Georgia, however, there never was much of the activity of powerful vitality and certainly there was never anything immense and fecund. . . . It is not a scene in which the visitor steeps his imagination.
W. Stevens.

and I convince myself that if I do not I shall feel abominably cut up; and no doubt I shall. I think I shall have to use the tactics approved of by the novelists— feigning indifference & the like. But then I'm going home for Thanksgiving which is only a short time away & I think my real feelings will explode all fake ones then. Our letters seem to have wrought changes. It will be like two new persons facing one another. Will it be two happy ones?" (*SP*, 143). Since they had known each other for some sixteen weeks by then, he had received fifteen letters from her and apparently had written many more than that to her. By March 5, 1905, he summarizes his daily life: "Work, concerts, letters from Elsie, books, jaunts around town— these are what I seem to live for" (*SP*, 144).

His letters to her took up the time he would have devoted to writing in his journal, and on April 10, 1905, he notes, "I fear that the habit of journalizing has left me" (*SP*, 144). On September 15, 1905, he writes, "No letter from Elsie for nine days. If I get none tomorrow, hanged if I'll be in haste to write again. This cannot be a caprice—too much is excused on that ground, anyhow" (*SP*, 154). On November 14, 1905, he reports "a month of bitter far niente" that included "writing and receiving love-letters" (*SP*, 154). On December 9, 1905, he says, in a fragment of a notation, something very similar to what he had said about his father after a long discussion of what he should do with his life: "She is quite right. Even reason aids her." But he goes beyond what he said about his father: "She touches all my subtle stops" (*SP*, 155).

Elsie's Book

{Page 1.}

Excerpts from letters of Wallace Stevens

from 1904

with this memorandum:—

In an answer to a sonnet written by Wallace Stevens while at Harvard University—in which he took the point of view of a man whose impulses to good found their source "say in Nature," George Santayana wrote: "the church is one's guide through the conflicting labyrinth of Nature and the inconsistencies of natural laws."[3]

3. In the *Harvard Monthly* 28, no. 3 (May 1899): 95, Stevens published the unsigned Italian sonnet with the first line "Cathedrals are not built along the sea." Santayana answered this sonnet with his "Answer to a Sonnet," which eventually was published in *A Hermit of Carmel and Other Poems.* Both Stevens's sonnet and Santayana's answering sonnet, in each author's handwriting, are laid in Stevens's copy of Santayana's *Hermit of Carmel* at HEH. Just before Stevens left Harvard for New York in 1900, as he writes in his hand in his copy of Santayana's *Lucifer,* he and Santayana discussed the matter a final time: "I said that the first suggestion of the organ-pipes [in Stevens's sonnet] came from

"Sentimental things are things to cherish—not to speak of."

"I mean to keep as busy as I can, so that in the end I shall have something to show for the trouble of keeping alive."

"A single tone of voice, a single color in the cheek, a single gentle act."

"not that you ought not to know things and people as they are, for you ought to—and the worst are only a very little from the best."

{2.}

"So long as the work is profita[b]le and leads to something, I love it. The desperate thing is to plod, to mark time, to stand still. This I cannot endure."

"I wanted to understand you, to give you confidence enough to make you reveal yourself."

"The truth of ourselves must guide us—or else we shall deceive each other horribly."

"The only brilliant things in life are friendship, self-denial, and similar evidences of civilization, as far as men are concerned."

"A world of our own—certain scenes with which we shall associate one another, certain mornings, certain afternoons, certain nights."

"I should like to make a music of my own, a literature of my own, and I should like to live my own life."

"Doves murmuring all day long."

"Few people have spirit enough to know when they're

{3.}

content. But Elsie does."

"The world is only a trap. It can hardly have caught you yet."

"We long ago passed into a world of our own, away from this one. I do not think you can fail to see why I write, or why I wait so impatiently to hear from you."

"Epistle of Saint Wallace to the Philistines, Chapter 1, verse 1: —A pearl is finer than a diamond, yet a rose is finer even than any pearl."

---

the wind. He said that the wind was then a stimulus—the organ-pipe—a result, etc. We both held our grounds. We smoked cigars, drank whisky etc until eleven when we broke up. I shall probably not see him again" (*SP,* 68–69).

"Still, you too, must be in sympathy with change, with restoration, or perhaps I should say restitution. I grow infinitely weary of accepting things, of taking things for granted and so on. I sicken of patterns, and trite symbols, and conventions and the lack of thought."

"One of my ideals is to make everything expressive, and thus true. I would like to get out of line."

{4.}

—"the family to whom I send bulletins in regard to my progress. They call it progress. It is really nonsense. Once one is born, one does not progress again until one dies. The rest is all a waste of valuable time—or so it seems."

"I believe that with a bucket of sand and a wishing lamp I could create a world in half a second that would make this one look like a hunk of mud."

"—for if two people ever sincerely care for each other, they will care always."

"Six months more or less ought not to be the extent of our good will. We cannot be so shallow or changeable as that."

"I like to think that I do not bring a jaded fancy, or a cunning hand into this Solitude of ours. It is as new to me as it is to you, and that is why, regarding it as a new world, its colors are still bright and its horizons still wonderful."

{5.}

"Perhaps I do like to be sentimental now and then in a roundabout way. There could be no surer sign of it than in my sending verses to you. I certainly do dislike expressing it right and left."

"I long for Solitude—not the Solitude of a few rooms, but the Solitude of Self. I want to know about myself, about my world, about my future when the world is ended."

"I feel as if I could begin to write all over again—it is almost self-communion with me."

"Heaven is home, and the world is, all in all, only a doll's house. But the Strong spoil most of the fun for the weak, and the Weak disgust or bore the Strong. There is only one good thing in it from the beginning to the end, and that is friendship."

"Think what a refuge affection is—from evil, from Selfishness, from helplessness, and from adversity."

{6}

"November 1st—All Saint's Day—the day for communion with the Spirits of "just men made perfect."[4]

"To be happy today, not to expect to be to-morrow."

"Conduct—mental conduct, moral conduct, social conduct—is everything, and one's self is nothing."

"The young man with his star, or the young woman with her dreams are not as happy as the man with his cow—and the woman with her knitting."

"If I were at your elbow, I should prompt you. I'd say "Tell him to keep himself straight-forward, and to work hard.""

"I could imagine how anxiously you watched the time go by, expecting my step.["] "It made me quite wretched."

"— and that we must now consider how to be loyal and serviceable to one another."

{7} [1905]
"But in a book I escape realities."

"—for there is no merit in our virtues except out of our wish for them."

"It seems insincere, like playing a part, to be one person on paper and another in reality. But I know that it is only because I command myself there."

"You said sometime ago that you did not believe that one lived for a single friend alone. But I do not think so. There is a part of one's self that only one other can share; and one lives most for that other, cherishing him, and desiring for him all good things and all pure things. That desire is nothing more than loving."

Package No. 4:

"Let us have faith together in the maxim that there is no good thing to be had without effort—without pain."

4. From the Epistle of Paul to the Hebrews 12:23. All of Stevens's biblical references are from the King James version of the Bible.

{8}

About T. Hardy's books: "If you should come to regard him as not as interesting as he might be, read his "Under the Greenwood Tree" before you give him the sack. It is pleasantness itself."[5]

"How inseparable Memory would make us!"

"—and I should wish you to be as wise as you are good."

"Are you really fond of books—paper valleys and far countries, paper gardens, paper men and paper women? They are all I have, except you; and I live with them constantly."

"intoxicated with language"

"Sometimes it seemed to me as if I were the only person who really knew you."

"I shall always have an answer to gossip."

"You have too good a defense against gossip in your own nature."

{9} [1906]

"I trust you, and I have trusted you always—from the beginning, because you understand instinctively that conduct, good or bad, is the source of happiness or unhappiness."

"Peace is what you want, not pleasure; and peace is a matter of Conduct."

"The music you desire, I think, is the music that takes the spirit away from its surroundings and ministers to it. Many simple things will do that—songs in particular."

"To practice an art, to need it and to love it, is the quickest way of learning that all happiness lies in one's self, as Omar[6] says it does."

"I know that you judge me not from what you read in my letters, but from what you feel from them."

---

5. In his journal for December 31, 1905, Stevens records his reading of Hardy's "Trumpet-Major."

6. This casual form of reference to the central voice of the *Rubáiyát of Omar Khayyám* (Fitzgerald translation of 1859) was used (and explicitly defended) by Fitzgerald throughout his introduction and notes, and it thus became common at this time; one of Stevens's favorite poets of the time, Bliss Carman, refers to "Omar" four times in the three Vagabondia volumes.

"I thought today that our letters were like some strange instrument full of delicate and enduring music—music just a little haunting, on which we played for each other[7]

{10}

in turn."

"Let us both hope that I have the strength to be earnest—not earnest for a day or two, but always."

"We have turned a whole Country into a home and had sunsets for hearths, and evening stars for lamps."

"Ointment and perfume rejoice the heart; so doth the sweetness of a man's friendly counsel."[8]

"Life seems glorious for a while, then it seems poisonous. But you must never lose faith in it, it is glorious after all. Only you must find the glory for yourself. Do not look for it either, except in yourself; in the Secret places of your spirit and in all your hidden senses."

"There is a new moon in the evening sky—it nourishes beauty and the desire for beauty; but you must go to it with a pure heart, with a passion for it—else it does not exist." Look for

{11}

it. Then the glory will come back. And so with many things, in Nature and in men and women. Never give up."

"It will be part of a secret world far dearer than you and I could ever create, however much we might love each other."

"Whoso keepeth the fig tree shall eat the fruit thereof; so he that waiteth on his master shall be honored."[9]

"As in water face answereth to face, so the heart of man to man."[10]

7. This excerpt is very similar to a journal entry Stevens made some time in the summer of 1906: "It struck me that our letters were like an instrument full of delicate & enduring music—music just a little haunting" (SP, 168).

8. Proverbs 27:9 reads, "Ointment and perfume rejoice the heart: so doth the sweetness of a man's friend by hearty counsel."

9. Proverbs 27:18.

10. Proverbs 27:19. This proverb is also given in SP, 169, in an entry just prior to July 22, 1906.

"We have proof of that in ourselves; for if you and I had not answered each other—"

"Music is not life—it is only one of the needs of life. Have the courage for all of life—for disappointment, for sorrow even—but all of it, good and evil."

"Love is a burden, like anything else; but a burden not to be cast off, but to be carried gladly."

{12}

"Love is not love which alters when it alteration finds."[11] "I abominate quotations; but that is one we need."

"We cannot count it adversity, when we feel sure of each other's loyalty, not only when we cannot help it, but always—and when we need it."

"A man wants the woman he loves to have true things and beautiful things. He doesn't want her to know what a jack-a-knapes he is, because if she loves him too, it will be like taking her behind the scenes when she discovers it."

"Perhaps love is not so much adoration as understanding and being faithful nevertheless."

"I should come to you clapping my hands, because you have made me feel so much the lover."

{13}

—"for already you act the woman's part when you give comfort, and that is just what you do now."

Package No 5.

"This is our story, I hope—all there is of it."

"Men and women may always be kind."

"—writing to you is like whispering to you."

"Something speaks for us and it is all music like an air from the joyous isles. How often we have listened to it together!"

"—for we are not studying each other in other people's books, but in ourselves. We are far better authorities."

---

11. Sonnet 116 by Shakespeare.

"I want you so much to <u>desire</u> to be good. That is the main thing. I don't mean religious or priggish—but kind, patient, unselfish. To be good, that's just what I want to be more than anything else."

{14}

"—makes me want to stand between you and everyone else[.] — I want to be the only person who knows what you really like and think and are. Then you would be my Elsie in reality, and alone."

"It is my way of trying to make a world of our own, a place for us to dwell in: our first house."

"But I want you to feel that when it is over you will go home with me and be glad of it. Oh, more than all the rest, I want you to be glad of it."

"—say to myself quietly "She loves me, Elsie loves me." It is a kind of thanksgiving. I never wanted you to love me just to have you love me; but because I love you."

"I realize that I have a second self in you[.] — When I shake off sentiment, you are still my Elsie; and that is as sweet and as welcome to me as the other mood."

{15}

"Now it really isn't polite in us to wonder what will happen when our castles fall. They never may. But if they do, you will still be with me, won't you?"

"The top of a house in the suburbs is about a[s] comfortless a place as there is in the world. It is part of my probation, however, and I shall have to think of it as amusing."[12]

(In October 1906 Wallace made up his mind to come to see me in Reading every month.)

"—conscious that the sounds beat on last memories that just fail of coming to the surface" (on seeing a Shakespeare play, or listening to a spinet or a lute.)

"If I consider <u>that</u> being worthy, don't you think you are worthy already? What makes one worthy is goodness and kindness."

"Be good to yourself; be kind to others—but be kindest of all to me."

12. This reference to the suburbs might date from the time he lived at two different addresses on Halsted Street in East Orange, New Jersey, the second half of 1905 and possibly through early September 1906.

{16.}

"Surely nothing could be kinder than to be content—and we are content."
"Kindness is death to tragedy and all the elements of tragedy."

Read letter dated November 1, in package No 5—read it often.[13]

"—and have you playing with my watch-chain and eyelids and buttons."

"You are infinitely more a part of me than my family, or than any friend I have ever had. So that you <u>must</u> be constant."

"Aren't we happiest of all when we identify ourselves so that we live and think for each other? You are all that I have. If I could say to myself "Elsie[14] will stand by me always.""

"Yet one enjoys the kindness of it."

{17.}

Package No 6.

"If I love thee, I am thine;
But if I love thee not,
Or but a little—let the sun still shine
On palaces forgot.

For me; be thou no more
Attendant on my way.
My welcome one will not, like thee, implore
No never! He will play

Brave dulcimers and sing
In darkness, not repine;
And I shall leave all the dreams and closer cling
And whisper, "I am thine.""
"for my collection of "Songs for Elsie.""[15]

13. This is the first of five letters in these excerpts singled out for this or a similar comment. The year for this letter is 1906.
14. This word is partly written over and obscured.
15. This poem is the only evidence of this "collection"; it recalls Stevens's "Song" ("She loves me or loves me not") in the *Harvard Advocate* 67, no. 2 (March 13, 1899): 150:

> She loves me or loves me not,
> What care I?—

"You and I can have each other—if we must desire, do not let us desire other men and women, but—pictures and chateaus and honors and other desirable but unnecessary things."

"Sleigh-bells! That's a welcome chord coming out of confusion. Elsie! That's another—my little girl. Clear air—all good elements."

{18.}

"My thoughts just drifted so; but now, as at the end of our evenings at home, they flock about you. Leaving you, or finishing a letter to you, is always like lifting sail in the only haven one has ever known, and departing."

"Good-night Elsie. That is like a call to me. It calls you to me."

"Don't you like the idea of people who give up everything wildly, as Sylvia and Hilton did? Instead of hanging on to dreary safety, they take a tremendous fling. That seems to be the New York idea. I'm glad some people do it though I shouldn't do it myself—nor recommend it."

"The right side of my face throbs with a new tooth. You must forgive me, therefore, if I am a little derelict in my letters."

"Perhaps I am not always a greenwood sort of fellow. After all I'm not one thing or another, but this thing today, and that, tomorrow."

{19.} [1906]

"Respect breeds respect, desire breeds desire, affection breeds affection, goodness breeds goodness."

"—picture of an old man, still strong, full of patience, a man who knows Life and has beaten the devil."

"We shall always be what we are now, —perhaps not to each other, but to ourselves."

"If you had asked me for the deepest pit we could dig for ourselves I should have said that it was: feeling free to do as we like."

The depth of the fields is just as sweet,
And sweet the sky.
She loves me or loves me not,
Is that to die?—
The green of the woods is just as fair,
And fair the sky.

1907: "I know perfectly well that to live in town would be a cruel disillusion to you."

"Surely, I am falling into bad habits when I go about peeping into forbidden doors, and tomorrow, and all tomorrows are forbidden doors."

"I'd like something that couldn't be bought."

{20} [1907]

"I wish no one knew about us. That would make it infinitely sweeter."

"It is painful to me to think that you fear I am criticizing you. And why should you not satisfy me? If there were anything to criticize, I hope you would find me true enough to defend you, rather than criticize you. My criticizms are only grotesque amusement to me. —They are instinct, no more."

"Tonight I took dinner down town. There were twelve people—four of them girls not much older than you. They played and sang and were pretty and had pretty manners. They were all rich, I suppose, and they will all be sought for. They satisfied me in the way you mean; but they are not different from you. They have only had a great deal more experience. At heart each one of them is as simple and personal as you."[16]

"Let us be ourselves and not study contrasts."

{21}

"—but sometimes when I am in a haughty humor the parable of the sower that sowed on barren ground repeats itself to me, and in my gorgeous pride I cease to sow. But one seed must have fallen on good ground for your last letter was like good fruit in a wilderness."[17]

"Let us be humble with each other. We have nothing to quarrel about and we can live our own lives in our own way—you and I."

"Drone, dove, that rounded woe again
　　When I bring her tomorrow.
The wood were less a happy place,
　　But for that broken sorrow.

Tell her in undertones that youth
　　With other times must recon [*sic*]:

---

16. She does not skip lines between these excerpts separated by the paragraph break, perhaps suggesting that they are from the same letter.
17. This parable is given in Matthew 13, Mark 4, and Luke 8.

That mist seals up the golden sun,
    And ghosts from gardens beckon."[18]

"An old song: but that is the way Wallace sang it for Elsie. Have I sent it to you before? I think not."

{22.}

"What interests me is your thoughts and your feelings—to know that I possess them a little and that you are glad of it."

"Critics are busybodies and you and I are quite capable of minding our own affairs."

"Facts are like flies in a room. They buzz and buzz and bother."

"It was written when you would not let know that you cared. The first verse amounted to this: That it was unnecessary for you to tell me, and then the last verse ran:
    For muter to my muter call
      Come magic means;
    Now the enchanting measures fall—
      A spirit intervenes."[19]

Package No 7.

"To be alone is, for me, to be happy."

{23.}

"Unless I like a person, I see all his faults and none of his merits. It is the other way when I like him. Such a person does not make many friends."

"I should not like luxury, but I do desire freedom from pinching, and I'm sure that will come in time. I should like to live easily, without thinking of ways and means."

"My thoughts are my heart."

"—I am not in the least religious. The sun clears my spirit, if I may say that, and an occasional sight of the sea, and thinking of blue valleys, and the odor of

18. This is poem XIII, "Adagio," in the "Book of Verses" presented to Elsie on her twenty-second birthday, June 5, 1908 (*SP*, 194).

19. This is the second stanza of poem XV, "Damask," in his 1908 "Book of Verses" for Elsie (*SP*, 194–95). There the beginning the first of these lines is correctly given as "For mutely to my muter call." See the complete text below after the last of "Elsie's Excerpts."

the earth. Such things make a God of a man; but a chapel makes a man of him. Churches are human."[20]

"Judge me by yourself: we are too much alike for that test to fail. We could not be more alike if we were brother and sister."

{24}

"Just to have written last night was like recovering a part of myself that had been lost for a little. Do you realize how much a part of each other we have become?"[21]

"Each time we get a hair's breadth apart, we come closer together than ever before; and so it may be that your occasional defiances are only tricks that Nature plays on us—and so with my mistakes."[22]

Package No 8.

"Earth and the body and the spirit seem to change together."[23]
"Every Spring I have a month of so of semi-blackness—perhaps, a revulsion against old things—habits, people, places—everything."[24]

(Read letter dated March 22, 1907 often.
(Read letter dated March 25, 1907 often.[25])

{25.}

"—and I wondered how to tell you of it so exactly that you would know what I meant."[26]

"—the little wilderness all my own, shared with nobody, not even with you—it made me myself. It was friendly, so much deeper than anything else could be."[27]

---

20. Starting with "My thoughts are my heart," all of this material is from WAS 1777 March 10, 1907. This is the first excerpt from an extant letter; others will be identified by WAS number and date.
21. WAS 1780 March 18, 1907 contains this excerpt; in the second sentence Elsie replaces the pronoun "we" with "you."
22. WAS 1780 March 18, 1907.
23. WAS 1783 March 21, 1907.
24. WAS 1783 March 21, 1907. She has left out a number of words in this passage.
25. There are no extant letters of these dates, but it is likely that she is referring to the letters dated here as March 21 and March 24, since their postmarks are for March 22 and March 25.
26. WAS 1784 March 24, 1907, published in *LWS,* 99.
27. WAS 1784 March 24, 1907. The comma after "friendly" was added by Elsie.

"You know that in every essential I am your own."

"One can walk in a wood, dim and full of music; and one can walk on a road dusty and bare. Long ago you and I chose the wood and lost ourselves in it."

"When she to time has paid her due,
May I still be her mirror true."[28]

"It is only one's thoughts that fill a room with something more than furniture."[29]

"We are in a strange situation, understanding so well, saying so little."[30]

{26.}

"You have a strong, vigorous and <u>cheerful</u> disposition, and that is an immense advantage. The aid and stimulus of that disposition is one of the things you have to give, one of the things you wondered about. Then you like to enjoy yourself. Thank Heaven!"

"Soon we shall be actual people."

"I want to be a new person, a person separate from my tedious self, for you. I want your mere name to be a motive to me. I want to give you the last bit of good that is in me—whatever it may be: love you and never scold."

"Please, Elsie, learn to swim. This is one of the most important things you can do. I used to have an intense fear of water, because I had several adventures that taught me how helpless I was in it, then I took lessons and kept at them until I could swim."

"We'll both put our boquets there to ornament it."

{27.}

"Whatever binds us to each other is magic. Otherwise you could not possibly love me, if you knew me. What is there in me to love? What is there in any one to love?"

"But of two lives, I should rather live the life of the bee, than the life of the ant; and so would you."

"Pity me that I am so shallow in gratitude."

28. WAS 1773 April 12, 1907 (not a letter but a separate poem in an envelope).
29. WAS 1790 April 16, 1907.
30. WAS 1789 April 14, 1907.

Oct. 4, 1907: — "I have determined to go ahead without the rum-bowl for a year—and probably always. The thing has never had any hold on me—it is a mistake to trifle with it."[31]

"The stenography too is not so bad.[32] —The main thing is not to get into idle habits."

"On the whole, I think we should not live too much in villages, after all— but live there most; and include cities in one's life, as one includes great ideas, great feelings, great deeds: that is from time to time."

{28.}

"You are an excellent walker and I think that a walk is better, almost, than sleep—and sleep, you know, is the great medicine."

"The last days of Summer are too precious to waste. September sunlight is a very special kind of sunlight. Sit in it if you can and see. It gets into the body like a fine spirit. The warmth is purely planetary. Its whole effect is un-earthly."

"Last night was my last night at Mrs. Jackson's[33] and tonight I sleep in a new bed. After paying all my debt to her I find myself with exactly a quarter. But somehow I do not care; and I speak of it so that you may laugh at it too."

"Well here's news: I'm determined to go ahead without the rum-bool for a year—and probably always. I continue not to smoke but without making any resolution about it. It is an evil. All this self-control will make me a regular Roundhead—an old maid."

31. This resolution is repeated on the next page of the excerpts, with the spelling "rum-bool"; both of these spellings may refer to "rumbo," defined in the *Oxford English Dictionary* as "a kind of strong punch, made chiefly of rum." In his journal for April 12, 1907, Stevens had written, "I have caroused. Not wildly—yet my nerves are absolutely at rest. It is only ten o'clock—a walk, four glasses of [here the word "whiskey" has been crossed out] rum! ["rum" has been underlined twice], three cigars" (*SP*, 145). Elsie's opposition to drinking anything alcoholic was a long-term point of contention in this relationship.
32. 1907 was the first of the three consecutive years that Elsie was listed as a stenographer in Reading's city directory.
33. The last clear reference to Stevens's living at this address occurs in WAS 1791 for April 19, 1907. However, a letter from his father (WAS 2165 Nov 17 [1907; year from envelope]) suggests that Stevens may have remained at Sedgwick Avenue until he took his "temporary 'situation'" with the law firm of Eustis and Foster in early November 1907: "Dear Wallace: Glad to hear from you and to have your new address."

{29}

Package No 9.

"You say I should take advice. One's life is one's own—or isn't it? Advice is thoughtless, it is chiefly criticism, well-mannered scolding. You must sympathize with me and be loyal in all your feelings."

"Don't let my spirit affect you, except for good, so far as it can."

"Let us say we are poor—<u>never</u> wretched."

"Another leaf on our green Tree, already so full of them, and so full of songs and little murmuring sounds. Master W. S. wants to climb up into that tree tonight, and loaf there, in the boughs—and listen and dream."

"And so when summer came, they went in a boat to [a] quiet island, and on the way, Pierrot pulled out a newspaper and read to Columbine a little news of the stupid world from which he was taking her. But Columbine didn't think

{30}

it stupid. So Pierrot turned the boat around, and they drifted back to town. Yet even while they were drifting, Columbine thought of the quiet island and she knew that Pierrot was thinking of it too."

(Commenting about a girl in Reading) "How little able she is, either by art or nature, to be the companion of any one, except the clods who are her present friends."

"We are content to think about unimportant things. It is useless to think about the important ones. We'll let the masters do that for us."

"Luxury is nothing to me—comfort is everything; show is nothing—quiet everything."

"Kindness, loyalty, love, honor, self-sacrifice—these are the things. Elsie and I must seek what is within our reach, no more."

"We'll make a dull world pretty for ourselves."

{31.}

"Lastly, dear sister, you may be sure that I shall be home for Christmas—and I shall have a present for you. <u>Please</u> have one for me."

"I would rather write to you than sleep."

"I want to set you an example (so holy I am) of writing after hours."

"Good hope, good will! May we have our reward bye and bye."

"I've been writing some verses to put in the first "Vagabondia" book. Here they are:

I

"For me, these little books contain,
(As if, like flowers, we put them here.)
Three odorous summers of delight,
(With withered leaves of day and night.[)]

II

These poets [*sic*] Vagabondian airs,
Recall how many of our own,
That sang themselves, without a rhyme
To stirrings of some sweet chime.

{32}

III

Our oriole sings, our wild-rose blooms,
Our azure river shines again,
Our moon returns. Dear Elsie, hark!
Once more we whisper in the dark."[34]

"What else have we to get and keep except each other's love?"

"We have only ourselves—and that is a very great deal—the most important thing in our lives."

34. Holly Stevens points out that these verses appear (under the title "To Elsie, Xmas, 1907, From a Vagabond") in Stevens's handwriting on the flyleaf of *Songs from Vagabondia* by Bliss Carman and Richard Hovey (*SP*, 186). She also says that *More Songs from Vagabondia* has the following undated inscription in Stevens's hand:

> With a heart of one's own,
> In a world of one's own,
> Clinging, or loath to cling,
> Why should one cease to sing? (*SP*, 187)

Holly further points out, "The third volume in the series, *Last Songs form Vagabondia*, bears the following in my father's hand on its flyleaf:

> Night stopped them here,
> One singer fell,
> Dark Vagabondia
> Lost her spell. (ibid.)

"The difficulty of using the word "love" or "dear" arose from a delicacy which, I am sure, neither of us would wish to feel had been lost. It has not been lost. We must treasure those words, don't you think? I mean the word "love" more than any other." — "my feelings are deep, and you are so truly dear to me."

"I am a man, after all, not a beau."

{33.}

"Politeness is the cure to subjection to moods—a desire to please others by anticipating their wants and wishes and studiously avoiding whatever might give them pain."

"Politeness is superior to moods, as it is to circumstances, and, indeed that being superior is the first condition of politeness.—"

Read letter dated Jan. 6, 1908 often.[35] [1908]

"—if all the machinery of Life could stop, —if people could lay by their work, and rest, and think, and recover all their lost ideals, they would all return quite simply to fundamental things—honesty, politeness, unselfishness, and so on—hiding in oblivion all the distortions that influence them now. Let the two of us always rely on those fundamental things."

"What all the world agrees is good, pure, and the like, is so, in the long run, and is the only law we have, and the only comfort."

{34} [1908]

"I have always one ally at home—Lady Nature, whose children we are, both of us, so completely."

"Do you know what I would do, if the world were made of wishes? I'd lock you up—in a large enough place, to be sure; a whole valley as big as a country, maybe—and I'd allow only the most unexceptionable people to come there."

"But here's Reality—what harm, when all is said and done, has it ever done you? You have always had your own path to find and certainly you have found it. It seems to have led you away, when the time came, from every peril, and I trust it, and you."

---

35. The only extant letters of 1908 are those from December of that year, as Stevens was preparing to bring the engagement ring to Elsie at the time of the Christmas vacation. For all of 1908, Stevens's journal has only three entries: January 2, January 5, and August 17, 1908. All three are brief, the first two dealing primarily with Stevens's visit to Reading for Christmas and New Year and the last simply stating that he has been working for the American Bonding Company of Baltimore since January 13, 1908.

"The blessedness of being quiet."

"It would only be proper for you to have your own private book of verses,[36] even if it were very small and if the verses were very bad."

{35.}

"So I write, calling you sweetheart, and again calling you darling—out of my heart. I do not want to feel that those words are lost to us."

"Night is a symbol of death. When one of the poets died Vagabondia lost its spell.[37] So much of which was in the [verses] were [*sic*] comradeship."

"Get Charles Lamb's essay called "Old China" and others—for the sweet temper of them."

"Look up John Burroughs. His pages are summer days, or like them.[']"

"Read Thoreau's "Week on the Concord and Merrimac Rivers"—and his "Walden.""

Package No 10.

"I would rather sit here, with this button, these letters and the thoughts of you, than dine at all the queer places between the Hudson and the Yang-sti-Kiang.[38] Give me something sweet and clean. It is so little to ask. I mean to have it."

{36.}

"Peace shall play the viol for us, and Quiet her small lute."

"Even if I did not know you, I should always find myself in what you are. I should be dreaming of some such—Elsie."

36. Though he has mentioned other collections of poems for her, this is Stevens's first mention (using the eventual title) of what is the first of the two surviving "books" of poems he wrote for her.

37. Richard Hovey, the coauthor with Bliss Carman of the three volumes of *Songs from Vagabondia,* died in 1900. Stevens's four-line verse tribute, in his own hand, is in the 1905 edition of this work, which is still in Stevens's library at the Huntington:

> Night stopped them here,
> One singer fell,
> Dark vagabondia
> Lost her spell. (*SP,* 187)

38. The name of the longest river in China is given in a number of different ways: Yangtze River (river of the Yang village, a British name), Ch'ang Chiang (long river), Ta Chiang (great river), and Chin Sha Chiang (river of golden sand).

"—The great trouble is to keep from being buried in work. It gives one a chance to "shine in use."[39] That remains to be seen."

(1908) "Try to stay home from now on. This summer we can tell your mother. You have so little a practical idea, or I think you have, of what home is. Goodnight my little girl."

"Our letters have told us more about each other than we could have learned otherwise. I shall always know how, back of one Elsie, there is another—and you will know all the Wallaces."

"Which is the more important—that in some little thing I have vexed you, or that I desire so much to please you?"

{37.}

"Love exaggerates the good in people."

"A good opinion is more valuable than rubies—and I will purchase your good opinion at any cost."[40]

"We are like spiders spinning an immense web (in our letters) that glistens sometimes and sometimes is all pitiful confusion. —However, it glistens again now, and I am only eager to forget the snarl."

"Back of all I say and do is the one desire that you should find in me, when you think of me, things to like."

"The fact is, most people are a great nuisance, and my own disposition is not remarkably lenient in such things. Perhaps that is why my own likes are more often for things than for people; because of intolerance."[41]

"My society has always been an airy thing, not of men and women; books,

{38.}

music, quiet places, ye blue bird, ye country garden, quiet Elsie."

"But since you call me knightly, my armor seems bright again."

"This is to be only a note—so small a celebrity must not come with too great a flourishing of trumpets." (Written just before a visit to Reading.)

---

39. Phrase from Tennyson's "Ulysses."

40. Twice in Proverbs (3:15 and 8:11) wisdom is said to be more precious than rubies.

41. This sentiment is similar to one Stevens expresses in one of the Adagia: "Life is an affair of people not of places. But for me life is an affair of places and that is the trouble" (*OP*, 185).

"Elsie is my glory."

"Shall I take off my purple and say, "I am what I am." —No I'll stand up in the purple you give me and say "I am what it pleases my Good Angel to make you think me.""

—"till I reach for my purple, and hide her in it"

"—little words, tricking me, tricking her, —what are you but little creeping shadows, little thieves, after all."

{39}

"I acknowledge how good it is in me to love you with all your faults. When I read one of your letters and come to the end smiling in spite of myself, I say, "How kind it is of me to like that so much!" Or when I see you and hear you, I say, "How nice it is of me to feel this way! How polite it is of my blood to do that! What pretty manners my heart has! It is all very remarkable."

"I don't believe in holding up the microscope to one's self, or to you, or to my friends, —but only to the dolts and others whom I dislike."

"Don't be too conscientious. I must have Elsie young and sweet and full of courage."

Letter dated March 9, 1908. Too bad! Too bad![42] I am ashamed.

"—writing to my Sylvia in the dead of night."

{40}

"Some power to make you love
The poor thing that I am, forgetfully
    If I were king."

"The truth is, I cannot endure friends whom I do not choose for myself, uncharitable beast that I am! But isn't it a sweet thing to have things one's own way— quiet, clean, whimsical?["]

"Trusting each other is the strength of us; and that too we must respect without failure. We must be able to say "Here we two stand together, and all that one is, the other is."

"I should rather have your letter than the sun every morning. It is true, it is true, it is true—but you won't believe it."

---

42. These exclamations are written directly above "I am ashamed." All of these words are Elsie's.

"In a little while, when it is warmer, they" (robins) "will warble at twilight with their red breasts turned toward the sunset. Does Elsie know that enchantment?"

{41}

"All of us want to express our moods: to be frank. It is not a brave or spirited thing to do. Silence is the better part. It is nothing to assert one's self."

"One's self is nothing—except in pleasing."

April 10, 1908
"Quick, Time, go by and let me to an end.
To-morrow, oh to-morrow! But today,
Poor draggling fag,—insipid, still delay,
Flat drudge. Now let my feeble earth descend
To violent night and there remend
Her strength, not for a dream's affray
But 'gainst slow death. Then up the sounding way
Where vivid reaches of new blue attend.

And many shadows of the whirling sun
To greet her exultation thunderously!
Let me be first of living men to throw
The weight of life aside, and there outrun
Even the magic light—so swift to know
Some passionate fate accomplished wondrously."[43]

{42.}

April 23, 1908
"Am I falling in love with you in some new way, from some new point of view? What a complication of motives!"

"Good-night, my dearest Lady—Lady Little Girl"

"Let there be a shower of grace because I want to sing for Elsie once more—be her Captain, King and Knight-At-Arms."

"I am so tired of holly sprays
And weary of the bright box-tree
Of all the endless country ways;
Of everything alas! save thee."[44]

43. This sonnet, not in any of the standard sources, including the Chadwyck-Healey English and American poetry databases, is possibly by Stevens.
44. From Ernest Dowson's "Spleen," which is the third of four poems under the general title "After Paul Verlaine."

"We two—Elsie and Wallace—I could not explain it if I wrote and thought all night. You are so much a part of myself. It is as if we were the same person, only that you are the brighter part."

{43}

"That elevated train, coming home with its negroes and cheap people! Dearest keep me from seeing all that. It is nonsense but it wrecks me. —It is a hideous, foolish, maddening world, and you are my only escape from it."

"Take possession of me, fill my mind, my thoughts—if you love me, it will be so easy, if you do not, so hard."

"I will sing for you, with the first bird you hear, and what he sings will be my song. I shall not be the mortal thing you think me, but that sudden warmth in your own heart."

"And when I kiss you, I shall lose all my thoughts—everything—just in kissing you."

"I do not get on well with my equals, not at all with my superiors. Ergo, I have no friends."

{44}

"Columbine and Pierrot. How aptly those two evanescent characters symbolize, in some aspects, ourselves![")

"It is such a blunder to call the main thing in you goodness. It is not that at all, but rather-delicateness. Certainly goodness would be very little alone. Perhaps it is both together."

"The idea of neat, clean, sweet contented poverty—I confess that seems one of the best things in the world."

"Write to me often and irregularly. If I may not have a letter every day, let me at least have the possibility."

"—an odd play that I have just finished. The best thing in it was the names of the women. I like Selysette and Bellangere most" —not as whisperable as Sylvia—nor as tinkling as Elsie."[45]

---

45. Maeterlinck wrote *Aglavaine and Selysette;* another play by him, *The Death of Tintag-iles,* contains a character named Bellangère; both plays were available in English translation in 1899.

{45}

"I have found another name for you—Isolde. Elsie <u>must</u> be a form of that old name.

Elsie, Ilsa, Ilsolde—Isolde. Sylvia—Yseult—to embrace so many famous histories in your name alone."[46]

"I have become an intense Arnoldian" (Matthew Arnold)— "You will recall his diary. Let me open it now and copy the first thing I see—

"The happiness of your life depends upon the quality of your thoughts; therefore guard accordingly. M. Aurelius." Good Emperor, I thank you."[47]

"—and to be poor, so long as you can be as rich as the richest, in having leisure and the feeling of home, is no deprivation. My earnest wish is that you remain at home, and do just what you are doing now."

"I was wishing for a wise shepherd for both of us."

"—a shepherd more human than Nature—some innocent and true Confessor, some vigorous and consoling guide to whom we could be gladly obedient, finding in such obedience irresistable

{46}

sustenance and consolation."

"Good-night, dear, good, happy girl."

"In all the world, I am the only man awake. The Quiet says: "Come, be part of me."

"but you will tame my savagery."

"It is useful to understand such men" (great men) as we understand other men[.] —Their works are distinct from them. There is no more reason for blinking at them in awe—at Keats for his poetry—than there is for blinking at a rose-bush for its rose. The poetry emanates mysteriously from some mysterious origin through Keats as, say, the rose emanates mysteriously from some mysterious origin through the rose-bush. It is all a delightful chemistry, to put it so."

---

46. The subject of naming is one of great importance to Stevens, both in this correspondence and in his life as a whole. It will become of intense interest to him in 1909 as he tries to get Elsie to invent "a name of one syllable only" (WAS 1802 January 7, 1909), a "knock-about-the-country name" that would contrast with their "polite names" (WAS 1804 January 12, 1909).

47. The respect for Matthew Arnold will remain for most, but not all, of Stevens's life, and this resort to sortes reveals his often-expressed love of maxims.

"The vital thing is that <u>Elsie</u> should be jaunty—well, happy, and think it a happy world, and never be sorry for anything—and now and then make dunce-caps for her lord. (I am, I am, I am.)["]

{47}

"I have been away from home for eleven years, half <u>your</u> life.[48] Yet it remains the only familiar spot in the world. My little sleepless trips home every little while do not get me in touch. I do not feel the strength of the place under me to sustain."

"Life is a very, very thin affair except for the feelings; and the feelings of home waters the richest garden of all—the freshest and sweetest." ["]Endure much for that."

"We all, men and women, want so much more affection than we get, from those around us. That, for example, is why my world centers about you— because you show me affection."
"—because I cannot help showing my affection—and LaRue,[49] because she shows hers."

"The deep center, of which you know, is under seal—except between two. It is the strange Law."

{48.}
"The house fronts flare
In the blown rain;
The ghostly street lamps
Have a pallid glare.

A bent figure beats,
With bitter droop,
Along the waste
Of vacant streets.

Suppose some glimmering
Recalled for him,
An odorous room—
A fan's fleet shimmering.

48. This reference indicates that this excerpt is from 1908.
49. Dorothy LaRue Moll (October 13,1902–September 30, 1973), Elsie's half-sister, later Mrs. Earl W. Weidner, will live her entire life in Reading and will eventually be Elsie's principal correspondent, after Stevens himself and her mother.

Of silvery spangle—
Two startled eyes—
A still trembling hand
With its only bangle."

"That is to be in my second "Book" for you, which you will not see for a year—or almost—on your next birthday.[50] But that's a secret."

{49}

"—It has become necessary to have you near, or to hear from you constantly. This is not only because I love you, but because you are, in such innumerable ways, my second self."

"In an essay on Octave Feuillet, some interesting notes on romance—and hence on you and me. "Romance is the taste for the extraordinary. It is imagination in revolt against reason." —"the souls a prey to its influence are perpetually unsatisfied and disconsolate."

"Adieu, dear Elsie (flippantly)—good-night (in plain song!)["]

"You must not let yourself think that I am all virtue, and you all mischief. We are both alike[.]— We can flippantly say to St. Peter that what we are not, we hope to become."

"Then I read that mystics have pointed skulls, that man raises himself above the earth by two wings: purity and simplicity."[51]

{50.}

"They have this drawback." (books): "They occupy your mind to such an extent that your mind ceases to be your own. But for a while, why not?"

"Columbine is (historically) the flower of youth and beauty. Pierrot was "pale, slender, dressed in white clothes, always hungry and always being beaten—the ancient slave, the modern member of the mob, the parriah, the creature, passive and disinterested who assists, gloomy and malign, at the orgies and frolics of his masters." "That was all changed. Pierrot powdered his face with flour.

---

50. Under the word "birthday" Elsie has written "(23rd)," which would make it 1908, but it is not in either of the collections of poems Stevens presented to Elsie. A somewhat different version of this poem, printed as "Chiaroscuro" in *OP* (rev. ed., p. 3), is based on a separate holograph manuscript (WAS 4120) at the HEH.
51. The second of these two noun clauses is the first sentence of part 2, section 4 of Thomas à Kempis's *Imitation of Christ*.

He wore many disguises. As a marquis, "all in white satin"—made love to Columbine in other people's clothes, kissed her, "grew drunk with glory."

"The plain truth is, no doubt, that I like to be anything but my plain self; and when I write a letter that does not satisfy me—why it seems like showing my plain self, too plainly."[52]

"To bring me back my pride—and to solace

{51}

me I tell you that:
    What I aspired to be
    And was not, comforts me."[53]

Package No 13.

"All the orchards are white—it is fantastic. Somehow, amid so many blooms, one longs for dark woods, rain, iron capes. There is a great white cherry tree just outside my window."[54]

Nov. 20, 1908 (About a diamond engagement ring for me)
"I shall not tell you, since it is unnecessary, that I should like to come in a week or two. The truth is, my dear, that I want to get you something for Christmas (it is no very great secret) which requires a considerable degree of modesty in the mean-time. Don't you think that we can deny ourselves this trip to make the one at Christmas all the better?"

"—But you are my "big tall girl" now, aren't you, and tall girls, you know don't bother tremendously about peace and dignity."

{52.}

"After dinner, Walter[55] came. We both felt like cocking our feet on the bureau and sitting still. Therefore, we went out." —"dashing through the upper East

---

52. This sentiment obviously informs Stevens's ars poetica.

53. This quotation from Browning's "Rabbi Ben Ezra" is also in Stevens's journal for May 14, 1909 (*SP*, 220) and is paraphrased by Stevens in his speech accepting the National Book Award for his *Collected Poems* on January 25, 1955 (*OP*, 289).

54. WAS 1843 May 9, 1909. Elsie is quoting Stevens, who is quoting from his journal for April 29, 1909, a passage that is no longer extant in the journals, as Holly points out in *LWS*, 142 n 5.

55. Walter Butler. In *SP*, Holly Stevens explains, "Walter had been a close friend of my father's from the time they first met, *ca.* 1905, when the Butler family lived in East Orange, New Jersey, not far from where my father lived" (202). She points out that he is eleven years younger than Stevens, and so he must have been born about 1890 and was thus eighteen at the time of this letter, fifteen at the time of their meeting.

side to the Park, around the Reservoir in quick time, then through the Park to Fifty-Ninth Street running part of the way. We ran from fifty-sixth to Forty-Second Street and from Thirty-fourth to Twenty-Third and from Eighteenth to Eleventh street. Well a cold bath and a brisk rub set me to rights. At tea I ate practically everything on the table."

"While I want to see you more often, yet I am not afraid that enforced separation temporarily can change us, as long as we have our letters, in which, for so many years, we have grown accustomed almost to live; and although it is a shadowy life at best, there is no evil in living it for a period, since neither of us mistake [*sic*] it for what it takes the place of."

"One's health should be one's primary care."[56]

"You climbed to Pulpit Rock without the least difficulty."[57]

{53.} [1909]
"Schubert's Unfinished Symphony—Tschaikowsky's Fifth Symphony—both old favorites."[58]

"We are a part of the world about us—that's the plot." Illimitable complications!"[59]

"It is heavy work, reading things that have so little in them that one feels to be contemporary living."

"—just so, people who live by the sea, have the brightest hearths in the stormiest weather."[60]

"The snow was just commencing to fall, blowing from the North, the direction in which I was going, so that my cheeks were, shortly, coated with ice, or so they felt. While I enjoyed that flow of North wind and the blowing snow, I felt as if I did not enjoy it quite as much as possible—as if (in so short an experience of it) it did not go the deepest possible. There is as much delight in the body as in anything in the world and it leaps for use."[61]

56. WAS 1796 Dec 14, 1908.
57. Ibid.
58. WAS 1802 January 7, 1909. Elsie is reporting information, not quoting, but Stevens does say, "Both pieces are old favorites."
59. WAS 1803 January 10, 1909.
60. WAS 1805 January 13–14, 1909, for these two excerpts.
61. WAS 1806 January 17, 1909, slightly modified.

{54}

"I still grapple with all the law business that comes my way, but it is surely the quaintest way of making a living in the world. Practicing law is only lending people the use of your bald head. It is silly."[62]

"I have never thought much about those early days and certainly never set them in order."[63] Read childhood and boyhood reminiscences in letter dated Jan. 22, 1909.

"Here is a classification of them by Tieck: "the war-like and pious Bavarians (we have many Bavarians at home)—the gentle, thoughtful and imaginative Swabians—the sprightly, gay Franconians—the upright Hessians, the handsome Thuringians=the Low-Germans, resembling in true-heartedness the Dutch, in strength and skill the English." The Low-Germans, too, are very common at home."[64]

"The day does not tire me in the least, but it occupies me so completely that the quiet of the evening seems diversion in itself."[65]

{55}
<u>Package No 14</u>
In a Garden.

["]Oh, what soft wings shall rise above this place,
This little garden of spiced bergamot,
Poppy and iris and forget-me-not,
On Doomsday, to the ghostly Throne of space!

The haunting wings, most like the visible trace
Of passing azure in a shadowy spot—
The wings of spirits, native to this plot,
Returning to their intermitted Grace!

And one shall mingle in her cloudy hair
Blossoms of twilight, dark as her dark eyes;
And one to heaven upon her arm shall bear
Colors of what she was in her first birth;

62. WAS 1807 Jan 19, 1909. From this point on, there is, above several of the excerpts, the correct letter date penciled in, in Holly Stevens's handwriting.
63. WAS 1808 January 21, 1909. In her note, the second sentence here, Elsie takes the date of January 22, 1909, from the envelope.
64. WAS 1809 January 24, 1909. "1/25/09" in Holly's hand.
65. WAS 1810 January 26, 1909.

And all shall carry upward through the skies
Odor and dew of the familiar earth."[66]

"I admit a measure" (of vanity—after reading a review of poetry in the <u>Post</u>) ["]in the writing of poetry. "But there is also a pure delight in doing it. How deeply one gets into one's mind! Poetry only lies in the remotest places of it."[67]

{56}

"I was not in good shape for walking. You have to keep it up to go ten miles in two hours—and run every mile or two. We played tag. (Walter Butler and W. S.) It was like a game between the elephant and the hare."[68]

"Only to see the rank, tempestuous, horrid temper—all nervousness and savageness—go like a black cloud, and to get back to quiet: it is next to a prayer with me now."
"Your letters were the first light—and a balmy light."[69]

"—a very fascinating observation. It makes one aware of the love of mystery among damsels. Collateral with that" —"should go the gallantry of youths; for from the two spring all that is enduringly fine and pleasant between them."[70]

"It is considered that music, stirring something within us, stirs the Memory. I do not mean the personal Memory of our twenty years and more—but our inherited Memory, derived from those who lived before us"—"whose lives have insensibly

{57}

passed into our own, and compose it."
"While I had always known of this infinite extension of personality, nothing has ever made it so striking as this application of music to it."[71]

"From my notes:
"O to cast off doubts, and fears!
To touch truth, and feel it true!"[72]

66. WAS 1812 January 31, 1909.
67. Ibid. "Remoter" in the original.
68. WAS 1815 February 6–7, 1909.
69. WAS 1817 February 15, 1909. "Feb. 15, 1909" in Holly's hand.
70. WAS 1821 February 28, 1909. Some material is omitted from original.
71. WAS 1823 March 3, 1909 (source identified there). A considerable amount of material is omitted and small changes are made.
72. WAS 1830 March 16, 1909 (source identified there).

Package No 15.

"In Japan the ladies of the court are kept in a palace with many gardens, where they never see any of the wretchedness of life=the princesses. They do not know that there is anything in the world except cherry-trees, and poets, and things of pearl and silk and ivory. As far as it is possible, I should like to do that for you."[73]

"There is something as complete defeat in this narrow, unfriendly life of boarding-houses."[74]

"Loveliest of trees, the cherry, now
Is hung with blooms along the bough."[75]

{58}
"Your loving,
               Wallace."[76]

"I feel, nevertheless, the overwhelming necessity of thinking well, speaking well."[77]

O World, be noble, for her sake!
If she but knew thee, what thou art,
What wrongs are borne, what deeds are done
In thee, beneath thy daily sun,
Knows'st thou not that her tender heart,

For pain and very shame, would break?
O World, be noble, for her sake![78]

"And always remember, dear, that I seem to have a way of saying things that I do not mean forever and ever and ever. One's thoughts are like flowing water

73. No extant letter contains this passage.
74. No extant letter contains this passage.
75. WAS 1839 April 28, 1909. Elsie is quoting Stevens correctly, but A. E. Housman's "Loveliest of Trees" has "bloom along the bough."
76. Stevens used this closing seven times between January 7, 1909, and May 26, 1909, in the following WAS numbers: 1802, 1817, 1839, 1840, 1845, 1846, and 1851. He had never used this closing before and he would never use it again. In WAS 1844 May 11, 1909, he used "Your loving, Caliban," and in WAS 1863 June 25, 1909, he used "Your loving Pen Man." He used some form of the word "love" in his closings many times before and after this period.
77. WAS 1840 May 2, 1909.
78. Was 1843 May 9, 1909. This is Laurence Binyon's "O World, Be Nobler." "May 1909" is penciled in above this poem in Holly's hand.

that reflects new objects at each moment. A letter shows the reflections of the moment when it was written. They may be quite different in an hour."[79]

"strawberry blossoms white as crystals."[80]

{59}

"The seventy palms of Elim are far better and I hope to find them some day. Next to palms are pools and wells. They speak of wells of sweet water in the sea. A well of sweet water in the sea would be pretty much what a palm would be to the desert."[81]

"—and I noticed the new moon—like this [☽]. Can you tell which part of the crescent (without looking, of course) is toward the sunset? Does it hang this way [☽] or this way [☾]? In other words do the horns point toward the earth or toward the sky—down or up?"[82]

"But goodness must be defined, since all people do not have vigilant consciences; and the tangle comes in different definitions."

"Serious views are an offense."

"I have, in reality, never read a great deal of poetry; and yet I could not get on without reading a little."[83]

{60.}

"Your suggestion about the locust tree is capital and we must start a special fund for that purpose one of these days. It would be fine to settle on some plot of ground, somewhere at home, buy it, plant it, and hold it as a place to build a little home for summers bye-and-bye."[84]

"Certainly death causes no greater loss, than when it takes away the scholarship of one wise head."[85]

"I wish, one of these days, in a few years, some capital opportunity would come up at home" (Reading) "it would be great fun to pack up one's things and come back—after twelve years of absence."

79. WAS 1845 May 14, 1909.
80. WAS 1846 May 16, 1909.
81. WAS 1849 May 21, 1909. With minor excisions (see Exodus 15:27, Numbers 33:9, and Job 38:16).
82. WAS 1850 May 23, 1909.
83. WAS 1851 May 26, 1909, for this and the two excerpts above it.
84. WAS 1853 June 9, 1909, with slight deletions and alterations.
85. WAS 1855 June 15, 1909.

"Washington Square keeps looking so full of interest, and actual charm and makes the other places struggle."[86]

"Moon's been hanging like this ∪. Bad Sign. Should hang like this ⊃. The Indians had a saying: "If you can hang your powder-horn to the moon, don't go hunting.""[87]

{61.}

Package No 16

"Constant observation of one's own moods is a distress. Be glad that you are beyond yourself—and never study anything, please, except combinations of colors—and other really interesting and amusing things.

I am pretty grumpy now and then—although always sorry when I am, and more sorry afterwards. The Dutch are all like that—as weird as the weather. We'll find a way, however."[88]

"Take a little walk on Sunday. Your flowers will take care of themselves."[89]

"I've started "Endymion" and find a good many beautiful things in it that I had forgotten, or else not noticed." I wonder if it would be possible for a poet now-a-days to content himself with the telling of a "simple tale." With the growth of criticism, both in understanding and influence, poetry for poetry's sake, "debonair and gentle" has become difficult. The modern conception of poetry is that it should be in the service of something, as if Beauty was not something quite sufficient when in no other service than its own.""[90]

{62.}

"Dear, I am afraid that I should keep all this a secret—especially since it is about myself; but if I share a secret with you, it is still a secret—and you have your charity in keeping it."[91]

"Being tired, seems to make me humble, don't you think?"[92]

"Relatives are queer people whom one meets at funerals. They seem to assert themselves only at such times—and sometimes at marriages."[93]

86. WAS 1856 June 16, 1909, for this and the excerpt above. Minor excisions.
87. WAS 1858 June 18, 1909. "June 18, 1909" in Holly's hand.
88. WAS 1860 June 22, 1909, with several omissions.
89. WAS 1863 June 25, 1909.
90. WAS 1864 June 27, 1909.
91. WAS 1866 July 6, 1909.
92. Ibid.
93. This is not in an extant letter, but in WAS 1982 June 27, 1916, he will express a similar sentiment: "Relations are stupid."

"It is great fun to lie on a rock and bask in the sun—notwithstanding that the July sun is not the basking sun—but the boiling. August is the baking and September's the basking."[94]

"The Chinese say that a half hour's reading gives savour to a whole day."[95]

—"the desire for new things—is a part of our need for stimulation."[96]

"As it is, he (Walter B.) [is] better off than many with more merit."[97]

{63.}[98]
"But tonight is set apart for the Mirror of Past Events."

"Tomorrow evening, you remember, I go over to Twenty-first Street to close the lease with Mr. Weinman. I shall be quite a citizen when that is done."

"—the poem by Chénier, in prose. I think it one of the simplest and most charming things: here is my translation:

The Flute
"This memory always affects and touches
me: how he, fitting the flute to my mouth,
laughing and seating me in his lap, close to
his heart, calling me his rival and already
his vanquisher, shaped my incapable and
uncertain lips to blow a pure and harmonious breath; and how his skilful hands
took my young fingers, raised them, lowered
them, commenced over again twenty times,
thus teaching them, although still backward,
how to touch in turn the stops of the deep-toned wood."
"What an old-fashioned and delightful picture!"

{64}
"an expression about rhyme being an "instrument of music," struck me as being so. In the "June Book" I made "breeze" rhyme with "trees," and have never forgiven myself. It is a correct rhyme, of course, —but unpardonably

94. WAS 1871 July 16, 1909.
95. WAS 1877 July 23, 1909.
96. Ibid.
97. WAS 1879 August 2, 1909. Name added.
98. WAS 1887 August 17, 1909. In pencil, in Holly's hand at the top of this page, is her correct identification of the letter from which this excerpt comes: "8/17/09 post-mark (entire page)."

"expected." Indeed, none of my rhymes are (most likely) true "instruments of music." The words to be rhymed should not only sound alike, but they should enrich and deepen and enlarge each other, like two harmonious notes."[99]

"if I do not smoke, my nerves tingle and I am full of energy: yes, tingle with it. And then I want to walk violently, work violently, read, write, study—all at a bound."[100]

"Take long looks at Reading while you can. Nothing there will ever be the same to you again—and resolve to be a patriot so far as the town is concerned." We shall probably not get back to it before Christmas—and then you will already be something of a New Yorker, and the little country girl you like to call yourself will have disappeared."[101]

{65}
"In any event, with loyalty and courage, we have nothing to fear."[102]

Package No 18[103] [1910]

(about President Taft) "but at the same time we all know him to be a man of much wisdom, patience and courtesy."[104]

"There are so many changes—so much at which we just look on, so much we endure. And the best treasure is to have familiar things to console and encourage us."[105]

"   :he is in her heart, and therefore he does not fear to be out of her sight."[106]

[1911]

"I am far from being a genius—and must rely on hard and faithful work."[107]

"But personally I find pleasure in too many things not sociable. This is largely the result of many years of isolation and tastes formed under such conditions."[108]

99. WAS 1888 August 19, 1909, with some modification. "8/19/09" in Holly's hand.
100. WAS 1896 August 31, 1909. "8/31/09" in Holly's hand.
101. WAS 1898 September 8, 1909. "Christ" added to "Xmas" and Stevens's usual hyphen dropped from New York.
102. WAS 1901 September 12, 1909.
103. The remaining excerpts come from after the marriage.
104. WAS 1908 May 30, 1910.
105. WAS 1911 June 7, 1910.
106. WAS 1912 June 10, 1910.
107. WAS 1922 August 6, 1911.
108. WAS 1925 August 16, 1911.

{66.}

"But all my hopes lead me to expect most from life in the end by doing as I am doing. For the present patience and good-will are our greatest virtues. And all the time you know how much I love you and how much we have in common deep down."[109]

～

Letters of 1907

Several times in his life, Stevens had to begin over again, and these seventeen letters represent one such time in his courting of Elsie by mail. Starting over in a continuing relationship should imply large change, such as a significant remaking of the personalities of the two people, something that is not often, if ever, achieved, and such will prove to be the case here. The year before, their relationship had almost come to an end, but now things were looking up, though their basic incompatibility remained. In the first of these letters, Stevens mentions this sense of new beginning, while at the same time hinting at a problem his thinking can not make go away, her sense that his expressions of feeling for her are "affected devotion," sham emotion. The next letter deals with a related problem, their "being easier" in their letters than they are when they are together. The fifth letter contains reverberations of the near breakup of "last summer" and notes that Elsie's "occasional defiances are only tricks that Nature plays on [them]." Their difference in age, almost seven years, is treated at some length in the first of the letters that has been abridged, a sure sign of some tension, some revelation that someone wanted hidden.

Perhaps the letter of March 24, 1907, best represents the clash in Stevens between his desire to be with Elsie and his desire to be alone. As he reports on a landscape that seemed to be "the face of [his] dearest friend": it was "a little wilderness all my own, shared with nobody, not even with you—it made me

---

109. WAS 1925 August 16, 1911. This is the end of Elsie's notebook of excerpts, WAS 1772, sometimes called "Elsie's Book" in scholarship on Stevens. The bottom two-thirds of this page is cut off. Also, it should be noted that the spiral that originally held this notebook together has been removed and so the pages are essentially loose. There are five blank pages remaining in the notebook. The back cover bears a pricing sticker with the following: "G. Fox & Co. Hartford, Connecticut 14/04 F7 62140 20." In addition to this document, there are ten three-by-five-inch note cards (Box 80, Folder 18, Wallace Stevens Papers, HEH) on which someone, presumably Elsie, has typed selections from Stevens's letters to her that are still extant. Six of the letters from which these selections were taken are from 1909, one from 1910, one from 1915, and one from 1931, this final one bearing this incorrect identification at the top of the note card: "Packet No. 28. April 4th, 1926." There are other, less-severe errors of dating, including the tell-tale "1959" on several cards. This material reveals the demanding nature of Elsie's enterprise of saving some memories for herself before she destroyed the rest. Doubtless, the ravages of her strokes prevented her from carrying out this vast and difficult task.

myself. It was friendly so much deeper than anything else could be. —You are different. I play a silver lute for you, when I am good, and Elsie is a soft name to sing, and you make a lover of me, so that I can be nothing else." This passage struck Elsie as being so important that she put it in her Book.

It is likely that this group of letters was from one or two of Elsie's packets of letters that were not destroyed; all of Elsie's excerpts on her pages 23 to 25 are from these letters.

All of the extant letters before Wallace and Elsie married, that is, those letters identified as WAS 1776 to WAS 1905 (March 7, 1907–September 16, 1909), are addressed to "Miss Elsie V. Moll, 231 South 13th St., Reading, Pa."

⌐⌐

[WAS 1776 March 7, 1907 New York][110]

Thursday Afternoon

My dear Elsie:—[111]

May I write from the office? I am going out to dinner this evening and it may be that I shall not get home in time to write to you. Your letter this morning made me call you my better self. At first I thought—my better half,

---

110. This is the first extant letter. Throughout this edition, the material not in square brackets is what Stevens himself put on the stationery on which he writes his letters; his positioning of greetings and salutations are particularly varied but will not be indicated here. Throughout the letters, he usually indicates only the day of the week and whether morning or evening; he puts dates only on letterhead stationery, a practice that becomes more common after he begins traveling for the Hartford Accident and Indemnity Insurance Company in 1916.

The first line of material in square brackets, derived from the envelope or internal evidence in the letters if there is no envelope, comes from the Huntington Library folder for each letter; this line gives the Huntington's accession number (beginning with WAS), the date, and the city from which the letter was sent. I provide the other lines of material, also in brackets, which are derived from descriptions of postcards or unusual stationery, especially letterhead of the companies for which he worked or of the hotels at which he stayed.

Before the time of the marriage in September 1909, the typical letter was written on eight-by-ten-inch stationery, folded once to make two eight-by-five sides, and contained writing on the front and back. That made for a typical letter of four pages, but sometimes Stevens used two of these sheets and thus wrote letters of eight pages. He tended not to leave pages blank. After his marriage, he changes to smaller stationery and a smaller envelope; however, he uses letterhead stationery with increasing frequency at that time.

Through 1911 (or until WAS 1927 July 7, 1912) all of Stevens's letters are addressed to 231 South Thirteenth Street in Reading, to "Miss Elsie V. Moll" before their marriage and to "Mrs. Wallace Stevens" after their marriage.

111. Stevens will use this pattern of indentation in only two other letters, WAS 2030 January 30, 1923 and WAS 2035 January 31, 1923. Throughout the correspondence

but that has a double meaning, and besides you are all of my better self, your panacea—cure-all, for the evils I conjure up, that is: not to think of them, is, after all, the wisest, isn't it (isn't for is'n't!)? You are perfectly right and yet you are the opposite of me in that respect, because I am naturally pessimistic while you, thank goodness, are naturally optimistic. But you will make me optimistic just by insisting on it, for it is a thing I love, and then you will be a princess in reality. They say that there is no evil, but that thinking makes it so:[112] thinking is the evil. So just be Elsie and you will be all that I could hope for, and more than I deserve. —I had intended to write a new kind of letter to you to-night; and may-be I shall on Sunday. It almost seems as if we had not been writing before, now that I have such pleasant and frequent letters from you; and we must be careful not to let anything interfere. Be yourself. I should like to see whether or not that included any of me, and I shall be able to tell. I could no longer be myself without you. That is not affected devotion; nor is any devotion I have ever shown you. You are sorry for that phrase, aren't you, Elsie? What need have we for affectation? But surely it was only something passing in your mind and you need not speak of it.

With much love,
Wallace

⌒

[WAS 1777 March 10, 1907 New York]

Sunday Evening

Dear Elsie:—

I've been shovelling snow and it made my arms so tired that now my hand shakes as I write. It has been snowing all day—confound it! This morning I thought I should have to stay indoors all day and so, after breakfast, I put on my loafing outfit and began to read a volume of new poems that I bought yesterday. But shortly after ten o'clock there was a lull and I started out. Good Lord, how I needed it! My blood leaped. I wanted to wash my face in the snow—to hold it there. I did let the wind **blow** through my hair. Then I ran a long way and towards noon, when it had started to snow again, I was on [the] Bronx River, or rather, along it. It was enchanting there. What is known as the Hemlock Forest was a huge clump of green and white. I stopped under an oak still covered with

until WAS 2005 January 17, 1919 (with the exception of WAS 1960 July 21, 1915, a letter he treated like a "little book"), he will not indent to indicate the beginning of a new paragraph. Until that time he seems to have used the dash, herein represented by an em dash, to represent the beginning of a new paragraph.

112. See *Hamlet* 3.2.245. He will repeat this idea in WAS 1922, the letter for August 6, 1911.

dead leaves and noticed a whispering noise as the snow fell on the leaves. And it was so quiet and lonely there. —Then I bounced out of that to the Green Houses,[113] and there it was mid-summer. All the larger palms, some of them much higher than your house, are gathered together in one room, under a dome. Some sparrows have built nests in the dome. When I got there they were just coming out of the sparrow church (probably in a banana tree) and they were all chattering at once—"So glad Spring is here!"—and outside there was a blizzard. In another room there is a collection of camelias. One bush from Japan was in bloom. It would have made you sing to see it. In the last room I shall tell you about, instead of a floor there is a pool, crossed by a little rustic arch. I stood on the arch and watched the fish flick their gold backs—it was almost insane. — Then, after dinner, I took a nap. Imagine! Well, I happened to be lying on the bed playing my guitar lazily and I remember leaning it against a chair nearby and then—it was six o'clock. It had stopped snowing. Usually I have to wade from this house to Mrs. Jackson's[114] so I went down to the cellar and got a shovel and shovelled until it was time for tea. —After tea, the first thing I did (not to include a lot of smoke and talk) was to fall down Mrs. Jackson's steps into the path I had made. But there was still enough snow there to save me. —And here I am—and you want me to take you into my heart! Oh, wonderful girl—you will have to turn into something else before I can take you into that little chamber—or strange forest, or whatever else it may be. What is it to be? My fancy is all snowed under to-night and I cannot think. But aren't you there already? I know you are in my thoughts, because I can see you and hear you there. How do you look in my thoughts? Oh, you would know yourself at once. You are looking at me and you are smiling and saying something. I can't really hear what you are saying because you laugh in a way before you finish. You are perfectly yourself and that is a little different I think, although not so very much, from the way you are sometimes when we are together. I wonder whether, in saying that, I haven't stumbled across the reason for our being easier in our letters than we are—when we are together. It must be because you are more perfectly yourself to me when I am writing to you, and that makes me more perfectly myself to you. You know that I do with you as I like in my thoughts: I no sooner wish for your hand than I have it—no sooner wish for anything to be said or done than it is said or done; and none of the denials you make me are made there. You are

113. In the New York Botanical Gardens in Bronx Park. In a letter of July 22, 1915, he will describe another visit to this extensive park, to both the zoological and the botanical sections.

114. Stevens's landlady when he lived on Sedgewick Avenue on Fordham Heights, from at least October 10, 1906 (according to *SP,* 171), to at least April 19, 1907, the last reference to this address in the letters to Elsie (WAS 1791).

my Elsie there. —Yet it is the real Elsie, all the time. I do not think you have ever said or done anything there that the real Elsie wouldn't say or do—only you have not made me beg so hard there. —Now have you seen into my heart? And haven't you seen your own eyes looking out at you—and laughing at you? My thoughts are my heart. —I was more interested than you may believe in what you said about religion. A. T.'s[115] opinions are quite elementary. I have never told you what I believe. There are so many things to think of. I don't care whether the churches are all alike or whether they are right or wrong. It is not important. The very fact that they take care of A. T.'s "stupid" people is an exquisite device. It is undoubtedly true that they do not "influence" any but the "stupid."[116] But they are beautiful and full of comfort and moral help. One can get a thousand benefits from churches that one cannot get outside of them. They purify a man, they soften Life. Please don't listen to A. T., or, at least, don't argue with her. Don't care about the Truth. There are other things in Life besides the Truth upon which everybody of any experience agrees, while no two people agree about the Truth. I'd rather see you going to church than know that you were as wise as Plato and Haeckel[117] rolled in one; and I'd rather sing some old chestnut out of the hymn-book with you, surrounded by "stupid" people, than listen to all the wise men in the world. It has always been a particular desire of mine to have you join [the] church; and I am very, very glad to know that you are now on the road. —I am not in the least religious. The sun clears my spirit, if I may say that, and an occasional sight of the sea, and thinking of blue valleys, and the odor of the earth, and many things. Such things make a

115. Alice Tragle and her sister Clare were with Elsie when she met Stevens for the first time. See above for the whole account, which is also published in Brazeau's *Parts of a World*, 255. The following information on Alice Tragle comes from the *Graduate Catalogue of the Reading High Schools: 1856–1905* (Reading, Pa.: Alumni Association, 1905), class of 1901: "Alice Amanda R. Tragle, 1510 Perkiomen Ave., Reading, Pa. First Honorable Mention, Alumni Essay Contest, 1900" (239). Frances Claire Tragle (same address as Alice) is listed as a graduate of the class of 1902, with no additional information (250).

116. Stevens may have in mind this famous line from Lucretius: "Tantum religio potuit suadere malorum."

117. Ernst Heinrich Haeckel (1834–1919), a widely read early and ardent supporter of Darwinian evolution, applied evolution to philosophy and religion in *The Riddle of the Universe* (1900, translation of *Die Welträtsel,* 1899). He also applied this reasoning to the cause of German nationalism. Stevens, in his journal for some time after May 29, 1906, and before July 22, 1906, makes the following observation: "Lodge & Haeckel. These fellows lose themselves in the technology of philosophy and science. For example, I have been thinking lately that men & women were the precipitates of some force— well, that turns out to be Monism. Perhaps, one ought not think of such things without reading, too: but thinking is superb, the reading preposterous" (*SP,* 168).

god of man; but a chapel makes a man of him. Churches are human. —I say my prayers every night—not that I need them now, or that they are anything more than a habit, half-unconscious. But in Spain, in Salamanca,[118] there is a pillar in a church (Santayana told me) worn by the kisses of generations of the devout. One of their kisses are worth all my prayers. Yet the church is a mother for them—and for us. —There is a noise on my windows as if it had started to rain. Poor March! Poor Elsie! You are so glad that Winter is gone—and then it isn't. But it is; for the cold is gone, and a few days will melt everything. —Just to see green grass again—a whole field of it, shining in the light. Grass! How sweet and strange it seems—better than anything else—Spring's "light green dress."[119] —I have just been looking at your picture. I could look at it and look and look, without thinking of anything at all. You hold yourself as if you knew I was going to look at it—or don't you want me to say that? —Suddenly the idea of a hay-field comes into my head and I imagine myself lying on a pile of hay watching swallows flying in a circle. Let that be my last thought to-night.

> Affectionately
> Wallace.

◞

[WAS 1778 March 12, 1907 New York]

> Tuesday Evening

Dear Elsie:

Since it is almost two o'clock, I suppose I ought to say "Wednesday Morning." Mr. Driscoll,[120] of Reading, came to see me this afternoon and we took dinner together and went to the theatre and then talked until after midnight. It was a disappointment not to be able to stay at home and write to you, particularly as it was only last Thursday that I had another excuse. But if I write to you so late and send you —say, two Spring kisses, won't you forgive me, and accept, for once, the wish to write in place of the writing? I am not sleepy, but I have so much to do tomorrow that I ought to go to bed. Besides, I have promised to spend to-morrow evening with a fellow who wants to show me

---

118. This famous pillar, in a church in Saragosa, is still a famous place of pilgrimage and annual celebration. Santayana mentions this church and its specialized cult in *Reason in Religion,* in the section titled "Catholic Piety More Human than the Liturgy." Stevens is making the same point as Santayana about the human comfort offered by the traditions of the church.

119. See Keats's sonnet "Keen, fitful gusts are whisp'ring here and there" for his reference to Petrarch's "lovely Laura in her light green dress."

120. Daniel J. Driscoll (1862–1919), a Reading industrialist who founded the Delaware Seamless Tubing Company, lived near the Stevens home, at 224 North Fifth Street in Reading.

some new books—and to talk and smoke,[121] and, of course, I must try to be entertaining and chipper, as they say. See how many excuses I have for not writing to you! Yet I <u>am</u> writing and not only because it is my night to do so, but because I want to. You have been so perfect in your letters lately that it keeps me bubbling over. You haven't missed <u>one</u> and each of them has been so full of confidence and affection. Do I spoil it by saying so? It is only my desire to thank you, not for alms, but favor; just as Pierrot[122] kisses the hand of Ninette. It is high time for me to come to see you again—or else to write you madrigals and sonnets. Spring is getting into my blood and as your poet I ought to celebrate you. But there are other means than rhymes. If only I could dream of you! Unfortunately, I sleep like an animal all night long.[123] Do you ever dream of me? Impossible question.

Affectionately,
Wallace.

⌐⌐

[WAS 1779 March 14, 1907 New York]
[Stationery of the Hotel Astor, Times Square, New York.]

March 14, 1907

Dear Elsie:

One o'clock and I haven't even started for home. I am overwhelmed with things to do; and expect to be for the next few days. Do not mind, dear, if I write these flighty notes; and write to me just the same. Your letter this morning was the dearest and tenderest you have ever sent me—and here I am half-blind with smoke and the need of sleep. I must write an important business letter, and then I'll be free till morning. Good-night—you will have my very first possible minute.

Affectionately,
Wallace

⌐⌐

121. After the *s* of "smoke," a *p* is crossed out and an *m* is written above it, one of very few such corrections in all of the letters to Elsie.

122. For two treatments of this important figure in Stevens's poetry, see Bates, *Wallace Stevens,* 56–59, 115–16, and Robert Storey, *Pierrot: A Critical History of a Mask* (Princeton: Princeton University Press, 1978), 167–92.

123. In his journal for April 10, 1905, Stevens had written, "I dream more or less—often of Elsie" (*SP,* 144), but this could refer to daydreaming.

[WAS 1780 March 19, 1907 New York]

Wednesday Morning[124]

Dear Elsie:

It is just twenty-five minutes to three as I commence to write. I have had a long conference with some gentlemen tonight (one of them from Reading), and it has been slow work getting home. But here I am and I mean to write to you before going to bed. It has been snowing and raining all day and now the wind has come up and the stars are out and I know that I am alive. Even you are tight asleep. It seems strange to write to you and think of that—it is like talking to you without your listening. To-night I am more like myself. Just to have written last night[125] was like recovering a part of myself that had been lost for a little. Do we realize how much a part of each other we have become? Do you know how we should feel if I were to come home without seeing you? If I were to come and you were to have other engagements—what a vile fancy! You have always welcomed me. I shouldn't know what to do if you were to change. If I were to come and they told me that you had gone out for the evening, I cannot imagine what would happen. Surely these are nightmares. People never really know about themselves. They find out innumerable unexpected things every moment: but we have been through it all once, a year ago. Last summer it seemed impossible that we should ever get where we had been before. Oh, but we were nowhere, compared to where we are now. Each time we get a hair's breadth apart, we come closer together than ever before; and so it may be that your occasional defiances are only tricks that Nature plays on us—and so with my mistakes. Yes: we must blame them all on Nature, our witch as well as our fairy god-mother. I shall be home at Easter—Sunday after next; and if the ground is not too wet we shall have to go walking: not up our old hill, but to some new place. We are not so old and reminiscent that we cannot continue to explore, and it may end—by [our] having two hills instead of one. I should like to walk up the Tulpehocken.[126] The glimmer of the water will waken us, and we should probably see more green things along water than elsewhere. Then at Van Reed's paper mill we can climb the hill there and see a part of the country that must be new to you. Suppose it happened to be a warm, brilliant day—with the sky high and blue and clear! But I forget: I am no longer a poet. Yet it may be that the sight of Spring waters will restore that faculty, with many others.

124. Stevens is writing at 2:35 A.M., and the letter is now with an envelope post-marked 11:00 A.M., March 19, a Tuesday, so he was probably writing on Tuesday, mislead by the lateness of the hour.
125. There is no extant letter between March 14 and 19, 1907.
126. This tributary enters the Schuylkill River near Reading after running through the heart of the Reading quadrant Stevens and Elsie often explored together during the years of their courtship.

You must be my poetess and sing me many songs. I shall hear them in strange places and repeat them afterwards as half my own. —Good-night, dear poetess! The wind storms around my windows like the violent wings of Night. You can see that already I am half-dreaming.

With much love,
Wallace.

〜

[WAS 1781 March 20, 1907 New York]

to[127] dinner once, except on Monday evening and I worked tremendously. But for the present, that is over. —And I am glad that you wrote faithfully all the time. How can you ever doubt me, Elsie? I mean my loving you and desiring you. —But I shall not speak of that. You are my chief possession, since you <u>are</u> my own; and if you regarded yourself as a stranger and looked on at Wallace and Elsie, not as one of them, you would appreciate it better. When I thanked you for favors I was attempting to be frivolous—was it too unexpected? Long ago when young men and maidens did not have their own sweet will, as we do, it was regarded as a favor for any woman to look at any man; and if she accepted him, she might expect a long speech of thanks in the man's best rhetorical manner. Since then we have grown less stiff and more sincere, thanks to orchards and twilights and summer moons. Yet I know I was in the mood for thanksgiving when you first let me know. (Now you say, "<u>Have</u> I let you know?") It made me so happy. —Do <u>you</u> feel that I am not myself to-night? There is no sentiment in me, no color—nothing at all. Yet you will be expecting my letter with especial curiosity—and when it does not come to-morrow, you will say, "I wonder if that boy has been foolish enough to do as he did last year." That will never happen again, dear. Think—you will be twenty-one in June. It makes me feel as if you were getting nearer to me[.] —I was twenty-five when we met, but then you were only eighteen. Eighteen! I was at college at that age, writing sonnets by the yard. In October I shall be twenty-eight. Great Caesar! Can't we stop it somehow? You will be twenty-three when I am thirty, thirty-three when I am forty, forty-three when I am fifty. Well, when you are forty-three, I shall cease to worry—but not a day before; yet even then, in New York, you may find some means to make me hot and cold—unless I keep you thoroughly terrorized. —This must be Spring fever and these the visions of fever. —Pray that the ground will dry and that the last pile of dirty snow will melt and that the grass will brighten—and that Elsie's world will come back, new and beautiful. Everything is so pitiably dingy now. The

---

127. This is the first incomplete letter. What remains is the normal folded sheet and its four pages of text; thus what is missing is probably another sheet with four pages of text.

birds sing a little in the morning, but not the night birds. Listen for the robins' four and five notes. They used to sing them marvellously at Cambridge in the evenings, long before the leaves came. I long for that. How content I was to love it. Now I am no longer a poet, and only a poor lover, at least to-night. We shall soon be together again and then you must deny me nothing. At the last moment, I am in a sorry humor. Write me a cheerful letter and scold me for being so dull and believe me to be always yours.

> With love
> Wallace.

⤶

[WAS 1782 March 20, 1907 New York][128]

> Wednesday Evening

This is a picture of the house in which I take my meals. My room is in the house to the left and you can just see one corner of it opposite the little arrow (:⌧)[129] Of course the snow is pretty nearly all gone now but you can see that there was once a good deal of it. I go from one house to the other by way of the front steps—a short but muddy trip. —To-night [over to back] I am so sleepy that I am going to bed just as soon as I can. To-morrow is the first day of Spring: the greatest day of the year for us, don't you think? And imagine— Barnum & Bailey's Circus opens in the afternoon in Madison Square Garden! That is a <u>better</u> sign than blue-birds or crocus-es.

> Wallace

⤶

[WAS 1783 March 21, 1907 New York]

> Thursday Evening

Dear Elsie:—

I am so full of misery tonight that I am ridiculous. Every Spring I have a month of so of semi-blackness and perhaps the mood is just returning. Perhaps, it is simply a revulsion against old things—habits, people, places—everything: the feeling the sun must have nowadays, when it shines on nothing but mud and bare trees and the general world, rusty with winter. People do not look well in

128. This, a postcard with no cancellation on it, pictures a two-story house in deep snow. The beginning of Stevens's text is written beside the picture and concluded on the reverse side, which would have carried only the address if it had not been mailed in an envelope (not extant). The date is written in pencil, not in Stevens's hand but probably Holly's. It is reproduced in volume 1 of Richardson's *Wallace Stevens*, between pages 192 and 193.

129. Stevens's arrow here represents the arrow in his left margin pointing to the house on the postcard.

Spring. They seem grimy and puffy and it makes me misanthropic. —Spring fills one so full of dreams that try one's patience in coming true. One has a desire for the air full of spice and odors, and for days like jewels[130] of changing colors, and for warmth and ease, and all the other things that you know so well. But they come so slowly. —Earth and the body and the spirit seem to change together, and so I feel muddy and bare and rusty. —I'd like to wear a carnation every morning and I'd like to see other people decorating themselves like good children. —The winter-nights leave a mark in their faces: the beer and the smoke and the late reading and talking! It makes me want to plunge them all in a crystal pool and bring them out rosy and sparkling. Some of them are young and have gray hair and round shoulders[.] —I'm thinking of one. How lost he would be in our Eden! Elsie (now I could add so many, many more names)—you will never grow old, will you? You will always be just my little girl, won't you? You must always have pink cheeks and golden hair. To be young is all there is in the world. The rest is nonsense—and cant. They talk so beautifully about work and having a family and a home (and I do, too, sometimes)—but it's all worry and head-aches and respectable poverty and forced gushing. Still you must not remember this against me. By gushing, I mean: telling people how nice it is, when, in reality, you would give all of your last thirty years for one of your first thirty. Old people are tremendous frauds. The point is to be young—and to be a little in love, or very much—and to desire carnations and "creations"—and to be glad when Spring comes. Three cheers for it. —You remember my telling you about Miss Schmidt in the German picture on the wall over my table. She looks wonderfully chubby and golden to-night and she is quite right to stand on her sunny rock so tranquilly week after week. —Some of us used to lie in the sun at Kissinger's Locks[131] a whole summer long, going home only for meals and to sleep. I can feel the warmth now and remember the laziness of it. Was that in this world—so cloudy and cold and full of winds? —I lost a world when I left Reading. You and I only sip it—I lived in it. —Once last summer I went to the level where we ate our lunch—and went swimming in a secluded spot. I left myself float under the water (left should be let, of course) and looked at the blue

---

130. *LWS* (97) reads this word as "junk," and the word is indeed crowded against the margin and thus difficult to read. The letters *ewel* occur several times in Stevens's use of the word "farewell" (he does not use the word "jewel" anywhere else in this correspondence), and the pattern there is the same as the pattern here: four upward peaks followed by the letter *l*. Stevens forms the *s* in "jewels" exactly like the nonvertical half of the letter *k*. It is thus easy to see how Holly read this word as she did.

131. This lock and dam of the Schuylkill Canal is located at the foot of West Douglas Street (originally Centre Street), not far from Stevens's childhood home. See *Passing Scene* 1:198–203 for information about this lock, complete with pictures of boys diving and swimming there.

and brown colors there and I <u>shouted</u> when I came up. —So there is still some of the foolishness and delight in me. —Yet here I am, twenty-seven, practicing law in New-York, and writing letters to <u>my</u> princess. But I am glad to be

Your
Wallace.

↬

[WAS 1784 March 24, 1907 New York]

Sunday Evening

Dear Elsie:

Was this the day you joined the church[132]—or is it next Sunday? I thought of it before going over for tea. You have kept so quiet about it. Well, if it was, I salute you no longer as a Pagan but as just what you ought to be. I read <u>Proverbs</u> in bed this morning and marked this verse in the thirtieth chapter:

"Remove far from me vanity and lies; give me neither poverty nor riches; feed me with food convenient for me."[133]

So I send that verse to you, as a good desire. —But, principally, I have been walking in the rain. I let it rain on my head and in my face. You know all my similes, yet once more it was like a spring in a desert. I seem to get more good from raw weather than from mild weather. Then, I saw a blue-bird and threw a kiss to him. On Saturday morning, at East Orange,[134] walking before breakfast, I saw my first robin. There was pussy-willow everywhere—and mud and mist, to-day. The wind drove the mist in sheets over the fields. You would have enjoyed it—just to let the rain gather in the rim of your hat and to hear the water squeaking in your shoes and to have your clothes hang on you, heavy and cold. It would have blown all your powder away, but you would have been glad of that: the blood would have made your cheeks hurt. —I found a new road through new woods. The bushes seemed full of song—sparrows, singing songs they sing in August. Once I stopped and smelled the earth and the rain and looked around me—and recognized it all, as if I had seen the face of my dearest friend. I said to myself, "It <u>is</u> like seeing the face of a friend," and I wondered

132. According to Elsie's records, as given in "A Branch of the Bright Family" mentioned in the introduction, she was confirmed by her pastor, Reverend William H. Myers of Grace Lutheran Church, on March 24, 1907. Only two weeks earlier Stevens had encouraged her to join the church (see WAS 1777 above).

133. Proverbs 30:8.

134. According to his journals, Stevens went to live in East Orange, New Jersey, in May 1905 (*SP*, 147), and he lived there until October 11 of that year (*SP*, 154). A reference on May 2, 1906, could imply that he is still living there or at least outside New York: "In town, I lunched with Walter Arensberg at the Harvard Club" (*SP*, 167). At any rate, he is living on "Sedgwick avenue, Fordham Heights" by October 10, 1906.

how to tell you of it so exactly that you would know what I meant. The sheets of mist, the trees swallowed up at a little distance in mist, the driving cold wind, the noisy solitude, the clumps of ice and patches of snow—the little wilderness all my own, shared with nobody, not even with you—it made me myself. It was friendly so much deeper than anything else could be. —You are different. I play a silver lute for you, when I am good, and Elsie is a soft name to sing, and you make a lover of me, so that I can be nothing else. —But today I escaped and enjoyed every breath of liberty. And now that I have come back it seems as if I might play my lute more sweetly than ever, and more gladly. —There's a sonnet by Andrew Lang that might serve as a text for all this and explain my sense of liberty; and perhaps it will be new to you—so here it is:

> As one that for a weary space has lain
> Lulled by the song of Circe and her wine
> In gardens near the pale of Proserpine,
> Where that Aeaean isle forgets the main,
> And only the low lutes of love complain,
> And only shadows of wan lovers pine,
> As such an one were glad to know the brine
> Salt on his lips, and the large air again,—
> So gladly, from the songs of modern speech
> Men turn, and see the stars, and feel the free
> Shrill wind beyond the close of heavy flowers,
> And through the music of the languid hours,
> They hear like ocean on a western beach
> The surge and thunder of the Odyssey.[135]

To-day was so much of an Odyssey for me that you must forgive my truancy and, also, because I am penitent now. —That is such a long quotation that I promise not to quote again for a long time: quotations are fatal to letters. —It may be possible for me to come on an early train next Saturday and even if I came on the train leaving New-York at five o'clock, it would be uncertain when I could meet you, because that is a most uncertain train. How nice it would be to have you meet me at the station! No one has ever done that; but my stuff would be in the road and I might like to put on a clean collar, besides. So that, after all, it seems easiest to meet you at your house. We need not stay there, you know, for we can run out immediately and go where we like, if the weather is what I hope for. We shall be having moonlight, shan't we? I think so.

---

135. *LWS* (99) points out that this sonnet, "The Odyssey," is found in a book still in Stevens's library: *Sonnets of This Century* (New York: Walter Scott, n.d.). It is also in *The Oxford Book of English Verse.*

Then, if you met me somewhere else you might not know me without my moustache. I shaved it off this morning and the absence of it makes me look rather queer. —It is nearly time for me to move again. Yesterday it was fairly warm and my room, when I came home, was like an oven. What will it be like in July and August? If I can find a pleasant place out on Long Island, not too far from town, I might try it, as soon as affairs at the office become settled. As they are now, I don't know whether I shall be there one week after the other; and it is a very difficult thing to make an advantageous change late in the season. Sometimes I think that if things do not go well soon, I'll pack up and go to California or some other outlandish place. There is so little in New-York that I desire enough to work for: certainly I do not desire money, and yet my thoughts must be constantly on that subject. It is active, gay (at times), powerful, interesting and full of people who say that they would rather be lamp-posts on the Bowery than cedars in Lebanon. But, of course, I'm of the cedary disposition. —Did you laugh at my black mood? Please do, if you haven't already—because it is such absolute barbarism to say such things to you. Alas! I say so many things to you, that I ought not to. Sometime ago I promised not to scold and to-night I promised not to quote (for a while) and now I promise to be cheerful. The ink gets into my blood—I'll draw a line through black[136] and write blue, white, pink, violet, purple, red, bronze, orange, brown—and ring the bells in my fool'scap. Hey, ding-a-ding! Be a merry fool, Wallace. This lady is neither widow nor orphan—but a gentle maiden. Oh, maiden, we are still in the land of the living, we are still in the sun. Let us wear bells together and never grow up and never kiss each other : but only play, and never think, and never wish, and never dream. —Will that stop Time and Nature? —Let us hate[137] Nature, this cruel mother, whose hand you have just taken, and whom I have known a little longer. —They say it is to be clear in the morning. I feel as if I could sit up all night to see the sun again—but that would be a great excess. Good-night, dear stranger, dear E. V. K., since you call yourself that (and are). I shall be so glad to see you again, and to walk with you or talk to you, or do anything else in the world <u>with</u> you.

Your affectionate, troublesome,
good-intentioned, nonsensical
Wallace.

⌒

---

136. He draws a line through the word "black."
137. In *LWS* (100), Holly reads this word as "trap."

[WAS 1785 March 26, 1907 New York]

Tuesday Evening

My Dear Elsie:—

This is another one of my after-midnight letters. It was half-past twelve when I got home and then I sat down and lit a cigarette and read <u>two</u> Heralds[138] and saw in one of them the name of Elsie Violet Kachel. It is really Elsie Viola[139] Kachel, isn't it? There were forty-three others—but there was just a baby thrill in seeing yours. What a darling you are! —I cannot understand the weather you are having. It is still quite cold here. At all events, it does not seem like Spring. It is quite wonderful to see you taking such delight in it. I believe I care more about that than about Spring itself. Do you feel as I used to feel—almost a part of the light and the warmth? The next few years are the best of all. I haven't really changed—only there are bars in front of all my windows now. If only I could get out where you are. In a week I should be writing verses and singing to myself. —Now, <u>you</u> are singing for me. I thought of that this morning and it made me read your letter over and over again. Of course, you are not an angel, as you say; but aren't you different to me than to anyone else—aren't you just a little like (in spirit) the "young-eyed cherubim"?[140] Mind, I say in spirit, so as to say a thing you cannot laugh at, or think silly. —Sing to me all Spring and Summer and, perhaps, during my vacation, my own voice may return. —If you were here tonight I should kiss you like a madman. What a fate! But I should not be able to help myself.

With all my love,
Wallace.

---

138. The *Reading Herald* was established in 1881. In *Passing Scene* 7:113–14, there is an article from 1909 describing the history of this newspaper. However, it was with the *Reading Times* that the Stevens family had the closest connections, through the friendship between its editor and well-known local poet, Col. Thomas Zimmerman (whom Stevens refers to in his journal as the "author of 'Olla Podrida'"; *SP,* 140), and Stevens's father.

139. This is the correct form of her name at birth. He writes a very large "a" here, over another letter in Viola.

140. Lorenzo, in Shakespeare's *Merchant of Venice* 5.1.58–65 speaks:

> Sit, Jessica. Look how the floor of heaven
> Is thick inlaid with patines of bright gold:
> There's not the smallest orb which thou behold'st
> But in his motion like an angel sings,
> Still quiring to the young-eyed cherubins;
> Such harmony is in immortal souls;
> But whilst this muddy vesture of decay
> Doth grossly close it in, we cannot hear it.

⟅

[WAS 1786 March 29, 1907 New York]
[Much smaller than normal stationery, small handwriting.]

Good Friday, 1907

My Dear Elsie:

I expect to get away early to-morrow so that I shall be with you early, say between half-past seven and eight o'clock. I missed your Tuesday letter. Did you avoid writing just to punish me for the "liberty" I took? But do not punish me when I am at home. Why should you ever? Let us keep such things for mid-winter.

Hastily
Wallace.

⟅

[WAS 1787 April 1–2 1907[141] New York]

Monday Evening

Dear Elsie:—

This morning, on the train, I thought that we were like two people in a dark room groping for each other. Once in a long while our hands touch and we get a glimpse of each other. Then we are lost again. —It is very hard to lose you this time, harder than ever before, because we both feel that we are becoming "all letters," as you said. —I can think of at least one way of changing that and, to say it at once, it is this: when I come, be all the time what you are on the sofa. You know how quickly we change on the sofa, and that is because you are yourself there, as you are in your letters. <u>Honestly,</u> are you yourself when we sit so primly, talking like strangers? I am not myself. I am "making a call." But you might laugh and talk just as you do on the sofa, and just as you would do with one of your friends. You must let me know you. —When we were walking along Mineral Spring[142] road, I said to myself, "I will never love anyone that does not love me. I will never try to make anyone love me that does not. All the delight of love is being loved in return." —If you love me you will not wish to hide it. If I am your lover and if you are glad of it, you will give yourself to me, and not fear to let me know. You think that if I know, I shall cease to care. The truth is that if I do not know, I shall cease to care. If I did not love you, it would be just the opposite. —Now, I must try not to speak of this again. It is unpleas-

---

141. In his journal entry for this same visit, Stevens simply wrote, "April 1 [1907]. Just back from a trip to Reading for Easter. Family about as depressing as usual; Elsie more or less unmanageable" (*SP,* 174).

142. Broad Road (near Elsie's home) that runs between the lower, joined slopes of Mount Penn and Neversink Mountain.

ant to me to speak of love. It is a thing not to be communicated in words, and words are like thorns in its wings. Poets and rhetoricians give it words. Men and women, who are not poets and rhetoricians, do not. Let us hide it, not from each other, but from words. How subtle and sweet it was! We must keep it so. We must say that there has been a little winter in us, and we must watch it grow new and clear and wonderful again. You must return to the Elsie I knew and I must become the old Wallace. It must be Spring for us as well as for the fields.

Tuesday Evening.

I have been reading all evening and it has refreshed me so, that, when I took up this letter again, it seemed a little lifeless and stale. — Then I happened to see in a bowl of odds and ends on my table the carnation you took from the table in your dining-room the last time but one that I was home—and that you gave me. It is quite dry. I picked it up and smelled it and—there was still an odor of faint spice. So there is still life in what I wrote last night. I want Elsie to love me. How many, many times I have said that to myself. I want Elsie to love me—always. This quiet evening at home, with my lamp, is half-empty without you. If you were here, I should still be quiet. But you would be here. —I am in the mood for reading some big book and for looking up and seeing you here. —Was it the sunset that made me so? It was clear and quiet and soft—like the shore of some island of adventure; and I looked at it for a long time.

Your
Wallace.

⌣

[WAS 1788 April 9, 1907[143] New York]

Tuesday Evening

Dearest—(Isn't it enough to say just that?):—

Your quotations always interest me, because I like to see the things you like well enough to make note of. Your quotations, too, are proofs to me of the naturally sensitive sympathies of your mind, if you will let me say that. Yet I do not need proofs beyond your willing love of delicate skies and delicate flowers, and everything that is beautiful in the sun, or moon. —The love of books for the thoughts in them is like the love of the earth for its seas and distances. We must talk about books sometime when we are together. That will be quite as good as a walk on the hill, if we talk about the right ones. —Yesterday I bought a little vol-

---

143. In Box 80, a box of ephemera, there is an empty envelope addressed to Elsie in Stevens's hand, mailed and received April 8, 1907, the day before this letter. This empty envelope is evidence of a missing letter, since WAS 1788 has its own envelope, mailed on the morning of April 10 and received in Reading at 10:00 P.M. that night.

ume called the "Note Books" of Matthew Arnold.[144] It is made up of quotations jotted down by him from day to day, and of lists of books to be read at various times. The quotations are in a half-dozen different languages. (It gives me a sort of learned delight to guess at the Latin ones; and last night I hunted all through Dante for translations of several Italian ones.) Here is a Latin one: "Angelica hilaritas cum monastica simplicitate"; and here is what I guess it to mean: "Angelic hilarity with monastic simplicity." And here is an English one: "A merry heart doeth good like a medicine, but a broken spirit drieth the bones." — I also bought a volume of lectures on greek subjects.[145] If there were some book about Greece in the library at home to which I could refer you, I should do it and plead all evening with you to read it. The impression of Greece is one of the purest things in the world. It is not a thing, however, that you get from any one book, but from fragments of poetry that have been preserved, and from statues and ruins, and a thousand things, all building up in the mind a noble conception of a pagan world of passion and love of beauty and life. It is a white world under a blue sky, still standing erect in remote sunshine. —But I am bookish to-night. It must be because winter has suddenly returned. It has been snowing all day. Down town the streets grew dark early, and there was mist and wind; and when I came home this evening the ground was covered with snow. Everybody is laughing about it. It is so unheard-of at this time of the year. They called the last storm the onion snow. This must be the strawberry snow. —I wish you had sent the odds and ends you changed your mind about. Before I read the postscript, I looked in the envelope for them and thought that you had forgotten them. Can't we send each other what we like? Lately I have been wishing for a new photograph of you—one looking at me. This one is looking away, and it makes me want to turn its head, so that I can see all of you, as I sometimes turn your head at home, when you look away. Do you think you will be having any taken this

---

144. This volume is no longer in the Stevens library, though there is a copy of an edition of 1952. This respectful attitude toward maxims (which was a constant of Stevens's intellectual life for many years to come) contrasts with Stevens's letter of June 8, 1953, to Barbara Church concerning the recent publication of a new edition (Howard Foster Lowry, Karl Young, and Waldo Hilary Dunn, eds., *The Note-Books of Matthew Arnold* [London: Oxford University Press], 1952) of this volume: "I used to have a book containing a collection of aphorisms on which Matthew Arnold's soul depended. Recently his entire collection of notebooks was published. I started to read them as I once read the lesser volume but lost interest. One good saying is a great deal; but ten good sayings are not worth anything at all. Anyhow, it may be that I don't belong to that church anymore, or that I don't care for conversation with that particular set of gods; nor, perhaps, with any" (*LWS*, 780).
145. This is probably a reference to S. H. Butcher's *Harvard Lectures on Greek Subjects* (London: Macmillan, 1904). The University of Massachusetts–Amherst has Stevens's copy of this book with a considerable number of marginal markings in it by Stevens.

Spring? (If you cared for one of me, it might persuade me to have one taken, though I have a horror of that sort of thing.) Often one forgets that a photograph is a photograph. Your own often brings you to me. But it is such a pity that you should always be looking away. —Do you remember when I came to see you the morning after your letter last summer—at the office? You looked at me then as I wanted you to. I remember how large your eyes were and how they smiled. —If you go to Allentown for any length of time, will you write to me from there? I wish you could go and have a change.

With love,
Wallace.

↪

[WAS 1773 April 12, 1907 New York][146]

> Elsie's mirror only shows
> Golden hair and cheeks of rose.
>
> It is like a glimpse of skies,
> Whose early stars are Elsie's eyes;
>
> Or like a faintly silver shade
> That shines about the magic maid.
>
> When she to Time has paid her due,
> May I still be her mirror true.

WS

↪

[WAS 1789 April 14,[147] 1907 New York]

Sunday Evening

My dear Elsie:—

A day of Spring sun and Winter wind. Arthur[148] came up at noon and took dinner with me. In the afternoon we walked North and South criticizing all the architecture in the little world we saw. Home again in time for tea—and a crimson and yellow and blue sunset—and here I am, sitting in a new chair, with the

---

146. This poem is dated only by the postmark on its envelope.

147. *SP* (176) incorrectly indicates that this letter was written on April 7, 1907.

148. Daniel Arthur Clous was in Stevens's class (1897) at Reading Boys' High School. He is mentioned in Stevens's journal for the first time on September 26, 1904, indicating that they are planning to share a room in New York. In the *Graduate Catalogue of the Reading High Schools: 1856–1905*, he is listed as a draftsman for Howells and Stubbs, Architects, of 100 William Street in New York, an address near which Stevens worked for the law firm of Philbin, Beekman and Menken (52–54 William Street; see *LWS*, 93).

wind crying around the chimneys and rattling the windows. Next Sunday I am going to the country, and on the Sunday following I am going to the country, too, — your country and mine, god willing, as the sailors say—to see you. Last night I was home (Saturday nights down town are out of the question) and I read the "Letters of John Keats"[149] until early this morning; and there is a page full of news. I have been wanting to read Keats' letters ever since I knew there were such things. They are mere chatter (as they ought to be) with only a little observation here and there. The other evening I bought Boswell's "Life of Johnson,"[150] an enormous affair in three volumes. Have you ever read it? It is one of those books one is always going to read, but which one never does. Lately, I have been buying almost any book that struck my fancy. I wish I might line my walls with them and devote myself to study, or rather, reading; for if I have ardor left for anything at all, it is for books. The book stores in New-York are a distress to me: they are so <u>un</u>bookish. I like to drop into a dusty-looking basement shop and find odd volumes of the old English poets or of the old French ones for all that. I'd like to find a volume of Marot or Villon; but the books one does find are the most utterly common-place, trashy things under the sun. In Boston and Philadelphia it is different; and they say that in the bookstalls along the quays of Paris, it is different, too. And how different it must have been in Florence at Franceschini's. You remember the clipping I sent about him. — One gets in a way of looking at people (those beastly blobs [two small smudges on the letter paper] must stay; I have nothing to remove them) as one does of looking at houses or fields or stones and of feeling about them impersonally. But when you think that some old bald-head in a car may be humming:

"ce doulx parler, ce cler tainct, ces beaulx yeulx"[151]

149. This volume is still in the remains of Stevens's library at the Huntington: *The Letters of John Keats to His Family and Friends,* ed. Sidney Colvin (London: Macmillan, 1891). This book is signed by Stevens and dated "4/1907" at Fordham Heights.
150. These three volumes are in the remains of Stevens's library at the Huntington: James Boswell, *The Life of Samuel Johnson L.L.D.,* 3 vols. (London: Macmillan, 1906). Volume 1 is signed by Stevens and dated "4/1907" at Fordham Heights. Volume 3 is dated "5/30/07."
151. His handwriting is quite clear at this point; the extra *l*s are clearly there before each *x,* an implicit acknowledgment of the difficulty of reading his handwriting and the certainty that he intended this older spelling. He may be quoting anyone from Villon (c.1431–after 1463) to Marot (1496–1544), perhaps Charles D'Orléans (1394–1465), whose rondel ("Le temps a laissé son manteau") he and Elsie read in a translation by Andrew Lang. (See WAS 1887 August 17, 1909, for this reference.) Ronsard also has many examples of these phrases in these spellings in his work, and it may be that Stevens is putting these three phrases together from more than a single source.

that is: "that sweet speech, that clear skin, those beautiful eyes," and know that he got it from a book: don't you feel ready to believe that men and books—life and books are all a wonderful jumble by this time? I wish I could fan the little flame for books that must be born-in you. Then our winters would be as full of Small miracles as our summers; and our summers would be more and more what they ought to be: a thousand summers in one. There are so many illustrations of that; but illustrations limit the imagination. But suppose on a summer day I quoted:

"Rest, and a world of leaves, and stealing streams."[152]

I should be adding another day to the real one, don't you think? So I might ramble on, only suggesting things, not completing them. I do that too much; and I am afraid that sometimes you must be at a loss for a meaning in my scribble. —What will you do when you find the first line in your forehead? You know that you cannot possibly be old at twenty. No one says a girl is old until <u>she</u> says that she is twenty-five. That is why she never says it. You are too young to be anything but a girl; but, of course, you are not really a little girl, except in the sense that every woman is always a little girl, and that every man is always a little boy. That, however, is sentimental. Would it be also sentimental to say that I hope I shall not always be writing you letters until you are old? Need I speak of this now any more clearly than we needed to speak during our first summer? We do not understand each other the less, I hope, for not speaking. You know. I have a special dread of speaking of it to-night, because Mrs. Jackson had a piece of beef for dinner to-day that cost $2.25 and some asparagus, for salad, that cost .85 a bunch. Oysters are .15 and oranges .40 a dozen. It is frightful. Whenever the desire becomes so strong as to make me unreasonable, I find it a great help to inquire about the price of eggs and pine-apples and coal. And you cannot get a cook under $25. a month; and (and, and) one <u>must</u> have a cook; at least I think so now. But you know my views. Meditate on the figures—and then put your right hand in my left and let us call down the wrath of heaven on all butchers, grocers, landlords, laundresses, tailors, seamstresses, and so on; and thank good-ness that for the present we can be happy without them. You must not scold me for saying all this. I think our notion of waiting until everything is ready, before speaking of it, is, <u>also,</u> sentimental. I have all manner of plans and as soon as vaca-tion time comes around, we must put our heads together. —Now, surely I have said enough, without running the risk of stirring your old-time rebelliousness; if,

152. He may be referring to "Rest" by Margaret L. Woods, a twenty-line poem in *A Victorian Anthology: 1837–1895,* ed. Edmund Clarence Stedman. Originally published by Houghton, Mifflin in 1895, this work was reprinted in New York by Greenwood Press in 1969. The second line of this poem is "Silent besides the silent-stealing streams."

indeed, you still set any store in that green mood. At all events, no more to-night. ——[153] I have been dreaming since writing the last sentence. Will you be able to imagine what it was about? Or will you refuse to imagine and think me impudent for such liberty? But we are in a strange situation, understanding so well, saying so little. —After all, it is only myself that I understand. When I say "us," it can only be I. No: I remember things you have said. We must settle it all between ourselves. —The wind is still blowing hard. It is a sign of my great age that I pay so little attention to it. If I were still young, I should listen to it, won-dering. Children dream in the wind. It makes a warm room sweet to them. It turns a rug by the fire into an Arabian Nights' carpet. —My adventures grow few and far between; but it is a great adventure to be writing to you to-night, calling you my little girl, yet knowing that you are a woman, almost—not that I should ever use the word. To think of you one way to-day, helps me to think of you another way to-morrow.

With my love,
Wallace.

⌁

[WAS 1790 April 16, 1907 New York]

Tuesday Evening

My dear Elsie:—

We have been having that roast-beef at Mrs. Jackson's, about which I wrote to you, at every meal—warmed over, cold, <u>in formâ</u> hash; but to-night I objected. —But you see that there are still possibilities, since one piece of beef can go so far. —I hesitated about sending the last four pages of my Sunday evening letter. Your last two letters, however, written apparently (I hope I am not unjust) in such careless haste, almost excuse me. Sometimes it seems as if special states of mind in me wrought a contrast in you. When I am really full of you, you are as indifferent as a coquette. Therefore, to be spiteful and Dutch, I do not altogether regret writing about roast-beef instead of about pomegranates and apple-blossoms. —The deuce with being spiteful and Dutch! Life is too short, as the washer-women say. What I say is that Elsie calls herself my own and that that is enough. Nevertheless a long letter makes me happier than a short one. Now, you will not think me trying to vex you, will you? I am in such a quiet mood to-night that I would not vex anyone. Perhaps, it is because this has been a quiet day—nerveless. This morning the clouds were low. It made me wish to be an artist. I saw a goat tied to a tree and everything was so dull that I felt it would be interesting to sit on the curb-stone and make a sketch of the goat and the tree and the bank of grass. —This evening I read a London weekly that

153. Stevens puts an extralong dash here.

I have been getting and took a placid sort of pleasure in reading about English politics, Egyptian politics, Russian politics and a raft of other things. Then I cut the pages of some new books. Then I listened to the rain on the windows and fretted a little about it until I remembered that I still have two umbrellas. —I ought to tell you what Arthur said on Sunday. After we had been walking, he said, "Why don't you ask me what I think of Elsie?" Well, he said that you went beyond his expectations! Remember that his expectations were high. He liked your voice and your manner. So he said! I shall not tell you what more he liked, because little girls should not hear such things about themselves. —Late at night mice run about my room and make a rustle among my papers. I hear them now—their rustle and the hissing of an engine and the abstracted buffeting of the wind on the windows. How full of trifles everything is! It is only one's thoughts that fill a room with something more than furniture. Startling reflection! —One more cigar and an hour's reading and then I shall go to bed. Last night I read Ruth, Ecclesiastes and the Song of Solomon (and much besides that was not so sanctimonious). The verse about the voice of the turtle is in the Song. The one that follows it runs,

> The fig tree putteth forth her green figs,
> And the vines with the tender grape
> give a good smell. Arise my love, my
> fair one, and come away.[154]

If you lived in a house with a balcony under which I could serenade you, that would make a pleasant serenade in two weeks time.

Affectionately,
Wallace.

↩

[WAS 1791 April 19,1907 New York]

Friday Evening

My dear Elsie:—

Last night was house-cleaning night with me. I went through my things (as you went through yours not long ago) and threw away a pile of useless stuff. How hard it is to do it! One of the things was my Bible. I hate the look of a Bible. This was one that had been given to me for going to Sunday-school every Sunday in a certain year. I'm glad the silly thing is gone. There are still a few odds and ends that I keep for sentimental reasons: my college books, my father's copy of Burns' poems, and so on. They'll go, too, when my courage is at its height.[155]

---

154. Song of Solomon 2:13.
155. There is no book by Burns in what survives of Stevens's library.

Everything looks prim and old-maidish to-night and I half like it for a change.
—Yet I wrote to you last night. It was a disquisition on April star-light, very
poetical—and I tore it up and went to bed. Don't you think I was wise? No: I
didn't go to bed at once. I put out my lamp and loafed in a chair in the dark
looking out at the moon and I smoked, too. Then this morning! But hang the
weather. Now the moon is out again, looking as innocent as if nothing had
happened. It looked fairly brilliant as I came home at nine o'clock. Mrs. Jackson and I and an old maid with golden hair had been talking since dinner-time,
like three gossips, about South America, and Life(!), and our neighbors. I had
intended going down-town to see some pictures; but it was so comfortable sitting there, with a pocketful of cigarettes, that I thought it would be too much
trouble to go anywhere. —This morning the desire to move came over me
again. I thought of moving into what was once called Greenwich Village. It is
very far down-town, on the west side. It was all owned by Queen Anne in the
eighteenth century. She granted it to Trinity Church, which owns most of it
now. It still looks like a village, notwithstanding it is in the heart of town. But
it is forlorn, out-of-the way, a little quaint, and I should be sure to like it for a
while. It was only the hope of Spring that kept me here, and since this morning's snow has taken away that hope, there is no reason to stay. —To-morrow,
as you know, I am going away over Sunday. But I shall write to you Sunday
evening, unless I should get home unexpectedly late, when I shall write on
Monday, and I hope I shall have a great deal to tell you, because this trip
threatens to be something of an adventure. —I wish you could see my new
books. They make me as proud as a peacock. My room is so large that the
books seem lost in a thundering big space, but I suppose that by and by they
will amount to something. I want to surround myself with them. It was
thoughtless of me to recommend them to you. Most of mine would bore you
terribly. Besides I ought not to thrust my own tastes on you. I am quite content to have you write of blue clouds. <u>Blue</u> clouds! There must be blue ones,
after all, at twilight. I am waiting for a long letter from you. Perhaps, it would
be better not to say so, and to wait patiently. I shall do that. If the letter that
comes to-morrow morning is a short one, I shall be more disappointed than I
can tell you.

Affectionately,
Wallace.

[WAS 1792 April 22, 1907[156] New York]

Monday Evening

My dear Elsie:—

This might well be a wonderful letter because Sunday was a wonderful day. The house, where I visited, is in the midst of a wood, but the house was quite as fascinating as the trees. On Saturday evening, we sat by the fire and talked and read until almost midnight. The room was full of pretty things—every picture, every lamp, every chair. We slept late. When the church-bells began to ring at nine o'clock, I was still dozing, or else half-listening to the frogs whistling, or whatever it is they do. After lunch, we walked to the Sound with two dogs, passing all manner of pleasant houses on the way. We basked in the sand, and loafed on a point of rocks, looking out over the empty water, blue and tumbling.[157] It makes me feel now as if I had been away for a month or two. My room was unwelcome when I returned. So, at noon to-day, I ran up-town and (to do what I could) bought a large photograph of one of Rembrandt's paintings. It is a portrait of himself and of his wife Saskia—and she is sitting in his lap![158] I might just as well have chosen a Madonna, but now I am glad I chose this, because it [is] just what I needed. And of course I bought a few more books: some pamphlets of lectures delivered at Oxford, and a translation from the Greek—Propertius. (Maybe it's from the Latin—I know it's about love, and that is really all I know).[159] Thus, you see, I have been having an

156. Since this is the last letter of this period before the nineteen-month gap, it might be helpful to note that the address on the envelope for this letter is marked through with a single red line and replaced in the left margin in Stevens's hand the following address: "641 Penn-St." This is probably the address of the "office" mentioned above at which Elsie worked as a stenographer.

157. This visit, to Charles Dana, a friend since law school, is also mentioned in his journals: "On the 19th, snow all day. —But today [April 21] it was blue & gold again. Have been to Darien, Connecticut, walking with dogs, loafing along the Sound. Mrs. Dana very attractive. Beautiful little house" (*SP, 177*).

158. This painting, *Self-portrait with Saskia,* hangs in the Gemäldegalerie in Dresden. It is listed as no. 30, with the title *Self-portrait with the Artist's Wife,* in the A. Bredius edition of *The Paintings of Rembrandt* (Great Britain: Phaidon Edition), which identifies it as no. 334 in the *Hofstede de Groot Descriptive Catalogue*. In a letter some forty years later, February 17, 1950, Stevens expresses a different attitude toward Rembrandt: "Rembrandt, I must confess, has never stimulated me a great deal. I bow to him. But he leaves me, somehow or other, indifferent. The sense of his greatness is something I have to read about: I do not feel it" (*LWS, 668*).

159. This Latin poet, who is known to have looked back to Greek models, may have eventually influenced Stevens; for example, the third section of Stevens's "Le Monocle de Mon Oncle," the one that emphasizes hair, may have in mind the Propertius poem that begins "Quid invat ornato procedure, vita, capillo."

exciting time. After dinner to-night, Professor Lamb[160] and I took a walk (to Hop Sing's for some collars of mine) and we noticed a cloudy ring around the moon. Therefore, it will rain to-morrow. But at all events, it is not raining now, and that is something to be thankful for in April. I came home alone, through the grounds of the University,[161] not at all a bad place at night. There is a dome there, and there are pillars and arches and quiet shadows and a suggestion of dark nobility. I wished you were there, just to feel as I felt—and you would have felt so; only, it is a feeling you can never have in Reading, where there are neither domes, nor pillars, nor arches. —I shall come over on Saturday afternoon,[162] but whether early or late, it is too soon to say—but early probably, and sometime surely. If I do not come early, I shall come late. The desire to see you burns especially this time. You must be my "gracious lady" in every way, because I have been so well-behaved of late (perhaps, not in my letters, but actually). We have almost outrun Spring, because we welcomed it long before it came. On that account, let us consider it as the first touch of Summer—that Summer which, to you, is four seasons in one. I shall write again on Wednesday evening.

With love,
Wallace.

〰

A Nineteen-Month Gap in the Correspondence

The only break in the following silence of nineteen months in the correspondence (from April 1907 until December 1908) is, in addition to the excerpts Elsie made of Stevens's letters to her, and the poems he wrote for her birthday in 1908, a postcard from Elsie addressed to "Mr. Wallace Stevens, 84 William

160. In WAS 1806 of January 17, 1909, Stevens will refer to "an engraved invitation" from "my friend Lamb" for a large ceremony honoring Edgar Allan Poe. Albert R. Lamb (1881–1959), a 1903 graduate of Yale, received the M.D. degree from Columbia's College of Physicians and Surgeons in 1907, after which he served there as an intern and later as a member of the faculty for many years.
161. Columbia University. In his journal for June 20, [1900], Stevens had given his first ecstatic impression of the school: "Also went out to Columbia College at Morningside Heights—a delightful place. The Seth Low library has a great deal of grandeur to it—its approach consists of terraces of granite stairs rising to a domical building with a porch of lofty columns. There are roses and evergreens planted here and there on adjacent terraces. Their scents filled the hot, motionless air that hung about the structure. Inside is a huge dome supported by encircling galleries and alcoves. From these, I could hear the song-sparrows singing in the foliage without" (*SP,* 75).
162. This would have been April 27, but there is no information about this visit because the nineteen-month gap in the correspondence begins after this letter.

Street, N. Y. City, N.Y.": "Just received telegram. —Seeds were thrown away this morning. A post card! E." (WAS 4035 August 24, 1908).[163]

The primary sources of information about Stevens for 1908, at the end of which he and Elsie will become engaged, are scant: three brief entries in Stevens's journal (*SP,* 188–89), five letters from his father (from January 27 to May 13), eight letters from Stevens to Elsie at the end of the year, the excerpts in Elsie's Book, and Stevens's "Book of Verses" presented to Elsie on June 5, 1908, for her birthday. Although the following poems are printed in *Souvenirs and Prophecies* (190–96), they are given here because they were an integral part of this correspondence as the references to some of them have shown.

There is some evidence that the Book of Verses Stevens presented to Elsie on her twenty-third birthday was begun in 1907, and that the poems in that collection represent a selection and not a totality of the poems he wrote for her. One of her excerpts from 1907 is the poem that begins "If I love thee, I am thine," about which Stevens wrote, according to Elsie's excerpt, "for my collection of verses for Elsie." This poem is not in either of the two collections that still exist and therefore was not selected to be included in that first group of twenty poems. Two of the other poems that are excerpted by Elsie and are in the 1908 collection, notably "Adagia" and four lines from what would be "Damask," are in the excerpts from 1907. Other poems of 1907 in the excerpts and not in Book of Verses include the three quatrains Stevens wrote for her at Christmas 1907 in the flyleaf of Carman and Hovey's *Songs from Vagabondia* (as well as a quatrain for the flyleaf of each of the two following volumes by Carmen and Hovey: *More Songs from Vagabondia* and *Last Songs from Vagabondia*). In what seems to be early 1908, an excerpt reads, "It would only be proper for you to have your own private book of verses, even if it were very small and if the verses were very bad." Some time after March 1908, Elsie excerpts three lines of verse—"Some power to make you love / The poor thing that I am, forgetfully / If I were king"—lines not in the 1908 collection. An entire sonnet dated April 10, 1908, with the first line "Quick, Time, go by and let me to an end," is also left out of the 1908 collection.

---

163. This card is identified as Mt. Penn Boulevard, Reading, Pa. It shows a generic dirt road, lined on one side with white posts and a single white rail, curving uphill past pine trees. This address would be a business address for Stevens.

"Book of Verses"[164]

I

One day more-
But first, the sun,
There on the water,
Swirling incessant gold—
One mammoth beam!
Oh, far Hesperides!

II
New Life

Noon, and a wind on the hill—
Come, I shall lead you away
To the good things, out of those ill,
At the height of the world today.

I shall show you mountains of the sun,
And continents drowned in the sea;
I shall show you the world that is done,
And the face of the world to be.

III
Afield.

You give to brooks a tune,
A melody to trees.
You make the dumb field sing aloud
Its hidden harmonies.

An echo's rumor waits
A little while, and then,

164. This is the title from one of the excerpt above; the poems were for Elsie's twenty-second birthday, June 5, 1908; they were published in *SP,* 190–96 (WAS 24, Box 2, HEH). The title may allude to the following famous lines, the twelfth quatrain of Fitzgerald's translation of the Rubáiyát of Omar Khayyám:

> A Book of Verses underneath the Bough,
> A Jug of Wine, a Loaf of Bread—and Thou
> Beside me singing in the Wilderness—
> Oh, Wilderness were Paradise enow!

In Stevens's holograph text, each poem is centered on a separate page, and his use of the period after titles (and once after a roman numeral) is not consistent.

I hear the water and the pine
Take up their airs again.

IV

Hang up brave tapestries:
Huntsman and warrior there—
Shut out these mad, white walls.
I hate a room so bare.

And all these neighbor roofs
With chimney and chimney above—
Oh! let me hear the sound
Of soft feet that I love.

Then fetch me candles tall,
Stand them in bright array,
And go—I need such lights
And shadows when I pray.

V.
In a Crowd.

So much of man,
The wonder of him goes away!
The little art of him returns again
To struggling clay.

Come one, alone,
Come in a separate glory keen;
And sing, on shores of lapislazuli,
A song serene.

VI
On the Ferry.

Fog, now, and a bell,
A smooth, a rolling tide.
Drone, bell, drone and tell,
Bell, what vapors hide.

Lights, there, not of fire,
Unsensual sounds, yet loud,
Shapes that to shape aspire,
In that encumbered cloud.

Toll, now, a world resolved
To unremembered form.
Toll the stale brain dissolved
In images of storm.

VII
Tides.

These infinite green motions
Trouble, but to no end;
Trouble with mystic sense
Like the secretive oceans—

Or violet eve repining
Upon the glistening rocks;
Or haggard, desert hills;
Or hermit moon declining.

VIII
Winter Melody[165]

I went into the dim wood
And walked alone.
I heard the icy forest move
With icy tone.

My heart leapt in the dim wood
So cold, so bare—
And seemed to echo, suddenly,
Old music there.

I halted in the dim wood,
And watched, and soon,
There rose for me—a second time—
The pageant moon.

IX
Sonnet.

Explain my spirit—adding word to word,
As if that exposition gave delight.
Reveal me, lover, to myself more bright.
"You are a twilight, and a twilight bird."

165. A separate holograph copy in Stevens's hand of this poem at HEH (WAS 4105)
has the title "Ancient Rendezvous."

Again! For all the untroubled senses stirred,
Conceived anew, like callow wings in flight,
Bearing desire toward an upper light.
"You are a twilight, and a twilight bird."

Burn in my shadow, Hesperus, my own,
And look upon me with triumphant fire.
Behold, how glorious the dark has grown!
My wings shall beat all night against your breast,
Heavy with music—feel them there aspire
Home to your heart, as to a hidden nest.

X

Song.

A month—a year—of idle work,
And then, one song.
Oh! all that I am and all that I was
Is to that feeble music strung,
And more.

Yes: more; for there a sound creeps in,
A second voice,
From violet capes and forests of dusk,
That calls me to it without choice,
Alone.

XI

After Music.

The players pause,
The flute notes drop
To the song's end,
And, trembling, stop.

The harper's hand,
Reluctant, clings
To the hushed strain,
Of muffled strings.

The sounds die out,
And dying, free
The thoughts of all
You are to me.

XII
Twilight.

Here the huge moth
Whirled in the dusk,
The wearied mammoth reared
His reddened tusk.

The rank serpent stole
Down golden alleys,
To the envenomed trees
Of jasmine valleys.

Lark's clangor rang,
In haggard light,
To giants, crouched in fear
Of fearful night.

XIII
Adagio.

Drone, dove, that rounded woe again,
When I bring her to-morrow.
The woods were a less happy place,
But for that broken sorrow.

Tell her in undertones that Youth
With other times must reckon;
That mist that seals up the golden sun,
And ghosts from gardens beckon.

XIV

There is my spectre,
Pink evening moon,
Haunting me, Caliban,
With its Ariel tune.

It leads me away
From the rickety town,
To the sombre hill
Of the dazzling crown.

Away from my room,
Through many a door,
Through many a field
I shall cross no more.

After man, and the seas,
And the last blue land,
At the world's rough end,
If, perchance, I should stand

To rest from long flight—
Pale evening moon,
I should never escape
That wild, starry tune.

XV
Damask

You need not speak, if that be shame.
I need no voice.
Nor give to bright cheeks brighter flame:
I can abide my choice.

For mutely to my muter call,
Come magic means.
Now the enchanting measures fall—
A spirit intervenes.

XVI
Rest.

Glimpses of Eden for the tired mind,
The misty vale, the bending palm,
Bright Orient reefs in Orient oceans rolled,
That never lose their flooded calm.

Oh! large and glorious, the quiet star
Lighted beyond the half-seen trees.
Sweet is their comfort, but for dear repose,
You by my side are more than these.

XVII
In Town

It's well enough to work there,
When so many do;
It's well enough to walk the street,
When your work is through.

It's night there that kills me,
In a narrow room,

Thinking of a wood I know,
Deep in fragrant gloom.

XVIII
Meditation

There were feet upon the waters in the morning,
Like a golden mist that came from out the deep—
The feet of spirits lost in many a circle
Of winding dance, as if in wavering sleep.

They move away in quiet in the evening,
Lingering yet in a slow-ending round,
Faint lustres, rose and gray and purple,
That vanish soon in the devouring ground.

XIX
Home Again[166]

Back within the valley—
Down from the divide,
No more flaming clouds about—
Oh! the soft hill side,
And my cottage light,
And the starry night!

XX
What have I to do with Arras

Or its wasted star?
Are my two hands not strong enough,
Just as they are?
Because men met with rugged spears,
Upon the Lombard plain,
Must I go forth to them, or else
Have served in vain?

And does the nightingale, long lost
In vanished Shalott's dew,
Sing songs more welcome, dear, than those
I sing to you?

---

166. This poem was published, with "From a Junk," as one of "Two Poems" in *Trend* 8, no. 2 (November 1914): 117. It is the only poem from this first book of poems for Elsie that Stevens published.

2

Engagement

December 1908–September 1909

The letters[1] of this period are a unique resource in the study of the personality of Wallace Stevens; they are a large body of self-revelation from a concentrated period and are addressed to the single person who would be the most important stimulus of the psychic energy that went into the writing of his poetry. Although Stevens has probably been considering marriage to Elsie for several years, they are only now officially, though not very publicly, engaged. He has just made the commitment to get married, a commitment he considered desirable for many years, since his self-analysis on July 26, 1900: "I am certainly a domestic creature" (*SP*, 81). He believes that marrying Elsie will make him happy beyond his wildest imagination. He believes that he is marrying someone who is essentially a second self to him, someone who will "make a fuss over" him. He pays careful attention to the stories of marriage by those he knows in New York, and he has notions of chivalry in his mind that determine what he writes to Elsie and what he expects of her.

In these letters, Stevens gives rare expression to a sincere part of himself. There is little conscious irony in what he says in them. This is a final attempt to be honest and to keep under control the "perfect rout of characters" he believed was "in every man" (*SP*, 166, April 17, 1906). Though he brings several of these characters into the open in order to entertain and charm Elsie, there is no attempt here, as there will be later, to believe in any one of these fictions. His letters and his poetry before his marriage are completely different from those after the marriage, and in this difference one sees more directly than ever again the most "real" of "all the Wallaces," his own phrase, which Elsie selected for one of her excerpts of 1908. After the marriage, Stevens will invent a Wallace that came to be seen as *the* Wallace; that Wallace will write poetry we appreciate infinitely more than that written by the "real" Wallace before

---

1. There remain, from this brief period, 113 letters, 8 in December 1908 and another 105 of 1909, up to the time of the wedding in September of 1909.

the marriage. Yet the Wallace revealed in these letters is always a part of whatever Wallace is on stage at the moment.

Though he approached this marriage with doubts and fears, he tried to do everything he felt would ensure his happiness and thus Elsie's. He controlled every aspect of their marriage, including the determination of the wedding year, the non-announcement of their engagement, the severely restricted number of people at the wedding (which excluded his own family), and the tight schedule that fitted the ceremony, the reception, and the boarding of their train into the period from 10:30 until 12:19, one hour and thirty-nine minutes. He picked out their apartment without input from Elsie, and he seriously misled her as to the possible return to Reading in a few years. In these letters, he preserved the memories of their time together, and he had plans for the editing of those letters when they would look over all of them at once. He left nothing to chance and very little to Elsie to decide. The "Philadelphia jaunt" is a small example of his organizational efficiency, a prelude in February of the larger demonstration to be given in September.

Until his marriage, he deeply believed, as his upbringing, religious and social, had taught him, in the power of the will to determine one's fate and one's happiness. When he says this in one of his letters to Elsie, he is being as honest and as candid as he can be. He is, one might say, the Crispin at the beginning of "The Comedian as the Letter C," the person who believes that "Man is the intelligence of his soil." He believed that he and she would, through the exercise of their wills, eventually triumph over circumstances, certainly over all incompatibilities between them. He believed that Elsie would become a true New Yorker and respond to the attractions of the city as he had done. He thought that all of her past resistance to his wishes was a simple whim that language and their time together would straighten out.

He was unable to see the great degree of disparity between his rather literary imagination and Elsie's reality, and he was particularly blind to the degree to which he was misleading her about the possibility of their returning to Reading. As early as 1907, in an excerpt from a letter no longer extant, he writes, "I know perfectly well that to live in town would be a cruel disillusion to you." On June 9, 1909, he declares, "Your suggestion about the locust tree is capital and we must start a special fund for that purpose one of these days. It would be fine to settle on some plot of ground that we should like to have, some where at home, buy it, plant it, and hold it as a place to build a little home for summers bye-and-bye. Both of us, wherever we may be, will always return to our native "land" as the best place (for us) in the world—and it would be pleasant always to think of some country patch there as entirely our own. But that is one of the things we may keep to dream of" (WAS 1853). It is significant that this passage was selected by Elsie for her Book, her excerpts from Stevens's letters. Shortly after this letter, he is even more encouraging about the possibility of a return to Reading: "Yet a much better idea would be to move the office to Reading during the summer—up on the hill! I wish, one of these days, in a few years, some capital opportunity would come up at home. Really, it would be great fun to pack up one's things and come back—after twelve years of absence—with the feeling that one was going to stay" (WAS 1856, June 16, 1909). That this suggestion was merely a verbal construct designed to ease over differences between them and not a true plan for future developments did not occur to Elsie, and passages like this might have sown the seeds of serious future discord.

Stevens's mature poetry seems to be a product of that discord as much as any direct inspiration by Elsie as a mythical muse. One constant source of discord is the long passages of earnest sermonizing or moralizing that were a regular part of these letters of 1909. Those letters that were most clearly on the subject of morality were those most likely to be partly or totally excised. These letters continue a long meditation on the subject; his journal entry for June 1903, in a highly excised section, asserts, "Moral qualities are masculine; whimsicalities are feminine. That seems hardly just but I think it is exact" (*SP*, 114). A journal entry of April 27, 1906, the crucial year in which their relationship almost ended, contains more of his basic thinking on this subject (this is the last use of the word "moral" in *SP*):

> There are no end of gnomes that *might* influence people—but do not. When you first feel the truth of, say, an epigram, you feel like making it a rule of conduct. But this one is displaced by that, and thus things go on in their accustomed way. There is one pleasure in this volatile morality: the day you believe in chastity, poverty and obedience, you are charmed to discover what a monk you have always been—the monk is suddenly revealed like a spirit in a wood; the day you turn Ibsenist, you confess that, after all, you always were an Ibsenist, without knowing it. So you come to believe in yourself, and in your new creed. There is a perfect rout of characters in every man—and every man is like an actor's trunk, full of strange creatures, new & old. But an actor and his trunk are two different things. (*SP*, 166)

Stevens's small lessons to Elsie are of large importance in revealing his basic personality as a teacher, a preacher, a prophet, a rabbi, a philosopher, and a poet, all of which were synonymous terms for him. The letter of February 28, 1909, serves as almost a gloss to "Sunday Morning," that great pagan sermon, as he imagines "temples, bound to be built some day, when people will seek in a place not specially dedicated to religion, those principles of moral conduct that should guide us in every-day life—as distinct, say, from the peculiar life of Sundays. — My mind is rather full of such things to-day, and so resembles the mood that

fastened me, a year or more ago, so intently on Matthew Arnold—and Maxims!
. . . —To think occasionally of such things gives me a comforting sense of balance and makes me feel like the Brahmin on his mountain-slope who in the
midst of his contemplations—surveyed distant cities—and then plunged in
thought again." This passage shows his deep love of generalizations and abstrac-
tions, the peace he feels that such abstract statements bring him, the sense of
control and protection from accidental intrusions and wrongs, indeed, the home
that he seeks.

In another letter, he rues this penchant for preaching: "It worries me to be so
much of a moralist, as I might seem to be from the sheets I sent you. I don't
want to seem priggish, and yet it is a little hard to take anything back without
being—confusing. You know that the love of maxims is one aspect of Idealism—
of which I am not ashamed provided you understand that in my case (as I understand it to be in yours) the Idealism is accompanied by a love of milk and honey,
of moon-light nights, of good, red earth, and a good many human frailties. I am
not going to moralize for a long time. It is a creepy occupation" (WAS 1828
March 14, 1909).

The next letter of the very next day is on this same subject and, significantly,
only a fragment of it remains: "It is just as well that I tore up my last, because it
had more about moralizing in [it]—and I prefer to regard that word as tabooed.
It is insulting, impertinent, ill-mannered, low-spirited, creeping, flat, weak, like
the thing (not 'think,' bejabers) it represents. Ugh! —But no more of it" (WAS
1829 March 15, 1909). The letter on the following day continues this subject so
crucial for Stevens and for his poetry:

> "My green cap is hanging behind the door, tonight, and I have on my
> wig—because I am not quite through with this disturbing subject. —
> When you consider the reverence we feel for all Wise Men, at least for
> such as have spoken wisely of the life and destiny of men and women, it is
> apparent that their Wisdom is something different from Morality. I want
> to preserve all the reverence due to Wisdom, however much I may
> malign Morality. —By Morality I mean that nagging voice that approves
> or disapproves of what one does: that lectures one. It is Morality that vexes
> you with the accusation of being selfish now and then (according to your
> letter), that speaks slightingly of the pretty variety of clothes, that does any
> one of a number of things. —Morality would make us all old maids.
> Eschew it! —But Wisdom is another thing. To think and to philosophize
> is an exciting delight and they are only the lesser exercises of Wisdom. —
> But that is not what I want to say. I want to distinguish Wisdom from
> priggish Morality—as different as a goddess from an old hen in curl
> papers—and tell you that while I am ashamed of having ever recognized

Morality I am prepared to bow to the ground at sight of t'other. —Think
of Buddha directing millions of aspiring souls, fashioning a happiness for
them; think of Plato with his powerful, clear thought. —Well you've
never read 'em (no more have I). —But I swear I feel a holy élan toward
them. Élan, according to my French dictionary means "spring; start;
bound; flight; soaring; burst; sally; impulse"; etc, etc. —I propose, then,
still to worship the Wise and reverence Wisdom, or as Solomon says, to
"get Wisdom, get understanding." —Look for me in Sacred Pagodas; in
shadowy Temples; in groves hallowed by ikons and—the voice of
Socrates; by Ilyssus. (WAS 1830 March 16, 1909)

The letter of May 2, 1909, continues this subject, coming ever closer to the spirit
of "Sunday Morning":

Today I have been roaming about town. In the morning I walked down-
town—stopping once to watch three flocks of pigeons circling in the
sky. I dropped into St. John's chapel an hour before the service and sat in
the last pew and looked around. It happens that last night at the Library I
read a life of Jesus and I was interested to see what symbols of that life
appeared in the chapel. I think there were none at all excepting the gold
cross on the altar. When you compare that poverty with the wealth of
symbols, of remembrances, that were created and revered in times past,
you appreciate the change that has come over the church. The church
should be more than a moral institution, if it is to have the influence that
it should have. —The space, the gloom, the quiet mystify and entrance
the spirit. But that is not enough. —And one turns from this chapel to
those built by men who felt the wonder of the life and death of Jesus—
temples full of sacred images, full of the air of love and holiness—
tabernacles hallowed by worship that sprang from the noble depths of
men familiar with Gethsemane, familiar with Jerusalem. —I do not wonder that the church is so largely a relic. Its vitality depended on its association with Palestine, so to speak. —I felt a peculiar emotion in reading
about John the Baptist, Bethany, Galilee—and so on,[2] because (the truth
is) I had not thought about them much since my days at Sunday-school
(when, of course, I didn't think of them at all). It was like suddenly
remembering something long forgotten, or else like suddenly seeing

2. These geographical references and Stevens's emphasis upon them might be an
indication that the "life of Jesus" he has just read is that of Ernest Renan, in which the
geographical emphasis is also heavy because Renan was physically in the Holy Land
when he wrote his book. The importance that the word Palestine will have in "Sunday
Morning" could also point to this conclusion.

something new and strange in what had always been in my mind. —
Reading the life of Jesus, too, makes one distinguish the separate idea of
God. Before to-day I do not think I have ever realized that God was distinct from Jesus. It enlarges the matter almost beyond comprehension.
People doubt the existence of Jesus—at least they doubt incidents of his
life, such as, say, the Ascension into Heaven after his death. But I do not
understand that they deny God. I think everyone admits that in some
form or other. —The thought makes the world sweeter—even if God be
no more than the mystery of Life. (WAS 1840)

This letter may have ended this subject for a while, and the word "moral"
does not appear again in Stevens's letters to Elsie. After their marriage, the topic is
largely moot, largely irrelevant in their relationship, though the desire to explain
"How to Live. What to Do" will always remain with him. His moral lectures to
Elsie are precursors of all the moral lectures he will deliver in his poetry, from
"Sunday Morning" to "Aphorisms on Society" (finally called "Owl's Clover")
to "Notes Toward a Supreme Fiction" to "An Ordinary Evening in New Haven"
and "The Rock."

⌇

[WAS 1793 December 2, 1908 New York]

A Winter Night

Dear Lady:

Behold this sheep at your cottage door again—after a ramble through many a
dark 'n gloomy valley; for Monday night was sacred to Blackness and last night I
wept at my forlornness (as I looked down from the gallery at all the wonderful
people—on the stage and off—at one of the theatres). "I am better now," as the
old man said in the story—except, of course, for this sheepish feeling. —Yet I
wonder that I am better. I wonder that I am anything at all after an argument I
had at the table to-night. The subject of the debate: Why is it that school-boys
who win gold medals (the little Jews!) never amount to anything afterwards? Pop
out of the box they brought up Lincoln. Groans from my end of the table, etc. I
denied that gold-medal boys never amounted to anything afterwards, said that
So-and-So was a nobody. Everybody horrified—a tempest among honest minds.
—It is such an odd thing that bright boys should be expected to be successful[3]
men. Brightness is so small an element of success. Brightness disillusions. —Shall
I go into it? Fiddlesticks! The educated man or woman is simply that. People
look for so much more, just as if knowledge involved ambition, tenacity, character.

---

3. Richardson, *Wallace Stevens,* reproduces the first page (which goes through "successful") of this letter (vol. 1, facing p. 193).

—I think only the learned know the uses of learning—they alone understand their own position. —The fact that Cromwell or Napoleon were dull scholars is not an argument for dull scholars. It is not an argument for anything at all. It is an idle fact. —But these school-teachers and clerks guage everything by brains. Is there nothing in the world but the weariness of brains? Whatever is active makes its mark: industry, desire, temper; and so on. —But they are all snug in their dingy rooms now, saying, "Mr. Stevens will learn"; and here am I saying to myself, "The dunces!."[*sic*] —The proper thing to do is to read one's paper at the table and pay no attention to them. —Poor old Lincoln (the boarding-house Lincoln, not the historic one) drives me out of my wits with his anecdotes. He caps everything with a story. Tonight he said, "Well, Mr. Stevens, Stephen Douglas thought that Lincoln had no ability, but he changed his mind. When Lincoln was inaugurated he stood beneath him and held his hat." At that, all the school-marms glared. Piffle, piffle, piffle! What had Lincoln's immense ability to do with gold-medals? —When I came up-stairs, I noticed a dispatch in the Sun[4] about the typhoid epidemic at Reading. I had heard about it before but did [not] know it was so serious. Is anyone down with it in your neighborhood? Please tell me, dear. I think you ought to boil all your drinking-water. Do you? Let me know what care you take. I never drink anything but spring or distilled water. I always have several bottles of distilled water in my room and have now. Don't run any risk. Tell me in just what parts of town people are being taken sick. Above all, don't drink any milk. That is one of the most common sources of infection. If you want to take something to build you up (nearly everyone "takes something to build them up") let it be eggs, or plenty of meat and potatoes, and the like. — Don't forget to write to me on this, because I shall think about it until you do. — It was pleasant to have you speak of the saxophone. It whisks one away to a kind of German or, rather, Dutch Arcadia. I have no doubt that Dutch satyrs play the saxophone. —And then that being afraid. You deserve a kiss for being so nice and timid. But, my dear, I know all about that—not only about the frightful next room, but also about the fat men that chase around the wall, and the skinny men that chase around the ceiling—and the two men downstairs putting the silver in a great, big bag—and the footsteps in the yard—and most of all the delicious relief of the family finally coming home, when you say "Hello!" and they say, "Were you afraid?" and you say, "Afraid? What a silly question! Did you have a good time?" —I haven't always been the abandoned animal I am now, you know— living in a corner of a hostile house. There used to be halls and stairs and vacant

---

4. Popular New York "penny" newspaper that was founded in 1833 and that in 1897 published the famous editorial that began "Yes, Virginia, there is a Santa Claus" in answer to the letter of Virginia O'Hanlon. Stevens will refer to this newspaper a number of times in his letters of 1909.

rooms—and a cellar <u>full</u> of tramps and people prowling around, waiting to <u>jump out</u>! —But I haven't told you about "The Prima Donna"[5]—except to say that I wept, and that my tears looked like a chandelier. You know they rub it in here: Fritzi Scheff, and an unsurpassed chorus; book by Henry Blossom; music by Victor Herbert; wigs by Hepner; shoes by Dazian; scenes by Perlstein, Goldstein, and Katzenstein; Mme. Scheff's pearl dress by Mrs. Osborne; her pink dress by Henriette, her black dress by Heléne; hats by Cobber and Dobber; gowns for the chorus by Fobber and Gobber; the programme by Nobber and Popper; the house perfumed by Ed. Pinaud; doctors in the audience will please leave their names at the box office; carriages for 10.45. —Well, it was very tame. Mm. Scheff trills and trills and trills and the chorus marches and sits around and there is a joke to each act. At all events, it passes the time; and last night I was too tired to think of anything else. —There has been only one truly great event and that is the cold wave. It was the chatter of the breakfast table. When I went out I found it to be an ordinarily brisk day with a high wind—no more. I hate high winds[.] They blow up one street and don't touch the cross-streets. You walk along—zip! —In Martinique, the wind breaks down iron doors. Here it blows your hat into an ash-barrel. —Why, I must be an ill-natured crow to quarrel so with everything. (That is one of the things that moved my self-contempt last night.) Tell me that I am not ill-natured—so that I have some solace from my own thoughts. — On Saturday evening, I am going to take old Mr. Maitland to the Murray Hill[6] for dinner. We have been planning it for a week or more. He is going to bring some of his cigars—oh, they are as dry as dust, and perfect. —I wish you would write me a letter telling me everything you do some day from the time you get up until you go to bed. Don't take a special day, but just one out of a hundred— take Friday. Tell me what you wear—what time you get my letter—where you read it—every little thing. I want to have a peep into one of your ordinary days—as if I were watching you without your knowing it. No embellishing, mind you. —Couldn't you have a photograph taken for me for Christmas? It need not be a large one—just one of those inexpensive small ones, because they are all the same when framed. I shall have it framed here afterwards. I should like to have you facing me but not looking right out of the picture—and (if I may suggest it) in the simplest dress you have. There is something disturbing about pictures that look right out, just as there is in too formal dresses. Will you do it? I

5. Comic Opera in two acts by Henry Blossom and Victor Herbert, produced November 30, 1908, at the Knickerbocker Theater. Photo of Frizi Scheff as the Prima Donna and a review of the play in *Theatre* 9 (January 1909): 1, 2.

6. The Murray Hill Hotel on Park Avenue between Fortieth and Forty-first streets, completed in 1884, was patronized by such famous people as Mark Twain, Senator George Hearst, Jay Gould, Diamond Jim Brady, and Presidents Grover Cleveland and William McKinley.

should like to have that most of all.[7] —You may even have a hat on, if you wear the one with the black thing-a-ma-jig on it—not the one with the wide brim. There is something quaint about hats as they go out of fashion—when people no longer wear anything like them. They get to be like the clothes one sees in groups of college classes fifteen or twenty years ago—strange, curious. They mark an era. —What a to-do about a little picture! —Do you realize that it is only three weeks to Christmas? It falls on a Friday, I believe. No doubt, I shall be able to come on Thursday evening and stay until Monday morning—three whole days. Write me long letters in the meantime, Elsie, so that we may forget how long it is since we have been together. Upon my soul—it is half-past ten. I have been writing since a little past seven—so that you know how I have spent one evening at least. To-morrow evening there is going to be a musicale at a house nearby at which all our artists are to perform. Do you think I shall go? On the contrary, I shall be just where I am now—drat 'em. (Forgive the 'em.) —I must keep myself in good form for Saturday evening, of course. —I've a notion to run over to the Library some night a take a look at the <u>Journal des Débats.</u> One must keep in touch with Paris, if one is to have anything at all to think about. — There is an old church on my favorite Varick street which the <u>Post</u> announces is to be torn down. The organ, which is a hundred years old, was built in Philadelphia and while being sent to New-York on a vessel, was captured by the British in the war of 1812 and taken to London, where it was kept for two or three years. So that I was not wrong, after all, in taking a fancy to Varick street.

With much love,
Sambo.

⌒

[WAS 1794 December 7, 1908 New York]

Monday Evening

My dear:

I was delighted to get a letter from you this morning. Indeed, if there had been none, I should have sent you a telegram. I thought that you might be sick. Yesterday I went up-town and bought some <u>Eagles</u> to try to find out about the situation; but they were dreadfully stupid and had no news at all in them. I am certainly relieved to know that you are all right and I trust that you will take

---

7. In *SP* (200), Holly says, "But she did have a photograph taken. It shows her facing to the right, though not full profile, wearing a simple white, high-collared dress and a gold locket, with her long blond hair drawn to the back of her neck, where it is bound with a ribbon. It was as my father had wished (apparently it was taken almost immediately after she received his letter), and it was used as her wedding photograph in the local papers when my parents were married the following September." This photograph is reproduced in volume 1 of Richardson's *Wallace Stevens*, opposite page 384.

<u>every</u> precaution. If you go to visit your grand-mother or anyone else in the dangerous part of town be careful not to drink anything. Here's a kiss for you— a real one. —I forgive the neglect—you <u>have</u> neglected me, Miss Shameless, but it is all right. I mean I am too glad about the other to care much about this. —It is good news, too, to hear about the picture. I am sure I shall like it. After you are through with them, couldn't you send me the proofs? Or would that be looking too soon? Perhaps, it would be better to wait. —Another thing, you <u>must</u> let me see your hair with a ribbon in it. <u>Please</u>! And when I am at home at Christmas. <u>Please</u>! —Bye the bye, I ought to apologize for not writing last evening. But if you were sick, I did not want to write. I should have gone home at once. —I spent the evening reading the last volume of "<u>La Chartreuse de Parme.</u>" In the afternoon Walter Butler[8] and I took our usual walk, up to Grant's Tomb and back. It was beastly cold— my hands were swollen with it. But the air poured into us like light into darkness. In the morning I read the newspapers—mountains of them. On Saturday evening I had old Maitland out to dinner. He is a fine old fellow—outrageously polite. His grandfather was vice-president of the Bank of New-York when Alexander Hamilton, who founded it, was President. Maitland has a portrait of him painted by Gilbert Stuart, who, as you know, painted Washington and numbers of other important people of the days of the Revolution. I remember a whole wall full of Stuart portraits in the Academy at Philadelphia. In fact, when I was there last summer I made rather a study of them, observing, as the ignorant and untutored amateur always does, a ridiculously unimportant thing that pleased me—that is, the manner of giving expression to the eye; of putting light and intelligence into it. Stuart paints his eyes blue or black or whatever the color may be. That, of course, leaves the eye blank. Then he adds a little white dot—and that makes all the difference in the world. —I should like to see if Maitland's grand-father's eyes have the white dots. No doubt. —And on Saturday afternoon (you see, I am progressing backwards) I walked hard for two hours to drive the smoke out of my blood. All my valleys were lost in mist and my sparkling hill-tops were miles in the dark. They remained so. —But the moon of the external world was sparkling enough; and, in the vivid twilight, the early stars were like incessant scintillations. The sky was June; the air was deep December. —The rest of the week before that—after the writing of my last letter, was nothing at all, except routine days and evenings in my room. —Only one thing of interest appeared. J. P. Morgan, the banker, has a very celebrated collection of manuscripts.[9] Among

---

8. See chapter 1, note 55, above.

9. On a visit to Hartford two years before he moved there, Stevens (see WAS 1958 August 11, 1914) visited the cemetery in which he knew J. P. Morgan was buried, the same one in which Stevens himself was eventually buried (see note in *LWS,* 182).

them is the original of Keats' "Endymion." This is now (or was last week) on exhibition in the library of Columbia University. You know the beginning—

"A thing of beauty is a joy forever."

I wanted to get up to look at it on Saturday afternoon, but was unable to get away from the office before four o'clock and then a walk was imperative. If I can manage it next Saturday afternoon, I shall do so. —The winter pressure begins to make itself felt at the office. Business is at a high pitch and I have my hands full. There is a little law business, too, now and then, but law is mostly thinking without much result. It consists of passing one question to take up another. —There was a little, weazened fellow in to see me today who has his links with the Duke of Hamilton. Well, I suppose it is true. He sat at my desk, waiting for something, and talked to me when he could—with astonishing frankness. One comes to regard frankness as a phase of the simplicity that marks people of good-breeding—either dairy-men or dukes. It is generally the unimportant people who are secretive and full of dignity. They must be to hide their unimportance. —We gabbled about Michael Angelo—he, for—I, against. And don't you agree with me that if one could get the Michael Angeloes out of our heads—Shakespeare, Titian, Goethe—all the phenomenal men, we should find a multitude of lesser things (lesser but a <u>multitude</u>) to occupy us? It would be like withdrawing the sun and bringing out innumerable stars. I do not mean that the Michael Angeloes are not what they are—but I like Dr. Campion, I like Verlaine—water-colors, <u>little</u> statues, small thoughts. Let us leave the great things to the professors—substitute for majestic organs, sylvan reeds—such as the shepherds played on under cottage windows—

In valleys of springs of rivers,
By Ony and Teme and Clun.[10]

A fancy, at least. I need not agree with it to-morrow, if I do not care to. —But there are many fancies. They do not last. —Tonight, after dinner, for example, I thought I should like to play my guitar, so I dug it up from the bottom of my wardrobe, dusted it, strummed a half-dozen chords, and then felt bored by it. I have played those half-dozen chords so often. I wish I were gifted enough to learn a new half-dozen. —Some day I may be like one of the old ladies with whom I lived in Cambridge, who played a hymn on <u>her</u> guitar. The hymn had thousands of verses, all alike. She played about two hundred every night—until the house dog whined for mercy, and liberty. —Alas! It is a sign of old age to be so full of reminiscences. How often I have spoken of Cambridge

10. Holly Stevens identifies this as number L in Housman's *Shropshire Lad,* a copy of which Stevens inscribed "Elsie from Wallace / September 1, 1906" (*LWS,* 110).

and Berkeley! Here are two of my college notebooks that came to light with the guitar. You know the things one writes—scribbles—on margins. Mine are abominably serious—I can't find any fit to copy. Yes: here's one:

> Jack and Jill went up the hill
> To fetch a pail of water.
> Says Jack, "I think we ought have beer";
> Says Jill, "Why so we oughter."

Here is a verse I wrote because I liked it, read it somewhere, and remembered it:

> "As the lone heron spreads his wing
> By twilight, o'er a haunted spring."[11]

Let that mirror be black. I have not looked into it for a long time. . . . I have been far afield, wandering through my eternal journal. It is the most amusing thing in the world—that long record of states of mind—and of historic events, like the famous night when I read "To Have and to Hold"[12] until half-past three in the morning. I had completely forgotten it. Is it worth remembering? . . . I have [been] wandering so long that I must sit under this green tree and refresh the universal traveler. . . . (Most worshipful punctuation!) . . . As I live, here she comes tripping up the road. Pink slippers, too, with pom-poms. What d'ye think of that? And white gloves—and a proud air, the like of which was never before in Vagabondia..[13] And where are you going, my pretty maid? —("I'm going to ignore you, sir," she said.) —And when you've ignored me, what then, what then? "Now, Marse Sambo, don't lie under that tree making eyes," sez she. And up jumps Master Sambo, and politely taking her parasol, offers her his seat, which she takes, after carefully spreading her dress on the grass. —Then he comes up the road under her parasol. "Hello, young feller," sez she, just like that. "G'long with you," sez he. "Gimme that parasol!" "Come and take it." Constable, constable, constable! —A treacherous tree to dream under, don't you think? —Good heavens! That sounds like a paragraph from one of the letters I write on the ceiling. I must be careful, because they are full of just such scandal—and, if you read a whole one, you would never sleep another wink, not even if your hair was stuffed full of ribbons. —It is time for me to pull on my own nightcap. It is too late to post my letter to-night and so I shall take it with

11. These are lines four and five of section XXIII of Canto Fourth of *The Lady of the Lake* by Sir Walter Scott.
12. Novel by Mary Johnston (1870–1936), published in 1900 by Houghton, Mifflin.
13. A double period is used here in this letter, one in which Stevens makes punctuation a matter of comment.

me in the morning, and you will have it on Wednesday. —Try to write me another long letter soon—about anything at all, you know. I like to see you dusting and that kind of thing—seriously. Do you wrap your head in a piece of white cloth? —Tum-ti-tum! Forgive me. You are the best of girls, and the dearest—and if I could, I should kiss that disdainful [.] —But that is not fair to you. —Be <u>sure</u> to write during the week; because you were really—well, you have two demerits. This morning's letter does away with one.

With much love, your
Wallace.

⌒

[WAS 1795 December 8-9, 1908 New York]

Tuesday Evening

My dearest Elsie:—

Here I have been sitting for an hour writing "The Book of Doubts and Fears." Bang! I'm not a philosopher. —Besides, it did not seem desirable to disclose so much of my own spirit. —And, while I cannot pretend to any mystery, yet it seems just a bit more cheerful not to go on with that book. —Pooh! Dear Two-and Twenty, what solemn creatures we are! Here's a list of Pleasant Things to drive dull care away, my lass, oh, to drive dull care away— and a jig, and a jig, and a jig, jig, jig:

> black-birds
> blue-birds
> wrens
> crocks of milk
> pumpkin custards
> hussars
> drum-majors
> young chickens

My dearest, dearest Elsie—please do stop having doubts about me or yourself or anything—and give me a kiss—and learn as much as you can about pumpkin custards. I will never love anybody but you—<u>bad</u> as you are—why it would be impossible, dear. I simply couldn't—wouldn't know how. And we are not shadows at all. We won't be the least strange to each other—unless we think we will. There is really no good excuse for my not coming more often. I know it. —And yet there is one. Surely, I need not humiliate myself by going into it. —I feel the deprivation of not seeing you intensely at times. But there is no need of explaining that. You believe me. Do not reproach me for a thing I do against my wishes. I shall try to tell you at Christmas. Notwithstanding, when all is said, there is really no good reason—and yet there is. —I am very much of a stranger in Reading. It has grown to be like going to a strange place, especially in the winter time. Sometimes, even, I resent the familiarity of those I once knew well enough, just as one would resent the familiar greetings of strangers. —I wish I had you here. I wish you were nearer—then you would see. —But it is eleven o'clock and I promised myself to go to bed early.

Wednesday Evening

> Rig-a-jig-jig
> And a jig-jig-jig—
> Apple-blossoms
> Moon-light on roofs,
> Fairy-tales,
> Bon-fires,
> Three-volume novels,
> Poplar-trees
> Lanterns on dark roads.

I defy you to think of anything more pleasant than a lantern twinkling toward you along a dark road. —But I must hurry over this page. It will be like starting anew to leave what I wrote last night around the corner—Now, quick, for a change of masks—so that as you follow me around you only find—[14] Tom Folio[15]—a lazy-bones in an eighteenth-century pair of knee breeches, with a long-tailed coat, holding his large spectacles to the sun as he looks for the dust on them. In one hand he has an umbrella, neatly rolled up, and under his arm is one of the early editions of nothing less than the never-ending "Book of Doubts and Fears."

Elsie. Look'ee, Tom Folio, why do you stand there in a decent body's road wi' that clumsy book under your arm?
Tom. Oh—oh—Mistress Elsie—I was just cleaning my specks before taking a peek into that very book.
Elsie. Out upon you, you drudge, you idle, good-for-nothing, useless slow-poke. A fig for doubts and fears! Tell me, have you seen a melancholy fellow flying up the street?
Tom. Softly, dear Lady. He passed by a minute's space ago.

14. Here the letter continues on the back side of the paper, the fourth page of this eight-page letter.
15. In *Brewer's Dictionary of Phrase and Fable:* "Tom Folio: Thomas Rawlinson, the bibliomaniac. (1681–1725.)" Addison's *Tatler* for April 13, 1710, describes him as a particularly aggressive book buyer at auctions.

Well, pursue me. Hurry by the baker's, the butcher's, the milliner's, around the next corner—[16] and find Dick Lovelace, a descendant of the gallant colonel, in the baggy clothes of Colonial days.

Dick. A curtsey to you, my dear.

Elsie. Sir, you are a rogue.

Dick. Fie, damsel.

Elsie. Sir, you take liberties. Dare to touch me, and I shall call for assistance. Help! Help!

At that moment, a tall form, in a ridiculous hat, jumps from behind a tree and twists Master Lovelace around his little finger.

Elsie. At last! . . .

And what does all that mean? I'm sure I don't know. —I have been drawing up an agreement full of "Whereas" and "Now, Therefore" and I thought I'd take a fling—to prevent myself from growing too sedate. —It has been a terrific day at the office, and I am really too tired to bother with things that mean anything and all the blessed commas and exclamation points. Hey-ding-a ding. —Now you have a blue ribbon in your hair and I have on slippers and I don't see why we should be prim and prudent and proper. —Once upon a time there was a beggar who scraped together a living by juggling, and that was all he could do. One day he thought it would be easier for him to become a monk, so he entered a monastery. Being a man of low degree, he knew of no way to worship Our Lady except to juggle before her image. And so, when no one was looking, he did his few tricks and turned a somersault; and thereupon, Our Lady, being much pleased by his simplicity, smiled upon him as she had never smiled on any monk before.[17] —Now, suppose that, instead of doing his best, he had grieved about his short-comings, and offered only his grief. Would the image have smiled? —And a jig—and a jiggety-jigetty-jig. There is my juggling, my dear—and my somersault. I inscribe a record of it in the last chapter of "The Book of Doubts and Fears." —And for yourself—never look "in a cracked glass." —The theory that this is the best of possible worlds was short-lived; but for all that, no one ever doubted that two sinners could make each other happy and so forget themselves. —I am tempted now, after having been so wise and so foolish by turns, to go on with my jig, and finish to the sound of the fiddle, the saxophone, and the flute—with undertones of tinkling glass. —Everything I have ever seen or heard or thought rushes through my head—as if I were agreeably mad—the memories of my quarter-of-a-century, and more, just as if this were a special occasion.

16. There is another page break here, and the letter goes on to page 5.

17. This famous fabliau, *Le Tombeur de Notre-Dame,* was retold by Anatole France as *Le Jongleur de Notre-Dame* in *L'Etui de nacre,* published in 1892. It is also the subject of a comic opera by Massenet.

Toot,
Flute!
Bellow,
Mellow,
Saxophone!

The music is over—and done. I must collect myself, and put order in this jumble, if I can. But I think you will gather my meaning—and my mood; and then forgive me for being so flighty. It would have been just as easy to have been parsonical. Perhaps, I shall write again to-morrow evening—so carefully, with reverence for the dusty grammarians. —Good-night, dearest Elsie—wave your hand to the grammarians, just to give them courage and self-respect.

Toot,
Flute!

What a dazzling melody! I think I shall be humming it to myself all day to-morrow. —I arranged today about coming for the three days at Christmas—reaching home on Thursday evening of the week after next. But let it remain a little remote, otherwise we shall grow impatient. —I must begin to get ready next week.

> With much love,
> Wallace.

∽

[WAS 1796 December 14, 1908 New York]

Monday Evening

My dearest Elsie:—

Last evening I was too "distraught" to write you. —I had had an afternoon full of violent walking and running that made it impossible for me to gather my wits; and so, after trying, and getting as far as the second page, I gave it up and read a little of Meredith's "Rhoda Fleming," and then went to bed. —I am quite forgetting the out-door world, if, in fact, I ever knew it at all in winter. And yet I recognized the gray river with its dusky barges and tugs—and the white roads in the Park. I haven't seen stick or stone of the country since my last visit to you. —Next Sunday, however, Walter and I hope to get over to Jersey for the day. I must do something, you know, to whip up my sluggish blood, so that I may be in high spirits when I come home. —I have just written for my room and to Miss Keeley.[18] But

---

18. Sarah D. Keeley ran a boardinghouse in her home at 144 North Fifth Street in Reading, two blocks from Stevens's parents' home (see Boyd's *Reading City Directory* for 1902). Stevens did not stay with his family on this visit, during which he would become engaged.

that is unimportant. —There were doubts if I could write even to-night. My musical neighbors have been at it hammer and tongue (literally) for two days. There is nothing to do but move. They are merciless; and as soon as I can after New Year I shall be off to new quarters. I think I know where I shall go. —One of them is a cripple. I met her on the stairs to-night and was more or less shocked at the look of her. I shall not complain any more. —It was pleasant to have a letter from you this morning and to notice that, once more, there was an odeur de sachet—that feminine fragrance has been missing for a little while—and this is quite frail and piquant, becoming to the idea of my girl—unlike the violet and musk of long ago (although goodness knows I liked that, too—immensely.) —I wish that where you wrote, "I send my love to you, monsieur, which you must not treat lightly" you had written, instead, "I send my love to you, Wallace, which you must not treat lightly." There is a difference to my ex-acting mind? Don't you, too, observe it? Besides, my dear, it is unnecessary to warn me that I must not treat it lightly. What is so sweet to me needs no more guarding that what I give it with delight. —However, I know that you do not send it lightly, nor ever will—not even a kiss that is not meant—nor a name that is not felt. —They all have their separate value and rememberance. — Did I tell you (and may I, without provocation) that when I read one of your letters lately I said to myself, "I may believe every word of this, and just as it is written?" How much happiness there is in that! —What I meant was that it put invisible doubt to flight. (Do not entangle me. You understand just what I mean.) —I am glad to know that the fever epidemic is on the wane, as they say. But you must still be careful, and, indeed, ought never to drink raw water. In the cities it is very seldom done except by the poorer classes who are always neglectful of themselves. One's health should be one's primary care. The English are perfectly right about "good bread and good beef"—and about their baths and fresh air. But whatever it may be that leads to a strong body and strong spirits should be the guide. Strength is a delight. —I am always glad to hear of your walks. I remember once when you told me of a long ramble around Rosedale. —And that was really a splendid walk we took from Sinking Spring to Adamstown, at so perfect a time of day. You climbed to Pulpit Rock without the least real difficulty except for your skirt. — Walter Butler is a capital walker. He is good for an entire day at a high rate with occasional half-mile runs, and since finding it out I think quite differently of him. We are just about evenly matched —though I can still beat him two times out of three. We ran all the way around the Reservoir yesterday, upwards of a mile and both of us were like rags when we passed the lamp-post at which we had started— puffing and blowing like porpoises.[19] —You and I must get the sharp air of the hill next week—and <u>on foot</u>—unless the roads should happen to be muddy. —We

19. On page 52 of her "Excerpts," Elsie has copied Stevens's account of a similar, though much longer, run through New York with Walter Butler.

might try a trip up the Tulpehocken and then cross country—fields, fences and everything else—hurrah! to Leesport, and come back by train—you with your cheeks bright red and with sparkling eyes—and deliciously tired—so tired after all, that you would consent to rest a little against me in the train. —Bosh! I'm a dreamer. Of course, you wouldn't. Or would you? Lud! I wish it was <u>this</u> Thursday that I was coming, instead of Thursday a week hence. I shall come on the train leaving here at five o'clock and I shall be at your house at almost nine o'clock or a little after. Even if I should be very late, I hope you will wait. Wait even until eleven o'clock, <u>will</u> you? You know all kinds of things might happen, and those holiday trains are always slow anyhow. —I am getting too far ahead. I ought not to be writing this until next week—but there, it is written. —Are you going to have a ribbon on for me—the very first night? Please do—a pink one, because pink is your color, your best color, I mean. —Is there—no: a secret, my dear. Well, you are a dear. —Are you making any Christmas cakes? Are <u>you</u> making them? Imagine having a plate-ful of Elsie's own backing. I shall expect them—backing—what a singular word—bakeing or baking or whatever it is. The deuce with or-tho-graph-y. Cakes are much more important than spelling. —I picked up some "oaten biscuits" from the English Reading at Park & Tilford's grocery store to-night. They also make excellent graham crackers there, and if I have room I shall bring some for you next week. —Hélas! I must be posting this if you are to have it to-morrow. I shall write several times during the week and hope that you will write as often as you can. I could not write last Thursday evening because I was at the office until ten o'clock catching up with my desk. I hope you were not disappointed.

With love (not "as always" but
with love, and a kiss)
Wallace.

↶

[WAS 1797 December 16, 1908 New York]

Wednesday Evening

My dearest Elsie:—

I meant to write you last evening but neglected to bring home a fresh supply of paper. But I detest explanations, apologies, excuses, etc., etc.; so here's to it. —Miss Keeley has replied to my note of Monday evening to say that she can accomodate [*sic*] me. That disposes of one branch of the thorn-tree. No doubt, the other inn-keeping Miss will reply by morning. —I am most impatient to come, and I do not know how I am going to get over the interval. —Happily the novel I happen to be reading is one of the maddeningly interesting kind. There is little of it left. Perhaps, there will be another. —I think it would be nice if we could just spend our time together quietly without attempting or wishing to do much, so that the time itself would seem longer. But that is always so difficult. —I want to steep myself in you, if I may use so extraordinary a term—as if you were a South wind and as if I were, well, a dingy fellow, as I am. —You will not be too terribly ironed, will you? Just have a few comfortable things—perhaps, pink slippers quite late, and that plate of cakes—so that I won't feel at all as if I were making a call. —Suppose we could pass quickly through some gate of the imagination and find <u>ourselves.</u> Yes: we must do that, at once. —You must not look at me as if you had not seen me for a long time—or anything. (A mandoline passes in the street.) —Yet it is silly to lay down so many rules. They'll all be broken. —There seem to be reservoirs concealed in all of us, even the most sedate, that break unexpectedly. I do not say they will break at this time or that. Folly! I simply say that they are concealed and that they break unexpectedly,—and so much for rules. —You will say, "The lazy vagabond wants his Princess to salute him in the manner of a vagabond and not in the manner of a Princess." Oh, my dearest Elsie, what a fib! I never said it, and I shall be as royal as the occasion requires. —Still I shall want very much that pink ribbon and the pink slippers—or if you would rather be a snow-maiden, white ribbon and white slippers, and, maybe, a little white daub on the tip of your nose. —Yes, Yes, Yes. However, it is a week away. I could count the days. Fortunately Sunday intervenes and will break up the week. Then Monday, Tuesday, when I shall begin to be ready, Wednesday, when I shall be almost ready, and Thursday, when I shall start—hours before the train. Doesn't it make you tingle? —One ought not to think of it. I shouldn't specially except for you. —You are right in saying that the day itself is a kind of anti-climax. Yet it depends on the attitude of mind. —I wonder if I could keep my presents until the day. No: I should be afraid to carry them through the streets—especially that big one that comes in that wonderfully large bundle! Sh! Not another word. This is only to excite you and to try to make you feel as I do. Acknowledge that you do. How delightful that would be. —Come, do throw your hat into the air—or do whatever you do in lieu of that. —The Fast is over—the Dry Season—the Period of Penitence, or whatever you choose to call it. And in a week I shall have you again. Cry "Good Riddance," to this last month and more. —But I'm a vain, assuming, dreaming—no: too late for that, and it's <u>rubbish</u> anyhow. —And we don't really care about the ins and outs of it, do we Elsie? I come unabashed without any philosophizing and proclaim myself,

Your impatient,
Wallace.

↩

[WAS 1798 December 20, 1908 New York]

Sunday Evening

My dear Elsie:

Here come the noise-makers up the stairs just as I commence my letter. —I
have not been very well during the week. On Thursday evening I was in bed at
twenty minutes to seven and had a feverish night. I had caught a cold all over my
body—probably in that icy morning tub with the broken pane of glass in the
room. Friday and Saturday I was quite myself again with a bit of neuralgia (or
what felt like it.) —This afternoon I had my usual Sunday afternoon airing with
W. B. and I feel perfectly well again and hope that I remain so. Of course, I
shall. To-morrow morning I mean to get back to the icing process again just to
keep my hand in. —It was an exceptional day. The dark blue wintry clouds
seemed to be tinged with crimson all afternoon. The water in the reservoir blew
against the wall as if it were full of icy needles. There was the usual parade of carriages and machines in the Park. —In one smart Victoria there were four fat
chorus girls with their lips carmine—and furs and feathers and everything else.
No doubt they had all "chipped in." —We saw a parakeet in a tree. It must have
escaped from one of the houses. It sat high up, pure red, making a slight clack.
—Coming home, down the avenue, the churches were just emptying, and we
ran into a multitude. —Walter wanted to go out to dinner but I persuaded him
to wait until—next year. —To-morrow, Miss Summer, is the shortest day in
the year, and after that the days begin to move the other way. I remind you of it,
because you will be glad. In two months, and less, it will be noticeable. One
always notices it early in February. —At the same time, for some planetary reason, it commences the coldest quarter of the year. January is twice as cold as
December, and February is horrid to think of. But then they're not here yet. —
I went through some book-stores yesterday afternoon, without finding anything that interested me. —There was a volume called "Teuton Studies." It
turned out to be economic things, etc. —I should be glad to have a series of
sketches of the Germans describing their <u>character.</u> It helps one to understand
one's own. —The problem is solved. I have thought of the very book and I shall
bring it for you.[20] —Odd, that it did not occur to me yesterday. —But I intend
to run uptown at noon before I come home and I shall have ample opportunity
to get it then. It is entertaining—very, as they say. —Time drags along most
slowly. The inn-keeping Miss has approved my application, so that everything is
ready. It came out very nicely. —Thursday evening, remember, Elsie, early or
late. I could give you a big hug right <u>now.</u> Be careful that you do not take a cold
or anything because we must have the best possible time. —(I thought you were

20. From references in his letters after Christmas (January 5 and January 7, 1909), this
is probably *Wind in the Willows* by Kenneth Grahame.

going to be so sick this winter! All one's romantic whims remain whims—and one goes on growing "healthy, wealthy, and wise"—in a fashion. It is one of the blessed ironies of fate. Poor Red-Cheek!) Lord! I wish the next three evenings were over and gone. —I must find something else to read, to make that wish come true. —Forgive me, if I do not write a long letter. I cannot write easily when I am so soon to see you—at least, I cannot spread those airy wings of purple and gold and at will when I have a destination. —So Good-night, dearest. Send me a little letter. I have had none for three or four days.

Your
Wallace.

↩

[WAS 1799 December 22, 1908 New York]

Tuesday Evening

Dearest:

On my way to the honest shoemaker's (a German with a fat dog and three canaries)—surely, on such a cold night, a capital opportunity to tell you that you have divined one of the embarrassing influences—in those bundles! You are spiritual and have the perceptions that make meetings more than "How d'ye do?" So I shall leave the bundles for morning: not bother with them the first night—I think. There is nothing to wonder at. —I am glad you do not imitate my habit. —Let me scourge the country-side and bring home what spoils I can; and you stay at home and be good, and have fun. —Besides, it is so much easier to give presents than to receive them. Odd, but true.

Your
Wallace

↩

[WAS 1800 December 28, 1908 New York][21]

Monday Morning

Dear Elsie:—

Reminder: do not forget, please, to call up Miss Sarah Keeley, —say that I shall be back on Friday morning. The lady may think, otherwise, that I have

---

21. This letter is written on stationery of the American Bonding Company of Baltimore with the following names on the top:

Jas. L. D. Kearney　　　　　　Wallace Stevens
Res. Vice President and Manager　　Res. Asst. Secretary

embezzled her turkey and cranberry sauce. Met Arthur Clous[22] on the train. Isn't it a corking day?

Your
Wallace.

~

[WAS 1801 January 5, 1909 New York]
Here begins the year 1909. And
a voice cried out in the wilderness,
saying:
O Muse:

Sweet is the memory of Geranium-at-the-Window-ville—sweetest of all when thought of here in Blind-at-the-Window-town, and on such a torpid night, with its muggy rain. —I'd give much for a long season there, to go about making notes, to study the forlorn Human at his forlornest—say, when perched on a hill-side making laws for empty piano boxes, or when conducting a livery—hiring plugs to villainous strangers about to kidnap a fair innocent. —But I am not sincerely mirthful, for last night's endless sleep has clapped me in a mental cellar, and I shall need a day or two to get back to daylight—and more until I reach the ancient crystalline tower. —I do not return placidly, as if it had never happened. —I do not attempt History. I shudder at Art. —I only write turbulently to say that I am back again—and that I wish you were here with me—wish it immensely. — I could say more—there is a great sleepy jumble in me seeking to be arranged, to be set in order, and then to be spoken. —But if I pull Silence over me like a cloak and retire to a corner I am not less stormy; and this little letter is my corner, for the minute. —I will not flatter my paper. —Hidden in that cloak I make ready for the next stage of the Inky Pilgrimage—through snow, through wind, through rain, through early warmth, through May and June and summer—until the Pilgrimage is over. —I was a grim companion for Arthur [Clous] on the train. He looked excessively doleful at the starry hour, and I felt so—snoozing in my sleeves. Last night I went to bed long before eight o'clock and slept until seven this morning. I walked down town in an intermittent rain trying to get back to consciousness, without any real success. Kearney[23] has been in Baltimore, for a funeral; but

22. Identified in note to WAS 1789 for April 14, 1907.
23. James L. D. Kearney was the resident vice president and manager of the American Bonding Company of Baltimore, the company Stevens had joined on January 13, 1908 (*SP*, 189). Kearney would eventually bring Stevens to Hartford in 1916 to join the Hartford Accident and Indemnity Company, of which he headed the Bond Department. In an administrative coup, in which Stevens acted as Kearney's ally, Kearney became president in May 1934 and Stevens was finally promoted to vice president.

returns to-morrow. And we have been otherwise upset. Holidays play hob with the serene mind. Shortly, however, the adventures will cast longer shadows of silver and then for History—and Art—the Art of recalling the day colorless except for the shadows of silver—white and blue—snows and sky,—and silver itself—on the icy crests of high fields. —I need meditation for that. —Yet forgetting all that, and thinking only of yourself—the cloak <u>must</u> shelter me, to-night at least. —The newspapers, with their "white sales," the President's messages, the news from Italy seem like tedious messages from earth to a blazing inhabitant of Mars—or of some planetary <u>Terra</u> <u>Incognita,</u> where only Elsie lives always, and where I visit and have become half-native with her. —But I cannot, and will not, enter so lofty a serenade; and promise you only the plain contents of an idle spirit and, bye-and-bye—inquiries regarding Moly and Mr. Toad.[24] —How soon we came together—after that first conquest of myself, so necessary to be made by me. Could you fail to see the prim letter-writer being mauled by the more vigorous warrior—yet still clinging to his wig? —Now the wig is resumed. We exchange the lamp for the sun. We exchange paper for what paper can only paint. —But I warn you the warrior with his button-hole bouquet is the stronger and the prim scribbler will come to a bad end. You will see. It will exceed all Faery. —Adieu! Another night and I shall be more myself. I have been sketching plans for winter evenings—going so far as to think of skipping through all of Shakespere. But that will come later on. I could not read a legacy to-night, nor a patent of nobility— nor a recipe for cinnamon tarts, nor anything—ahoy! And so good-night!

Your own
Wallace

⌐◡

[WAS 1802 January 7, 1909 New York]

Thursday Evening

My Dear:

Was my highly figurative frame of mind the other evening appalling? —I am once more what I was <u>lang syne,</u> and this evening I have been idling with newspapers and pamphlets for several hours—noting a concert to be given next Saturday evening which I think I shall go to. They are going to play Schubert's Unfinished Symphony. I have not heard it since I left Cambridge, where I saw Professor Norton[25] listening to it in the college theatre—twirling his forefinger

---

Brazeau, *Parts of a World,* 59–61. On February 11, 1937, Kearney resigned this position. *Hartford Agent* 28, no. 9 (March 1937): 170.

24. Two of the main characters of Kenneth Grahame's *Wind in the Willows* (1908).

25. Charles Eliot Norton (1827–1908) was a professor of art history at Harvard from 1873 to 1898.

around his thumb by way of expressing his pleasure. Tschaikowsky's Fifth Symphony is on the same programme. Both pieces are old favorites. I want to go to the Academy of Design in the afternoon. It is the last day of the winter exhibition, which I never fail to see. There are several galleries of German pictures at the Metropolitan Museum[26] that invite me—and down town there is another exhibition. —On Sunday morning I have an appointment to work over a case with a friend of mine. In the afternoon, I shall, very likely, resume my rambles with W. B. who telephoned anxiously the other day. —I was very glad to have your letter this afternoon—yet a little sorry to hear that you had already finished off Mr. Toad—and to learn that the hat is all right once more (that is, that it <u>stays</u> turned up a little.) The truth is, I like as much as you to talk about such little things—over-shoes, slippers, and so on. —And if I wondered why, I should have to be most wise and think like an owl. So I don't wonder. —Only you don't seem so awe-inspiring then. (It's like sitting at the foot of the throne and talking about the weather.) —The weather-prophets, by the way, have been trying to frighten the life out of us about a cold wave, which, when it came, was nothing at all: and already they predict mildness. —Last evening I went to the Columbia Club for dinner with a friend of mine. He has been married for about a year, and his wife is away on a visit. I had him tell me all about it. It is thrilling! Then we went to the Automobile Show, which I thought tiresome beyond measure. — But the walk home alone made up for it. The night was perfectly clear and the moon as round as an ideal circle. I thought of writing a page or two to you, but the clock in the Jefferson Market tower near by shook both its hands at me, and so, of course, I went lazily to bed. —I have been trying to think of a name of one syllable only to call you by—some name between ourselves. It must be something natural, you know. Can you think of one? Perhaps, you would not care to have me do that, however. But have you ever had such a name? —Send me the folk-song you liked. The book is practically unknown to me, although I have parts of it in other books. You may depend on it that almost anything greek is beautiful. —Moreover, quotations have a special interest, since one is not apt to quote what is not one's own words, whoever may have written them. The "whoever" is the quoter in another guise, in another age, under other circumstances. Now you will be afraid to quote! Because I send you a short letter to-night— is not to be taken as what I shall do. —Let us compare letters to those mystical lanterns with their low lights set in the dark gardens of the Japanese for the guidance of spirits. You will see the application. —And meeting by this second one, in this new garden, let me return the two kisses you sent me to-day.

Your loving
Wallace.

26. This exhibit opened January 5, 1909. See article in *New York Times,* January 4, 1909, p. 8; see also *Times* of January 17 for illustrations.

⤸

[WAS 1803 January 10, 1909 New York]

Sunday Morning

My dearest Elsie:—

The appointment with the legal gentleman has been put over until to-morrow evening. So that I have the morning to myself. Butler and I thought of walking all day, but there is a small drizzle in the air and so we agreed by telephone to loaf this morning and to roll around the Park this afternoon. —Last evening I took him to the concert with me. It was all that I expected, except for an atrociously dull concerto on the cello. I cannot imagine a man writing such a thing. The cello is an important instrument enough, doubtless, in an orchestra—but alone, it sounds like the long-drawn croaking of a summer frog. —In the afternoon, I went by myself to the National Academy.[27] It is refreshing to pass through galleries so multi-colored; but the pictures, taken one by one, were hardly worth the trouble. There was a picture of the interior of an English inn with a group of Red-Coats around a table interrupted in their boozing by the voice of a woman singing, to which they are listening. Another of a boy leaving home to join his regiment—the horse at the open door, the father with his hand on the boy's shoulder, the mother with her face in her hands, the sisters hovering around. Another of a widow in a pew at church praying with <u>such</u> pretty eyes. Another of a field of tulips in Holland. Another of fish on a table. Fiddle-faddle! The artists must be growing as stupid as the poets. What would one lover of color and form and the earth and men and women do to such trash? —There was a bust of John La Farge. Looking at it one thought of more things than the entire exhibition contained. —And this is the common opinion. —This afternoon I hope to see the German pictures at the Metropolitan. I know almost what to expect—I <u>do</u> expect pleasure. The Germans have sense enough to paint what they like. —So you see I've had rather a lively Saturday—a kind of pool on the edge of the desert. By the way I meant to drop into Schirmer's for your music, and shall the next time I am near. I have learned of another little thing that seems to be suited for the refining ear—acute for melody first of all. —Only a half-hour ago I was downstairs picking out snatches of last evening's Schubert.[28] Do-do-dodódodí![29] —It is ten years since I heard it. An echo ten years old—surely the

---

27. The National Academy of Design was located at this time at the corner of Twenty-third Street and Fourth Avenue. Walter Pach, who designed the set for Stevens's play *Bowl, Cat, and Broomstick* in 1917 as well as an illustration for "Earthy Anecdote" in 1918, was a student at the Art Student League associated with the National Academy.

28. Here he sets up a key signature for music in four-four with three sharps.

29. The first and second "do" are joined by curved lines above and below.

world is a magical place. But think of music a hundred years old. —There is a difference between the thought of motion long ago and the thought of sound long ago. I think of the siege of Rome, say, simply as motion, without sound—take an ancient siege. The trenches are dug, the guns are brought up, the regiments manouvre, the walls tumble. It is all visionary. The firing of the guns is merely a flash of color—a flick in the mind. The regiments are as quiet as leaves in the wind. The walls fall down mutely as all things happen in times far off. —But let sound enter—the hum of the men, the roar of the guns, the thunder of collapsing walls. The scene has its shock. —So that ten-year-old do-re-mi-fa reanimates—and by closing the eyes—it is ten years ago. —Another sensation (one depends on them): one of the pictures yesterday had been exhibited in Paris. It had the number of the Paris exhibition on its frame and bore the "Medaille" mark—an honor picture. By looking at that, and at nothing else I could imagine myself in Paris, seeing just what any Parisian would see. —I laughed in my sleeve at New-York, far out on the bleak edge of the world. —That particular picture was a sunset from the roof of an Oriental house, so full of burning light, that it looked like a city drowned in the Red Sea, perceived through placid water. —There is a church in the neighborhood that has the grace to ring its bell on Sundays. It has just stopped. It is so pleasant to hear bells on Sunday morning. By long usage, we have become accustomed to bells turning this ordinary day into a holy one. The general absence of that familiar ringing here makes the day half a waste. —Toll the pious forth—saintly Belinda in modified Directoire and honest John in his stove-pipe. —Has the cyclamen lived out the week? I have seen pussy willow in the florists' windows since coming back. Of course, it is from the South. I must not think of anything but winter for certainly three months to come. The florists are all topsy-turvy anyhow. The first of the tribe must have been a most devoted fellow, don't you think—an idealist of immense proportions, with infinite satisfaction in the success of his labor of love. —Or did it all come about by chance? Were flowers merely left at the window—and the discovery lazily made? —In some Visigothic chaumière, perhaps—some wattled hut in Mérovingia, —a field for research. But it is not a task for a Sunday morning to trace the connection between our flippant florists and the Visigoths. —I reserve it for one of the learned volumes I mean to write when I have time. —Yet one might easily be learned in such learned weather—the sky is as gray as a bald head, and the world beneath is all frown, like the solemn phiz of a Doctor of Philosophy. The Earth—old Tellus[30]—in his wintry wig—his red fez and his green cloak—even his yellow night-cap—blown into the void. Tall talk, my dear—but do you expect me to sit—There!—and read my letter as if it were a note from Aunt

---

30. Tellus (or Tellus Matera) is the earth mother. Saint Augustine assaulted the logic of gender in Roman divinities, including Tellus, in his *City of God* 7:23–28.

Tabitha[31] to Young Jemima, if you can. —Make your eyes round as the roundest saucers and marvel at the moon-colored night-cap and all the candles set round the bed. —(That all came from looking out of the window and feeling a shade bored by the mist and the possible rain—mist drives the wind back. Hence the confusion.)— . . . We begin to disperse for the day. Footsteps on the stairs. The other foot-man will soon be here. —The Park will be— like a stage set with trees full of smoke—as if a duel had just been fought with pistols—and the orchestra will be the sound of horses' hoofs and the slippery sound of automobiles. —We may go to the Murray Hill for dinner. I promised to do so a month or more ago and it was spoken of last night. It won't be a bad idea to get rid of all those odds and ends of promises and then to settle down to the bare mode of life that is, after all, so much more satisfactory in the long run than any other. The objection to such bareness is that it ends by making the smallest indulgence an affair of the conscience, and so—a bugbear. One is not a monk to live on bread and water, with parseley on Sundays. Only the monk—in the long run—comes out of it so nobly, so liberated, so much the master of himself. I say—three months of winter, of stern conduct—of work—and I start off with a dinner fit for a Bishop. —Sometimes it is frivolous to be so much the master of ones' self—the isolation is keen and clear—but the plot is pitifully thin. We are part of the world about us—that's the plot. Illimitable complication! —But why think it all out? The disorder is the mystery—the darkness we sit in to catch the dramatic beyond the foot-lights. A lighted theatre is no theatre at all. —We walked no farther than the Museum. How many senses the pictures touched! I am German to the utter-most. All the exiled ancestors crowded up to my eyes to look at the <u>Vaterland</u>— to see those goslings in the water by the fence, the man and woman and baby trudging home through the rainy twilight, the meadows with the meadow trees, the oddities of undeveloped imagination, the infinite humble things. —There was at least one picture not at all German: two little girls in large dresses, one olive, another lavender, singing to the music of a violinist crouching at their feet—as I remember it. —The crowd was particularly large and seemed, too, particularly German. —One would like to understand the Germans. They seem like a nation of peasants. All their qualities seem to be primarily, essentially, peas-ant qualities. They are as much what they are as the Japanese are; but it is hard to see it distinctly. —I escaped the dinner fortunately, and shall have the evening at

31. Woman, "full of good works and almsdeeds," who was raised from the dead by Peter (Acts 9:36–42). This name was popular among Puritans and dissenters from the seventeenth to the nineteenth century. Dorcas (small gazelle or deer), the Greek trans-lation of this Aramaic name, was applied to Dorcas Societies that made and provided clothes for the poor throughout the nineteenth century. Jemima was the first-named of the daughters given to Job after his terrible ordeal with God (Job 42:14).

home. The need for reading begins to make itself felt, and I must look through my books for something new—almost a hopeless task. —Will there be a long letter for me to-morrow or the day after? Full of little things, remember, —about going to the store, and so on, so that I can see you. —And have you thought of that name yet? It must be inspired or it will never do.

Your
Wallace

⌒

[WAS 1804 January 12, 1909 New York]

Tuesday Evening

My dear Bo:—

To-night you must come to no serious purpose—come as Bo-Peep—(I do not say it boldly.) —Imagine my page to be as white as the white sheet they use for magic-lantern shows, and suddenly see your changeful self appear there in the ribbons and flowers of the damsel that lost her sheep. I point and say (not at all familiarly)—"ma chère Bo!" And you vanish. —But it really isnt so frightful when I say it again, and perhaps you would not always vanish. —Elsie is such a pleasant name and means so many different things. —I am only looking for an everyday name, keeping Elsie for Sunday. —At college my own name was Pete! Bo-Pete is not so far from Bo-Peep, do you think? —The change is tremendous. But try it in your next letter. I bow to the shock. —So, when you put on one of those fresh white dresses and I come as creased as a Major we can pop out our polite names. —Bo is quite simple in slippers. We'll call them our workday, knock-about-the-country names. —The christening over, a word of news. After working without dinner last evening until eight o'clock, I went home with my fellow-slave. His wife had roasted two chickens for us and I think I am responsible for one of them and for a mountain of apple-jelly. We smoked and talked until almost mid-night. Not at all a bad evening—and one fairly likely to dispel the horror one has of working when no one else does. —The verse you sent was perplexing. Just what was it that was discovered? But the mental scene of many rowers at sea at night lit by a starry flash was suited to remembrance. I say it priggishly—words have that faculty. —And as a mental scene, aside from remembrance, the verse had its value. —From one of many possible figures— regard the mind as a motionless sea, as it is so often. Let one round wave surge through it mystically—one mystical mental scene—one image. Then see it in abundant undulation, incessant motion—unbroken succession of scenes, say. — I indulge in heavenly psychology—I lie back and drown in the deluge. The mind rolls as the sea rolls. —Bo-peep passes with her crook tending only young lambs with silver bells around their necks,—a golden valley sparkles through me—twilight billows in a dark wave—and the foam of the next motion is all starlight, or else the low beam of the rising moon. —The mind rolls as the sea rolls! I must save that for a rainy Sunday.[32] It is preposterous on a Tuesday evening, and while one is so white awake. —The magic-lantern show continues: (that "white awake" up there ought to be "wide awake"—you see it back a line or two—it is so learned to be correct) —what's this? (We concern ourselves only with the marvellous.) —A yellow mountain-side in the background, its outlines dissolving in soft sunlight. In the foreground, sits a pilgrim, resting and gazing at the mountain before him. Near-by, on quiet feet, a group of maidens dance, as yet unseen. It is the <u>Pays</u> <u>du</u> <u>Plaisir</u>—the Country of Good Pleasance. The pilgrim sings:

> Under golden trees,
> I might lose desire;
> Rest, and never know
> The mortal fire.
> In that golden shade,
> I might soon forget;
> Live, and not recall
> The mortal debt.

The slide is removed. Before the next can be inserted a clock strikes quickly—as if a spider ran over one's hand. A nice, harmless spider—but disconcerting. —And when the pilgrim was at his saddest. We shall have more of him, and it ends gaily—otherwise, how account for the maidens dancing so near. You'll see. —Yet last night's revelry requires a balancing to-night and besides it is too thrilling to give it all to you at once. —A kiss—and more than a bird-peck, too. Good-night!

Your
Jack-o'-Lantern

~

[WAS 1805 January 13–14, 1909 New York]

Wednesday Evening

Dear Bo:

(You must <u>dash</u> it off, like that.)— I hope you were not giving me a beating with your "Dear Germany." I said I was German to the uttermost. Look at my letter, please. —And I am glad. —Peasants are glorious. Think. Who inhabited

---

32. Stevens may have had this passage in mind as he wrote a number of his poems: "The Place of the Solitaires," "The Comedian as the Letter C," "Sea Surface Full of Clouds," "Two Versions of the Same Poem," "Page from a Tale," and "Prologues to What Is Possible."

Arcady? Who inhabited Sicily? —You see the oration I might make. —I do not mean your staring, open-mouthed, poor devils. The cottage has been the youthful ideal of all men. I suppose that by peasants one means cottagers of one kind or another, people who dwell—

> Where morn is all aglimmer
> And noon a purple glow
> And evening, full of the linnet's wings.[33]

Briefly, English and French artists do not find picturesque the same things that German artists do. The catalogue speaks of "maternal soil." That is what is commonly called by the ugly name of Nature. Some of the pictures: "Farm in Snow," "Foggy Evening at Dachau," "Field Loneliness," "Burgomaster Klein," "Portrait of Dr. Schnitzler," "Feeding Hens," and so on. —But it is all figgish-ness as you say. —I paint a picture of the every-day Wallace, as he sat in his room this evening: leather slippers—the kind they wear with snow-shoes—these are shoes in reality, but without soles like shoes—I bought them in British Columbia—old trousers, sweater without a neck (of course), woolen shirt with the collar turned up, one leg over the arm of an easy rattan chair, the Post in one hand, a perfect Havana in the other. —I read, and then I said, "I'll write poetry. Young men in attics always write poetry on snowy nights, so—I'll write poetry." I wrote,

> Only to name again
> The leafy rose—"[34]

To-to-te-tum, la-la-la. I couldn't do another line—I looked up at my ceiling, frowned at the floor, chewed the top of my pen, closed my eyes, looked into myself and found everything covered up. —So, sez I, I'll have a little argument about peasants and stuff. But you must not argue with green ink. It does seem absolutely green by lamp-light.[35] —Well, about that dance. I think I probably said, "Oh, my!" and sighed. But that was in New-York. It made no impression at all in Reading. The grief-stricken dancer at the Academy was worse, compara-tively. When she walked—you saw the physical peacock at every step. —Let the lady dance for the gallery. —The dance itself: imagine Anna Rigg[36] doing it—

33. In Yeats's "Lake Isle of Innisfree," the first of these lines is "Where midnight's all aglimmer."

34. These lines are used in "The Little June Book" of 1909.

35. This ink is a lighter shade and is a bit greenish.

36. Anna B. Rigg is listed in *Boyd's Reading City Directory* for 1902 as a "saleslady" at 442 Penn Street, the C. K. Whitner and Company Department Store. Elsie is also listed as a "saleslady" for that year at that store. Anna Rigg was also one of Elsie's bridesmaids at her wedding (cf. Brazeau, *Parts of a World,* 256).

leaning back or swinging by the neck. What a sweet, pastoral way of passing the time! It is simply an exhibition. —But it makes all the difference who is doing it. The same thing in a cake-walk would be dull. —The dancing of the day is not a fireside matter. This dance was part of the general rage. It is the only one I saw. —I saw none of the Salomes, or the rest. It may be that I'm an old prune, but there you are. —A propos of the last point raised by you in regard to the life about us. Of course, we are, as I said myself. But I find in one of the Sacred Books[37] the following weighty remark written one April day at East Orange:

"It is chiefly in attics that one dreams of violet cities."

I certainly do not exist from nine to six, when I am at the office. To-day was the anniversary. The year has been marked by important advances, —but to-night I could not write a single verse. There is no every-day Wallace, apart from the one at work—and that one is tedious. —At night I strut my individual stage once more—soon in a night-cap.

Thursday Evening

Our first day of snow, although, in fact, it has been thawing since morning, and most of the day it has been dropping rain. I left the office at five and went to several book-stores for something to read. The shops were just closing and the crowd, the lights, the cars, the machines and horses in the street, together with the mist and the casual rain, made a flawless city night. —I imagined (if I might, Bo) that I was going home to you. No such luck. But I picked up a novel and finished cutting the pages and expect to dip into it to-night. Last night I read Coleridge until midnight, after writing a little to you. —It is heavy work, reading things like that, that have so little in them that one feels to be contemporary, living. My novel is Henry James' "Washington Square." I think I'll send it to you if it is good. It was written almost thirty years ago, when Henry James was still H. J. Jr. and had tales to tell. —We ought to be sitting together. I should read for you, gladly. Weather so dismal here must be barbaric in the country. —But out of perversity, it heightens my spirits, puts me in fine spirits. —Just so, people who live by the sea, have the brightest hearths in the stormiest weather. Bye-bye.

Wallace.

↪

[WAS 1806 January 17, 1909 New York]

Sunday Evening

My dearest girl:—

The Park was turned to glass to-day. Every limb had its coating of ice and on the pines even every needle. The sun made it all glitter, but then the sun did not

37. He quotes from his journal for April 27, 1906 (*SP*, 166).

shine directly and it was twilight before it was really clear. —It would have been wonderful if there had been a moon tonight. —At a distance clumps of trees looked like winter clouds. —And the wind made the trees jingle. —Very bad walking, however—in spite of the snow-plows. There were pools over your ankle. We went through them, depending on a change when we reached home. —At twenty minutes to six it was still fairly light—a visible lengthening of the day, which makes one indifferent to hateful February, whose end is signified before it has begun. —Call this the thirteenth month of the year, February the fourteenth, and so on. —Yesterday afternoon I went a-Parking, too. The snow was just commencing to fall, blowing from the North, the direction in which I was going, so that my cheeks were, shortly, coated with ice—or so they felt. —It would be very agreeable to me to spend a month in the woods getting myself trim; for while I enjoyed that flow of the North wind and the blowing snow, I felt as if I did not enjoy it quite as much as possible—as if (in so short an experience of it) it did not go the deepest possible. There is as much delight in the body as in anything in the world and it leaps for use. I should like to snow-shoe around our hills—from Leesport to Adamstown, from Womelsdorf to East Berkeley— long trips made at a jog that would pull the air down and give one life—all day trips, hard, fast; and I could do it very well except for the need of being here. — Last night, sitting at home, with a file of the Law Journal, with the snow blowing gustily against the window, I wanted very much to be in your parlor with you. I had intended not to say so; but I want you to know, dear, that I do not accept these fearful absences without feeling. They call for absolute faith in each other: and particularly, on your part, for faith in me. Do not let any doubt, even the smallest, creep in, Elsie. It is simply extraordinary that I cannot see you more often: but let us make the most of what we have and be happy with that. Fight the thought of absence. I have both your pictures in front of me, and they are there every evening. The new picture has changed considerably for me. I can see one of your smiles flicker over it every now and then. I do not think you know that if you have looked at it only critically. And when that happens, it is just as if you were here and had said something or other. —About a trifle: I am rather glad that you do not want that song. It isn't really pretty enough, notwithstanding it gets into one's ears. There is something else that I have heard of. I may send you a package in two or three weeks. —The "Washington Square" was not especially good: altogether an exhibition of merely conflicting characters. It is such an old story that the neighborhood was once suburban but that with the growth of the City has come to be very much "down-town"—the very last place, in fact, in which people live, all below it being exclusively business, except for the tenement intermissions. —Yet it was balm to me to read and to read quickly. I have such difficulty with Maeterlinck. He distracts by his rhetoric. Indeed, philosophy, which ought to be pure intellect, has seldom, if ever, been so among moderns. We color our language, and Truth being white, becomes blotched in transmission.[38] —I think I'll fall back on Thackeray. —There is a celebration of Poe in the air. He lived at Fordham Heights, you know, for a period and the people up there have gone in for a tremendous ceremony on Friday, I believe, of this week. My friend Lamb[39] sent me an engraved invitation as big as a bill-board. —By the way, did I ever tell you that Poe once wrote to someone in Reading offering to lecture there and that the original letter is on sale at Richmond's now? The committee was unwilling to pay what he asked, so that he never came. — Nowadays, when so many people no longer believe in supernatural things, they find a substitute in the stranger and more freakish phenomena of the mind—hallucinations, mysteries and the like. Hence the revival of Poe. —(I have just interrupted my letter to you to thank Lamb for his prodigious invitation.) —Poe illustrates, too, the effect of stimulus. When I complain of the "bareness"—I have in mind, very often, the effect of order and regularity, the effect of moving in a groove. We all cry for life. It is not to be found in railroading to an office and then railroading back. —I do not say the life we cry for is, as a question of merit, good or bad. —But it is obviously more exciting to be Poe than to be a lesser "esquire." —You see the effect of the railroading in my letters: the reflection of so many walls, the effect of moving in a groove. —But books make up. They shatter the groove, as far as the mind is concerned. They are like so many fantastic lights filling plain darkness with strange colors. I do not think I complained for myself, but for the letters. Do you remember—(if it matters)? —I like to write most when the young Ariel sits, as you know how, at the head of my pen and whispers to me—many things; for I like his fancies, and his occasional music. — One's last concern on a January night is the real world, when that happens to be a limited one—unless, of course, it is as beautiful and as brilliant as the Park was this afternoon. I did not tell you that we counted eight ducks flying rapidly through the air. Walter said, "I wouldn't have missed that." —It was just what was needed. —A squirrel chasing a sparrow over the snow, which we had seen before, was tame by comparison. —Wild ducks! We followed them. A policeman shouted and we came meekly back to the walk. The police are as thick as trees and as reasonable. But you must obey them. —Now, Ariel, rescue me from police and all that kind of thing. —"She doesn't like to be called Bo," he whispers. —Don't you? Is that why you signed your last letter with "Elsie"? Oh, but Elsie is always a sweet name to me—and I will not call you Bo. It had no reason

38. Stevens seems to have in mind a philosophical rather than a dramatic work by Maeterlinck, and his reference to the "treasure of the humble," in his letter of May 17, 1909, seems to confirm this assumption.

39. This is probably the Professor Lamb with whom Stevens took a walk in WAS 1792 for April 22, 1907.

and no appropriateness, for where were the sheep you had lost—what were we to think of when we thought of the sheep? Perhaps, the folds of hair in the old picture. I can see now why that way of doing your hair would possibly look a little out of place now; although sometime you must do it that way just once more for us both to see and only for us. It looks perfectly old-fashioned already, in so short a time—and, after all, it was only a way for a girl not yet in her twenties. I like it immensely. "She doesn't like you to talk too long about that," comes this small voice. "But, my dear fellow," I reply, "that is not talk, but meditation." —There is a creaking and rattle of trucks in the streets and shouts of "Gid-dap!" Already, the week has commenced. An incalculable element in the activity and the variety of the town is made up of the traffic. During the day, on Sundays, one seldom sees a wagon and, no doubt, it is because of the carriages in the Park and on the Drive that people, missing something elsewhere, go there in such droves. —Now, it is quiet again, as a valley in Eden—our old Eden, deep in snow and ice. —I expect to read violently all week, but what—remains to be seen—and to stay at home every night. It is the easiest way to be content in winter. —Write to me as often as you can, and I will to you—no matter what just so I hear from you. —It is half-past eleven and time for me to stop. —I send you a real kiss.[40]

And more—
Wallace.

∽

[WAS 1807 January 19, 1909 New York]

Tuesday Evening

Dearest Bo:—

Ariel was wrong, I see. So you make Bo-Bo of it, do you? Let's keep it, after all. Only you must not spell it Beau! But Bo is my Beau—as much as Elsie. —Your letter this morning was simply bully, as they say. It made Old Prune quite playful. We could have a dandy time to-night if we were together. I'd have you practice the piano for seventeen hours and so massacre the noodles next door—one of whom played like a mad-woman a half-hour ago. —I walked down-town this morning, leaving my razor at a barber's on the way. It was as dull as a stick of wood. Yesterday morning at breakfast my phiz was wooly. And to-night I came up part way in the Subway and then walked for an hour trying to pick up something to read. New-York has everything except good book-shops. Very few of the people read. —In Boston, on the contrary, it is all you can do to keep your money in your jeans. —I picked up several novels—and a box of cheap cigars and a seven-cent apple and an Evening <u>Post</u> and then came home. There,

40. Very atypically, Stevens closes this letter at the top of the page; in almost every other letter, he uses up all the space on the page.

you have all the scandalous details. —The air was as raw as snow, East wind, fog and evening could make it. But the tedious prophet spoils it all by forecasting a rise in temperature for to-morrow. —Last night I wrote two pomes —and to-morrow night old Wolfinger[41] from Reading is going to be here. We shall take dinner together and waste the evening prattling about his musty old law-suit. — I still grapple with all the law business that comes my way, but it is surely the quaintest way of making a living in the world. Practicing law is only lending people the use of your bald-head. It is silly. —I don't really think that anything at Stony Creek is too familiar. —The whole back of the mountain,[42] which we have come to know so well, is one of the quietest places. In all our walks there we have passed probably only a half-dozen people—and never a motor at all. — There is still one walk that you know nothing about, I am sure. You go East from Rosedale over the first hill and turn to your left into the woods. Yet we may have gone there—on second thoughts. I think we did—one Sunday. —Do you remember the last walk along the ridge north of Mc Knight's gap[43] when the first warmth made us both so languid and heavy? I felt like an old horse, going up the side of the hill. —To-night I could have run up, for I have felt on my metal all day. In fact, I felt like dashing up to Union Square at noon—only conscience would have had me in its coil: one likes to work in working hours. So I had my usual sand-wiches and milk and apple-pie and was back in the office before you could say Jack Robinson—very often. —About two o'clock I went out on an errand and cast an inspecting eye on the damsels gadding about. I swear they dress as fashionably as if they could afford it. Let us catalogue the observation under the title, "Gallantry of Human Nature." —I regard old clothes (except on Sundays and holidays) almost as a point of honor—I don't mean rags. —Surely the Gods, looking down on maidenly clerks in Empire and Directoire laugh in their sleeves. —The men, too! We have a clerk in the office who shines like the bearer of glad tidings. —Oh, but they get nothing else out of it. —Suppose they met the youthful Keats tramping in dilapidated shoes, crumpled clothes, without a hat. Pooh! —The supposition is unfair. —Well, I say it is cheerful anyhow. They deck the streets, just as they hope to do. —I wish you would let me know

41. This is most likely a reference to William D. Wolfinger, who had run a wallpaper establishment in Reading since 1877, though there were other members of this family in business in Reading at this time. Stevens's father had written to him about Wolfinger in 1908. Perhaps Stevens's meeting had something to do with the A. W. Wolfinger Company, manufacturers of Fine Hosiery, which was established at Walnut and Rose streets in Reading in August 1909. See *Passing Scene* 7:130.

42. The reference is to the east side of Mount Penn, the side away from Reading and looking toward Oley.

43. This is a gap, just outside the city limits, in the ridge of which Mount Penn, which runs north-south as the eastern boundary of Reading, is an extension.

which of the Nevin[44] books of music you do not have. I should like to get some new things together for you. But now that I go so seldom to concerts it is rather hard to pick up just the thing one wants. On the face of the Tschaikowsky or Paderewski piece that you have there is a list that makes the ears burn as I remember it. Is there anything there that looks good? Nothing hard or showy, you know. The hard things are made for women with glasses and men with long hair. "In Arcady" is exactly the kind of music I like.[45] Music in minor tones is ——[46] but in major tones it delights. —So of all things, cries the Devil of Sermons, within me. —Your letter was in major, the weather is in major. Your Spring is buoyant minor, and Autumn minor all in all. —Fiddlesticks is major, so I say Fiddlesticks! —Bo is major—Major Bo. Old Prunes is major. The Golden Treasury[47] is major. Rub-a-dub, rub-a-dub-dub-dub! We'll soon be marching up and down the hall. —I suppose we'll have to find that old tin hat and use it for a drum. —In a window to-night I saw a hat-box called a "tire-box"—as they called it a few generations ago. Well, the tin-hat is in its tire-box to stay, after all. —Good-night, old Bo-Bo. I'm not going to end my letters so ceremoniously any more—just a kiss and a touch of the winkling device—and good-night!

Wallace.

⌒

[WAS 1808 January 21, 1909[48] New York]

Thursday Evening

Dear Bo-Bo:—

Secret <u>memories:</u> go back to the bicycle period, for example—and before that to the age of the velocipede. Yes: I had a red velocipede that broke in half once going over a gutter in front of Butcher Deems (where the fruit store is now, beyond the Auditorium)—and I hurt my back and stayed away from school. —On Sundays, in those days, I used to wear patent leather pumps with silver buckles on 'em—and go to Sunday school and listen to old Mrs.

---

44. Ethelbert Woodbridge Nevin (1862-1901), American composer of sentimental songs and piano pieces.

45. "In Arcady (An Idyl)" has music by Joseph McManus and words by Carolyn Wells: "As I came dancing through a grove, / In Arcady, in Arcady, / I fashioned me a lady love," with prominent red cheeks, golden hair and "eyes of cornflow'r blue"; and when he finally embraces her in the second verse, "somehow, she was you."

46. Longer-than-usual dash as if it stood for the elision.

47. Stevens's signed copy of Francis Turner Palgrave, comp., *The Golden Treasury of the Best Songs and Lyrical Poems of the English Language* (London: Macmillan, 1896) is in the remains of his library at the Huntington.

48. On page 54 of her excerpts, Elsie reminded herself to "read childhood and boyhood memories" in this letter.

Keeley,[49] who had wept with joy over every page[50] in the Bible. —It seems now that the First Presbyterian church was very important: oyster suppers, picnics, festivals. I used to like to sit back of the organ and watch the pump handle go up and down. —That was before John McGowan, the hatter,[51] became a deacon. —The bicycle period had its adventures: a ride to Ephrata was like an excursion into an unmapped country; and one trip to Womelsdorf and back was incredible. —In summer-time I was up very early and often walked through Hessian Camp before breakfast. Sometimes I rode out to Leisz' bridge and back. —I remember a huge cob-web between the rails of a fence sparkling with dew. —And I had a pirate period somewhere. I used to "hop" coal-trains and ride up the Lebanon Valley and stone farm-houses and steal pumpkins and so on—with a really tough crowd. —Then I took to swimming. For three or four summers I did nothing else. We went all morning, all afternoon and all evening and I was as black as a boy could be. I think there are some photographs of all that at home— somebody had a camera. I must try to find them. —I could swim for hours without resting and, in fact, can still. Bob Bushong[52] and I were chummy then—and Felix North and "Gawk" Schmucker.[53] —We used to lie on the stone-walls of the locks and bake ourselves by the hour, and roll into the water to cool. —I always walked a great deal, mostly alone, and mostly on the hill, rambling along the side of the mountain. —When I began to read, many things changed. My room was the third floor front. I used to stay up to all hours, although I had never, up to that time, been up all night. I had a pipe with a very small bowl and a long, straight stem. There never was a better. —Those were the days I read Poe and Hawthorne and all the things one ought to read (unlike "Cousin Phillis["]54—the book I am reading now.) —And I studied hard—very.

49. Mrs. Keeley was an old family friend; in a journal entry for June 25, 1912, Stevens reports that on her deathbed, his mother "asked for Mrs. Keeley, an old friend, who came to see her" (*SP*, 254).

50. Holly Stevens reads this word as "pap" (*LWS*, 125), but other instances of the word "page" in Stevens's handwriting closely resemble this one.

51. John G. McGowan, an 1875 graduate of Reading High School, ran a men's shirt, finishing, and hat store at 630 Penn Street in Reading and lived at 1915 Perkiomen Avenue.

52. Robert Bushong Hoff of 722 North Fifth Street was in the class of 1999 at Reading Boys' High; he earned a bachelor of arts degree from Princeton University in 1904 and then became a law student in the office of Cyrus G. Derr of 542 Court Street in Reading. *Graduate Catalogue of the Reading High Schools: 1856–1905*, 215.

53. The two previous names do not appear in the *Graduate Catalogue of the Reading High Schools: 1856–1905*.

54. *LWS* (125) identifies this as by Elizabeth Cleghorn Stevenson Gaskell (New York: Macmillan, 1908).

—You know I took <u>all</u> the prizes at school![55] (Isn't it an abominable confession?) No doubt, mother still has the gold medal I won for spouting at the Academy— picture in the Eagle, and all that—just as the school-boy orators of today are puffed up. —At High School, I played foot-ball every fall—left end. We gener- ally won at home and lost when we were away. In one game at Harrisburg the score was fifty-two to nothing, against us. But the other team was made up of giants. —The only other member of the team that I recall is "Tod" Kaufman,[56] a half-back. He has something to do with the <u>Herald</u> and still calls me Pat, which was my name then. Most of the fellows called me Pat. —I never attended class- meetings and never knew any of the girls belonging to the class. Well, perhaps I did; but they do not come back to me now. —I sang in Christ Cathedral[57] choir for about two years, soprano and, later, alto[.] —Worked at Sternberg's for two weeks, once—at the Reading Hardware Company for two months. (Father was an officer of the company—my working did not interfere with swimming.) — And I went to the World's Fair, and to school in Brooklyn[58] for a while, and sometimes to the Zoo in Philadelphia. —When I was very young, "mamma" used to go shopping to New-York and we would meet her at the station—and then there would be boxes of candy to open at home. We used to spend months at a time at the old hotel at Ephrata, summer after summer, and "papa" would come on Saturday nights with baskets of fruit—peaches and pears, which would

55. Jerome M. Edelstein gives the following: "'Greatest Need of the Age.' Reading (Pa.) *Eagle,* December 23, 1896, p. 5. An essay for which WS received a prize given by the *Eagle* of Reading, Pa., and the Alumni Medal for Oration at the Reading, Pa., Boys' High School. A sketch of WS appeared in the *Eagle* the following day." Edel- stein, *Wallace Stevens: A Descriptive Bibliography* (Pittsburgh: University of Pittsburgh Press, 1973), 189. Stevens also delivered the commencement address: "'The Thessal- ians,' Reading (Pa.) *Eagle,* June 24, 1897, p. 5, col. 1" (ibid.).

56. He is listed with the class of 1897 at Reading Boys High School: "Stanley Reber Kaufman, 114 West Oley Street, Reading, Pa. Circulation Manager *Reading Herald. Graduate Catalogue of the Reading High Schools: 1856–1905,* 197.

57. The Christ Episcopal Church is located on North Fifth Street near Court Street, just a couple of blocks from Stevens's home. Its choir was very active and well known in the area; in 1890 and 1891, members from this choir and from another Episcopal church in Reading performed *The Mikado* seven times at the Grand Opera House and at the Academy of Music (see *Passing Scene* 1:62).

58. In the Williamsburg section of Brooklyn, Stevens attended the parochial school of the prominent St. Paul's Lutheran Church, where his uncle, Henry Baptiste Stro- dach (1847–1900), who was married to Stevens's mother's sister, Mary Louise Zeller, was the pastor. See Stevens's journal for June 22, 1900 (*SP,* 76) for an account of his revisiting this school on June 22, 1900. A lead story in the *Reading Eagle* for January 27, 1900, recounts the life of Reverend Strodach and the details of his death from a combi- nation of a concussion and exposure, both suffered after he had wandered away from the hospital to which he had been admitted in a delirious state two weeks earlier.

be given to us during the week. —Sometimes an uncle from Saint Paul[59] visited us. He could talk French and had big dollars in his pockets, some of which went into mine. —Then there was a time when I went very much with Johnny Richards and Arthur Roland.[60] They were "bad": poker (for matches) and cigarettes. —The truth is, I have never thought much about those early days and certainly never set them in order. I was distinctly a rowdy—and there are still gossips to tell of it, although Aunt Emmy Schmucker[61] who had all the scandal at her fingers ends no longer lives to tell. When Jones', near you, moved into their new house, they gave a blow-out which Aunt Emmy attended. She ate so much that she was sick the next day and stayed in bed. After that she never got up. Soon she knew she was dying. She asked mother to ask me to see her and when I went she kissed me good-bye. —With her, went infinite tittle-tattle. But she made the most of life, while she had it. —My first year away from home, at Cambridge, made an enormous difference in everything. Since then I have been home comparatively little and, but for you, I think I should have drifted quite out of it, as the town grew strange and the few friends I had became fewer still. —But the years at college will do for another time. —Your own recollections interested me so much that I have followed your lead. Bye!

Pat.

∽

[WAS 1809 January 24, 1909 New York]

Sunday Evening

Dear Bo:

The clouds have been down to one's hat for three or four days. —In other words, we are all cloud-capped. A quip, as I live. —But let me roll in on you like a salt wave—for I have been at sea half the day, or as good as that. In such atmosphere, land and sea are indistinguishable. —W. B. and I crossed the Forty-Second street to Hoboken: no—Weehawken and walked to Edgewater. Such perfect sloppy mud and black snow. The Jersey lanes were all mist, black trees,

---

59. Identified in *LWS* (126) as James Van Sant Stevens (1846–1917), a bachelor brother of Stevens's father who was in a "business related to art in Saint Paul." See the letter of June 27, 1916 (WAS 1982), for an account of how Stevens avoided meeting this uncle on the street.

60. Neither Richards nor Roland is listed in the *Graduate Catalogue of the Reading High Schools: 1856–1905*. The *Boyd's Reading City Directory* for 1902 lists Arthur Roland as a clerk at 19 Fifth Street; the same directory lists five John Richardses, with the following occupations: butcher, laborer, stonemason, painter, and salesman.

61. One of the three sisters of Stevens's mother, she is probably the person listed as Emma Schmucker living at 302 North Fifth Street in 1902 (Boyd's *Reading City Directory*) and buried in the Charles Evans cemetery (1850–1904).

puddles, snow-furrows, gutters, and so on. —It was as good as mid-ocean. —It is the first time I have been away from the streets since my last trip home. —And afterwards, we had that great dinner at the Murray Hill, stuffing ourselves beyond speech. —We walked down the Avenue together. There is a beastly drizzle—but I don't care a rap. It may drizzle and rain all week, if it likes. —Next Sunday we must make a whole day's trip. It saves my blood from turning into ink. —And there you are swimming in a salt wave—way up! —I did not get my Saturday afternoon walk yesterday, but stayed at the office until five o'clock talking to a bore, who didn't know where to begin or where to end his story. At five, I walked him out of the office and then rambled up empty Broadway. My coat was heavy with rain. —In the evening I read Scribner's for February. There are some capital serious articles in it, one on contemporary German art.[62] You know I am still hammering at them, trying to get the feel of them. Here is a classification of them by Tieck: "the war-like and pious Bavarians (we have many Bavarians at home)—the gentle, thoughtful and imaginative Swabians—the sprightly, gay Franconians—the upright Hessians, the handsome Thuringians—the Low-Germans, resembling in true-heartedness the Dutch, in strength and skill the English." The Low-Germans, too, are very common at home. True-heartedness surely describes them. I love them, my dear. You must not think that I do nothing but poke fun at them—in spite of Theresa Powdermaker or Antoinette Himmelberger. —I felt my kinship, my race. To study them is to realize one's own identity. It is subtly fascinating. —In Scribner's, there is a picture of an iron foundry. The mass of the machinery, the hot iron, the grimy workmen—I looked at them for a long time, they were so familiar. —There was also a picture of two old women sitting in a field, tending geese. The hard faces full of suffering endured revived the old puzzle: what do old people think? —Only the moderns reflect much on old age. The Greeks shuddered at it. In that respect I am Greek. To live while one is strong—that is enough, I think. No race has ever occupied itself with the realities of life more than the Germans. —I should rather spend a year in Germany than in any other part of Europe, provided, of course, I had the facilities for getting into the life and thought of the day—and wandering through the villages and the smaller towns. —Cities, I imagine, are more or less alike the world over. —You speak of the people here. It is one of the oldest of observations that, in a city, one does not know the people around one. It is not the people you know that count, but the people you don't know—who don't know each other. It is the mass. —The simplicity of the society of the smaller places gives way to formality. There are

62. Holly Stevens's helpful note (*LWS*, 127) is "Christian Brinton: 'German Painting of To-Day,' *Scribner's*, XLV (February 1909), 129–43. The Tieck quote is from this article."

few intimacies. —You lose your individuality in a sense; in another sense you intensify it, for you are left to your own devices to satisfy your desires, without the interest or encouragement of friends. You become what you desire to be. — It will make a great difference to you coming here. For you will find immediately the necessity of adjusting yourself to many things now unknown. You will find your character either a torment or a delight, and <u>which</u> will depend entirely on your strength. —It will be an immense pleasure to you, I think. I have never doubted your courage, or your will—so far as they will be called on. —But higgeldy-piggeldy, I'm not writing to Joan of Arc, or to anyone but my Bo. What the deuce! Courage and will—and the life of the city—nonsense. I'll take care of her, and she won't have anything to think of, if I can help it. Bother! — We'll have a little place of our own and do what we like—and once a year we'll go to the theatre, and on Christmas I'll give you a box of cigars. —Bye the bye, I'll send the music and so on next Saturday. Thanks, dear, for your suggestions. There will be some things that I have not mentioned, too. —Your description of the Thackeray makes me think that it is the same edition as my own. Look on the title-page and see if it was published in London by Smith, Elder & Co. about 1869.[63] I have the complete set in I-don't-know-how-many volumes—they are packed away. —Thackeray is old-fashioned now, or is called so. But he has so much human nature at the tip of his pen, and so much fun, that he will never be left unread. I read "Vanity Fair" while I was waiting for the time to pass to come home at Christmas; and I have "The Newcomes" at my elbow now, although I have not yet started it. There is one called "Beatrix Esmond" or "Henry Esmond" or Esmond something or other which you should read without fail. It is one of the best novels ever written. —I have finished "Cousin Phillis." It was a poor kind of thing as novels go, but written perfectly. —I must not forget to tell you how glad I was to have your long letters during the week. In return for your verses, I send you one of my own

> Now, the locust, tall and green,
> Glitters in the light serene.
> Leafy motions shake around
> Brilliant showers to the ground.
> At a dart, an oriole sings,
> To glimmering of yellow wings.
> Sunlight in the rainy tree
> Flash Two-and-Twenty back to me![64]

63. Though this whole set of books in not in the surviving part of Stevens's library, two of these volumes are at the Huntington: *The Christmas Books of Mr. M. S. Titmarsh,* and *The Four Georges: The English Humorists of the Eighteenth Century.*

64. This is number VII of "The Little June Book" of June 5, 1909.

Think of me scribbling at that for a whole evening. Well, I did—to the accompaniment of a line of Bliss Carman's:

June comes, and the moon comes.[65]

I hummed that for a day—and then scribbled. —You will like Robert Louis Stevenson's "Child's Garden of Verses"—and you will recognize many things in it. They must have it at the library. —The gelatine sounds good. Do you eat it with thick cream? They flavor it with coffee—and that is very good with cream. Just put a cup of coffee in it, I suppose—or perhaps not so much. — The desserts[66] here are things like cottage pudding, pie and the like. I detest pastry for dessert. They have rice pudding, too, which has a very queer taste in the evening. But on Wednesdays and Sundays they have ice cream! They give you a square piece. I like it in mountains. —Have you had all this raw weather we have been having? Keep yourself warm when you go out—and don't forget those over-shoes. Just the time for a bad cold. Mind! Have you heard anything about the exhibition of pictures they have in Philadelphia every winter at the Academy of Arts?[67] It would be fun to have you meet me there some Saturday afternoon and then we could have dinner together and go home in the evening. If you hear of it let me know, and I'll make arrangements.

Affectionately—

Wallace.

~

[WAS 1810 January 26, 1909 New York]

Tuesday Evening

Dear Bo:—

I ran up-town at noon and bought some music which you will receive, no doubt, to-morrow. I mailed them in tubes. If they are all crumpled up put them under that big Bible under the table at the foot of the stairs. They were too large for a package. I had meant to send you two of Kenneth Grahame's books but they will do for another time. I sent the "Sketchbook" of Nevin's, with Mac-Dowell's[68] "Marionettes," an album of short pieces by Arthur Whiting and

65. From "May and June" in *Last Songs from Vagabondia* by Bliss Carman and Richard Hovey (Boston: Small, Maynard, 1900), 3. This poem was written by Bliss Carman.

66. The second s was added after the fact here and in the next "dessert," one of his very rare emendations.

67. This is the first mention of what will become an important episode in Stevens's relationship with Elsie, important enough to influence at least one poem thirty years later, "Arcades of Philadelphia the Past."

68. Edward MacDowell (1860–1908), of whom Rupert Hughes in 1900 said, "An almost unanimous vote would grant him rank as the greatest of American composers."

Henselt's "If I were a bird, etc." (si j'étais oiseau—)[.] Arthur Whiting is quite as good as Nevin. Tell me what you think of him, in a week or so, after you have gone over his book. The Henselt piece is very well-known. Gabrilovitch, the Russian pianist, played it at his last concert. It was so well spoken of that I made note of it for you. —I hope it is suited for our little collection. —I'll watch out for new things. —Before I forget it—Wolfinger was taken sick shortly after he reached New-York and went home at once, so that I did not meet him. I was at home here that evening. —The fact is I am glad to loaf in the evenings. The day does not tire me in the least, but it occupies me so completely that the quiet of the evening seems diversion in itself. —My principal regret is that I do not have sufficient books—but hang books for a change. —Another thing: I am not really impatient for Spring to come. I shall probably move when it does come and at present I'm too lazy to think of such a thing. It would be impossible for me to pass the Summer in so small a room. But that is all far enough away. —Yet the weather is exciting. There seems to be a special light for Spring (for every season) and this morning I saw that light. —February may, of course, be as mild as May. One begins to think so, for in another week it will be here. —But for the present, let us confine ourselves to black and white, and keep radiance only for dreams. To-morrow it is to be freezing, and I, for one, should be sorry if it were <u>not</u> so. Winter braces us all. Only the snow and the mud and the damp are unbearable. But these are not here, so a salute to Master Zero, and wish him well. —It is almost time for me to be going to some theatre again. I have not been since before Christmas. Maxine Elliot [*sic*] has a new theatre[69] of her own which is said to be the best in town. And last night a new English musical comedy, "Kitty Grey,"[70] started at the New-Amsterdam.[71] The English musical shows are quite likely to be amusing. They are not so beastly elaborate, the music is agreeable, and the people are bright. A New-York show is always stuffed with Jewesses singing solos and making dull remarks. And the English shows are English—clean, original, and so on—but English. —You get to know even second-rate actors here. Often, you see a man or a woman that you remember. It is tiresome. —But the English companies are all new. They bring over the whole business from the

---

Gilbert Chase, *America's Music from the Pilgrims to the Present,* 3rd ed. (Urbana: University of Illinois Press, 1987), 344. Nevin's *Sketch Book* (1888), Opus 2, included five piano works: Gavotte, Love Song, Berceuse, Sereneta, and *Valse Rhapsodie.*

69. Named Maxine Elliott's Theater on West Thirty-ninth Street, between Broadway and Sixth Avenue, this theater (725 seats) opened at the end of 1908.

70. Musical comedy in three acts, adapted from the French by J. M. Pigott. Music by Lionel Moncton and Howard Talbot. Produced January 25. Review in *Theatre* 9 (March 1909): xiii–xiv.

71. New Amsterdam Theater: Forty-second Street between Seventh and Eighth avenues.

funny-man to the obscurest girl in the chorus. —Perhaps, I'll call up W. B. to-
morrow and get him to go in the evening. One need only ask him—poor Youth!
—Anything like a serious show would bore me to death. —Bernard Shaw has
just brought out a new thing in London called "The Admirable Bashville."[72]
There is no scenery and the actors act in their every-day clothes. It is a burlesque
of Shakespeare, I believe. —Wouldn't it be nice to live in London and go—say,
on Saturday evening? We'll be going over there one of these days, I hope. I
should mope in Paradise (possibly) if I were to die without first having been to
London.[73] —On Sunday, it was Berlin. —I have had my hours for Paris, too—
when I could see the Street of Little Stables, and the Street of Beautiful Leaves,
and the Bridge of Arts, and the Church of Our Lady, and the Arch of Triumph—
as clearly as I can see you looking out of that frame. —Good Fortune, send us to
them all. We'll save for that. It isn't so impossibly expensive, you know. People
who go once, go often—unless that <u>once</u> they go in state, foolishly.[74] —It seems
much nearer, too, when the steamers start from the foot of your own street, as
they do here. I was well aware of that the other night in the fog, when there was
a continual whistling and bell-ringing all night long. —Perhaps, it was <u>that</u> turned
me into that salty billow, rolling so far inland—foaming over the dazzling white
shutters opposite you—white as blinds in, say, Algiers (where they are, doubtless,
green or brown.) —So you have been sending kisses to me each night! My dear,
I have sent you many—very often. But I must remember that you send them as
you do, and wait for them—and send others in return. I have been thinking lately
so many pleasant things of you. That will only be another. Bye!

Wallace

⌒

[WAS 1811 January 29, 1909 New York]

Friday Evening

Dear Bo:

I'm in the midst of a fit of dissipation. When I have saved and cooped myself
up for a month,

There comes a night
When we all get tight.

72. This play, published in New York by Brentano's in 1909, did not come to New
York at this time.
73. Stevens never made a trip to Europe; his foreign travel was limited to Canada,
Cuba, and the Panama Canal.
74. Stevens and Elsie took but one foreign trip in their lives, the trip from New York
to San Francisco by way of Cuba and the Panama Canal from October to December
1923.

Well, I haven't been doing that, of course, but I've been to the theatre twice and am going again to-night, and to-morrow night too, possibly. It will be a good plan to see everything good this month and then not go again for a long time—say until April. And that is my plan. —I'll tell you all about the things I've seen on Sunday. One of them, "The Blue Mouse,"[75] was as funny as possible. — It puts one all up in the air and I feel as if I had been raising the deuce. —But if I stayed home always I'd be as tame as a cat, and that would be tiresome. — Suddenly I feel like staying home. But they'll be drumming the piano in a moment and it will be the same old bother all over again. —Beginning with the first of the month, I'll be old prune again. I think it will be "Kitty Grey" to-night, though Maude Adams[76] pulls me toward her—See the lights go down!

Sh!

Wallace

⤺

[WAS 1812 January 31, 1909 New York]

Sunday Evening

My Dearest Bo:

Once more I wanted intensely to see you last night. I wanted to send you a telegram at the last minute that you would get at your supper time, when you would have no time to get ready. But I didn't start. Instead, I passed a reckless afternoon at the Library and an even more reckless evening at the Museum with the German pictures. —The theatre on Friday evening disappointed me—so I stopped a day earlier. Three shows in a row—that's quite enough. The tiresome one was "Kitty Grey," which I thought immensely stupid. The dresses were pretty—but the music was thin and there was nothing in the least amusing. "The Blue Mouse," on the other hand, was <u>very</u> amusing—all kinds of mistaken identities, and so on, and everybody in hot water all the time. "The Easiest Way"[77] was interesting and well-acted. It was in a theatre new to me—I think the most attractive theatre in town. The ceiling is low and full of designs in

75. Comedy in three acts, adapted by Clyde Fitch from the German of Alex Engel and Julius Horst. First produced on November 30, 1909, at the Lyric Theater. Reviewed in *Theatre* 9 (January 1909): 5, xi, and photographs of scenes on 29.

76. Maude Kiskaden (1872–1953) took her mother's maiden name as her stage name, which she made famous. Stevens first mentions seeing her "as the Duke of Reichstadt in Rostand's *L'Aiglon*" in his November 10, 1900, journal entry. In that entry, he says, "There's something about Maude Adams that wrings a fellow's heart" (*SP,* 89).

77. A play in four acts by Eugene Walter; it opened at the Stuyvesant Theater (Forty-fourth Street, east of Broadway) on January 19, 1909. After 1910, this theater was known as the Belasco. *The Easiest Way,* about a woman who unhappily trades her favors for wealth, was popular and ran until the end of the season.

wood—no: just one design repeated, made of beams. Set in it are squares of stained glass with lamps behind them—and so on. I am not able to give you a picture of it. —Why I should so suddenly have taken to going to the theatre is beyond me. But I have already stopped going so it does not matter. —I shall settle down more easily to February, which seems ready to make its customary icy entrance, to judge from the hard cold of this afternoon. I went walking alone— literally driven from the house by the pitiless caterwauling in the next room. I crossed the street and inquired for rooms there and then gave notice here that my patience had been worn out for a long time and that I should give up my room the moment I found another—and that will be very soon. Then I went up to the Park and looked at the camels and the China pheasants and the polar bear—but principally at the new snow and the bright sunlight shining on it and the country-like sky. It was a perfect winter-scene. —W. B. did not turn up. — I felt fairly brisk coming home and threw off the bad conscience that follows indulgence. What a dunce a fellow is to feel that way about going to the theatre! —Yet I am never so thoroughly content as when I pass my evenings quickly (and, say, usefully) at home. It is wild dissipation to go to bed at midnight, what- ever you have been doing—at least, when you have to be at an office the fol- lowing morning, and to keep up all day with the rapid complications of so disturbed an organism. —A fresh start to-morrow! I saved a good deal. I am satisfied. —It is a bother to have to save at all sometimes. At other times, for weeks at a stretch, it is the spice of the whole game. It becomes second-nature. (You must not comment on this, please.) —My letters to you, however, have not prospered. Forgive that, Bo-Bo. The fresh start is to include an amendment in that respect, too—beginning to-night. I could love you for your letters alone; for nothing gives me more pleasure, or shows you to me more clearly as I like to see you than they do. —Aren't you overdoing the gelatine—just a little? How many times last week? Doesn't your father look at it and holler, "What! More gelatine!" Put raisins in it for him if he does. Raisin-gelatine! —By the way, I don't in the least mind what your grandmother said either about her relatives or mine. It is amusing to think of that washer-woman. Mother must be worried to death when she thinks of her. You know she is a Daughter of the Revolution and traces herself through two or three generations to an officer in the American army. You can imagine her crowding out the details. Father once told her that she was a shoemaker's daughter and he was a farmer's son.[78] That is true. But her

---

78. *LWS* (3–4) quotes a May 3, 1943, letter by Stevens as saying that in the 1856–57 directory of Reading, John Zeller is described as a shoemaker, but he is quick to indi- cate that "he himself was far above the average from the point of view of ambition and the will to get on." Brazeau has a very thorough discussion of the passion Stevens him- self would develop for genealogy: "Over a third of Stevens' voluminous archive

father was an excellent shoemaker and his father was an excellent farmer—not at all the kind of man we call a farmer at home, but a man of ability and character. They both belonged to large families and both were poor. It is very silly for people in a country town to bother about such things. Besides, you can't get around a washer-woman. —On the other hand, we all have poor relations. — And as a last refuge, we can say that individuals rise or fall on their own merits. Their families are nothing. —The whole question is one of respectability. —We both come from respectable families—you and I. What more is there to be said? The rest depends upon ourselves. —What we inherit in our characters presents a question. What we inherit otherwise is unimportant. Nothing is more absorbing than to trace back the good and evil in us to their sources. At the same time, nothing is more unjust or more ungenerous. Our spirits are what we will them to be, not what they happen to be, that is if we have any courage at all. —I hate a man that is what he is—the weak victim of circumstances. That involves occasional hatred of myself. For example, no one loathes melancholy more than I, yet there are times when no one is more melancholy. And there are other traits besides melancholy. No one likes good manners more than I, or appreciates them more, and yet when I am blue—Lord! how blue, and bearish, and ill-mannered I am. —In defense: this is, quite likely, true of everyone, in a measure. It is particularly true of idealists,—idealism being, perhaps, the most intolerant form of sentimentalism. —By contrast, one likes those plain characters, always equable, that accept things as they are. Their simplicity seems so wise. — Unfortunately such characters commonly develop only in maturity and even in age. —The young are incorrigible. Personally, I am still decidedly young—not nearly so competent as I have an idea of being some day to be superior to circumstances. —But there's no end to this. Let us avoid the beginning, therefore. —At the Library yesterday, I skipped through a half-dozen volumes of poetry by Bliss Carman. I felt the need of poetry—of hearing again about April and frogs and marsh-noises and the "honey-colored moon"[79]—of seeing—

---

testifies to the strength of this passion: some 2,500 genealogical items in the form of letters, documents and the multivolume work-in-progress, as he called his history of his Stevens, Barcalow and Zeller lines" (*Parts of a World,* 270). Though this effort was disinterested in part, it focused on gaining entrance to the exclusive Holland Society of New York; however, Stevens had to settle for the less prestigious Saint Nicholas Society (Brazeau, *Parts of a World,* chap. 8, "Family Ties"). The letter of June 21, 1944, from this society telling Stevens that he has been elected a member of the Saint Nicholas Society is at the University of Massachusetts at Amherst.

79. From poem LXXXII of Bliss Carman's *Sappho: One Hundred Lyrics* (London: Chatto & Windus, 1921), 96.

"oleanders
Glimmer in the moonlight."[80]

You remember the fragments of Sappho. Carman has taken these fragments and imagined the whole of the poem of which each was a part. The result, in some instances, is immensely pleasant—although distinctly not Sapphic. Sappho's passion came from her heart. Carman's comes from a sense of warm beauty. Sappho says, "Sweet mother, I cannot weave my web, broken as I am by longing." Carman, on the contrary, has his morning planet, his garden and <u>then</u> his longing. —There is a sonnet of my own that I have not sent you, that I wrote last week. At Berkeley I used to jot down lines as they came to me. Looking over my diary recently I found the line

Oh, what soft wings shall rise above this place—[81]

And so after ten years I wrote the rest:

In a Garden
Oh, what soft wings shall rise above this place,
This little garden of spiced bergamot,
Poppy and iris and forget-me-not,
On Doomsday, to the ghostly Throne of space!

The haunting wings, most like the visible trace
Of passing azure in a shadowy spot—
The wings of spirits, native to this plot,
Returning to their intermitted Grace!

And one shall mingle in her cloudy hair
Blossoms of twilight, dark as her dark eyes;
And one to Heaven upon her arm shall bear
Colors of what she was in her first birth;
And all shall carry upward through the skies
Odor and dew of the familiar earth.

The <u>Post</u> reviewed some recent poetry last evening and said that the writing of poetry nowadays was partly an exercise of vanity. <u>Partly,</u> that is, no doubt, true. And it is just in the measure of the vanity that we laugh at poets. Well, I admit a measure. Let the admission excuse the vanity. —But there is also a pure delight in doing it. How deeply one gets into one's mind! Poetry only lies in the remoter places of it. —It is vanity all the same. Vanity, vanity, vanity. No

80. Also from Carman's *Sappho,* here poem XIII on page 19.
81. This entry for August 1, 1899, is in *SP,* 51.

hypocrisy! —I am going to be at it again soon. It passes an evening. <u>Very</u> soon, for I am in the same old condition of having nothing to read. —I am tempted to study Italian. What with my whirling enthusiasm, first for France, and then for Germany, I may expect sooner a later to be as interested in Italy. The books are here—it is only a matter of opening them. —I remember a book on modern Italian poets in the Library at home. It is a little blue book, a few shelves up from the floor, upstairs, to the left, in the alcove facing the second window on the Fifth-Street side. There is a sonnet on "Rome" by Carducci[82] (I think) worth looking all morning for. —Could you send me a copy of it? —What dress do you wear mostly now-a-days? The black one? And the hat I like? Tell me so that I shall know how you look when you go down town shopping. —Do your cheeks still—of course, they do. Paint a little picture for me so that I can see you. —I still wear that abominable hat—and the dark suit: it is the warmest. The weather has been so mild that I have not needed an over-coat, although to-night it is really as cold as you please, and to-night, it took me a half-hour to get my fingers nimble. —As a matter of fact, I am out-of-doors very little except on Sunday afternoons. —I have fallen into the habit of reading the papers on Sunday mornings—and a chapter or two of whatever book happens to be in the way. Even so, that longest of mornings seems very short. We have dinner at one—and everybody goes at once—particularly the people who missed breakfast. I did myself this morning, but went out to a place not far away where Charlie Dana,[83] an old friend of mine, used to go years ago—and told me how good it was. It is really rather fair. —Two fat red apples wink at me from my bureau. I seem to think of apples at ten o'clock every night. As a clock strikes then, so something in me says, "Apples." —So, appleward. And a few more pages of "The Madonna of the Future" by Henry James. Good-night, dear. Stop for a minute just here. . . . (Did you notice it?) Bad girl! Try again.

With love,
Wallace

⌒

82. Giosuè Carducci (1835–1907), an Italian poet who won the Nobel Prize in Literature in 1906. Richardson gives this poem and an English translation (*Wallace Stevens,* 1:326, 560–61.)
83. Charles Dana was a friend from Stevens's law school days. There are references to him in Stevens's journals for September 8, 1902 (*SP,* 109), March 11, 1904 (*SP,* 129), a long account of a rather rowdy, drinking weekend with him for May 23, 1904 (*SP,* 135), and a visit to him and his wife in Darien, Connecticut, for April 21, 1907 (*SP,* 177), on which occasion he says, "Mrs. Dana very attractive." (For a longer description of this visit, see WAS 1792 above.)

[WAS 1813 February 2. 1909 New York]

Tuesday Evening

Dearest:

I noticed that the exhibition in Philadelphia opened yesterday but beyond the mention of the prizes there was little of interest. Later on, I expect, there will be critical articles. I have not yet found out in what part of the town it is being held. It remains open until the middle of march. Washington's birthday [Feb 22] falls on a Monday. I shall come home for it—in less than three weeks. Let us do this: I'll get over to Philadelphia about two o'clock in the afternoon of the pre-ceeding Saturday [Feb 20] and you meet me there, in the station. Find out what trains on the Reading road get to Philadelphia about that time—unless, of course, you'd like to go down in the morning. I'll send the spondulix[84] for the ticket. I have always wanted to see one of these Philadelphia exhibitions. They are said to be ahead of those here. We could run out there and you could be back home in time for supper, or we could have supper in Philadelphia and go to some theatre afterwards, or a concert or something. There is a late train from Philadelphia that gets to Reading a little after one o'clock and you would be home by half-past, or about that. Don't you think it would be fun? Just say, "Yes!" and tell me what time you would meet me so that I can arrange my own train from New York. —Exhibitions are quite different from museums, you know. Everything is fresh and interesting—and it has an effect. —The latest bul-letin from the field of battle: the landlady has put her foot down on the piano "forever." It has been as quiet as a chapel for two nights and I have been peace-fully reading Dr. Campion and Oliver Goldsmith. Yet they are noisy devils, to speak mildly, even without music. —I have been studying apples. The Italian at the corner sold me some poor ones on Sunday night, I think, and yesterday, at noon, I ran down to Washington Market and spread confusion among the apple-women. Such beauties! To-night, I went to a place on Madison Avenue and picked up some "Arkansas Blacks!" They are as black and ruddy as black cherries. The man who kept the store (it was a small place) was a marvel of attention. I noticed stuffed prunes, and so on—jars of marrons, figs—fresh peaches, fresh strawberries, melons, and the like. —I've got to keep an iron hot—whether in theatres or fruit stores. By the way, I didn't see Maude Adams.

---

84. According to the *Oxford Dictionary of Americanisms,* this word is slang for money or cash, as in *Huckleberry Finn,* chap. 13: "I'm derned if *I'd* live two mile out 'o town[,] . . . not for all his spondylicks." Thanks to Paul Zall, senior research fellow of the Hun-tington Library, for considering several different spellings of this illegible word until he discovered the right one. With Stevens's difficult handwriting, one has to have a hunch in order to read unusual words; Paul had the hunch, when I did not have a clue.

Her play: "What Every Woman Knows"[85] is said to be only so-so. There is something about the lady I do not like. She has such a silly voice—or something. I have only seen Maxine Elliott once, long ago. In fact, all the better known American actresses—Viola Allen,[86] Virginia This and That, Julia Marlowe[87]—I have never seen, and have no curiosity to see. So with Faversham,[88] and his ilk. I have no feeling about them, only they do not interest me. They are popular, and that is sufficient criticism. —They are not the subtle, dynamic creatures they should be. They invoke images of rouge, of painted scenery, of "the play of the day"—and I have a contrary way of desiring something more vital, something with more illusion. —The stage is Imagination, in a way. With them it is Invention. —It is curious to think of the wide-spread, deep interest in the theatre. The greatest minds coöperate there with the greatest spirits—at its best. But when it is mediocre the interest suffers constant obstacles. —Yet at its worst it is still something. —Human nature, which is always the primary concern of any art—no: of literature and largely of the drama, is distinctly <u>not</u> the concern of the theatre in New-York. —I suppose that thesis would not be universally accepted. I am not prepared to debate it. Let it pass. —The theatre is a puzzle. —If we are to believe in the theory that we are never anything but children (a theory supported by Fashion, Sport, our houses, Work—everything)—then the theatre becomes no more than the most dazzling toy ever devised. —The most dazzling toy, the most absorbing plaything! —The frowning mask of Tragedy and the smiling one of Comedy—put them by: they are the conceptions of a sincerer and less knowing age. —Good heavens, yes! I'm content with "The Blue Mouse" sort of thing. The rest is all pretence now-a-days. —And I like musical comedy immensely. The tragedies of the Greeks with their invocations and prayers and solemnities have evolved into "The Three Twins"[89] and "Mr.

85. Comedy in four acts by J. M. Barrie. Produced December 23, 1908, at the Empire Theater. Reviewed in *Theatre* 9 (February 1909): 38–39. Full-page photo of Maude Adams as Maggie Wylie in *Theatre* 9 (January 1909): 17.
86. Viola Allen (1867-1948) was born in Huntsville, Alabama. Most active in the New York stage from 1882 through 1912, she was known for her intelligent acting.
87. Stage name of Sarah Frances Frost (1866-1950), who was appearing in a notable series of Shakespeare's plays at this time.
88. English actor William Faversham (1868-1940). After he made his American debut in 1887, his career peaked in the next decade; he was having trouble finding the appropriate vehicle by this time.
89. Musical play in two acts by Charles Dickson, adapted from Mrs. R. Pacheco's farce *Incog*. Lyrics by Otto A Hauerbach, music by Carl Hoschna. Produced by Joseph M. Gaites at the Herald Square Theater on June 15, 1908. After a fire at this theater, the play was reopened at the Majestic Theater.

Hamlet of Broadway."[90] It is superb. It is modern. Sparkling dresses, Frenchmen acting the dunce, pretty songs, choruses like Persian armies—that's the ticket. I mean it. —I hate solemn things—unless there is enough genius to make them real. But all the genius lies the other way. Hence Broadway.

Affectionately,
Wallace.

↩

[WAS 1814 February 5, 1909 New York]

Friday Evening

My dear Bo:—

Brutal February is as mild here as it is in the Bahamas. I write with my window open. Last night, too, was horribly stuffy, and I went to bed with a headache that lasted until almost morning. A rank day at the office—business is slow—very. At five o'clock Walter called up and said that he would be down after dinner to-night to take a walk; and I expect him any moment. —I think it would be as well to drop into some theatre, if the evening is to be fribbled away. Anyhow, I feel like fribbling. —I felt quite piqued about your letter until I knew what all that diligence was about and then I was amused. So you didn't want me to think that Mrs. A. had taught you to embroider! Not that: you didn't want me to think that I knew. I bow my head, my dear. —But if you really embroider much, I shall have to call you Tabitha, for it is the chief art of aunts and things. —But bells, of course, are different, especially when they are of leaves and flowers. Only no "God Bless our Home," you know. — I wish B. would come. He's dragging it out so that we'll be too late to do anything but walk around and gobble apples, and I've eaten so many apples recently that I hate the name. The "Arkansas Blacks" were sweet as the honey—comb or the melon hangin' on the vine. —Here he is—soft shirt, old hat, and so on. Dead set against the theatre. Well, it might be worse. Perhaps it will be just the thing to ramble about absorbing the moist air, premonitory of starry May.

With love,
Wallace.

↩

90. Musical comedy in two acts. Book by Edgar Smith. Lyrics by Edward Madden. Music by Ben M. Jerome. Produced by Sam S. and Lee Schubert at the Casino Theater on December 23, 1908.

[WAS 1815 February 6–7, 1909 New York]

Saturday Evening

My dear Bo:—

That was disagreeable of me last night and I <u>am</u> <u>sorry.</u> We walked far up-town until we were thoroughly tired and then came home. We stopped at the fruit store on Madison-Avenue—Plumbridge's—and bought some apples and stuffed prunes—and were favored with a taste of very special ginger by no less a person than the admirable Plumbridge himself—and looked on grapes from Belgium, peaches from South Africa, melons from Egypt—and more. —This afternoon I went to Pratt Institute[91] in Brooklyn to see some paintings by Charles Warren Eaton. They concerned Bruges, the Belgian Bruges, chiefly, although there were many interesting and pleasant landscapes of a general character, as one might say. —Bruges appears to have a central square (Grande Place) with a monument in it and a church on one side and markets on another side! Well, it is true that that <u>is</u> common enough—but they have such moonlight in Bruges—Flemish green nights when the slender trees are black and the bridges throw arched reflections in[92] the canal. I suppose people pass the time in Bruges examining reflections—by sunlight as well as by moonlight. —Beyond Bruges the canal winds in large curves through flat fields. On each bank, it seems, there is a single row of a [*sic*] tall trees, with foliage high in the air. These make a line of superb grace, whether by day or night. Witness: Canal near Bruges: Morning (all greyish, silvery mist) and Canal near Bruges: Moonlight (trees in an ame-thystine sky.) —And the wharves at Bruges! There is one that is called "Le quai du Miroir"—the quay of the mirror—a dock of glassy tranquility, with forms of blue and amber and rose swimming around idle sloops. —Bruges becomes important to me. I must whirl away there to-night in my chariot and never rest until I touch the Pont Flammand. —Coming home I walked across the Brook-lyn Bridge. It was clear and marvellously mild, except for a high wind. The harbor is certainly one of the great sights. To the Southwest it was a monstrous glare of sunlight on water—and then the innumerable ships, the fort, the huge silhouette of the city in the twilight. —I wanted to go up to the Columbia Library to-night and play a bit—it is so beastly hot here. The house is like a sun-baked rock. But they look askance on the rank outsider up there, so here I am. —I read with relief that it is to be freezing to-morrow. —

Sunday Evening

Not freezing, actually, but fresh.

---

91. Private college in Brooklyn (founded in 1887) that had the first public library in Brooklyn and the first manual high school in New York.

92. The first page of this letter ends with "in," and the next page begins with a repetition of this word.

As the clock struck three
Along came W. B.

We took the Elevated through Brooklyn to Cypress Hills, then the trolly to Jamaica and from Jamaica we walked home. At Cypress Hills there is a Jewish Cemetery.[93] They pack them away like things in a box. I never saw graves so close together. A large number of stones run So-and-So born in Bavaria, or born in Hesse-Darmstadt and the like. It is something to think of. —At Jamaica we ran in to see Arthur Clous. He lives as severely as a saint—in a dismal frame house—in a room that looks painfully bare. He paid no attention to us and so, after smoking a pipe of his tobacco, we started for home. New-York lay directly Westward ten miles away. As we came near to town we could see the lights from the hill-tops. That is new—for there are very few hill-tops to look from. —The Brooklyn Bridge was brilliant with its hundreds of lamps. And the Singer building with its lighted tower shows far more beautifully in the vague light than you would expect.[94] —It was much too late to go home and so we went to the Murray Hill grill once more and did the usual stuffing. — Then we walked down to Calvary church getting there a few minutes before the recessional, which happened to be the glorious

"The daylight slowly fades."[95]

It is the finest hymn in the world—the music of it. I wonder if I could get a copy of it for you. I must try. —I was not in good shape for walking. You have to keep it up to go ten miles in two hours—and run every mile or two. We played tag. It was like a game between the elephant and the hare. —There was no letter from you yesterday although I expected one. But perhaps it will be at the office in the morning. I am anxious to hear about the Philadelphia jaunt. Madame Nazimova[96]

93. In this border area between Queens and Brooklyn, sometimes known as "the city of the dead," there are twenty-four cemeteries, of which the following are Jewish: Salem Field, Ahawad Chesed, Washington, Machpelah, Mount Nebo, and Union.

94. At 612 feet, this skyscraper at 149 Broadway (not completed until 1911) remained the world's tallest building until the completion of the Empire State Building.

95. Calvary Episcopal Church is located on Fourth Avenue at Twenty-first Street. The Hymn Society of America was unable to find these exact words as the beginning or title of a hymn but suggests two close alternatives as candidates: George Washington Doane's words and Carl Maria von Weber's music in *The Hymnal: 1940* of the Episcopal Church, "Softly now the light of day / Fades upon my sight away," or Christopher Wordsworth's words to Henry Thomas Smart's music in *The New Baptist Hymnal* of 1926, "The day is gently sinking to a close, / Fainter and yet more faint the sunlight glows."

96. Alla Nazimova (1879-1945), Russian born and trained, made her New York debut in 1905 and became famous as an interpreter of Ibsen.

will be playing Comtesse Coquette[97] that night and there will be a play by Clyde Fitch: The Happy Marriage.[98] Nazimova is clever and Fitch is clever, too. And you could wear the new belt.

With love,
Wallace.

↜

[WAS 1816 February 10, 1909 New York]

Wednesday Evening

My Very Dear Bo:

A rank, tempestuous, horrid day—and I am going to bed in a moment and put my head under the pillow—and just snooze. —I am so glad that you will meet me in Philadelphia. It doesn't matter at all about the evening, because the Exhibition is the principal thing and a few hours of looking at pictures will quite satisfy me. But we can, as you say, make up our minds on the spot. —You have said nothing about the trains. I think I can find out just as well here and I shall, therefore, look up a Railway Guide and see what may be convenient. —The only event since my last letter has been an exhibition of Spanish pictures by Sorolla at the Hispanic Museum.[99] They show marvellously the reality of sunlight—as one sees it on the beach at Valencia (chiefly). But I have not really thought much about it. —I have no interest in the technical side of painting. I look only for things I know—to recall them—as one recalls "the beauty of morning," or "Hesperus, gloaming's prime cheerer"[100]—or any such common-place—to recall them and feel their eloquence. —You will find a new delight. —But I am desperately tired, dear. —Good- night—and a kiss.

And my love—
Wallace

97. This comedy in three acts by Roberto Bracco (trans. from Italian by Dirce St. Cyr and Grace Isabel Colbron) and starring Alla Nazimova had opened in New York at the Bijou Theater on April 12, 1907.

98. This play opened in New York at the Garrick Theater on April 12, 1909, but Nazimova was not in the cast.

99. This exhibition of 356 paintings by the Spanish painter Joaquín Sorella y Bastida (1863–1923) was held from February 4 to March 9, 1909, by the Hispanic Society of America on 156th Street, west of Broadway. At this time, Sorolla was considered one of the great contemporary painters. In *SP*, 213 (March 7, 1909), Stevens writes a paragraph about this exhibition.

100. It is known that the English painter Turner liked to call the sun the "prime cheerer," and others have referred to the light or to hope in the same terms. Stevens uses Hesperus twice in his 1908 verses for Elsie's birthday; and William Morris, someone Stevens was reading at this period in his life, regularly referred to Hesperus.

〜

[WAS 1817 February 15, 1909 New York]

Monday Evening

My dearest Bo:—

I had <u>two</u> letters from you this morning—to make up for your wicked neglect—and I was very, very glad to have them. —Since that rank, tempestuous, horrid day I have been in a rank tempestuous, horrid humor, beyond control—but I can hide that by not speaking of it. —We make a great deal of Lincoln's birthday here, although it is not altogether a holiday up-town. I took an all day walk in the country, the first for many months, and alone. It was a perfect winter day, with patches of long-forgotten snow in sheltered banks. —Saturday afternoon was another of the many spent in galleries and so on, looking at paintings and etchings—the last by Meryon[101] at Keppel's.[102] —Yesterday I met W. B. at the Fort Lee ferry[103] shortly after ten o'clock and we had a bully time of it until five in the evening—without a crumb to eat—just hammering along. The air was to me what cream is to peaches or oatmeal. —I saw—(hold your breath)—a—a—bluebird! And pussy willows! So you see that Spring <u>is</u> not so far away after all. The roads were heavy and the air raw. We had on only the oldest of old clothes—and were spattered with mud up to our knees. —Afterwards, when we had gone home to prink, we met at the Murray Hill and had a thundering dinner. Walter was so exhausted, however, that he was unable to eat more than some soup and an alleged squab. I did much better. —Then I had some papers to look over, which required an answer this morning, and when I had finished that it was after ten o'clock. —But the principal reason why I did not write last evening was because I wanted to let you know about the trains on Saturday. —You might like to start early and run into Wanamaker's[104] before you meet me—or some such place. The trains for that leave <u>Franklin</u> <u>Street</u> at 9:28 (express) reaching Philadelphia at 10:50, and at 10:18 (local) reaching Philadelphia at 12:02. But if you do not care to go earlier, there is a train at 12:22 (express) from Franklin-Street reaching Philadelphia at 1:50. I shall take a train reaching Philadelphia about 2 o'clock. The time-table I have does not show all

101. Charles Meryon (1821–1868), a French artist whose reputation rests on twenty poetic etchings of old sections of Paris.

102. Keppel, an important print dealer located at 4 East Thirty-ninth Street, began the *Print Collector's Quarterly* in 1911.

103. This crossing from 125th Street across the Hudson to Edgewater, New Jersey, took them to the area Stevens extensively explored in his earliest years in New York; see, for example, *SP*, 79, 108ff, 127.

104. Trend-setting department store in Philadelphia (1876; branch in New York in1896) founded by John Wanamaker (1838–1922), who was famous for his creation of Bethany Bible Union and for his generous support of the YMCA movement.

the expresses between here and there. One train starts at 11 and arrives at 1:23, another starting at the same time arrives at 1:36. Probably there is one that starts at 12 and arrives at 2. I shall see—and let you know. And you let me know, too, please. —Just go in the waiting room at the Terminal—the big one that every-body uses—and I'll look for you. —About the weather: bad weather doesn't matter at all to me, because we shall hardly be on the streets much. —The Exhi-bition is only a short walk up Broad-street. —I shall enclose some money for your ticket, which I shall have to ask you to buy for yourself. I send enough to take care of any emergency, —your lunch and so on, if anything should happen. The rest we'll spend for catalogues, etc! —About the evening: the Philadelphia Orchestra plays (by the greatest chance in the world) Schubert's Unfinished Symphony, which I heard here some weeks ago. It is worth waiting for. Or if you would rather go to the theatre—and I should not wonder (rascal)—why, Ethel Barrymore will be playing "My Lady Frederick"[105] and Madame Nazi-mova "Comtesse Coquette" —and—I believe that's all that is of any account. —But what <u>have</u> you been doing to keep you up so late? I must call on Hawk-shaw the detective.[106] —Don't say that I have had my revenge—dear. (A queer place—to say that.) I had not thought of that. I have been such a nuisance at the office that I do not want to think of such mischief-making. —Only to see the rank, tempestuous, horrid temper—all nervousness and savageness—go like a black cloud, and to get back to quiet: it is next to a prayer with me now. —Your letters were the first light—and a balmy light. —Let us think only of each other. The thought has become a large part of us (at least of me) and the chief comfort. And only good thoughts—like lovers of goodness, as we must be, if we are wise. —Sometimes I am terribly jangled, full of clashing things. But, always, the first harmony comes from something I cannot just say to you at the moment—the touch of you organizing me again—to put it so. —I have such a hatred of com-plaining and quarreling—and there has been such a deuce of a lot of it all around me—and I in the midst of it. —Your voice comes out of an old world. That is not eloquence. It is the quickest way to express it. It is the only true world for me. An old world, and yet it is a world that has no existence except in you. —It

105. *Lady Frederick,* by W. Somerset Maugham, a comedy in three acts with Ethel Barrymore in the title role, opened in New York at the Hudson Theater on November 9, 1908.

106. A detective in the play *The Ticket-of-Leave Man* (1863), by the English dramatist Tom Taylor. The *Oxford English Dictionary* (2nd ed.) cites a use of Hawkshaw to mean detective in 1903.

is as if I were in the proverbial far country[107] and never knew how much I had become estranged from the actual reality of the things that are the real things of my heart, until the actual reality found a voice—you are the voice. —What I mean is that these hideous people here in the house (it is not polite to say so) and the intolerable people that come and go all day at the office—they make up the far country and occupy me so much that I forget that I am not one of them and never will be. —What am I then? Something that but for you would be terribly unreal. A dreamy citizen of a native place—of which I am no citizen at all. Sometimes I am all memories. They would be all dream except that you make them otherwise. You are my—you know what I want to say—what in the fairy tales is called the genius—the thing that comes in smoke a-building marble palaces— thing for the mystery of it. But that mood works itself out as I write of it. —Do you remember the verses in "Songs" no: "Harps Hung up in Babylon"—

> "Though palmer bound, I shall return
>
> ———
>
> From Eden beyond Syria."[108]

Well, I feel as if I had been returning to-night—from very rough water to the only haven I have. —I cannot tell how hard it has been at the office—the work staggers one. But pooh: I'll not think of it. —Oh! I forgot to tell you that on Saturday night I went to the theatre, after all. Walter came down in the evening and we went, against his will, to see Maxine Elliott in "The Chaperon."[109] It is an extremely light affair. Maxine Elliott is advertized as a stunning beauty. She is not, however —I should say. She is getting large—very. But she has a pretty voice and a pretty accent and all that is pleasant. I suppose I'll see Maude Adams again, too, one of these days, just because I said I wouldn't. —We had our usual baked apples after it was over, and so made ready for yesterday's long fast. —It is apparent that February is going to be quite harmless this year. No doubt the weather had its influence on me. —The blue-bird should cure all that, and I must say "Blue-bird!" instead of "Blue!" —The medicine was news to me. So

107. In his journal for April 27, 1907, Stevens refers to Elsie as "*une vrai princesse lointaine*" (*SP,* 146). Holly Stevens was told by Claire Tragle [Bauer] that Stevens used to refer to Elsie as his "princesse lointaine" (*SP,* 145), a term he possibly got from the title of Edmund Rostand's second play, *La Princesse lointaine* (1895), the story of the troubadour Rudel and the Lady of Tripoli.

108. In *LWS* (132), Holly points out that this is from "The Return" in Arthur Willis Colton's *Harps Hung Up in Babylon* (New York: Holt, 1907).

109. This production of Marion Fairfax's play was designed to showcase the popular beauty Maxine Elliott and to open (December 30, 1908) the new theater named for her (paid for by J. P. Morgan); though reviewers concentrated their attention on the new playhouse, the show ran for eight weeks.

long as it does you no harm I hope it will do you good. Personally I think one should only take prescriptions—nothing else. However, too many doctors are as bad as too many cooks, so I don't prescribe, particularly as I do not know the complaint. —But I continue to harp on the advantages of walking on bright days, more especially when you feel least like it, for then you need it most. —This, I recall, was the winter you feared. Now, that it is almost over—and that frogs are waiting to trill—you must not be behind them in celebrating. Yet leaves are two months away—leaves and shadows—for this is the shadowless season. —I have not been reading in the least and in fact I don't, all of a sudden, feel especially like it. —To-night I bought some apples. The apple era of two or three weeks ago already seems historic. —<u>Be</u> <u>sure</u> to write me several times this week, and I shall write to you. —And send me a kiss.

Your loving
Wallace

↫

[WAS 1818 February 16, 1909 New York]

Tuesday Evening

My Dear Bo:

A word from under my night-cap. —There <u>is</u> a train from New-York at twelve which reaches Philadelphia at two. I shall take that. Your train reaches there ten minutes before. So that is arranged. —I was dragged to a lecture on "The Savage South Seas" tonight. —It is the day of lectures on far-away places, but the lecturers are bold youths with familiar airs who do it because they need the money. —The lecture was given at the American Institute in 44th Street. It is the oddest place for New-York I have ever been in—looks exactly like a lodge-room or library in a small town. I liked it. —I went with one of the men in the house. We walked home and dropped into a restaurant back of the Jefferson Market police court[110] and talked until almost midnight with a lad back of the counter who was in a confiding frame of mind about his prospects. —But I write now only to let you know about my train—and to return that tiniest of kisses hidden under the last line in this morning's note. I love you for that, dear—and I do return it

With love
Wallace

↫

110. This market at Greenwich Lane and Sixth Avenue, a civic complex in High Victorian Gothic, included the Jefferson Courthouse, voted one of the ten most beautiful buildings in the United States in 1885.

[WAS 1819 February 17, 1909 New York]

Wednesday Evening

My dearest Bo:

You must not disappoint me Saturday. I am impatient to see the real Bo once more and there must be no "if I come." Please—because it will be a little fun for you; and besides, everything is just right—the Exhibition, the concert, and so on. Do you know anything about Philadelphia? It is all as dark as Carthage to me. We'll do some shopping together, to see how it goes, perhaps for apples—most likely for candy, because I shall not bring any from New York. —If it rains you can use my umbrella—so throw yours out of the car-window as soon as you are on the train. —The sky cleared this afternoon and let in a crisp, brilliant day which entirely revived my shattered spirits. —I have been going more slowly at the office and curiously I seem to accomplish just as much—and not to get wicked at all. —Allah be praised! —The clipping about Kuechler[111] showed some of the geniality that exists even in "crabbed, old age!" Kuechler was just the man to go with a bottle of Claret on an autumn day—provided, of course,

---

111. A native of Switzerland, Jacob Louis Kuechler (1830–1904) ran, for many years, a place of entertainment known for its homemade wine on the east slope of Mount Penn in Reading. It catered to a German clientele and was frequented by Stevens's father. After Kuechler's death on January 2, 1904, Stevens's father had the *Reading News* for January 7, 1904, print the following four paragraphs of eulogy Stevens had written to him about this genial man, referred to as a "hermit" in a promotional booklet about Reading published by the *Reading Herald* in 1909 (see *Passing Scene* 1:189–97 and 7:173):

And so the genius of the mountain woods has flown! He was such good company, and has gone to join such good company that one catches himself wishing, wishing he might be there, too.

There must be an end of names and of dignities and whatsoever is of the earth. Where is Mowbray? Where is Mortimer? Nay! What is more, where is Plantagenet? They are entombed in the urns and sepulcres of mortality.

His death leaves the loved hill as a desert to me now. Reminiscences (older than his wines) have, through the years of absence, refreshed me: the airs of his Aeolian Harp! the new blossoms from his mountain garden; his dim lamp lighting up the "Roost!" his kingly face rimmed with royal beard! I even recall the tones of his guarded voice, tuned low and sweet, as he recited from Schiller some loved line. Ah! he was charming: and his "Geist" was real to him. The sprites and fairies and goblins were his familiars, and no worldly fellows should have invaded his sanctuary thinking this king served for aught but for good company's sake.

He will meet the Foozgängers in Paradise, in the Ivory Tower with Michael and Peter and Gabriel and it is not for the busy and vain to say he was foolish. For under the stars that hung so close to his humble home, he seemed to be communing with spirits: the mere pleasure-seeking idler could not understand. Tell Tom I love him for the nice things he wrote of him.

that one was young enough to believe in him. Like all Germans he felt sensitively what people thought of him and he tried to live up to it. Hence his poetry. At the same time, he had a sure character of his own. I wrote a French verse in his book, just to be one of his masqueraders. —Bye-bye. Remember: about two o'clock in the waiting room at the terminal. —gid-dap, Time!

Your
Wallace.

⌒

[WAS 1820 February 25, 1909 New York]

Thursday Evening

My Dear Delight: —

My pen has grown musty and I am an evening behind-hand—for all of which I ask forgiveness. —On Tuesday evening, I went to bed at about nine o'clock, although it had not been a specially tiresome day in spite of the wakefulness of Monday night, and a particularly chilly ride before breakfast, as far as Philadelphia. —Walter came in last evening and wanted me to go home with him and, of course, I did. They are all greatly distressed, and it excited me very much to meet them, under the circumstances. I spent the evening with them and, when I came out, walked home—a matter of almost seventy blocks—in order to divert myself. —And this morning, with the wind turning, I walked down to the office. At noon I walked around the Battery; and this evening, before dinner, from Seventy-Second Street, through the Park, to the house; and after dinner, to a store near Twenty-Third Street to exchange a particular something with which you are familiar, and then to the Astor Library[112]—where I found the same old nuisances coughing over the same old magazines in the same old corners. —So that I have apparently not been diligent with my pen; but what I called you at the beginning of my letter has, nevertheless, been on my lips many times. —Darling! You were really patient with me when I was in Reading. —And it was so nice of you to wear the slippers—and then not to let me see them except by chance. It wouldn't have been Elsie if you had let me see them—and that is additional reason for calling you my dear delight. —I love you so very much for just that kind of thing. —Lent began yesterday and Easter is, therefore, forty days away. We must think specially good things of each other in this season. And we ought to do some trifling thing. I am going to do without cigars and without cakes or apples, etc. at night. Won't you, on your part, and

112. Opened in 1854 on Lafayette Street near Astor Place and the Cooper Union, this library of 100,000 volumes open to the public eventually became the nucleus of the present New York Public Library. Stevens first visited this library on June 18, 1900 (*SP*, 75), and many times thereafter.

for your own comfort, take a brisk walk for an hour each day? —Walking becomes an ecstasy, you will find. The body answers good treatment and proper care, like a fine instrument. —Besides, all the world admits that as an exercise there is nothing superior to walking. —It would make me particularly proud to think that you had made a plan to do this and then resolutely carried it out. —It would bring you through March winds and April showers in high spirits. —We have had all the winds of March to-day—two or three days ahead of its being March itself. Isn't it odd that it should blow like the deuce about this time every year? I suppose there's some ridiculously simple explanation for it as there is for everything else. —It has grown cold, too. But it doesn't matter for by the middle of March, cold weather is always over—really cold weather. —To-morrow evening I am going to read, and on Saturday evening I expect to go to a lecture on something about the government of the city by a man I have been hearing of ever since I came to New-York. But about Saturday afternoon I don't know. If I look respectable I may continue to look at pictures. Otherwise I shall read or tramp—although hardly tramp, since I am quite sure to do that on Sunday. —Enclosed is a clipping from the <u>Post</u> containing an amusing thing about Goethe.[113] —Finally, about our letters, my dear. We have enough confidence in each other—or enough knowledge of each other—to write whatever we like and so I hope you will let me hear from you as often as possible. —I want so <u>very</u> much more of you than I get. Here we are beginning another long separation! Send me many little letters—or long ones—with a kiss in each.

With much love,
Wallace

⌒

[WAS 1821 February 28, 1909 New York]

Sunday Afternoon

My dearest Bo-Bo:

"The distant sounds of music that catch new sweetness as they vibrate through the long-drawn valley, are not more pleasing to the ear than the tidings of a far distant friend." —So said the Chinese philosopher. —To-day, then, for a change, I am loafing in my room. It is a good enough day for my usual walk,

---

113. Text of clipping: "One day an English traveller tried to force his way into Goethe's house at Weimar in order to see the poet. Goethe ordered his servant to let the man in and then planted himself in the middle of the room, rigid as a statue, his arms folded; his eyes fixed on the ceiling. The Englishman came in and showed some surprise at first. Then, in the most matter of fact way, he adjusted his monocle, walked slowly all around Goethe, looked him over from head to foot, and walked out without saying a word." There is no date or source on this clipping.

and I could walk if I wanted to, but I did so much of it last week, that it seems pleasant for a change, to stay here. —Every now and then the sky darkens, and lights up again, and just to sit here and be aware of that, almost unconsciously, is agreeable. —Yet this morning I went to church near-by. On one of the windows (there is a way for such things) were the words "In loving memory of Charles Hammond Little, who fell asleep December 27, 1894." I mused on that, and thought of the great multitude of those that lie sleeping. Isn't it odd to think of them all as sleeping? They rest in the sea, in the Memphian desert, by Gangâ, in all the innumerable little grave-yards of civilization—all asleep. And only to name them makes it stranger still—Lorenzo di Medici sleeping in his beautiful tomb, Ophelia sleeping so softly near her willowed stream, and her tragic Hamlet at rest without dreams—I could name all those that ever lived, who gave up in sorrow, or otherwise, the same idle sunlight that shines now on the houses opposite—all asleep. —A proper Lenten meditation! —You know it is very impressive to go to church if you do not go mechanically, and especially to an old church full of memorials. —After church I read for an hour or two, and then after dinner I opened my trunk to look for a pipe and fell to looking over the general contents. —In a little envelope, I found two things that you know: one a piece of lace that you tore from a skirt in a field, (I can see where your foot caught it) and another a gold tassel,[114] or whatever it should be called, from one of your dresses. There were many things besides, and it was quite late before I finished looking at them. —I think that when we see all our letters, and think of the last few years, since we have known each other, we ought to—I do not know just what; but I am glad—very glad—that we shall soon be together. — Last night I thought of you, too, and longed to have you with me. I had spent the afternoon and evening at the Astor Library looking through the books of Paul Elmer More, one of the most discriminating, learned and soundest critics of the day. He has a very marked tendency to consider all things philosophically, and that, of course, gives his views both scope and permanence. I quote a thing quoted by him—in Latin for the sound and sight of it:

> O vitae Philosophia dux! O virtutum
> indagatrix expultrixque vitiorum![115]

Oh, Philosophy, thou guide of Life! Oh, thou that searchest out virtues, and expellest vices! —That struck me as such an admirable inscription for the

114. He will save this gold tassel in his final house cleaning before the marriage. See WAS 1901 for September 12, 1909.
115. Stevens will put this quotation, which he gets from Paul Elmer More's "Thoreau," in his journal for May 14, 1909, three months after this letter. See SP, 220. LWS (133) identifies it as from Cicero's Tusculan Disputations 5.2.5.

façade of a library—or of one of those temples, bound to be built some day, when people will seek in a place not specially dedicated to religion, those principles of moral conduct that should guide us in every-day life—as distinct, say, from the peculiar life of Sundays. —My mind is rather full of such things to-day, and so resembles the mood that fastened me, a year or more ago, so intently on Matthew Arnold—and Maxims![116] —But each for himself, in that respect; and I do not, therefore, make a point of what may not interest you. — To think occasionally of such things gives me a comforting sense of balance and makes me feel like the Brahmin on his mountain-slope who in the midst of his contemplations—surveyed distant cities—and then plunged in thought again. —To plunge in another direction: More, speaking of the herbalists, botanists and the like who go about examining Nature with microscopes, says, —"I sometimes think a little ignorance is wholesome in our communion with Nature; until we are to part with her altogether. She is feminine in this as in other respects, and loves to shroud herself in illusions, as the Hindus taught in their books."[117] I think that that is a very fascinating observation. It makes one aware of the love of mystery among damsels—and accounts (although you would not admit it) for a certain pair of hidden slippers—that would have looked so pretty coming down the stairs. Bo-Bo is nothing if not feminine. — Collateral with that love of mystery among damsels, should go the gallantry of youths; for from the two spring all that is enduringly fine and pleasant between them. —And while this would be dull stuff to Princes, I think it is a pardonable subject for speculation, on a Lenten Sunday, on the part of one neither born nor bred a Prince, and yet a willing courtier and aspirant. —The sunlight is gone, and I must light my lamp. . . . [118] —The ceremony of taking tea is gone, too. —Ought I not suddenly pull off my black wig and black gown and put on a white wig, full of powder, and a suit of motley—or maybe, the old costume of Pierrot? For when I sit at the window and write, I look out on real things and am a part of them; but with my lamp lighted and my shade down—there is nothing real, at least there need not be and I can whisk away to Arcady—or say Picardy. Yes: Picardy, and sit there in the rose, misty twilight and watch the gold, misty moon come up over the trees—

> Till, in late starlight,
> The white lilies creep,

116. Stevens quotes Arnold's *Notebooks* in his journal for February 21, 1906 (cf. *SP*, 160). In WAS 1788 for April 9, 1907, he told Elsie that he had just bought a copy of this work. See there for Stevens's later attitude toward this work.

117. *LWS* (133) identifies this as from Paul Elmer More's "Thoreau" in his *Shelburne Essays*, first series, vol. 1 (New York: Putnam's, 1909), 4.

118. He is dramatizing his going from page 4 to 5, thus to a second sheet of paper.

Like the dreamt dreams
Of Columbine, asleep.[119]

That's from the interior of the magic trunk! —Are you able, by the way, to
recall any of the pictures we saw at Philadelphia? One of the strange things about
that kind of thing is the difficulty of bringing the things one has seen back to
one's mind. There were so many! —With the catalogue, it is not so hard—and
portraits and pictures of scenes are not so hard. But pictures of landscape, like
landscape itself, disappear without a trace. The only one that comes to me now
is that green river bordered by green trees, all suffused in green light—and that
sparkles. —I think I remember two of the Picardy scenes—the moon rise, and
the church. —There is not likely to be any notable exhibition here until the
Water Color Society's show late in April. That is always one of the best things of
the year, because in water color artists attempt less ambitious things than in oil
and content themselves, often, with the fleeting impressions that, for most of us,
are all there is of artistic perception. —Next year you will see for it yourself. —
In poetry, anyone sensitive to beauty or emotion feels the beauty or emotion
that the poet desires to communicate. That, I mean, is the common experience.
Curiously, this is not true of painting, quite probably because painting does not
make an altogether objective impression: that is, instead of seeing the thing seen,
you see the thing itself. The result is that the appreciation of painting is not as
acute as the appreciation of poetry. It is not as common, nor as just. People's
pleasure in good poetry is simple pleasure. But people's pleasure in good painting is a timid, unbelieving thing, involved somehow with the idea that the pleasure is incomplete without some understanding of the technique of art. We see
people admire painting in a mysterious way—whispering about it—venturing
remarks on the "drawing," the "color," the "composition," the "style." That is
all nonsense. A good painting should give pleasure, like any other work of art.
—The same people who consider a painting so professionally ought, logically,
to consider a pretty girl's "pattern" —"design" —and so on. —I used to think I
was putting on airs to pretend to like a picture. But I am satisfied now that if it
gives me pleasure, I am right in not caring about "scale," or "balance of tones"
or anything of the kind; just as I can boldly enjoy the lines:

"This thou perceivest, which makes thy love more strong,
To love that well which thou must leave ere long"—[120]

---

119. Searches of the American and the English Poetry Full-Text Database by Chadwyck-
Healey and searches on the Internet failed to find these lines; they may be by Stevens
himself.
120. Shakespeare's Sonnet 73.

without knowing that they are a Shakespearean couplet composed of deca-syllables. —I say all this to give you confidence, if, in fact, you need it; because I do not want you to be frightened away by other people's mystery from one of the greatest things in the world. —So let us call that golden, misty moon rising over Picardy our own—and see the elves dancing on the leaves in its beams—and forget the wise and their folly. —And suppose we could really meet there at such an hour—and by chance—and when we happened to be thinking most of each other. —Would I need to touch you to be happy? Only to know that you were there would be enough to fulfill that

> "Rose and gray,
> Ecstasy of the Moon."[121]

Oh, but I think of a real evening—a real summer night when we lay in the clover and wild yarrow and watched that soft witchery expand and fill a famil-iar valley—and I kissed you so often! —That seems like some sweet, imagined irreality. —Yet the best of it is that Bo and I may do it again, since our world is so quiet a one, and so unchanged. But we must not think of it, or of anything, too intently, "as the Hindus taught in their books." —I have no plans for the week, except to read nightly. I have a new fairy-tale for you the next time we are together. You must ask for "The Ancient Tale of the Blue Cat that Swal-lowed the White Mouse with the Green Eyes, and why, and what followed." —But I must post this for you. I want you to have a letter to-morrow, if pos-sible, because you had only one last week—and that was a bit hurried. And remember, Bo,—you promised to write to me often.

With much love,
Wallace

∽

[WAS 1822 March 2, 1909 New York]

Tuesday Evening

My Dearest:

It was a diversion to have those "sea-blue eyes afire for war" look out at me unexpectedly from your letter on Monday morning. —I have just seen the glazed eyes of the blind described as "blind eyes like pearls" —and we may add all this to our memories. —I find that I was all wrong (according to my latest reading) in saying that the function of art was to give pleasure. It seems that "the pursuit of beauty as something unconnected with character is a most insidious

---

121. Exact matches of these lines have evaded searches. However, a translation of "Mandoline" by Verlaine speaks of "the ecstasy of a rose and gray moon" and may have been the source that became rephrased in Stevens's memory.

danger,"[122] which "must inevitably become corrupt"; and that, in a way, art is "the desire of select spirits to ennoble and make beautiful their lives!" Remember that, dear Bo-Bo, the next time you find yourself carelessly taking pleasure in a Picardy moon-rise, and be humble. —Certainly, such a desire accounts for all these Madonnas and other holy pictures that bore me so perfectly. But there is much to be said. I refer to the matter only to convince you of my own humility. —I am struck, more deeply, by the observation of Dr. Goncourt, who said, "The torment of the man of thought is to aspire to Beauty, without having any fixed and certain consciousness of what Beauty is." —That, if I were a man of thought, would, I think, be my peculiar torment. —So much for a tedious matter. I am still reading Paul Elmer More, and expect to do so all week. I imagine that his limitation is to be found in his learning: his philosophical bias. —One does not invariably care to have the simple pleasures of life discussed with such importance. —It is always a relief to know that the great poets and the great artists were not such devilish scholars. —Your lines from Ada Negri[123] do, without a doubt, express a feminine emotion—not altogether unknown to men. We all know that there are women who pity themselves, just as there are men that do. But, on the other hand, it was a woman who said, "The joy of the spirit is the measure of its force."[124] You will recognize the truth of that. —But I shall not philosophize, although it is a night when one might very pleasantly consider ideals, out of contrast to the murky quiet that clings to the streets like moss to a stone. —You must not be jealous of the Brothers. I have a confirmed notion that they are now what they seemed to be at the time of my breach with them. I say very decidedly that they are unpleasant—excepting Walter, who is undeveloped. They are grasping, selfish and ambitious. But I am sorry to speak ill of them. —The truth is they are a different race. Frances'[125] plan is to get some

122. Throughout the first half of this letter Stevens is quoting from different parts of "Tolstoy," one of Paul Elmer More's *Shelburne Essays,* first series; this first quotation is from page 212, the next one ("desire of select spirits") from page 209, the Goncourt quotation from page 210 (in French there), and the quotation from "a woman" from page 216. The last of these quotations, from Ninon de l'Enclos, an influential French courtesan (c. 1620–1705), is identified by author and given in French in Stevens's journal entry for May 14, 1909 (see *SP,* 220). Another passage from this More essay on Tolstoy will be quoted in WAS 1845 for May 14, 1909.
123. Ada Negri (1870–1945), an Italian poet whose *Fatalità* was translated as *Fate and Other Poems* in 1898, became the first woman member of the Italian Academy in 1940.
124. This is his translation of a sentence by Ninon de l'Enclos that he had put into his journal for May 14, 1909: "La joie de l'esprit en marque la force."
125. This is most likely the Frances Butler, Walter's sister, whom Holly mentions meeting in *SP,* 202. See the original note to Walter Butler at Elsie's extract 52. There is no more information about this emotional episode than appears in this letter and in hints from later letters such as WAS 1833 of March 13, 1909, and WAS 1879 of August 2, 1909.

dashing clothes, get into a rich family as the companion of somebody or other and marry somebody connected with it. If you can imagine anyone of your acquaintances scheming like that you will understand her. —You must not wonder, however, that I should have felt any excitement at their sincere distress after such a sudden and complete shock. —I offered to do any legal work they might need with reference to Hugh's estate. Their desire to conceal the smallness of it will probably send them to a stranger. —Yet this is all pitiable stuff and no concern of ours. —Your description of Mr. Austrian's[126] bower is more interesting. One does not often find a Jew in a nook; and that there should be one so near home is attractive, in that it shows the softening influence of our green vales on one of the exiles from Jerusalem. Only the gold lettering in front of the cottage betrays the Hebraic occupant. —I believe he married a Christian. The fancy revolts at a Christian and a Hebrew billing and cooing among the vines. —Still, that, too, is no concern of ours; and if the Lady loves her Israelite, we must leave her to her fate. —Some day, when good roads have been built back of the mountain there will surely be many cottages there, and the Sunday morning services at Spies' Church will be as smart as those in a Parisian chapel. That day lies deep in the mist, but will shine in time. —I am glad you are taking walks. It becomes a habit that you cannot break, and it is one of the few good habits that fix themselves easily. It should be very simple to fall into it this month and next when the desire for rambling asserts itself so naturally. —But I need not make such an ado about it. —You are perfectly right in saying that we are going to be good children; for nothing gives me more delight—and as a token I send a kiss—or two—or three—and my love.

Your own
Giant.

∽

[WAS 1823 March 3, 1909 New York]

Wednesday Evening

My dearest Bo-Bo:—

A little fantasy to beguile you—a bit of patchwork—and about music. . . . What is the mysterious effect of music, the vague effect we feel when we hear music, without ever defining it? It is considered that music, stirring something

---

126. Born in 1870 in Reading and educated there, Ben Austrian was a self-taught artist who exhibited his work in Paris and London, becoming famous as the painter of the chick ("Hasn't scratched yet") in the Bon Ami cleaner ads. He had a summer studio, "Cleverly," on the slope of Neversink Mountain and a winter studio on Perkiomen Avenue in Reading. See Judith M. Hartman, "Ben Austrian: 1870-1921 and 'The Chick that hasn't scratched yet,'" in *Historical Review of Berks County* 47, no. 2 (Spring 1982): 47–51, 64–65.

within us, stirs the Memory. I do not mean our personal Memory—the memory of our twenty years and more—but our inherited Memory, the Memory we have derived from those who lived before us in our own race, and in other races, illimitable, in which we resume the whole past life of the world, all the emotions, passions, experiences of the millions and millions of men and women now dead, whose lives have insensibly passed into our own, and compose them.[127] —It is a Memory deep in the mind, without images, so vague that only the vagueness of music, touching it subtly, vaguely awakens, until

> "it remembers its August abodes,
> And murmurs as the ocean murmurs there."[128]

But I need not solve any theme—so I drop poetry. There is enough magic without it. —I hang prose patches to my introduction and say that "great music" agitates "to fathomless depths, the mystery of the past within us." And also that "there are tunes that call up all ghosts of youth and joy and tenderness; —there are tunes that evoke all phantom pain of perished passion; —there are tunes that resurrect all dead sensations of majesty and might and glory,—all expired exultations,—all forgotten magnanimities." And again, that at the sound of Music, each of us feels that "there answers within him, out of the Sea of Death and Birth, some eddying immeasurable of ancient pleasure and pain."— While I had always known of this infinite extension of personality, nothing has ever made it so striking as this application of Music to it. . . . So that, after all, those long chords on the harp, always so inexplicably sweet to me, vibrate on more than the "sensual ear"—vibrate on the unknown. . . . And what one

127. This entire letter is essentially a summary of Paul Elmer More's ideas in his "Lofcadio Hearn," in *Shelburne Essays,* second series. In *SP,* for May 14, 1909, Stevens gives part of this prose material and says that it is from Paul Elmer More (220). James Longenbach, "The 'Fellowship of Men That Perish': Wallace Stevens and the First World War," *Wallace Stevens Journal* 13, no. 2 (Fall 1989): 108n43, points out that in this passage Stevens is paraphrasing More's "Lafcadio Hearn," in *Shelburne Essays,* second series (Boston: Houghton Mifflin, 1905), 46–72. Stevens continues quoting from this essay after the verse quotation from Landor.
128. From Walter Savage Landor's *Gebir,* bk. 1, lines 175–76. These two lines are a part of a famous quotation about a sea shell:

> But I have sinuous shells of pearly hue
> Within, and they that lustre have imbibed
> In the sun's palace-porch, where when unyoked
> His chariot-wheel stands midway in the wave:
> Shake one, and it awakens; then apply
> Its polisht lips to your attentive ear,
> And it remembers its August abodes,
> And murmurs as the ocean murmurs there.

listens to at a concert, if we knew it, is not only the harmony of sounds, but the whispering of innumerable responsive spirits within one, momentarily revived, that stir like the invisible motions of the mind wavering between dreams and sleep; that does not realize the flitting forms that are its shadowy substance. —A phantasy out of the East wind, for meditation.

—With love,
Wallace.

[WAS 1824 March 7, 1909 New York]

Sunday Afternoon

My Dear Bo-Bo:

Overlook the phantasy! It was true—but—well, it's a by-gone. —I wonder today has not called up something equally strange, for it has been a day full of mysterious weather. This morning there was snow and mist and gloomy darkness. I walked up Eighth Avenue to the Park, skirted that, then went down to Riverside Drive and at noon reached the Hispanic Museum where the Sorolla pictures are. The exhibition closes tomorrow and I wanted to get a last glance. The crowd was dense. —I am spending the afternoon at home, partly to write to you, and partly to read, and partly to have a little leisure to think about things. I saw so many pictures yesterday and it seems indispensable that I should give a moment's thought to them and to the painters: to arrange them in the mind, to appreciate and understand them. —And then it is very pleasant, too, just to go over the things read during the weeks—to think about them, or, perhaps, just to remember them. I make notes as I read on little slips of paper[129] which, it is true, I throw away before long, but which are interesting for a while. —For instance, last night I saw something about "March wind-mills" and promptly jotted it down—because it is amusing to sit here and think of all the wind-mills in a Dutch village whirling madly in a March gale and sparkling in the crisp air—or clattering all night long while the people in their nightcaps listen and wait for the morning. —There was also an Irish poem:

> O, to have a little house!
> To own the hearth and stool and all![130]

---

129. George S. Lensing, in *Wallace Stevens: A Poet's Growth* (Baton Rouge: Louisiana State University Press, 1986), 158–200, prints Stevens's notebooks that contain similar jottings and shows how they were incorporated into Stevens's work.

130. Padraic Colum's poem "An Old Woman of the Roads," which is in Palgrave's *Golden Treasury*.

—that made me think of something you said not long ago, although you were not thinking of just those things at the time. And another line from another poem:

Withers once more the old blue flower of day.[131]

That is so old an idea, and yet so charming. "Old blue," that's quaint—isn't it—and "old blue flower"—it makes one think of morning-glories with films of spider web in them. Only it is impossible to think of anything blue as old—and it is quite impossible to think of morning-glories as old—even those close to the ground and deep in the shadows that remain open and fresh all day long, if ever they do. —I have just begun Thackeray's "Newcomes." —The truth is, Thackeray seems like a waste of time. I like to be anything but entertained when I read (everything is entertaining, of course)—and Thackeray, I fear, sets out to amuse his reader. That seems perfectly defensible—but just now I feel so abundantly able to amuse myself. Poor, old Thackeray! I mustn't be too severe! There are so many things I want to know about in preference to that "most respectable family";[132] but I must be satisfied with the books I have for the present. —During the afternoon it has gradually grown clear, as very often happens after mornings of extraordinary horror. It is fairly cool, not cold, and even the cab-horses must know that the earth is out of its wintry orbit and has begun to run a friendlier, and longer, course around the sun. A month of daily snow would make no difference—because the change is certain—and the actual Spring, the actual budding is very sudden and very short. Birds come one by one, warmth settles, and the leaves come over night, or so it seems. —It is half-past five now, a little shadowy, but quite light enough to write. I shall send you only a short letter to-day, Bo,—because I am not satisfied to be so invincibly pompous when I ought to be—your giant. —I meditated on the difference between champagne and sparkling Burgundy and how you had come by the knowledge of it. (She starts!) — But, of course, from the top of my hat you could see that as well as anything else. Bye!-bye!

Your
Solemn as Solomon

〜

---

131. From "The Great Breath," by George William Russell; see his *Collected Poems* of 1935.

132. The full title of this 1853 novel is *The Newcomes: Memoirs of a Most Respectable Family*.

[WAS 1825 March 8, 1909 New York]

Monday Evening

Dearest Goose:

Fie on you, to call yourself a spinster—and then to speak (or even think) of kisses! We shall see. Shall I call myself a bachelor? Yes: yours: And you, my spinster. —I took a long walk before dinner to-night, feeling quickened by the freshness of the air. And at seven o'clock I met an old friend of mine with an odd name, Witter Bynner,[133] and we went to the Player's Club[134] for dinner—rather, I met him there. It is one of the pleasantest places in town. They have cabinets full of memorials of the stage: the swords of Edwin Booth, his crowns, the gowns of Juliets dead and gone, endless pictures, endless relics. It is very quiet, very comfortable. After dinner, we talked until almost eleven o'clock, about fellows we know, and about books, and so on, and then I walked home. He lives in Vermont, and is on his way to Florida, to spend two months in a bungalow. He has promised to write me a descriptive letter, which I shall like— and if it is interesting I shall send it to you. By the way, Arthur Whiting lives in his town—he knows him and thinks him likeable. —I had meant to read to-night, but this put me off. —I think my girl has taken up poetry again—as Spring comes on. —Bynner had some Japanese prints, full of the eerie poetry of Japan. If he can get more when he is passing through Boston, he will—I should like to have some for you. —There is a Japanese store in Boston: Bunkio Matsuki's[135] that is one of the best in this part of the world. —Your link from Ugo Flere's "Necklace" (whatever that may be) was quite in the Greek manner, like a verse from the Anthology. —Turn to the Golden Treasury and look for Browning's

133. Stevens had known Bynner (1881–1968) since they were at Harvard, Bynner in the class behind Stevens. In an editorial of March 10, 1900, as editor of the *Harvard Advocate,* Stevens welcomed Bynner to the staff; Bynner himself was the editor from 1900 to 1902. To see what the two men said about each other in their journals, see James Kraft's "Biographical Introduction" to *The Works of Witter Bynner* (New York: Farrar, Straus, Giroux, 1978), 1:xl–xliii. The two men exchanged letters as late as 1954-55 (see *LWS,* 859–60).

134. Stevens had first visited this club with Arthur Goodrich of Macmillan on June 15, 1900, soon after arriving in New York from Harvard (see *SP,* 72). Incorporated in 1888 in a brownstone on Gramercy Park, and designed in the style of an Italian Renaissance palace, this club contains a working library of the theater and quotations from Shakespeare on the walls of all the rooms.

135. Bunkio Matsuki, a Japanese Buddhist monk from a family that dealt in art, came to Salem, Massachusetts, in 1888 and eventually developed a Japanese department in Salem's largest store; his success helped to bring "the Japan craze" to America. He was one of the important dealers who provided Charles Freer with Japanese prints for his famous collection, which was given to the Smithsonian.

Oh, to be in England,
Now that April's there.

It was written for you, Bo-Bo, my dear, and you should memorize it for next month. —I am glad (although I am ashamed to say it—a little) that you did not go to the theatre. —But aside from that, and not thinking of it, a kiss for Good-Night—and another for To-Morrow Morning.

Your
Unwilling Bachelor

—

[WAS 1826 March 9, 1909 New York]

Tuesday Evening

My Bo:—

A kiss for you and now imagine that I am talking to you. —It is worth at least one night's studious candle to understand Spring—to realize that the sense of coming into one's own that grows, as the season grows, is only the increasing gratification of the senses. They understand the senses better in the orient (and hence, understand Spring better). Bare Winter beats with thin shadows, small colors. The raw form of the Earth is lost sight of. The haze turns pink, blue, vivid green, golden—the April moon shimmers in a vague sky. —The emotions (which are only the effect of the senses) stir—and suddenly one's old spirit returns, subtly as

The mystic dew
Dropping from twilight trees.[136]

—My nightly sprig from the Holy Hill of the Muses. —But did I ever talk like this? —Pshaw, I meant only to send you a kiss and I did that first of all—and

---

136. Stevens is quoting "The Gift" by A. E. (George William Russell):

I thought, beloved, to have brought to you
A gift of quietness and ease and peace,
Cooling your brow as with the mystic dew
Dropping from twilight trees.
Homeward I go not yet; the darkness grows;
Not mine the voice to still with peace divine:
From the first font of the stream of quiet flows
Through other hearts than mine.

Yet of my night I give to you the stars,
And of my sorrow here the sweetest gains,
And out of hell, beyond its iron bars,
My scorn of all its pains.

then wandered off on the influence of color on the senses, and of the senses on the emotions. —Yet it is worth pondering on, as you take your daily walk. — And this, too, is ponderable: the adaptation of clothes to character. —One can see oneself in a pile of clothes as plainly as in a mirror. (The idea is as dusty as the man who first conceived it.) We read a knight in his armor, a bride in her veil, —and so on. —We must amuse ourselves by reading our friends in their— clothes. —I read E. V. M. I see her in the rain in a green coat. It is puzzling. — Or in a certain dress—(I spare you the adjectives, Bo.) —Or crossing a field with flowers at her belt and in her hair—as a part of her—costume. —If you read me, please do not consider these tan shoes. They grow darker slowly. By the way, I bought cherry, etc. to-night for myself. How do you like yours? You have not told me. If you like it and will need more at Easter, let me know, please. —Time to be asleep. Snuff the candle. . . . Night!

> Your
> Wallace

~⌐

[WAS 1827 March 11, 1909 New York]

> Thursday Evening

Dear Bo Bo:

I wrote last evening, but afterwards I thought of doing what I was going to do to-night, and so did not send my letter. By mailing this now, too, you will not miss a day. —I am only going to send you a few things for your mirror—the corner of it. Do not read them all at once. Put one in each morning and do not read it before it is there. —Then read it while you prink and fix your hair. It will be no fun at all if you read them first. —And each morning crumple up the old one and throw it away. That is part of the game. Hear and obey. —In my copy of the Greek Anthology I found these climber roses which you may only look at and sent back to me—look at, remember! They will remind you of last summer for a moment and bring it before your eyes. What a goose you are to think that I should tell you of any faults, if I knew of any. On my honor, I do not; and I do love you every day—a little.

> Your
> Mister.

~⌐

[WAS 1828 March 14, 1909 New York]

> Sunday Evening

My Dear:

I am in one of those wild frames of mind in which I start a new letter every few minutes. —It worries me to be so much of a moralist, as I might seem to be from the sheets I sent you. I don't want to seem priggish, and yet it is a little hard to take anything back without being—confusing. You know that the love of maxims is one aspect of Idealism—of which I am not ashamed <u>provided</u> you understand that in my case (as I understand it to be in yours) the Idealism is accompanied by a love of milk and honey, of moon-light nights, of good, red earth, and a good many human frailties. I am not going to moralize for a long time. It is a creepy occupation. Forgive me if I write only a note to-night. I wanted to say just one thing and make it memorable by saying that and nothing more—and there it is. But I shall write more to-morrow.

With love
Wallace

↩

[WAS 1829 March 15, 1909[137] New York]
[Fragment.]

—To-gether—take a tremendous leap, out of all extracts, quotations, parables, maxims, precedents, proverbs and the like—and do not come down until you've found some grove of oaks, full of leaves, and of windy motions, of blue-sky full of boughs, and sweet with fragrant warmth. Now, old bogies, get ye behind us. We only want to have a good time. See that cap? Now you don't. See it now? P-r-e-s-t-o! Now you don't. —Are you fond of butter? I'll just hold a butter-cup or two, and then a dandelion or two, under the chin of this poor philosophizing head. —She loves me.
[Other side.]

I wish I could write as fast as I think, but often while I am writing one thing my mind darts to another, and the queerest jumble results. —It is just as well that I tore up my last, because it had more about moralizing in [it]—and I pre-fer to regard that word as tabooed. It is insulting, impertinent, ill-mannered, low-spirited, creeping, flat, weak, like the thing (<u>not</u> "think," bejabers) it represents. Ugh! —But no more of it. Heads up, Bo-Bo-and Mister! —Now for my green cap, like Robin Hood's—and for some bright-colored dress of yours. (I do like certain clothes immensely: that light dress with the
[End of fragment.]

↩

---

137. This letter has been cut up; all that remains are the front and back of a single sheet of stationery. It is dated from the envelope.

[WAS 1830 March 16, 1909 New York]

Thursday Evening

Dear Bo:

My green cap is hanging behind the door, tonight, and I have on my wig—because I am not quite through with this disturbing subject.[138] —When you consider the reverence we feel for all Wise Men, at least for such as have spoken wisely of the life and destiny of men and women, it is apparent that their Wisdom is something different from Morality. I want to preserve all the reverence due to Wisdom, however much I may malign Morality. —By Morality I mean that nagging voice that approves or disapproves of what one does: that lectures one. It is Morality that vexes you with the accusation of being selfish now and then (according to your letter), that speaks slightingly of the pretty variety of clothes, that does any one of a number of things. —Morality would make us all old maids. Eschew it! —But Wisdom is another thing. To think and to philosophize is an exciting delight and they are only the lesser exercises of Wisdom. —But that is not what I want to say. I want to distinguish Wisdom from priggish Morality—as different as a goddess from an old hen in curl papers—and tell you that while I am ashamed of having ever recognized Morality I am prepared to bow to the ground at sight of t'other. —Think of Buddha directing millions of aspiring souls, fashioning a happiness for them; think of Plato with his powerful, clear thought. —Well you've never read 'em (no more have I). —But I swear I feel a holy élan toward them. Élan, according to my French dictionary means "spring; start; bound; flight; soaring; burst; sally; impulse;" etc, etc. —I propose, then, still to worship the Wise and reverence Wisdom, or as Solomon says, to "get Wisdom, get understanding."[139] —Look for me in Sacred Pagodas; in shadowy Temples; in groves hallowed by ikons and—the voice of Socrates; by Ilyssus.[140] —Now, then, Master Green Cap, attend me. A curtsey to the Noble Lady Wisdom—and bid her adieu for the evening. —I've been galloping

138. Clearly a reference to the subject of morality in the cut-up letter of March 15, 1909 (WAS 1829).

139. Proverbs 4:5: "Get wisdom, get understanding: forget it not; neither decline from the words of my mouth," 4:7: "Wisdom is the principal thing; therefore get wisdom: and with all thy getting get understanding," and 16:16: "How much better is it to get wisdom than gold! and to get understanding rather to be chosen than silver!"

140. The Ilissus, a river in Attica, is part of the setting and the discussion between Socrates and Phaedrus in Plato's *Phaedrus,* a dialogue Stevens will draw upon again for his essay "The Noble Rider and the Sound of Words" in 1942. Also, in his preface to Paul Valéry's *Eupalinos,* published in *Dialogues,* the last of four volumes of Valéry in the Bollingen series (New York: Pantheon, 1956), Stevens is, at the very end of his life, discussing this work and this setting: "What, then, are the ideas that Valéry has chosen to be discussed by the shades of Socrates and his friend Phaedrus, as they meet, in our time, in their 'dim habitation' on the bank of Ilissus?" (*OP* 2:292).

through books. One was a long poem by So-and-So, full of excellent lines and images. From my notes:

> "O to cast off doubts, and fears!
> To touch truth, and feel it true!"[141]

(The second line is capital, I think.)
and

> "The charm of deeming nothing vain"

And as images:

> "Out of suspended hazes the smooth sea
> Swelled into brilliance, and subsiding, brushed
> The lovely shore with music"

and

> —"soft as moths asleep
> Come moonlit sails."[142]

The last is <u>very</u> charming—or whatever the appropriate language is. I am about to begin a bundle of books by Kakuzo Okakura! He's a Japanese who has written some rather thoughtful things about this, that and the other - and it soothes me to think that I'm reading the latest Japanese author.[143] No: the fact is, it is all enchantment—it is all wonderful, and beautiful and <u>new</u>—what a fine opal would be after a season of pebbles. I shall send you any interesting ideas that may occur. —But I s'pose you are really thinking about Spring Hats. There's a thrilling thing in this Evening's Post that ought to set your blood on fire. It doesn't read like anything in "the ancient books of the Hindus" but it seems thoroughly maddening. I send a little of it, for the sensation. —Think how reasonable Wisdom would be about all that, and how cross and narrow

141. Lyric XXVII from "Midsummer Vigil" in Laurence Binyon's *Lyric Poems,* published in London in 1894.
142. In his journal for May 14, 1909, Stevens says he "gone through the books of Laurence Binyon," and he quotes all of these lines from Binyon's long poem "Porphyrion" (*SP,* 223).
143. On May 14, 1909, Stevens, in a list of notes he had taken at the Astor Library in New York, says, "Kakuzo Okakura is a cultivated, but not original thinker. His 'Ideals of the East' was interesting" (*SP,* 221). In *The Ideals of the East with Special Reference to the Art of Japan,* a book he wrote in English and published in 1903, Okakura stresses the unity and primacy of Asian culture. He also wrote *The Book of Tea,* published in 1900, which Richardson (*Wallace Stevens* 1:555) believes Stevens probably read.

and mean Morality would be. —Oh, Wisdom we both salute and offer allegiance. Adieu!

Your

Green Cap.

↶

[WAS 1831 March 18, 1909 New York]

Thursday Evening

My dear Rose-cap:—

It was a disappointment to me last week not to have written you a letter "for Saturday and Sunday." To-morrow evening I expect to go to the Academy of Design.[144] Therefore I must write this evening, to avoid a repetition of last week. It is just twenty-nine minutes of twelve! Fancy sitting down to write a letter—and a longish one at such an hour. But I want you to have a letter. — You wonder what I have been doing to-night. Well, I continued my superficial study of Mr. Okakura's book, and read a great deal besides. Then I went to an exhibition (getting there at nine.) It was an exhibition chiefly of tapestry. But there were some antiquated musical instruments that were amusing. One had sixteen strings. There were lutes inlaid with mother of pearl and there were French cornemeuses. —I saw two cabinets of carved jade—whatever that may be. I know it is highly prized but I don't altogether see why. — Shall I send a picture or two to make a private exhibition for you? Well, here they are, and all from the Chinese, painted centuries ago:

> "pale orange, green and crimson, and white,
> and gold, and brown";

and

> "deep lapis-lazuli and orange, and opaque
> green, fawn-color, black, and gold";

and

> "lapis blue and vermilion, white, and gold
> and green"

I do not know if you feel as I do about a place so remote and unknown as China—the irreality of it. So much so, that the little realities of it seem wonderful and beyond belief. —I have just been reading about the Chinese feeling about landscape. Just as we have certain traditional subjects that our artists

144. The National Academy of Design was founded in 1826 and dedicated to promoting and exhibiting the works of living artists.

delight to portray (like "Washington Crossing the Delaware"[145] or "Mother and Child," etc., etc.!) so the Chinese have certain aspects of nature, of landscape, that have become traditional. —A list of these aspects would be as fascinating as those lists of "Pleasant Things" I used to send. Here is the list (upon my soul!)—

> The Evening Bell from a Distant Temple
> Sunset Glow over a Fishing village
> Fine Weather after Storm at a Lonely Mountain Town
> Homeward-bound Boats off a Distant Shore
> The Autumn Moon over Lake Tung-t'ing
> Wild Geese on a Sandy Plain
> Rain in Hsiao-Hsiang[146]

This is one of the most curious things I ever saw, because it is so comprehensive. Any twilight picture is included under the first title, for example. "It is just that silent hour when travellers say to themselves, 'The day is done,' and to their ears comes from the distance the expected sound of the evening bell." And last of all in my package of strange things from the East, a little poem written centuries ago by Wang-an-shih:[147]

> "It is midnight; all is silent in the house;
> The water-clock has stopped. But I am
> unable to sleep because of the beauty of the
> trembling shapes of the spring flowers, thrown
> by the moon upon the blind."

I don't know of anything more beautiful than that anywhere, or more Chinese—and Master Green-Cap bows to Wang-an-shih. No: Wang-an-shih is sleeping, and may not be disturbed. —I am going to poke around more or less in the dust of Asia for a week or two and have no idea what I shall disturb and bring

145. A reference to *George Washington Crossing the Delaware* (1851), by American painter Emanuel Gottlieb Leutze (1816–1868).
146. *Night Rain over Hsiao Hsiang,* by the artist-monk Mu Chi of the period of the Southern Sung Dynasty, dated c. A.D. 1100, can be found on the Internet.
147. Here and in the list of "pleasant subjects," Stevens is quoting from Laurence Binyon's early pioneering work *Painting in the Far East,* published in 1908. This work is extensively noted by Stevens in his journal for May 14, 1909, a date on which he copied notes from a winter of readings (see *SP,* 221–22). The poem by Wang An-shih is not set off in lines of verse. (Wang An-shih [1021–1086], a native of Lin-ch'uan, Kiangsi, China, a statesman and a leader of the reform party, held the highest post in the government during the reign of Emperor Shen-Tsung, who reigned 1067–85.) There are also numerous references in Binyon's work to several of the books of Okakura and a brief discussion of Okakura.

to light. —Curious thing, how little we know about Asia, and all that. It makes me wild to learn it all in a night. —But Asia (a brief flight from Picardy—as the mind flies) will do for some other time. —I expect to read the week out and to walk on Sunday. Finer than all books is this full, gusty air. How specially bright it blows the stars in the first hour of evening! I noticed it to-night, just as it was growing dark. There were at least a dozen big, golden stars—that seemed to belong to March, more than to the general sky. —And I wish my Sunday walk might be with you. You said in your letter to-day that if it was more convenient for me not to come at Easter—why, I should tell you. You are not twitting me, Bo-Bo, are you?

Your
Wallace

⌒

[WAS 1832 March 21, 1909 New York]

Sunday Evening

Dearest Bo-Bo:—

One of these days you will vanish—fade like a too delicate color into this rude canvas on which you are painted! —Stay real for me—send me, besides your letters, a pinch of sachet, for the odor of you, a thread from a dress, for the touch of you, another leaf, for the world about you. —I have been so far away all week, in books and pictures. Only the hard March sky, blue as a vault of blue marble, brought me back to earth to-day. —I have been in the Sixteenth Century, and in China, and in Spain—and this afternoon I've had my nose buried in my French dictionary looking up unfamiliar words—to get the full meaning of some very interesting essays on a certain painter. —Forgive me! But you know you sent me only two brief notes last week, and those early in the week. I wish that just for one week you would send me a word each day—or could you not send a parcel of slips such as I sent you, with something of your own for each morning? —That would make breakfast, say, like one of those old-fashioned bon-bons with a motto wrapped around it. —A quaint device—but why not? —It is not so much that I have been so far away that made me begin as I did, as that I have been so long away. I had a feeling that—well, so long as you do not misunderstand it, and I am confident that you do not, my feelings may be regarded as imaginary. —We know each other too well to have any misgivings, and we must trust to the loyalty of each others thoughts. —While it is only three weeks until I shall see you again, yet those three weeks must be added to those that have already passed— and then I shall see you only for a day or two. —However, nothing is to be gained by laboring the thorn. I promise never to let so long a time elapse again. I promise myself as well as you. Twice I have been on the point of coming over, but that is neither here nor there. We must not think of it—and try to be happy (as I am) and content (as I am not) with our letters. —What I fear is that it may give rise to some misconception in your mind—that you may think that since I ought (judging by the theories expounded in the novels) to come more often, there is a mysterious reason (as, in the same novels, there would be) why I do not. There is, of course, a reason; but it is not a mysterious one, and you know what it is. —The vanishing is only an idea, not a feeling; and as an idea, it is only one of the "multitude of my thoughts within me."[148] Yet it should make that capricious pen of yours less fickle! Two weeks! —Oh, Bo-Bo, and with April in the air—with the robins already meditating their Aprilian chants in the twilight—with the crocus up, and violets stirring under the leaves— with the sun pouring out its large Spring lights—and Master Green-Cap scribbling verses for you to make up a second June book, bye-and-bye. —(Be kind to us both, who want it so much, dear Guardian—and especially inspire Bo-Bo to write to me, even when her hair is in curl-papers—as, of course, it <u>never</u> is.) —Wouldn't it have been nicer to turn a pumpkin into a chariot and to have taken a ride in it to-night than to have written as I have? Gid-dap, grass-hopper, and Squirrel, and Fairy, and you Swallows. Take us—or the Fancies of us—into some warm Woodland—and show us the first pink, the first spear of yellow, the first blade of new green—and while we ride let the blue-bird whistle and the sparrow sing its brief melody. —All we need now, since the light is here (and that is worth worshipping) is—warmth to make the ground swarm with life. —But it was really cold this morning, when I took a long walk from the house, through the Park, and along Riverside Drive. At church-time, the bright-colored dresses looked vivid in the clear air. They need shadows and a softer atmosphere. —In the afternoon I stayed at home to complete some reading—and smoked for the first time, this evening, in eight days! —To-morrow evening I expect to take dinner with two fellows at the Harvard Club[149]—the rest of the week is veiled in darkness. — I started one of Thackeray's thousand-page novels a few weeks ago—but it is the least important reading I have to do, and the book seems interminable. —Have you read R. L. Stevenson's "Virginibus Puerisque?"[150] I thought of it for you some time ago, but forget to tell you.

With much love,
Wallace

148. Psalms 94:19.
149. A club formed in 1865 with a handsome clubhouse at 27 West Forty-fourth Street designed by the firm of McKim, Mead, and White.
150. This volume of essays, published in 1881, includes many passages that are echoed in Stevens's letters and poetry. The first essay, presenting a witty assessment of marriage that must have interested Stevens as he himself was moving toward this state, defined it "a sort of friendship recognised by the police," a definition that Stevens may still have in mind in his late poem "Anglais Mort à Florence."

∽

[WAS 1833 March 23, 1909 New York]

Tuesday Evening

Dear Bo-Bo:—

I have a wild night (as they go, nowadays) to account for. Two friends of mine and I took dinner at the Harvard Club last night. We sat close to an open fire—and just when we had got started on some really remarkable cigars I had to run away to meet Southworth[151] at the Belasco Theatre. We had some business to do there, and after it was over the manager asked us to see the evening's performance—an invitation we very agreeably accepted. Blanche Bates in "The Fighting Hope"[152]—the actress handsome but nervous, the play well-written and somewhat absorbing, when all is said. Afterwards we went to a restaurant where I had a big cigar, a sandwich and two (count 'em) bottles of . . . ginger ale. —It is a long time since I have sat around in the smoke like that. It was one o'clock when I reached home. —Candidly that kind of a thing is a bore and cannot possibly interest a student of Chinese antiquities. But it was a wild night, not in itself, but by contrast with the long studious evenings I have been indulging in—with so very much pleasure. —You mention the B's.[153] I haven't seen them at all—except for the call I made after H. B.'s death—and I don't know anything at all about them. Walter will turn up when he has nothing more amusing to do. Just now there are horses for him to ride, and so on, at friends' houses in the country—and I suppose we all agree that a good horse is better than—walking. —The letter I had from you yesterday was "most welcome," my dear. I am glad to know all about the plants—transplanting and so on—oh! but there was affection in it, and that is such an infinite blessing, wiping out all distance between us. Dear, dear, dear Bo- Bo! —Don't let's bother

151. Edward B. Southworth Jr. served as an officer in the American Bonding Company of Baltimore, Stevens's employer at the time. Both of their names appear on the letterhead stationery for the company at this time in 1909. Brazeau's *Parts of a World* has helpful information on Southworth: "In February 1914, as [James L. D.] Kearney was leaving Equitable Surety for a better job and Southworth was named to succeed him as manager of its New York office, Stevens was tapped to fill Southworth's former position as resident vice-president and second in charge of Equitable's New York branch" (6). Stevens will go to see Southworth, one of his "oldest friends," in his final fatal illness in 1949. See Beverly Coyle and Alan Filreis, eds., *Secretaries of the Moon: The Letters of Wallace Stevens and José Rodríguez Feo* (Durham, N.C.: Duke University Press, 1986), 171.
152. Play in three acts by William J. Hurlbut. Produced by David Belasco at his Stuyvesant Theater on September 22, 1908, and moved to the Belasco Theater on January 18, 1909. Blanche Bates played Anna, the wife of Robert Granger, a bank cashier she wrongly believes innocent of the fraud charge for which he went to prison.
153. Walter Butler and his sister.

about my last letter—just throw me a kiss—and never remember anything I say.

With love,
Wallace

⤳

[WAS 1834 March 26, 1909 New York]

is[154] expected to do. Be quite certain that your parents will not grudge you their aid. —I hope, too, that you have told your mother of our plans. Take her entirely into your confidence, if you have not already done so. —I am putting aside money every week and by September I shall have all that we shall need to start with—and we must have some. Rely on me, trust in me. I do not care that you write, "I do not intend to marry one who is only <u>nice</u> to me,"[155] because I know that I love you—if that is what you mean. What nonsense about Abe Lincoln! Shame on you, to say such a thing. Oh, please, <u>never</u> say things like that, and do not think them. I should not think of marrying you, no matter what had occurred, if I did not expect to be happy. . . .
[Other side.]

Be kind to yourself and to me, darling. Do not vex yourself. Live your own life, and try to perfect it—by living unnoticed and kindly and faithfully. I will not protest that I love you, you will know whether or not I do without my telling you. And believe, besides, in my friendliness and in that of your parents. —I am not blind to the embarrassments of your position—but endure it, because it is best. It will soon be over. —Remember that you are <u>not</u> a stranger in your own home, and it is your home. —I am so sorry that you cannot be spared these anxieties—but they are unreal. Don't allow yourself to brood. Keep up your friends, walk, read, work at home—<u>learn to make your own life.</u>

With my love, and all of it,
Wallace

⤳

[WAS 1835 March 26, 1909 New York]

Friday Evening

My Very Dear Bo-Bo:—

Send a kiss to me before you read another word. . . . I was so glad to get your note this afternoon. It came shortly after I had posted your "Saturday and Sunday"

154. This is a fragment. The envelope shows that it was mailed at 2:00 P.M. on a Friday, a most unusual posting time for Stevens. That he also wrote the next letter that same evening indicates the crisis nature of this exchange.
155. This rare surviving sentence from Elsie's half of this correspondence suggests the "barbarous strength" of Stevens's Penelope in "The World as Meditation."

letter, which, I fear (alas!) will be very dull reading. Gobble, gobble, gobble! But isn't it just a little your fault? Well, whosever fault it is—don't read it twice. Please be dreadfully frightened—and go on making spice cake and all the known varieties of gelatine—and get up on your right foot every morning. —Depend upon it, those two bottles of . . . were really ginger ale, nothing more. I'm a prune in that respect. —I imagine we've been sharing the same weather. To-night it is clear and there's a new moon—always a pleasant companion. I expect to take a day on the road on Sunday—I need it greatly. Think of me, then, as in Vagabondia. Here's a kiss for each cheek and one for—just a touch!

With much love, dearest
Wallace

↬

[WAS 1836 April 6, 1909 New York]

Tuesday Evening

My Dear Bo-Bo:—

The deuce with Mr. Black-Eyes. —My plans are simple: to come on Satur-day afternoon, on either an early or late train, and to be with you once more, and certainly, on Saturday evening. —And I hope you have on either the new brown dress, or else that nice old whitish one with the flowers—you know. And if you haven't found contentment by that time, I'll stand on the piano and call you a silly <u>goose</u>—and preach, and shake you, and scold you, and kiss you. Perhaps I'll bring a rabbit along.

With love,
Wallace

↬

[WAS 1837 April 18, 1909 New York]

Sunday Evening

My dearest Bo-Bo:

I sent you Rubinstein's "Kammenoi Ostrow"[156] on Friday. No doubt you have it by this time. I am tremendously fond of it, but never knew the name of it until a few days ago. —During the week I have been especially busy in the eve-nings with "The Little June Book."[157] When I was home I was only at No. 7 but

---

156. Opus10, Number 22 of Russian pianist and composer Anton Gregoryevich Rubenstein (1829–1894), published in 1855, became very popular.
157. This collection of twenty poems he is writing for her birthday on June 5 parallels the collection of twenty poems (called "Book of Verses") for the year before. Both col-lections are given in Holly Stevens's edition of her father's journals, *Souvenirs and Prophe-cies* (190–96, 227–34). Five of the poems for this "June Book," those numbered III, VIII,

I am now at No.15—and some of them are just as I want them. I want to get them all finished a month or so before I send them so that I can hum them and study them and so get them as nearly desirable as possible. —Yesterday afternoon (the first <u>time</u> I could call my own since my visit) I walked up town and through the Park. The forsythia is bright yellow, although not yet fully opened, and the trees have a green shade. The Park was crowded. I spent the evening at home—meditating! —This morning I went to two churches—St. Luke's and St. Peter's. St. Luke's is a little chapel, full of ceremony, in old Greenwich Village, the part of town I live in. St. Peter's is an old church, not chapel, in old Chelsea village, a part of town a little to the North-West. The windows in St. Peter's were rather good, and the choir decidedly so, of course. I saw only a part of the service at the second church. I went largely out of curiosity. —In the afternoon I crossed the new Queensboro Bridge over the East River. This leads from one of the crowded parts of town to Williamsburg, which is more a name, at this point, than a place. Then I walked out into the country and turned around at four o'clock to look at New-York as a whole—a huge city. One understands its being one of the largest cities in the world. —During the week I expect to move. This house is going to be vacated on May 1 and I have, therefore, had to get another room in the neighborhood: in the same block. The house is very nice although I have not yet seen the room. It comes on faith. —It was pleasant to have your note—although it made me puzzle my head to think what it was that I had written that you agreed with. I remembered the main part and knew, of course, that you felt about that as I did; and that was enough. It would be nice to go up the Maidencreek[158] on Sunday, if the weather permits. If you have kept up your walks, you would find it an easy jaunt: to go from Blandon to the Stone Bridge and then North until we were ready to turn back. Would you care to walk? We might be able to pick up a horse at Blandon but that is not half so fine as walking. Or, we might walk back the way we went—in the other direction—summer before last. It would be fun to start early on Sunday morning (with even a bit of lunch.) I leave it to you, because you can tell about the weather. I shall come on Saturday afternoon, on the early train no

---

IX, XVII, and XIX, were published as parts of a group of poems titled "Carnet de Voyage" in *Trend* 7, no. 6 (September 1914): 743–46; the nineteenth poem of the group of twenty presented to Elsie in June 1908 was published as "Home Again" in *Trend* 8, no. 2 (November 1914): 117. Holly says that Elsie's later aversion to the publication of Stevens's poems came from the fact that Stevens had "published 'her poems'; that he had made public what was, in her mind, very private" (*SP,* 227).
158. Maiden Creek (spelled thus on maps) flows from the north into the Schuylkill just north of Reading; Stevens and Elsie spent less time in this quadrant of the countryside around Reading than they did in the more westerly one through which Tulpehocken Creek runs.

doubt. —But I shall be writing to you in the meantime so bother trains. —I'll come on <u>some</u> train. —You will have lots to tell me if you do not write!

With much love,
Wallace

↩

[WAS 1838 April 26, 1909[159] New York]

Monday Morning

Dear Bo-Bo:

I had your key after all—but in another pocket. Sorry to have taken it away. I shall write in <u>extenso</u> later.

Bye!
Wallace.

↩

[WAS 1839 April 28, 1909 New York]

Wednesday Evening

My dearest Bo-Bo:—

I take my rusty pen in hand. —On Monday evening, with the aid of two English sailors, whom I picked up, I moved to my new room. It is almost three times as large as the old one, with a closet, <u>two</u> windows, a fire-place and so on, and altogether a great advance on the one I left. And I have a small table to write on, too—instead of a suit-case on my knees. I have grown so accustomed to having your letters come to the office that I think I shall ask you to send them there. But my address here is Number 117 East—No: 117 <u>West</u> Eleventh Street—in case of emergency. Everything is already in order. Only the bed has a board or something running from side to side which rather gives me a kink—and I must investigate it one of these days. —Last evening Southworth and I went to dinner at a fellow's house. He was married in December and the dinner was a matter of pride in his wife and her cooking. It was a capital dinner. I had intended writing to you afterwards, but it was almost twelve o'clock when I reached home (in a shower)—and so I tumbled into bed—and said I was sorry. —I wonder why newly married people always have roasted chicken at their dinners. Is it because the damsel knows it will taste good—and because the youth can display his carving? Anyhow, they always do, and it is always good. We had some home-made marmalade with the cheese. I wish you knew how to make marmalade. The kind they have at the stores is perfectly good—but I thought last night's just about the

---

159. Written on American Bonding Company stationery, listing the following officers: Jas. L. D. Kearney, Resident Vice-President and Manager; Edward S. Southworth Jr., Resident Vice-Pres.; Hulbert T. E. Beardsley, Attorney.

best I had ever had. —Have your cheeks got over the chafing the wind gave them on Sunday afternoon? I have been feeling just as if I had been sunburnt—and in fact I looked decidedly sunburnt on Monday. —It was a pity I didn't have any old clothes with me. I should like to romp over those fields if I had it to do over, in my oldest duds. Then I could really swing you over fences as you should be swung. They had a windy day here on Sunday. The result is that it has been like March ever since and to-night the <u>Post</u> says that it is to be colder to-morrow. Dear me! But we shall get around to it—since there are only two more days of April. On May 1, I begin to take cold plunges in the morning—naturally, therefore, I am interested in the thermometer. —As the county gets to be what it ought to be, you must let me know. I never tire of hearing news about growing things, as they are called. So much thinking about them is likely to change them into thoughts, to such a degree that the reality of them undergoes a change. The reality I think seems less delicate, less fantastic than the images. But the reality has an immensely more powerful effect. —Possibly one reason why fields full of flowers, such as we saw along Maidencreek, are so delightful, is that such fields fulfill the fancy. —Yet how pleasant they are without any reason at all! I like to think of you gathering up so many more flowers than—you had thought of.—

> Loveliest of trees, the cherry, now
> Is hung with blooms along the bough.[160]

Two happy lines to have come across just at the right moment. They applied to nearly every tree we passed. I wish we had seen a tulip tree. I have never seen one in bloom. You should walk out Fifth street. There used to be two magnolias near Walnut Street that were always worth seeing. No doubt, they are in bloom now. —Have you started house-cleaning? It must be horrid work—except that your house is always so spic-and-span. They do not do that over here. It is a fine old Dutch habit, I think. —I have put away the second picture and have gone back to the white dress and shining hair. Isn't it tempting the way it hangs down over your temple—and what wouldn't you give just to brush it back? Dear Bo-Bo! I shall be so glad when I have you here. I must look around. It has always been my plan to make observations this summer on Saturday afternoons and on Sundays and I must soon start. There is a place in Washington Square—but there are many, many places—and I shall look at all of them. I wish we could do it together; and of course we will before we come to a decision.[161] —But that is another story.

Your loving,

Wallace.

---

160. "Loveliest of Trees" by A. E. Housman, from *A Shropshire Lad* (1896), has "bloom along the bough." This poem is in Palgrave, *Golden Treasury*.
161. Stevens will eventually choose their apartment by himself.

⌒

[WAS 1840 May 2, 1909[162] New York]

Sunday Evening

My Dearest:

"How sweet are thy words unto my taste! Yea, sweeter than honey to my mouth."[163] That is à propos of your last letter. I cannot tell you better how glad I was to hear from you. To have a letter so rich in what I desire. Oh, I love you very much, my dear. —Today I have been roaming about town. In the morning I walked down-town—stopping once to watch three flocks of pigeons circling in the sky. I dropped into St. John's chapel an hour before the service and sat in the last pew and looked around. It happens that last night at the Library I read a life of Jesus and I was interested to see what symbols of that life appeared in the chapel. I think there were none at all excepting the gold cross on the altar. When you compare that poverty with the wealth of symbols, of remembrances, that were created and revered in times past, you appreciate the change that has come over the church. The church should be more than a moral institution, if it is to have the influence that it should have. —The space, the gloom, the quiet mystify and entrance the spirit. But that is not enough. —And one turns from this chapel to those built by men who felt the wonder of the life and death of Jesus—temples full of sacred images, full of the air of love and holiness—tabernacles hallowed by worship that sprang from the noble depths of men familiar with Gethsemane, familiar with Jerusalem. —I do not wonder that the church is so largely a relic. Its vitality depended on its association with Palestine, so to speak. —I felt a peculiar emotion in reading about John the Baptist, Bethany, Galilee—and so on,[164] because (the truth is) I had not thought about them much since my days at Sunday-school (when, of course, I didn't think of them at all). It was like suddenly remembering something long forgotten, or else like suddenly seeing something new and strange in what had always been in my mind. —Reading the life of Jesus, too, makes one distinguish the separate idea of God. Before to-day I do not think I have ever realized that God was distinct from Jesus. It enlarges the matter almost beyond comprehension. People doubt the existence of Jesus[165]—at least

162. This letter is misdated May 3, 1909, in *LWS,* 139, which omits the first six sentences.

163. Psalm 119:103.

164. These geographical references and Stevens's emphasis upon them might be an indication that the "life of Jesus" he has just read is that of Ernest Renan, in which the geographical emphasis is also heavy because Renan was physically in the Holy Land when he wrote his book. The word Palestine occurs twice in "Sunday Morning" and nowhere else in Stevens's poetry (or published letters and essays).

165. Stevens, a close student of Emerson, may have his "Divinity School Address" in mind.

they doubt incidents of his life, such as, say, the Ascension into Heaven after his death. But I do not understand that they deny God. I think everyone admits that in some form or other. —The thought makes the world sweeter—even if God be no more than the mystery of Life. —Well, after a bit, I left the chapel and walked over the Brooklyn Bridge. There was a high wind, so that I put my hat under my arm. I imagined myself pointing things out to you—the Statue of Liberty, green and weather-beaten, Governor's Island, the lower Bay. Then I rambled up one street and down another until I had a fair idea of the neighborhood. It isn't very promising. —Took the Subway back to Union Square, Manhattan, and walked across Fourteenth-Street. It is lined with the windows of cheap photographers, and I must have looked at thousands of photographs. How silly people are! They curl their hair, put on large white shirts, boutonnières and the like and then have their pictures taken. Such idiot's sights! —After lunch, I walked up-town to the Exhibition of the Water Color Society. It isn't at all a good show—there's nothing fresh, nothing original—just the same old grind of waves and moonlight and trees and sunlight and so on. Yet there are some interesting etchings of New-York—pictures of out-of-the-way corners, that will be more valuable in the future than they are now. I am always especially interested at these water-color shows in the pictures of flowers—bowls of roses and the like. It would be pleasant to make a collection of them. There was one picture of a glass vase with six or seven cyclamen in it that was particularly good. There is something uncommon about cyclamen, something rare, if not exceptionally beautiful. —Then I walked down-town—catching a glimpse, on Madison Avenue, of a yard crowded with tulips. —I dropped into a church for five minutes, merely to see, you understand. I am not pious. But churches are beautiful to see. —And then I came home, observing great masses of white clouds, with an autumnal shape to them, floating through the windy-sky. —To-night, it is blissfully quiet—and, as I went for a cigar, I saw the moon, large and full of lustre, shining around the sky. —I fear it is too late to make history of last Sunday. I like to do it while the pageant is still in mind. But for the Muse, I note that we met early, hurried down-town, caught a car for Blandon, crossed the country to the Stone Bridge and then went Northward along the bank. We found the water green, we heard it ripple over the shallows. Bo-Bo ran across a wobbly bridge— gathered cow-slips and what-d'ye-call-'ems—heard robins—saw dandelions. We passed through Evansville on foot—left the creek—and climbed up a field to a hill-top, where there was a <u>very</u> remarkable view. But the wind took hold of Bo-Bo and shook her out of all dignity—so that we rested in a corner of a fence while the damsel fixed her hair. Next, on the road, she rode a little way on the giant's shoulder (pretending not to like it)—getting off just in time to avoid a meeting with four Italians (who would have been enormously astonished). — We crossed a field on a foot-path, and then skirted one that had been plowed by picking our way along the fence. We inspected a lime-kiln. We climbed over a fence into a grove and there we sat with our backs against a tree and made a combined assault on a box of rolls, some with tongue, some only with butter, eggs, tangerines, pickles, and two kinds of cake. —It was a most excellent grove, well-suited to a whole day's idling. —Another fence—a kiss in the lane on the other side of it—a drink from a goblet at a farmer's pump—two immense willows (under which the cows stand in July and August switching their tails)—a bit of rough walking—a glimpse of blossoms—the trolley once more—a blue-bird racing beside the window—The End. —O, Muse, look back on that page in our Book only with kindness. (—I called you Bo-Bo when that was written. You had pink cheeks and light brown hair and soft hands. You were twenty-two. You wore a black dress—that old black dress—and slippers—I think.) It hardly seems as if that could have happened a week ago, with all the snow, and rain, and hail, and fog that we have had; but so it was. —Or have we been to Florida in our dreams? That seems most likely. I do not think the weather will have done any damages. The magnolia trees here look rather bedraggled but not injured and the window boxes of geraniums and tulips look none the worse. —I wish I could spend the whole season out of doors, walking by day, reading and studying in the evenings. I feel a tremendous capacity for enjoying that kind of life—but it is all over, and I acknowledge "the fell clutch of circumstance."[166] —How gradually we find ourselves compelled into the common lot! But after all there are innumerable things besides that kind of life—and I imagine that when I come home from the Library, thinking over some capital idea—a new name for the Milky Way, a new aspect of Life, an amusing story, a gorgeous line—I am as happy as I should be—or could be—anywhere. So many lives have been lived—the world is no longer dull—nor would not be even if nothing new at all ever happened. It would be enough to examine the record already made, by so many races, in such varied spaces. —Perhaps, it is best, too, that one should have only glimpses of reality—and get the rest from the fairy-tales, from pictures, and music, and books. —My chief objection to town-life is the commonness of the life. Such numbers of men degrade Man. The <u>teeming</u> streets make Man a nuisance—a vulgarity, and it is impossible to see his dignity. I feel, nevertheless, the overwhelming necessity of thinking well, speaking well. —"I am a stranger in the earth."[167] —You see I have been digging into the Psalms—anything at all, so long as it is full of praise—and rejoicing. I am sick of dreariness. —Yet if I prattle so much of religious subjects, Psalms and things, my girl will think me a bother; and so, no more, as we used to say when we had stumbled across something

---

166. A phrase from William Ernest Henley's poem "Invictus," which is in Palgrave's *Golden Treasury*.
167. Psalm 119:19.

unpleasant. —Progress with the June Book is a bit delayed, but I am at number nineteen. I think I shall stop at twenty, because that was the number last year. But I may have a tuneful[168] week and never stop at all. —Keep the Shropshire Lad[169] until sometime when I am at home. I have enough books, and to spare, without it. —Besides the change in my room, there has also been a change in my arrangements for meals. I am taking them next door to the old place with pretty much the same people. There is a new woman to my left—very fat, very refined— Irish, musical and gray-haired. Next to her is a young fellow named Robinson, about four feet high, as gentle as a lamb, a novel-reader, whom an ogre would have for dessert. There is another woman near-by, who reads the dictionary and tells of its contents—rather a dry, withered old-maid. She lives here—on the same floor. —But it is the usual story. You probably know the kind of people that infest boarding-houses—and it isn't a very diverting subject. —I smiled at the dinners and suppers you have been making. How fine that is! No one has a better spirit than you—and I must try with all my might to be equal to you. I am afraid I should grumble a little. I cannot think of anything besides marmalade just now, unless it should be stewed rhubarb—and I suppose anyone understands that. And rhubarb pie would be very nice for Sunday evenings, instead of corned beef and biscuits and cocoa. Sunday tea is a thing everyone makes at home here. It is such a bore to go out—it is like breakfast. —But I've written you a longish letter and it is time for me to stop, else I shall have nothing to say next time. Only letters do not depend on news. If they did! —Did you put in your last letter what I asked you to? Of course! Well, I <u>think</u> there is one in this.

Your loving,
Wallace.

⌐

[WAS 1841 May 4, 1909 New York]

Tuesday Evening

My dear Bo-Bo:

The June-book is finished! Now for the polishing—the correcting—humming—erasing—rewriting—and so on. You've no idea how hard it is to write these little verses. —It keeps me up to all hours, too. —Same old routine since Sunday—days at the office, early evenings at the Library, late evenings at home—looking at the ceiling in search for poetry. —Coming home from the Library to-night I looked at the moon over Cooper Union and thought that

---

168. Holly Stevens, *LWS,* 141, reads this as the pun "Juneful," which the handwriting does not support.

169. This book is still in the remainder of Stevens's library at the Huntington, inscribed "Elsie from Wallace / September 1, 1906."

the next time I saw it like that, so round and bright, would be almost the time of your birthday. And then, too, this strange weather will be over and, perhaps, we shall be wearing straw hats and wondering at the heat. —But what is the mysterious announcement in the <u>Eagle</u>? You kill me with curiosity. Don't forget to tell me. —I am going over to Brooklyn again on Sunday morning with a man who knows the beastly place. Manhattan seems more and more attractive by comparison. But we shall see.

Your
Wallace

⌐

[WAS 1842 May 7, 1909 New York]

Friday Evening

Dearest:

The clipping[170] was a charming surprise. I had no idea of it, upon my word. I had heard he was looking Westward but no more. —And imagine John's being a party to an announcement! But that, of course, is as the lady wishes, as they say. Personally, I am more secret. I should like our own engagement to remain our own secret, except in our families, and among the one or two; and I think that my desire and your desire are birds of a feather. —Well, we had a summer day yesterday—two straw-hats, and the like. This morning before going downtown I walked over to Union Square and walked around it, stopping at the beds of pansies, to study the little faces, and to look at the colors. In the middle of the Square (as in the middle of any Square) there is a large fountain with a circular basin. The basin is surrounded by tulips—yellow and crimson. —Over the Bank of the Metropolis was a great furry cloud, very fine to see. —Then I dropped into the Subway and sped to the office underground. —This evening I walked home, through Lafayette street, which runs parallel to Broadway, an old route with me. Then through Washington Square, where there were more tulips. — There is an apartment house on the West side of Washington Square, where I often imagine we live. You often sit in the window-seat about six o'clock and I can see you as I come home, reading some wicked novel[.] You were there tonight, and looked up, and I waved my hand, and you threw me a kiss. —The fountain in that delectable spot has been cemented and looks quite handsome. How many times I have loafed there—reading the inscription on the Arch: "Let us raise a standard to which the wise and honest may repair. The event is in the hand of God. —Washington." One would have to look far and wide for the wise and honest that <u>have</u> repaired. —But it is a pleasant Square and a noble

---

170. Probably announcing the engagement of his younger brother John (1880–1940), who married Elizabeth (Bess) Hatch of Illinois (1875–1934) in 1909.

Arch. —Is Bo-Bo going to have a new dress? The hooks and eyes! Won't that keep her busy! —There is a cat and dog fight going on under my window— probably a wise cat beating an honest dog. —Good-night, dear Bo-Bo. Let me give you just one kiss—oh!

With my love,
Wallace[171]

[WAS 1843 May 9, 1909 New York]

Sunday Evening

My dearest Bo-Bo:—

It has been a dull day. The sun has been half-hidden, and the air has been heavy and cold. This morning I loafed and read a chapter or two of "The Great

---

171. The Huntington folder for this letter has the following article:

Once an American City."
To the editor of the Evening Post:

Sir: I had determined to revisit old St. Mark's, a famous American church. On my way, I wandered through Union Square, passing many doing the same or seated on the benches. There was much voluble talking, but not a word of English did I hear. The only thing that looked like an American was General Washington.

Then, reaching Astor Place, once well known as a part of America and New York, I sighted my church in the distance. Wending my way along, I passed many people—hundreds, but not an American face, and not a word of English. At Third Avenue, I was startled by seeing a very small group huddled around the American flag, held proudly aloft. This group was surrounded by a wild-eyed foreign mob. I realized it all in a moment: this was the last stand of America—of Manhattan against the foreign invasion. It was the glorious End. There was nothing else for one to do than also to die there with that little group of patriots. I hurried forward, pushing to the right and left the makers of cloaks and pants, and reached my brothers—when, lo: it was nothing but a Salvation Army squad trying to lure these Yiddishers from their synagogues.

After the service at St. Mark's, I passed up Second Avenue in search of a newspaper. I soon found a stand stacked with daily papers of many kinds. There was not one of English print among the lot.

And there stands old St. Mark's! Let us start a subscription for erecting around it ramparts of steel, topped with sixteen-inch rapid-firing guns, and then, waving over it proudly every day, the American flag, defy the foreigners forever. And thus we will keep this spot in memory of what was once a city that we old codgers used to call New York.

Instead of having a Hudson celebration, I think we better have solemn mass for the soul of the departed American city of Manhattan Isle.
M.
New York, May 2

Hoggarty Diamond."[172] After dinner, I walked up Sixth-Avenue slowly, looking at millinery, postal cards, shoes and so on, going East, and then West, and
then North, and finally I reached the Park, where I ran into a Dutchman with
a red beard exercising his little girl, and we sat down on the grass and talked
about fees and other matters interesting to lawyers, until five o'clock, when I
said "Adieu!" and came home on a car and read a little more in my novel, until
it was time to go to tea. Such a shabby tea! Corned beef, cold salmon, dry biscuits, cocoa and chopped pine-apple! I hate that kind of thing. Cold meats are
the saddest thing in the world to eat—and on the saddest evening in the week.
—You wonder why I didn't go into the country to see apple-blossoms and the
like. The truth is, or seems to be, that it is chiefly the surprise of blossoms that I
like. After I have seen them for a week (this is great scandal) I am ready for the
leaves that come after them—for the tree unfolded, full of sound and shade. I
remember a passage in my journal written when I lived at East Orange. It is
dated April 29, 1906:

> "All the orchards are white—it is fantastic. Somehow, amid so
> many blossoms, one longs for dark woods, rain, iron capes. There
> is a great white cherry tree just outside my window."[173]

The following year I lived at Fordham Heights, and on May 22, I wrote:

> "This morning I walked down Aqueduct Avenue to the bridge.
> There were lilacs, gray and purple, in the convent garden. The
> corner of a stable was hung with wisteria. —This evening, as I
> passed the same way, a warm scent drifted out to me.[174]

That shows the difference. I am eager for the warm scents. The white and
pink of blossoms is delicately beautiful, but they beautify a chilly season. Late
May brings grass in luxury, and a general luxury of leaves and warmth and fragrance. If there is anything more luxurious than warmth and fragrance I do not
know it. And so, long for lilacs, purple and gray. —My journal, bye the bye, is
in sad neglect. I have not written two pages this year. I wish I could put into it,
without too much trouble, even a small part of the notes I have made at the
library. Let me preserve one by putting it in our annals:

172. This novel, *The History of Samuel Titmarsh and the Great Hogarty Diamond*, was
originally published by Thackeray in 1841 under the pseudonym Michael Angelo Titmarsh.
173. In *LWS*, 142, Holly Stevens has "iron cages," and in her note 5 she points out,
"This entry no longer appears in the Journal where part of this page has been excised."
174. This passage from Stevens's journal for May 22, 1907, is in *SP*, 179.

O World, be noble, for her sake!
If she but knew thee, what thou art,
What wrongs are borne, what deeds are done
In thee, beneath thy daily sun,
Knows'st thou not that her tender heart,

For very pain and shame, would break?
O World, be noble, for her sake![175]

"For very pain," etc. should be "For pain and very shame" —I hate erasures, just as I do corned beef—and saxophones. And since the mood to quote is here, why, here's another, picked up one learnèd night:

Ask me not, Dear, what thing it is
That makes me love you so;
What graces, what sweet qualities
That from your spirit flow:
For I have but this old reply,
That you are you, that I am I.[176]

They are both by Laurence Binyon—a very clever chap, who is attached to the British Museum, in London.[177] —Scraps of paper covered with scribbling—Chinese antiquities, names of colors, in lists like rainbows, jottings of things to think about, like the difference, for example, between the <u>expression</u> on men's faces and on women's, extracts, like this glorious one from Shakespeare: "What a piece of work is man! how noble in reason! how infinite in faculty!"[178] and so on; epigrams, like, "The greatest pleasure is to do a good action by stealth, and have it found out by accident"[179]—(could any true thing be more amusing?)—lists of Japanese eras in history, the names of Saints: Ambrose, Gregory, Augustine,

---

175. Laurence Binyon's "O World, Be Nobler" is in Palgrave's *Golden Treasury*.

176. *LWS*, 143, identifies this poem as Binyon's "Ask me not, Dear" from his *Lyric Poems* as published in London in 1894. Montaigne gave a similar explanation for his love for his friend, Étienne de Boétie: "Parce que c'était lui; parce que c'était moi."

177. Laurence Binyon (1869–1943) was important to Stevens at this time, both as a poet and as the author of *Painting in the Far East* (London: Edward Arnold, 1908), a work from which Stevens took many insights and quotations that appear in these letters.

178. *Hamlet* 2.2.315. Laurence Binyon (in *Painting in the Far East,* 23) quoted this passage right after another passage that Stevens copied into his journal for May 14, 1909 (see *SP*, 221).

179. Charles Lamb, "Table Talk by the Late Elia," *Athenaeum*, January 4, 1834. Richardson, *Wallace Stevens* 1:555n40, points out that this passage is quoted in Kakuzo Okakura's *Book of Tea* (see note to WAS 1830 March 16, 1909). Stevens had recorded this quotation in his journal for May 14, 1909 (*SP*, 223).

Jerome; the three words, "monkeys, deer, peacocks"[180] in the corner of a page; and this (from the French:) "The torment of the man of thought is to aspire toward Beauty, without ever having any fixed and definite standard of Beauty";[181] the names of books I should like to read, and the names of writers about whom I should like to know something. —The quotation from Shakespeare is particularly serviceable to me now, for I have lately had a sudden conception of the true nobility of men and women. It is well enough to say that they walk like chickens, or look like monkeys, except when they are fat and look like hippopotamuses. But the zoölogical point of view is not a happy one; and merely from the desire to think well of men and women I have suddenly seen the very elementary truth (which I had <u>never</u> seen before) that their nobility does not lie in what they look like but in what they endure and in the manner in which they endure it. For instance, everybody except a child appreciates that "things are not what they seem";[182] and the result of disillusion might be fatal to content, if it were not for courage, good-will, and the like. The mind is the Arena of Life. Men and women must be judged, to be judged truly, by the valor of their spirits, by their conquest of the natural being, and by their victories in philosophy. —I feel as if I had made a long step in advance: as if I had discovered for myself why Life is called noble, and why people set a value on it, abstractly. It is a discovery, too, that very greatly increases my interest in men and women. One might say that their appearances are like curtains, fair and unfair; the stage is behind—the comedy, and tragedy. The curtain had never before been so vividly lifted, at least for me; and my rambles through the streets have been excursions full of amateur yet thrilling penetration. I respect the chickens; I revel in the monkeys; I feel

180. Here he is quoting from his journal for May 14, 1909, and the reference is to the types of subjects that Laurence Binyon says Maruyama Okio (1733–1795) could paint peerlessly (see *Painting of the Far East,* 2nd ed., 233–34).

181. Paul Elmer More quotes this line from "the Goncourts in their Journal" in French in his essay "Tolstoy; or the Ancient Feud between Philosophy and Art" in *Shelburne Essays,* first series.

182. Longfellow's famous "Psalm of Life" includes this clause; the first two stanzas are:

> Tell me not, in mournful numbers,
> "Life is but an empty dream!"
> For the soul is dead that slumbers,
> And things are not what they seem.
> Life is real! Life is earnest!
> And the grave is not its goal;
> "Dust thou art, to dust returnest,"
> Was not spoken of the soul.

most politely toward the hippopotamuses, poor souls.[183] —I had ground for thinking well of them yesterday afternoon, too, for different reasons. After leaving the office, I went to Flatbush, which is part of Brooklyn. After looking at all manner of apartments, I walked over to Prospect Park. The flowers were more than beautiful—immense beds of tulips, gigantic vases of pansies, beds of wonderful trees. At the entrance to the Park, there is a large Arch, surrounded by bronze figures—horses, and a flag of bronze flying in the air. Nothing could be finer. And from the Plaza surrounding it, I could see the stupendous bulk of the new Manhattan Bridge in the distance. It is a mass of steel, suspended over the East River by steel cables attached to two lofty steel towers. A chant to the builders![184] —I think that if people went more often to points outside of the city from which they could look back and see the magnitude of it, and the immensity of some of the structures, they would feel more awe for it than they do now. It is superb. It may not be beautiful, but in force and strength it is superb, yet I think it is beautiful. Its power is inspiring. —We talked of the bridges last night—a friend of mine and I. He has been all over Europe—knows London Bridge, the Pont des Arts (Bridge of Arts) at Paris, the Ponte Vecchia at Florence, and the rest. But these Cyclopean monsters of ours springing from one city to another, and making them all one, require no explanation. They speak for themselves. — I had not expected to spend the evening talking of bridges. In fact, I had thought of going to the theatre, and I walked indifferently through the theatre district looking at the electric signs— "The Candy Shop," "The Beauty Spot," "The Fair Co-Ed," "The Girl from Rector's," until I found myself in utter darkness, far uptown. Afterwards, I came home (talking on the way) and read late—and that is, no doubt, the reason why I knocked about from pillar to post to-day, instead of going to some far-off place—near-by. It would have been nice to be at home, but it would always be nice to be at home. It would have been nice, too, to hear you play "A Shepherd's Tale"—a hundred times, for surely I have hummed it and whistled it (to myself) that many times to-day. It is such a blithe, saucy, little air. —Do you remember—saucy—and the three brown books—and have you read them? —And do you remember "Under the Willows"? I think I shall bring more of Grahame's books the next time I come—at the end of the month—to-morrow will be the tenth—already, as they say, you know where. It is getting to be such a strange place to me. To-night, I can hardly remember it—

183. Stevens had a similar sympathetic epiphany in his journal for April 1903: "There was a time when I walked downtown in the morning almost oblivious of the thousands and thousands of people I passed; now I look at them with extraordinary interest as companions in the same fight that I am about to join" (*SP*, 114).
184. Stevens may be imitating the voice of Walt Whitman "singing and chanting the things that are part of him" (*CP*, 150).

oh, yes: parts of it, scenes. But to remember the market-wagons, the working-men with their kettles or pails, the families shopping on Saturday nights, the white dresses—that's the thing. If I remember these, how much, after all, have I forgotten? The market-wagons—isn't that fine? That sound of a horse, the squeaking of a wagon, the clear sound of the car-tracks—early in the morning, long before it is light, when you lie awake—and feel a companionship in the sounds, and a relief, and say, "It will soon be morning"—and fall asleep, as if "the waters of night" had carried you into some haven. —And the white dresses on the children with their well-soaped faces and hair brushed tightly back. There is nothing like that here. At least, I have never seen it. —But this is a melancholy pleasure. What is over, is done—and good-bye! —Yet we shall speak of such things often. —And so, dear Bo-Bo, of the sloping shoulders, and the shining hair, once more Good-Night! —And the soft hand—but that is not in the picture. But there never was one more soft—and you must take good care of it, unless the house-cleaning is finished, as it very possibly is by this time. You will want a long breath of air after it, and therefore I hope for a real May morning—blue as the sea, and full of green hills—and whisk your image to me as you walk and let me ride above you, in the only cloud. A fantastic promenade!

> With very much love,
> Wallace

↬

[WAS 1844 May 11, 1909 New York]

> Tuesday Evening

My dear Bo-Bo:—

Just home from Daly's where I sat in the top gallery and saw rather a queer comedy called "The Climax."[185] After dinner I sat down to read <u>Life</u> and in its "Confidential Guide to the Theatres" I saw this stated as a "delightful and unassuming comedy, with a tinge of music"—and after an unusually brief struggle with temptation I gave up and made goose-tracks for the theatre. —It was all about a girl from Azalea, Ohio, who wanted to sing Carmen. An old friend from Azalea wanted to keep her off the stage, and a new friend wanted to get her on. The old friend did something to her that took her voice away (the scamp!)[.] Bye-and-bye, on their wedding-day, while the carriage, that was to take them to the Alderman's office, was waiting at the door, she found him out: that is, he told her . . . the beast.[186] —Suddenly her voice returns and she whoops it up to a thing called "The

185. Play in three acts by Edward Locke, incidental music by Joseph Carl Breil. It opened at Weber's Theater on April 12, 1909, and moved to the Daly Theater on April 26, 1909.
186. Stevens has the two closely spaced dots before "the beast." This is the first instance of this mark of punctuation to represent a pause.

Song Divine" (which is peddled at the door after the performance.) But all is o'er. Her voice didn't stay. She marries the youth from Azalea, who meant well all the time—packs her trunk right on the stage, and takes the chew-chew train—and it is fair to assume was as happy as could be expected without singing Carmen. —Not delightful at all, but certainly unassuming. —At one point, the hero says, "God put love in my heart," etc. Isn't that kind of thing abominable? I cannot endure allusions to God in that way—and cries of "My God!" or "Oh God!" make me shudder. —There was also a good deal about that old thing—the artistic temperament. Such a tiresome affair! The pole-axe for temperaments—poison, sudden death for temperaments. —I think a very pretty comedy could be written showing how people suppress temperaments. In proof, I send a clipping from the aforesaid Life.[187] —But it grows late, as the villain says: and I have a chapter or two to read in that thrilling book "The New Testament." That is my latest hobby. Extraordinary things like casting out demons, raising the dead, turning two fishes and five loaves of bread into enough to feed a multitude, and so on. —I know of nothing like this even in Jules Verne or the Arabian Nights. And so—ahoy!

Your loving
Caliban.

⌒

[WAS 1845 May 14, 1909 New York]

Friday Evening

My Dearest Bo-Bo:—

Dante's "New Life" is a strange book. I have had it for a long time, looked through it often—and never read it. But I know what it is about. In copying my notes into my journal, I came across this paragraph,—

> It was the mission of the new faith to promulgate the distinctly feminine virtues in place of the sterner ideals of antiquity—love in place of understanding, sympathy for justice, self-surrender for magnanimity,—and as a consequence the eternal feminine was strangely idealized, giving us in religion the worship of the Virgin Mary, and in art the raptures of chivalry culminating in Dante's adoration of Beatrice.[188]

Thus it appears that the "New Life" is one of the great documents of Christianity. It is very strange to read, as I am reading now, the <u>chief</u> document—the

---

187. No longer with this letter.

188. In his journal for May 14, 1909, Stevens says this passage comes from Paul Elmer More (*SP*, 220). It comes from More's "Tolstoy" in his *Shelburne Essays*, first series, an essay Stevens quoted several times in WAS 1822 for March 2, 1909.

New Testament—and to consider the growth of our Western religion. St. Matthew opens with a list of the families from which Jesus descended as if to impress
the fact of his humanity. And then follows, as I said the other night, a narration
of the most incredible adventures that ever befell a human being. The Catholic
church, for reasons of its own, has made much of the Virgin, and when I have
finished my reading, I must meditate on it and try to find the reason. Twenty
centuries of Christianity have made life quite different for women (as for men,
too). It may be that Christianity is a feminine religion.[189] That, too, is worth
thinking about. —But I have been far from such thoughts this week. The truth
is, Spring has been in my blood, and I have been restless, and unable to sit at
home. The night before last I went to "The Candy Shop"[190] and last night to
"Havana."[191] They were both pretty poor—and I sat in cheap seats—but they
seemed to exhaust me, and I think I can get back to books and my attic again in
peace. In fact, to-night I felt like plunging into some book and reading until
morning. Only my own books are too familiar and dull so I have been having a
pleasant time with old notes—and things. —No: you must not have the June
book until the day comes. It is only a little thing—but it took a month to write
it. I have decided on one or two changes. —And I cannot let your birth-day be
just like any other day. Fie! We shall have a celebration—a parade around the
parlor, and the porch—and I shall have some memento—and "not all the king's
horses, and all the king's men" shall stand in the way. —It will be only for the
two of us, and why shouldn't we? —By the way, I heard a piano in the house
grinding out "O Belle Nuit"[192] to-night. I couldn't think what it was at first.
They played as if it was intensely hard, and I said to myself—"You should hear
Bo-Bo play that." To-morrow afternoon I hope to get the first fresh air I have
had in seven days, and on Sunday, if I am not too lazy, I shall take a walk in the
country—for the good of my soul. The other evening I noticed the trees in
Madison Square, fat with green. It was gorgeous. They seemed like the scenery

189. Santayana makes this point, among many others about the church, in his *Reason
in Religion,* in the section titled "The Episodes of Life Consecrated Mystically": "Christianity . . . was democratic, feminine, and unworldly."
190. Musical play in two acts. Libretto by George V. Hobart, lyrics and music by John
L. Golden. Produced at the Knickerbocker Theater on April 27, 1909, with a very
large cast.
191. Musical comedy in three acts. Book by George Grossmith Jr. and Graham Hill.
Revised by James T. Powers. Lyrics by Adrian Ross and George Arthurs. Produced by
Sam S. and Lee Schubert at the Casino Theater on February 11, 1909.
192. From Jacques Offenbach's *Les Contes d'Hoffmann,* "O Belle Nuit" has such a
familiar melody that it was once a staple of simplified piano music, with the name Bar-
carolle, after the type of music it represents, and with words of innocence rather than a
song of the experience of a "nuit d'amour."

of some magnificent stage. —And, after all, to go back, I haven't really forgotten Reading. Yet when you have been away from it for twelve years— as I have— it can't help having grown a little strange—a little unknown—a great deal more, perhaps, than I appreciate. To lose it entirely would be like losing everything— because the thought of it is always with me. There are fugitive moods when it seems quite gone. Afterwards, it comes back as vividly as ever. —And always remember, dear, that I seem to have a way of saying things that I do not mean forever and ever and ever. One's thoughts are like flowing water that reflects new objects at each moment. A letter shows the reflections of the moment when it was written. They may be quite different in an hour. —But I insist on the market-wagons. They come in town at three and four o'clock. There is a lantern on the seat. The driver is huddled up half asleep. The horse slaps his feet on the asphalt. —It is novel, and fascinating. And I agree about the kind-hearted, respectable people—good luck to them—and to everyone. —The clocks strike— ten. Time for the mail-box, and bed.

Your loving
Wallace

⌐⌐

[WAS 1846 May 16, 1909 New York]

Sunday Evening

My dear Girl:

What a day this would have been at Lenhartsville! I lay on the edge of the Palisades basking on a rock and I thought of the top of the Pinnacle—and then of the panorama below. It must be exquisitely green—for the green now is exquisite, so young, so fresh it is. Yet it has been a half-misty day, a steamy day, a day for vegetating. I noticed that the grass has come out of curl and stands high and straight. And such a multitude of flowers—wild honey-suckle, wood-violets, purple and white, strawberry blossoms white as crystals, dande-lions, buttercups—wonderful to see. The dogwood trees were sheer white and the lilac-bushes sheer lilac. I shall put in this letter two flowers the names of which I do not know.[193] I climbed a little way down the side of the Palisades to get them—because I thought that if you had been there you would have asked me to—and so here they are. —And then to lie in the sun for two whole hours in a quiet place and listen to the birds—the bold call, the sweet answer, no less bold, but softer. The woods rang with songs. It was <u>delicious.</u> —There were green beetles crawling around and red ants and fat bumble-bees and mosqui-toes and everything. I ought to write you a long letter and tell you all about it, but I am sleepy, Bo-Bo—and tired. After tea, I went to church, chiefly to rest,

---

193. These blossoms are preserved in the folder for this letter at the Huntington.

but I think bed is the best place—and I shall try to do better to-morrow, or Tuesday. On Saturday afternoon I walked around Prospect Park in Brooklyn—around the outside. It is very large and quite different from Central Park. There was a great patch of peonies that will soon be in bloom. You ought to see the red birds coming out! I remember another patch—two of them—at the entrance to Washington Bridge, that I must pay a visit to next week. —I think they will celebrate Decoration Day on Monday.[194] It falls on Sunday, you know. If they do, that will give us an extra day. Have you seen that they are going to dedicate a new monument at Gettysburg that day? It is to be to the soldiers of the regular army, and the President is going to make an address, and so on. —Is there going to be a parade at home? I should like to see our veterans march once more. There must be few of them left—and it is impressive beyond description. —Good-night, dear.

Your loving,
Wallace

⤳

[WAS 1847 May 17, 1909 New York]

Mon. Evening (or Tuesday morning
—I'm afraid to look at my watch.)

Dearums:

Very flowery—our letters. But mum's the word: and you may send me all of that kind you like. The honey-suckle you enclosed is exactly the kind I saw myself. I don't remember having seen it at home. —You spoke of dogwood the last time we were together. Do you really have that? I never knew of it before I came here. —I've been reading, all evening, a batch of sketches by Richard Whiteing[195]—very light, and in spirit a little disheartening. Whiteing lives in London and I think that one is likely to get these depressing notions more keenly in London, and New York—and in big cities generally, than elsewhere. The conditions of life are so much harder. It is pleasant to think of the sunny villages at home, at intervals along the different roads, by contrast. It is such an enormous relief—yes: enormous! —The truth is, it gets to be a terror here. Failure means such horror—and so many fail. If only they knew of the orchards and arbors and abounding fields, and the ease, and the comfort, and

---

194. Decoration Day (now Memorial Day), first proclaimed on May 5, 1868, by Gen. John Logan, was first observed on May 30, 1868, when flowers were placed on the graves of Union and Confederate soldiers, though the South at first recognized its dead on another day.

195. Richard Whiteing (1840–1928), originally a successful journalist, wrote *The Island* in 1888 and its sequel *Number 5 John Street* in 1889, both critical of accepted social values.

the quiet. —One might preach the country as a kind of Earthly Paradise. —I was very much struck by your remark about knowing people. It was just the wholesome and pleasant kind of thing that is agreeable to hear. What you call my critical spirit is my greatest enemy—and I say most sincerely that anything that helps me get the better of it is balm to my good will. Sophocles, I believe, based everything on knowing one's self and you know the result, the cry

I would I might forget that I am I.[196]

The answer that Jesus made to the lawyer

Thou shalt love thy neighbor as thyself[197]

seems wiser. It is pure sweetness to the critical sense to think of the patience, the endurance, the kindness,—briefly, the virtue—of men and women. And one gets an idea of all that most easily by knowing them. —If I were not so much of a hermit, this primary truth would have been known to me long ago. Loving one's neighbor involves knowing one's neighbor. —It is probably true that the qualities I have mentioned are the "treasure of the humble";[198] but they are treasure for all that. —Indeed, I am getting to a point where I consider that it would be a sufficient achievement to make a little circle happy—so important it seems to me to fix on the essential success, as distinguished from the various vexing objects of ambition. What a pity that wealth and position should confuse us so! —An innocent reverie in the month of May—yet it is the truth. I should be glad, at all events, if that idea stayed with me for a while, as a pause to anxiety (which, of course, is not very pressing at the moment.) —You are invariably right in regard to such matters and I bow to you for not humoring me in cynicism. Just to look at your picture shows how much <u>braver</u> it is to keep one's thoughts to one's self—and to be pleasant. I have a rage for being pleasant—for saying pleasant things. And it is a job for a spiritual Hercules with me. —Whenever you come across sayings that would be useful (I am perfectly serious)—like "Keep a civil tongue in your head" and "When in doubt touch your cap"— send them to me <u>please,</u> so that I may think about them; for I have that part of life to learn—from the alphabet. —You are a dear about La Rue,[199] and her

196. This is sonnet number VII from Santayana's *Sonnets and Other Verses* (New York: Stone and Kimball, 1906); Stevens cites this poem again in WAS 1860 June 22, 1909. Stevens's copy of this Santayana volume, inscribed in his hand ("W. Stevens. / Nov. 22. 1899. / Cambridge."), is in the remains of Stevens's library at the Huntington.
197. Matthew 19:19. God gives the same commandment to Moses in Leviticus 19:18.
198. Maurice Maeterlinck published a metaphysical and somewhat mystical essay "Le Trésor des humbles" in 1896. Stevens's reference to Maeterlinck on January 17, 1909, seems to be to this work.
199. Elsie's half-sister Dorothy LaRue, identified in more detail in chapter 1, note 49, above.

white and blue socks, and all that. Oh, but you are a dear anyhow, Bo-Bo, and if you will take a kiss from such a poor dunce as I am—why, here it is—and more than one. —At least, I can kiss you happily without thinking about it—and it is such an infernal bother to have to think about everything. I wish that old bug-a-boo, Life, took care of itself, or else that one's guardian angel gave one a set of Rules and Regulations at an early age. The philosophers have them all so jumbled up that you can't tell head from tail. —If they keep it up, I shall have to hoist sail for some distant isle and occupy myself with other matters—say, putting salt on elephant's tails, and that kind of thing. —The man at the stamp window has my very best compliments.

Your own
Wallace

⌇

[WAS 1848 May 19, 1909 New York]

Wednesday Evening

My Dearest—

What? Columbine? Well, for auld lang syne[.] —It is such an admirable evening, cool and bright—starry—that I feel a bit like Pierrot—for the moment. And I've been such a sad dog with das Bibel. —I've just come from the Princeton Club[200] where I had dinner with a friend of mine—Reynolds; and afterward we eat [sic] and smoked some very good cigars and talked about fellows we know, and how they are getting along. Then I walked home by way of Union Square (where the benches were cluttered with loafers, snoozing.) —I noticed as I came in that the front of the house is covered with ivy or something like ivy. There is a lamp-post just in front of the door and the under sides of the leaves, looking up, were lampy, and pleasant—and this is a nest after all. —Nothing could be more agreeable than an evening spent in small talk after these rather dull evenings with books. Reynolds is an excellent fellow who keeps up his friends and speaks well of them, which makes it pleasant to know him. He is with Eaton & Lewis—the old firm that I used to be with. —I find that Decoration Day is to be celebrated on Monday—the day following, so that the office will be closed and we shall have an extra day together—and then I shall be back on Saturday of the same week for our own ceremonies. Please put away the pink dress and keep it until then—and that sun-hat, which I have never seen. — I wish I had had a letter from you to-day—a long one, for I should like to read one now, full of fancy and pleasant thoughts. Instead, I'll think them as I drop

---

200. Incorporated in 1899, it occupied the former home of the architect Stanford White in Gramercy Park at this time.

off to sleep—deep down in sleep, out of light, in some cavern. Come like a mermaid, with seaweed and shells, and sing a small romance in that restful cave.

Adieu!

Pierrot

⌐◝

[WAS 1849 May 21, 1909 New York]

Friday Evening

My Lady:

   Third attempt—and it is almost time for the last collection to be made.[201] The other two were not very valuable contributions anyhow, so don't regret them. The first was—you know: dull; the second was—it was all right, but down on the second page I said something twice and—zig!-zag! The truth is, it is a particularly stupid evening—cold, blowy, rainy, what not? And I started wrongly after dinner by reading a book quite empty of inspiration. When there's nothing in a book, one gets nothing at all out of it, like a newspaper. It steals away one's time. The seventy palms of Elim are far better and I hope to find them some day.[202] Over we go.[203] Next to palms are pools and wells. They speak of wells of sweet water in the sea—many more than seventy.[204] I remember delighting in the thought, because a well of sweet water in the sea would be pretty much what a palm would be to the desert. And there you are. (I insist on writing a letter in this tone to keep the rain out of mind—and the window-pane.) —Oh, Lady. Lady, how sick I am of separation—<u>sick.</u> I will not say that I wish you were here—or that I send you a kiss—or that I hope to see you soon. —I am sick of being away from you. —I am like a prisoner deprived of Liberty: you are just that—and all that it means. —Patience—and my love.

Your own

Wallace

⌐◝

201. The envelope for this letter shows that it went out at 2:00 P.M. from the Hudson Terminal Station, a common mailing point for Stevens.

202. Exodus 15:27 (also Numbers 33:9): "And they came to Elim, where were twelve wells of water, and threescore and ten palm trees: and they encamped there by the waters."

203. To the back side of the page.

204. Job 38:16: "Hast thou entered into the springs of the sea? or hast thou walked in the search of the depth?"

[WAS 1850 May 23, 1909 New York]

Sunday Evening

My dear Bo-Bo—

I don't think I did my share of letter-writing last week. It was a deuce of a week, anyhow—with all that cold weather and rain. For all that, it was cold all day to-day—and an unexampled day (at this time of year) for walking. I went out to Englewood first. A little way beyond that village I saw a redbird, or a tanager, or a cardinal-bird. At all events it was a crimsonish red with black wings and a black tail. I sat down to watch it. It seemed to be having a stupid time—rather; —once it sat on a bush for at least ten minutes and did nothing at all. By and bye, I saw a second one—the mate. They seemed marvellously tame—allowed me to walk within four feet of them without flying away. Then I made for some hills and rambled among them all day. About half-past four, when I thought I had been walking Eastward (towards home) for some hours, the sun suddenly came out just in <u>front</u> of me and I realized that I had been walking Westward. Upon inquiring, I was told that I was twenty-eight miles from New-York. I had not had anything to eat since breakfast, it was twenty minutes to five, and I had exactly forty-cents in my pockets! I managed to reach Paterson in a little less than two hours hard walking. From there I went by trolley to Undercliff and crossed the river at 130th Street—with five cents left—To get down town with—and for dinner. Fortunately, I know a fellow on 121st Street. He had just paid the cook! (or so he said). Well, I scraped a little together—enough for this, that and the other—and here I am none the worse. —I had expected to find all the blossoms gone, and they were from the fruit trees. The cherry-trees, in fact, are full of green cherries so soft that you can bite right through what will some-day be a stone. But the dogwood was as fine as ever. There were a number of pink trees which I took for pink dogwood—but they were on lawns and I could not get near enough to them to look at the leaves. —In some out of the way place, there was a really old-fashioned garden, a little gone to weed. Around it was a hedge of <u>arbor</u> <u>vitae</u> high enough to lean against—and strong enough, I really believe, to sit on. In one corner, there was a bush of shrubs—with the richest smell, a thicket of honey-suckle, and a tree hung with wisteria. —But there were many such things—and besides, I was gladder to see the farms in the valley of the Hackensack—to see the market-gardners filling up the lettuce barrels or standing by the barn-doors smoking their pipes and looking over their farms—and to smell the odor of the cows—which I pronounce to be heavenly, nothing less. —Have you noticed how high the wheat is? A little warmth and it will ripen. —Towards evening it grew clear—wonderfully—and I noticed the new moon—like this ☾. Can you tell which part of the crescent (without looking, of course) is toward the sunset? Does it hang this way ☾ or this way ☽? In other words do the horns point toward the earth or toward the sky—down or up? —And the new moon means that we shall have moonlight on both my trips—and long evenings. —During the week I came up here after dinner: it is a bore to walk the streets—and thus I have not appreciated the evenings as they passed—that long hour or two of pure tranquility. But this evening was memorable, particularly for a reflection of orange sunset in a stretch of marshy water. —Ah! but it's Manhattan again—and four millions of us once more. How happy I should be never to see it again! I hate it with particular glee after such a day as this. —Forgive my notes of last week. It was one of those weeks when ink stands still in the bottle. Is that why I didn't have a letter yesterday? —I shall come on Saturday afternoon in time to be up early in the evening, which we can spend for the first time in the open air.

With my love Bo-Bo,
Your Wallace

⌐

[WAS 1851 May 26. 1909 New York]

Wednesday Evening

My own Elsie:—

I've been frivolling at the Phi Gamma Delta Club or something—and walked home, feeling as if I should have had a much better time with Hans Andersen's fairy tales, which I am reading now-a-days. —Different people bring out different things in one and so knocking about has its excitements; yet how few people, after all, bring out anything but gabble and gossip! —I had an argument about religion, my present <u>bête</u> <u>noir</u> (black beetle, says the dictionary.) and it ended as all such arguments ended: in a cigar. —Goodness—that's enough religion—provided, of course, that one has a vigilant conscience. But goodness must be defined, since all people do not have vigilant consciences; and the tangle comes in the different definitions. —I walked home by way of Broadway— same old automobiles, same people along the curb leaning on bamboo canes, same electric signs—and when I turned my final corner, I thought more of the misty moon over the dark house-tops, and offered a little petition to the Weather for fairness at the end of the week. I shouldn't like it to rain; but let us prepare our souls for such a misfortune—for the days have been treacherously fine. —Try to think of some excursion that we can take—some walk, if possible; because I think we enjoy walks best, when they are not too long. And when the first languor of Spring is gone, as it is by this time, walking never tires. I know of one trail we have never followed, up the Tulpehocken to Van Reed's paper mill and then across country to Leesport. Or we might go by train to Womelsdorf and then walk down the Tulpehocken to Bernville and drive from there to Wernersville. But it doesn't matter. The principal thing for both of us is to be together. What a full week of it we shall have! And you will see how glad

I shall be to see you again—even if I should be pompous at first. You won't let me be pompous, will you? I don't want to be. I'm not going to think that I haven't seen you for more than a month. I'll imagine that it was only last week. Don't forget to wear the white dress on Saturday evening. That's the one I like best. Well, I always like you in white best, for all that. —I liked your poetess, although her name was new. The "silver net of rain" was a pretty image; and, as poetry goes, a pretty image is a great deal. It seems, however, that what counts in poetry, is the "noble elucidation of a difficult world," the noble "criticism of Life." The fortunate do not bother their heads about all that. I mean they are fortunate because they don't. Serious views are an offense. Therefore, "silver net of rain" is quite good enough from any point of view. —I have, in reality, never read a great deal of poetry; and yet I could not get on without reading a little. A little satisfies me. In fact, a little of anything satisfies me. There are so many things and I am too curious about all of them to spend much time on one. — Lately, I have thought about Painting. There are pictures quite as wonderful as poems. It seems a tremendous discovery. Some time, when it is possible, with the photographs in our laps, we can make researches together. There is a painting called "La Zingarella" by Correggio,[205] of which I have a photograph, that will be to you, one of these days, when you see it, what that volume of Keats was on the river. Do not look for it. Let me show it to you, by and bye. You will understand then how nice it is for young rabbits to eat wild flowers—in the innocence of their hearts. —But Adieu! That hollow sound of the Elevated late at night comes in at my open window—and my pillow is Peace.

Your loving
Wallace

⌒

[WAS 1852 June 1, 1909 New York]

Tuesday Evening

Dear Buddy:

The tireless Historian traces the plot from its beginning—from the forgotten ride to Riverside and the walk home, to the walk under the locusts, odorous as Asia, under the tulip-tree, up the high hill, beside violets, over the clover-field, down to the cold spring with its roof of spiders, up to the observatory and its airy box of sunlight (a thing to think of in January) where you lay back and looked at the sun through golden eyelids—quickly towards another observatory surrounded

---

205. After this painting, also known as *Madonna del Coniglio* ("Gypsy Girl," or "Madonna of the Rabbit") and *Madonna and Child,* was restored in 1965, the rabbit Stevens refers to was removed. See Cecil Gould, *The Paintings of Correggio* (Ithaca, N.Y.: Cornell, 1976), plates 23A and 23B.

by savage rocks (that eat shoes)—back to a wind-mill and up in the air, where we saw the shadow of the wheel whirling on the trees—toward a bush of yellow roses, guarded by a grand-mother—to stone-house-building with the sandy-haired—to a tea of sardines and bottled milk (in my native land, oh, woe is me!)—to the timely descent into the Valley of Moonlight, to the tale of Big Claus and Little Claus[206] in the arm-chair (where we say—and have said, how often,—"Adieu!" to the rest of the world—the chair of sweet forgetfulness—our Oriental Divan)—to a pleasant morning on the hill, to a pleasanter after-noon behind Mary,[207] the fat and foamy, when we hunted Bob White, and saw and heard him—"Bob White!"—to a walk up to the dark Pagoda,[208] black in a night full of mysterious calm and heavenly beauty (heavenly, of course, as descriptive of the scene), to a memorable smelling of the black-berry blossoms that shone whitely in the shining air, to the old prose of the Springs—and back to our own old comfort—and what one day's absence makes wonderful, and not to be spoken of. I salute you, dear, distant Buddy—as Sleep struggles with me—and send you, if I may, a kiss—quick as thought.

Your own—always your own

W.

The Little June Book[209]
W. S. to E. V. M.[210]
June 5, 1909

I

Morning Song

The blue convolvulus,
Less flower than light,
Ghostly with witchery
Of ghostly night,

Trembles with silver
And magic and dew,

206. This is a reference to the story of this name by Hans Christian Andersen.
207. Their rented horse.
208. The Chinese Pagoda raised on Mount Penn in 1908 is clearly visible in Reading from the main shopping street, Penn Street, as one looks east.
209. These poems were published in *Souvenirs and Prophecies,* 227–34. They are WAS 25 in Box 6, HEH.
210. Stevens always addressed his letters to Elsie V. Moll, her mother's last name after she remarried, but he will decide on Kachel for her last name for the initials on her wedding ring. About the Viola, her middle name, he was not completely certain as late as March 26, 1907.

And the lark sings
On twinkling wings.

O sun, O melting star,
Some sense supreme
Flashes inglorious Life
To glorious dream.

II

If only birds of sudden white,
Or opal, gold or iris hue,
Came upward through the columned light
Of morning's ocean-breathing blue;

If only songs disturbed our sleep,
Descending from that wakeful breeze,
And no great murmur of the deep
Sighed in our summer-sounding trees!

III
A Concert of Fishes

Here the grass grows,[211]
And the wind blows;
And in the stream,
Small fishes gleam:
Blood-red and hue
Of shadowy blue,
And amber sheen,
And water-green,
And yellow flash
And diamond ash;
And the grass grows,
And the wind blows.

211. When Stevens published eight poems (the first poems of his mature career) as "Carnet de Voyage" in *Trend* 7, no. 6 (September 1914): 743–46, five of them came from this "Little June Book": III, "A Concert of Fishes," was published under the title that comes from its first line—"Here the Grass Grows," the third "Carnet"; VIII, "Man from the Waste Evolved," the sixth "Carnet"; IX, "She that Winked Her Sandal Fan," the fourth "Carnet"; XVII, "I Am Weary of the Plum," the fifth "Carnet"; XIX, "Chinese Rocket," the seventh "Carnet." See Edelstein, *Wallace Stevens,* 194–95, for all of the "Carnet de Voyage" titles. "Carnet de Voyage" is published in *OP,* 5–8.

IV

Life is long in the desert,
On the sea, and the mountains.
Ah! but how short it is
By the radiant fountains,

By the jubilant fountains,
Of the rivers wide-sailing,
Under emerald poplars,
With the round ivory paling.

V
Vignette

This, too, is part of our still world:
Night, like a cloud, upon the sea,
Far off from us, full of the stern
Possession of deep-rolling waves;
A broken ship, with empty deck,
Sinking in darkness, all night long.

VI

This is the lilac-bush
Full of the cat-bird's warble,
The singer drunken with song
Of his heart's distillation,
Falling from azure tuft,
From violet spray, and jade,
Down through the dusk of the bush,
To rest in a grassy shade.

Soon again, the happy sound
Will enchant the purple ground.

VII
Noon-Clearing[212]

Now, the locust, tall and green,
Glitters in the light serene.

Leafy tremors shake around
Brilliant showers to the ground.

212. This poem, without the title, was in WAS 1809 January 24, 1909.

At a dart, an oriole sings,
To fluttering of yellow wings!

Sunlight in the rainy tree,
Flash Two-and-Twenty back to me.

VIII

Man from the waste evolved
The Cytherean glade;
Imposed on battering seas,
His keel's dividing blade,
And sailed there, unafraid.

The isle revealed his worth:
It was a place to sing in
And honor noble Life,
For white doves to wing in,
And roses to spring in.

IX

She that winked her sandal fan
Long ago in gray Japan—

She that heard the bell intone
Rendezvous by willowed Rhone—

How wide the spectacle of sleep,
Hands folded, eyes too still to weep!

X

Only to name again
The leafy rose—
So to forget the fading,
The purple shading,
Ere it goes.

Only to speak the name
Of Odor's bloom—
Rose! The soft sound, contending,
Falls at its ending,
To sweet doom.

XI
Shower

Pink and purple
In water-mist
And hazy leaves
Of amethyst;
Orange and green
And gray between,
And dark grass
In a shimmer
Of windy rain—
Then the glimmer—
And the robin's
Ballad of the rain.

XII
In the Sun

Down the golden mountains,
Through the golden land,
Where the golden forests lean,
And golden cities stand;

There I walked in ancient fire,
To many a shining place;
And found around me everywhere
A new, a burning race.

One from hidden capes come home,
One from incessant seas,
One from valleys lost in light,
And all with victories.

No man was hampered there at all,
But lived his visions out.
There was no god's necessity,
Nor any human doubt.

XIII
Song

This is the house of her,
    Window and wall,

More than the house of her:
> Rare omens fall

From the dark shade of it,
> Pleasant to see;
And the wide door of it
> Opens to me.

XIV
In April

Once more the long twilight
> Full of new leaves,
The blossoming pear-tree
> Where the thrush grieves;

Once more the young starlight,
> And a known mind,
Renewed, that feels its coil
> Slowly unbind

Sweeping green Mars, beyond
> Antique Orion,
Beyond the Pleiades,
> To vivid Zion.[213]

XV
Eclogue

Lying in the mint,
I heard an orchard bell
Call the ploughman home,
To his minty dell.

I saw him pass along.
He picked a bough to jog
His single, loathful cow,
And whistled to his dog.

I saw him cross a field,
I saw a window glint,
I heard a woman's voice,
Lying in the mint.

213. At the bottom of one copy of this poem, Stevens lightly penciled in "The Imagi-nation Revised" (*SP,* 232).

XVI

He sang, and, in her heart, the sound
Took form beyond the song's content.
She saw divinely, and she felt
With visionary blandishment.

Desire went deeper than his lute.
She saw her image, sweet and pale,
Invite her to simplicity,
Far off, in some relinquished vale.

XVII

I am weary of the plum and of the cherry,
And that buff moon in evening's acquarelle;
I have no heart within to make me merry,
I read of heaven and, sometimes, fancy Hell.

All things are old: the new-born swallows fare
Through the Spring twilight on dead September's wing.
The dust of Babylon is in the air,
And settles on my lips the while I sing.

XVIII

An odorous bush I seek,
With lighted clouds hung round,
To make my golden instrument's
Wild, golden strings resound,

Resound in quiet night,
With an Arab moon above,
Easing the dark senses need,
Once more, in songs of love.

XIX

There, a rocket in the Wain
Brings primeval night again.
All the startled heavens flare
From the Shepherd to the Bear.

When the old-time dark returns,
Lo, the steadfast Lady burns
Her curious lantern to disclose
How calmly the White River flows.

XX
Pierrot

I lie dreaming 'neath the moon,
You lie dreaming under ground;
I lie singing as I dream,
You lie dreaming of the sound.

Soon I shall lie dreaming too,
Close beside you where you are—
Moon! Behold me while I sing,
Then, behold our empty star.[214]

&

[WAS 1853 June 9, 1909 New York]

Wednesday Evening

My dearest:
    Ten o'clock already and I intended to write to you all evening. After dinner
I gossiped for an hour about Niagara Falls, Queen Wilhelmina of Holland, and
everything else under the sun. Then I came over here and read the Post—and
then tried to think of things for us to remember; additions to the laurel and the
wild strawberries. I could recall only that train of chickens and blackbirds following a plough, and the corn-flowers or poppies (whichever they were) in
the green wheat. We might, possibly, make a special memory of that pond on
the hill, with its population of frogs. It was the typical woodland mirror,
reflecting an over-leaning tree. There was a group of reeds in it. And here and
there were goggle-eyes looking over the calm surface, apparently blind to our
being there. —On Monday night when you and M. S. and A. R.[215] were rambling about, I was sound asleep, for I went to bed at a quarter past eight and fell

214. These poems, written for Elsie's twenty-third birthday, about four months before
Stevens's thirtieth birthday, in the midst of the most thoroughly revealed personal context for any poems Stevens will ever write, are not without the indirection he will more
thoroughly master for the major poems of his career. He has already written fifty letters
in this sequence, and now he will write fifty more letters before being married.
215. Mary Stoner and Anna Rigg, in Elsie's "A Branch of the Bright Family," are
listed as the two bridesmaids at the wedding on September 21, 1909. Mary Ella Stoner
was an 1894 graduate of the Reading Girls' High School, graduate of Bryn Mawr College in 1898, and college instructor in charge of the English and German Department
of The Woman's College, Frederick, Maryland, 1899–1901. Two brothers named
Rigg, living at 220 South Fifth Street in Reading, graduated from Reading High
School in 1891 and 1898, and both became doctor of medicine from the University of
Pennsylvania.

asleep as I pulled the covers over myself—so tired I was. On Tuesday I was as heavy as lead—mentally—and felt incapable even of History. But to-night I begin to feel in possession of myself once more. —It was very pleasant to have a letter from you this morning, and I am glad you wrote without waiting to hear from me—especially such a spirited letter. Curiously, I do not have your feeling about my trip having been long ago (as I sometimes do.) It seems to have been only the other day and it is all perfectly fresh in my mind. Sunday's walk was one of the best we have ever taken and we may both be glad that that lame livery-man was afraid of the mud. No doubt, cherries are already coming into the market and yet the weather can have been of little help. To-day, at least, was pretty much like Friday of last week, although I managed to walk both to the office and from it—with rather muddy shoes (to tell the truth.) —I hope that you will read "The Little June Book," now that it is in your possession. It represents a really considerable amount of pleasant work—and poets, you know, find the greatest delight in giving it. —Your suggestion about the locust tree is capital and we must start a special fund for that purpose one of these days. It would be fine to settle on some plot of ground that we should like to have, some where at home, buy it, plant it, and hold it as a place to build a little home for summers bye-and-bye. Both of us, wherever we may be, will always return to our native "land" as the best place (for us) in the world—and it would be pleasant always to think of some country patch there as entirely our own. But that is one of the things we may keep to dream of. —By the way, I have tried to find out about candy-tuft without much success. It is a branch of the ginger family—whatever the ginger family may be. A lady told me it was like sweet alyssum, but then I do not know what sweet alyssum is like—so there you are. —Flowers are like fairy-tales to me here in New-York: they exist only in books—and florists' windows (which I seldom see.) —Don't you feel as if you would like to stop these long days from ever going? In two weeks they will be growing shorter—not visibly, but on the calendar. That always seems to me like the beginning of another year. —Adieu!

With love,
Wallace

෴

[WAS 1854 June 14, 1909 New York]

Monday Evening

My Lady:—

My pen has rusted in idleness—vile weather—what not. Yet you sent me a letter on Saturday (with tokens of the season.) —Yesterday I went to West Nutley, over in Jersey, and spent the day with Sam Poole and his wife (one of the Sheridans of East Orange) whom I had not seen since their marriage, almost two years ago.[216] They live in the country, next door, in fact, to a large farm, where they get fresh eggs and vegetables. Mrs. Poole does her own cooking—spent most of the day at it, I regret to say. She makes <u>very</u> good muffins in a jiffy. —It was after eleven when I got home, and I was sincerely ashamed that I had not written to you,—and that it was too late to do so. —But now I will settle down after so much gadding about and truancy. —Vile weather, I said, and say again; for to-night it is soggy and hot and full of the feeling of rain. We go by the moon at this season: when the moon changes, the weather will change. —This kind of thing is much worse here than it is in the open air. I mean here in town, where there is no such thing as open air. Whenever I go into the country, I notice how rich and sweet the air is—the open air, by comparison. —And then there is something benumbing-deadening about the evenings. The same people take the same places on the same steps—the library is too stuffy—one doesn't care to read at home. Do you wonder that I have been really homesick? On Saturday I wanted to come home, in old clothes—without all that getting ready—and find you (without thinking of even one kiss) and go off into that ever-dear wild-wood—and have fun with you. And so to forget myself, and the contemplation of men and women and all that kind of thing—to forget every <u>stale, old</u> thing—and be young. —There goes a Catholic church bell—or is it, after all, the Presbyterian one in Twelfth Street? —I need an immense period of country-life—a period long enough to make New-York seem as far off as Boston seems, after ten years. I think I could quite easily sit in my room and do nothing at all except to look at the floor or the ceiling, night after night, waiting for the time to pass. —Now a band is going up Sixth Avenue, with drums and cymbals and horns, and I can hear a mob of boys shouting as they follow it. To-day has been Flag-Day, I believe.[217] The office buildings were all decorated and here and there were men in uniforms. Perhaps, this is the climax of it. —Will you do something for me, Bo-Bo? I wish you would write down for me everything you do—say on Wednesday. Take any day you wish. I asked you to do that once and you did it, and now I am anxious to watch you once more all through one

216. In his journal for February 6, 1906, Stevens writes, "Spent the evening smoking cigarettes with Sam Poole" (*SP,* 159). This is someone he seems to have met while he lived in East Orange, New Jersey, in 1905–6, possibly a fellow boarder. On August 17, 1906, Stevens also wrote, "Last night Poole & I went to a band concert in Brook Branch Park in Newark" and "Tonight—after dinner a harp, a violin, a bad piano, Mrs. Yeager and Louise singing hymns, my rusty guitar in vindictive opposition, bawling crickets, Poole, & Gillis piled up—I fled to the park" (*SP,* 170).

217. June 14, the date on which the Stars and Stripes was adopted as the national flag, was widely celebrated at this time, though Flag Day was not proclaimed nationally until 1916 by President Wilson; in 1949, President Truman signed an act of Congress designating June 14 as Flag Day.

of your ordinary days. It will be like spending something besides a holiday with you—and it will quicken a dull week—I know this one is going to be dull. — Forgive me for being so atrociously stupid to-night. I am not going to stay so, very long. You will see. To-morrow, I am quite sure, I shall be able to send you a wonderfully frivolous letter. I wish I could tonight. But Adieu!

Your

Wallace

⌒

[WAS 1855 June 15, 1909 New York]

Tuesday Evening

My dear:

When I reached the office this morning I said, "I have forgotten to bring Elsie's letter." I thought that I had left it here on my table—and I was glad, after all, because it was to give me a chance to write you more pleasantly than was possible last evening. But alas! I had only forgotten that I had posted your letter last evening and probably you have been wondering to-day (after reading it) what in the world "has got into me." To-night I am greatly improved—for I haven't smoked all day and do not intend to smoke again until next month. Smoking is really the source of all crankiness with me—the root of all evil. Well, why not stop? Because, if I stop, there is that constant thought of it—and abstinence makes me deaf. That sounds strange. But I am quite sane. Yet I will not smoke now for a period no matter what happens. —I have been sitting here reading the <u>Athenaeum,</u> a weekly published in London— "a journal of—Literature, Science, the Fine Arts, Music and the Drama."[218] London continues to be the ultimate point of romance to me. I wish there was some chap there to whom

218. Stevens is reading No. 4257, the issue for May 29, 1909, with a review of *The Springs of Helicon: A Study in the Progress of English Poetry from Chaucer to Milton* (London: Longmans, Green, 1909) by J. W. Mackail (1859-1945) on 640-41. The rest of this material is reported in No. 4258 for June 5, 1909: the report of the Japanese prints at the Fine-Art Society's Galleries on 679; the death of Michiel Johannes de Goeje, "the greatest European Arabist of our time," on 672-73; and the election of Dr. Rendel Harris to an honorary fellowship at Clare College on 675. On at least two more occasions in the future, Stevens will cite from Mackail's *Select Epigrams from the Greek Anthology* (London: Longmans, Green, 1908): in "A Note on Martha Champion," in 1935 Stevens's comments in *Trial Balances* (*OP*, 215-16n328), an anthology of thirty-two young poets paired with an established poet or critic (e.g., the anthology in which Marianne Moore introduced Elizabeth Bishop); and, using the same epigram, three times in "The Effects of Analogy" in 1948, published in *The Necessary Angel.*

I could write for things.[219] I have for a long time wanted a photograph of Professor Mackail, of Oxford. And now they are having an exhibition of Japanese Prints at the Fine-Art Society's Galleries with a catalogue, with notes by Mr. Arthur Morrison, a most important authority on such things. Frankly, I would give last winter's hat for a copy of that catalogue.[220] —The <u>Athenaeum</u> contains a note on the life of a great student of the Arabian, who has lately died—Monsieur de Goeje. It also announced that Clare College has elected Dr. Rendel Harris to Honorary Fellowship, and says that he "is a man of great learning." Such gossip gives me no end of sheer pleasure. —I worship learning in Dr. Harris and I lament the loss of it in Monsieur de Goeje. —Certainly, death causes no greater loss, than when it takes away the scholarship of one wise head. —But speaking of scholars, I note that our ancient L. T.[221] has been awarded honors "in disputation," and has been elected to Phi Beta Kappa, a group of wiseacres, at todays commencement at Princeton. This (owing to my impressions of him) was altogether a surprise. I must moderate my ideas. —Yet it is not all scholarliness with me to-night for I have been looking at a long poem full of

> "The yellow apple and the painted pear."
> in "a land the fairest" where
> "—many a green-necked bird sung to his mate."[222]

Don't you like "green-necked"? It is the best thing of its kind I have heard for a long time—unless "the painted pear" (however old) is better. But all that imagination—how fickle! The delights of the mind seem as little related to its resources, as, say, the windows of a Cathedral to its structure. Pooh! It doesn't matter. —When I read the shining wish at the end of your letter of Sunday afternoon, I regret more than ever that stupid letter of last night—and the general numbness. Forgive it, and forget it quick, dear Bo-Bo. —and think only of "the actual soft, sweet, starry evenings" that we shall have—so soon again, when

219. This wish anticipates Stevens's later practice of having people (from Ferdinand Reyher in England in the late teens to Harriet Monroe's sister in China in the twenties, Leonard van Geyzel in Ceylon in the thirties, and the Vidals in the thirties, forties, and fifties) send him things from many foreign locations, including London.

220. Holly Stevens, in *SP,* points out that "by August he had obtained one, for he inscribed the date on the flyleaf" (235). This catalog is now in the Huntington Library's collection of books Stevens owned.

221. This person will be discussed in more detail in Stevens's letter of June 21, 1909 (WAS 1859).

222. William Morris, *The Life and Death of Jason,* bk. 14, lines 514, 502, and 521.

absence (and its troubles) will be things to forget. —A little kiss, if I am [good] enough,—and my love.

Your
Wallace[223]

⌒

[WAS 1856 June 16, 1909 New York]

Wednesday Evening

My dear Bo-Bo:—

Let us assume that the post-man has forgotten the three packages that came at once, one day last week; for here I am, ready to send my souvenirs of the day—not that this sixteenth day of June has, in any sense, been immortal. No: most fugitive, in fact. Only the morning walk down-town and the evening walk up-town marked it; and those are not specially distinctive markers. —The days are like waves—they roll, and roll, and roll, up the beach, down the beach, out of the sea, into the sea. —Suppose I send you a few of the things that come into my head. I thought of an elm-bordered village-street. That means comfort and quiet and liberal thoughts. It means space to think in—and I greatly fear that young men in attics are desirous of space to think in. They do not have the mild distraction of the people lower down in the house. —I thought, too, (as often as one thinks of a tune) of "green-necked birds." Such a fascinating adjective! I thought of rhymes. There are certain words that have been rhymed together so often that when you hear one you expect the other. It is considered innocent to use them still. For example, "breeze" and "trees." But the critics are too severe in that case. There is only "bees, fleas, sneeze," etc., etc. It is a point in poetical fashion, worth observing. —But these are small things with which to make one day different from another. Usually, the work at the office begins to grow lighter as summer comes on. This year, however, it seems to be growing heavier. I hope that it is a sign of growing business. —They think of closing the office during July and August at half-past four in the afternoon. —Nothing would be more agreeable than a longish walk before dinner: or even if it were impossible to get away from the office with the others, there would still be the pleasure of working there in quietness for an hour or two. —Yet a much better idea would be to move the office to Reading during the summer—up on the hill! I wish, one of these days, in a few years, some capital opportunity would come up at home. Really, it would be great fun to pack up one's things and come back—after twelve years of absence—with the feeling that one was going to stay. June makes me home-sick,—so does July—and August—and September—and October.

---

223. Lack of space at the bottom of the page led Stevens to put his name next to the closing.

After that, and until May, I am perfectly content here—very much so. —Next Saturday I must resume the search for a befitting home. Last Sunday (on the way to Jersey) I came across just the thing—but it is filled up, and there is a waiting list. It is wonderfully difficult to find a nice neighborhood, a nice house and a possible price all together. But of course I will find them before much longer. — The trouble is that Washington Square keeps looking so disreputably full of interest, change,—and actual charm and makes the other places struggle. —I have started to read William Morris' "The Earthly Paradise." It is a tale, more or less—and, like others, has to be well under way, before it becomes readable. —I am sorry I have no candy-tuft to put in my letter—not even a daisy—not even the fiddle-sticks daisy.

Your
Wallace.

⤶

[WAS 1857 June 17, 1909 New York]

Thursday Evening

My lady:

The sweet sound of the down-right rain changes the city into something very much like the country—for rain falls on roofs, pavements, etc. with pretty much the same sound with which it falls on trees or fields: no, trees; for surely it falls on fields (and the grass of them) with a softer sound than this. —So much for the sweet sound of the down-right rain! —The whistles on the river are drowned in it, the noise of the Elevated is swallowed up, a neighborly mandoline is quite lost (except in snatches.) —One long, unbroken, constant sound—the sound of the falling of water. —A sound not dependent on breath. One sound made up of a multitude. A dark chorus blending in wide tone. A numerous sound, to speak so (and it wouldn't be shocking at all.) —A sound native to the mind, remembered by the mind. —Therefore, the ancient and immemorial sweet sound of the down-right rain. —Perhaps, a certain damsel, sits in her porch to-night, with her chin, say, in the palm of her hand and watches—the leaves wet in the lamp-light, the shining street, the water flowing down-hill. —Perhaps, (on the other hand,) she is at her piano— improvising—a "song to a lute at night." But surely there never was a more melodious fall of rain than this—more musical than winter's music-box. —It has been preparing all day. A clear morning drifted into an obscure afternoon and that, in turn, into a cloudy, misty evening—the color of November. At all events, it was interesting, if not exhilarating. —At seven o'clock the top of the Metropolitan Tower (the subject of study just then) was as cloud-capped as Fujiyama, or any marvellous mountain; and it was new to watch the wraiths drift through the upper scaffolding. —Later on, it was new to read of the day's celebration at Dayton, Ohio, to the Wright Brothers, the aeroplanists. The days approach when the aeroplane (it is imaginable) will be "as common as can be"—no more can possibly be said. But these are not especially sacred observations—remunerative, let us say, instead of sacred. It may be, after all, (since the truthful scroll of the day shows it to have been so close to bare existence, compared with zestful living—just as the truthful annals of the world might make similar revelations in glorious history)—it may be that things possible exceed in magic things actual; again, that the journalist, like the novelist, to be most fascinating, should search his heart and not his mind. —It is all a grotesque puzzle. But the heart is the most obstinate thing in the world—and will never pour itself out in ink, as it should, and when it should—for which The Heavens be praised. —"Old Dry as Dust!" cries the crowd. No: only Harlequin, in a poor light. —Perhaps this is not clear. A little mystery, then—deluged with a sound that, all the while, has never stopped—to say it again, the constant murmur of down-falling rain. Only now it seems to grow a little lighter, a little softer—so that there is a path through the weather to the letter-box. Let this bring with it a little of a whole evening's leafy noise—and always the same delight in it.

Your

W.

⌒

[WAS 1858 June 18, 1909 New York]

Friday Evening

Dear Miss Over-the-Hills:—

An old fellow this morning, in Washington Square, said, "Bad spell of weather, eh? Looks better, now the moon's changed. Moon's been lying like this ∪. Bad sign. Should hang like this ⊃. The Indians had a saying 'If you can hang your powder-horn to the moon, don't go hunting.'" —A turquoise sky all day—it seemed as if it might be like the sky of the West Indies. And at noon the light in Nassau street was beautifully bright. —This evening, too, Eleventh Street streamed with gold (and last night's rain seemed imaginary.) —A walk led me through Washington Square. From the easterly side, it was miraculous, with the fountain white in the strange air. Then through the East Side—the junk-shops, fruit-stands, bakeries, clothing stores, bird stores—through Jews, Italians, Roumanians, Galatians—through countless children (one does not usually get beyond middle life down there)—out and up and over the Williamsburg Bridge. —It was just like climbing a ladder and so getting out of a mob. How wretched! Here's what it was like—since it led into the sunset—it was like the experience of whoever-it-was that was carried up through the air in a chariot of

fire.[224] Especially coming from the Brooklyn side back to the New-York side—
it was altogether like a chariot of fire. —And such a stupendous survey as it gave
of other sparkling bridges, grey towers, the whole silhouette of the western city.
—In all the windows (at about eight o'clock) there were cadelabra [sic]. To be
correct: they were on tables in the centre[225] of the rooms. Around the tables sat
the fat elders—observing the custom. To-morrow, you understand, is Sunday
for them; and it commences at sun-down tonight. You have a clear description:
the neighborhood twinkled. It suggested a mid-summer Christmas. —How
true it is that the sun "makes bliss of all"! If it shines to-morrow as it did to-day,
will there be a soul left under cover? —One can fancy the green snoozers in the
depth of the sea, smitten by unaccustomed beams, groping with starry snouts in
water the color of smoke. But it is not our affair to follow the beams of the sun,
which, quite likely, do not limit their adventures to falling on the gross serpents
of submarine slime! —Oh, enough trifling. It was much nicer with the candles
and the candle-sticks and the chariot of fire and the new moon. —But since we
have spoken of sea-ful things, observe

> How nigh to Cyprus, ruddy as the rose,
> The gold sea grew, as any June-loved close.[226]

We are never so <u>very</u> far from each other, and our own country—let's call
<u>that</u> Cyprus—full of June—loved closes. —But now to be reasonable and
clear: Saturday is to be for rambling in search of the befitting home, and Sunday is to be filled with a sacred walk (with every-day excursions into cherry-
trees, if any should appear.) —Adieu, then, and remember that you, too, must
sun or be sunned upon, or whatever it is they say. Report the blazing hour. —
You will have burning volumes from

Your own

Scribe and Learned Hand.

⌒

224. In 2 Kings 2:11: "And it came to pass, as they still went on, and talked, that, behold,
there appeared a chariot of fire, and horses of fire, and parted them both asunder; and
Elijah went up by a whirlwind into heaven."

225. An important street near Stevens's boyhood home was named Centre, and thus
he spelled the word all his life. In a letter to his editor at Knopf as late as January 27,
1950 (WAS 3305 at HEH), Stevens says, "Center is correct. One of the principle
streets in the place where I come from is called Centre Avenue. I have never quite been
able to shake it off."

226. In WAS 1860, Stevens will indicate that "June-loved close" came from William
Morris's *Earthly Paradise*. Part 4, lines 155–56 of that work are "How anigh Cyprus,
ruddy with the rose / The cold sea grew as any June-loved close."

[WAS 1859 June 21, 1909 New York]

Monday Evening

My dear—Bo-Bo:—

Not a bad Saturday afternoon and Sunday. To report on the befitting home: it must, I fear, be up-town. The place I wanted to have you see in Washington Square is quite out of the question; and inquiry at neighboring places makes them seem equally prohibitive. —It is tiresome work, especially when you know beforehand that the nicest places are only made to look at, like bakers' windows. —So that it is only a report of progress, with nothing definite. —On Saturday evening I went to the Astor Library at seven and read for an hour—including the definition of candy-tuft in several dictionaries. Candy doesn't mean candy—it means Candia, which was a name for the island of Crete. Candy-tuft is, therefore, Candian tuft or Cretan tuft. There were pictures of the plant, of the flower, and of the seed—and I don't care for any of 'em. A little after eight I thought of Sir Charles Wyndham who was playing a little comedy called "The Mollusc"[227] at the Empire; so I hurried over to Broadway, took a car and shortly "found myself" au théâtre. It was an amusing little play, principally concerned with a woman requiring a good deal of waiting on—and the breaking of the habit. Wyndam is over sixty and Mary Moore: the mollusc, is about fifty-eight. There were only four people altogether in the cast—and the same scene all the way through. —And when Sunday morning came around I didn't in the least feel like taking that long walk in Jersey. I loitered over breakfast and then wandered up town until I was near the Park—entered it, made a circle in it and came back to my room to read the papers. —Then, after dinner (you do not mind my making a chronicle, for a change, I hope) I went to the Park in Brooklyn. They have a rose garden there very much worth while—like this.[228] The three round rings are three fountains, or basins of water. The things around them are beds of roses. The thing marked x is a rose arbor. It is just like a long grape arbor only covered with roses. The whole garden is surrounded by heavy foliage. The air is sweet—distinctly; and it is a beautiful place to see. —Near-by is what is called the Vale of Cashmere. In the centre is a fountain. The sides are slopes planted—like a jun-

227. Comedy in three acts by Hubert Henry Davies, produced at the Garrick Theater on September 1, 1908. "Sir Charles Wyndham's London Company played 'The Mollusc' for two weeks at the Empire Theatre, New York, beginning June 7, 1909." *The Best Plays of 1899–1909,* ed. Burns Mantle and Garrison P. Sherwood (New York: Dodd, Mead, 1944), 566–67. The play had been revived so that New Yorkers could see the original London cast: Wyndham as Tom Kemp and Mary Moore as his sister, whom he forces into activity.

228. Across the width of his page, he draws a diagram with three one-quarter-inch circles in a line, each with three or four shapes like *p*s arranged around their periphery; under these circles, he gives dotted parallel lines with an *x* between them.

gle of rhododendrons. Again—it is a beautiful place to see. —I crossed from the Park to the Brooklyn Museum and looked at an exhibition of water-colors by Sargent. He is the man that painted the lady in the brilliant dress at the Philadelphia exhibition. —They were interesting and full of bright color—scenes in Portugal, Spain, Italy, Turkey, Africa. But museums are stuffy at this time of year and I didn't stay very long. —I went down to Brighton Beach (with dusty shoes) and saw two memorable things, first: the sea full of bathers (memorable because unexpected); and, second: a sea of green parasols (last year's perhaps) around a band-stand where a large band was grinding out Wagner. —I followed the board-walk to Coney Island where I went to catch a train—and incredible as it may sound I was home again in time for tea. —At the tea-table some one said that it was the longest day in the year. To-day was, in fact, but I thought yesterday was until I saw this mornings paper. A celebration seemed desirable; so I went uptown to get the long sunset—and took all evening to get home. —There was an air-ship over the Palisades. —And at ten o'clock I was home in bed trying to get to sleep. —The longest day in the year—and the first day of summer. How long a wait we have had for it to come! —Yesterday I found some cut grass that dried in the sun and, while it was warm, smelled of August—the dry season. Dryness has a welcome sound after all our showers. —In two weeks more I shall be home. Do you think we could arrange an "outing" somewhere? I wish we could go away for a few days. But, of course, we couldn't, since we shall have only two days. But why not take down a map of old Berks and see if there isn't some fascinating place to go to—North, South, East or West. Whatever else we do, we must certainly have a picnic: old <u>clothes,</u> you know—and bread and butter. We might make that long-talked of trip along the Tulpehocken. We could take a train to Womelsdorf and walk from there to Bernville in one day. At Bernville you could (or couldn't you—or wouldn't you care to) stay with "those people" and I could go to the Eagle Hotel or Mansion House, or whatever it is.[229] Then on the following day we could continue our trip. I think that would be lots of fun—no white gloves, no parasol, no powder-puffs, or things. What do you say? You know, if we stay in town, it isn't such indescribable fun on the Fourth of July. Or we might get Mrs. A. or somebody and go to that place we were last Fall—upon my word, I forget the name—if Benj.[230] and Mrs. Benj. and the Benj. maids and dogs and chickens, etc., etc. can be got to agree. You remember that they were in a dozen different frames of mind last year. You would have to call

---

229. Robesonia, near Womelsdorf, had both an Eagle Hotel and a Mansion House hotel at this time. See *Passing Scene* 9:194. A streetcar line went from Reading to Womelsdorf, about fifteen miles. This suggested walk would have been on the banks of the Tulpehocken Creek, their favorite area for excursions.
230. This seems to be an abbreviation, perhaps for Benjamin.

them up on the telephone and make arrangements. —Or have you thought of something better than all this? If you can, do. —I know just what people are doing in Reading to-night. They are sitting on steps and porches—wishing for things. "I wish I was in Mars." "I wish I had all the money in London." "I wish," etc., etc. Only the old people no longer wish, but say, "John married Mary Hinkle's sister Kate and moved to Philadelphia. I remember, etc., etc." How well content I should be to sit with you, Bo, and overhear all that—the peculiarities of Effinger's grand-pop, the strange adventures of a friend of a lady "whom I knew" (cries the mistress of the saxaphone.) —That was a gorgeous letter you sent me— on Saturday. You say L.I.T.[231] But this youth's name was Ralph L. T. and he was from Lewisburg, Pennsylvania.[232] Perhaps, it was altogether another T. Permit me to say (without the slightest feeling) that I should be greatly surprised to have L. I. T. distinguish himself. Even if this was the same T. my surprise remains. He struck me as particularly—bother with him. And what the deuce is "disputation?" —But adieu! adieu! "The conspirators are at hand! Quick! Quick! My Lady. The secret staircase." _ _ _ _ _ _ A breeze has sprung up, most pleasantly. They all complain of the heat. It has not seemed bad to me. —Heat is infinitely more to my taste than cold—and I think to yours, too, isn't it? But why discuss it? Adieu!

Your

Wallace

❧

[WAS 1860 June 22, 1909 New York]

Tuesday Evening

Dear Beauty:

Think of it! Your rose had little yellow things in it—that gave one a creepy feeling. They all do unless you watch them, powder them, wash the leaves off, etc. But then you're not a gardener. —It was like getting close to you again to have a letter from you, nevertheless, —and a letter written in good spirits. (I do

231. Elsie has probably guessed someone near her age, Llewellyn I. Thomas of the class of 1905 of Reading Boys High, listed on page 273 of the *Graduate Catalogue of the Reading High Schools: 1856–1905,* as being from Burnham, Mifflin County, Pennsylvania, and attending St. John's College in Annapolis, Maryland.
232. Ralph Llewellyn Thomas (1887–1965) is not listed as a graduate of the Reading High Schools, but he graduated Phi Beta Kappa and near the top of the Princeton class of 1909, did graduate work in electrical engineering at MIT in 1911–12, and had a distinguished career as an executive in the electric power industry. His connection with Elsie and Stevens might have come from the fact that his father was the pastor of the Presbyterian Church in Lewisburg, Pennsylvania, and that he had two sisters and three brothers. (The Reunion Books for the class of 1909 and the student folder for Thomas at Princeton provide more information on him.)

not mean to say that they are not <u>all</u> written in good spirits. But you know what I mean.) —One point: you may be glad that your feelings are beyond analysis and description. What is it Santayana says—

> Wretched the mortal, pondering his mood.[233]

There is little dispute that anything like constant observation of one's own moods (experience being what it is) is a distress. My journal is full of law on the subject—only it is too warm a night to cite authorities for anything. —Be glad that you are beyond yourself—and never study anything, please, except combinations of colors, varieties of powder—and other really interesting and amusing things. —Whatever life may be, and whatever we may be—<u>here we are</u> and <u>il faut être aimable:</u> we must be amiable, as the French say. —The dickens with moods. That will be your chief difficulty with me. I am pretty grumpy now and then—although always sorry when I am, and more sorry afterwards. —The Dutch are all like that—as weird as the weather. —We'll find a way, however—and perhaps it won't even be necessary. —The dickens with that kind of thing, too. It is much better to try to hide our weaknesses than to point them out and say—"Beware." So, kind Miss, forget that I am "pretty grumpy now and then"—and depend on it that you will never find out. —(Do you remember that scandalous afternoon when we walked over Mount Penn and rode on the side of the sleigh? Phew!—give me a kiss, Bo-Bo,—I am really quite sorry.) —But the dickens, the dickens, the dickens—I haven't any faults, and I'm not sorry about anything at all, and it would be too hot to say so even if I were. —Fe, fo fum! The Tulpehocken walk would be too much I think. Don't you think <u>two</u> picnics would be better—one, say, up the Maidencreek—and the other somewhere else—and then we could get home for the evenings. —Can you preserve cherries? That's a perfectly nice thing to do. Why don't you preserve about a dozen jars—for Sunday nights next winter? That would be lots of fun. If I were in Reading I think I'd preserve 'em myself. (You don't like me to say 'em, do you?) —And what were you reading the other afternoon in the hammock? I'm still at "The Earthly Paradise" and if I come across any more phrases like "June-loved close" I shall send them to you. At noon to-day I went up town to get some lectures delivered at Oxford—but they wouldn't interest you, I imagine. If my books were unpacked I think I'd read Hardy again. As it is, I have every intention of reading "Endymion" before I come home—and perhaps not much more. —I love to loaf on summer evenings, but I cannot do it with any pleasure among strangers; and so this summer I shall keep close to my room.

With love,
Wallace

233. From sonnet VII in Santayana's *Sonnets and Other Verses,* cited above in WAS 1847 May 17, 1909.

⤙

[WAS 1861 June 23, 1909 New York]

Wednesday Evening

My Dearest:—

Ten o'clock—and I must be lively, if this is to reach you to-morrow. This evening three of us walked up-town. One of the three was from Baltimore. He is going to move to New-York and I was showing him likely places to live. Then we went to the Lafayette and had dinner together—and afterwards I smoked a big Havana cigar, the first one in ten days. But I shall go without again to-morrow. It is very <u>much</u> better to go without in such weather. And after dinner, we rambled around until a few minutes ago. —I need not say how hot it is—and I wish I might borrow your dozen clouds to sleep in (provided, of course, they were cool clouds—and pleasant.) How pretty that part of that letter was! It will be great fun one of these days to look through our <u>nice</u> letters. The bad ones (mine) we must have the courage to destroy. —I am thinking of going to Manhattan Beach next Sunday for my first swim. The sand is always as hot as an oven, and the water as cold as a Polar stream; yet between the two one winds up feeling like a lion—or a modern Samson. —If I may say so, the water in the tub is still really chilly and my plunges in the morning are as bracing as if I took them in a mountain pool—as I wish I did—one those rushing pools in the Rockies filled with water from the melted snow on the peaks—always strong and rushing towards the end of the day. —The wheat will soon be yellow and the corn is undoubtedly high and the birds of high color are in the Northern woods—in Canada and the forests of Labrador. But those at home, in their new nests, will be company enough for us. —Good night—dear Bo-Bo. A real kiss.

With love, your
Buddy

⤙

[WAS 1862 June 24, 1909 New York]

Thursday Evening

Dear Bo-Bo:

You ought to receive in the same mail with this some new post-cards, just from Europe, which Mr. Stryker[234] brought along from Baltimore for me, and

234. Heber H. Stryker, a colleague of Stevens's at American Bonding Company, would move to Hartford by 1913 and play a role in Stevens's social life and in his move there. Brazeau says that through Stryker (with the help of the Heubleins), "Stevens had an entrée to Hartford's social and cultural elite from the outset" (*Parts of a World,* 241). In 1913, Stryker was a vice president and secretary of the First Reinsurance Company of Hartford, and he later (at least by 1930) became its president. Stevens visited the

which I send you in a separate envelope.[235] —The one called "Puente de Alcán-tara" shows a very famous and beautiful bridge—"The Alcántara Bridge" at Toledo in Spain. Note the beautiful arch at the right hand side. The tower at the left hand side was, doubtless, fortified. Nothing could show better the parched, half-desert condition that is so common in Spain. A team of donkeys is drawing a big-wheeled Spanish cart over the bridge. The houses of the town seem to be all white, with low roofs. —Biarritz is one of the great watering-places of Spain. "A travers les tamaris" means "Through the tamarisks." Tamarisks are, of course, trees. They grow in this country, in the Adirondacks, and in the Rockies, although I have never seen one so large as the one in the picture. Look at the sea-wall and rocks and the sails bleaching on the sand. The second card from Biarritz shows the rocky coast. "La loge de théâtre" means "the theatre box" and the cave is certainly placed very much like a box at the theatre, don't you think? —I remember a very striking picture by Sorolla at the exhibition of his paintings here in New-York last winter—full of celestial sunshine. —And I remember that Bismark, the great German statesman used to go to Biarritz and loaf in quiet corners on the shore to rest. —The last card merely shows an hotel in Paris. Yet it shows, too, one of those long streets lined with trees for which Paris is (among other things) celebrated. I have no doubt that we shall see Paris together one of these days and, perhaps, stroll along this very <u>Avenue Friedland.</u> —I had a letter from you this morning. We will do whatever you like when I am at home—although I hadn't really thought of much walking in the sun. The Bernville trip was, after all, entirely too ambitious. If we could go somewhere in the cool of the trees—that we both should like. I am never tired of pic-nics— and it is never an old story. Yet even if it was an old story—going pic-nic-ing, why "all things are old" and it is only the pleasant choice that we happen to make, in this, or that, or anything, that amuses; and on holidays one desires to be amused. —What were you doing when you almost—? I cant imagine—unless it was stirring up those cherries, or bending over a new waist! Tell me. We have

---

Strykers often enough to get familiar with their neighborhood, and from 1924 until 1932, Stevens and his wife lived in a two-family house at 735 Farmington Avenue in West Hartford, just around the corner from Arnoldale Road, where Stryker and his wife lived when they first came to Hartford. (See *LWS*, 169, and the note on 242; also see *All in the Family*, the monthly publication for representatives of the Fidelity and Deposit Company of Maryland and the American Bonding Company of Baltimore, vol. 11, no. 6, June 1930, for a description of a reunion of American Bonding Company alumni and an extensive list of important people in surety and casualty, including Stryker, Kearney, Collins Lee, and Paul Rutherford, as well as a few judges such as Arthur Gray Powell of Atlanta. Stryker, one of the organizers of this reunion, is described as "a master of anecdotes.")

235. These cards are not in the Huntington folder for this letter.

had the same weather here, for three or four days, and to-day was the hottest of all. My room is a furnace as usual—but then I haven't got everything I own on at the moment—oh, far from it, and that makes a difference. The "paper" says that we are to have rain—probably to boil us, after we have been roasted. Yet I can say quite honestly that I prefer this, hot as it is, to anything else—not so much in town, it is true—but how splendid it must be at the sea-shore, and in favorable places in the country. In town, in fact, the weather doesn't make a great difference, because there is no time to think of it—and besides, it is always decent at the office. —After dinner to-night I sat out-doors for a while. A man with a harp came along and played across the street—and may be playing yet. Yet a harp is a poor thing to play in the street. No one could imagine, to hear it, how wonderful it is in an orchestra—in good music—when, for example, there is a pause and suddenly (while you wait for the next sound) arpeggios and long runs thrill over it—and the violins begin again, and all the rest. —Music is far away. I wish I could remember "La Crepuscule"—but everything turns into "A Shepherd's Tale" sooner or later. Jot down two bars for me—like this, a, b sharp, a, d, etc.—whatever it may be, so that I can pick it out. Don't forget because I want something new to hum. This is the season for humming—and humming. —Did La Rue "get promoted"? I hope so. —Good-night, Bo-Bo.

With much love,
Wallace.

⤳

[WAS 1863 June 25, 1909 New York]

Friday Evening

My dear:—

A thunder-shower at the end of the day (as I came up town) has cooled the air out of the house—and I sat gossiping with two <u>white-haired</u> school-teachers until nine o'clock. They are both very agreeable—one of them spent several months at Wernersville, for her health, a number of years ago, and likes to praise the beauty of the country there. She remembers that it is "frightfully cold" there—in the cold season. —At noon I bought two boxes of cherries and this evening I gave them one—and they made lemonade in return—very tart. —In a boarding-house, you know, the people talk about one another. The great question with us is whether or not a certain Captain Ffolliott is going to marry the landlady. He is a book-keeper and has jaundice and it would be a very good match for him ("a place to hang his hat") and an abominable one for her. He brings her a bouquet every Sunday and they spend their evenings together—and it is a long story about two quite ordinary people. —When I was buying the cherries I noticed peaches, plums, apricots, fresh tomatoes and all the usual things. Decidedly, a market is a pleasant place with its stalls of silvery fish, red fruit—and so on; and I do not wonder (altogether) that people have painted such things almost as frequently as they have painted the shadows of poplars, of which you spoke. —But it has been too hot for anything to happen. I am impatient for Saturday afternoon and Sunday to come around, so that I can get into shape again. Yet they are almost the hardest part of the week to get through because one never knows just what to do—and not to do anything at all would be disappointing "beyond all whooping."[236] —Anyhow, I shan't go house-hunting, which can very well go over until after my trip to you, for even if I found what I wanted I shouldn't know what to do with it a whole summer ahead of time. My rambles are chiefly to find out where to look when the time comes. —Take a little walk on Sunday. Your flowers will take care of themselves. Adieu!

> Your loving
> Pen Man

∽

[WAS 1864 June 27, 1909 New York]

> Sunday Afternoon

My dearest girl:—

A day meant for a country ramble (an old thing—old as the hills—but always a pleasure) has been spent here in my room, at work for five hours on a tangled piece of business, to the accompaniment of thunder, lightning, rain, heat, canary birds, pianos, mandolines, and talking machines. One of the machines has been singing, "Oh, you'll have to sing an Oirish song if you want to marry me";[237] and now it is grinding out a bass solo, with a sound like a whale in agony. —But yesterday afternoon Kearney and another fellow and I went down to Manhattan Beach and had a swim. The water was cold—too cold to stay in; and the sand wasn't much better. You can imagine what a crowd had gone down on account of the heat. There wasn't a foot of room to spare on the raft. —The showers have made it a little cooler this evening (it is about half-past five) and as it is more or less clear, I think I shall take a walk up to the Park, after we've had tea, then come home early and go to bed. —I've started "Endymion" and find a good many beautiful things in it that I had forgotten, or else not noticed. I wonder if it would be possible for a poet now-a-days to content himself with the telling of a "simple tale." With the growth of criticism, both in understanding

236. Possibly an allusion to Celia's speech to Rosalind in Shakespeare's *As You Like It* 3.2.191–93: "O wonderful, wonderful, and most wonderful wonderful! and yet again wonderful, and after that, out of all whooping!"
237. This was the hit song of Florenz Ziegfeld's *Follies of 1908,* sung by Nora Bayes (1880–1928), a popular vaudeville singer and comedienne.

and influence, poetry for poetry's sake, "debonair and gentle"[238] has become difficult. The modern conception of poetry is that it should be in the service of something, as if Beauty was not something quite sufficient when in no other service than its own. —There has been a popping of fire-crackers for a day or two, a sure sign that the Fourth is on its way. It is like reading the future to see it coming—rather, to hear it. —More anon.

Your
Wallace

∽

[WAS 1865 July 2, 1909 New York]

Friday Morning

My dear Bo-Bo:

I've been keeping in the dark all week so as to be more mysterious to-morrow. This is a word before breakfast to say that I shall come on the train that leaves here at five o'clock to-morrow afternoon. That will put me home about half-past eight and I can come up at once. Don't you think that that is better than to meet you somewhere—especially as I cant think of any place? It will be dark except for the first beams of the lantern of the m—n. —This is the earliest letter I have ever written, I think.[239]

Yours
Wallace

∽

[WAS 1866 July 6, 1909 New York]

Tuesday Evening

My dearest:

(So much dearer than I express—believe it—please). —I have been worried to-day by the thought that, perhaps, I made a bad impression on you last night after we had reached home, and particularly while we were saying, "Good-bye." I do not know just what it was: something vague. —You saw me thread-bare—for I am thread-bare when I stand beside you, dear, spouting those long sentences. You don't say much, but I don't believe the smallest thing escapes you. And I don't like to be seen thread-bare. —The purple robe must, of course, be laid aside now and then; but never, I hope, entirely lost sight of. — But if this is all my own imagination, re-assure me in your first letter. I shall send

---

238. This phrase is from Keats's "To one who has been long in city pent."
239. Postmarked at 10:30 A.M. and received in Reading at 7:00 P.M. (as stamped by the post office on the rear of the envelope), this letter would let Elsie know on Saturday morning that Stevens would be arriving that evening.

this to-night, so that you will have it to-morrow, before you write. —After all, let these little moments be swallowed up in our great ones. (Confound it, how is a sleepy fellow to write to the tune of a street-organ and a bag-pipe? Does Puck, the comic spirit, intervene to spare further melancholy? A bag-pipe is the acme of silliness.) —It is, no doubt, best; and I turn from my woe-begone self to that immense scene we drove round-about in for two days—a pleasanter thing to observe than the compunction of an uneasy lover. In May, it was a place of new green; in June, of new flowers; in July, of wheat and wheaten-fields—the first fruits of the ground which seems not so long ago to have been all snow, or all cold, barren rain. Sing a hymn to Ceres, the goddess of wheat and wheaten-fields—she that follows the plowman and goes before the reaper; and to Priapus, the rugged god of gardens, now in his season of plenty; —and to all gods of summer and the long season, just beginning, that never goes before the hunter's horn challenges. —Yet it is true that the whole heart (in me) no longer joins in such a hymn:

> Art thou less beautiful, or I more dull
> O Nature, once my passion and delight,
> How shall I win thee?—
> By me thy skiey splendours are unwatched,
> By me thy changeful year unheeded flies—
> Time was, I thought, that thou to me hadst given
> The dearest boon imparted from above,
> The greener meadow and the bluer heaven,
> With the deep heart of wonder and of love,
> But now, the sharer of a common lot,
> I only wonder that I wonder not.[240]

I could say two things of this, first: that it is not altogether true of me; and second that nothing could be more true. Holly-hocks, such as we saw, should be more than French-looking and pretty; and roadside patches of white roses should have more than a white smell. Yet should they? Should they or shouldn't they? I think I could argue <u>successfully</u> either way. —And our two July morns— one blazing like the very crown of heaven—one as red as the shield of the god Mars. Yet I felt quite tranquil at the sight of them—even at the sight of the Silver River and the immense multitude of stars. —But I swear this is all nonsense. No: I swear it is the truth. Yet we both saw:

The greener meadow and the bluer heaven

---

240. "Omnia Mutantur" by E. H. Brodie, from his *Sonnets* (G. Bell & Sons, 1885). Stevens will quote a line of this just below.

I would give a year of life to spend this summer at home with you—so that I might fall back into that "passion and delight"—in so many well-remembered places. Books are a vexation, thought is a waste, work is idleness so far as living is concerned. Suppose I could waken in the country in the morning—to-morrow—and know that morning after morning I should do the same. O Nature, (horrid word,) then I should win you! One small indigo bird would be no more than one of all the birds of summer. —Dear, I am afraid that I should keep all this a secret—especially since it is about myself; but if I share a secret with you, it is still a secret—and you have your charity in keeping it. —Pshaw! What cannot be, cannot be; and I mean to go to bed early to-night and be at the office early to-morrow and toss things around. At thirty (or almost) one has to be practical. The deuce! —I am going to write to you a little every day—not a word about myself for a long time—and so gossip with you, if I may. I want to do it, and I am glad you liked it before, and I hope you will write very often to me. —By the way, if I said anything about September that you wish I had not said, believe that it was entirely thoughtless and I am sincerely sorry. I do not quite understand why we should not talk over even the small details together and be absolutely in each other's confidence. But we agreed not to, and it was an offense to have done so after that. You must forget it. —I expect to come again towards the end of the month—just when, I'll hide and surprise you, Bo-Bo. —Being tired, seems to make me humble, don't you think? And so, humbly, I send you a good-night kiss, and every bit of my love.

> Your
> Wallace

↩

[WAS 1867 July 7, 1909 New York]

Wednesday Evening

My dearest:

I read in "Endymion" before breakfast

> A homeward fever parches up my tongue
> Oh let me slake it at the running springs!
> Upon my ear a noisy nothing rings—
> Oh let me once more hear the linnet's note![241]

Yet that mood had been considerably eased by last night's long, solid sleep. —True, my fancy still dallied, as ever, with "noisy nothings"; but the streets were cool and full of people—and they enlivened me. —To-night I went up to Central Park and walked around the reservoir. Once as I stood looking at the

241. Book 2, pp. 320–23.

reflection of the sunset in the water a fish leapt above the surface after a fly—and later, farther away, after another. —It looks like another perfect night, and like another perfect day to-morrow. —Pete and Kate must wonder where we are—in their dark, cool stalls, and wish we'd turn up for another jaunt along the country roads. The next time we go we must take some apples along for them—unless you have a little loaf of sugar. I should think that sugar might be welcome after a few quarts of oats! —I enclose an extract from an address by M. Jusserand, the ambassador from France, made at Ticonderoga yesterday, at the celebration of the discovery of Lake Champlain, which I think will interest you. It seems to me to be a model of what such an address should be.[242] —There were other incidents but these you can look for in the Eagle. —By the way, was that noise

---

242. This address of M. Jusserand concerned principally the history of battles between the French and English, in years gone by, in this vicinity, and the bravery of Montcalm, the French soldier and victor of Ticonderoga, 150 years ago. He said in part:

In this same month of July, three centuries ago, this lake with the fine forests bordering it then on every side, was seen for the first time by a white man, as good a representative as one could wish of the white race, Samuel de Champlain, the navigator, the explorer, the honest man, the founder of Quebec. In this same month of July, a century and a half ago, was fought, on this same spot, one of those battles where so much valor was shown on both sides that the vanquished carried away with him, while leaving the field, the esteem and admiration of the victor. In the long wars between France and England, whatever may have been the changeful issues of each contest, such an occurrence was the usual one. The two nations could detest, they could never at heart scorn each other.

The winner of Ticonderoga was one of the soldiers France can be most proud of—Montcalm, whose life was short, but every day of which was spent in the service of his country. He belonged to a fighting race. He was, however, one of those soldiers who believed that to be a good fighter, one did not have to be necessarily ignorant, and that one could enjoy the beauty of a verse without the edge of the spirit being blunted.

Another charming trait in Montcalm's personality, was his fondness for his mother, for his wife and children. Married young and the father of ten children, he kept his wife informed of all that happened to him, in witty, good-humored letters, recalling those of another young French officer, Lafayette, was to write later to his own wife, also from America.

The French are sometimes said to like to brag; great Shakespeare is somewhat hard on them on this account. The taunt may, however, well be disputed. It certainly does not apply to Montcalm, either living or dead; modest enough is what our best books of (those from which the public at large gather their information) have to say concerning what happened on this spot a century and a half ago. In his hour of triumph, Montcalm had rendered full justice to his enemies. When he fell, his enemies nobly requited him; they gave him an equal share in the honors rendered to the memory of their own Gen. Wolfe,

we heard on Monday night the bursting of our jug of wine, as I thought? —I hope I shall have a letter for you to-morrow, with full accounts of the sun-burn and so on. My own face is all crinkled up. —I expect to take dinner to-morrow evening with E. Bechtel,[243] a fellow from Reading, at the Harvard Club, and so assuage the "homeward fever."

Your

Wallace

⌒

[WAS 1868 July 8, 1909, New York]

Thursday Evening

Dear Bo-Bo:

Bechtel told me a good story to-night. It was about a Pennsylvania Dutch-man that went to the World's Fair. When he had been there a day he wrote a post-card to his wife; and this is what he said:

---

and the same column commemorates in Quebec the similar virtues of the two opponents. On the tomb of Montcalm, in the Ursulines Convent at Quebec, one of the finest inscriptions ever devised for the sepulture of a hero has been engraved: it is in French and it means: "Honor to Montcalm. Fate, while deny-ing him victory, has recompensed him by a glorious death." What true insight into a hero's heart is shown by the choice of that word "recompensed." The inscription is due to Lord Aylmer, Governor of Canada in 1831.

Years have passed; on these happy shores guns have long been silent; the feeling around the just-now rebuilt fort of Ticonderoga have changed; the colonists of yore, who had played an important part in the fight, now belong to a great and independent nation, the United States, the friend of the former enemies, those two liberal countries, France and England.

As for France and England themselves, they have, of late, given to the world the example of settling all at once the whole series of their secular quar-rels and difficulties, without even having recourse to arbitration. In medieval times, France and England have known the horrors of a hundred years' war. The time is not far distant when they will be able to celebrate the completion of a hundred years' peace.

243. Edwin deTurk Bechtel, class of 1898 at Reading High School, lived at 347 North Thirteenth Street in Reading. He took first prize in debate, delivered the class oration, attended Harvard on a need-based scholarship, became a lawyer, and after an interval of four decades became an important friend to Stevens for the rest of his life. When Henry Church was looking for a lawyer in 1943 to help establish a philanthropic foundation, Stevens made the following recommendation: "I think that, if you call on Edwin deT. Bechtel, of Carter, Ledyard & Milburn, 2 Wall Street, New York, you will find exactly the man you want. . . . Mr. Bechtel is one of my oldest friends. I won't waste time rec-ommending him beyond saying that I know of no abler lawyer and no man of finer character. I use him from time to time on our own things in New York" (*LWS,* 440).

Dear Maria: —I-yi-yi-yi-yi! <u>I-yi-yi-yi-yi</u>! <u>I-yi-yi-yi-yi</u>!
Sam.

That's the best story I've heard for a long time. We had a pleasant dinner and a chat afterwards—although he is rather a poor talker. —When I came home I read both of your letters over again. You grow sweeter every day to me, dear. The first reading of them made me warm all over—I was so glad to get them, and so glad to read what they contained. I shan't put them with the others just yet, because I shall want to look at them again.[244] You know that I love you, Bo-Bo, and have for a long, long time and I cannot think of anything happier for me—than such letters. But no more. —I think I exaggerate my interest in "grub" when I am at home. Why I chatter so much about it when I am with you is beyond me. Depend on it, I shall keep it out of my letters. When a boy comes home from college they stuff him day after day with the things he used to like, and after a while he begins to look forward to the stuffing as much as to anything else. That was my case, I fear, and, maybe, that accounts for my gossiping about currant pies and frogs' legs and so on. —I think you will find your willingness to play coming back bye-and-bye. At least don't give the piano away! —Do you remember our seeing Richmond Jones[245] sitting on a terrace before his house near the Green Tree[246]—smoking a cigar and gazing at Reading in the valley at his feet? I thought of that today, and wondered what his thoughts were. To look at the home of a hundred thousand men and women from a high place—to see their chimneys, their spires, their multitude of roofs and walls and windows, ought to provoke considerable lofty philosophy and broad meditation, in a man who is growing old. I envy him the contents of his mind—a little god-like, if his cigar happened to be an agreeable one. —But was

244. The letter of February 28, 1909, indicates that he expected to go over all of their letters with her after their marriage.
245. A prominent citizen of Reading, a soldier in the Civil War, a lawyer, and a member of Congress, Jones was married to the daughter of a prominent ironmaster and had a home, Merioneth, on a hill overlooking Reading. There is a page or two about him in Morton L. Montgomery, comp., *Historical and Biographical Annals of Berks County Pennsylvania: Embracing a Concise History of the County and a Genealogical and Biographical Record of Representative Families,* 2 vols. (Chicago: J. H. Beers, 1909), which is now on the Internet, put up by the Historical Society of Berks County (Pennsylvania, Stevens's home county).
246. This well-known hotel in Cumru township, across the Schuylkill River from Reading, celebrated its centennial in 1905, and an article about it at that time mentions that "immediately beyond the property is the splendid estate of Richmond L. Jones, with its well kept lawns and boulevard, its stately mansion, well-equipped stables and its beautiful flowers" (from the *Reading Weekly Eagle* for July 8, 1905, as quoted in *Passing Scene* 9:174).

his meditation any broader than that of two people, whom we know, as they sat on the hillside looking at the same home on a holiday night, full of fire-works, and then looking at the whole round of July stars—and one, so large and luminous, that led all the others around their eternal circle. —The moon, later, didn't really look like the shield of Mars to me. It looked like one of those large paper rings that the clowns jump through at the circus. And I don't think I should have been greatly surprised if one had jumped through when we saw it; since what I saw in my mind, as I saw that, would not have been over-marvellous in reality. —But we must let this trip (during which we didn't waste an hour) pass like the others into History, and begin soon to think of the next. —Let the last record of it be a note on crossing the Maidencreek in a small scow with the aid of a pole—as they used to do in the days of Nebudchadnezar. You have seen me as a gondolier. And I have seen you in a gondola, after a fashion. —I notice that the ceremonies at Lake Champlain keep going on. There was a capital speech by the British Ambassador to-day in which he remarked that when Champlain paddled into the lake three hundred years ago, the nearest white men were in Virginia. You know Henry Hudson discovered the Hudson River in the same year—1609. They are going to have a great celebration here in the Autumn, when a boat built like Hudson's "Half-Moon" will sail up the river accompanied by men-of-war of different nations. I hope you will be here in time to see it. —We continue to be busy at the office and instead of closing early in the afternoon we seem to wind up later than ever—and I believe the boys are working there tonight. But Saturday and Sunday will be here in another day and then there will be a bit of respite. —It is almost half-past ten and time, therefore, to be taking this to the mail-box. The collector must wonder who E. V. M. may be. If he knew as much as I—! Good-night, Bo-Bo.

Your
Buddy.[247]

247. The following clipping is in the folder for this letter at the Huntington, and though it is not mentioned in the letter, it could well have been included since it is about the area in which Stevens and Elsie will eventually live from 1909 until 1916 (across the street from the seminary mentioned):

RECALLS OLD CHRISTMAS POEM
Site of Clement C. Moore's Garden, in 22d Street, Leased
    A small plot of ground in 22d street, near Tenth Avenue, which was leased yesterday by James N. Wells's Sons for the Moore estate, recalled to many minds memories of days long ago in the Chelsea district. Near the site rented was the house owned and occupied by Clement Clark Moore, author of the famous poem, "A Visit from St. Nicholas," written in 1844. The first four lines of the poem are:

⇝

[WAS 1869 July 9, 1909 New York]

Friday Evening

Dear Bo-Bo:—

I came across some interesting notes about Master Bob White in a newspaper—they call him the bobwhite. The bird is considered "the most valuable wild fowl in existence for the American home, garden and farm." That is because it seems to live on the most pestiferous insects and on the seeds of specially troublesome weeds. One bird ate in a single day "300 seeds of smartweed, 500 of sheep sorrel, 1000 of ragweed, 5000 of pigeon grass, 10,000 of pigweed, a tablespoon of chinch bugs (whatever they are,) and over one hundred potato beetles." Another one ate 1268 rose slugs; another "5000 plant lice and 568 mosquitoes in two hours." I suppose we'll have to believe it because no one would say "1268 rose slugs" unless they had been counted. 1268 is a very exact figure. They have such queer appetites: for cut worms, cucumber beetles, squash bugs, grasshoppers, crickets, Hessian flies. And here is a little more:[248]

We must remember all this and make use of it one of these days at Phosphor Farm—when our ship comes in. What with our researches into the subject of

---

'Twas the night before Christmas, when all through the house,
Not a creature was stirring, not even a mouse.
The stockings were hung by the chimney with care,
In hopes that St. Nicholas soon would be there.

The site leased formed a part of the farm owned by Mr. Moore, and some years before his death, on July 10, 1863, he had it made into a flower garden, it is said, and spent many hours there. He gave to the General Theological Seminary the site it occupies, at 22d street and Ninth Avenue.

248. There is a blank spot for a half of a page where the following clipping had been glued by using the adhesive edge of stamps, a bit of one of them remaining:

The bobwhite is naturally a sociable bird, and this characteristic makes it a most companionable and charming household pet. It "homes" about the house and garden, if protected; and, if petted a little, becomes much tamer and responsive than the domestic fowl. The first pair of these pets which the writer had, produced twenty eggs, laid in a cage in a dining room window. In one season his hens averaged fifty-eight eggs apiece, and at the Massachusetts State Fish Hatchery one bobwhite hen laid 100 eggs, practically all hatchable. This gives some hint of how soon we could have these cheerful birds common in every garden in the land if we could all work together.

The greatest obstacle to bird protection is the uncontrolled cat. The writer had eleven bobwhites killed by one cat in a night. Another point to guard against is disease. The common fowl carries an internal parasite fatal to the turkey and the bobwhite. We should be careful to keep our bobwhites on ground uncontaminated by common fowl.

candy-tuft, etc. we ought to [be] pretty fair amateurs bye-and-bye. —I thought of writing you a little fairy tale for Sunday, but I shall have to defer that for some other day—perhaps I'll think of one on Sunday, when I expect to walk in the country—certainly, if the cool weather keeps up. —I saw an odd fellow on Eleventh Street to-night smelling—pshaw! I mean <u>selling</u> catnip. He had a big burlap bag of it swung over one shoulder and carried a bunch of it in another hand—at least in a hand. Every little while he cried—"Green catnup"—not nip but nup. —But in our neighborhood, with the views we have about cats, he was not likely to sell anything to give them pleasure; and I am sorry to say he took away all that he brought. —He should have tried a street full of old maids. — One of <u>our</u> old maids wrote a poem today!

"He shakes his head, this stalwart chap,
And says he doesn't care a rap,
Nor give a single finger snap,
For all this wearisome clap-trap."

but

"just beware for you will find
He's pessimistic still in mind."

Time must hang heavy on her hands.

"Is there a cure for Mr. S—?
We all unite in saying "Yes!"

There, you see what they think of me. She is the German school-teacher, whom I admire so much for her cheerfulness and good-will. But I shall have to make a shocking "Valentine" and pass it around the table in revenge. —And that gives you a glimpse of boarding-house life, too. —Next to me at table is a very stout woman who affects daintiness. I told some one that she reminded me of an elephant with a little red ribbon tied in a bow around its tail—and they threaten to tell her. That would mean a lingering death. —But I'll pull the curtain down over such trivialities. They are the common-places of daily life and not specially amusing. —There will be a letter for me tomorrow I am sure, and I shall be glad to have it. —Bye-bye, Bo-Bo.

Your
Buddy.

[WAS 1870 July 13, 1909 New York]

Bo-Bo and her Buddy[249]

enjoying the country.

Dearest:

I'm not <u>nearly</u> tired of talking about country things—and since you ask me—
"What do you see in the country there—cherry-trees, too?"—I'll tell you. The
first thing is that there are no country roads leading into town. At home, we have
the road from Kutztown, the Harrisburg pike, the Lancaster road, the Philadelphia pike and so on. There is nothing like that here. People come to New-York
by water. Things [empty space here since this was the back where the pin holding the clipping had been] are shipped here. We don't grow anything to speak of.
—What few farms there are, are vegetable farms. These are generally run by
foreigners—Italians and Germans. —You never see a wheat-field, or a corn-field
or a barn. —The kind of farms we have at home are unknown. —What we call
country is'n't [*sic*] at all what you call country. —Your wide fields, and white
houses, and large barns with cows and pigeons and chickens—my dear girl, they
don't know what such things are, here. The country here is <u>simply a place where
there aren't many houses.</u> As a matter of fact, New-York makes itself felt for
many miles in every direction. —And one can't say that the people are nicer.
There are so many of them. —There is one fundamental difference that has
nothing to do with the difference in the country itself. I am not emotional; but I
am aware that I look at the country at home with emotion. The twenty years of
life that are the simplest and the best were spent there. It has become a memorable
scene. But I do not look at the country here with emotion. When it is beautiful I
know that it is beautiful. When the country at home is beautiful, I don't only
know it; I feel it—I rejoice in it, and I am proud. —But the deuce with all these
buts. You will understand without more ado. —Besides I have two red bananas
to eat and I am determined to read at least ten pages of Endymion—and I'd much
rather be amusing for a while, since I'm bound to be so serious later on. —I went
to another apartment house after dinner to-night. Really, you'd be shocked at
the black little rooms. I wouldn't go into one of them if we had to live in a tent as
an alternative. —I think I'll take a look up-town next Saturday afternoon. I want
so much to be able to stay in this general neighborhood, but it looks to be impossible. Everything fit is beyond me; and everything unfit is, of course, unfit. —
These jaunts after dinner, followed by a half-hour with the <u>Post,</u> and an hour
with you, make up my evenings. —Aren't summer evenings rather difficult
things to dispose of? One hates to come up stairs at once—it is such a bore to sit

---

249. At the top of this sheet of stationery, something had been pinned to the paper;
now this comment is all that remains.

here when the weather is fine. —But red bananas and Endymion are a partial solution. I begin:

> Increasing still in heart, and pleasant sense,
> Upon his fairy journey on he hastes—[250]

And so on.

With much love,

Buddy

⌣

[WAS 1871 July 16, 1909 New York]

Friday Evening

Dear Bo-Bo:—

On Thursday evening I went with a fellow to visit a friend of his who is a doctor in one of the hospitals on Blackwell's island.[251] It was eleven o'clock when we got back and as we were walking along we ran into those automobile 'busses that make a midnight trip through Chinatown and the Bowery, and both of us, without any special reason, hopped on board. Chinatown is pitifully dull. They take you through a few stores, give you a cup or two of tea and some so-called Chinese dishes and then dash homeward. But it was three o'clock as I crawled into bed. Last evening I was so tired that I went to bed before eight o'clock. —So you see that I have been misbehaving instead of just reading and writing. Only, reading and writing make Jack a dull boy. —Nor has to-day been inspiring. We have had showers and rain-bows and clear skies and a twilight filled with golden clouds but it is just as hot as ever—at least, here in my room; and I wish very much that I didn't have to go to the office in the morning. —Or, since I must, I wish that, like you, I could get up early, get a bite of breakfast, and go for a long, quiet walk in the cool air of some morning-like place. The desire

> For to admire and for to see,
> For to be'old this world so wide[252]

was on me strong to-day and at lunch-time I got a map of the Provinces and spent a half-hour to-night, after reading the paper, studying rivers and lakes and

---

250. *Endymion,* bk. 2, lines 351–52.

251. At this time, the three hospitals on this long, narrow island in the East River (crossed by the Queensboro Bridge in 1909) served those who were insane, indigent, or infected with smallpox. In 1921, it was renamed Welfare Island, and in 1971 it was given its present name, Roosevelt Island. The friend might have been the Albert R. Lamb, a physician of Columbia University he mentioned in WAS 1792 (April 22, 1907) and WAS 1806 (January 17, 1909).

252. Kipling, "For to Admire," lines 9–10 and 53–54.

steamship lines and all that. I should like to see Quebec and the St. Lawrence and the bay of Fundy (where the tide falls seventy-five feet and people get off boats by ladders.) —What sport it would be to knock around up there for a few months—in real woods, hunting and fishing. One of these days! When I have seen London and the rest. —We must save for London together. —There isn't a blessed thing to do in town. In a week or two there will be three people out of eight at my table at the boarding-house and in this house I now have the whole floor to myself. There is something uncanny in that after one has become accustomed to two or three people in every room. Yet I like it, of course. I can sleep and all that with my door open. —I do not know just what I shall do over Sunday—probably take pretty much the same walk I took a week ago. It is great fun to lie on a rock and bask in the sun—notwithstanding that the July sun is not the basking sun—but the boiling. August's is the baking and September's the basking—when the air is so full and warm without being tropical, as it is now. — I do not expect to be home again until the end of the month: the week after next. But I shall write often and come two or three times in August. You know that I wish I could come every week. August is a better month for outings than July, anyhow. I can probably arrange next time to come on Friday evening although we continue to be as busy as ever. One thing, I shall not stay at the office any more on Saturday afternoons. There is a great pile of stuff on my desk but to-morrow at one I'll be off with the rest. —But where? —Perhaps to Manhattan Beach for a swim with thousands of others—and a loaf in the sand. Anything. —And so bye-bye, dear—and a kiss. Oh, I wish you were here—so that I might give it to you really.

Your
Buddy.

⤸

[WAS 1872 July 18, 1909 New York]

Sunday Evening

Dearest:

Spent a horrid Saturday—at the office, after all; for I couldn't think of a thing to do. In the evening I read. —But to-day has been pleasant enough. In the morning I walked to Englewood. There I picked up some post-cards which I shall send you to-morrow. I had intended to go far up the river and take another sunbath on a rock but it grew very threatening at noon and I came back to town, expecting to be kept indoors all afternoon by bad weather. Yet when I had had lunch (in a little place in Harlem) I thought that since I was in tramps' clothes I might as well risk it, so I went directly to Long Island City and took a train for Rockaway. —I hadn't been there for two or three years. It is an exceptionally long beach of white sand. To-day there were thousands of people there, as you can imagine. At first glimpse, it looked like a field of orange and blue umbrellas. An enterprising hatter had distributed them and each one bore his advertisement in large letters: "Wear Young's hats. None better made."[253] I swear the whole beach proclaimed "Wear Young's Hats"—except in one spot where a group of yellow and blue umbrellas gave notice that "All cars transfer to Bloomingdale's." I saw just one umbrella, a large yellow one, without an advertisement on it. —By umbrellas, I mean sunshades—the large ones, such as drivers put over their seats. —All the familiar sights and sounds. —The upper end seems to be patronized exclusively by Jews who don't look at all well in the water. Some of 'em were as big as elephants. —There were patches given up to children—summer outpourings from the slums. One crowd of Italian boys were as brown as the proverbial berries. But a crowd of Jewish girls—five, six and seven years of age—or about that—looked to me to be beyond "the healing of the sea"[254]—poor things. —After I [had] gone from one end to another, I left the crowd and found a more or less solitary pier running out into a bay and I loafed there on the rail for a half-hour, enjoying the wind and watching the boats, until train-time. —And promptly at nine o'clock to-morrow the stale round of the office will commence all over again and I must grind for six days before I can get back to the sun—darn it. Yep: darn it. —Your letter of Thursday evening made me feel particularly cheerful. I'm such a contrary affair that when anybody else is blue—it always makes me feel in high feather. As a matter of fact, you have probably felt the same thing by this time, for uncommonly low spirits are usually followed by a reaction to uncommonly high ones; and, as likely as not, I shall have a letter from my girl to-morrow in which she snaps her finger at that letter. I know that that feeling, which we all experience, does not last long with you and that you have too much good will to let it influence you. —About those dark rooms: you may depend upon it that I didn't look twice at them. We shall certainly have light ones—more than one. Rascal! But I was glad to have you say that, because I do not want you to expect too much. More than one, and yet not too many, because I do not want to get a lot of furniture at once. I think that after you have had a year or two in town and have got to know your way around, you will be glad to go to one of the suburbs, and come to town only to shop, and so on. New-York isn't at all a place for people to live in unless they are well-to-do, and not even then, if they are young. But of

253. Postcard number 09348 of the Detroit Publishing Company shows a picture of the Italian market on Mulberry Street, New York, between 1900 and 1910 with "Wear Young's hats" on an umbrella and "Avalone, 71 Mulberry St." on a sign. This postcard may be accessed at http://lcweb2.loc.gov/ammem/detroit/dethome.html.
254. This phrase was used by James G. Blaine near the end of his eulogy, delivered February 27, 1882, for the assassinated President James A. Garfield.

course you will have to make up your own mind about that. I understand that women like it much better than men. —How did you get through the day to-day? Don't you wish we could have gone up to the Tower[255] together and read the Sun —or something? And doesn't it seem much more than two weeks since we drove to The Plough?[256] Jove! It seems months.

With much love, dearest, from
Your Buddy.

ᦔ

[WAS 1873 July 18, 1909[257] New York]
[Postcard: "The Palisades, Hudson River, Englewood, N.J."]

Sunday July 18, 1909

There are three roads along the Palisades. One is at the foot along the water. It is stony and not often used. Another is on the top along the edge. It is a foot-path from which there are all manner of fine views. The last is on the top about a hundred yards from the edge. This one is the road for carriages, etc. It is the prettiest road near New-York and yet one seldom meets people on it—probably because you must cross the river to get to it.

W

[Postcard: "Clinton Point, Englewood, N.J."]

Sunday. July 18, 1909

This is about an hours walk up the other side of the Hudson: the Western side. The river flows toward you as you look at the card. You are, therefore, looking up the river. Yonkers is on the right hand side. The left hand side is, of course, a part of the Palisades. The picture seems to have been taken in the winter-time from the top. —The other card shows pretty much the same thing. Only it seems to have been taken in the summer-time from the foot of the rocks. The rocks are the result of an ancient glacier.

W

ᦔ

255. The Mount Penn Tower was the main attraction for riders on the loop made by the gravity railroad from Reading from 1890 until 1923.
256. The Plough (also spelled Plow) and Harrow Hotel in Reading became the Merchant's Hotel, but the reference is probably to The Plow hotel in Robeson Township (which includes the village of Gibraltar) about ten miles south of Reading.
257. These two postcards were probably sent in an envelope that is not extant. Stevens wrote the day and date on the back of each card.

[WAS 1874 July 19, 1909 New York]

Monday Evening

My dearest:—

An October day. You felt that the sky was blue, when in fact it was gray. This evening, however, it <u>was</u> blue, and gold, and rose, and yellow and violet, and purple, and—black, with a new moon, looking very keen and beautifully welcome. —If the beastly hot weather could, possibly, be regarded as at an end, I should rejoice. But, at best, this can only be a change. —I came home by way of the new tunnel under the river, which was opened to-day.[258] It is like any other tunnel to look at. But it is a great work, enormous in labor and art—the part of it one cannot look at. —From the Jersey City end I took the Twenty-Third Street ferry—a longish ride—and then came back to Eleventh-Street by trolley. —A little walk to Madison Square after dinner and then back here to the stale newspapers. I think I'll drop newspapers for a while. There's nothing in them at all at this time of the year. —Then I read few pages in a book I borrowed this afternoon. A new book is a real pleasure to me. I like to read for a long stretch at a time; and I like best to read what are called "instruction" books, or else poetry; and yet I cannot possibly read either of those for more than an hour, if that. — This is a book of essays on progress, money, Hope, fashion and all that kind of thing, written from the socialistic point of view. I find it interesting. —To tell the truth, I should be glad to stumble across a good novel—not a love story— something larger. —But I have been wonderfully listless—feeling pretty much about books, I imagine, as you have been feeling about the piano. —Indeed (as they say) I wish we could just sit around together and not do a blessed thing— except, perhaps, to gossip a little. The days run on so heavily and the nights seem so intolerably long. —To-morrow I shall spread wing and send you a letter from the clouds. Haven't we had enough from this tiresome room? I don't mean spread wing—but escape from—things. —I wish I had done it to-night, but it is too late, alas. —Send me a kiss, Bo-Bo, in your next letter—a <u>good</u> one. ++++ I have lots and lots of them for you.

With much love,
Wallace

〜

258. In an elaborate ceremony on July 19, 1909, the Hudson and Manhattan Railroad began operations between lower Manhattan and lower Jersey City. This ride was famous for taking only three minutes.

[WAS 1875 July 20, 1909 New York]

Tuesday Evening

My Very Dear—Sylvie:—

Two letters from you, to-day! I was <u>delighted</u>—and could give you a good squeeze if you were here. My dear, dear girl. —It was very amusing to read about the wind blowing your writables about. I could see it—especially the blotter blowing just out of reach. —And I am so glad that you were glad to get my letter yesterday. I could see that too. But. . . . One always hears the wind first—even before the stage is lighted. Imagine, then, a leafy rustling as the scenes change, in darkness—change because we are going to forget all old things to-night and. . . . A mysterious voice cries, "Have a stout heart against Fortune":[259] a familiar thing, an old thing (to speak the truth)—but the best possible counsel when one is about to start on an adventure. . . . Aren't dots like that the most thrilling and fascinating things? —But I cannot dream. I cannot altogether spread wing—I am dragged down by this strange book I have been reading. — When will young writers remember that politeness is the attitude established by twenty centuries of brave men and women? —The book is impolite because it comments on irremediable things as if someone were to blame. —I might have wept over my seller of catnip. We might all weep daily. . . . But beyond the slums there is an endless round of green fields, where sellers of catnip might do very handsomely as shepherds or gardeners and the like. I wish to Heaven they did and that these fearful books with their fearful thoughts were all at an end. — . . . The pressure of Life is very great in great cities. But when you think of the ease with which people live and die in the smaller places the horror of the pressure seems self-imposed. — — — After all, a stout heart anywhere and everywhere! — — — Now, I wish we could rest after so much disquisition and listen to what we have never heard. The wind has fallen. The moon has risen. We are where we have never been, listening to what we have never heard. We are in a dark place listening—contentedly, to—well, nightingales—why not? We are by a jubilant fountain, like the one in the forgotten "June Book," under emerald poplars, by a wide-sailing river—and we hear another fountain—a radiant fountain of sound rise from one of the dark green trees into the strange moonlight—rise and shimmer—from the tree of the nightingales. —And is it all on a stage? And can't you possibly close your eyes and, by imagination, feel that it is perfectly real—the dark circle of poplars, with the round moon among them, the air moving, the water falling, and that sweet outpouring of liquid sound— fountains and nightingales—fountains and nightingales—and Sylvie and the

259. This is a translation of a French proverbial expression Stevens recorded in *SP* for March 4, 1906: "Le mieux est de faire contre fortune bon coeur," now available in the *Dictionnaire de L'Académie française,* cinquième édition, 1798, on the Internet.

brooding shadow that would listen beside her so intently to fountains and night-ingales and to her? —If only it were possible to escape from what the dreadful Galsworthy calls Facts—at the moment, no more serious [than] that[260] neigh-borly bag-pipes and a dog singing thereto—. All our dreams, all our escapes and then things as they are! But attend to that mysterious cry: "Have a stout heart against Fortune." Meditate on it long after ghostly fountains and ghostly night-ingales and [sic] have ceased their ghostly chants in the ghostly mind. Yes: for flesh and blood: "Have a stout heart against Fortune." — The curtain falls. The brief flight is at end. —I cannot tell you, dear, how glad I have been for these last two bracing days—the weather, I mean—to be sure. I remember reading a description by Lafcadio Hearn of the effect of tropical weather on the mind and spirits—the lassitude, the diffidence. —Really I feel as if I had been half-unconscious for a month and as if I were now about to recover and get back into shape. —Yet, as I said last night, this is only fugitive; for at noon to-day, it was pretty much what it has been for some time. —Tell me, Bo-Bo, do you have any trouble to read my hand-writing? This looks as if it might be pretty bad. Sharp pens are always too hard for me to write with; but I think I could get a better one than this if it bothers you. —Both of your last letters seem to have been written in good spirits—especially good; so I shall completely forget the piano letter. You're a great girl! —Write to me soon.

> With love — very much
> Buddy.

࠻

[WAS 1876 July 21, 1909 New York]

> Wednesday Evening

My dearest Bo-Bo:—

I feel as if last night's fountains and nightingales had not been very convincing. —But as a diversion! —I walked down to the office this morning. At noon, instead of going to lunch, and with the idea that I should enjoy the air more, I walked up to Ninth-Street and back within the prescribed hour. And this evening, before dinner, (in spite of being a bit hungry,) I walked from the office up to Forty-Second Street and then back to the house, about five miles, judging by the time it took. — So you see that I have been energetic in taking advantage of the fine weather. —This evening I have been reading "Endymion." How full it is—of wonders! —I am still in great need of a good novel and have strong hopes of finding what I want shortly. —But this is only a note—about a pleasant day.

> With love, as always,
> Buddy

260. Stevens actually wrote "that that" instead of "than that."

~

[WAS 1877 July 23, 1909 New York]

Friday Evening

Dear Bo-Bo:—

My novel goes along well. —The Chinese say that a half-hour's reading gives savour to a whole day. —Certainly it stimulates me. I remember that a few nights ago the little things on my table—my writing-table—seemed stale. —I read for an hour to-night. They seem far from stale: the row of books— "Tom Jones," "The History of Early English Literature," "Geological Sketches," "Whitney's German-English and English-German Dictionary"[261]—the four or five pictures, and so on. —Observe how the things around one cease to stimulate after a while. (That is why kings are bored—and like Haroun-al-Raschid assume nocturnal disguises.) — The desire for new things—is a part of our need for stimulation. And what more restless motive is there, since that need is so constant, than the desire for new things? —When a thing is stale it is done for. —When a thing is new it has the world at its feet (I am careless of rhetoric.) It stimulates —that's <u>why.</u> — Hence air-ships, wireless, the morning newspaper, the "extra," the interest in the theatre, fashions, etc. —Man flies from nothingness. Not less than nature he abhors a vacuum—or what is the same—staleness. —All that speculation springs from a "known mind renewed," to cite the "Little J. B."[262] once more (and finally, for the time being.) —I hope for a vigorous and pleasant Sunday. —Nine chances out of ten, you shared our rain to-day, and heard how good a thing it was for crops. —The instructive barber informed me to-night that corn should have been in the market long ago, that carrots were the size of your little finger and that all fresh "produce" was high. —A scintillating subject. I vibrate with concern about the carrots. —The truth is I saw a man eating a carrot for breakfast in the street the other day and it was as thick as a thumb! What lying knaves barbers are! —But he was quite right about corn. We must take a walk next week and investigate. —I am rather sorry, in fact, that we haven't been walking more. I think one gets more details that way—although one covers less ground. Six of one, half dozen of the other, as they say. —Don't bother about the letters you would have written if——. One word in this morning's was enough—the first. You remember it. —I looked at your picture and thought of it—the word—and I know how deserving I must <u>try</u> to be. You would be the last person to use such a word unless it was in your mind. —Oh, I

261. This dictionary is the only one of these books still in Stevens's library at the Huntington: William Dwight Whitney, *A Compendious German and English Dictionary* (New York: Holt, 1887).
262. This quotation is from the fourteenth poem of "The Little June Book" (1909) that Stevens wrote for Elsie.

could quite easily make a wonderful letter out of that single word[263]—just by thinking of it—and of your voice saying it. —But, my dear, I feel very brisk and lively to-night, and I say no more. —Be sure to tell me on Sunday what you've been doing all week. I don't think you have. —My walking to-day was much cut down by the weather—but I came up on foot to-night under my umbrella in a down-pour. Hence my slippers.

Your own
Buddy

⌣

[WAS 1878 July 25, 1909 New York]

Sunday

Sweet:

(It takes a bold youth to write the word now-a-days. It was commoner in cleaner and less sentimental centuries—to which I prefer to belong at the moment.) I happen to have spent the whole day—a gorgeous, blue day—in my room, reading some of the French poets of the sixteenth century; and that is why I happen to like—for the moment, again—such great antiquity. In fact, I have spent the afternoon, translating a sonnet by Joachim du Bellay. I do not know how much French you will recognize with a translation by its side. At all events, on the next page is the original; on the next is a translation by Austin Dobson; and on the last is the one I made this afternoon. Du Bellay was the cousin of the Cardinal and Sire de Langey. The chief event of his life was a residence of three years in Rome, as intendant to the cardinal. He died at the age of thirty-five in 1590. —You can find the "proper names" mentioned in the sonnet sometime at the Library. —This will make a scholarly Monday for you.[264]

Your
—Bold Youth!

[On page 2 of this letter is the French text of Du Bellay with Stevens's notes at the bottom:]

Sonnet des "Regrets"

Heureuse qui, comme Ulysse, a fait un beau voyage,
Ou comme celui-là qui conquit la toison
Et puis est retourné, plein d'usage et raison,
Vivre entre ses parents le rest de son âge!
Quand reverrai-je, hélas, de mon petit village

263. Several of the words in this part of this letter are uncharacteristically carelessly made, with extraneous or anomalous marks.
264. This note is written in perhaps the clearest manner of all the letters.

Fumer la cheminée: et en quelle saison
Reverrai-je le clos de ma pauvre maison,
Qui m'est une province, et beaucoup davantage?

Plus me plaît le séjour qu'ont bâti mes aïeux,
Que des palais romains le front audacieux:
Plus que le marbre dur, et beaucoup davantage
Plus mon Loire gaulois, que le Tibre latin,
Plus mon petit Lyré, que le mont Palatin,
Et plus que l'air marin la douceur angevine.

In the eleventh line "et boucoup davantage" should be "me plaît l'ardoise fine."

Lyré, bye-the-bye, is a little hill near Du Bellay's home. It is not likely to be in the books.
[Page 3 of this letter is the Austin Dobson translation.]

Regrets
Happy the man, like wise Ulysses tried,
Or him of yore that gat the Fleece of Gold,
Who comes at last, from travels manifold,
Among his kith and kindred to abide!

When shall I see from my small hamlet-side
Once more the blue and curling smoke unrolled?
When the poor boundaries of my house behold, —
Poor, but to me as any province wide?

Ah, more than these imperious piles of Rome
Smile the low portals of my boyhood's home!
More than the marble must its slate-roof be!

More than the Tiber's flood my Loire is still!
More than the Palatine my native hill,
And the soft air of Anjou than the sea.

                                        Austin Dobson.[265]
[Page 4 of this letter is Stevens's translation.]

Sonnet from the Book of Regrets.
Happy the man who, like Ulysses, goodly ways
Hath been, or like to him that gained the fleece; and then

265. Holly Stevens, in *LWS*, 151, points out that this translation by Dobson is in a book still in Stevens's library: *The Sonnets of Europe,* ed. Samuel Waddington (London: Walter Scott, 1886), 130. It was signed by Stevens and dated March 10, 1898.

Is come, full of the manners and the minds of men,
To live among his kinsmen his remaining days!

When shall I see once more, alas, the smokey haze
Rise from the chimneys of my little town; and when:
What time o' the year, look on the cottage-close again,
That is a province to me, that no boundary stays?

The little house my fathers built of old, doth please
More than the emboldened front of Roman palaces:
More than substantial marble, thin slate wearing through,
More than the Latin Tiber, Loire of Angevine,
More, more, my little Lyré than the Palatine,
And more than briny air the sweetness of Anjou.

WS

⌐

[WAS 1879 August 2, 1909 New York]

Monday Evening

My dear:

Feel like a scare-crow on a rainy day. —It was a terrible tug to get up this morning. I fell asleep almost before the train started and woke up in the Terminal. —After I had changed to the New-York Express, I had breakfast and then went into the baggage car and smoked a pipe until the sign-posts said "63 M. to N.Y."; "62 M. to N.Y." —and then I went back to my seat and read a few chapters of Galsworthy's "Country House"—pretty poor stuff. —A very pleasant trip—only that horse "Charley" has seen the last of us. I like "Kate," the white mare that we had up the Tulpehocken best of all. —One scene goes into History: the road-side blue with corn-flowers and—the green shadows under the corn with the crumpled cups of pumpkin-flowers—yellow as pumpkins themselves. —And perhaps I should memorialize for the wastes of old age the wide golden sheet of cloud (before it had cleared) when the moon was a quarter of the way up the sky: seen from the porch of Schwartz's hotel as we started for the car.[266] —I wish I could say one more thing—for your most private ear—and have you believe it: and that is that I thought all your dresses charming! Bloody butcher-knife! —All white—well, but that's mere gossip, isn't it? But you must

---

266. Schwartz's Summit Hotel on Mount Penn was contiguous to the Tower (not the Pagoda) referred to above (in the letter of July 18, 1909), both of which were reached by the "Mount Penn Gravity Railroad," the car of which would have brought them back to a point not far from Elsie's home. For photographs and a history of this entertainment complex, see Meiser and Meiser, *The Passing Scene*, 1:229–47.

believe it, you know, to find it pleasant. —And I should like to sing another compliment—(yes: a compliment from Buddy) only such things are not good for little girls. But for my lady? Another time. —I had rather a surprise this afternoon. Walter Butler came in to see me. Money matters—I was icy—Arctic—and he must have decided to postpone negotiations, for he went with a woeful look. I suppose I'd have to if he asked. He ought not to ask—for as long as things went well he never came near me. —His new friends have left town and he's lonely, poor chap. He must expect to endure what we all do. As it is, he is better off than many with more merit. It is not necessity with him but mere desire I am sure—hence the regretted iciness. —The next two weeks I shall pass as in a cloister. The pipe is to go on the shelf—there will be translations, (at least, of Chénier's "La Flûte" —with its beautiful last line

"A fermer tour à tour les trous des bois sonare") and

I solemnly promise a fairy tale—about golden hair and blue eyes—and how they came to be so. They might just as well have been green hair and opal eyes—such as mermaids have—except for the reason which I heard one feather tell another feather in my pillow once upon a time. The feathers in my pillow, by the way, once covered the bosoms of two birds that—but I shall tell you about them one of these times. —I hope you gave La Rue lots of the caramels (if there were lots) to comfort her for a whole day's solitude. —Time for bed. A long night to make up for three hours. —A kiss for you, dear.

Your own
Wallace

⌒

[WAS 1880 August 3, 1909 New York]

Tuesday Evening

My dear:

This is the story of how golden hair and blue eyes came to be so. —A good many years ago, long before Malbrouck went to become a soldier, and yet not so long ago as the days of Hesiod (in fact it is a little uncertain when) two pigeons sat on the roof of a barn and looked about them at the yellow corn-fields and the cows in the meadow and the church-spire over the hill and did nothing at all but murmur "Coo-coo-coo," "Coo-coo-coo" "Coo-coo-coo."[267] It was the end of the summer and the air was so full of the dry fragrance of harvest that the young King of the country, who was riding along, felt happy at so much sweet plenty

---

267. Stevens's coo, both here and in his poetry much later, might bear some of the resonance of Edward Fitzgerald's note to the twentieth quatrain (second version, that of 1868) of his *Rubáiyát*:

and looked up at the pigeons and smiled and answered them, as any foolish young fellow would, and said "Coo-coo-coo." Now, it happens, that the farmer's daughter, who had been gathering berries in some bushes by the road-side, heard what the King said (without knowing who he was) and pushed the bushes aside to steal a look, out of curiosity. The King noticed the bushes move and looked that way and as soon as he had done so he saw the girl and felt himself suddenly grow light as air and then heavy as lead. He wanted to dismount and run toward her, but all he could do was to sit perfectly still and stare. She was the most wonderfully beautiful creature he had ever seen. He noticed that she had eyes as black as black shadows and that her hair was like a shining black cloud from which those shadows fell. And all the time the two pigeons kept murmur-ing their soft "Coo-coo-coo," "Coo-coo-coo," like a bewitching music. Then they stopped and opened their blue wings and flew close by over his head. He glanced at them. When he looked back at the bushes, the girl was gone. He was off his horse in a twinkling and although he didn't lose a second and looked and ran this way and that, the girl was no more to be seen. Then the King, filled with disappointment, went to the farm-house and asked to see the farmer. The farmer had gone to the next town, however, to sell some cattle at a fair and was not expected to return for three days. The farmer's wife, who recognized the King, said that she had no idea who the girl was, because she was afraid that the King, who, like all young men, was said to be no better than he ought to be, might do her daughter some harm, if he found her. Farmer's wives, you know, always think that. But the King was far better than his reputation, and had broken only two hearts in all his life—and those not particularly strong ones: one of them belonging to the widow of a general in his army, and the other to a very senti-mental young person who had seen him at court, but to whom he had never even spoken a single word. So the King went back to his horse and rode away with a heavy heart. Bye-and-bye the girl came back and asked her mother (pre-tending that she did not know) if anyone had been there.

> The Palace that to Heav'n his pillars threw,
> And Kings the forehead on his threshold drew—
> I saw the solitary Ringdove there,
> And "Coo, coo, coo," she cried; and "Coo, coo, coo."

Fitzgerald states, "This Quatrain Mr. Binning found, among several of Hafiz and others, inscribed by some stray hand among the ruins of Persepolis. The Ringdove's ancient *Pehlevi Coo, Coo, Coo,* signifies also in Persian '*Where? Where? Where?*' In Attár's 'Birdparliament' she is reproved by the Leader of the Birds for sitting still, and for ever harping on that one note of lamentation for her lost Yusuf." *The Rubáiyát of Omar Khayyám* (New York: Walter J. Black, 1942), 70, 162–63.

"Why no," said the mother, "Nobody, except the butcher's boy from T——, who brought some veal cutlets."

"Was he on horseback?" asked Rosalind, for that was her name.

"Yes," said the deceitful woman.

At this, Rosalind ran upstairs and threw herself on her bed and cried—and cried—and cried, without knowing why, except that she was sorry that it had been a butcher's boy. And while she was crying, the pigeons flew onto her window sill and began to murmer "Coo-coo-coo," "Coo-coo-coo," "Coo-coo-coo." She listened to them and felt a great deal of comfort in the sound and after a while she dried her eyes and went down-stairs to her mother and baked forty loaves of bread without saying a word. That evening when the field-hands and the milk-maids were gossiping and singing and dancing, she felt so lonely and so sad that she went back to her attic and cried again and then, try as she could, she was unable to fall asleep. Soon the pigeons came and cooed and kept her company; and, after a while, when it was quite dark they flew into the room, without her knowing it, and settled on her pillow. Each one plucked a blue feather from its breast and each one put the feather on one of Rosalind's eyelids. The feathers were so light that she did not know they were there. And so she fell asleep. But the pigeons still made their cooing sounds. . . . Well, early in the morning, when the birds were twittering in the tree-tops, and just as the sun cast its first beam into the valley where the farm was, Rosalind got up and walked across her room to the little cracked mirror on the wall by the aid of which she was accustomed to put up her black hair. She rubbed her eyes sleepily, and then started—and rubbed harder, and then looked, and rubbed even harder than before, and looked again. There could be no doubt of it! Her eyes were as blue as the wings of a pigeon. Not knowing what to do, and feeling frightened, she ran down-stairs and out of the house, where to her astonishment she found all the men and the milk-maids already up and gathered about a bold-looking man on horseback who was telling them that he was a messenger from the King and that he had been commanded to seize any girl in the kingdom with black hair and black eyes and bring her safely to the King at C——. They all marvelled greatly at this. It was at this moment that Rosalind ran among them and one of the milkmaids, who was jealous of her, cried out to the messenger that Rosalind, pointing to her, was such a girl. The bold fellow quickly came toward her and took her by the arm and looked at her closely.

"By my faith," he exclaimed, "she has the most beautiful black hair, but her eyes are not black. They are blue."

"Blue?" whispered the crowd, "Whoever heard of blue eyes?"

They crowded around Rosalind and looked at her. No one had ever had blue eyes in that kingdom before—and they seemed as strange as they were beautiful. Roselind was so frightened that she ran away from the crowd, without even staying for breakfast, and never stopped until she came to a field far away, which was filled with sheaves of wheat. There she lay down on a big sheaf to get her breath and rest awhile. Poor child, she had never had so many adventures in all her eighteen years, as she had had in the last eighteen hours. Tired and hungry, she soon fell asleep. While she was sleeping, the messenger from the King came along and being a heartless brute, who wanted to do his best, he knelt down beside Rosalind, loosened her hair and cut it off with his dagger, intending to make a wig of it for his own daughter who had black eyes—but hair as fair as gold. That was a strange combination. The messenger thought that with the help of the wig he could make his daughter, who was more or less an object of ridicule for her very peculiar looks, appear to be the girl the King desired. He strongly suspected that the King was in love and hoped, by his cunning, to make his daughter a Queen. So the messenger returned to C——, and made a wig of Rosalind's hair and put it on his daughter and presented her to the King. Of course, the King recognized the fraud in an instant, and filled with wrath and believing that the messenger had slain the girl he had been sent to bring ordered the messenger to be put to death and turning on the daughter cut off her golden hair with his sword. The messenger was a bold fellow, as you know, and told the King that he had not slain Rosalind and that if his life was spared he would take the King to her. The King eagerly agreed to this and they set out at once. They found Rosalind lying on the sheaf of wheat and near her were two pigeons cooing softly, "Coo-coo-coo," "Coo-coo-coo," "Coo-coo-coo." Her head was so deep in the wheat that you could not see that her hair was cut off. Instead, she seemed to have hair of the color of the soft gold of ripe wheat. The King looked at her lovingly, with a full heart, and knew her face at once. He was about to leap from his horse when her eyes opened. He was the first young man in the whole world who had ever seen blue eyes and golden hair together and I will not attempt to describe his feelings at the sight. He bade the messenger leave him. After he and Rosalind had talked in each others arms for a long, long time, he lifted her onto his horse and they rode back to the castle to-gether, she with her arms around his waist, to hold on better. When they had arrived at the castle the King as punishment to the messenger's daughter would not give her back her hair but gave it to Rosalind. The court Magician soon had turned it into Rosalind's own and you would never have known that it had not been hers always. The King put the black hair in a silver box and kept it in his treasury. — And when Rosalind's father came back from the fair his wife turned up her nose at him and told him that while he had been making a few pounds of money, <u>she</u> had succeeded in marrying their daughter to the King. —

W.

[WAS 1881 August 4, 1909 New York]

Wednesday Evening

My dearest:

Once more the soft monotone and sweet sound of falling rain—the constant, consoling, sonorous noise—as if it were the earliest autumn storm. —It will be pleasant to go on with my novel to-night, especially as the heroine has just dropped a mysterious letter in the box fastened to the door of the hero's studio, and then ran away. What a singular thing to do! I wonder. —Both of your letters came to-day—and another one from a landlord who wants me to come to see an apartment that I had inquired about. I have written to say that I would come next Monday evening. It is a splendid house—just what I want. But, of course, it all depends on the rooms. I shall let you know the result. —I sent you some post-cards this afternoon, one from India, and I expect to have a very rare one in a few days from North Cape, in Norway I think. —Adieu!

Yours truly,

Patsy Dooley.[268]

⤳

[WAS 1882 August 5, 1909 New York]

Thursday Evening

My dear Bo:

My third start. The others were evidences of the commercial spirit—which I suppress. —I've been out walking—looking in shop-windows at shoes and pictures and fans—at fruit-peddlars' wagons, at towers, band-concerts, stars, new buildings, apartments, advertisements, restaurants, orange-colored clouds, people. —I suppose I ought to be able to make quite an Odyssey of it—but haven't I? They've painted the ceiling at Martin's (where I bought a cigar) and the Metropolitan Tower[269] is almost finished and the widening of Fifth Avenue is still under way, and so on. That's what one notices on these walks. —I am meditating another fairy tale—if you liked the last. This one is to be about High Hats and

268. To this letter he attaches, by means of the border that holds stamps together, this small newspaper clipping:

EGGS.—Pennsylvania and nearby hennery whites, fancy 30a32c.; do., gathered whites, fair to choice, 25a30c.; do., hennery browns, fancy, 28c.; do., gathered browns, fair to choice, 24a27c.; Western, extra firsts, 23a25c.; do., firsts, 22a33c.; do., seconds, 20a21c.; lower grades, 15a19c.; dirties, 15a19c.; checks, 12a17c.; very inferior, per case, $3a4.

[Under this clipping he writes:] "The latest in eggs!"

269. The Metropolitan Life Insurance Company Tower (designed by Pierre Le Brun) at 1 Madison Avenue, completed in 1908, became a well-known landmark.

it has ghosts in it! Only you must be a <u>very</u> good girl and write often if you want to hear it—one of these days.

With love,
Buddy

⏝

[WAS 1883 August 9, 1909 New York]

Monday Evening

My dearest Bo:—

Well, I think I have found the befitting home. They have given me until one o'clock to-morrow to think it over; but my thinking is all done and I am going to say "Yes." It has everything in its favor and I <u>know</u> that you will like it. —My only hesitation was due to the fact that I thought you might like to look around for yourself. But I am sure that nothing better could be found and I have come to the conclusion that I must take this bull instantly by the horns. It is too good an opportunity to let go by. There are two very large rooms with abundant light (they occupy almost an entire floor.) The front room looks out over the General Theological Seminary—a group of beautiful buildings occupying an entire block. It is all freshly painted and papered—has hardwood floors—open fire-places—electricity, etc.[270] There is also a corking kitchenette—clean as a whistle—white paint, etc. And a corking bath-room with a porcelain tub, a large window, etc. Then I saw at least three large closets for clothes. There can be no question about it—fine-looking house with perfectly-kept hall, and all that sort of thing. It is pure Providence to have found it. I shall have to sign a lease for a year. But, of course, that would have to be done anywhere. —So let us regard it as all settled. —The lease will commence September 1, and I shall move my books over before you come. But I shall not get anything in the way of furniture or anything else, because we shall want to exchange ideas and go for such things together—and besides it will be fun for you. —By the way, two rooms may sound crowded. Not at all. They are larger than any room in your house, except possibly the parlor and I shouldn't be surprised if each of them was as large as that, only square. —Hurrah! It is like getting rid of a great burden to have found <u>just</u> what I want. And you will be delighted—especially when you have seen what other people have. —I must tell you why I did not write on Friday night. Our agent at St. Louis has been in town and I have been taking him around to the theaters, etc. On Friday night we went to "The Motor Girl"[271] and on

270. This apartment at 441 West Twenty-first Street would be their home from September 1909 until the spring of 1916, when they moved to Hartford.
271. Musical comedy in two acts, book and music by Charles J. Campbell and Ralph M. Skinner, at the Lyric Theater from June 15, 1909.

Saturday night to "The Midnight Suns."[272] —Yesterday I took a sail to Rock-away Beach and stayed there on the sand until long after dark. It was half-past eleven before I reached home and too late, therefore, to write. The good news I have just given you, however, ought to be some compensation. —I shall give you more details on Saturday. As usual, I shall come on the early train and be up about half-past seven in the evening. —I am going to write to the Mansion House and ask them to call up that livery-man and ask him to keep "Pete" or "Kate" for us on Sunday. "Charlie" is too full of loose ends. "Kate," the white mare, is the best horse we ever had, don't you think? Offer the customary prayer for good weather. —I shall write again—and hope to have a letter from you in the morning. . . . Good-night, Bo.

> Your own
> Buddy.

↜

[WAS 1884 August 11, 1909 New York]
[American Bonding Company stationery.][273]

> Wednesday Afternoon

Dear Bo-Bo:

Didn't you get my letter of Monday evening? I <u>have</u> been very bad—and to make matters worse, I shall not be able to write this evening because I am going out to Whitestone on Long Island[274]—with the possibility of remaining all night, although I have said that I would not stay. My second visit to the apartment last night more than satisfied me that we could not do better and so I closed the matter, paid a deposit and gave my references. If I go through, the lease will be signed this week and we shall be just so much ahead. —We can talk it all over on Saturday. I feel <u>most</u> guilty, sending you only a note; but forgive me.

> Your
> Buddy

↜

272. Musical play in two acts by Glen MacDonough and Raymond Hubbell, opened May 22, 1909, at the Broadway Theater.
273. Listed on the letterhead are Jas. L. D. Kearney, Resident Vice-President and Manager; Edward B. Southworth, Res. Vice-Pres; Wallace Stevens, Res. Asst. Secretary; and Hulbert T. E. Beardsley, Attorney.
274. In this neighborhood in Queens (which the trolley reached in 1909 and where the waters of the East River and Long Island Sound mingle) at this time there were mansions of wealthy New Yorkers as well as rowdy excursion parks. It is not far from Bayside (mentioned in Stevens's next letter), also a neighborhood of mansions at this time.

[WAS 1885 August 12, 1909 New York]

Thursday Evening

My dear Bo:

I was glad to have your letter this morning—even if it was only a word. —I expect to hear to-morrow about the apartment, finally. —I thought just what you thought—but I thought more of our good fortune in finding something so perfectly what we want. —Stayed at Whitestone all night last night. We drove to Bayside and back—it was cold. —Lying in bed, I could hear the surf on the beach near-by—and, in the grass and trees, all the familiar August sounds. —But I slept poorly; for on Tuesday I caught an abominable cold, which is now at its height. I am going to bed in a very few minutes and to-morrow night I shall go to a Turkish bath[275] with the hope of breaking the thing up before Saturday. — Colds in the summer-time are always so hard to shake off. —The fact is, I find this cool weather tiresome. The hotter, the better—in August. —Bo-Bo, I know I have been writing you poor letters this week—and it is so unpleasant to do that. Please forget it and think only of our excursion together on Sunday. I feel like writing more now than when I started; but my very bones feel disturbed—and a long night under lots of cover will make all the difference in the world, I hope. —I send you many kisses, and my love.

Your own,
Buddy.

⌒

[WAS 1886 August 16, 1909 New York]
[American Bonding Company stationery.]

Monday Afternoon

My dearest Bo:

To bed at twenty-minutes of three and up at twenty minutes after four! Then at the station they announced that the train was an hour late. I was dizzy with sleep on the first train—wide-awake on the second. When I reached New-York there was a down-pour, and I took a hansom to the office. —And now I am perfectly wide-awake—thanks to a series of violent cigars. —I think I should have written to-night, in spite of it: but the sheets of rain would make it horrid to run to the box. So I'll go to bed at once, after catching up with the news. We had a marvellously good-time—which I shall flash up for Memory to-morrow evening in the unfailing Mirror of Past Events. <u>Much</u> love.

Your
Buddy.

---

275. One of the best-known baths in the city was the Russian Turkish Baths on Tenth Street between Avenue A and First Avenue.

[WAS 1887 August 17, 1909 New York]

Tuesday Evening

My own Bo-Bo:

A cricket chirps in the rain. —I walked up-town tonight with a fellow, dur-ing a lull, and he asked me to go to a Chinese restaurant. We had Chinese noodle-soup, chop-suey with bamboo and mush-rooms, rice, ginger in syrup and rice cakes. —But to-night is set apart for the Mirror of Past Events. This time it dis-closes, not a patch of flowers, or a colored cloud, or pigeons in the air; not a lot of little things; but a winding drive—a long serpentine tour behind "Kate" around and around: up the Tulpehocken with a glimpse at swimming ducks and at the site of the ancient mule bridge, and across the Red Bridge, with its new roof, up hill and across country to Leinbach's and the high church there and the chestnut tree, down a dip to Stoudt's Ferry and over the blue river, Southward to Tuckerton, Northward to Ontelaunee, where we had lunch on the dry grass, Westward to Temple—no: Eastward, and then into the back-country beyond it, along a mountain road, where we had a shower of a few drops and put up the top of the wagon and pulled a checkered robe over us—when the showers stopped, along the Kutztown road, past Hampden, through the Park—and home again, laden with dust. —We were fortunate to have been able to go at all, when you think of the rain yesterday and to-day. —I have been looking at my calendar. It will be more convenient for me, Bo-Bo, if you do not mind, to come in three weeks instead of two. Besides I think that the first Monday in September is Labor Day, and, therefore, a holiday, although I am not sure. If it is, so much the better. That will be near enough to the time set for my vacation for us to talk about our final plans. We must not leave them until the last minute. —Oh! But such things must be mentioned only in whispers. —I hope you will not be <u>much</u> disappointed about the two weeks, dear. Don't scold me, or any-thing. I thought I would let you know at once. I feel guilty about it, and all that—<u>really.</u> But-but-but-but. —To-morrow evening, you remember, I go over to twenty-first Street to close the lease with Mr. Weinman.[276] I shall be quite a citizen when that is done. —Then, I expect to come back and translate that poem—the rondel by Charles D'Orléans—the translation of which by Andrew Lang we read to-gether on Sunday evening:

276. Adolph Alexander Weinman (1870–1952), an important American sculptor, was born in Germany but came to the United States in 1880 and studied with Augustus Saint-Gaudens. In addition to designing the half-dollar and the dime, for which Elsie served as the model, and which was in use in the United States for most of her marriage to Stevens, Weinman produced large monuments for sites all across the country.

Le temps a laissé son manteau.

Here is my translation of the poem by Chénier, in prose, which I spoke about. I think it one of the simplest and most charming things: the poem (not the translation)—

The Flute

"This memory always affects and touches
me: how he, fitting the flute to my
mouth, laughing and seating me in
his lap, close to his heart, calling me
his rival and already his vanquisher,
shaped my incapable and uncertain lips
to blow a pure and harmonious breath;
and how his skilful hands took my young
fingers, raised them, lowered them, commenced
over again twenty times, thus teaching
them, although still backward, how to
touch in turn the stops of the deep-toned wood."

What an old-fashioned and delightful picture! —My friendly cricket still chirps—but not in the rain, for that seems to have stopped, for a time. I want very much to see the sun again. Three days of darkness in August are more than enough. —And I should like to take a long walk under a clear sky. —Write to me soon, my girl—anything that comes into your mind.

With Love,
Buddy

⌒

[WAS 1888 August 19, 1909 New York]

Thursday Evening

My dear Bo:

I was glad to get your letter this morning but shocked to hear of the death of your neighbor. You must try not to think of it. It seems so very sad under the circumstances, as I remember them. —I wish I had written you a long letter last night to help you forget. Willie Carrel, whom I had not seen for a long time asked me to go to dinner with him at a club.[277] Afterwards, we sat and smoked and talked over old times and old friends until almost eleven o'clock, when I

---

277. In his journal for August 17, 1906, Stevens writes, "Tuesday night at Sheepshead Bay with Carrell. Rowed out to sea and bathed from the boat. There were rose waves and gold—and gnats" (*SP,* 170). In WAS 1942 (August 12, 1913), Stevens will again mention Carrell with two *l*s, probably the same person in all three references.

came home, tired, and went to bed. —Earlier in the evening, before meeting
him, I settled our affair with the "landlord"—signed the lease and set that much
in order. It is a great relief to me to have it disposed of. —And this evening, I
drifted, in the aimless fashion of the novels, into the Astor Library, which
seemed strange to me after so long an absence, and read for an hour and a half—
I don't know what—but a good deal of poetry. It is astonishing how much
poetry I can read with sincere delight. But I didn't see much that was "new or
strange"—except an expression about rhyme being "an instrument of music"—
not that that was "new or strange"—but it struck me as being so; and it was a
pleasant thing to think about. In the "June Book" I made "breeze" rhyme with
"trees"; and have never forgiven myself. It is a correct rhyme, of course,—but
unpardonably "expected." Indeed, none of my rhymes are (most likely) true
"instruments of music." The words to be rhymed should not only sound alike,
but they should enrich and deepen and enlarge each other, like two harmonious
notes. —We shall get the ever-greens, I think, sometime when we are home
together. I am afraid that if we took them at once they would dry up before we
could get around to them, because we shall have so many other things to look
out for at first—curtains, rugs, chairs, candle-sticks, andirons, patented coffee-
making machines (for breakfast,) pin-cushions, towels, shoe-boxes, tables, etc.,
etc. And all the time the trees would be lying in the corner, wishing they were
back on the river-bank or hill-side. But we will get around to them. —Let us try
to make our plans as simple and as sensible as possible, because, after all, we have
only ourselves to please. Besides, I think it would be the nature of both of us to
wish it so. I hope that on my next trip, we shall be able to determine them—so
think hard, Bo-Bo. —My cold is still with me and giving me bit of a headache. I
always take so long to get rid of a cold altogether. But if a long walk on Sunday
will do it, then I ought soon to be in shape, for I expect to go off somewhere for
the whole day—probably up the river, since I know no walk to compare with
that. —I have translated the "Rondel," but I am not yet ready to send it to you.
Also, I have written to Walter Butler for that song about the two men that went
to the circus. —Bye—bye, dear. — —

Your
Buddy

∽

[WAS 1889 August 20, 1909 New York]

Friday Evening

My dear Bo:—

There is something quite new in town. On top of the tower of the Metropolitan Life building, in Madison Square, are four great bronze bells that ring every
quarter hour. To-night I heard them for the second time—but really for the first

time to listen to them. They are immensely high up in the air. It is splendid. —I have been rambling around to-night. I walked through Twenty-First Street to see what it was like at night. Our block is very quiet and respectable and well-lighted. I had an idea that it might be dark. Not at all. —I thought about the furniture we shall want. Don't you think that instead of getting what are called "suits" (horrid!) it would be pleasant to get only what we need to begin with and then pick up odd chairs and things that we see and like as we go along? In other words—to make haste slowly.[278] The selection of a lamp, for example, would of itself be a great affair, where one has such an extraordinary choice. We should want to see those at Yamanaka's, and at Vantine's, and at Higgins & Seiter's, and so on! —And chairs are a world in themselves—not those of Commerce, but of Art—to put it so. We must not deprive ourselves of the excitement of choosing by choosing too soon. —These are the idle thoughts of an idle youth. Youth! Jove, I forgot—but fe-fi-fo-fum—the cat jumped over the Chinaman's thumb,—and the cow of the ballad, came down in the salad—fe-fi-fo-fum. —It has been a busy week and I am <u>glad</u> that to-morrow is Saturday—although I expect to-morrow's letter will give me a deserved scolding for putting my next trip off a month.

With much love—and a kiss from

Your Buddy

🙣

[WAS 1890 August 23, 1909 New York]

Monday Evening

My dearest Bo-Bo:

I am quite shattered by the walk I took yesterday—not less than thirty miles. The walks up and down town keep me in condition; but they have been rather few and far between of late. I ought not, therefore, have gone so far yesterday; for I have been as stiff as if all my "j'ints" were rusty. —Yet it was, as you say, such a glorious day: almost a September sun (I know them all)—when the earth seems cool and the warmth falls like a steady beam. It was the old route along the Palisades, interrupted at noon for a sun-bath on a rock at the edge of the cliff—basking in full air for an hour or more—unseen. —The woods along the side of the road looked at their height. And yet at twilight, in the neutral light, as I looked over the edge, I observed, meekly, that what I had thought to be various shades of green, were, indubitably, green and brown and yellow—oh, the faintest brown and the faintest yellow, yet brown and unquestioned yellow. You see! — I did not altogether respond— my sensibilities were numb—emotion sealed up. It is true. — But when the sun had set and the evening star was twinkling in the

---

278. The Latin, *Festina lente,* is attributed to Suetonius, *Divus Augustus,* 25.

orange sky, I passed a camp—where gypsies used to camp a few years ago. There were two or three camp-fires and at one they were broiling ham. Well, Bo, it may sound absurd, but I did respond to that sugary fragrance—sensibilities stirred, emotions leapt—the evening star, the fragrance of ham, camp-fires, tents. It was worth while, by Jupiter! Not that I give a hang for ham—horrid stuff. But it was the odor of meat—the wildness or sense of wildness. You know—when you camp in wild places—and come in at the end of the day, you always find venison over the fire, or a dozen trouts—and then, there is hot bread, and your pipe afterwards, and then you roll up in your blanket—and the fire begins to fall together—and you fall asleep, so tired, so contented.[279] —I am glad I passed the camp—and I am glad they were not eating boiled potatoes. —And when I reached home I was too dusty and worn out to write, which you will forgive I know, now that you know the reason. I fell all over the bed in a lump. —Next Sunday I hope to do the same thing. —Although I had no letter from you on Saturday, I did not care when I got your letter this morning. Bo-Bo—here are three real kisses for you—silly or not. You are perfect. —I say no more, because I cannot. Only, you do make me tremendously happy—and if you vow to be a bother, why I'll vow to try with all my might to take the best care of you. It seems wonderful to think that you are coming—in a month. I shall have to buy a cane, I suppose, to live up to it. —But I'm not going to think about it, or about anything—only keep on getting ready—although there's really nothing to do, except to look out for nice things—and to know where to go for them. If there is anything I can do for you, you must be sure to let me know. —It is only nine o'clock, but I'm such a battered hulk that I'm going to bed as soon as I have posted this. —Write to me as often as you can.

Your own
Buddy

⤳

[WAS 1891 August 24, 1909 New York]

Tuesday Evening

My dear Bo-Bo:—

Here's a kiss to start with. Oh, you've missed it! (Better look sharp next time.) —It is a very warm kind of evening—and I suppose you have on a white dress and are sitting on the porch—with Mr. Bell. Fe-fi-fo-fum—the sailor from Cadiz cried "Boo!" to the ladies, who wished him in Had-um-um-fe-fi-fo-fum. —I wish I was coming on Saturday. It is so pleasant to see the moon getting rounder and rounder and to think that it will probably be full then—and

---

279. Stevens is thinking back to his hunting trip to British Columbia in August 1903. See *SP,* 117ff.

that the nights will be all gold and silver and lapis-lazuli and mother-'o-pearl and all the rest:

> A caravan from China comes;
>   For miles it sweetens all the air
> With fragrant silks and dreaming gums,
>   Attar and myrrh—
> A caravan from China comes.
>
> Oh merchant, tell me what you bring,
>   With music sweet of camel bells;
> How long have you been travelling
>   With those sweet smells?
> O merchant, tell me what you bring.[280]
>
> The little moon my cargo is,
>   About her neck the Pleiades
> Clasp hands and sing; lover, 'tis this
>   Perfumes the breeze—
> The little moon my cargo is.[281]

(Beastly Pen.) Under my window, the little cricket that sang in the rain—so long ago, it seems—chirps, chirps, chirps—like—well, like an old clock; and I have been sitting here reading and looking at pictures—in the "Studio," a magazine you will know and like one of these days. I have been reading about votes for women, languidly, and then—one of those malicious articles that the English like to write about the Americans: "the sheer, stark, staring madness of the Americans," "the witless Americans." Last week I read a letter by an Englishman in which he said that there were "300,000 inhabited, windowless rooms" in New-York City alone. Jove! What a fib! —I always feel sensitive to this kind of

---

280. Under "merchant," Stevens draws a quarter moon, horns left, and underlines it.
281. *SP* (241) identifies Richard Le Gallienne as the author of this poem. Stevens omits the title, "After Hafiz," and substitutes the word "lover" for "Hafiz" in his line 13, and omits two five-line stanzas in which the merchant identifies his cargo:

> A lovely lady is my freight,
> A lock escaped of her long hair,—
> That is this perfume delicate
> That fills the air—
> A lovely lady is my freight.
> Her face is from another land,
> I think she is no mortal maid,—
> Her beauty, like some ghostly hand,
> Makes me afraid.

thing, notwithstanding it is such awful rot. But the kind of Englishman that makes such remarks must be as much of a bounder in fact as he is in print; and while the desire is to give him a black eye (if I may say so,) the proper thing is to chuckle and enjoy the show. —But you can hardly care about all that; and no doubt, you wonder why I write of it. . . . The cricket must have reminded me of it—chirp, chirp, chirp, chirp, chirp, chirp. . . . It reminds me of a Russian symphony I heard a winter or two ago—by Glazounoff,[282] I think. One movement was a reminiscence of crickets, as I recall it, and throughout that movement the violins kept up an unbroken imitation of these two monotonous notes—monotonous and drowsy and agreeable and companionable and frail and—like the sound of the ponds late in March—chirp, chirp, chirp, chirp, chirp, chirp, chirp. —I want you to hear it—not that buzzy thing (probably a locust)—not your katy-dids and tree-frogs on the noisy hill-side. Last night's long rest patched me up and to-day I felt pretty much myself. By to-morrow I shall be all together again. —You can imagine what Sunday's walk really was— long runs—and so on. I did not tell you of a vegetable garden I saw—rows of celery, rows of tomatoes, a patch of squashes, and the like. It was almost forgotten. —What an answer to pessimists it is to be able to point to things growing— and not only growing, but ripening, too! If the odor of ham under the evening star failed to enchant them, that patch of yellow squashes would. What a delightful poem that is, too:

> A caravan from China comes;
> For miles it sweetens all the air—
> Good-night, my dearest Bo-bo.

With much love,

Wallace—no: —you know+

↩

[WAS 1892 August 25, 1909 New York]

Wednesday Evening

My dear Bo-Bo:

Here are two exceptionally pretty post-cards—Japanese—for that young amateur;[283] and a clipping from the <u>Sun</u> for you[284]—and I have only a rather

---

282. In *SP* (160), the journal entry for February 25, 1906, Stevens reports attending a concert of the Russian Symphony in which he heard a symphonic arrangement: "'From the Middle Ages,' by Glazunoff, that contained two most *encorable* movements."

283. Elsie's sister LaRue. The cards are not extant.

284. This clipping contains a flippant five-hundred-word essay, "The Call of the Kitchen," that, after mentioning Kaiser Wilhelm's admonition to German women that

seedy envelope from the office of the right size to hold them. —These are almost school-boy scraps to send you, I am afraid—yet I think they will pass five minutes for you pleasantly. —It is June weather all over again, except for the shortness of the evenings. To-night, as I walked after dinner, I thought it would never be half-past eight, the time I had fixed for coming in. The streets are so tedious when it is dark. I was tempted to go to the theatre; but there is nothing here that is good that won't be here for a long time to come; so I'll wait. —I hope there will be a letter for me to-morrow. Send me one about things out of doors—the looks of the country, if you have seen it.

With love-
Buddy

⌁

[WAS 1893 August 26, 1909 New York]

Thursday Evening

My dear Bo:

I've been looking around for a pen—and this is my third start. I cannot endure my hand-writing as affected by a stub-pen. The letters and words are as stiff as wax-works. —I had two letters from you today, my dear. I couldn't possibly be sentimental enough to tell you how pleasant it was; but it <u>was</u> pleasant, especially since they were full of what is so sweet and welcome to me. —Don't think that I didn't see that signet in the middle of one of the inside leaves! Rascal. —It has been one of the most uncomfortable days. To-night, the caravan from China was only half-visible through the heat mist in the sky. This is the great moon of the year and I follow its growth as a devout poet should. —I noted that they are stringing thousands of bulbs of electric lights along Fifth-Avenue. That is for the Hudson-Fulton celebration next month, which you will be in time to see.[285] It is going to be one of the greatest affairs of its kind that we

---

"'Kinder, Küche, and Kirche,' that is children, cooking, and church" should be their motto, and after citing various sexist sentiments by Metchnikoff, Dr. H. W. Wiley, Byron, and Schopenhauer, concludes by emphasizing cooking alone:

> If the call of the kitchen rings out its clarion clear note, then in the name of all the master cooks of history answer the call and fry the doughnuts as mother did! But don't let either Dr. Wiley drive you to the kitchen or feminine politics drive you away from your post; for while your hand may some day control the destiny of the nation, it must never be too far away from the pot that boils over.

We leave the two other "Ks" of the Kaiser in peace.

285. The huge Hudson-Fulton Celebration, September 25 to October 9, 1909, was commemorated with special U.S. stamps (one for Henry Hudson's *Half Moon* of 1609

have had for years. —But it is really very dull, all in all, and I hardly know what to do at night. It is much too hot to read. My lamp throws off waves of heat like a tempestuous volcano. —Bye-bye.

Your own

—Giant

⤺

[WAS 1894 August 27, 1909 New York]

Friday Evening

My Dear:

The sky is purple tonight and in the East there is a great golden star. I have been up to the Park wandering around in the—moonlight. There is a reservoir there a mile around. The water was as quiet as a mirror, and it was, in fact, very much like a mirror altogether. Then the shapes of the trees were so splendid against the sky—the flat, palm-like boughs of the pines, the round, graceful elms, the tall, slender white birches. It was after ten when I came in. Will you forgive me if I send only a word? I shall do better and deserve better on Sunday. I feel too tired to take the walk I had planned; but a cool Saturday may make a difference.

Your

Buddy

⤺

[WAS 1895 August 29, 1909 New York]

Sunday Evening

Dear Bo-Bo:—

I feel my notes of the past week have tried your patience. But I feel invincibly languid and dull. I did not realize how much I might be disappointing you, day after day, until today, when, thanks to more agreeable weather, I find myself remorseful. —After tea, this evening, I pulled my chair close to the window and spent a half-hour in so-called reflection and then my crimes as a letter-writer haunted me. —The last Sunday in August: the last vacation Sunday in the minds of most people—or many people. I spent it here at home—in this very chair, reading the Times, the Sun, the Studio, the Athenaeum. There is such a funny story about the Atheneum. It is, as you may know, a weekly devoted to litera-ture, music, art and the drama. It is able and complete but prodigiously dull. Stevenson, the novelist, mentions a sporting man who picked the paper up and

---

and one for Robert Fulton's steamship *Clermont* of two centuries later), the closing of the New York Stock Exchange (September 25, 1909), and an elaborate Reception Day. The young FDR was a member of the Hudson-Fulton Celebration Commission, and war ships from all over the world made appearances in New York.

said "Golly, what a paper!" —That amused me immensely. —The sky was too threatening to think of a walk. I waited until the last minute for breakfast, and came back here, feeling indescribably lazy and tired. In fact, the mere idea of moving made me sigh. —But that singular lethargy has been decreasing all day. At four o'clock, I walked up and down the streets, getting as far North as 34th Street, before it was time to return to the house. There were many interesting things in the windows, which I made note of, although I really know, without looking, just where to go for anything I want. Yet one makes discoveries. In a general way, I knew where to go for coffee machines, for example; but today I found a store that deals in them altogether. That is one of the first things we shall need, because, while we won't want to bother about little dinners for ourselves, for the present, we shall have to get our own breakfasts. Everybody does, that lives that way—and it is great fun. The coffee makes itself (in the machine,) while you thrill over the morning paper. —What I meant by "suits" of furniture was—furniture that matched—furniture in sets. Where there is only one floor (as there will be with us,) it will be very much more interesting to have odds and ends. I think that we shall enjoy the mere largeness of the rooms. —By the way, the lease commences next Wednesday. But I do not intend to move in. We'll move in together. But I shall have to have a few book-shelves made and put up and that I shall attend to at once. And I may get one or two other things. But the place will be <u>absolutely bare</u> when you come and you will have to jump right in and fill[286] it up. —I wish to-morrow was going to be a holiday. By morning, I shall be thoroughly rested and ready for the exercise I scorned to-day, and all my energy will have to be expended on the work at the office. With half the people away on vacations, that particular spot is very much of a nuisance. —Yet my days and nights are just a continual to and fro from it. To-morrow I must resume my walks which have (to tell the truth) been few and far between, of late. Also, I came across a swimming pool not far away, where they give you what is called a "Scotch scour," which I have a notion to look into. —But it is all grist that comes to the mill.

Your own

B.

⏝

---

286. It looks as if Stevens originally wrote "fill" and then crossed the first *l* to make an *x,* or originally wrote "fix" and added an *l,* leaving a composite word that could be either "fill" or "fix." His final intention is not clear.

[WAS 1896 August 31, 1909 New York]

Tuesday Evening

My own Girl:—

I <u>did</u> mind your not writing on Sunday very much. Did I show it in my letter last night? I tried not to. . . . The real reason my letters were so bad last week was that I was depressed from too much smoking. Often, when there is a great deal to do at the office, lots of people to see, and so on, I smoke incessantly to quiet my nerves. The result is, that, when the day is over, and the strain is gone, I find myself in a kind of stupor and find it very difficult to do anything at all. I do not even feel like reading—unless it be the newspapers. —On the other hand, if I do not smoke, my nerves tingle and I am full of energy: yes, tingle with it. And then I want to walk violently, work violently, read, write, study—all at a bound. The trouble is, however, that I am intolerably irritable at such times and make life miserable for everybody who must assist me and am apt to be very short and sharp to people with whom I must do business. That, of course, is impossible. For example, I didn't smoke at all on Sunday. On Monday I did mountains of work and had everybody on tip-toe. To-day I started my third day without a cigar and behaved outrageously; so that at lunch I smoked—and have been like a lamb all the rest of the day. —Yet if I go without smoking for three of four days at the end of that time the irritableness disappears and I am as agreeable as the next man. —I wonder if you know that I always stop smoking a few days before I come to see you. I will not smoke to-morrow, nor at all until after our holiday. —I wanted to break myself of the habit entirely, but it is a terribly insidious and seductive thing and, if one could indulge in it mildly, quite harmless. To-morrow commences a new month and I am going to try to go through it without a single puff—or if I must smoke, at least try to limit myself to one cigar a day, which I think I could do. . . . So much for a thing that causes me more regrets than anything under the sun. But was there ever a smoker who was not bidding farewell to the weed with one hand and reaching for a perfecto with the other? I doubt it. —Pshaw! What a thing to write about! —I am <u>really</u> impatient to see you again. There are so many things to arrange, and we must settle on them in advance. Try to settle in your own mind the way you would like this and that to be done, because I want you to please yourself. That will be happiest for both of us. —I shall come on Saturday afternoon and be up reasonably early in the evening—before eight. —All your letters of late, long or short, have been very sweet to me—because I know you do not say things you do not feel. They make me feel both humble and glad. Yes: it is true—and I send you my love, over and over again, in return. —Let us not think of it. We'll be driving on Sunday, wondering at the ripeness of grapes, and the redness of apples. —Adieu!

Your
Giant

[WAS 1897 September 2, 1909 New York]

Thursday evening

My dear Bo-Bo:

The news of the discovery of the North Pole seems to have brought a bit of polar weather with it. —Last evening Kearney came back to town from his vacation. He wants to devote a few days to finding an apartment. He and Mrs. Kearney have lived in a single room over a millinery shop in Brooklyn since their marriage. He wanted to see what I had found and as I was proud to show him, he and Stryker and I walked up town and dropped off at the apartment. Such shouts of envy! Kearney offered me a prize to give it up. I had not been there myself for some time and I swear I was more than ever pleased with it. You will like it immensely. —Then we had dinner together and went to see a very amusing comedy called, "Is Matrimony a Failure?"[287] One of the most entertaining things I ever saw. —And afterwards, I walked home <u>smoking a cigar.</u> How the deuce could I help it—after such a riotous evening! —A fellow might as well be a priest as keep all his beastly resolutions. But heigh-ho, the cat and the fiddle, and the tiger asleep, with 'em both in his middle. —So you're going to be too busy to write to me any more this week. B-e-w-a-r-e! —But then there's only another day, isn't there? I'll be so glad to get home again on Saturday that I suppose I'll have to overlook it this time. —Now, if you wait a moment, while I put on my overcoat, ear-muffs and fur cap I'll run out into the wintry air and post this at the corner. —When I posted the last one, the other night, I saw an air-ship, with a light at each end—at least it was something. —I sent a few stray post-cards this afternoon for La Rue.

Bye-bye—

George Washington

[WAS 1898 September 8, 1909 New York]

Wednesday evening

My dear Bo-Bo:—

Here is the penman at his pen again. You ought to have had a letter day today. But last night I went to East Orange to be measured for some clothes,[288] and

287. Comedy in three acts by Leo Ditrichstein, from the *Die Thue in Freie,* by Oscar Blumenthal and Gustav Kadelberg, produced at the Belasco Theater on August 24, 1909. The first big hit of the season, it ran for 183 performances.
288. This same tailor, Axel Lofquist of 14 Washington Place (or after his retirement, his son, Spencer Lofquist), made Stevens's suits from 1905 until his death fifty years later. He had met this tailor in 1905 while he was living in East Orange, New Jersey (cf. *LWS,* 682n6).

then I went around to Lee Smith's[289] to pick up a deer head that he has been keeping for me. I am going to have it tinkered a bit—it will be just the thing for the wall over the fire-place in the sitting-room. Well, it was ten o'clock when I reached home and as I had had less than two hours sleep the night before, I jumped right into bed—and now I hope you will excuse me. At noon, I ran up-town to Potter's and saw about having my easy chair done over. Also arranged with "Madame Pauline," a cleaner, to take care of my hunting blankets, and make them "sweet" and clean again. And this evening I had a long dicker with a cabinet-maker and ordered two book-shelves from him, one for each side of the fire-place. I want to get the books moved and in order before you come because they are a great nuisance to take care of—although pleasant enough, once arranged. It takes a week for everything, so you see that I have no time to lose. To-morrow I shall have to go up to Tiffany's, because there will have to be an inscription made and for all I know, that may take a week too. There are always so many people ahead of one. I got a very pleasant letter from the landlord the other day (to whom I had written that we would not move in until the end of the month) saying that he was sorry we were not coming sooner, and that he hoped we would be comfortable. So that you see that all the arrangements are going ahead diligently. Next week sometime I shall write to Dr. Myers[290] to remind him and I'll tell him definitely the hour—Tuesday, the twenty-first, at half-past ten. That will give us both plenty of time to get into travelling togs and get to the Franklin street station for the 12:19 train. I hope you are making your dress-maker hurry and that you will have your things done in time just as you want them. Don't forget, in packing your trunk, to pack only those things that you will not want right away—like that pink dress (the every-day one.) We can forward the trunk by express after I have come over to Reading, in my name to

289. In a journal entry for December 27, 1898, Stevens refers to Lee Smith (cf. *SP*, 25). On July 21, 1899, he compared a Miss Benz to Lee Smith in her "gulping her literature from magazines and the latest novels" (*SP*, 47). In his journal for October 1, 1902, Stevens mentions that "Lee Smith [is] in England" (*SP*, 109). Lee Keely Smith, in the class of 1891 at Reading High School, lived at 144 North Fourth Street in Reading. The entry for him in the *Graduate Catalogue of the Reading High Schools: 1856–1905* reads, "Lee Keely Smith, . . . 59 West Seventeenth St., N. Y. City. Graduated with Merit Salutatory. Registered as a Law Student in Philadelphia, 1892. Attended the Harvard Law School, Cambridge, Mass., 1894–95. Organist, Christ Protestant Episcopal Church, East Orange, N. J. Instructor, voice, Piano, and Organ" (154).
290. Reverend William H. Myers of Grace Lutheran Church in Reading. In her "Branch of the Bright Family," Elsie outlines her connections to this church and this pastor: "Elsie V. Kachel became a member of Grace Lutheran Sunday School, and attended Sunday School until about 1900. She became a member of Grace Lutheran church, and was confirmed by the pastor Rev. William H. Myers, on March 24th, 1907." Stevens had urged her to join the church in his letter of March 10, 1907.

the house. The other things, of course, will have to go in a suit-case. You will have to have things enough for about a week—because we shall go to Boston and then to the Berkshires in Western Massachusetts and then to Albany and down the Hudson by daylight—and I think it will take about a week. —Do you feel excited about it? I don't at all. My feeling is just gladness that you are going to be with me—and pride. I must think hard how to take care of that shadowy Elsie of long ago who is going to come to me. Take long looks at Reading while you can. Nothing there will ever be the same to you again—and resolve to be a patriot so far as the town is concerned. We shall probably not get back to it before Xmas[291]—and then you will already be something of a New-Yorker, and the little country girl you like to call yourself will have disappeared. —By the way, Lee Smith has a fireless cooker. It looks like quite an idea. But one would care to use it only for certain things—such as baked potatoes for breakfast, and all that kind of thing. Perhaps you won't care for one, but I'm sure you'll be interested to see such a queer affair. —Well, this is a queer jumble of stuff I'm sending you. There's so much to tell you that I got it out all higgeldy-piggeldy. But it's all here, after all, and that's the point. Haven't you a hundred and one things to think of? There are so many that I am sure something will be forgotten. —If you haven't much time, only write me notes so that I know you are all right.

With much love, your
Buddy

↩

[WAS 1899 September 9, 1909 New York]

Thursday Evening

My dear Girl:—

The ring is arranged for. —It has a ferociously legal look. In fact, it's a regular chain. But I got the lightest one I could get. They are all heavy—so that the lightest one isn't saying much. —Well, it will serve it's [*sic*] purpose—and I should like you to have it, whether or not you wear it afterwards. —I am having our initials put in it and the date. I did not know quite what to do about your initials; whether to have E. V. M. or E. V. K., but as I had to decide, I decided on E. V. K.[292] because those are the correct ones. It will not be ready until next week. —A number of odds and ends went for repair, etc., today and when

---

291. This is his first use of this abbreviation in his letters to Elsie; the word Christmas will not appear again.

292. Elsie's last name was never legally changed to Moll, though Elsie's mother, Ida Smith Kachel, married Lehman Wilkes Moll in 1894, when Elsie was eight years old. When Lehman Moll died in 1952, Elsie did not attend his funeral but did send her daughter Holly to represent herself and Wallace. See *LWS*, 747.

finished will be sent to the new house—like the deer-head. I have decided to keep only one of my rugs—a tawny red one which I am fond of. It goes to the cleaners tomorrow for complete renovation. —Then to-day, also, I procured a number of boxes, in which I intend to pack books on Saturday afternoon—no: I think I'll have to let it go until Sunday, although I want to get off for a walk on Sunday, if possible. To-morrow evening I must go out to East Orange to try on my clothes. Queer place to go for clothes—only I think the tailor there is the best one I ever had, or know of. —Really I have to keep a list of places where things are and when I am to be here and when there. The man that is making the book-cases called up at the office to-day in great excitement to know something or other—and so on. —I suppose you are in the same boat, poor girl. —It will probably be much worse when we start to get furniture, so we should regard all this as a mere preliminary. —Don't work too hard over your dresses. Spare a little time for exercise and take a little walk each day. —I walked uptown myself to-night and never enjoyed it more. There was a very clear autumnal feeling in the air.

With love,
Wallace

⌒

[WAS 1900 September 10, 1909 New York]

Friday Evening

My dear:

Wretched weather all day—heavy rain and mist. Tried to get out to East Orange and back before dinner, but got home just too late. I went to an Italian table d'hote on Tenth-street. The sort of crowd seemed familiar. It is a long time since I have been to such a place. —East Orange, in the wet, dismal twilight, looked indescribably gloomy. But then the truth is that it is not often wet, and even less often dismal. —This is the very kind of rain that sets the leaves going. In Spring it brings them. In Autumn it takes them away. —Everything goes along just as it should (and as it is bound to do if one pays attention.) Yet we may take a little recess to-night and not speak of plans—although anyone coming into my room would know at once that a change is pending—bare floor, pile of boxes—and so on. —I wish it was to-morrow that I was going home, instead of a week hence. Next week will hang on me like lead, because of the week to follow. —As I look over my things, there are a good many odds and ends that I want to throw away, I find; and it is the hardest thing in the world to make up my mind to do so. My old trunk, which has been through a score of boarding-houses is sure to go. It is a most disreputable-looking piece of baggage. Then there is a batch of papers—college note books, etc., which have a sentimental interest, yet ought to be sacrificed, it seems to me. I hate to throw them away. At the same time, I hate to have all that junk tagging after me. I'll make up my mind on Sunday. —I should like to start with everything fairly new—not necessarily new-looking, but fresh; and I am going to get rid of everything possible. —But weren't we going to take a recess? It seems difficult to think of anything else, and you must overlook it. Thus we train ourselves in the grace of forbearance—the salvation of all offenders! —There will be a letter for me tomorrow I hope—just a little one. I haven't had a letter from you all week—but never mind, dear. Here are a hundred kisses for you—and my love.

Your own
Buddy

⌁

[WAS 1901 September 12, 1909 New York]

Sunday Evening

My dear Bo-Bo:—

Whenever I move I have a house cleaning and I have been having one all day to-day. First I packed the books, dusting them first. They are now ready to be moved. When I get them over, and when the new shelves are ready, I am going to fill the shelves and then throw away a good many of those that remain and for which we shall have no room. The ones to be thrown away are the old ones, some of them in bad condition, and others which no longer interest me—chiefly historical and similar books. —This evening (it is after ten o'clock) I went through my trunk and threw away practically everything that was in it. Then I had a great batch of papers in connection with legal matters which I have reduced from a pile two feet high to two small packages in envelopes. It has been my habit to save everything that might be useful and the result was an appalling litter. It was high time that something was done. —For example, at college, where the instruction is given by lectures (instead of recitations) I took notes on what was said. So did everybody else. It was part of the system. —Well, my note-books were scandalous affairs, full of pen-and-ink sketches of queer noses, the backs of heads and so on. These note-books, which seemed to have a sentimental interest, have always survived previous cleanings; but to-day I found courage to dump them one and all in the overflowing waste-basket. —Of course, I have kept my diaries, and my priceless poetical scribblings, and other odds and ends—but the whole business can be carried now in one hand, instead of blocking up closets and corners. —Among the things I saved was a gold tassel[293] from a certain blue dress—and an equally mysterious bit of lace, of which I send you an inch or more to remind you of a Spring walk we took long ago. Also I send you a little picture in which I appear

---

293. Such a gold tassel is first mentioned in WAS 1821 of February 28, 1909.

to have dropped down from a balloon. I seem to be taking the visit with uncommon seriousness. —All that remains now is to tackle my collection of medicines for burnt hands, colds, and so on—and throw the whole thing away, since hereafter I am to have a nurse. —I was very glad to have your little letter yesterday. What a pity it is that you cannot finish what you planned. But, after all, you will have the essential things. —Don't worry about my being able to take care of you. That will be very simple—provided we are content to live modestly and without envy of other people. I do not, however, propose to think of such things until the time comes. —In any event, with loyalty and courage, we have nothing to fear. —I do not know if I can get the early train on Saturday. I want to go to the new house and see that its bareness is, at least, neat. If the book-shelves are delivered on Friday, I can do it on Friday evening. Otherwise I should have to go on Saturday afternoon. But I will let you know in time. —Have you been taking a walk to-day? As you can imagine, I have been indoors all day to my regret. But the result satisfies me.

> With much love, dear,
>
> Your
>
> Wallace

⟿

[WAS 1902 September 13, 1909 New York]

> Monday Evening

My dearest:

Yesterday's disorder has turned into the strict arrangements of emptiness. The room looks prim and spacious as empty rooms are apt to. —Everything is going perfectly. Mrs. Jones, the washerwoman, black as an African thunder-cloud, came in person to bid me adieu. —Thus the farewells commence. Stryker, to-day, starting for the shore, cried "Good Luck!" —But I keep it pretty much a secret. —I am glad you have two such steadfast friends as Mary and Anna to assist you (and, no doubt, tease you a little.) They must both come to see us when we are settled. Tell them so. —Don't allow yourself to grow nervous, Bo-Bo. Everything will be, to use your own expression, as easy as pie. I remember that Dr. Myers suggested that we walk down the aisle together. But that would be making a march of it. There will be only a handful of us and I think we should confine the solemnity to the ceremony proper. The simpler the better, don't you think? —I have decided to get along without a best man. There is no one at home whom I should care to ask, or, in fact, of whom I can think. And if I asked any one from New-York, we should have to come back with them or him. I shall be obliged to look after the baggage myself, but that will not be difficult. By the way, will you take more than a suit-case or bag? I think I can put all the stuff I'll want in a single suit-case. —We should go as lightly laden as possible, because

I hope to get some candle-sticks in Boston, and there may be other odds and ends—especially in some of the little shops around Boston Common. —It will be all right to wait for a drive until Sunday evening. Anyhow, we could hardly go on Monday because I have an engagement with Dr. Hickman[294] in the morning, and then must go for the license (horrid affair) and then take it to Dr. Myers, so that he can prepare himself. I shall see the florist on Saturday evening. You will want a bouquet—and then we shall both want some things on the altar. —I got the ring to-day at noon. It is better than I expected. —Also (this is a queer jumble) I looked at the bookcases. They are quite large. Decided to have them a mahogany[295] stain, instead of white—they'll wear better. They are to be finished by Thursday. —On Wednesday I go to East Orange to take the last fling at the tailor. I swear I'll be as dressed-up as a trick pony. —By the way, are you going to ask your father? It would be pleasant to have him—for then I should not feel so much like the captive of four ferocious women—and he and I could support each other. —Was there ever anything so higgeldy-piggeldy as this letter? —This afternoon I sent a last batch of post-cards for La Rue. Some of them are souvenirs of that hunting trip to British Columbia—and probably smell of the camphor in which they have been so long preserved. —So you are only a simple damsel, are you? Well, you will be ten thousand times happy, then—for the simple are as blessed as the pure in heart. I am perfectly sure that we shall be a great deal happier than we can imagine now. To have you always! What more could—no: just a kiss—and my love—always—

> Your
> Buddy

↬

[WAS 1903 September 14, 1909 New York]

Tuesday Evening

My dearest:

I begin to feel restless at the office—but to-morrow will be the fourth day of the week. My work is in good order. So that there may be no great rush at the end of the week I am disposing of matters in a high-handed way. Friday is usually the busiest day. —Today has been like August all over again and after dinner tonight I loitered until half-past eight before coming up-stairs. Besides, it is not comfortable up here with only one chair to sit on, and that one not particularly easy. —The preparations for the Hudson-Fulton celebration are going ahead at

---

294. Glyndeur Hickman, a prominent Reading dentist, had his office at 35 South Fifth Street, just a few blocks from the Stevens home.

295. This word has been obviously altered (the second letter changed from an *e* to an *a*), one of the rare corrections in the letters.

a great rate. Fifth-Avenue begins to look gay with courts of honor and electric lights. —This is the week, as well, of the Mardi Gras at Coney Island. By the time you come, that strange place will be closed for the season—although I believe there is always more or less activity there. —But you will not miss that, for Dr. Cook and Commander Perry, the discoverers of the North Pole, will be coming to town in a few days and give every promise of making things even livelier than they are at Coney Island. —Then the election will be commencing—for mayor: and, on the whole, there will be no lack of excitement. —You will think New-York, under such circumstances, much wilder than it really is. Yet, at the worst, it can hardly be as bad as Penn Square[296] was on Labor Day, when the fat man passed with his trained goat in harness. —To-morrow we say adieu to straw hats—and the stores begin to annoy one about fall (or Fall) fashions. —But all this is neither here nor there, except as it gives me an opportunity to say a word to you. Bye-bye!

Your own
Buddy

⌒

[WAS 1904 September 15, 1909 New York]
[Stationery of the Princeton Club, New York.]

Wednesday Evening

My dear Bo-Bo:

After the visit to East-Orange (where I made all manner of trouble for the honest tailor) I hurried back to town and took dinner here with a friend of mine. Afterwards, we walked over to the apartment, where I had some arrangements to make about the receipt of packages, turning on the electricity, and the like. Everytime I see it I like it more, and the fellow I was with thought it splendid. Then we walked back here, to smoke a bit and gossip—with the understanding that I was first to have an opportunity to write a little note to you. One's friends marvel at the matter of marriage, and act as if they were seeing me give up the delights of "single blessedness."[297] But they do not know of

---

296. The central business and ceremonial area in Reading.
297. Stevens is using an often-repeated phrase first used by Theseus as he explains to Hermia her options about obeying her father near the beginning of *Midsummer Night's Dream:*

> Either to die the death or to abjure
> For ever the society of men.
> Therefore, fair Hermia, question your desires;
> Know of your youth, examine well your blood,
> Whether, if you yield not to your father's choice,

the delights I look forward to, and that all men look forward to in their turn. I only wish this old week were over and that we were together. But then we shall be in <u>less</u> than a week—and in Boston at that—and I don't know of any place that I should rather be with you, unless it were in a sofa of our own by our own fire. And that, too, will come before we know it. —This is only a word to keep in touch with you.

With much love,
Wallace

⤸

[WAS 1905 September 16, 1909 New York]

Thursday Evening

My dear Bo-Bo:

I shall be very glad to see your two supporters on Sunday evening. We can then complete our arrangements. I have already written to Dr. Myers reminding him of the time. —The books were moved to-night, and to-morrow night I shall unpack them and put them on the shelves, which were also completed and delivered to-day. —The people at the place where I take my meals decorated my chair. Fortunately, I did not get home until after seven o'clock, and ate dinner down-stairs—to the intense discomfiture of the celebrants. —Afterwards, I took a peek and have promised to sit on the throne at breakfast. Imagine! The chair is all white ribbons, with roses at the top. Ridiculously funny—but permissible, I suppose. —It may be that I shall not be able to come on the early train on Saturday. But if I do not, I shall come on the one that leaves here at five o'clock, and shall be up as soon as I can after reaching home. But only for a little while; for, since travelling tires one, we shall have to keep good hours until we start. And that, I think, would be your own desire. —I was glad to have a letter from you this morning, which I was not expecting. Are you still so busy with the dress maker? I am all ready and could start at a minute's notice. No: there are still some things to be done, but only odds and ends. — Everybody is very nice—full of advice and good wishes—and for so much

---

You can endure the livery of a nun,
For aye to be in shady cloister mew'd,
To live a barren sister all your life,
Chanting faint hymns to the cold fruitless moon.
Thrice-blessed they that master so their blood,
To undergo such maiden pilgrimage;
But earthlier happy is the rose distill'd,
Than that which withering on the virgin thorn
Grows, lives and dies in single blessedness.

kindness, one must be grateful. It is pleasant—although I feel flitting regrets for the old-time secresy. —Why should we limit ourselves to such tiny kisses? When I think that you are coming at last, I feel really <u>humble</u> and then I want to cover you with kisses.

With love, all of it,
Your own,
Buddy

3

First Years of Marriage
New York, 1909–1916

The letters of this period, until Stevens begins his first travel for the Hartford in the spring of 1916, are all occasioned by Elsie's absences from their apartment at 441 West Twenty-first Street, at first as she extended the Christmas holiday for several weeks with her family in Reading and then, in following years, as she was sent to stay at resorts during the hottest months of the summer.

The newspaper account of the wedding presents a remarkable portrait of normality, but it omits the news that no one from Stevens's family was present, that he had, in fact, made a large and unbridgeable gap between his old life and his new one:

QUIET WEDDING IN GRACE LUTHERAN CHURCH
Miss Elsie Viola Kachel Becomes Mrs. Wallace Stevens of New York

A quiet church wedding was solemnized in Grace Lutheran Church at 11 o'clock this morning, when Wallace Stevens, son of Garrett B. and Mary C. Stevens, 323 North Fifth street, and Miss Elsie Viola Kachel, daughter of the late Howard I. Kachel, who resided with her mother, Mrs. L. W. Moll, 231 South Thirteenth street, were united in marriage. The ceremony was performed by Rev. W. H. Myers and was witnessed only by the immediate relatives.

There were no attendants. The bride was attired in an embroidered crepe de chine dress over white taffeta and carried a shower bouquet of lilies-of-the-valley. Immediately after the ceremony a reception to the relatives was held at the home of the bride. Mrs. Schroeder was the caterer. The Moll home was beautifully decorated with palms and cut flowers.

At noon the couple left on a wedding tour to Buffalo, Boston and other points in Massachusetts. On their return they will go to house-keeping at 441 West Twenty-first street, New York city.

Mr. and Mrs. Stevens are very popular among a wide circle of friends and received numerous telegrams of congratulation. The bride is an accomplished musician. Mr. Stevens is a graduate of the Reading High School, Harvard College and the New York Law School. He is a member of the New York bar and is assistant manager of the American Bonding Company of New York. The couple were accompanied to the train by a number of friends.[1]

This seriously flawed account allows only one hour (Stevens had scheduled an hour and forty-nine minutes) for the ceremony, the reception, and the catching of the train, one of its less misleading statements. Its truest suggestions are the word "quiet" and the absence of attendants. Stevens's mother's first name is wrong, his degree from Harvard is wrong, Buffalo is not on the itinerary, and the popularity of the couple seems somewhat exaggerated. The reference to "immediate family" is frankly misleading.

The church in which the wedding took place is the same one Elsie had joined at the urging of Wallace in WAS 1784 March 24, 1907. She tells of her connection with this church in her typescript "A Branch of the Bright Family," cited in the general introduction above, and then she gives her account of the wedding: "On September 21st., 1909, we were married by Rev. William H., Myers, in Grace Lutheran church in Reading, attended by the bride's parents and two bridesmaids, Miss Anna Rigg, and Miss Mary Stoner."

After their honeymoon trip to Boston, Stockbridge, Albany, and then a boat trip down the Hudson to New York, they each wrote a message to her mother and family on a postcard of the Chapel of the Good Shepherd at the General Theological Seminary, Chelsea Square, a card on which an arrow points to their apartment (in the background):

Our house is under the mark. Our floor is the next to the top. Therefore, we face the chapel, which is only across the street. Chimes every evening. We are not a part of the chapel—but apart from it. Hence, the word apartment. Hope this is clear.

Wallace is crazy. Don't mind him. But this is the house, as much as you can see of it. (*SP*, 246)

The sons of their landlord later informed Holly Stevens that Wallace used to stand in one of the couple's closets and recite poetry and that Elsie would sometimes "pace through the apartment slamming doors vigorously, including closet doors" (*SP*, 247). Elsie's brief paragraph about this part of their lives

1. *Reading Eagle,* Tuesday, September 21, 1909.

gives the important basic facts and also a touch of reality from her point of view:

> After his marriage in 1909, [Wallace Stevens] and his wife occupied the top floor of 441 West 21st Street, N. Y., a studio house owned [and occupied] by the well known sculptor [and his family], Mr. Adolph Weinman. [; with the exception of the two top floors, a tenant also occupying the floor below ours.][2] There were four flights of stairs to reach their apartment, the house entrance being lower than the sidewalk. While there was no elevator, there was a dumbwaiter on which they pulled up their mail, packages and ice. The corner grocery store made no deliveries, so the writer carried the groceries home.

One visitor to their apartment in those days, Frances Butler, the older sister of Walter Butler, whom Stevens had met when he lived in East Orange, New Jersey, and to whom a number of the letters of 1909 refer, reported that the apartment "was rather sparsely furnished, and that the evening she was there Wallace sat in a corner reading, while she talked with Elsie." At that time Elsie also told Frances that "she wanted a child" (*SP,* 247).

Because Elsie spent most of each summer away from Stevens and New York, he wrote to her, letters addressed to her at her old home in Reading (1910 and 1911), at Vinemont, a rest resort near Reading (1912), at Pocono Manor in Pennsylvania (1913), at her old home again (1913 and 1914), and, finally, at Byrdcliffe in Woodstock, New York (1915). After the move to Hartford, this pattern will be basically reversed, with Elsie remaining at home and Stevens writing to her from places on the road for the Hartford Accident and Indemnity Company.

Two important deaths occurred during this period, that of Stevens's father on July 14, 1911, and that of his mother, just over a year later, on July 16, 1912. Stevens, in his journal (*SP,* 253–55), gives a strong reaction to the final illness and death of his mother, one line of which is revealing in the light of his rejection of "imperishable bliss" in "Sunday Morning" just three years later: "All the feelings that are aroused create a constant desire or hope of something after death." Nothing contemporaneous survives of what he thought about the death of his father, though he did leave, in a letter of September 13, 1943, to his niece

---

2. From "A Branch of the Bright Family." Elsie's greater specificity about the floor on which they live seems to override Stevens's possibly ambiguous reference above to their floor as "next to the top." However, Stevens's clear reference in WAS 1907 December 28, 1909, to hearing "the Rudolphs moving about upstairs" opens up the possibility that they moved from one floor to the other during their more than six years at this address.

Jane MacFarland Stone, a touching statement about his father that probably applied as much to himself:

> I think that we have to take him as he wanted to be. He wasn't a man given to pushing his way. He needed what all of us need, and what most of us don't get: that is to say, discreet affection. So much depends on ourselves in that respect. I think that he loved to be at the house with us, but he was incapable of lifting a hand to attract any of us, so that, while we loved him as it was natural to do, we also were afraid of him, at least to the extent of holding off. The result was that he lived alone. The greater part of his life was spent at his office; he wanted quiet and, in that quiet, to create a life of his own. (*LWS*, 454)

The period in which Stevens wrote these letters (1909–16) is arguably the most important in his life, if for no other reason than he wrote "Sunday Morning" during it. This poem continues to strike students of Stevens's work as an unprecedented and startling achievement right at the beginning of his real poetic career. How did he get from the conventional poetry written for Elsie in 1908 and 1909 to the mastery of "Sunday Morning"? Robert Buttel devotes an entire helpful book to this question.[3] Many have pointed to the possible influence of the famous exhibition in New York of European art at the Armory Show of 1913 and to Stevens's meeting leading members of the avant-garde, about which Glen MacLeod is particularly helpful; James Longenbach will suggest that Stevens's reaction to World War I made "Sunday Morning" possible; Milton J. Bates suggests that poetry will replace Elsie as the interior paramour.[4] All of these factors contribute powerfully, but the letters of Stevens to Elsie allow us to follow another factor, his emotional life, rather closely, because Elsie represented a reality at this time far more important than anything else in his life. The great adjustments he had to make in his optimistic expectations of bliss with Elsie, and his concomitant readjustment of his religious belief, profoundly changed his poetry.

The tone of these letters for the first two years, 1910 and 1911, is unlike the tone of those in 1909; Stevens is experiencing pain. He, with a transparent gallantry, defends Elsie from the gossips in Reading, in language that will be reflected with bitterness in "Arcades of Philadelphia the Past" thirty years later: "And why should a girl not go home for two or three weeks and be at ease and

3. Robert Buttell, *Wallace Stevens and the Making of Harmonium* (Princeton: Princeton University Press, 1967).

4. See Glen G. MacLeod, *Wallace Stevens and Company: The Harmonium Years, 1913–1923* (Ann Arbor, Mich.: UMI, 1983), 3–41; James Longenbach, *Wallace Stevens: The Plain Sense of Things* (New York: Oxford, 1991) 44–82; Bates, *Wallace Stevens*, 68–82.

think pleasant things in the Spring? Oh, because her lord and master cannot care for her if he gives her such liberty. But, ladies, the damsel is not my prisoner, nor my slave. Oh, because she ought to be busy with pots and pans, just as we are. Honorable ladies, there ain't no pots and pans—we live on strawberries, etc., etc., etc." (WAS 1912 June 10, 1910).

However, it eventually became apparent to Stevens that Elsie did not appreciate New York as much as he did, and that she actually preferred to stay away from New York, and Stevens, as much as possible. The pattern of separation is repeated the following Christmas and summer, and Stevens's tone of gallant approval is replaced by one of diminished confidence and increased perplexity. Several communications at the end of 1910 convey this darkening attitude, and in two successive pieces of correspondence, January 2 and January 8, 1911, Stevens writes the identical lines—"I shall wait for you in Jersey City"—the second time implying that Elsie had not shown up for the first appointed time on January 5. (One might even speculate that the poem "Loneliness in Jersey City" is not completely unrelated to this memory.) By July 1911, disturbed but calm, he writes to Elsie in Reading, "I shall be quite comfortable and you must try to have a pleasant visit and not think too much about me. I mean to spend my evenings at home reading and trying to think a way through the future, that will lead us all through pleasant places. Be sure to let me hear from you." Finally, the letter of August 6, 1911 (WAS 1922), contains one of the most direct and dispirited lines in all of Stevens: "It is not hard to see why you are discontented here. It is undoubtedly lonely— and if by nature you are not interested in the things to be done in a place like New-York, you cannot, of course, force your nature and be happy."

The problem was basic, not casual; it went far beyond the fact that Stevens loved the city and Elsie could not. He had to accept the possibility that Elsie's basic nature might be largely beyond possible modification by his words and even beyond Elsie's control. Later in his career, recognition of that reality will be expressed as a basic theorem of human nature: "The truth is that a man's sense of the world dictates his subjects to him and that this sense is derived from his personality, his temperament, over which he has little control and possibly none, except superficially."[5] Stevens's desire for a quiet sanctuary in which he could think or write in peace, while Elsie stayed just out of communication in the same room, was not going to be realized.[6]

---

5. *The Necessary Angel: Essays on Reality and the Imagination* (New York: Knopf, 1951), 122. From "Effects of Analogy," originally published in the *Yale Review* 38, no. 1 (September 1948): 29–44.

6. He expresses this desire in WAS 1787 of April 1–2, 1907:

I have been reading all evening and it has refreshed me so, that, when I took up this letter again, it seemed a little lifeless and stale. —Then I happened to

The letters Stevens wrote to Elsie in 1912 as she is in Vinemont, not much far-ther from Reading than many of their pre-marriage countryside walks and rides together, reveal the beginning of his more active social life, especially as a guest of the Strykers.[7] They are helping Stevens to respond more to the immediate and to put the ultimate aside for the moment. His letter of July 7, 1912, reporting on several dinners with the Strykers, has one sentence that anticipates, with its accep-tance of a truce in his lifelong habit of moralizing, the first sentence of "Sunday Morning": "You know, all this meditation on old age, death and the other bare-bones of the scheme of things, would be dissipated in easier surroundings."

Despite changes and disappointments, he is able to project an image of domes-tic tranquility in one of the few surviving early letters to his sister Elizabeth:

> In my own case, life runs along obscurely. Nothing picturesque. We
> have been keeping house. Elsie is a stunning cook—quite the best in my
> experience. . . . We've been to a raft of plays—"The Lady & the Slip-
> per," "Oh, Oh, Delphine," and "The Merry Countess" all in less than a
> week, and I have had to say that there would be no more theatre-going
> for a while. . . . —Neither of us reads particularly. I've dozed over "The
> Winter's Tale" for weeks. Goodness knows, as the saying is, what we do
> with ourselves, but we're alive and perfectly well and happy—and so I
> suppose the lack of incident may be excused.[8]

---

see in a bowl of odds and ends on my table the carnation you took from the table in your dining-room the last time but one that I was home—and that you gave me. It is quite dry. I picked it up and smelled it and—there was still an odor of faint spice. So there is still life in what I wrote last night. I want Elsie to love me. How many, many times I have said that to myself. I want Elsie to love me—always. This quiet evening at home, with my lamp, is half-empty without you. If you were here, I should still be quiet. But you would be here. —I am in the mood for reading some big book and for looking up and seeing you here.

A similar case of approach-avoidance comes at the end of "No Possum, No Sop, No Taters," when the speaker records the call of the crow in the landscape of negation and "joins him there for company, / But at a distance, in another tree" (*CP,* 294).

7. Heber H. Stryker was one of the early American Bonding Company alumni to leave the company and move on to higher positions in the insurance industry; and moving to Hartford three years before the Stevenses, he will play a large role in intro-ducing Stevens to the society of that city and influencing the change in Stevens that will lead to his first mature poetry. For more about Stryker, see note to letter of June 24, 1909, and references to him in Brazeau's *Parts of a World.*

8. See *LWS,* 177–78.

All that is left out of this account is the reality of his emotions, which he could of course share with no one, until he discovered how to make such revelations in his poetry, in a language he created especially for that purpose.

In the twenty-five letters of 1913, a new tone of insouciance and emotional distance dominates, one in which the agonizing self-analysis of 1911 is forgotten. This tone represents the more familiar Stevens, the man in control of himself and his language. In 1913, he is very socially active, spending weekends with the Strykers and their prominent friends, such as "The Miss Trumbull" and the Hubleins. Stevens is so impressed with a mansion he visits in Great Barrington, Massachusetts, that he draws a floor plan for Elsie and then negotiates the purchase of a used baby grand piano from the people of this milieu. He discusses golf and encourages Elsie to play, whereas six years earlier he was urging her to join the church.

There are only two letters of 1914, one telling of a trip to Hartford to see the Strykers and another ruing the fact that his poems (five of which are "Elsie's" poems from the Little June Book) have not appeared yet in the *Trend,* edited by one of his most important friends from Harvard, Pitts Sanborn. Stevens has begun his most intense period of literary networking, becoming a member of the Arensberg Circle, which would make it possible for him to know Marcel Duchamp personally and to establish relations with the founders of several of new magazines in which he would publish his earliest work.[9] He is responding rapidly to his new opportunities, and in November of 1914, he goes beyond the circle of his friends and publishes a collection of rather conventional war poems, "Phases," in Harriet Monroe's relatively new but already very important *Poetry.*

However, he has been writing poetry of a very different type and reading it by the end of that year, to members of his group of sophisticated friends. Fortunately, we have an account of his reading "Cy Est Pourtraicte, Madame Ste Ursule et Les Unze Mille Vierges," a poem that Elsie does not like because it is affected, a word that she had used to apply to Stevens's expression of love in 1907.[10] Perhaps emboldened by the positive response of his friends, he submits a second set of poems to Harriet Monroe, who quickly rejects them as "recondite, erudite, provocatively obscure, with a kind of modern-gargoyle grin in them— Aubrey-Beardsleyish in the making." And she told him to "chase his mystically mirthful and mournful muse out of the nether darkness."[11] Stevens responded to this rejection by sending his most daring work, such as "Cy Est Pourtraicte,

9. For extensive detail on these developments, see MacLeod, *Wallace Stevens and Company*.

10. See Van Vechten's "Rogue Elephant in Porcelain," 41–50.

11. This note of rejection to Stevens, dated January 27, 1915, is cited in Bates's *Wallace Stevens,* 74.

Madame Ste Ursule, et Les Unze Mille Vierges," to *Rogue* and "Peter Quince at the Clavier" to *Others* for the next several years.[12] But "Sunday Morning," his most serious statement to the world, one that summarizes his life up to this point, one that demonstrates an assumed insouciance, a new sophistication, his lifelong love of aphorism, and his developing sense of drama, he sends to his "Chère Alma Mater" Monroe at *Poetry.* He is so eager to publish this magisterial poem in the right place that he accedes to her heavy-handed demand to cut three of the eight stanzas and to rearrange the order of those remaining. He even agreed to rewrite a line she found obscure.

⮑

[WAS 1906 December 23, 1909 New York][13]

Thursday Morning

My dearest Bo-Bo:

I found the kiss last night—and put the things on the dumb waiter—and tended to the plants this morning—and have been a very good boy: got all those black marks off the floor in the sitting-room and made the front floor a little better. Here is a little clipping[14] for you. Home to-morrow.

With love—and a kiss
Buddy.

⮑

[WAS 1907 December 28, 1909 New York]

Tuesday Morning

My dearest Elsie:

The mileage book was on my desk when I reached the office yesterday, although, it only came the same morning. The town is white with snow—as white as the country was from the car-window. I found everything all right at home, although it was very lonely without you—especially when I heard the Rudolphs moving about up-stairs—and I shall be very glad when you are back

---

12. See John Timberman Newcomb, *Wallace Stevens and the Literary Canons* (Jackson: University of Mississippi, 1992), 35–38, for a discussion of this temporary split with *Poetry* and Stevens's reputation as an *Others* poet for much of the 1920s.

13. American Bonding Company of Baltimore letterhead, stationery Stevens often used during this period. Addressed to "Mrs. W. Stevens, 231 South 13th Street, Reading, Pa." Subsequent correspondence will be to this address until Elsie goes to Vinemont in the summer of 1912.

14. The clipping, once listed as part of the contents of the folder for this letter, is no longer in its folder at the HEH.

again. I read until midnight. Have as good a time as possible—don't forget the preserves (and some cakes.) With all my love—

Buddy.[15]

↶

[WAS 1775 February 14, 1910][16]

A Valentine
Willow soon, and vine;
But now Saint Valentine,
To whom I pray: "Speed two
Their happy winter through:
Her that I love—and then
Her Pierrot. . . . Amen."

W. S.

↶

[WAS 1908 May 30, 1910 New York]

Monday Evening

My own Bo-Bo:

I've just come in—after dropping you a postal (so that you might have a word, at least, in the morning.) It is rather wet and rainy, and I've taken a cold bath and am ready for a long evening. Yesterday, as I was going to the 23rd Street Ferry, I had the good fortune to see Curtiss in his flying machine pass down the river—[17] you ought to have been there. An inspiring sight! I wanted to see just exactly what kind of a place it was directly across the Hudson from our neighborhood. Found it to be a very dull place, indeed—but I walked all day—lay on the Palisades and looked at the City opposite—first, a warship in the river, then the smoke of a great fire on the East Side, then the peculiar million-windowed, walled mass of the whole vast exterior. At home, I read Keats:

It is a flaw
In happiness, to see beyond our bourn,—

15. The day of the week, the greeting, and the closing are written in much lighter ink than the body of this note, as if they were done separately. American Bonding Company stationery.

16. This poem is on a separate sheet of paper, not with the letters. It is given in both *LWS,* 166 and *SP,* 248. This is the last mention of Pierrot in this correspondence, and it is not mentioned in *LWS* after this date.

17. Glenn Hammond Curtiss (1878-1930), New York, May 29, 1909. When the *New York World* newspaper offered ten thousand dollars for the first successful flight between Albany and New York City, Curtiss won the prize money and national recognition.

It forces us in summer skies to mourn,
It spoils the singing of the Nightingale.[18]

And bye-and-bye—it was so quiet—just when I ought to have begun a little letter to you, my head began to nod and I stumbled in to bed. —This morning, I walked up Riverside Drive to see the parade, and stood for a long time opposite the reviewing stand, where President Taft stood taking his hat off to Hebrew Orphan cadets, negro soldiers, police companies and the like. His Excellency looked stupid to me. His eyes are very small—his hair is white with a yellow tinge. He is very heavy but not in a flabby way, specially. I say he looked stupid; but at the same time, we all know him to be a man of much wisdom, patience and courtesy. —At noon, a heavy shower fell and I ran into the library at Columbia College, where I read for an hour or two. Then I walked down through Central Park, which seemed to be the scene of a universal picnic. The trees were as full of voices as a bush is full of leaves—thousands of children everywhere—the children of the Jewish slums, largely. —The rain filled the Park with fresh odors. Saw great numbers of orange-blossoms. —But this is only the news of a holiday in town. How about the holiday in the country? Aren't you glad to be home again? Tell me all about it—where you have been and whom you have seen. Sometimes, a trip home is a little depressing at first, for many reasons. But in the end, it opens the heart and one longs to stay. In our simple lives, these desires and feelings are, comparatively, matters of great importance. Have a good time, dear, and be a good girl and think often of your Buddy. —Everything is in good order here. The plants have been in the rain. I left them out all night to strengthen them—and they look grateful. —Remember me to your mother and father and tell La Rue I shall bring her some molasses candy.

> With much love and a kiss
> —and still another kiss.
> Wallace

∽

[WAS 1909 June 2, 1910 New York]
[American Bonding Company stationery.]

Thursday Evening

Dear Bo-Bo:

I am so disappointed not to have heard from you during the week. This is only to let you know that I shall come on the Penna. R. R. to-morrow night.

---

18. From Keats's March 25, 1818, verse letter to John Hamilton Reynolds.

The train reaches Reading at 9:55 —foot of Penn street. Tell the family not to stay up.

Your

Buddy

❧

[WAS 1910 June 6, 1910 New York]
[American Bonding Company stationery.]

June 6. 1910—

Monday

Dear Bo:

Reached home after a desolate ride. My head—the inside—resembles an old Dutch painting of flowers, long-covered with dust and grime, newly cleansed— fresh-shining. Here is the mileage book with almost two hundred miles in it— plenty. Write to me for the middle and end of the week. I have a sad pile of law Journals for to-night.

Ajoo!

Buddy[19]

❧

[WAS 1911 June 7, 1910 New York][20]

Tuesday Evening

My dearest girl:—

Your letter came this morning—with its house-wifely injunction about camphor, etc.! I had thought of it myself, but forgot to get the camphor to-night. Moth-balls are better, since camphor sticks fast to things. I needed the blanket on Sunday night, when it stormed all night long. —To-night I went back to Mrs. Hillary's for dinner. The same people were at the table—but I felt as if I had been far away from them. Only, in the narrow life of a boarding-house, they do not change much—probably they were wearing the same clothes, with a new stitch or two. —But how much I miss you! Such a vacation makes one realize how precious a prize companionship is. We have never been in the habit of saying this or that—yet I wish I could say how sweet you seem to me. I don't say it mind you—I only know that it makes me happy: I just say that I am happy, and you will know why I am. —So you sit at your old window, looking at our old scene, and thinking old-far-off thoughts. Think kindly of your buddy. —It is an important thing to keep a true home in the world. There are so many

---

19. Ghosts of this handwriting indicate that Stevens sealed it before the ink had been blotted or had dried.

20. Small plain stationery.

changes—so much at which we just look on, so much we endure. And the best
treasure is to have familiar things to console and encourage us. We have more of
life ahead of us than after. Therefore, cherish that old scene and those old
thoughts. If I wanted to think all of life over, I think I could do it best up the
Tulpehocken, or sitting on a fence along the Bernville road. The Colisseum by
moonlight would be a distraction by comparison. Native Earth! That makes us
giants. —There was more of Spring in the few weeks we spent in Baltimore
than the whole season here has shown. To-day, instead of that golden freshness
of June there was a gray-blue in the air and the sunshine that was autumnal. And
the roses and peonies at home became little groups in florists windows. I like it
so. The country is one thing, the city another—I like them well-defined, separate. It is sentimental to mingle them. —Blackberries and plums are on the
stands—stony peaches—canteloupes—occasional watermelons. Those mark
our "perfect days."[21] —Have a good, quiet, comfortable time. That last bit of
dress-making left you a shade pale—your mother thought so and then I did, too.
And try to complete your summer things, so that you feel free. I shall send you
anything you want. Everything here is in good order, except, possibly, your
violet, which seems to be losing flesh. My pine is bright with new moss. The
ferns are strong-looking. The ivy was never better. —But I have discovered that
dust is a huge matter. It settles as calmly as "water falling down"—as continu-
ously, as finally. A little thing—but a huge matter. Thus, one learns day by day
things unexpected and amazing!

> With much love—
> Your—learner—and
> student of
> dust

⌒

[WAS 1912 June 10, 1910 New York][22]

Friday Evening

My dearest:
     Don't let that scare-crow next door worry you. I know what is in your mind
and it only amuses me. Why in the world Mrs. Althouse or Mrs. F. or Mrs.
Long-nose or Mrs. Long-ears should gossip as they do is beyond me. Such rot!
Tell them that, if they want to know it, I think more of my girl than I could ever

---

21. James Russell Lowell's "What Is So Rare as a Day in June" begins "What is so
rare as a day in June? / Then, if ever, come perfect days." Extensive marginal commentary by Stevens in his two volumes of the *Letters of James Russell Lowell*, ed. Charles
Elliot Norton (New York: Harper, 1894), amounts to small essays in some cases.
22. Extremely small plain stationery.

think of them by the thousands; and be content in feeling that I love you with all my heart, and am proud of you and that I don't care a crumb what they think about it. The truth is that people only see in other people what they see in themselves. They do not, and cannot see, the little more or the little less. Nor would they recognize it if they did. You remember who it was that said you were not affectionate. Pshaw! The old lady who said you were "sweet"—what a blessed old lady to be able to see it! But I will not tell you what you are. It is a balmy thought; but balmy thoughts sometimes make nervous reading. —Sweet— sweet—sweet—

> You give to brooks a tune
> A melody to trees.[23]

I never felt free, or strong, until I had cried "Farewell to my elders!" and their beastly ideas. . . . And why should a girl not go home for two or three weeks and be at ease and think pleasant things in the Spring? Oh, because her lord and master cannot care for her if he gives her such liberty. But, ladies, the damsel is not my prisoner, nor my slave. Oh, because she ought to be busy with pots and pans, just as we are. Honorable ladies, there ain't no pots and pans—we live on strawberries, etc., etc., etc. Then her lord should be with her. Most noble ladies, he is: he is in her heart, and therefore he does not fear to be out of her sight. — — — We have been having a storm from the North East, raw, heavy, damp. If you would like to go up the Tulpehocken, why do; because once you are back in town, you will not be getting away for more than a few hours before late in the summer. I wanted you to have a week in the country, if possible, and to luxuriate in it. This is the very best part of the year for it. And if it will not be convenient to go before the time you mention, wait till then. The longer you are away, the more I desire you—I think that you will be all the gladder to get back then. Don't let Dr. Hickman put in a gold[24] cap where it will show <u>under any circumstances.</u> If it will show, require porcelain. And don't let him tinker with front teeth.[25] And finish with him. You will be glad when it is done. —Everything is running along as it should. Things look clean and orderly and it's no trouble. I have a new straw hat and am going for some other stuff to-morrow afternoon. I shall send you something to-morrow

---

23. He is citing his "Book of Verses" of 1908: III, "Afield."

24. In late November 1904, Stevens had a dentist in Reading put in "two gaudy gold teeth" (*SP*, 143).

25. Carl Van Vechten, in "Rogue Elephant in Porcelain," 41–50, indicates that (in 1914) Elsie's "teeth were an unredeeming feature." Reprinted in Ehrenpreis, *Wallace Stevens*, 32.

which will reach you Monday. I would to-night but I think I have a better envelope at the office.

Your own, loving
Buddy

↪

[WAS 1913 June 14, 1910 New York]

Tuesday Evening

My own dear Bo-Bo:

   Why don't you write to a fellow? I had hoped for a letter to-night—probably there'll be one in the morning. I spent Sunday at home, on account of the miserable weather, but took plenty of exercise by clearing camp—chasing dust, that is. To-day, for the first time in more than a week we have had bright sunshine. How cool it was, indoors, when I came home to-night! I have been taking breakfasts of coffee and rolls at a place on 9th Avenue. Such light breakfasts are agreeable, but make one hungry for an early lunch. I generally go to Mrs. Hillary's for dinner, but like to feel free. Saturday evening I read, (I think.) Sunday evening ditto ("Legends of the City of Mexico,") last night I worked, to-night I am going to a Turkish bath—the first since Xmas, as a preparation for hot weather. Also, I have a pair of slippers and shouldn't be surprised if I went further. Is there anything special you have seen at home, that you want? I might be able to send a little extra. I want very much to hear from you, Bo-Bo—write often. Mrs. Duff didn't come for the things on Monday, so I dropped in on her this evening—and arranged to have her come probably Thursday of next week. If you are going to stay next week (and I want you to have a long loaf,) by coming back on Saturday afternoon of that week—getting here about four or five o'clock in the afternoon, if there is a train—you would give me an opportunity to brighten things up a bit. It is so much better to find things shining,—cheerful, etc. You will have to go shopping, once you are back, for screens, etc. However, be that as it may, everything goes smoothly—except for the fact that you write such few letters.

Your
Buddy
+ + + +

↪

[WAS 1914 June 17, 1910 New York]

Friday Evening

My dearest:

   I was very glad to have your long letter when I came home this evening—after a particularly tiring day. The weather has just cleared, by way of preparing

for Roosevelt's home-coming to-morrow.[26] There is to be all manner of excitement, which I shall probably not see on accounts of engagements at the office.
In the afternoon, I <u>may</u> go out to Hempstead Plains where there are a number
of air-ships—(bi-planes) to be on exhibition. Air-ships are thrilling beyond
description—and when you are home again I must try to take you to see a flight.
That sight of Curtiss coming down the river from Albany remains vivid. —
There is something extraordinarily listless about Saturday afternoon and Sunday
in New-York in the summer. On account of the <u>bad</u> weather, the beaches are
not open yet. And a day like to-morrow, so early in the season, looks quite
blank. Hence, airships are a treasure. —You know, the stores close at twelve
o'clock, most of them—so that there is no such thing as wandering around. —
Somehow, I do not feel like reading. It isn't in the air in June. But I <u>do</u> like to sit
with a big cigar and think of pleasant things—chiefly of things I'd like to have
and do. I was about to say "Oh! For a world of Free Will!" But I really meant
free will in this world—the granting of that one wish of your own: that every
wish were granted. —Yet so long as one keeps out of difficulty it isn't so bad as
it is. For all I know, thinking of a roasted duck, or a Chinese jar, or a Flemish
painting may be quite equal to having one. Possibly it depends on the cigar. And
anyhow it doesn't matter. —Whose girl? You darling. —This is a very poor
pen, I <u>vow.</u> There will be another installment of spondulix in Monday's mail.
Daren't send it before—because Saturday night in Reading plays hob with that
kind of thing. —Write on Sunday—and send your love to me. You have all of
mine and many kisses.

Your
Buddy

↩

[WAS 1915 June 22, 1910 New York][27]

Wednesday Evening

My dearest:

After sending that post-card, I came home and took a cold bath and was just
about to start my letter when Mrs. Weinman sent up yours of yesterday. It had
not been on the table as I came upstairs. It has been so hot here all week (and quite
likely will remain so) that I hesitate to ask you to come back. Certainly, it would
be a hundred times better for you to be in the country, in good air, having a good
time. At the same time, I should not like you to go alone. Come and see how

---

26. When Roosevelt left the presidency in 1909, he went on a one-year African
safari from which he returned in June 1910. While in Africa, he killed hundreds of animals, and he described some of his killing, for example a bull rhinoceros, in detail.
27. Very small stationery.

comfortable you can be and perhaps we can find some place near-by for you to spend a week or so. As a matter of fact, New-York is no worse than Reading in the summer time. One cannot be comfortable anywhere except in the country or at the shore and since we cannot spend the time there, let's be cheerful and happy at home here. The weather does not last for more than a month or two and your long visit ought to have given you strength. Of course, if you can arrange a few days in the country, you know that I should be happy to have you go. Otherwise, come and give life to these quiet rooms and take care of me for a while. You can go some other time, you know. I want to have you here again. It will be like beginning anew—won't it? And now that you have had long evenings (last night was the longest in the year) and have seen Spring change into Summer, (and have finished with Dr. H.) I think you'll be glad to be back in your nest. Mrs. Duff comes to-morrow to make it shine—and I hope that you will come on Saturday afternoon to see it—just the same place, but your own. Let me know in due time what train you will take and what time it reaches Jersey City and I'll meet you there and take care of your baggage—and we'll go off somewhere for dinner and enjoy ourselves. Don't forget my cap and the photographs and anything else that may have been left behind. Be sure to invite your mother and father and La Rue to come to see us some time this summer—and tell them how fortunate they are to live among so many mountains and so much pleasant country—and how much you thank them—and come to your Buddy with the knowledge that he will do all he can to make you happy. Here are many kisses and all my love.

Your
Wallace

꙳

[WAS 1916 December 28, 1910 New York][28]

Wednesday Evening

My Dear Bo-Bo:

Went to the Murray Hill Hotel for dinner last <u>evening</u> (after looking around Madison Square for a place for both of us) —and then to "Pomander Walk,"[29] which is a most amusing affair. We must go together without fail. I have arranged to send the big brown rug in the sitting room to the cleaner's. It goes to-morrow morning and is promised for Tuesday next. I think that you better stay until Wednesday of next week—so that you do not come back to a bare floor. The palm was quite dry, but is soaking up water now like a sponge. The Japanese pine is done for—dry as a match. It seems to be very dull around town, although, at

---

28. American Bonding Company stationery.
29. Comedy in three acts by Louis N. Parker, at Wallack's Theater on December 10, 1910. A musical version of this play in 1922 was called *Marjolaine* after the heroine.

the office, there is plenty to do as usual. Take this opportunity to rest and breathe native air—and don't be restless, please. I expect to spend the evening at home with a book. It is raining now.

> With much love,
> Your
> Buddha.

⸙

[WAS 1917 December 30, 1910 New York]
[Night Letter, Western Union]

> 1 Ny Fr 36 Paid Night Letter
> CW New York Dec 30th 1910

Mrs. Wallace Stevens
221 South 13th Street
Reading Pa

Surprised and very sorry to hear of your grandmother's death.[30] Think you should stay until Thursday at least. Shall write on Sunday. Am perfectly well but rather at a loss for something to do at night.

> Wallace 716 AM (Dec 31st).

⸙

[WAS 1918 December 31, 1910 New York]
[Night Letter, Western Union]
13NY-DA-9NL-
Received at

> Cw–New York–12-31-10

Mrs. Wallace Stevens,
231 South 13th Street

A hundred happy returns of the day with love.

> Wallace 741am(1st)

---

30. The following account of this grandmother is in Elsie's "Branch of the Bright Family":

CATHERINE ANNE BRIGHT (1836–1910), was born on March 23, 1836, in Reading, Pa. She received her education at the Reading Female Academy, a private school located at Fifth and Walnut streets in Reading, where the courses included music, needlework, and cooking. She was a member of the Universalist Sunday School, and of the Universalist church, "The Church of Our Father."

Her summers were spent on the family farm at Monocacy, Pa. and here she met GEORGE WASHINGTON SMITH, who was the station agent and telegrapher at the Monocacy station. Although he was ten years her senior, they were married on October 27th, 1856, by Rev. Asher Moore, in the Universalist church in Reading, when she was 20 years of age.

⌒

[WAS 1919 January 2, 1911 New York][31]

Monday Afternoon
January 2. 1910[32]

My dearest:

A most dismal day it is—and was yesterday. On New-Year's eve, I looked at the clock in the Metropolitan Tower, (it is illuminated), at about half-past eleven, and I remember how bright the stars were. And yet when morning came there was a deluge of rain, that kept me indoors until evening. Then I went out only for dinner, and afterwards, read and studied a little. This morning there was a heavy fog filled with mist. It was impossible to see Tenth-Avenue from our door. Across the street, the trees were like a charcoal <u>sketch</u> of trees. However, I was in great need of a walk and, therefore, started for the Metropolitan Museum. They are showing some new things—one a small bronze by Bouchard: a girl feeding a faun, I liked particularly. There is some new Japanese armor. I have no sympathy with those who go in for armor. —There is a bronze bust of John La Farge, which I hope to see often. —Walked down Fifth Avenue to Madison Square and, after lunch, went into the American Art Galleries, where, among other things, they are showing some Chinese and Japanese jades and porcelains. The sole object of interest for me in such things is their beauty. Cucumber-green, camellia-leaf-green, apple-green, etc., moonlight, blue, etc., ox-blood, chicken-blood, cherry, peach-blow, etc. Oh! and mirror-black: that is so black and with such a glaze that you can see yourself in it. —And now that I am home again, and writing, in semi-obscurity, lights lit, boats whistling, in the peculiar muteness and silence of fog—I wish, intensely, that I had some of those vivid colors here. When connoiseurs return from the pits of antiquity with their rarities, they make honest, every-day life look like a seamstress by the side of Titian's daughter. —I have sent you during the last few days several messages. I shall not be certainly ready for you before Thursday. It is quite likely that the rug may be a day late and the place looks quite shocking without it. Unless I hear from you to the contrary, I shall expect you on Thursday evening. The train leaves the <u>outer</u> depot at 5:57. I shall meet you in Jersey City. —Enclosed

31. This letter was sent special delivery (as indicated in Stevens's hand) and carried ten cents of extra postage in addition to the normal two cents. This ten extra cents got this letter carried from Station E to Hudson Terminal Station by 11:00 P.M. that night, for there is a stamp to that effect on the back of the envelope. Thus, this ten cents assured Stevens that Elsie would get the letter the next morning; it was stamped as received in Reading by 8:00 A.M.

32. Stevens wrote the year as 1910, but the envelope and internal evidence (i.e., mention of the rug) show that it was 1911.

is the money for your ticket and Pullman. It is a little more than necessary. Handle with care: for I shall be hard up for a little while to come. —If you have time to write a letter, I should be glad to get it, for I always enjoy getting letters from you and now that the opportunity for them is infrequent, why, improve it. — Give my respects (and good wishes for everybody for the New-Year) to those who may be interested in receiving them—and as for your self: love (much of it) and many kisses.

> Your
> Wallace

⤶

[WAS 1920 January 8(?), 1911[33] New York]
    I shall meet you in Jersey city. Glad you're coming.

> W.

⤶

[WAS 1921 July 22, 1911 New York][34]

<u>Saturday</u>   July 22. 1911

My dear Bo-Bo:
    I arrived safely and found the enclosed letter from your mother. You waited for it so long and so patiently that I send it to you in spite of the fact that you have seen her since. The apartment looked a little dusty and was as hot as India. But I "dusted" a bit last night and before breakfast this morning <u>swept</u> the middle room and the bed-room. Wasn't I a good boy? I shall be quite comfortable and you must try to have a pleasant visit and not think too much about me. I mean to spend my evenings at home reading and trying to <u>think</u> a way through the future, that will lead us all through pleasant places. Be sure to let me hear from you.

> With much love, your
> Buddy.

⤶

33. The exact date in January 1911 is uncertain because the stamp for the digit of the date is superimposed over the dark "M" of "Private Mailing Card"; however, the *8* is quite legible. The picture side of this card ("The General Theological Seminary Chelsea Square, New York Showing West Building, White and Lorillard Halls"), with Stevens's message written at the top (and an arrow Stevens drew to their apartment building in the background), is reproduced in the first volume of Richardson's *Wallace Stevens,* opposite page 384.
34. Stationery of American Bonding Company of Baltimore.

[WAS 1922 August 6, 1911 New York][35]

Sunday Morning

My dearest Bo-Bo:—

I was so glad to get your letter last night and to find you in such good spirits. —I was in rather low humor, to put it so; for I had learned during the day that Connie Lee had got a fairly good thing that I was after[36]—although Lee and Kearney and Stryker do not know that I know it.[37] Yet, to be honest, you will recall that I always said that Lee stood in my way—and I know that they are all loyal friends of mine. Only now that Lee is taken care of, I should be next in line. However, the assistance of friends is at best auxiliary; and progress depends wonderfully on one's own energy. —Your dream of a home in Reading is most fanciful. To be sure, if I succeeded here, we could have an inexpensive place there in summer. I think that possibly I should have been well advanced if I had stayed in Reading. If I were to come back, I should want to go into a business— and that requires capital and experience and a willingness to make money 1 3/4 cents at a time. I fully intend to continue along my present line—because it gives me a living and because it seems to offer possibilities. I am far from being a genius—and must rely on hard and faithful work. —It is not hard to see why you are discontented here. It is undoubtedly lonely—and if by nature you are not interested in the things to be done in a place like New-York, you cannot, of course, force your nature and be happy. If I could afford it, there are many things you might do. But there are many thousands of us who do not look too closely at the present, but who turn their faces toward the future—gilding the present with hope—to jumble one's rhetoric. And then you know, there is no

35. The pre-marriage stationery.
36. A 1904 graduate of the University of Maryland, J. Collins Lee began working in the home office of the American Bonding Company in 1905, and on July 1, 1914, he joined the Home Office staff of the Hartford Accident and Indemnity Company and was instrumental in the expansion of the Hartford's agency base. When Stevens was hired by the Hartford in March 1916, Lee was promoted to the rank of the executive officers as assistant secretary, a position to which he returned in early 1919 after a leave of absence to serve as a captain in World War I. In 1920, he was elected secretary. Throughout the 1920s, he was listed as secretary of the Hartford Accident and Indemnity, and on September 4, 1928, he was promoted to vice president and secretary, a position he held until the reorganization on August 14, 1934, that brought James L. D. Kearney to the presidency and Stevens his promotion to vice president. After this time, Lee is not listed among the company officers. Brazeau says that the "good thing" that Lee got here was the position "as surety manager of a large New York insurance agency, Whilden and Hancock" (*Parts of a World,* 5).
37. All three previously published versions of this letter (including *LWS,* 170) put the "yet to be honest" at the conclusion of the sentence expressing his disappointment. However, the capital *Y* in "Yet" is clear.

evil, but thinking makes it so.[38] —I hope to make next winter a little more agreeable for you. —There's the sexton announcing morning service with his bell. After an hour at church, I am going out into the country somewhere—haven't had any fresh air for a long time. I may go to Yonkers, cross the river and walk down the Palisades among the locusts.

With my love, Your
Bud.

Wuxtra![39]

There were no locusts. I saw <u>one</u> thing distinctly pleasant. A path in some woods was surrounded by black-eyed Susans—(flowers, of course.) Three yellow birds in a group were swinging on the yellow flowers—picking seed, or something, and chattering. —But in mid-summer grand-mother Nature is not specially interesting. She is too busy with her baking. —To-night as I came out of the Earle, I saw the moon, beautifully soft over Washington Square. The Weinmans have been up on the roof—gazing. —Such nights are like wells of sweet water in the salt sea (to repeat an ancient fancy)[40]—like open spaces in deep woods. —Why cannot one sit in such rich light and be filled with—tableaux! At least, why cannot one think of new things, and forget the old round—past things, future things? Why cannot one be moonlight through and through—for the night? —The learned doctors of men's minds know the reason why. I read it all once in the <u>Edinburgh Review.</u> Psychologically, the obscurity of twilight and of night shuts out the clear outline of visible things which is a thing that appeals to the intellect. The clear outline having been obliterated, the emotions replace the intellect and

> Lo! I behold an orb of silver brightly
> Grow from the fringe of sunset, like a dream
> From Thought's severe infinitude— —[41]

I swear, my dear Bo-Bo, that it's a great pleasure to be so poetical. —But it follows that, the intellect having been replaced by the emotions, one cannot think of anything at all. —At any rate, my trifling poesies are like the trifling

---

38. He first used this quotation from *Hamlet* in his letter of March 7, 1907.
39. This begins a second sheet of paper, the fifth page in the old pattern of the eight-page letter.
40. He had referred to this fancy in WAS 1849 May 21, 1909.
41. *SP* (84) points out that these lines are from David Gray's sonnet that begins "Lying awake at holy eventide." Stevens's journal for August 3, 1900, records his finding "some things in these [Gray's] sonnets which bring tears to one's eyes—David Gray is in them." Gray lived in Scotland (1838–1861), and his collected works are *The Luggie and Other Poems,* ed. Henry Glassford Bell (Glasgow: James MacLehose & Sons, 1886).

designs one sees on fans. I was much shocked, accordingly, to read of a remark made by Gainsborough, the great painter of portraits and landscapes. He said scornfully of some one, "Why, the man is a painter of fans!" —Well, to be sure, a painter of fans is a very unimportant person by the side of the Gainsboroughs. — I've had one of the candle-sticks over at the table to write by and find the wax has been melting over the table. Poor table-top—as if all its other afflictions were not enough! —Adieu, my very dearest—and many thoughts of you—and kisses.

W

꩜

[WAS 1923 August 6, 1911 New York][42]

Have a letter for you at home. —But I want to add a post-script and will, therefore, not post until morning.[43]

Wallace

꩜

[WAS 1924 August 10, 1911 (Highbridge, New Jersey)][44]

Came out here on business to-day. Beautiful country.

Wallace.

꩜

[WAS 1925 August 16, 1911 New York][45]

Wednesday Evening

My dearest:

I am writing by candle-light. The electric light, you remember, does not reach the table. —I found your letter, as I came upstairs. Just so you are happy. Only, you must not allow yourself to think too badly of us over here. We lead rather severe lives! Who in the world would see the truth in that remark? People in the country think it is one unbroken round of holidays here. The fact is, it is all work. The amusements are all "quick": —grab a bit of fun and then back to work—to use such language. . . . But personally I find pleasure in too many things not sociable. This is largely the result of many years of isolation and tastes formed under such conditions. . . . (Notice my Frenchy way of punctuating?

---

42. Hand-colored postcard of "The Bowery New York," showing people, a trolley, and horse carts under an elevated train.

43. Thus this card was written between the two parts of the above letter.

44. Postcard of "South Branch Raritan River, High Bridge, N.J." Above the 321 South Thirteenth Street address, a number and a word that seem to be "323 North" have been crossed out, as if he had started to write his old home address in Reading.

45. Pre-marriage stationery, large hand.

Très chic, n'est-ce pas?). . . . But for all that, I see your side of it, too. The society of friends is the sweetest of all pleasures—and the one you enjoy most. My
dear, you know I do not willfully forego all that. But all my hopes lead me to
expect most from life in the end by doing as I am doing. For the present patience
and good-will are our greatest virtues. And all the time you know how much I
love you and how much we have in common deep down. . . . I had thought of
running over to see you but will not do so at present. There are so many things
we need here and so much besides that it would be agreeable to have. I don't
think I have seen Mrs. Weinman since the day I came back. They use the porch
in the evenings—I mean the roof. If we had some place out-of-doors to loaf in
on summer nights a part of our problem would be solved. You would be surprised to find how pleasant a candle on this table makes the room. It gives such a
quiet, uncertain light—very favorable to meditation and the likes o'that. —
Have a good time, Bo. We'll have a good time when you come back, depend
on it. Remember me to your mother, please, and to the rest of the family.

Your own,

W.

⌒

[WAS 1926 August 20, 1911 New York][46]

Sunday Evening

My dear:

   I was late in getting up this morning and went out at once for breakfast and
then to church. Such a thundering good sermon! Then I walked up the West
Side of the Park and dropped into that confounded museum—just to see the
new things. There was an interesting picture of skating on canals in Holland by
a monkey whom people called Beerstraaten (1622–1666.) One Dutchman is
pushing a fat Dutch woman on a sled on the ice. He pushes into a stump and the
lady spills out on her nose. Near-by is another Dutchman—drunk. His friends
are trying, as usual, to persuade him to go home. . . . Then, although I fully
intended to go walking, I turned down-town and went into that old Library
where I had a charming afternoon. I fell asleep over a French book and had the
most delightful dream. . . . Yesterday I walked from four until seven, and after.
To-day I was a bit stiff. What really discouraged me, however, was the thought
of the crowds in the country near-by, the automobiles, etc. The solitude I
desired came on the roof at sunset to-night. There was a large balloon hanging
like an elephant: bait, I suppose, on the hook of some inhabitant of Mars, fishing
in the sea of ether. Bye and bye, the stars came out—and down by the docks, the
lanterns on the masts flickered—and there was a tolling of bells. . . . There

---

46. Pre-marriage stationery.

wasn't much to think of up there, after all—although I always have the wise sayings of Mêng Tzù and K'Ung Fu-Tzù[47] to think of, and the poetry of the Wanamaker[48] advertisements to dream over. In addition, I had this clipping from "The Noble Features of the Forest," etc. (which must be a very interesting document) to console me. . . . [49] Two recent storms have cooled the air. Always, towards the end of August, there are cool days; and then the warmth returns— chastened. The days that follow are the choicest of the year. Why shouldn't the golden glow still parade along your fence? There will be flowers of one kind or another for two months to come—and more. . . . I suppose in another week or two things will be more lively here as the children return for school. It is abominably dull—and everyone seems to be a stranger. The sight-seeing 'busses groan. People sit about on fire-plugs dashing off souvenir post-cards—and the cheap restaurants flourish. —I wish I had a good novel.

Your own

Wallace

47. K'ung Fu-tzu (c. 552–479 B.C.) is known in the West as Confucius. Meng Tzu (fourth century B.C.), a Confucian philosopher and defender, is known in the West as Mencius, and his sayings are collected in a very influential volume that bears his name.

48. The Wanamaker store was famous its use of advertisements; that these advertisements reflected the art of the times is clear in Carl Van Vechten's description of the impact of *Nude Descending a Staircase* in the Armory Show of 1913: "It was cartooned, it was caricatured. . . . John Wanamaker advertised cubist gowns and ladies began to wear green, blue, and violet wigs, and to paint their faces emerald and purple." From Van Vechten, *Peter Whiffle: His Life and Works* (New York: Knopf, 1922), quoted by MacLeod, *Wallace Stevens and Company,* 6.

49. Kuo Hsi (c. 1020–90), a great landscape painter of the Sung period in Chinese art, wrote this famous essay, which Laurence Binyon analyzed in *Painting in the Far East* (see note above to WAS 1843 May 9, 1909) and which the newspaper clipping that follows this letter will quote:

> Nearly a thousand years ago the critic, Kuo Hsi, in his work, "The Noble Features of the Forest and Stream," expressed once for all the guiding sentiment of Chinese landscape painting. He takes it as axiomatic that all gently disposed people would prefer to lead a solitary and contemplative life in communion with nature, but he sees, too, that the public weal does not permit such an indulgence.
>
> This is not the time for us [he writes] to abandon the busy worldly life for one of seclusion in the mountains, as was honorably done by some ancient sages in their days. Though impatient to enjoy a life amidst the luxuries of nature, most people are debarred from indulging in such pleasures. To meet this want, artists have endeavored to represent landscapes so that people may be able to behold the grandeur of nature without stepping out of their houses.

~

[WAS 1927 July 7, 1912 New York][50]
[Small stationery, folded to very small envelope.]

Sunday Evening

My dear Bo-bo:

   "The Patricians"[51] came Saturday morning in very good order. It is still at the office. I shall read it within the next day or two and then return it to the Strykers. I have been to dinner there two or three times. How nice it is of them to ask me, particularly since I so much like to go! Last time, about a week ago, we talked about the advancement of women until mid-night. Mrs. Stryker is very <u>live</u> on that subject. My dinners have been a great bother to me. The office closes too early for me to stop down-town; and I cannot bring myself to go to the cheap places up-town; so that I've been going to pretty stiff places for an entrée and a dessert. But bosh! I like variety and I think I may telephone the Earl to-morrow and go back there. The thought of the iced-tea would, of itself, tempt one. — To-day I had a slapping walk. If you care to you can read about it when you come back because I've taken to my journal again.[52] —Last night (for the first time) I went to the Library, particularly to read some French poems of the Comtesse Mathieu de Noailles.[53] I knew one of her poems and wanted to look through her books. I noticed an expression: "j'ai le gout de l'azur"—"I have the

---

   In this light painting affords pleasures of a nobler sort, by removing from one the impatient desire of actually observing nature.
   Such a passage yields its full meaning only upon very careful reading. One should note the background of civilization, quietism, and rural idealism implied in so casual an expression as the "luxuries of nature." Nor should one fail to see that what is brought into the home of the restless worldling is not the mere likeness of nature, but the choice feeling of the sage.

Much of the essay by Kuo Hsi is in Ernest F. Fenollosa's *Epochs of Chinese and Japanese Art* (London, 1912), 2:12–19. Fenollosa calls him (Kuo Hsi) Kakki.

   50. This is the first letter to Elsie somewhere other than her old home in Reading. Addressed to "Mrs. Wallace Stevens, Park Mansion House, Vinemont, Penna. Berks county." All of Stevens's correspondence of 1912 will be to this address.

   51. *The Patrician* (1911), a novel by John Galsworthy.

   52. There is no entry for this date in Stevens's journal, but Stevens is speaking in more general terms, referring to entries about the death of his mother in June and July 1912. See *SP*, 253–55.

   53. Anna de Noailles (1876–1933), a French poet originally from Romania whose *Le Coeur innombrable* was published in 1901, was a close friend of Marcel Proust, who also admired her poetry. *LWS* (174) provides the title of this poem, "Exaltation," and the entire line 32: "J'ai le goût de l'azur et du vent dans la bouche," from *Le Coeur innombrable* (Paris, 1921), 19–21.

taste for the azure" <u>literally.</u> The expression came back more than once today: "j'ai le gout de l'azur." The poems were mostly about Nature. Well, this taste for the azure, or of the azure, is just the desire to savour the charm of the many beautiful things about us. The charm! —When I am in town I have only the crowd to respond to. But in the country I have the sky, etc., etc. to respond to. And it is a response to charm: now, in summer. —Nothing makes that clearer than the poems I read. Nothing proves it more certainly than the charm I felt all day to-day. I sated myself in it. — — —You know, all this meditation on old age, death and the other bare-bones of the scheme of things, would be dissipated in easier surroundings.[54] — —So with you, now that July is coming on, and the earth is sweet with sweet breaths, sweet fruits, sweet everything, make the most of it. Love it and store up the love of it. —But hey diddle-diddle, who would think that I had been to the Murray Hill for dinner to-night. I drank a whole carafe of water—and walked home feeling like a camel starting over the Gobi desert. —I went up on the roof. The tent is not finished and I imagine the Weinmann's are much vexed. Mrs. Weinmann showed the baby to me a few days ago. And yesterday I saw the maid with the baby in one arm doing her duty to a pancake on the stove with the other. Am I to have no postals? —I wanted to sleep on the roof. It was so cool there. And after a while a star began to dodge in and out among the four corners of the tower in the chapel opposite. So I came down-stairs, bathed and began my letter.

With love,
Wallace

⤸

[WAS 1928 July 15, 1912 New York]
[American Bonding Company stationery, addressed to Vinemont.]

Monday:

My dear bud:

Park & Tilford are to send by express to-day some lotion to you at Vinemont. Very likely it will be at your hotel when you reach there. This is so that you will inquire and not miss it. Got back safely after an inexpressibly boresome ride on the train.

With love,
Wallace.

⤸

54. The dissipation of this mediation anticipates the first sentence of "Sunday Morning," and the "sweet fruits" below are a preview of its final stanza.

[WAS 1929 July 17, 1912 New York][55]
[American Bonding Company stationery, addressed to Vinemont.]

Wednesday

My dearest Bud:

I opened this by mistake, that is: I cut the envelope, then noticed that it was not for me. I have not read it, nor even had it out of the envelope, so it is all a secret in spite of the cut in the envelope. —Your letter came last evening. I am always glad to hear from you. Don't stop eating meat. You've gained two pounds on it, haven't you? Don't adopt other people's ideas about your own food. You need strength and blood, and you'll get them from meat, not from string beans. Will write some evening soon.

With love,
Wallace

[The following is on a second sheet of American Bonding Company stationery.]
Later

I have just received a telegram from John telling me of the death of my mother last evening (Tuesday)[.][56] The funeral will take place on Saturday. I shall send you a telegram to Vinemont because I believe you are going to Mt. Penn to-morrow. I shall go over to Reading this evening. Telephone me on Thursday or Friday so that I can make arrangements.

Wallace

⌐

[WAS 1930 July 29, (1912)[57] New York]
[Pre-marriage stationery, addressed to Vinemont.]

Monday Evening
July 29th.

My Dearest:

It was only a week ago that I returned to town. For several evenings I sat around, thinking chiefly of my poor mother. Then I drifted to the Library to

55. Volume 1 of Richardson, *Wallace Stevens* (photographs between pages 384 and 385), reproduces this letter. Richardson incorrectly implies that he wrote this part of this letter after hearing of his mother's death; the second half of this letter, on a second page of American Bonding Company Stationery, is headed "Later," and only this part is written after he heard of his mother's death.

56. Stevens's mother died on July 16, 1912, a year and two days after his father's death. In his journal, he describes his mother's final sickness in two moving passages, for June 25 and July 1, 1912, his last extant journal entries. See *SP*, 253–55.

57. There is no envelope for this letter, so the year is determined by the reference to the death of Stevens's mother. The envelope in the Huntington folder (addressed to "Mrs. Wallace Stevens, Park Mansion House, Vinemont, Penna. Berks County") is of August 6, 1912, a date for which there is no extant letter.

read a little about a painter—Delacroix. And late in the week Stryker asked me to
dinner. On Saturday Ward[58] asked me to go for a swim and we spent the afternoon and evening together. We watched a moon-rise over the sea. On Sunday I
walked to Sea Cliff, (a walk I am proud of.)[59] I did not get home until after ten
o'clock. By the time I had taken a bath (my legs were caked with dust and my
feet resembled Lady Mary Wortley Montague's upon her return from the East—
pardon my boasting: boasting! drat the pen)[60] it was time for bed. This morning I
had to go out to Morristown to see about a road, which we shall have to repair,
and while I was there I dropped you a postcard, meant to be an apology for not
writing last night. From Morristown I went to Hopatcong and from there, by
trolley, to Dover, and from there, by train, viâ Boonton, back to town. So that
with my walk yesterday, and my trip to-day I have seen quite a little country
myself. And to-night, I bought myself a cigar, which I am smoking as I write. It is
the first time I have smoked at home since January, 1911. Perhaps I shall smoke a
little next month, too; but not after the 1st of September, until next summer. As
you know, I make great ado about such things. . . . But during all this, I have not
forgotten you. I had many thoughts of you and wished for you often. Only, for
the present, I desire you to be where you are, and to enjoy yourself. So sorry
about the buck-board! I'll come to the rescue on Thursday, when I shall send
you Forty dollars. This you will need to pay this week's bill and the bills for the
next two weeks to come. That will leave you only Ten dollars for your laundry
and pin money. But I want you to try to make it reach. It will if you are careful
and independent. If it does not, let me know promptly (do not be afraid to) for I
do not want to think you are pinched and more particularly I do not want you to

58. After passing the New York Bar in the spring of 1904, Stevens had formed a
short-lived partnership (about one year) with Lyman Ward (c. 1877–1937), someone
he had known at Harvard. In a letter of April 4, 1937, to Philip S. May, Stevens gives a
description of Ward soon after he had died following an automobile accident: "Ward
was an extremely attractive fellow, who never got anywhere except to hold the jobs
spoken of in the clipping, because he knew nothing about making money. As you will
see, he was a bass soloist. If he had been the train dispatcher in the Jacksonville terminal,
the announcement of the departure of a local would have sounded like the bombard-
ment of Madrid" (*LWS*, 317). In a subsequent letter, Stevens suggests that Ward's
problem in the business world was to take people at their word, and then he commented on his voice for a last time: "I have always imagined that the basses in the heavenly choir were probably not as numerous or as effective as the other voices; Ward's
coming will make a vast difference" (*LWS*, 318).
59. A town on Long Island sound considerably beyond the eastern border of Queens,
perhaps twenty-five to thirty miles from the Stevens apartment.
60. There is a blob of ink on the first "boasting." *Letters during Mr. Wortley's Embassy
to Constantinople,* by Lady Montague (1689–1762), was published the year after her
death and followed by another volume in 1767.

borrow or to run up bills. Mind! I may be able to run over to see you about the middle of August but I cannot possibly arrange to do so before. Even then, perhaps, I should stay in Reading and come up to Vinemont for Sunday, all day. Our old home will, no doubt, be broken up for good, after thirty-five years, at the end of the summer; and I should want to spend at least a few hours there, among its familiar objects. This you will understand. . . . I can tell from the tone of your letters that you are in high-spirits. As soon as the weather settles into the August calm, you will have [the] quietest and softest of all the months of the year to enjoy.

With much love, from your own

Bud

⌐⌐

[WAS 1931 August 11, 1912 New York]
[Addressed to Vinemont.]

Sunday Evening

My dear girl:

No walk to-day. Last evening it blew as if the house was afloat in mid-ocean; and at two in the morning we had a down-right deluge. This morning the air was discouragingly like vapor. I lay late; and then went to St. Bartholomew's Church[61] for the morning service. I was so bleary that one of the hymns quite affected me, and I even thought the sermon good, when it wasn't. Then I bored it through the Park to the M-tr-p-l-t-n M-s—m of -rt (I hate the place). My hobby just now is the 17th Century, a very remarkable period in modern history. Fancy my pleasure then in realizing that <u>all</u> the pictures in the Flemish room and in the Dutch room were 17th Century pictures. I was perfectly enchanted with two—or by two—of them by Cornelis de Vos (the elder). Such fresh color: one of a woman with two children (one of the children very pretty, with a dish of bright flowers); the other of a girl of about fifteen in a brown dress. I looked at several cases of English silver and Sheffield plate, because I have just learned how supreme the English were in the matter of silver ware. Then I plodded down to the L-br-ry, because I wanted to find out who the devil Saint Anthony really was (I only found out that I <u>could</u> find out in the unreadable works of Saint Athanasius!) and who Saul was (confound my ignorance) and the story of Jacob and Esau—and I fell asleep over the Jewish Encyclopedia. I remember something about Jacob's ladder and Esau's mess of pottage and how the amiable tortoise Jacob beat the disagreeable hare Esau, all of which is portrayed at large in a sermon on Saul preached by Archbishop Trench of

---

61. Episcopal church at Madison Avenue and Forty-fourth Street at this time, with one of the wealthiest and most fashionable congregations in the city.

Dublin at Cambridge University. . . . [62] Aint this the most brilliant picture of an August Sunday? I feel like jumping out of my skin. I shall be sincerely glad to be at the office to-morrow and hope I shall find a mountain of work there. Recently, I spoke of coming to Vinemont next Sunday; but I cannot possibly spare the money. The events of July set me back so much that even as it is I shall be able to make progress only by making use of every dollar. I tell you this so that you will understand that I do not come because I do not want to, but for an excellent reason, as the saying is. If I keep quiet here I shall have plenty. It was pleasant to have your post-cards—two of them together [at] once.[63] The country at home seems far away to me. Some day I shall leave this monastic life here and see all your leafy roads again—and, of course, like the saintly Anthony shall have been so preserved by my love of good things that the roads will be a good deal more withered than I. Certainly my feelings do not wither—whatever may be said of that monster, the body. To-night the monster is full of capon and fresh peach pie.

With love
Wallace

⌣

[WAS 1932 August 26, 1912 New York]
[American Bonding Company stationery; no envelope.]

August 26, 1912

My dear Bo-Bo:

I walked from Van Courtland Park (the Broadway end of the Subway) to Greenwich, Connecticut—say, by my route, and judging by the time it took, roughly, thirty miles. It makes me feel proud of myself. This morning I am a little stiff here and there, because I am not in the best possible condition, but, on

---

62. Richard Chenevix Trench (1807–1886) wrote "On Some Deficiencies in Our English Dictionaries" (1857) and books on the historical study of English words that helped start the movement for, ultimately, the *New English Dictionary* (or *Oxford English Dictionary*).

63. One of these postcards, WAS 2051 Aug 9, 1912, is still extant; it pictures a house from above, with abundant foliage, especially vines, and is mailed to "Mr. Wallace Stevens, 84 William St., NYC c/o Bonding Co. of Balt." Elsie's text: "The top floor of this little place is the dance room. There is white netting stretched across the windows in the picture—but that has been taken out for the summer."

An earlier card of this series of three remaining cards from Elsie to Stevens at the same address is WAS 2050 July 30, 1912, "Park Mansion Facing South, Vinemont, Pa." Elsie's text: "This is a view of the house which I think you have not seen. My room is around on the other side of the main building. E." A later card, WAS 2052 August 30, 1912, pictures Galen Hall Bungalow in Wernersville, Pennsylvania. Elsie's text: "We walked over here again this morning —Had a perfect day. E."

the whole, I came through it very well. I got to Greenwich at about half-past seven, with the rising of the moon. Walking through the dark, to a strange place, with that mystical lantern in the trees, I could hear the early bells, calling for vesper-services. All day long, I had been reading scrawls on rocks in red paint: "Jesus saves"; "Prepare to meet thy God." . . . All told, you see, it was a devil of a solemn hour. And just then, there came along two creeking stages full of negroes, returning from a pic-nic, with their arms, etc. all intertwined. It was a chorus of barber-shop harmonies, horses' hoofs on the road, beating harness, crunching wheels, creaking stages. . . . I flitted along-side unseen, for a long time, like a moth. . . . I had my shirt turned back and my chemisette flung back, precisely like that corsair of hearts, le grand Byron, and I breathed! Of course, when I reached town, and its sorrows, and its civilities, I hid my exhilaration, put a noose around my neck, put on my coat and pattered, as neatly as anyone, along the route to the station. —In New-York, I bought a piece of meat (wow-ow-oo-oo-ruh-r-r-r!) and a Belinda perfecto and limped down the Avenue, looking like a Spanish gentleman, and blowing great rings of smoke, lighted home—still by that heavenly flame.

With love,
Wallace.

ᑌ

[WAS 1933 July 2, 1913 New York][64]
[Pre-marriage stationery, large hand.]

Wednesday Evening

My dear Bo:

I have an invitation to Hartford from to-morrow to Monday, which I have accepted. I had been wishing for it. It interests you, too, because the piano is involved. The washerwoman has not delivered my things and as it takes three days at the laundries, I face the prospect of wearing bath-towels, or nothing, unless I buy a lot of stuff (which I can scarcely do). —Yesterday Elizabeth[65] passed through town with half-a-dozen girls in pig-tails, bound, as I live, for the camp of Matilda Fairweather or Fayerweather or whatever her name is.

---

64. Addressed to "Mrs. Wallace Stevens, Pocono Manor Cottage, Pocono Manor, Monroe County, Pennsylvania." This is Elsie's address until WAS 1952 September 2, 1913, at which time she will be back at her old home in Reading.

65. His older sister, Elizabeth Banes Stevens (1885–1943), married George MacFarland (twenty years her elder) on September 20, 1917, and divorced him on June 20, 1927, charging desertion. Their daughter, Jane (MacFarland Wilson), born in May 1919, will become an important Stevens correspondent in the last fifteen years of his life, though she will not meet Stevens until she is 21, when Stevens will come to Reading for the funeral of his brother John's funeral in July 1940 (Brazeau, *Parts of a World,* 266).

What a ghoulish squeak for you! —I met them as a matter of fraternal courtesy to Elizabeth and showed them the Jewish synagogue at 43rd Street, the Library, the whale, etc. in the ceiling of the Grand Central—in the half-hour's time which was all I could spare. —Beastly hot here to-day. You could go trout fishing along my spine, I s'pose. —Did Mrs. Storms turn up? And are you making new friends among the young Quakers?[66] Let me know. I hope everything is perfectly all right. —This is just a note from the office at the end of the day. I found last night that you had taken the ink, etc. to the country with you. I had intended to write you more at my leisure then.

With love,
Wallace

∽

[WAS 1934 July 7, 1913 New York]
[Pre-marriage stationery, addressed to Pocono.]

Monday Afternoon. July 7, 1913
New-York

My dear Bud:

On the glorious Fourth, the Strykers, the celebrated Miss Trumbull (aged 50)[67] and I took an auto trip in the machine (a big six-cylinder car) of the people who live in the bungalow next to Stryker's house, and in the company of the bungaleers. We went about 65 miles going and the same distance returning—through Springfield to the Berkshires. We were, in fact, within walking distance of Stockbridge.[68] We pic-niced at a place in the Berkshires called Jacob's Well: a spread of chicken salad, sandwiches, cookies, watermelon, iced-tea, etc. The Miss Trumbull was, after all, a most agreeable person, with very pleasant manners and a sense of humor. She had tea with us. On Saturday evening we took dinner with her at the Hartford Country Club, an attractive place—dining in the open air. I need not (perhaps, could not) tell you how much I enjoyed the mint juleps and cigars.[69] We sat until almost midnight, with some quite reasonable talk. The

---

66. Pocono Manor had been founded in 1902 by a group of Friends of Philadelphia as a resort that was "conducive to the Quaker spirit of Peacefulness" (note in a brochure for the current Pocono Manor). Its first golf course (nine holes) was established in 1911; Holly Stevens reported that she and her parents took a vacation there in 1930. See "Holidays in Reality," 107.

67. Annie Eliot Trumbull (1857–1949) was a sociable poet, playwright, and novelist, who had once been a part of the younger generation of Mark Twain's Hartford circle and whose fame had been greatest at the turn of the century. Brazeau (*Parts of a World*, 114–16) gives an illuminating account of the Trumbull literary connections.

68. The Stevenses spent part of their honeymoon in Stockbridge.

69. The *s* on cigars has triple underlining.

rest of the time we loafed about on Stryker's porch and lawn. The walk to the house has an edge of blue lobelias on each side. Along the porch and around the front of the house are Canterbury bells and holly-hocks, in bloom, and various other things not yet in bloom. The long field which lay under the window of our room was full of newly-mown hay. Fancy how sweet the room was! And about a hundred black-birds were holding a convention in the field while I was there. The cats have grown very large!!! . . . I have not yet been home. Possibly, there will be a letter from you. I got your post-card just before I left the other day. How unpleasant Mrs. S. was after all her infernal invalidism! I am sure that by this time you know younger people and happier. I'll be along on the <u>Mountain Special</u> next Saturday afternoon; but since I'll be writing again in a day or two I can leave that until then. Did I tell you that the laundress telephoned me not to bother about my laundry until you returned? Does she know that you are to be gone for months? Isn't she the sweetest old devil ever? Cuss her.

With love,
Wallace.

⤚

[WAS 1935 July 10, 1913 New York]
[Pre-marriage stationery, addressed to Pocono.]

Thursday

My dear Bo:

I am coming on the "Mountain Special" on Saturday afternoon, reaching Pocono Summit about half-past five. Will you speak to the clerk at the Inn and make some arrangement for me? I want a single room near a bath to stay until Monday breakfast. Don't bother to come to the day-po, unless the impulse is irresistible.

Hastily,
Wallace

⤚

[WAS 1936 July 15, 1913 New York]
[Pre-marriage stationery, addressed to Pocono.]

Tuesday Morning

My dear Bo:

As I was leaving the cottage yesterday it passed through my head that I had not packed my razor; and last night, at home, I found, sure enough, that it was still either in the bath-room or in my bed-room—at distant Pocono. Interesting situation! I thought myself above such failings. Will you look it up and let me know if it has been found and, if it has, send it to me. . . . I had the pleasure of the oily chemist's company all the way to town. Blessings on us! He's a great swell, of course—automobiles, servants, twice around the world. But the fairies evidently don't like him; and I side with the fairies. What makes us happy is the goodness in other people and in ourselves. Isn't that true? Well, there's no good in that kind of a fellow. I was quite delighted with the children and old Mrs. Shipley.[70] And some of the other people seemed very pleasant. I wish you knew them.

With love, Wallace

⌐

[WAS 1937 July 17, 1913 New York]
[Pre-marriage stationery, addressed to Pocono.]

Thursday Afternoon

My dear Bud:

I have just finished my work. The razor came this morning just as I was leaving the house. I did not want to run back, so did not open it. No doubt, all is well! Then, too, Howard ran out to tell me that his father had returned yesterday and had brought him a British man-of-war. It is a beauty—nickel-plated guns—machinery between decks, etc. I expect they'll be having naval battles in the Park shortly. I have not yet seen Mr. W. The truth is, I got in at a sad hour last night. Walter Butler asked me to take dinner with him and his fiancée at the Park Avenue.[71] Who would ever think to look at that queer place (32nd to 33rd Streets facing Park Avenue—next to the Vanderbilt) that there is a great square court inside, with a fountain and a band-stand and a band and palms, bay-trees, poplars, flower-beds, etc.? And then during dinner somebody mentioned Lew Fields and we all went to the roof-garden on top of the new music-hall and saw "All Aboard"[72]—not a very amusing thing. —The girl is a rather nice girl and I hope they'll hit it off. But I cannot help feeling that poor Walter is the bulls-eye of several remarkable sharp-shooters. He spent enough last night to last me a long while: it made _me_ feel like a sharp-shooter. —I have not heard from the Strykers and so do not know what I shall be doing over Sunday. Perhaps, I'll hear in the morning. I was hoping that Stryker would be able to get a machine and that we could make a tour. —Nothing on for to-night, although I had half-expected to have dinner with Young. However,

70. Apparently, she was someone (possibly an amateur painter) from Philadelphia with whom Stevens seems to have made friends. See below, letters for August 26 and August 28, 1913.
71. Built in 1878, the stylish Park Avenue Hotel, popular for its palm court and band music, was demolished in 1927.
72. Musical comedy in two acts, book by Mark Swann, lyrics by E. Ray Goetz and Malvin Franklin, opened at the 44th Street Theater on June 5, 1913.

that has been put over until some evening next week. I shall, very likely, continue a book of Edmund Gosse's that I have been struggling with.

Your fat boy,
Wallace

⌒

[WAS 1938 July 30, 1913 New York]
[Pre-marriage stationery, addressed to Pocono.]

Wednesday Morning

My dear Bud:

Monday night I went to bed early to make up for the vicissitudes of two nights on a rather poor bed at Pocono. Last night, I felt much like going early, too; but shortly after I had reached my room Mr. Weinman came up. My head ached and I was not so friendly as I should like to have been; but I smoked many pipes of some very good English tobacco; and we talked until twenty minutes past eleven (by which time I was cock-eyed) about Paris, Rouen, London, steamers, etc. Mr. Weinman has a great collection of photographs, cards, etc. which we looked through. I think I got a better idea of the Louvre, the Pantheon, the Luxembourg, etc. than I ever had before. To have had one's attention specially focussed on the sculpture & all those things made them seem quite new. Mr. Weinman is full of feeling for Paris; but seems to have been left cold by London which, to be sure, has an interest of a different nature. This is only a note intended to reach you to-night, so that you may know that all is quiet and well.

With love,
Wallace

⌒

[WAS 1939 August 1, 1913 New York]
[Pre-marriage stationery, addressed to Pocono.]

Friday Afternoon.

My dear Bud:

To-morrow afternoon I am going by the Knickerbocker Limited (I say this just to rub it in) to New-London. There Mr. Heublein will meet me in a motor-boat and take me to his place at Eastern Point. Yes: the Strykers will be there. I stay until Sunday evening when I shall return to New-York by steamer from New-London. It is an all night ride on the Sound. Isn't this bully? I cannot understand why everybody and everything is (or are) acting so pleasantly. But after all, after so much, I suppose Fate seems obliged to be kinder. —And what a good time you are having! I am thoroughly glad to have your happy letters. I think all your friends are most interesting and they all seem so amiable, too. —I spend lots of time, now-a-days, looking at golf-sticks. Slazenger's have some very curious ones and I wish you'd need one—something for use on the green, say. The <u>Evening Post</u> contains accounts of a tournament in progress on the Shawnee links at the hotel you visited the other day. And only this afternoon I looked at some pictures of a water hazard on the links at Stockbridge. —Does this create a sporty atmosphere for you? —We shall both have lots to talk about next winter if we keep going to all these out-of-the-way places. —To-night I am going home until about ten o'clock and then I'm going to a Turkish bath for the night. I've been needing a good rub and mean to have it: so that I may shine like the rose over Sunday, to be sure. —Yesterday I was very much rushed at the office and hurried away without writing. It is impossible to write at home, so I dropped you a card. I hope to do better about my letters next week.

With my love, all of it,

Wallace.

⌒

[WAS 1940 August 4, 1913 New York]
[Pre-marriage stationery, addressed to Pocono.]

Monday Afternoon

August 4.

My dear Bud:

Got back this morning after a tedious ride. I came by rail instead of boat. . . . There is so much talk on these trips to the Heubleins that one doesn't have time to savour things. So much sea all around and all of it is missed because spray doesn't go well with clothes. We were under canvas or in the cabin most of the time. And then an immense deal of attention is paid to meals. However, I had a beautiful time. I think the Heubleins, personally, are uncommonly nice. But they had some other guests who were bores. (Pardon me for such bad manners.) Their cottage is quite a largish place near a very large hotel. On Saturday evening we went over to the hotel to a "Revue," which lasted until midnight. It was amusing. Rummy lot at the hotel. Everybody, men, women and children (excepting our superior party) in evening clothes. Afterwards, everybody went down to a grill-room and smoked and ate and drank, I suppose. Fortunately, there was no table for us and we went home. Sunday we cruised, so to speak, and went to Fisher's Island. After dinner we went to Watch Hill, in Rhode Island, I believe, but did not land. And then we came home to salvers of hard-shell crabs. Thoroughly stuffed, we sat on the porch listening to a Welte-Mignon. —To-day I feel cock-eyed and have been loafing shamelessly. But a good night, such as I mean to have, will fix me. I'll be out to the mountains next Saturday afternoon. If you can arrange for a double room and bath why go ahead. It will be like forty-eight hours of home.

With love,

Wallace

⌒

[WAS 1941 August 7, 1913 New York]
[Pre-marriage stationery, addressed to Pocono.]

84 William Street, New-York.[73]

August 7th 1913

My dear Bud:

I sit at home o' nights.[74] But I read very little. I have, in fact, been trying to get together a little collection of verses again; and although they are simple to read, when they're done, it's a deuce of a job (for me) to do them. Keep all this a great secret. There is something absurd about all this writing of verses; but the truth is, it elates and satisfies me to do it. It is an all-round exercise quite superior to ordinary reading. So that, you see, my habits are positively lady-like. Yesterday I went up to Goshen to examine some records and sent you a post-card. I actually saw the race-track, although there was nothing going on at the time. There is an Inn there called the Goshen Inn, very attractive, but right on the village green and not so airy. Got home after dark after a terrific ride on a rotten railroad. I had some tea in the diner. The tea pitched so in the cup that I could hardly keep it from dashing all over me. Then the train would stop for ages for no apparent reason. . . . To-day, too, I have been in the country, at Ridgefield, although it was gruesome there. —Mr. Jennings sent me a copy of the Public Ledger containing one of his letters. He is pro-suffrage. —Bought my ticket this afternoon. Too late for a Pullman. Thus, I shall be forced to come as I have long wanted to come. In the Pullman you always have the other fellows satchel, hat, knees, or feet either in your ears, eyes or pockets and it is as hot as the inside of a pie.

With love,
Wallace

⌒

[WAS 1942 August 12, 1913 New York]
[Pre-marriage stationery, addressed to Pocono.]

Tuesday Evening

My dearest: —[75]

As usual, on Monday evening, I went to bed at nine o'clock. I took up the clock to the man on 8th Avenue first; and afterwards did a bit of dusting. (It is growing heavy as snow.) It seemed as if bed-time would never come. This

---

73. This is Stevens's business address at the American Bonding Company.

74. As Eleanor Cook quotes this sentence, she adds "reading Marlowe, we assume." Cook, *Poetry, Word-Play and Word-War in Wallace Stevens* (Princeton: Princeton University Press, 1988), 98. She identifies the Marlowe play as *The Jew of Malta.*

75. This is the first use of this old, standard punctuation in several years.

morning I was in a police court and this afternoon I was way out on Long Island to look at a new sewer. At 6:30 this evening I dine with my old friend Jim Young. And to-morrow morning (Wednesday) before you have had your breakfast I shall be on my way to Troy (beyond Albany.) The beastly trip will take all day as I am going to try to make very short work of my business there. That is about as far ahead as I can see just now except that I expect to invite both Carrell and Southworth[76] to have dinner with me during the week. I owe both of them a dinner or two and it will be very nice to pay such agreeable debts. Well, I suppose when you came out-doors yesterday (Monday) morning you were as much surprised as I was to breathe that Alpine air. My train, by the way, was so late that I could not wait for it but took the next one! I had to wait more than an hour and wore a trail up and down the station platform. What a heavenly time we had—together. It was particularly nice not to have met <u>too</u> many new people. I wish, however, it had not been (as it was) too hot for us to exercise ourselves a bit. Exercise in the open-air is what both of us need most. I hope you'll do your golf as religiously as if it were medicine. This is an immense opportunity to learn. Most links are crowded with players and beginners always feel awkward and in the way. But that will not be your feeling at Pocono. . . . It may be that I shall not be able to write you to-morrow on account of trains; but I'll drop you a card at all events; and if possible, more.

With my love,
Wallace

↜

[WAS 1943 August 14, 1913 New York]
[Pre-marriage stationery, addressed to Pocono.]

Thursday.

My dear Bud:

I got back from Troy in time to have written (reaching home about eight o'clock) but I have no writing materials at home. It had been a <u>most</u> tedious day. So nice to have your letter—so full of pleasant things. To-day I have had a very decent day, which I am winding up by having dinner with Kearney and Southworth, somewhere or other. I have an invitation to visit some friends of Strykers at Great Barrington over Sunday, which I have just accepted. These are the people who have the piano that I want and I suppose that I'll know more about the chances this time next week than I do now. I really feel that I'd rather put the money into various other and more necessary things. It all depends on how much money is required; and, if they do not want too much, I don't know but

---

76. Carrell is probably (Southworth is certainly) a business associate, though his name never appears on letterhead along with Stevens and Southworth.

what I'll take the piano, because it would be a good thing for us both in the winter evenings. The people I am to visit: Signor Ferruccio Vitale, his wife and their little girl Giuseppina (!) are camping on a hill. There have a farm up there and I suppose the hill is part of the farm. It doesn't sound much in my line, does it? If it were not that I want to settle about the piano, I shouldn't go. I wanted to do nothing at all this Sunday, unless to take a walk near-by. But after all there will be plenty of time to look out of the window next winter and I ought to be glad to knock about. I am so thoroughly sick of railroad riding—the dust of it—the beastly Pullmans—[.] However, I'm going! I suppose, too, that I shall be delighted, after all, because I believe that the Vitales are uncommonly nice people. Only I wish they didn't live four hours away. Everything else is quiet and expensive as usual. I am glad Miss Custer was so nice. Pottstown seems so much warmer.

With my love,
Wallace

↩

[WAS 1944 August 15, 1913 New York]
[Pre-marriage stationery, addressed to Pocono.]

Friday Evening
My dear:

No letter from you last night. But I'm looking for one to-night. (There's more noise in this room than there ought to be. Kavanaugh[77] has been in and out all day. He has arranged a poker game for to-night with a crowd from Baltimore.) I've been looking up the place I'm going to to-morrow. It is apparently about ten miles from Stockbridge; but as my invitation read that we should be far from automobiles or horses I have no expectation of seeing that place of fond recollection.[78] I shall not get back to the office on Monday morning until after eleven, which is about the time I get there after the trips to Pocono. On Tuesday I shall be in Newburg, New-York, a little town up the river, where I have

77. In the *Hartford Agent* for December 1914 (vol. 6, no. 6), there is this reference to Kavanaugh: "William J. Kavanagh, who was with the Standard Accident Company's New York Office for about twelve years, and has been for the last three years manager of the liability department of the New England Casualty Company in New York City, has joined the New York Office of the Hartford Accident and Indemnity Company. In addition to having the liability and compensation underwriting, he will have charge of the automobile and specialty line of the Marine Department of the 'Hartford Fire.' Mr. Kavanagh is very popular both in and out of the insurance fraternity, and will make friends for the 'Hartford.' He is a 1st Lieutenant in Squad 'C,' the crack cavalry regiment of the National Guard."
78. This was one of the places they visited on their honeymoon.

some business. —Such a Dickens of a lot of traveling as I've had! —It's just like being a bag-man as they call them in England—traveling[79] with a strange line, however, for I go around to patch up trouble or else to cause it. How is the moon on your mountains? I should like to tramp your long porches, with a long cigar, in the clair de lune. Perhaps, my white tent to-morrow night, or summer shack, will satisfy the desire. I'll let you know all about it.

Your
Bud.

⌒

[WAS 1945 August 18, 1913 New York]
[Pre-marriage stationery, addressed to Pocono.]

Monday Afternoon.

My dear Bud:

I hope you're not cross about my going to Gt. Barrington. I had the most extraordinary time—and think the piano is ours. On Wednesday evening I am going to Vitale's for dinner and shall look the piano over and perhaps play a jig on it. It is a baby grand that cost about $1200 some years ago. It is now in its best condition. The terms are agreeable to me. The only thing is that you may want other things instead. Do you? I am wholly in favor of the piano. The other things we can get later on during the winter, possibly. I think, however, that a piano would make more difference to us than anything. It would help you through the evenings and be pleasant any old time. This is a great opportunity. Think it over. I shall not give an answer until I see you on Saturday; and I hope that by that time you will have made up your mind.[80] Do please decide in favor of the piano! The Vitales live on a hill-side just outside of Gt. Barrington. They have a little dago baby called Tobolina, which means little mouse. (Its real name is Josephine.) The house has huge dark pine groves on the West and the North. At the foot of the hill on the South is a lake. And before them on the East are the Berkshire hills. On the other side of Gt. Barrington is a place

---

79. Up until this point in this correspondence, Stevens spelled this word, and its variations, not in the accepted American way but in the accepted English way. In a letter of May 22, 1916, to Harriet Monroe about the publication of his play *Three Travelers Watch a Sunrise,* he corrects the proof by saying, "May I ask you to correct the proof of the title? It should be Travelers. The printer appears to believe that travelers are full of 1, so that he makes it travellers" (*LWS,* 194). After the date of this letter, he himself will double the *l* in this word. See below WAS 1983 for September 29, 1916. Thereafter, he remains inconsistent in his spelling of this word.

80. However, in a letter on Thursday (WAS 1947 August 21, 1913), two days before this promised deadline for deciding on the piano, Stevens reports to Elsie, "I bought the piano last night." See below.

called Brookside owned by a friend of Vitale's, Mr. William Walker.[81] It is by
far the most beautiful place I have ever seen. The house is on the banks of the
Housatonic (which we canoed on at Stockbridge.) You enter through beautiful gates, pass a lodge fit for a Duchess, and drive through stunning grounds.
[Here he draws the layout of the house and surrounding grounds.]

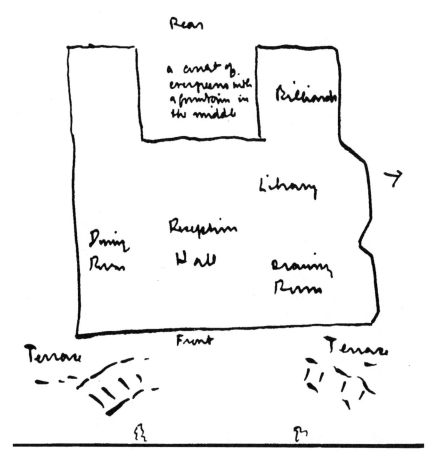

The house is a mass of beautiful things: $200,000 worth of rugs on the first
floor alone! In the library is a whopping organ. But bother all this. In front of

81. For photographs of and information about Brookside, see Carole Owens's book
The Berkshire Cottages: A Vanishing Era (Englewood Cliffs, N.J.: Cottage Press, 1984). It
is one of many mansions in the Berkshires, from Lenox south to Great Barrington, built
by people of great wealth. Brookside had been built by William Stanley (1858–1916),
inventor of the alternating-current coil and sold in 1908 to William Hall Walker, a
retired railroad man who brought Ferruchio Vitale from Italy to design the elaborate
gardens and grounds. Brookside is now the Eisner Camp, owned by the Union of
Hebrew Congregations.

the house is a circular garden full of seats, statutes [*sic*], flowers, a fountain, etc. I have shown the steps leading down. We sat here in the twilight. Old man[82] Walker showed me everything he had from dish-warmers to tapestries. My, my, your eyes would have melted. Then bye and bye, when the moon rose, we went in the direction indicated by the arrow on the right of the house and came to an Italian garden, bee-yu-tiful. The Strykers have given me some photographs so that you might see for yourself. I'll enclose them with this letter.[83] Take good care of 'em because I'll want them again. Mr. Walker has a big place (house) here in New-York. He gave me an invitation to visit him when he gets back to town. I'll arrange it for both of us and we'll toddle up there one of these fine days and weep with envy—sure as your [*sic*] born. I'm coming out again on Saturday and shan't forget the cucumber cream. Do you need anything else—not expensive, of course? But don't let them give me an expensive room again. They soaked me last time. Be sure I have a single room without bath. Must go home now and sleep up.

All my love, your
Old Man.

〜

[WAS 1946 August 20, 1913 New York]
[Pre-marriage stationery, addressed to Pocono.]

Wednesday.

My dear Bud:

To-day I went out to see a man at Belle Mead, Pennsylvania. This about completes my trips for the present. It seems as if I had been almost everywhere on the map. On the train to-day, I studied various ways of getting from the Poconos to Reading but fear I must leave it to you. If, however, you don't throw any light on the subject, I think I know how to do it. Let [me] hear from you regarding what the hotel people say. They ought to know. —To-night, I dine with Vitale and see the piano for the first time. It is in his house here in New-York and not at Great Barrington. I suppose I'll treat him to a sonata before the evening is over. . . . The particular merit of this particular piano is exactly its beautiful tone, I'm told. Well, must hurry. I only ran over here from the station to drop you a line.

With love,
Wallace

---

82. Volume 1 of Richardson, *Wallace Stevens*, reproduces two pages of this letter with both the drawing and the following text between pages 384 and 385. Richardson's reading of this word as if it were "mom" (416–17) is not supported by a careful examination of Stevens's handwriting.

83. They are not extant.

⤺

[WAS 1947 August 21, 1913 New York]
[Pre-marriage stationery, addressed to Pocono.]

Thursday Morning

My dear:

   This is just to say how glad I am to hear that you will stay another week. That is quite as I had planned. See you Saturday. . . . Also, I bought the piano last night. It is a beauty—a Steinway baby grand in an ebony case—gorgeous polish, etc. Of course, it shows that it is not pop out of the factory. But you will like it, I know. . . . We had a very pleasant dinner: Italian noodles instead of a soup, a glass or two of claret and some cigars. Vitale lives in one of those little houses in Grove street: the front covered with bay-trees, vines, window-boxes, etc. Very nice, neat garden in the rear, with a gravel walk bordered by rhododendrons, a plot of grass and a statue, more or less, in the middle of it. A good place for humming[84] soup whilst batting off flies from the neighboring stables.

With love,
Wallace.

⤺

[WAS 1948 August 26, 1913 New York]
[Pre-marriage stationery, addressed to Pocono.]
[No heading here; extremely rare.]
My dear Bud:

   I saw the bears on the way over to the station on Monday morning. Evidently your ankle is in good order, otherwise you could not have taken your walk in the afternoon. I smoked my head off and shant want to smoke again for some time. Indeed, it seems more than ever a poor habit. To-day I am just recovering from it and have a slight headache to help along. Have just written to Mrs. Shipley. So nice to have something of hers. Try to get some more everlastings. Our bunch ought to be about four times larger. Here is a dollar to help out. I find I must be economical. I arrive 12:13 Saturday and we both leave at 1:43. So be ready. You might ask Bob to make sure of the trains.

With love,
Wallace

⤺

84. This word looks exactly like "humming," as it occurs in normal contexts in both WAS 1841 May 4, 1909 and WAS 1862 June 24, 1909. However, the description of Stevens's handwriting by Hale Anderson Jr. as "an up-and-down series of V's" (Brazeau, *Parts of a World,* 23) applies in this case, and one is not certain.

[WAS 1949 August 27, 1913 New York]
[Pre-marriage stationery, addressed to Pocono.]

Wednesday Evening

My dear:

Lunch with Kavanagh to-day. To-morrow night Walter Butler and his fiancée have dinner with me and then we go to Potash & Perlmutter,[85] a silly show up-town. Don't like to do it but feel I should. Walter is a good sport, as the saying is. Am trying to find a woman to clean up next week since I do not wish to move the piano in until the place is clean. The piano is to be hoisted. Gosh! I never felt like less like writing a letter. There's a street piano playing away under my window and I cannot concentrate my thoughts. Went to the drug-store for your lotion this morning and shall get it on the way up-town. Fact is, I have been working on a Will all day and am just about done up. I suppose you'll [be] cross at such a hurried note. Forgive me. I'll be a better boy some other day.

Your
Bud

⌒

[WAS 1950 August 28, 1913 New York]
[Pre-marriage stationery, addressed to Pocono.]

Thursday Evening.

My dear Bud:—

I happened to be in the Grand Central Depot about four o'clock and stumbled across Miss Shipley and a cousin. I did not see Mrs. Shipley but suppose she was there. My time was too short to inquire. She said that she had received my note—Mrs. Shipley had. Invited us to see them in Philadelphia. Very agreeable friends, I think. Last evening I went around to Vitale's when he wasn't there and looked over the piano carefully. It is undoubtedly a very fine piano and I am perfectly satisfied. I expect to have it moved in next week some time and then to pass my evenings playing jigs until you come home. Mr. Corbett next door fills the street with his player piano every night. —We are going to "The Doll Girl"[86] instead of to "Potash & Perlmutter" tonight. I could not get seats for P. & P. which is said to be a great success. But then "The Doll Girl," which only opened the other night, is also well spoken of. I haven't blown myself this way

85. Play in three acts by Montague Glass, based on the stories in the *Saturday Evening Post,* opened at the Cohan Theater on August 16, 1913. With 441 performances, it had the longest run of any play that opened in 1913.

86. Musical play in three acts by Leo Stein and A. M. Willner, English version by Harry B. Smith and music by Leo Fall. It opened August 25, 1913, at the Globe Theater.

for years and heavens! how it hurts. I suppose I'll sulk like an old Dutchman until I have forgotten it. I imagine Miss Caird, whom Walter is to marry, might be nice for you to know.[87] Everybody helps in a way. —Well, I must be getting along, because I shall have to go home to prink and preen and prettify. See you on Saturday. Be all packed by twelve o'clock. I'll be there shortly after and we'll have no time to waste. Make arrangements about your trunk but do not check it. I'll attend to that. I mean: arrange to have it sent to the depot.

With love,
Wally![88]

⌐

[WAS 1951 August 29, 1913 New York]
[Pre-marriage stationery, addressed to Pocono address.]

Friday Morning

My dear Bud:—

Do <u>not</u> meet me at the station to-morrow morning. There is an hour and a half between the time when I come and the time our train starts for Stroudsburg. I'll come to the <u>Inn</u> for lunch; also to pay my bill. They haven't sent me the bill for last week so that it is quite necessary for me to go to the Inn.

Your
Bud

⌐

[WAS 1952 September 2, 1913 New York]
[Addressed to Mrs. Wallace Stevens, 231 South 13th Street, Reading. This address is used through WAS 1958.]

Tuesday Evening

My dear Bud:

Well, I suppose you think I'm a hyena in human form. I know just how you are thinking of winter things. It was simply a piece of bad luck to have this unseasonable cold snap right now.[89] However, this time next week, you'll be

87. Elsie seems to have become friends with Miss Caird after she became Walter Butler's wife because a Stevens letter of May 2, 1916, is addressed to Elsie in care of Mrs. Walter K. Butler on Long Island (WAS 1975).
88. Huge signature. This is the only time he will use this name in this correspondence.
89. Stevens may be talking about emotional and not physical weather; in WAS 1786 and WAS 1787 for late March and early April 1907, the word "winter" came to mean disagreement between Stevens and Elsie, and punishment. In WAS 1806 and 1810 (and in other letters), "winter" was clearly seen as a force that converted their apartment into a place of relative contentment. It seems likely that in this case he was, because of business pressure, unable to go to Pocono Manor to get her as planned, a failure for which he

here—and then all will be forgiven, I hope. I send you $5.00. Will you hold on to this as firmly as you can. I paid half of the price of the piano <u>to-day</u> and $5.00 looks like a six-cylinder motor car to me. I wish you would just keep it in your pocket so that it would be unnecessary for me to send more; but it will take almost that much for your fare and trunk. Write to me about this at once, because I'll have to send whatever else you need on Friday. Be brave, Missus, and make the most of the horrors of luxurious poverty; for when you hear the piano, you'll leap for joy. I hope you got my card from Albany and my note from the office later on. Wasn't it the limit about Mrs. Storms? Of course, if one really knew that such people were ill, it would be different. The truth is, I thought she was merely an old fuss. What a pity for her husband, too. He seemed to me to be wrapped up in her. Going to Newburgh early to-morrow. We have a very bad case up there which requires lots of attention. I like the town immensely. It seems so much what a small town ought to be. When I was there last week, the streets were full of school children and young men and maidens. Wished you could have been with me on the boat ride up the river the other night. Full moon. They had steam heat all over the boat and I woke up feeling like a piece of bacon. I haven't heard about Baltimore definitely but sincerely wish to work the trip off (if it must be taken) before you come. I do not want to go, because I have been up hill and down dale all summer.

You'll be a thousand times welcome when you come.[90]

Now I'm off to the Villa Penza for sphagetti.[91]

With love,
Wallace.

⌇

[WAS 1953 September 4, 1913 New York]
[Pre-marriage stationery, addressed to Reading.][92]

Thursday.

My dear Bud:

All is quiet along the Rappahannock. A Dutch woman turned up yesterday and made the front room shine. To-day she is wrestling with the rest of the place. Possibly she will be there to-morrow morning, too. I want to get everything neat

---

expected to be chided. The envelope for this letter, with no sign of cancellation or post-mark, is quite small (3-by-4 inches), as if designed for standard thank-you notes. Thus the stationery, which is of ordinary size, had to be given an extra fold along two sides.

90. This is the first indented paragraph in the letters, other than in first lines.

91. He partially prints this new word to his vocabulary as if to make it as clear as possible.

92. The archival folder for this letter contains two pressed leaves, possibly clover.

as a pin and then keep it so. . . . Pocono Manor, as I expected, sent along a little bill for my last week-end, which I have, of course, paid. And that cleans 'em up. . . . I have been somewhat out of kink since getting home, but expect to be all right again in a few days. The fact is, I think our bed better than a health resort. True. I swish around like a ship at sea before going to sleep. But when I sleep, I sleep like a monument. . . . And then it is so nice to look out and see a familiar chimney or two. . . What strange places one wakes in! Reading was very— unsympathetic, I thought. The trouble is that I keep looking at it as I used to know it. I do not see it as it is. I must adjust myself; because I do not intend to shut myself off from the heaven of an old home. How thrilling it was to go to the old church last Sunday! I had no idea I was so susceptible. It made me feel like Thackeray in the presence of a duke. The nobility of my infancy, that is: the survivors, all in the self-same rows. For me, a mirror full of Hapsburgs. . . . Je tremblais. Well, again, I do not intend to shut myself off from the heaven of an old home. And so, I keep recalling Du Bellay's sonnet in the Book of Regrets: for, when all is said and done, there is more for a common yellow dog like me in our Pennsylvania Anjou than in the "fronts audacieux" of New-York. Only, I never intend to admit that I'm a common yellow dog. Indeed, to-night I'd like to be in Paris, sipping a bock under a plane-tree, and listening to Madame's parrot from Madagascar.

With love,

W.

↩

[WAS 1954 September 6, 1913 New York]
[Pre-marriage stationery, addressed to Reading.]

Saturday Afternoon

My dear Bud:

The woman who cleaned was a real success. The place never looked so nice. I did not have the floors waxed, but washed. Everything is shining. The contagion spread through the house and Mrs. W. obligingly put up our winter shades. The job took three solid days. And the piano comes on Monday morning! And on Monday afternoon it is to be put in perfect tune!! The fact is, I cannot tell that it is out of tune (if it is at all, which I doubt)[.] But, of course, I want it to be at its best; and it will be. I shall be ready for you on the 16th; and shall send you money for R. R. on the 15th. If the weather brightens and you feel like lingering a day or two or three thereafter, right-o; but if the weather is still as rotten as it has been, then you might as well be here, for you'll be happier here (I hope.) I am going to be uncommonly hard-pressed until the 1st of October, after which things will run along as usual. This morning I went out to Brooklyn to see a contractor. In the Bay section, where there are open fields, etc., I noticed large flocks of birds, filling the air; and trees as full of birds as of leaves. It is a part of the psychology of all of us to feel a p-p-pang at all this—and to wish to spend the winter with the boids sunning on the equatorial wire. . . . However, as you begin to set your hands once more to house-hold affairs, cheered by the rivalry with your mother, you will grow forgetful of the equatorial wire; and it will be easy for you, when you have returned, to explore <u>new</u> cook books, <u>new</u> music, <u>new</u> stores (alas!)[.] Stern Brothers store, you know, is now on 42nd Street. They moved quickly to have a surprise for you (and ever so many other people) when you get back. Now, would Dives[93] do that? No—never. When I was home I felt that a good many people ought to imitate the store-keepers who are described as "Established 1807," etc. Yet Leon Buch has moved; but his old liquor store is still there, occupied by a thief from Bessarabia or Tyre, selling shoes, etc. Reading is too, too human and so set in its ways. I cast my shoes at it and empty my wash-pot upon it. But blessed be its name!

Adieu—
A plaintive spirit.

⟜

[WAS 1955 September 8, 1913 New York]
[Pre-marriage stationery, addressed to Reading.]

Monday Evening

My dear Bud:

The piano is now up at the house. To-morrow morning a man is coming to clean the inside. There's a little dust. In the afternoon, another man is coming to do the tuning. The piano people have this kind of thing down to a fine art and every time you think of something you'd like done it costs at least two and a half. They soaked me twelve simoleons to lift her in. And the men complained so grievously of the dry, hot weather that I couldn't resist a half-dollar for beer. I suppose the duster will discover something and the tuner something else. All I can see for myself is the need of polishing—thumb-marks, etc. I am going to try to do this myself. Mrs. Weinman has promised me some oil which she has used herself and recommends. The piano people want eight beans to do it. I may let them do it at Xmas, but not now. Besides, the thing looks quite stunning as it is, I think, and I am glad I've got it. You won't know the front room when you come. Now, no more about it. . . . Yesterday was my second Sunday in town since June. In the morning, after walking a while, I went to hear Albert Parker Fitch[94] in the

93. Prominent department store in Reading on Penn Street.
94. "The Reverend Albert Parker Fitch left Harvard at the same time as Stevens and Pitts Sanborn in 1900 and became a well-known minister and professor of religion. . . . From 1909–1917, Fitch was president of the Andover Theological Seminary in Cambridge, Mass.; from 1917–23 he was professor of the history of religion at Amherst

Brick Presbyterian Church. This man is one of the best preachers I ever heard; and, since he is to be here during September, I look forward to real elevation. I roamed around a while, afraid to do anything because it looked so much like rain; and finally I went home, where there was an awful racket on the roof. Bye-and-bye, it poured. I read, etc. until bed-time. I am wading through a French novel. Wednesday, I go to Newburgh. Friday, to Troy, again. And the rest of the week will be reasonably busy. I hope you will be sure to see Hattie[95] while you are in Reading. You will be glad to see her now and then in the winter—and must not grow too absorbed in putting up peaches—and the likes o' that. I hope that by the time you get back it will be cooler and brisker than it has been. That will be as it should be.

> Your,
>
> Rastus.

⇛

[WAS 1956 September 13, 1913 New York]
[Pre-marriage stationery, addressed to Reading.]

Saturday Afternoon

My dear Bud:

I am going to Albany by the night boat to-morrow (Sunday) night, in order to keep an appointment at nine o'clock on Monday morning, in Troy. So that when you sit down to breakfast on Monday morning, you can imagine me between a Jew and an Irishman, in Troy, trying to settle a claim. I have been in Newburgh twice this week. It is highly probable that I shall go to Baltimore next week for a day. . . . Last evening I had dinner with Mr. Vitale at his home in Grove Street. He told me how much the piano had been admired. There is nothing the matter with it. I asked the man who tuned it to leave word if repairs of any kind were necessary. He left word that he had examined it carefully and found that no repairs at all were necessary and that it was in beautiful condition. It gratifies me to have this opinion. I have about decided to have it polished before you come back. If you could stay until Monday, September 22, and come back on that day, it would just suit me. Couldn't you, Bud? Then I shall surely have it polished and have one other little thing done that I have thought

---

College." See MacLeod, *Wallace Stevens and Company,* 104–5. Reverend Fitch was, along with Stevens himself, one of the six people to whom Pitts Sanborn dedicated his volume of poetry, *Vie de Bordeaux,* in 1916. The other four were Donald Evans, Walter Conrad Arensberg, Carl Van Vechten, and Emily Latimer.

95. This is probably Harriet Heller, whom Elsie listed as one of the three friends with her when she met Stevens in 1904 (see note 5 of the Introduction, above). An unpublished letter at the Huntington from Alice Tragle to Elsie (WAS 2054 8/2/12) asks, "Do you see a great deal of Hattie? We hear from her often—she seems to be very well & contented in New York."

of. In fact, I think I'll have it polished anyhow—although it will make things close. I'm doing some very fine figuring. You have certainly been a real help by not wanting anything these last two weeks—just two weeks ago you left Pocono. (I suppose the Vegin's[96] are still there, since they were not to come back until Monday of next week[.]) —I shall send you a little Monday if I get back in time. Otherwise on Tuesday. I have been devilishly economical, too. Several times last week I went to dinner in an interesting Italian hole on Grand Street, called the "Villa Penza." I have been making researches in sphagetti. But I made up my fasts in Newburgh. The humors of practicing law in New-York! However, these ups and downs are the salt of life. They give a relish to the periods of indulgence. Personally, I do not mind in the least, since there is so much to gain; and I hope that you, too, between walks, etc. continue to be cheerful. . . . I suppose your affection for Reading has revived a little. It always does. Stevenson says that wherever we are our affections take root and spring up like flowers at our feet. But I was glad to have you say that you would be glad to be back. Last week, when it was so dismal and beastly, I wished for you often. Autumn will soon be here. It always seems so much as it should be to "come up to town"[97] for the winter when Fall begins. Mrs. Weinman is getting things ready. She has had all the carpets up on the stairs, and cleaned; and the steps, etc. have all been washed. She says that my cleaning up-stairs made her feel restless. Now, we smell like a rose-bush. . . . I enclose Miss Elliot's[98] post-card. The place looks quiet. Not a soul in sight. Notice the daisies northwest of the word Pocono. I intended to forward this before but have not had an opportunity. It was always up-town when I was down-town or the other way round. You're a nawfully poor correspondent. Am going to church again to-morrow morning.

> With love, your
> New-York Branch.

‫↬‬

[WAS 1957 September 20, 1913 New York]
[Pre-marriage stationery, addressed to Reading.]

> Saturday Afternoon

My dear Bud:

Yesterday, on the way up to town, I thought of not having written to you. But it is out of the question at home. And so you had no word to-day. When you wake up on Monday morning, I shall be in Baltimore. Am going down on

---

96. It looks as though he may have tried to erase the apostrophe.
97. This phrase is used in a couple of places in Wilde's play *The Importance of Being Earnest*.
98. There is a blob after the *o* and before the apostrophe, as if Stevens had originally written two *t*s. The card is not extant.

the sleeper Sunday night, but am coming back on Monday afternoon or Monday night. So that you'll be sure to find me in Jersey City when you arrive on Tuesday. Come on the train leaving Reading at 9.25 in the morning. Arrange with the Union Transfer Co. about your trunk. They are on North 6th Street on the right hand side going from Penn-St to Court-St. Tell them to come at 8 o'clock and tell them what train you want it on and then see Mr. Mengel at the station and make sure the trunk goes on the same train. Mr. Mengel is in the Baggage room. I knocked him unconscious with a brick once and we have been bosom friends ever since. I send 2.00. You will need almost 5.00 in all, for ticket, Pullman (.75, I think) and trunk transfer. See that your trunk is securely strapped. And come prepared to be hard up for a few days. . . . I had not expected the weather to be so beastly. No use to have the windows gone over again, etc. because it rains every night. Besides we look quite respectable as it is. Bought several waltzes for you yesterday. Tum-te-to! The polisher polishes on Monday and another fellow is going to look at something else. T'ell with expense. I think you're going to like the machine tremendously. I play for 7 hours every night. . . . Well, see you soon again and glad I'll be to have you back. Hope it clears up for you, although I have forgotten what good weather looks like.

With much love,
Wallace

↬

[WAS 1958 August 11, 1914 New York]
[Equitable Surety Company of St. Louis, Missouri, stationery, Branch office in New York; Stevens listed as Res. Vice-President,[99] E. B. Southworth Jr. as Manager and Vice-President, and Wm. R. Liedike as Asst. Sec.; addressed to Elsie at 231 South 13th Street, Reading.]

Tuesday

My Dear Elsie:

Very glad to find your letter when I reached home last evening. The bathroom curtains came but I shall not attempt to hang them. I intended to write you a good long letter last night but it was too hot to sit under the light. . . . My trip to Hartford was very pleasant. What a stroke of bad-luck that the Strykers should come to town just when you happened to be at home. Stryker has been ill—no: nervous, sleepless, full of the war, and wanted to forget it. . . . They have three children stopping with them. One is about sixteen, one, nine, one about six.

---

99. Brazeau indicates that Stevens was hired as resident vice president in February 1914. He will remain here after this firm "merges with New England Casualty Company of Boston on July 1, 1915, to become New England Equitable Insurance Company" (*Parts of a World,* xii).

They are all girls: daughters of a vagabond brother of Mrs. Stryker's, I believe. The two youngest are to stay permanently. They are robust looking but not well-colored. They are affectionate, as children are, and not at all rude—rather decent, I think. But I saw very little of them. Stryker and I walked the greater part of Sunday around the suburbs of Hartford, including an uninteresting cemetery in which lie the bones of J. P. Morgan.[100] On Sunday evening we sat at the edge of their meadow until one o'clock in moonlight and dew. It was astonishingly cool and fresh after a day of unusual heat. Then it was so nice afterwards to lie in my cool bed—cool! with the blinds drawn and the quiet moonlight coming through the blinds. . . . I have borrowed a half-dozen or more books from Stryker. And Mrs. Stryker gave me a necklace for you, which did not become her. It doesn't amount to much but will, I think, be useful: I mean you must not think it an expensive necklace. It is pretty. I should much prefer to have you come on Monday instead of Sunday. But why come at all? Why not spend a week or two, say, at Wernersville, Galen Hall,[101] or if you can find some other place not too expensive? Would you care to do this? If you feel inclined to do this let me know. But I do not want to be obliged to send any money before Saturday. I paid for the piano, finally, last week and it leaves my bank account looking like an airship or balloon, rather, on the way <u>down.</u> Anyhow, that's done and I needn't worry about it any more. . . . It would be the devil for you to be here just now. Do as you like, however. I am thinking only of your comfort and my own. We'll pull through the summer somehow, at all events. I hope you will write soon.

With love,
Wallace

⌒

[WAS 1959 August 13, 1914 New York]
[Same stationery and address as letter above; no envelope, but Elsie is apparently still in Reading.]

Thursday Afternoon

My dear Bo:

Business bum, Kavanaugh has been over this afternoon telling me stories (as usual.) Anyhow, I did more business than Southworth. It has been rotten for a

---

100. In *LWS* (182n4), Holly Stevens identifies this as Cedar Hill, where Stevens himself would be buried, according to the request he made in his final illness.

101. One of several resorts west of Reading, within ten or fifteen miles of the city center. A Galen brochure of the period gives some insight into the institution: "Those desiring the best home cooking, pure drinking water, invigorating mountain air and summer recreation will find them here, with exceptional facilities for rambles and open air sport; while those seeking rest and health find pleasant comfort on the extensive piazzas (700 feet), the near-by shaded seats, or in quiet hammocks beneath the trees."

week or more. By the way, they must have put off my stuff in the Trend[102] for a rainy day. I've been waiting (as one awaits the reading of a will) and only the other day they managed to get the August number out and then lo and behold you, I'm not in it. Well and all! —Pauline is up at the house to-day. She is getting impatient for Madame Stevens to get back to business, so I left a note for her to come next Tuesday. Heavens! That reminds me that I forgot to leave my key on the table for her to-day. Bless my soul! The poor Belgian has probably been wringing her hands; and I suppose it will rain to-morrow. I gave the geraniums a bath last night, washing the leaves, the pots, etc. Also soaked the fern-dish. One ought to know something about flowers to get any good out of them. What I'd like to know is how to make geraniums bloom. Could you find out from any one over there? Glad to hear you're coming back next Monday, and I hope the weather is better than it has been. Yesterday was painful.[103]

Yours, with love.
Wallace

〜

[WAS 1960 July 21, 1915 New York][104]

Wednesday Evening

My dear Bud:

Here's a little book for you to read.

The people below us now have ivy in their window boxes trained upward, so that they live in an illusion of the country. Very nice, eh? The plant in the painted

---

102. This is a reference to "Carnet de Voyage," a group of eight poems eventually published in *Trend* 7, no. 6 (September 1914): 743–46. Five of the poems in this group were originally in the "Little June Book" of twenty poems Stevens wrote for Elsie's twenty-third birthday; see note to WAS 1837 April 18, 1909.

103. At two different points in this letter, Stevens scratched out or altered a word, a freedom that is unusual for a man who had said earlier, "I hate erasures, just as I do corned beef—and saxophones" (cf. WAS 1843 May 9, 1909).

104. Extremely small pages made from two sheets of standard pre-marriage stationery; each sheet is torn carefully in half to form four sheets, and then these four sheets are folded in half to make eight pages. This would have taken an envelope considerably smaller than WAS 1952. There is no envelope, but the mention of Byrdcliffe puts it in the summer of 1915, and references in WAS 1961 indicate that this letter came before that one. The seven extant letters of this year (six of them with envelopes and thus addresses) indicate that Elsie was at Byrdcliffe near Woodstock, in Ulster County New York, from about July 17 to September 5, 1915. (The Stevens connection to this resort lasted at least six years. A letter from Stevens to Harriet Monroe, September 1, 1917, shows that Stevens and Elsie were back in Woodstock at that time, though there are no letters of 1917 from Stevens to Elsie at this location. See *LWS,* 202. *LWS,* 222, contains part of a letter of September 2, 1921, to Monroe; an excised part of this letter, at

pot is having a flower. It looks like a pale green pepper, half-open, with stamen of white (resembling the yellow stamen of a lily) about an inch long. I have put all these things on a table in the kitchen by an open window. Anna has agreed to run in whenever there is a shower and close the window. I talked to the florist about re-potting some of our things. He thinks it ought to be done in the Fall, not now.

I sent you the London Times (except the pages containing maps) this morning; and the other day, a letter from Frances Butler; and I shall send you, with this and with your calendar, in the morning, a letter from Mrs. Stryker, at Great Barrington. Will you let me know if these reach you? Your note to-day does not indicate that you had yet received my letter of Monday. The laundry came to-day and I am, for convenience, putting a few things in your bed-room closet until I hear from you about the key to the linen closet.

Mrs. Nürnberger gave herself the pleasure of telephoning me Tuesday. Dr. Lanson would be so pleased to have us buy, etc. She apologized for the weather when we were up there—and all that; warmly urged us to come soon again. Lord! Fancy staying at that miserable farm-house.

I have not yet gone to Washington Square for dinners. Perhaps I shall find some place nearer home. To-night I tried the Bellamar—the Spanish place on W. 23rd Street. Same old silver tureen, same old fish, same old roast beef, lettuce and ice-cream, same old coffee-pot. I wish one could find something new in these places. Washington Square is best after all, but it is so far down town that I get there long before dinner is ready and I have a horror, as you know, of killing time in that way.

Very likely, you have already commenced your studies with Mr. Schumacher.[105] You will soon get into the swing of it; and although you will, no

---

the University of Chicago, shows that Stevens and Elsie are on their way to Woodstock, and a letter of September 7, 1921, also at the University of Chicago, reports that Stevens and Elsie have returned from Woodstock.) This resort was quite different from either the restful atmosphere of Vinemont or the sporting atmosphere of Pocono Manor; it was an experimental art colony that was connected with the Art Students League of New York, and its living arrangements represented a somewhat communal experiment. Perhaps it was through Walter Pach, who studied with Robert Henri at the Art Students League, and who eventually illustrated Stevens's "Earthy Anecdote" (in *Modern School* 5 [July 1918]: 193), that Stevens knew of this summer art school. In a letter of July 17, 1944, to Harry Duncan of the Cummington School, whose small press published some of Stevens's work, Stevens describes Byrdcliffe: "When I was first married, my wife and I used to go to a place called Byrdcliffe, which was pretty much what Cummington is. There the driving force was Whitehead, an Englishman. The place is still in existence, but is now merely a collection of cabins in the woods on the hillside beyond Woodstock, N. Y." (*LWS*, 468).

105. See William R. Valentine, *The Frederick W. Schumacher Collection* (Columbus, Ohio, 1955) for a catalogue of his paintings.

doubt, feel a little lonely for a day or two, Byrdcliffe will soon be home (temporarily) to you. Go in for everything you can, my dear. I am sure that everybody there is nice—and to be enjoyed. I shall run up to see you in a few weeks.

I expect always to send your money Fridays or Saturdays so that it will reach you Mondays when your weeks end.

With much love,
Wallace

Morning

Ordered the <u>Tribune</u> this morning, daily & Sunday, for one month for you. Have been up every morning at half-past six. Breakfasts at home; fruit and coffee. Very <u>business</u> at the office.

W

∽

[WAS 1961 July 25, 1915 New York]
[Standard, white, pre-marriage stationery with envelope of Equitable Surety Company, addressed to:]

 Mrs. Wallace St[cut off here]
  Woodstock,
   Ulster Coun[cut off here]
    New-Yo[cut off here]
Byrdcliffe [written off to the left]

Sunday Evening

My Dear Elsie:

I went up to the Botanical—no: the Zoological Garden this morning to see a collection of birds that Professor Beebe has just brought up from Brazil.[106] There was a hyacinthine macaw, chiefly of interest because I could see what color hyacinthine really is! Then I went over to the Botanical Garden where I spent several hours in studying the most charming things. I was able to impress on myself that larkspur comes from China. Was there ever anything more Chinese when you stop to think of it? And coleus comes from Java. Good Heavens, how that helps one to understand coleus—or Java. There were bell-flowers from China, too, incredibly Chinese. I was able, also, to impress on myself the periwinkle—from Madagascar—pink or white or white with a red eye. The beds in front of the green-houses which were full of irises and tulips when we were up there sometime ago, now contain masses of phlox. There are patches of marigolds, portulaca, petunias, everlastings, etc. One or two things were absolutely new to me. One was a Chinese lantern plant. This is a plant about two feet high which bears pods, the size of peppers. The pods are green at one end and at the bottom,

---

106. C. William Beebe was curator of birds at the Bronx Zoo.

as they hang, are orange and yellow, so that they resemble lanterns. Another new thing was what is called swan-river daisies, from Australia. They are quite like the small flowers you got up on Madison-Avenue once. In fact, I rather think your flowers <u>were</u> swan-river daisies. Red yarrow and purple loose-strife were things that I have known for a long time but the names of which I did not know before to-day. After all this, I walked through the Bronx Parkway Reservation and then to Van Cortlandt and then to Spuyten Duyvill, where I sat on a fence and looked at some horses. Then I walked some little distance back to the subway and came down town, where I had dinner, and came home, getting here about six o'clock. Took a bath, finished this week's New Republic, and now I am writing this letter. . . . I have not looked up anybody at all since I left Woodstock. Pitts Sanborn[107] sent me a postcard from Paris, where he is just now. The Arensbergs[108] have dropped out of sight—in the country somewhere, of course. The truth is, I do not wish to see anyone but to be alone and quiet, so that I may, if possible, accomplish something. Everything is favorable: that is, there isn't the slightest distraction in town. Never knew it to be so dead and alien. Did you notice that Ivins[109] lost his father, who died suddenly during the

107. John Pitts Sanborn Jr., an unmarried acquaintance from Harvard, where he, too, had been on the staff of the *Harvard Advocate,* was at this time one of the editors of *Trend* and the music editor of the *New York Globe,* a position he held until 1923. In a letter to Harriet Monroe on September 23, 1922, Stevens says, "About the Crispin poem ["The Comedian as the Letter C"], Pitts Sanborn, one of my oldest friends, expects that he *may* be called upon to edit the Measure one of these days for a period and, as I am under many obligations to him, I have promised to let him have this poem if he wants it. During the summer, I re-wrote it and in its present form it would run to, possibly, the greater part of twenty pages of print. A long poem is what he wants, for of the three numbers that he would have to edit, this would account for one. And this promise I made to him long ago, when he went on that miserable sheet. So there you are. During the coming week, he sails from Havre bringing for me my autumnal bon-bons from the Place de l'Opera not to speak of a number of books etc. which he has picked up for me" (*LWS,* 229). "The Comedian as the Letter C" was not published before its appearance in *Harmonium.* Sanborn remained one of Stevens's most important friends until his death from a heart attack on March 8, 1941.
108. Another acquaintance from Harvard, Walter Arensberg (wife: Louise), a poet and wealthy art collector, played an important role in Stevens's early literary flowering and was especially instrumental in introducing Stevens to Marcel Duchamp and to the latest art movements of Paris. In a letter to Fiske Kimball on February 23, 1954 (*LWS,* 820–23), Stevens gives a very detailed account of his relations with Arensberg. See Macleod, *Wallace Stevens and Company,* 45–53, for another thorough account of their relationship and the group of which they were a part.
109. William M. Ivins Jr. knew Walter Arensberg and was thus a member of the "art crowd" associated with Arensberg during the years Stevens was writing the poems of *Harmonium.* See MacLeod, *Wallace Stevens and Company,* 3–31.

week? . . . I gather that the mail to Woodstock is irregular. Your letters reach me promptly. I have already replied to you about the powder and the watch (which cannot possibly be repaired and regulated under a week.) The Tribune ought to reach you. I subscribed at the main office. Did you fail to receive the London Times and New Republic which I sent last week. The current New Republic will be posted to-morrow. Had dinner at home Saturday evening: alligator pear.[110] I am sincerely glad to hear that you are enjoying yourself and are content. I have, of course, paid Dr. Whitlock.[111]

With love, Wallace

⌒

[WAS 1962 July 28, 1915 New York]
[New England Equitable Insurance Company stationery,[112] addressed to Byrdcliffe, Woodstock.]

Wednesday Evening

My dear Bud:

The girl at Park & Tilford's had some doubt about white powder. She was to telephone me if she could not get it at one of their other stores. Not having heard from her, I assume that she found a supply and sent it to you, as directed, by parcel post yesterday. Let me know if you do not receive it in the next day or two.

Mr. Mount came to New-York yesterday to buy his oldest boy (a fat animal, eleven years old) a silver watch and a cowboy saddle. I had dinner with him at the Transportation Club, (an excellent dinner, too—with alligator pear, again.) After dinner, we took a 'bus ride and I smoked two cigars—the first ones since returning from Woodstock. To-night, however, I shall be hard at work again. I am intent on having something to show for the summer, if possible.

Mr. Mount's boy complained that his eyes hurt. He had been wearing sun-glasses. I wonder if they are as good for the eyes as you think. They may be. If your eyes hurt, certainly you ought not to read much of anything, least of all in fine print. There are some collections of pictures in the shelves of the library at Byrdcliffe—the rear shelves—in large books: "Le Tapon," etc. which, it seems to me, ought to be far more fun and just as much discipline as Hyslop's "Ethics." One of the simplest things in the world is to look at a picture; one of the hardest

---

110. Avocado.
111. This last sentence is written vertically in the left margin of the last page.
112. This company took over the Equitable Surety Company of St. Louis, for which Stevens worked in 1914. The New England Equitable Insurance Company letterhead lists E. B. Southworth Jr. as manager, the only officer listed on the letterhead who has played or will play a role in these letters. Stevens's name is not on this letterhead.

things is to see it. I think that just as one acquires a taste and touch among books by reading them, seeing them, etc. <u>so</u> one acquires a taste and touch among pictures. From this point of view, nothing is more important than to study the albums—the good ones. Of course, they must not be spoken of as albums. People have a prejudice against the word. But they are albums for all that—wide paradises for rainy—even for clear—afternoons.

With much love,

Wallace.

∽

[WAS 1963 August 3, 1915 New York]
[Same size as pre-marriage stationery but very light green, addressed to Byrdcliffe, Woodstock.]

Tuesday Afternoon

My dear Bud:

Walter Arensberg telephoned yesterday afternoon and asked me to take dinner with him at the Brevoort with Marcel Duchamp, the man who painted <u>The Nude Descending A Stair-Case.</u> Duchamp is using the Arensbergs' apartment as a studio during the summer. Walter is in town for only a day or two. They have been in Pomfret, Connecticut, and did not go to Pocono. Mrs. Arensberg has just gone to visit friends for a month and Walter, who has been done up by the heat, is thinking of going to Pittsburg. After dinner, we went up to the Arensberg's apartment and looked at some of Duchamp's things. I made very little out of them. But naturally, without sophistication in that direction, and with only a very rudimentary feeling about art, I expect little of myself. Duchamp speaks very little English. When the three of us spoke French, it sounded like sparrows around a pool of water. . . . At the Brevoort, I caught a glimpse of Carl Van Vechten[113] sitting near-by. I did not speak to him. Walter says that Van Vechten bores him to death and he seems to feel even worse about Mrs. V. V. The two of them hurried out, passing near-by, studying the floor. Walter breathed a sigh of relief. V. V. is very much like Kavanagh in having absolutely no sense that enough is enough. There is no other gossip about that particular crowd. On Sunday, which was steaming hot, I went out to Long Beach, taking along the <u>New Republic</u> and a bottle of water, some biscuits, etc. It was incredibly fresh and

---

113. He had been editor of *Trend* and published some of Stevens's earliest poems. Because he had played an important role in the publication of *Harmonium*, Steven would write to him on September 11, 1923, "Dear Van Vechten: I am sending you a copy of Harmonium—since you were its accoucheur. Knopf has done very well by it and I am grateful to both of you. Very sincerely yours W. Stevens" (*LWS*, 241; original at the Beinecke Library at Yale). For a complete explanation of his role in Stevens's career, see MacLeod, *Wallace Stevens and Company*, 3–41.

cool there. I walked far up the beach, found an old log, sat on the sand, reading and enjoying what I read. Romain Rolland's "Unbroken Chain"[114] seemed uncommonly well written. Towards evening, the sky darkened and there was a good deal of thunder and lightning, but I reached home before the storm amounted to anything. . . . I walked the greater part of Saturday afternoon. I went to the botanical garden and found, in the rear of the green-houses, several large pools full of water-lilies of considerable interest and one or two that were beautiful to see. In the main flower-beds, the week had not brought out anything new, except a little cosmos. The weather had been too hot and the flowers were burned up. To-day we are having an Easterly storm. It is gusty and even bleak and it will be nice to be warm at home to-night. No doubt, to-morrow, or the next day, it will be blazing again. This is the great vacation month. People starting in such a storm must be wishing they had waited until Winter and had gone South. Well, what about this stationery.[115] I was at Brentano's at half-past eight yesterday morning for it! I sent you a package of magazines yesterday.

> With love,
> Wallace

⌒

[WAS 1964 August 5, 1915 New York]
[Same size as pre-marriage stationery but very light green, addressed to Byrdcliffe, Woodstock.]

> Thursday Evening

My dear Bud:

I shall come on the eleven o'clock train. This is the train that reaches Woodstock between 2 and 3, I think: the one on which we came up from Kingston. Don't bother to come over to the station (unless you want to, of course)—but if it is as good in the way of weather as it is to-day, it would be pleasant to meet you in the village on the arrival of the stage and walk up from Mrs. Parks to

---

114. *LWS* (186) identifies the issue: *New Republic* 3 (July 31, 1915): 330–33. Rolland's historical summary of the movements in nineteenth-century French painting posits that there is "an unbroken chain" that links the "masters of the Restoration to those of the Third Republic," and he maintains that Delacroix, "an entire world in himself," is a major part of this linkage. Other painters he praises and briefly characterizes are Ingres, Courbet, Manet, Monet (who "intoned an inexhaustible hymn to the sun"), Gauguin, van Gogh, Matisse (about whom Rolland quotes Maurice Denis: "The eye devours the head"), and, especially, Cézanne, with his "audacious dream . . . of enclosing the mobile forces of the world in a deliberate synthesis of all the forces of being."

115. Other than official business stationery, this light-green, felt-like stationery is the first that he has used in letters to Elsie that was not white. The final four letters of 1915 are written on this colored stationery.

Byrdcliffe. I shall be in need of exercise after three hours on the train. . . . If there is anything you want me to bring up with me, you will have to let me know by return mail, reaching the house on Saturday morning. I am not coming down-town on Saturday, and, very likely, will have time to stop off for anything on the way to the train. The weather has cleared and it is as cool as September. I am going to take a walk after leaving the office. In fact, I have been doing so quite regularly. The inability to do so during the last two days has thrown me quite out of gear and I feel as if I ought to walk a thousand miles to make up for what I have lost. . . . Mr. Weinman paid me a long call on Tuesday evening. After much coughing, blushing, etc., etc., he raised the rent <u>two</u> dollars. I thought he was going to make it one hundred dollars a month the way he started out. I had fully expected this, this year; and consider that we are in luck. Whoever heard of raising the rent two dollars? I told him, with smiles, that it was an outrage, but that under the circumstances we should have to do it, etc. . . . Last evening I read and wrote a little, as usual. I find it very slow work—getting anything done; but am keeping at it.

With love,
Wallace.

⌐⌐

[WAS 1965 August 29, 1915 New York]
[Same size as pre-marriage stationery but very light green, addressed to Byrdcliffe, Woodstock.]

Sunday Evening

My dear Bud:

It has been a rotten day here. It rained all morning (wherefore I stayed in bed) and drizzled all afternoon—drizzled and rained. I started to take a walk about two o'clock but my clothes got so full of the mist that I thought it would be agreeable to go up to the green-houses in the botanical park. Surely it would be warm and dry there. Nothing was ever more dismal. The rain leaked through the glass roof and the few people there walked about under the palms and banana trees with their umbrellas up. However I saw some in't'resting things, as the saying is— papyrus, various crotons, water-lilies, and one or two orchids. Afterwards, I came down town to the library and read more or less about orchids. Then I had an excellent dinner at the Holley and came home, with a copy of <u>Collier's,</u> which contains a letter from Turkey by Arthur Ruhl,[116] whom I know. —On

116. Arthur Brown Ruhl (1876–1935) became an important popular journalist. Stevens may have known him from Reading, though he is not listed in the *Graduate Catalogue of the Reading High Schools: 1856–1905;* however, a C. H. Ruhl had a law office at 534 Washington Street in Reading.

Saturday afternoon I went out to Rutherford, New Jersey, to see the nurseries and green-houses of Bobbink & Atkins and Roehrs & Co., large florists who supply most of the florists in New-York with flowers. Their places are huge and full of things worth seeing. Roehrs is probably the most important cultivator of orchids in America. I ran across a Mr. Muller, an Austrian, who spent several hours showing me around and, of course, I learned no end of things. We must go out there about the middle or end of October when the cattleyas and some of the other orchids will be in full bloom. Spring is the best time, I believe; but there are plants in bloom all winter. Muller told me that orchids will remain in bloom for a month on the plant and fresh ones will keep for ten days cut. You remember how long the green ones kept—cypripediums, I believe,—that we had last winter. There were some blue ones from Burma, at Roehrs, that were incredible. — Saturday evening I spent at home, writing a little. I am quite blue about the flimsy little things I have done in the month or more you have been away. They seem so slight and unimportant, considering the time I have spent on them. Yet I am more interested than ever. I wish that I could give all my time to the thing, instead of a few hours each evening when I am often physically and mentally dull. It takes me so long to get the day out of my mind and to focus myself on what I am eager to do. It takes a great deal of thought to come to the points that concern me—and I am, at best, an erratic and inconsequential thinker. —Here is a clipping[117] of this morning's paper to show that there is still a reasonable expectation of summer.

With love,
Wallace.

↩

[WAS 1966 August 30, 1915 New York]
[Same size as pre-marriage stationery but very light green, addressed to Byrdcliffe, Woodstock.]

Monday Evening

My dear Bud:

I shall post this to-morrow enclosing a check to Miss Hopkins for the week and five dollars for yourself. If you owe more (as for laundry) pay it out of the five dollars. It is perfectly all right for you to come home. Why should you feel bound to stay? Surely, I never was as stiff as that about it, was I? I'll come up for you on Saturday and we'll come down on Sunday afternoon. Will you arrange for the night with Miss Hopkins? I have, by the way, paid Mr. Schumacher to Sept 6 (inclusive.) Possibly he will refund this week's money—although it <u>does</u> take imagination to think so. Will you, in your sweetest manner, ask him? You

---

117. This clipping is not extant.

can have the money. If he starts to hem and haw—why not offer to swap the money plus your easel, paint-box, etc. for one of his smaller flower pieces. They're not worth a dollar more, in my opinion. I'd like to have one but I don't think that with his entire lack of reputation he ought to be fussy about it. To be sure, I suggest this only if you do not want the things. If you do, by all means keep them. Neither of us thought seriously of anything more than a summer's past-time. If he values his work as rubies and fine pearls and will not swap and if you do not care to take a few more mornings during the week why let him hold on to the filthy spondulix. Do as you like about it, any old way; and don't worry. Loaf in the sun a few days and then we'll come home together. I've been lonely for you anyhow—that's the truth. I think that it is not only my desire for solitude that suggests vacations to me. It appeals to my pride to be able to send you away. I have not made much progress, as the world goes; but I forget that, when I can feel that you are away in the country, like everybody else, doing pleasant things. When New-York is empty and dull, I should feel as though I were of no account to have you here and be unable to make things pleasant for you. The Barbers have been away for several weeks and the Corbetts who went before you did have not yet returned. Personally I think the whole trouble is with your eyes. The strain on them gets on your nerves and I'm a firm believer in the deviltry of the nerves. If you simply rest the balance of this week (and think a little kindly of your old man)—and try to get ahead of Schumacher or come out even with him—I think you'll be in much calmer condition by the time I come. I think it better to return Sunday than Monday, when the trains will be crowded. Monday is a holiday here. We can do as we like. —Cheer up anyhow and be easy in your mind.

> With love
> Wallace

～ 4 ～

Travel Separation

Hartford, 1916–1923

Stevens begins to write to other people more than he writes to Elsie. His letters are becoming much more complex, and his serious correspondents now include Harriet Monroe, added in 1914, and, as Stevens becomes a known poet, others connected with the world of small literary magazines: Rodker, Ferdinand Reyher, MacAlmon, and William Carlos Williams. With these correspondents, Stevens was perfecting his public persona, the drinking bon vivant, a creation in stark contrast to the staid reporter of travel details he remained for Elsie. The era of agonizing personal analysis in his letters to her is over. He is writing from the road as he begins his work for the Hartford Accident and Indemnity Insurance Company,[1] at first to Elsie still in their New York apartment, then, once, to Elsie as she is temporarily staying on Long Island with the wife of the Walter Butler, the younger man with whom he took vigorous walks in New York before his own marriage. This address alone confirms the strength of the relationship between Stevens and Butler, who was never again to be mentioned in Stevens's letters. A few later letters are to Elsie in Reading and to various temporary addresses in Hartford. However, throughout most of this period (from the beginning of December 1917 until the later part of 1924), they will be living at 210 Farmington Avenue, Apartment D1, of the St. Nicholas, "a large new building" (Brazeau, 242; see Brazeau for photographs of all of the Stevens residences).

Stevens's new appointment was announced in the *Hartford Agent* 7, no. 9 (March 1916): 347, in an article titled "Fidelity and Surety Expansion" (see "I. Introduction: Wallace Stevens and Elsie" above for the two paragraphs of this announcement). Although Stevens was hired to begin work at the Hartford on

---

1. The Hartford Accident and Indemnity Company was created by Richard Mervin Bissell (1862–1941), the newly appointed president of the Hartford Fire Company, in 1913; for many years thereafter, the two companies were known as "the two Hartfords." In this new company, the emphasis on fidelity and surety bonds grew considerably under James L. D. Kearney in 1915, and he brought in Stevens, whom he had known as they both worked for the American Bonding Company, the following year.

March 15, 1916, he did not move permanently to Connecticut until May. However, from the very beginning of his employment, he traveled for the Hartford handling fidelity and surety claims. Perhaps the best insight into the type of work he did for the company is in his own essay "Surety and Fidelity Claims" (*Eastern Underwriter*, March 25, 1938, 45), which is reprinted in *OP*, 237–39:

> You sign a lot of drafts. You see surprisingly few people. You do the greater part of your work either in your own office or in lawyers' offices. You don't even see the country; you see law offices and hotel rooms. You try to do your traveling at night and often do it night after night. You wind up knowing every county court house in the United States.
> (*OP*, 237)

In this article, Stevens first explains the basic categories of responsibility as "making sure that there has been a loss; that the company is liable for it; that you are discharging the liability by the payment, and that you are protecting whatever is available by way of salvage," and then he provides numerous examples of dealing with each of these categories, examples which doubtless owe something to his actual experiences. We know from Judge Arthur Gray Powell's account of first meeting Stevens one of the cases that took him to Florida so often early in his career with the Hartford:

> One winter, just as John Little and I and a party of our friends were about to leave for Long Key on a fishing trip, I got a telegram from Wallace Stevens, the untitled head of the Hartford Accident & Indemnity Company, which was the surety on the McCrary Company's contractor's bond [Stevens will mention McCrary by name in WAS 2041 February 8, 1923] in connection with their highway construction in the Everglades, asking me if I would not meet him at Miami for a conference with the County attorney.
> We had the conference with the County Attorney, and, while we came to an agreement with him, he told us that it would be several days before he could draw the papers necessary to be signed to carry it out. Barry and I persuaded Wallace to go to Long Key with us and wait there, instead of at Miami, for the papers. Billy Hardwick, who was the Governor of Georgia, was of our party, and when the Governor of Florida heard that he going to Long Key he sent him a number of pardons in blank. We issued Wallace one to make him feel safe and welcome.[2]

Judge Powell's account stresses the fishing and social aspect of this event, but the McCrary[3] surety bond was professionally important to Stevens from the time he

2. See the General Introduction, above, for an account of Stevens's first meeting with Powell and the tenor of those more social trips that probably began only in 1922.

joined the company, and it remained important for a number of years, at least through the time of the publication of *Harmonium*. Stevens's first trip to Florida in 1916 was doubtless to arrange the surety coverage for the McCrary Company as it contracted to build what will be known as the Tamiami Trail across the Everglades of Florida. This case represents the pragmatic world of Stevens, the early surety bonds troubleshooter for the Hartford Accident and Indemnity Company. It is not known how long Stevens continued to deal with the McCrary case after its "satisfactory adjustment" in 1922, but letters of 1923 show that he met with McCrary as soon as he returned from his trip to Havana (a meeting he arranged by telegram from Havana). It is perhaps relevant to note that the Tamiami Trail was not opened until 1928, and that Stevens did continue returning for years to Miami and the Florida Keys, sometimes clearly on other cases such as one involving a bank in Palm Beach. Judge Powell throws some light on this part of Stevens's business in Florida: "Following the collapse of the Florida boom all the Surety Companies were flooded with claims and litigations; and the Hartford was no exception. I have tried cases for the Hartford in Georgia, Alabama and Mississippi . . . but it was in Florida that Wallace and I, during the years immediately succeeding the collapse of this boom, were constantly in one part of the state or another adjusting, litigating and settling claims and law suits" (see Powell citation just above).

3. The J. B. McCrary Company of Atlanta, Georgia, won the $241,500 contract to build a portion of what came to be known as the Tamiami Trail across the Everglades of Florida, construction that raised the road bed on material extracted from a parallel borrow pit that became, in effect, a canal on which steam shovel could be floated on a barge. It was largely a matter of blasting, extracting, and reapplying the native rock as a straight road bed. The contract was signed on May 20, 1916, and a few days later the J. B. McCrary company filed a bond with the Dade County Commissioners with the Hartford Accident and Indemnity Company as surety in the sum of $120,750. In the following years, this contract had to be modified a number of times, and Stevens made several trips to Miami to monitor the situation, including the 1922 trip in which he went to Long Key with Judge Powell and others. In WAS 2028 of January 10, 1922, Stevens links the McCrary case to his trips to Florida: "On Sunday, we made a satisfactory adjustment of the case, which has been the reason for each of the three trips made by me to South Florida and I believe that the matter has now been finally disposed of." Between 1916 and 1923 (and beyond), the J. B. McCrary Company made several presentations before the Dade County Commissioners, usually making the point that the road was costing far more to construct than had been anticipated. On November 14, 1923, a long letter from the company, which was read to the commissioners, made the point that the costs as estimated in prewar conditions did not cover the greater expenses of wartime and postwar costs in labor and dynamite, the two principal components of the overall cost of the project (Minutes of the Meeting of the Board of County Commissioners of Dade County, Microfilm book 1–5, for April 17, 1914–February 17, 1931, passim).

In his 1938 essay "Surety and Fidelity Claims," Stevens explains his role and the role of his surety claim department: "The major activity of a fidelity and surety claim department lies, of course, in paying claims. This involves much more than merely drawing drafts. It involves making sure that there has been a loss; that the company is liable for it; that you are discharging the liability by the payment, and that you are protecting whatever is available by way of salvage. There is nothing cut and dried about any of these things; you adapt yourself to each case" (*OP*, 237). We can see in the letters of this period some of the tasks Stevens carried out in these cases, from spending days in court to spending hours on a porch in the rain waiting for a working man who owed the Hartford "a substantial sum of money," to threatening suit against a former agent of the company to recover seven hundred dollars, to one of the strangest stories in these letters:

> We are not quite finished at Miami but no person ever is quite finished at Miami where they can put more things off for a longer time and with less reason than one expects even of such confirmed lotus-eaters. We have been sitting around with almost one hundred and fifty thousand dollars in our hands for them and they have agreed to take it but, as yet, have not got to the point of saying <u>Now</u>! (WAS 2043 March 5, 1931 Key West)

A note by Holly Stevens in *LWS* (258) mentions a case in which Stevens was acting as the attorney for the Hartford in some sort of action against J. C. Penney. The clearest revelation of how Stevens combined business and pleasure on these trips is the series of letters he wrote in early 1923, a trip that lasted from January 22 to February 14, a trip that took him to his first real experience of a foreign country, Cuba: "The place is foreign beyond belief," he wrote to Elsie (WAS 2038 February 3, 1923).

Perhaps that foreignness was what led to his return to Havana with Elsie shortly after *Harmonium* was published on September 7, 1923.

⌒

[WAS 1967 March 20, 1916 St. Paul, Minnesota][4]
[Stationery of the Saint Paul Hotel, St. Paul, to their New York apartment.]

Monday Morning,
March 20, 1916.

My dear Bud:

I got here last night shortly after ten o'clock, took a tremendous bath to get the dirt off, went straight to bed and had a good night's sleep to make up for the restless night on the train. This is a capital hotel—just as good as any in

---

4. Stevens has been working for the Hartford Accident and Indemnity Company for five days.

New-York, and I am comfortably arranged. Instead of finding it piled up with snow, it is much milder here than at home. There is not a bit of snow on the ground. We had a snow-storm in Western Pennsylvania, but when I woke up in Indiana on Sunday morning I was in a different part of the world—dazzling sunshine and real warmth. I had an hour between trains in Chicago and took advantage of it to scurry around, along the Lake front, for exercise. The trip North, through Wisconsin, was uninteresting, and long drawn-out. There was no scenery and only a succession of farms and railroad villages interspersed with advertisements of Beech-Nut bacon and Climax Plug, the Grand Old Chew. I am not keen about either of these articles. I have been sitting still for so long that, before doing anything else, I am going to take a little walk, for an hour, to get my blood circulating again. I hope your mother and sister arrived in good order and that you are all having a good time. Water the plants.

> Yours,
> Wallace

↬

[WAS 1968 March 23, 1916 Minneapolis, Minnesota]
[Stationery of the Hotel Radisson, Minneapolis, to their New York apartment.]

> Thursday Evening

My dear Bud:

I do not expect to leave St. Paul until next Tuesday or Wednesday. I shall be obliged to spend a day in Chicago and consequently doubt if I shall be home before Thursday or Friday. I have been far busier here than I expected and my cases are only just beginning to get into shape. If your mother is thinking of going home toward the end of the week, it might be well, if you cared to, to go home with her for a few days. My address is in care of Cushing, Dunn and Driscoll, Endicott Building, St. Paul, Minnesota, for the present. I have not yet seen my uncle[5] for lack of time and also because I do not wish any personal matters to take my time until everything is in good order. I hope you have all been having a good time.

> With love,
> Wallace.

It is about 6.30. I have an appointment with two men at 7.30.

↬

5. This is the Uncle Van Sant Stevens from Saint Paul mentioned in WAS 1808 for January 21, 1909. See note there.

[WAS 1969 April 2, 1916 Chicago, Illinois]
[Stationery of the Hotel La Salle, Chicago, to their New York apartment.]

Sunday, April 2, 1916

My dear Elsie:

I am growing fairly keen to get home, yet I was not altogether disappointed in being obliged to stay here until to-morrow, as I telegraphed you yesterday, Chicago is new to me. It is much the same thing as New-York. I had dinner with Aunt Anna and Uncle Harry on Friday evening.[6] They asked about you and both of them expressed a desire to have you visit them. If they ever get around to asking you, you ought to come, because I am sure you would find much to interest you here. They wanted me to come out to their house to-day. At the time I had no idea that I was going to stay over Sunday. Kearney telegraphed me from Hartford on Saturday morning to do so. I ought to go out to-day. But there is so much to see that I have not the time. Besides I have a lot of papers to study this evening. I now expect to leave here Monday evening at midnight which would get me to New-York early Wednesday morning. Yesterday afternoon I took a trip down to the old World's Fair grounds, then looked at the University of Chicago, then crossed town to Edgewater and walked seven miles along the Lake Front. The Lake Front corresponds to Riverside Drive but is infinitely larger. In the evening, I went to the Chicago Symphony concert and almost fell asleep, I was so tired and the concert was so dull. This morning I have been exploring some of the western suburbs. It is a beautiful Spring day. I have just come in for my overcoat and am going down to the Lake Front again in a few minutes. The air out here is too good to be true. However, the spaces are enormous. One street is twenty-six miles long in an absolutely straight line as level as this page. They have an admirable park system but it is never-ending. I should not mind living here although, after all, New-York is much more varied, much older and far more full of the things I like. The Art Institute here does not compare with the Metropolitan Museum. It has some excellent things: a portrait of Manet by Fantin-Latour, four large panels by Hubert Robert and a loan exhibition of modern French paintings (Renoir, Monet, etc.) superior, as a group, to any in New-York.

With love,
Wallace

ᔑ

6. Anna Bluett Zeller, Stevens's mother's youngest sister (1862–February 9, 1919), was married to Harry Carle (died January 2, 1922, at age seventy-one). See genealogical material in Box 77, Folder 1, Wallace Stevens Papers, HEH.

[WAS 1970 April 15, 1916 Atlanta, Georgia]
[Stationery of the Ansley Hotel, Atlanta, to their New York apartment.]

April 15, 1916.

My dear old Duck:

I have had the most amazing trip. Dogwood, apple-blossoms, cherry and peach blossoms, irises in the gardens, laurel in the woods. The country is full of bare-foot boys, girls in white, boys in white trousers and straw hats. I am per-spiring as I write! But I am tired and sickeningly dirty and am going right up-stairs to bathe my weary hide and to sleep over the beautiful things I have seen. I shall write soon again.

With love,
Wallace

⤳

[WAS 1971 April 19, 1916 Jacksonville, Florida]
[Stationery of the Hotel Mason, Jacksonville, to their New York apartment.]

Jacksonville, Fla. April 19, 1916

My dear Bird:

After sending you a post-card I ran to the station to catch the 1.30 train which, however, does not start until 5.30. owing to delay somewhere or other. It is just as hot here as it is in New-York in August. It is decidedly hotter than in Atlanta. There it was spring. Here it is summer. This morning I crossed a public square where the path was covered by a wire tunnel, at least a block long, over which roses had been trained. They were in the fullest bloom, exhaling fra-grance. The gardens here are full of hibiscus, acacias, periwinkles, pansies, etc. Everything is absolutely out—no buds, but the biggest blooms. The trees are heavy with leaves. Jacksonville is a charming place and an excellent business town. The banks are just like New-York banks, and, in fact, you feel as if you were not far away from home. I go to Titusville this evening, then to Miami and then start for home. I doubt if I get home before Tuesday or Wednesday of next week. A great deal of time is lost making connections. I hope you are having a good time. Keep after the moving men.[7]

With love,
Wallace

⤳

7. This must be a reference to early preparations for the move to Hartford, since, according to Brazeau, "not until May were they ready to leave behind their apartment at 441 West Twenty-first Street for Hartford's Highland Court Hotel" (*Parts of a World,* 7).

[WAS 1972 April 21, 1916 Miami, Florida]
[Stationery of the Hotel Halcyon,[8] Miami, to their New York apartment.]

April 21st 1916
Miami

My dear Elsie:

This is a jolly place—joli. It is alive. It is beautiful too. The houses are attractive, the streets well-paved, the hotels comfortable and clean. All these things count quite as much as the tremendous quantities of flowers. This is almost four hundred miles south of Jacksonville. When I got here at midnight last night, the air was like pulp. But there is a constant wind that keeps stirring it up. To-day I expected to roast. It has, however, been cloudy. Besides I have spent the entire afternoon in an automobile with a hustling youth who represents us here. Through his kindness I have seen far more than I should otherwise. The town is situated on a bay which is separated from the sea beyond by a narrow beach. The beach is deserted at this season although the bathing establishments are open. I hope to bathe to-morrow. The best residence section is toward the South on the shore of the bay. The houses are not pretentious. Their grounds are full of oleanders as large as orchard trees, groups of hibiscus, resembling holly-hocks, strange trumpet-vines, royal palms, cocoanut-palms full of cocoanuts, which litter the ground, orange and grape-fruit trees, mangoes in bloom, bougainvillea, castor-beans, etc., etc. You soon grow accustomed to the palms. The soil is utterly different from ours. It seems to be all sand covered with sparse grass and the surrounding jungle. After all, the important thing in Florida is the sun. It is as hot as a coal in the day-time. It goes down rather abruptly, with little twilight. Then the trade winds quickly blow the heat away and leave the air pulpy but cool. They think they have about every-thing necessary to make Miami one of the great cities of the South and the way the natives praise the past, present and future is only approached by the gentlemen at Coney Island expounding the shows within. But it really must be great shakes here in the season when people from all over the country come very largely to raise the devil. This hotel is just about to close. The dining-room is already closed and I have to go around the corner to a tea-room, far better than most of those in New-York, for meals. It will be necessary for me to stay here over Sunday. I expect to start back for Atlanta on Monday, so that it will very likely be not until the end of the week that I get home. I managed to stick to my schedule by getting up at five twice and riding until all hours. But here I am compelled—alas, alas—to stay in one of the most delightful places I have ever seen.

With love,
Wallace

8. This important early Miami hotel announced that it was "on Biscayne Bay and the Sea."

◠

[WAS 1973 April 23, 1916 Miami, Florida]
[Stationery of the Hotel Halcyon, Miami, to their New York apartment.]

Easter Sunday, 1916

My dear Elsie:

Easter greetings, as the old song runs. There will be a stiff parade on Fifth-Avenue to-day. Here, people have been going by on bicycles toward the beach. It is difficult to believe in the absolute midsummer of the place. Miami is a small place. My hotel is opposite the Royal Palm Park. There is a church on the corner. In the quiet air of the neighborhood the voices of the choir are as audible as they used to be at Reading. Unfortunately there is nothing more inane than an Easter carol. It is a religious perversion of the activity of Spring in our blood. Why a man who wants to roll around on the grass should be asked to dress as magnificently as possible and listen to a choir is inexplicable except from the flaggelant point of view. The blessed fathers have even taken the rabbit, good soul, under their government. I lay abed this morning for a while listening to the birds. At eleven o'clock (notwithstanding that it is Sunday) I had a conference with some people. In the afternoon I expect to go to the beach for a swim. And at midnight I expect to start North by way of Jacksonville and Atlanta. Yesterday I went up to Palm Beach which is about as far from Miami as New-York from Philadelphia (in the time it takes to get there.) It is an interesting place. But it is absolutely dependent on the hotels, which are now closed. Miami is different in that respect. It has a life of its own. At Palm Beach, the coast is straight up and down. Near there the sea is pale blue shading as the water deepens to indigo. There is a trail through the jungle and a walk along Lake Worth under the palms. Then there are various walks among the cottages. But I suppose that even in the height of the season the people are pretty much dependent on the same things as in New-York: band concerts, tea-dances and, as my old shoemaker said, coffee-parties. You twirl your parasol and then you don't twirl it. . . . Florida is not really amazing in itself but in what it becomes under cultivation. To be sure I have seen merely this coast. Once a space has been given attention it turns into something extraordinary. But the ordinary jungle is not impressive. There are brilliant birds and strange things but they must be observed.

With love,
Wallace

◠

[WAS 1974 April 24, 1916 Jacksonville]
[Postcard: St. Augustine's "City Gate," to their New York apartment.]

Monday

Spent the afternoon in St. Augustine. Here between trains. Atlanta again to-morrow. Then home.

W. S.

↪

[WAS 1975 May 2, 1916 St. Paul, Minnesota]
[Stationery of the Saint Paul Hotel, St. Paul, addressed to:]
Mrs. Wallace Stevens, Care of Mrs. Walter K. Butler, Broadway-Flushing
Long Isl[cut off here], New-Yo[cut off here]

Tuesday Noon

My dear Bud:

I have just come in for lunch and find your note. I am glad that you wrote and am writing at once in reply. It is possible that I shall be leaving here to-morrow although I am not sure of my plans. In any event I shall let you know by telegram so that you can, if you like, make your plans accordingly. I shall telegraph you at home. Mr. Weinman would no doubt be glad to telephone my wire to you if you asked him to.

The ride out here was excessively trying. I came from Chicago by the Burlington which runs several hundred miles along the Mississippi. It rained like the deuce all day so that one could not see through the windows. It even rained on the table in the dining car. The river is flooded—houses floating off, etc. The train crawled along through water on all sides. However late we were in getting here, the fortunate thing is that we got here at all.

I got to work at once on Monday morning and have been hard at it ever since. The lack of exercise is deadly. Certainly before I start home I shall take time to do nothing but walk for a few hours. It is damp and cold. This makes Florida seem like a faded painting. But St. Paul is bracing. I think people here incomparably beyond those down there.

The neckties have not yet come. I bought a box of Redore from Golding owe[9] him 20 cents for it. Will you pay him? And will you pay the tailor and have him return my suit? I shall soon see you again.

With much love, Wallace

↪

9. The last lines of this letter and the closing are written vertically in the left margin of the second page.

[WAS 1976 June 19, 1916 St. Paul, Minnesota]
[Stationery of the Hartford Accident and Indemnity Company,[10] addressed to Elsie in Reading, with mistake in street number (239 instead of 231).]

Eminent Vers Libriste

Arrives In Town

Details of Reception[11]

St. Paul, Minn. July 19,[12] 1916. Wallace Stevens, the playwright and barrister, arrived at Union Station, at 10.30 o'clock this morning. Some thirty representatives of the press were not present to greet him. He proceeded on foot to the Hotel St. Paul, where they had no room for him. Thereupon, carrying an umbrella and two mysterious looking bags, he proceeded to Minnesota Club, 4th & Washington-Streets, St. Paul, where he will stay while he is in St. Paul. At the Club, Mr. Stevens took a shower-bath and succeeded in flooding not only the bath-room floor but the bed-room floor as well. He used all the bath-towels in mopping up the mess and was obliged to dry himself with a wash-cloth. From the Club, Mr. Stevens went down-town on business. When asked how he liked St. Paul, Mr. Stevens, borrowing a cigar, said, "I like it."

Dear Bud:

The above clipping may be of interest to you. Note my address. I am waiting for some papers to be typed—ah! give my best to the family.

With love,
Wallace

⌒

10. Three of the seven officers on the letterhead are R. M. Bissell, President; James L. D. Kearney, Secretary; and J. Collins Lee, Assistant Secretary. Also printed on this letterhead is "Cushing, Dunn & Driscoll, General Agents, Endicott Building, St. Paul, Minn."

11. Stevens is showing his excitement on winning the prize of one hundred dollars awarded by the Players' Producing Company for his one-act play in verse, "Three Travelers Watch a Sunrise," printed in *Poetry* 8, no. 4 (July 1916): 163–79. The donor and the staff of *Poetry* were the judges.

12. In *LWS* (196), Holly explains that the real date here is June 19 and that Stevens's error may have been caused by his obvious excitement.

[WAS 1977 June 22, 1916 St. Paul, Minnesota]
[Stationery of the Minnesota Club, St. Paul, addressed to Mrs. Wallace
Stevens, 231 South 13th Street, Reading, Pa.]

Thursday Evening

My dear:

Here I am in a great room with an open fire burning in the fire-place at one
end. Imagine that on the 22nd of June. It is the custom, in this club, for you to
order your dinner and then loll about in the lounge while it is being cooked.
Very nice idea—eh, what? You get time to glance at the evening's news or to
have a cocktail or whatever you wish to do. I am waiting for a mutton-chop. Last
evening was the longest in the year. I regret to say that it was not so long as I
expected. I looked out of my window shortly after nine and although I could see
streaks of light in the West, I can't say that it was anything extraordinary. Possibly
it is a clear half-hour longer than in the East. I had had a very pleasant hour's walk
and with a whole library of new books to draw upon I was content. The truth is,
I worked, and read very little. And so I have worked all day to-day until seven
this evening. There is a great deal that requires attention. I expect to be busiest of
all to-morrow, Saturday, Monday and Tuesday and then I expect to be able to
turn back, although it may be necessary for me to go to Sioux City and Omaha,
in Iowa and Nebraska, for a few hours. My cases oppress and depress me but I
shall be rid of these soon. Well, in about ten days we shall be settled in our summer home[13] and all our troubles will be over, for the summer, at all events.

With love, old dear,

Wallace

⌣

[WAS 1978 June 23, 1916 St. Paul, Minnesota]
[Stationery of the Minnesota Club, St. Paul, addressed to Mrs. Wallace
Stevens, 231 South 13th Street, Reading, Pa.]

Friday Evening
June 23rd, 1916.

My dear:

It is half-past seven, and I've just come in from a walk. Just before I started
out, shortly after five, I found your letter and I thought (after all the rain)—
"Well, this is as nice as hearing birds in the trees again." Then I thought, during
my walk, how to say place of existence in French, and my thoughts wandered in

13. They will be moving from Hartford's Highland Court Hotel, the Windsor Avenue "hotel for home lovers," as it liked to advertise itself, which had been their temporary residence for two months and into summer quarters close to the Kearneys' home in
Farmington village, a ten-minute trolley ride from town (Brazeau, *Parts of a World,* 7).

all directions. It has been a cool evening, rather damp, with enough wind to make the trees keep turning, turning, turning, as I do when I am trying to fall asleep. St. Paul is pretty much a park. To-morrow morning I am to have a conference with one of the State boards at the Capitol. On Monday and Tuesday I expect to be busy with creditors. So that I am afraid we shan't get started until the end of the week. I am glad you like the idea of a day at Atlantic City. We haven't been there for so long. There will be much for us to see. We might even take a swim. Exercise does one such incalculable good. Only this evening I was wishing I knew somebody here to take a long walk with on Sunday. There's a very decent chap here, whom I like; but he was obliged to go to the Coast a few days ago and will not be back until next week, about the time when I expect to be starting back. I want to see some of the lakes in the neighborhood. The Mexican wars[14] attract great attention here. Every morning now there are squads of recruits drilling in the square which this Club faces. I see them as I walk through on my way to the office. This is [a] capital place for young men and the recruits are husky fellows. I hope to see them in camp at Fort Snelling, but I have so much work to do that there is little time to spare.

Love, again, and always—
Wallace

⌐

[WAS 1979 June 24, 1916 St. Paul, Minnesota]
[Stationery of the Minnesota Club, St. Paul, addressed to Mrs. Wallace Stevens, 231 South 13th Street, Reading, Pa.]

Saturday Evening

My dear-O:

A billowy day. My morning made me as weak as a cat and my afternoon as strong as a wild dog. After lunch, I went out to Fort Snelling where the Minneapolis National Guard is to encamp. There was little to see. It is a regular army post, fairly extensive. But the way the wind rolled in the grass was better than the Russian ballet, although not unlike it. The first frame house West of the Mississippi was built by a Colonel Stevens in 1850. That came next, after the wind. Then the Minnehaha Falls. (Did you 'appen to know that Longfellow's poem concerning Hiawatha had its scene here?) Well, then I went into Minneapolis and walked along Stevens Avenue, and all that sort of thing, you know. I keep wondering which I prefer: Minneapolis or St. Paul. Minneapolis seems more friendly. You don't see people sitting in front of their houses, on porches, etc. in St. Paul, as you do in Minneapolis. I am quite tired now that I am back. I

---

14. Gen. John J. Pershing was leading a large force into Mexico on an unsuccessful attempt to capture Francisco "Pancho" Villa.

have a great deal of work to do to-night, and expect to be up late with it. But I can sleep late in the morning, in an excellent bed. I hope to get to Lake Minnetonka to-morrow. Although there are thousands of lakes in the State, I have not yet seen any of them. Since it takes two days for the mail to come, do not write to me after Monday.

Well, oh, Bud, g' bye
for the time being
Wallace

↬

[WAS 1980 June 25, 1916 St. Paul, Minnesota]
[Stationery of the Minnesota Club, St. Paul, addressed to Mrs. Wallace Stevens, 231 South 13th Street, Reading, Pa.]

Sunday Evening

My dear:

Here I am at the end of the long-wished-for day without having had any more exercise than a grass-hopper in rainy weather. The truth is, I worked until half-past two this morning, slept until half-past ten, and then spent the next two hours bathing, breakfasting, reading the news, etc. After that, about half-past twelve, I rode over to Minneapolis and to Lake Harriet, beyond the city. This is a Lake about half-mile long and something less than that in width. It is in a most orderly park. There were about three hundred canoes, not all in use, but on the banks, etc. I took a ride in a launch. Next I went to see an exhibition of peonies. They were beautifully open in the warm sunlight. Peonies seem to be particularly liked here. They are lusty and somewhat crude, like cabbages en masque. Cultivation seems to have done little for them. Yet one or two varieties were unusually rich or unusually delicate. Nearer the lake was a rose garden, not so extensive as the one in Elizabeth Park but of interest.[15] When I had walked a little around the lake, I took another car to Lake Minnetonka, about fifteen miles from Minneapolis. Here I took a steamer and rode around the lake for about two hours. The place swarms with summer homes, cottages, boat-houses, etc. It is about ten miles long in a winding course but it is not particularly wide. There were many kinds of boats skimming here and there. I left the steamer at Wildhurst because the sky had grown black. The rain fell like a tribe of Indians in a fight as we reached Minneapolis. I changed cars and got home about half-past seven, having dinner at the Club. I am thinking of going to bed early in

---

15. For all of his life in Hartford, this park would remain one of Stevens's favorite places, one through which he could walk on the way to work and in which he could spend time, sometimes with his wife and later with his daughter but most often alone. It is the park of one of his finest late poems, "Vacancy in the Park."

preparation for a savage day to-morrow. Possibly I shall read a little first. How-ever, the library here is horribly standardized—Thackeray, Dickens, Dumas, Stevenson, Kipling, etc.

With love,
Wallace.

⌣

[WAS 1981 June 26, 1916 St. Paul, Minnesota]
[Stationery of the Minnesota Club, St. Paul, addressed to Mrs. Wallace
Stevens, 231 South 13th Street, Reading, Pa.]

Monday Evening, June 26, 1916.

My dear Bud:

I was in the office all day to-day. Afterwards I walked for about an hour and a half. St. Paul is situated on the bank of the Mississippi, which at this point seems to run from Northwest to southeast. Well, there is a bluff that rises above the river, straight into the western sunlight, and this bluff is the residence section. (I wonder if the river doesn't run from southwest to northeast. I am terribly tangled.) And that is where I walked. It is amazing how well-kept and how flourishing everything seems. There are long streets full of unusually handsome houses. I know of no place like it in the East. But I have discovered one distract-ing thing and that is that these long, beautiful streets are solitudes. One never sees a soul—no children, no boys playing, no women sitting around. Everything in perfect order and nothing doing. Perhaps, all places are so. I can imagine a stranger in Reading walking through the better part of town and wondering where everybody had gone to. It is like New-York on a summer Sunday. Only here, the houses are not closed up. There is a certain amount of invisible life that fills such a vacuum; but for a while, at least, that remains unknown to one like myself. I relish enormously the trees, the gardens, etc. Zinnias are up and about their business here. The stems seem to be longer and the flowers smaller than with us. . . . So the artillery has left Reading. That's a sad business down there. It seems to me that the president ought never to have sent the army into Mexico, or, if he did, he ought to have declared war simultaneously. He has an unfortu-nate ease in getting into messes. A good fight would do him good. Why all this horror of what must be done? He is too much of a politician; and so is Carranza.[16]

Well, well—and my love,
Wallace

16. Venustiano Carranza (1859-1920) was the provisional president of Mexico at this time and later constitutional president from 1917 to 1920.

⌒

[WAS 1982 June 27, 1916 St. Paul, Minnesota]
[Stationery of the Minnesota Club, St. Paul, addressed to Mrs. Wallace
Stevens, 231 South 13th Street, Reading, Pa.]

Tuesday Evening. June 27, 1916

My dear Bud:

    This may be the last letter I shall write before starting for home. I expect to
leave here late to-morrow night—at the latest, Thursday night. I have not
accomplished a great deal, although goodness knows I have tried to. . . . As I
was coming uptown from the office this evening, I passed my Uncle Jim.[17] I
wasn't thinking of him at the time, nor he of me—and I didn't stop him. I
think he would be bored stiff—think I wanted money or some such thing. It
was very nice to see him and not to be recognized. Let it go at that. Relations
are stupid: I'm sure that after we had asked a few questions, there'd be nothing
in the world to talk about except Japan, and I don't feel the need of talking
about Japan. . . . I have the river straightened out now. It runs East and West.
Well, after coming up here to see if there was any mail, I crossed the river and
walked to the top of the high land south of the city. I got out as far as cows and
then turned back. The country here is full of dogs who make life miserable for
me. St. Paul doesn't look very striking from a distance. There is a Catholic
Cathedral that rises above everything else. It is a fairly distinguished piece of
architecture although it is so sophisticated that it doesn't quite carry. It seems
self-conscious. But it is architecture and that is something. It has a great deal of
character and you have a feeling that it is massive but you don't feel sure. . . . I
came back into town by a new bridge: new to me, and loitered there watching
some men pulling in a net. There were some river boats at a wharf that looked
as though a trip down the river to St. Louis might be agreeable. It takes a week
to make the round trip.

Adieu, ma cherie,
Wallace

⌒

17. James Van Sant Stevens. See WAS 1968 March 23, 1916, for an earlier reference
to him. A similar episode involving Stevens's passing his brother Garrett in Cleveland
without speaking is told in Brazeau, *Parts of a World,* 280 (see note 52, below).

[WAS 1983 September 29, 1916 Omaha, Nebraska][18]
[Stationery of the Hotel Fontenelle, Omaha, addressed to Mrs. Wallace Stevens, 594 Prospect-Avenue, Hartford, Conn.][19]

Friday, September 29, 1916

My dear Bud:

I have been travelling southward. I leave here at two o'clock this afternoon for Kansas City, where I change trains for Oklahoma City, arriving there at nine o'clock to-morrow morning. That is as far south as I shall go. After a day or two there I start to work my way back to St. Paul and so homeward. I have worked like an Italian and look forward to a long snooze on the train this afternoon. Caught a train at Marshalltown, Iowa, last night at 2 o'clock and was up again this morning at 6.30 o'clock. Have just finished a conference and have about two hours which I intend to use in getting some much-needed exercise. The weather is the most tempting in the world. They had frost last night: all the boards white, the roof of the train glistening in the lights, etc. And although there is still an edge to the sunlight, I have seen lots of things to remind one that summer was only yesterday: strawhats, for instance. Omaha is in the direct line of transcontinental traffic. It is active and powerful. But here and there the straw comes through and shows how recently it was a farming centre. It is five hundred miles west of Chicago. Oklahoma City is, goodness knows, still farther away: a land of mustangs, Indians, etc. I am glad to have a Sunday there. I shall, no doubt, be in Hartford by the following Sunday, among our new things. I imagine you as hard at work with curtains and things. And possibly you have asked Clare Batten to visit you, or somebody else. I gather that Madame Butler was unable to have company when you were there. Did you get the day bed? You might send me a letter to the St. Paul to meet me when I return there. I should so much like to know how you managed things. You will find a check for twenty dollars enclosed to cover living expenses. I hope that I am sending you enough. My address in Oklahoma City will be the Lee-Huckins Hotel,[20] but do not write to me there, for I shall be there only for a day or two. Well, my

---

18. On the envelope in Stevens's hand: "Return to W. Stevens c/o Hartford Accident & Indemnity Co. Hartford, Conn."

19. Brazeau says that the Stevenses had been living at this address since "late August" 1916 and that this apartment was in a new brick building in an affluent neighborhood in which "families such as the Heubleins were part of Hartford society" (*Parts of a World*, 241).

20. Six years earlier, in 1910, Governor Charles Haskell and a group of conspirators had gathered at this Oklahoma City hotel, then traveled over to Guthrie, Oklahoma, the state capitol, removed the state seal from that town, and returned with it to the Lee-Huckins Hotel, which Haskell then declared to be the temporary capitol building. It was still serving this function when Stevens was there.

dear, I shall soon be home again now, among the Courants,[21] the young men and maidens, etc., etc. Out here, everybody has the reputation of being as rich as the pope, but looks as if he had less than nothing. They live on "pigs feet, pigs tails, pigs ears and pigs snouts," according to a restaurant sign.

With much love, Wallace

↬

[WAS 1984 October 11, 1916 Kansas City, Missouri]
[Postcard: "In the Grand Lobby, Union Station, Kansas City, Mo.," addressed to Mrs. Wallace Stevens, 594 Prospect Avenue, Hartford.]

People who believe this part of the world to be rough and raw have much to learn.

Wallace

↬

[WAS 1985 October 15, 1916 Toronto, Canada]
[Stationery of the King Edward Hotel, Toronto; no envelope.]

Sunday, October 15, 1916

My dear Bud:

I had all arrangements made to be home last night but I met Lee[22] in St. Paul on Thursday. He asked me to do something which made it necessary for me to go to Milwaukee and then to Toronto. I now Expect to leave here to-morrow night for New-York, where I shall get the Seji ware[23] and, if all goes well, reach home Tuesday or Wednesday. I am getting impatient to be home to be quiet again and regular. This week I have spent every night except one on sleeping cars and I feel in need of a rest. The car last night was heated like an oven and I was wet through with perspiration. This morning I walked around Toronto to get back to normal if possible and I feel much better for it. Toronto is full of soldiers. They wear uniforms that make boot-blacks look like wild-cats or bullocks or something savage, although, after all, they can't be such tremendous warriors. I hope they are better ones than the Germans, at all events. This is the first time I have been in Canada for ten years and I find it most interesting. There are

---

21. The *Hartford Courant* newspaper.

22. J. Collins Lee, who had got the "good thing" Stevens had expected back on August 6, 1911, was now an assistant secretary at the Hartford Accident and Indemnity Company in charge of expanding the number of agencies that carried the Hartford line of insurance.

23. This type of pottery is generally known as celadon, from its green, jadelike glaze. In Japan, celedon porcelain is known as Seiji-ware. The French gave the porcelain the name celadon after a character in d'Urfé's novel *L'Astrée*. This ware originated during the period of the Five Dynasties (907–960) in China.

many touches that make it English, but on the whole it is American in most things. There are lots of things here I should like to have and to see. The Royal Ontario Museum looks as though it might be worth while and if I have an opportunity to-morrow I shall go to see it. This is an educational centre. The university buildings are large but entirely without style or charm. Yet on so perfect an autumn day, everything has more or less charm. I enclose a check for the coming week. Inasmuch as I shall be home in time for the rugs I am not sending a check for those. The last letter I had from you said that you had directed them to be shipped after the 16th—to-morrow. Well, my dear, we shall soon be together again. Kearney has promised that you shall go along on some pleasant trip soon.

With much love,
Wallace

⌒

[WAS 1986 January 21, 1917 Hartford]
[Addressed to Mrs. Wallace Stevens, care of Mrs. Lehman Moll, 231 South 13th Street Reading, Pa.]

Sunday Afternoon

My dear Bud:

This business of starting a letter on the last page is so English that I can't resist it. I have had two very nice notes from you. I hope that your mother is not seriously sick.[24] It seems to me that if she is in bed, her family might do something the days when your father finds it necessary to be in the country. Or is it customary in Reading to leave people, when sick, to the care of children? I cannot imagine that they know of her condition and permit that, or else it must be the case, as I hope, that there is nothing seriously wrong. And for the love of Mike, don't overdo things. I don't see why it should be necessary for you to carry coal from the cellar. I should think your father could get somebody to run in for the heavy chores. Another thing, don't worry about me. I am doing very nicely, I thank you. This place is full of restaurants, etc. and if I happen to bring a few lamb-chops home and cook them myself instead of going to one of the hotels, why, it is because I very much prefer to do so—enjoy doing so. I had dinner at Stryker's last night. Night before, I had chops, boiled potatoes, fried onions, celery, hot-house tomatoes, lettuce, etc., etc. Living like a prince. Now, don't bother about me. I don't expect you back until after the first of February, some time, unless, of course, you want to come back. Stay with your mother and don't plan as soon as you reach her to leave her again. As far as I am concerned, I have some work I want to do anyhow, so that about the first would be the earliest.

---

24. Elsie's mother died in an automobile accident in August 1940. See *LWS*, 364–65.

You understand, my dear, that I am not laying down the law, but merely trying to make you feel free to stay and be of use. . . . I had the piano tuned Saturday afternoon. Couldn't sleep nights for thinking it was so out of tune. This morning I walked through the reservoir and as usual saw nobody, didn't hear a bird, couldn't find even a shadow. This place is as cheerless as the catacombs. If I intended to stay here I'd set loose a herd of wild goats with bells around their necks to make the country more interesting. I hope you are making notes of all the gossip. If you need any money let me know. Did you give them kidney stew this morning? Eh, what? I know you can get lamb kidneys here. It has started to snow.

With much love,
Wallace

⌒

[WAS 1987 January 26, 1917 Hartford]
[Hartford Accident stationery, addressed to Elsie in Reading.][25]

Friday

My dear Elsie:

I am going to send you ten beans, in two envelopes. Here's one. Mrs. Heublein asked me to dinner last night. Regular blowout. Everybody dressed like a war-lord except myself—and I looked like old Quaker Oats. Among the people crowding around me was Mélanie Kurt,[26] one of the best singers at the Metropolitan Opera. She is visiting Mrs. Heublein. We must go over after you get back. Young Mrs. Heublein is not so attractive, to my mind, as the dowager; but she was very friendly, wants to see you and so on. I think I've about made the rounds now and I expect to settle down to a peaceful routine.

With love
Wallace

If you come Monday, telephone from New-York. Miss Reis will get me for you. You could take the morning train and have several hours in New-York, The five o'clock from N. Y. is a good train. Get your seat early. But you'd better wait until the 1st or 2nd.

[The second part of this letter, with Stevens' postscript, is also on Hartford Accident and Indemnity stationery.]

25. As a precautionary measure, Stevens is sending money in two envelopes. These two mailings are treated here as a single letter.

26. Originally from Vienna (1880–1941), Kurt made her debut at the Metropolitan Opera House in New York on February 1, 1915, as Isolde.

Be sure to get another pound of tea at Deans and possibly a can of oil at the Ven-
dome around the corner from Sloan's.

Wallace

See other letter

↩

[WAS 1988 February 18, 1917 Kansas City, Missouri]
[Postcard: "The New Union Station, Kansas City."][27]
    Kearney and I are on our way to Omaha. Thanks for your welcome wire.

Wallace

↩

[WAS 1989 February 21, 1917 Minneapolis, Minnesota]
[Stationery of the Hotel Radisson, Minneapolis, addressed to Mrs. Wallace
Stevens, 231 South 13th Street, Reading, Penna, without "in care of Mrs.
Moll."]

Wednesday, February 21, 1917

My dear:
    Kearney and I were unable to carry out our plans at Omaha and accordingly,
instead of staying there a week, as we had supposed, we left on Tuesday evening.
Possibly you wrote to me there. If so, I left before your letter came. But I left
word to forward it to me in Hartford. It is impossible to have it forwarded to any
address while I am travelling because my plans are subject to change and besides I
take long jumps. Before I start for home I expect to go to Houston, Texas which
is far south of Oklahoma; so that I shall be doubling on my trail. Here it is the ici-
est kind of mid-Winter: zero, high wind, snow, etc. My train should have
arrived here at 8.20 this morning. Instead, it arrived at 6. this evening. We had to
be dug out and then preceded by a snow plow. The drifts were nothing extraordinary. But the wind was incessantly violent. Of course, at Houston, it will be
just the other way. I expect to see flowers in bloom there. Unless I am called
back to Omaha, my plan is to go from here to Nebraska City, Nebraska, then to
Hamburg, Arkansas, and then to Houston, after which I shall start for home. I
expect that it will be a week or ten days, at least, before we can sit around our
own radiator again. No doubt you will stay where you are. I expect to wire you
in time to meet me in Philadelphia. But I think I told you this in an earlier letter.
I have been so knocked around that I scarcely know what I have written. Kearney is Eastward bound but has engagements of various kinds so that he is not

---

27. The address has been carefully scraped off, but enough remains to show that it
was sent to Elsie in Reading.

likely to be home much before Sunday. We were fairly successful in Oklahoma. The case there is wound up.

With love,
Wallace

⤳

[WAS 1990 February 26, 1917 Houston, Texas]
[Stationery of the Rice Hotel, Houston, to Elsie in Reading.]

February 26, 1917.

My dear:

If Oklahoma City reminded one of Easter, this reminds one of the Fourth of July. It is quite as hot here as it is in July or August in New-York. The grass is luxuriantly green. Everyone is in white. People go about in shirt sleeves and boys are bare-footed. The cats sleep in the grass. Bushes, like japonica, are a mass of bloom. And yet, unlike Florida, there is a visible Spring here. Some trees, like the red oak, are full of leaves; indeed, always are. But many trees are bare or fledged with green. Others, like peach-trees, for example, are in full bloom. As I walked about before dinner. the trees were resounding with birds. I heard crickets—saw people watering the grass, and so on. This is amazing, but it is true, of course. Only two or three nights ago it was below zero in Minneapolis; and to-day I wilted a collar and came home and took a cold bath to cool off. . . . All my things are now checked. I go to San Antonio on the midnight train. Then possibly to Cuero. Then to Chicago, Pittsburgh, etc. But I think of nothing except the incredible weather. One's very skin relishes it. Houston is decidedly a Southern City but it is not tropical. The vegetation looks much like our own. The palms in the gardens flourish but they are not natural, whereas in Northern Florida they spread themselves, by nature, all over the place. I can readily see that Houston has not always been as prosperous as it is now. There is an old part of town, not specially picturesque; and then there is a new part, a modern part, in which one finds buildings like this splendid hotel. Look at the picture of it and ask yourself if it represents your idea of Texas. It is stunning. This morning I went with our agent to the Rice Institute.[28] This is a college or university on the outskirts of town, established by a man who was murdered in New-York by a lawyer who tried to establish a false will. The college has a great fortune. It has erected a number of very beautiful buildings and will go on erecting others, as it grows. It has a faculty of young scholars from the East and will do an enormous amount to make sheep out of the prairie goats. It seems to draw its faculty from Oxford, Harvard, Princeton,

---

28. Though the Rice Institute (now Rice University) was chartered in 1891, the first classes were held just five years before Stevens's visit.

chiefly. This was the most interesting thing for me here. San Antonio will be equally interesting. It is a famous resort and an army centre. I shall not be too busy to see a bit of it. I may have to go to Cuero, but that will take very little time, so that I expect to be back here on Wednesday and then start back home. . . . You missed nothing by not being with me until to-day, and then you missed what would have given you extraordinary pleasure. But one of these days, I shall try to arrange it and it will be worth waiting for.

With much love,
Wallace

↩

[WAS 1991 February 27, 1917 San Antonio, Texas]
[Postcard: Mission San Juan de Capistrano, to Elsie in Reading.]

This town is <u>not</u> as advertised but it is interesting for all that.

Wallace

↩

[WAS 1992 November 7, 1917 Harrisburg, Pennsylvania]
[Stationery of the Bolton Hotel, Harrisburg, addressed to Mrs. Wallace Stevens, Highland Court Hotel, Hartford, Conn.][29]

11/7
Harrisburg, Pa., Wednesday Eve. 1917[30]

My dear Elsie:

I tried to get you on the telephone this morning, from New-York, without success. I am particularly anxious about what that man Phillips would do to our things if we allowed <u>him</u> to throw them from one room to another. It is certain that he would toss the bundles of books in a heap, breaking edges and corners. Moreover, I would not trust him[.] Even to carry the pictures. The point is that that is not his job. He will be ill-tempered about it and, therefore, careless. Now, it is perfectly possible to move all over the map without doing the least damage. I think that you should tell him that, if he will let you know when he is ready to finish the living-room, you will have some one move the things for

---

29. Brazeau explains this address and the need for Stevens's following instructions to Elsie: "In October 1917, the couple moved out of 594 Prospect Avenue and temporarily took rooms at the Highland Court, the hotel where they had first lived when they arrived in town. They remained at the Windsor Street hotel throughout November while their next apartment, much closer to downtown Hartford, was being readied" (*Parts of a World,* 242).

30. Because his "Wednesday Eve." took up all the space between the "Harrisburg, Pa." and the "19——" of the printed heading, Stevens put the month and day indication above the line.

him, he will be glad to let you do it. Tell him that you don't want him to do that part of the work. Then telephone King and have him come in and move everything, including the piano, into the dining-room. We can distribute things from the dining-room, having King come later to move the piano to wherever you want it. You will find King in the telephone book. It says "moving and trucking" after his name. When you telephone him ask him how much he will charge. It is worth about $2.50 but he may charge $5. which I should be willing to pay. His time is worth something. . . . I came through Reading this evening, and walked up and down the platform for a few minutes without seeing anybody I ever knew or heard of. The place looked forlorn. I don't wonder that you have no desire to go there even to visit your family. This is a miserable hotel. I have a room without a bath. But I expect to be here for only a few hours in the morning, so that it doesn't matter. I go from here to Philadelphia and start South from there some time to-morrow. I hope you can make yourself comfortable at the Highland Court for the little time it will be necessary for you to stay there.

> With much love,
> Wallace

⌒

[WAS 2018 November 16(?), 1917(?)[31] Tampa, Florida]
[Stationery of the Hillsboro, Tampa, Florida; no envelope.]

Friday Evening
My dear Elsie:

I suppose that it is a good deal like what they say of many Southern places here: hot in the sun, chilly in the shade. Nothing could have been lovelier than the weather to-day. It was perfectly clear and as warm as any day in the summer. When the sun went down, about an hour ago, the air immediately grew cool: not cold, far from it, but cool, as in August at home. I had a good deal of time free. I walked a little along the boulevard that winds around the bay—the bay glittering in the sunlight. And this afternoon, I walked for an hour around the town. There are many strange flowers. The poinsettia is everywhere, brilliant and fresh, with green leaves. Later the leaves fall, although the plant still blooms. Curiously, there are chrysanthemums. The stems grow as high as one's

31. These dates are conjectural. There is no envelope and no date given on the letter. Stevens had written a letter dated Thursday, Nov. 15, 1917, to Ferdinand Reyher from Tampa on stationery of the Hillsboro. For that reason, and the day indication from Stevens, it is likely that the date given (as determined by Roy Harvey Pearce in a note on pages 54–55 of his brief note on "The Emperor of Ice Cream" in the *Wallace Stevens Journal* 3, no. 3–4 [Fall 1979]) is correct.

head. There is a vine, with a flower the color of a rambler, but not in the least like it otherwise. I wished sincerely that you might be here. I shall surely take you to Florida when we can afford it. I expect to leave here to-morrow some time.

With love,
Wallace

↩

[WAS 1993 November 30, 1917 New York]
[Stationery of the New Weston Hotel, New York, addressed to Elsie at the Highland Court Hotel, Hartford, Conn.]

Nov. 30. /17

My dear Elsie:

I was obliged to come to New-York this morning hastily, without being able to let you know. I shall be through about 12 o'clock to-morrow but shall be down town all morning. I shall drop into the Little Gallery but do not expect to do any other shopping. The chances are I shall come up some time during the afternoon. Wish this had happened next week. I sent Cavalillo a check this morning for the December rent. I tried to get him on the telephone but could not. He was not at home. I shall bring a cake up so that we can at least have tea in our new domain on Sunday.[32] By Monday we can start with the iceman, the grocer, etc. all over again, at least for breakfast and lunch. Dinners we can take out for a while until the housework is disposed of. I thought you might be at Miss Alice's and telephoned there from the station. Poor Chip! I'm sure some poor Jew had him for Thanksgiving in the form of sossidge à la Mexicana.

With love,
Wallace

↩

32. According to Brazeau, they were in Apartment D1 of the St. Nicholas, "a large new building located at 210 Farmington Avenue, next to Jewell Court. (Stevens used both street addresses interchangeably during his years at the St. Nicholas, since Jewell Court and 210 Farmington Avenue were contiguous.) It was during the next six years, when apartment D1 was home, that the poet composed most of poems of *Harmonium*, published in September 1923, as his stay there was nearing an end" (*Parts of a World*, 242).

[WAS 1994 March 13, 1918 Indianapolis, Indiana]
[Stationery of the Hotel Severin, Indianapolis, addressed to Mrs. Wallace Stevens, 210 Farmington-Avenue, Hartford, Conn.][33]

Wednesday

My dear Elsie:

I am in Indianapolis to attend the funeral of our agent here, who died suddenly last Sunday afternoon. I do not leave for Chicago until late to-night. This rather throws my plans out of joint, since I had expected to be in Chicago to-day. It is amazingly hot, quite too hot to wear an overcoat, although I have been wearing mine all morning, to be safe. One does not think of So. Indiana as southern, but the grass is perfectly green, tulips are coming up: the stalks, forsythia bushes are bristling with green points. On the other hand, the weather has been cloudy, and this morning, when I counted on a long walk, it poured until about ten o'clock and drizzled the rest of the time. I walked out to the Art Institute. There is nothing there of any interest. It is much smaller and much more amateurish than one had supposed. A collection of cashmere shawls on the walls cannot possibly take the place of tapestries. But, to be sure, these things, too, must have their humble origins.

With love,
Wallace

⤸

[WAS 1995 March 14, 1918 Chicago, Illinois]
[Stationery of the Blackstone Hotel, Chicago; no envelope.]

Chicago, March 14—1918

My dear Elsie:

I arrived here this morning. When I left Indianapolis last night, it was so hot that I could not stand any cover. To-day, on the other hand, it has been snowing here. As I came into the hotel this morning, I met Mr. Bissell,[34] who had just arrived from San Francisco. I polished myself up and then went to the office. It

---

33. This is the first extant letter to this address; with the exception of the five final letters of this correspondence (those from the 1930s), all remaining letters (or those with envelopes) are to this address.

34. Richard Bissell (1862-1941) was the president and chairman of the board of Hartford Accident and Indemnity from its founding in 1913 until he was ousted in a company coup in 1934 that made Kearney president and Stevens one of four vice presidents. See Brazeau (*Parts of a World,* 59–61, 286) for this story and for a story of Stevens's brief portrait of Bissell, which was published in August 1941 in the memorial issue of the *Hartford Agent* on page 8. After this coup, Bissell remained the president of the far larger and more important parent company, the Hartford Fire Insurance Company.

will take me until Saturday certainly to finish up, so that I cannot possibly be home before Monday. This is [a] disappointment because I had hoped to be able to attend the Boston Symphony concert in New-York on Saturday afternoon. Everything seems to conspire against my hearing any music this winter. The concerts will be over in two weeks. Late this afternoon I went up to Poetry's office and saw Miss Monroe about my war-poems.[35] We went over them together and weeded out the bad ones. They will be published bye and bye. There is a chance that I shall meet Carl Sandburg, while I am here, although I am not disposed to see anyone. The trip to Indianapolis has, somehow, made me feel that I want to get my work done and get home. I am never much interested in old cases, like these I am handling here. But, on the contrary, like new ones, such as will, no doubt, be in the office when I am home. I hope that you are not lonely but manage to find something to do. I have wondered how it would be for you to put all your present music in the closet and start entirely with new ones. That would make the whole thing fresh for you and would excite you to practice, when you found time. There doesn't appear to be anything new here. Even the shop windows seem to contain the same old things. After all, this must be the effect of Spring on me. Perhaps one is influenced subconsciously by the advance of Spring, however invisible it may be. The bloody weather affects one more consciously. It is clear to-night and at twilight the side of the moon was apparent.

With love,
Wallace

⌣

[WAS 1996 March 15, 1918 Chicago, Illinois]
[Stationery of the Blackstone Hotel, Chicago, to 210 Farmington-Avenue, Hartford, Conn.]

Chicago, March 15, 1918

My dear Elsie:

This is really a cat's life. I have been bored unspeakably all day. I was at the office at nine, or shortly after, and was busy until about four. People save up their troublesome case until I come along and then expect the word of God to fall from my lips—as if I did not have to study and think, as everyone does. I leave here to-morrow or Sunday for Detroit where I shall be on Monday. I may be

---

35. "Lettres d'un Soldat," *Poetry* 12, no. 2 (May 1918): 59–65. None of these nine poems (based on quotations from Eugène Emmanuel Lemercier's *Lettres d'un soldat (août 1914–avril 1915)* was published in the first edition of *Harmonium,* though three of them (plus a fourth that *Poetry* had not published) were in the second edition of *Harmonium* in 1931. See Edelstein, *Wallace Stevens,* 199, for details.

home Tuesday, certainly, I think, on Wednesday. After a week of this special kind of thing, my one idea is to get home and sleep in a big chair over a big book. I went to the Art Institute for an hour after leaving the office but it did not interest me. Then I tried to walk but that did no good so I came back with an evening paper, containing nothing but advertisements. I might, possibly, have gone to the theatre to-night but everything here has been in New-York and kicked out. It is all so stupid one could cry like a widow. I shall be busy to-morrow morning but am afraid the afternoon will kill me. It is not like Florida, for example, where, between one's appointments, one can, at least, sit in the sun. Or Tennessee— although Nashville is probably the most trying place on earth. You will be needing a little money for the house, I suppose, and accordingly I send you a check for $10. After all, who knows, I may not be half so blue in the morning.

> With much love,
> Wallace

⌒

[WAS 1997 April 1, 1918 Nashville, Tennessee]
[Stationery of the Hotel Hermitage, Nashville, to 210 Farmington-Avenue, Hartford, Conn.]
here[36] in the morning. I have a number of appointments on Wednesday and may be able to start North Wednesday afternoon or evening. If I had stayed at home on Sunday for dinner, I should just be arriving here at the time I hope to be able to leave. I hope that your mother and sister arrived safely and that you are doing all that you can to make them happy. They might be interested in the flowers at Cromwell.[37] The trip would give them a glimpse of the river, which is, after all, a notable thing. But this is not quite yet the time of year to go sight-seeing and perhaps a good rest would do more good than an effort to unearth objects of interest which do not exist. There is a slight chance that instead of going directly from Nashville to New-York I shall have to go by way of Atlanta. That would delay me a day. The curious thing is that, while one is eager to be started on a trip, one is just as eager to be started home. The evenings in the hotels drive a fellow frantic, so enormous is the vacuum around one—a vacuum invaded only by the noise of keys slipping into near-by key-holes.

> Adieu, old dear, and with love,
> Wallace

⌒

36. This is the first extant page of this letter fragment. The date comes from the envelope.
37. Cromwell Meadows just north of Middletown, Connecticut, on the Connecticut River.

[WAS 1998 (April 27, 1918?) Chattanooga, Tennessee][38]
[Stationery of the Hotel Patten, Chattanooga; no envelope.]

Saturday Evening

My dear:

I arrived here at midnight last night utterly exhausted by the beastly trip. I have been at work in a law office all day, from ten in the morning until ten to-night, except between five and seven-thirty, when I took a walk and had din-ner. Although it is cool and rather damp, it seems like early summer. The season is at least a month ahead of the season at home. The roses are out. With us, that does not happen until Decoration Day. The trees are full of leaves which make the streets shadowy and, I must say, sweet. To-morrow I go to Knoxville, returning here on Monday evening or Tuesday. I begin to think that the trip may take all of next week, even with the greatest activity on my part. At the same time, I believe that this will probably be the last trip it will be necessary to make down here. There has been a great deal to do but I begin to see the end of it. I have always been of two minds about Tennessee. Sometimes I like it and sometimes I loathe it. This time I have seen so little of it, as yet, that I scarcely know what to think. I know well that I love the far South, along the Gulf, but this midway South is an uncertainty. I should really be glad to stay at home for a long time when I get back or, if I must go away, go, at least, to some new place. There are still a good many soldiers here. The streets are, in fact, crowded with them. There isn't a thing for them to do, except to walk up and down the few blocks on Market Street that amount to anything. They crowd into the hotel for meals—the officers; and a good many of them put up here for the night, on Sat-urdays, in order to sleep in good beds for a change. It is common gossip here that they are being sent abroad by the thousands and people begin to wonder whether our first million are not already in France. I hope so. Those that are here are splendid fellows. We cannot help doing well when we really start. I shall try to keep you posted regarding my movements. I shall remain in East Tennessee until I am finished here and then go to Nashville, probably returning by way of Louisville, Cincinnati, etc. That will make it unnecessary to return the way I came—one of the most boring trips I know of.

With much love,

Wallace.

⤙

38. This date, with the question mark, has been written in the blank (provided on the stationery) by someone other than Stevens, probably Holly Stevens since this date with question mark is given in *LWS*, 206.

[WAS 1999 April 28, 1918 Knoxville, Tennessee]
[Stationery of the Hotel Atkin, Knoxville, to 210 Farmington-Avenue, Hartford, Conn.]

4/29/18
Sunday Evening

My dear Elsie:

It was raining hard when I left Chattanooga this morning about eleven. I arrived here about three. It was clearing then, and now it is as fine an evening as any we have in June. There is nothing for me to do until to-morrow morning. I walked all afternoon and feel infinitely better for it, although I am tired. From Knoxville to the South East, one can see the Appalachian Mountains. Out near the golf club, at the Western end of the city, there is a really swank view. The Tennessee River makes a great bend through woods and cliffs and hills and on the horizon run the blue ranges of the mountains. I saw no end of irises in people's gardens. There were peonies, tulip-trees, locust trees and an unknown tree, very large and spreading, covered with purple blossoms. You remember, no doubt, the pungent, slightly acrid, odor of locust blossoms. I found lots of motherly old hens guiding their broods of ber-bers through the grass, already deep. And, of course, I saw many boys and girls, both black and white, loafing in pleasant places. I brought back some flowers to press and if they come out well I shall send them to you. Among them is a wild strawberry. I feel quite sure that I rather like Knoxville. The place is unfortunate in not having a decent hotel. This one is tolerable only because it is fairly well-managed. People in hotels of this sort are an amusing study on Sundays. They cannot make themselves comfortable either upstairs or down. Consequently, they loll about looking unspeakably bored. The town is now about what Reading was twenty years or more ago. There are a few rich people, but most of them are poor. The farmers in the market, which I shall walk through in the morning, are the most extraordinary collection of poor people, living off the land, to be found in the whole country. I hope you went out for a walk to-day. Do not neglect your exercise or your food.

With love,
Wallace.

⌒

[WAS 2000 April 30, 1918 Elizabethton, Tennessee]
[Stationery of the Lynnwood Hotel, Elizabethton; no envelope.]

Tuesday, April 30, 1918

My dear:

The inkwell here dried up some time ago. It is about four o'clock. I must wait until five for an auto-bus back to Johnson City, about ten miles away. It rains and rains and rains. Yet they have two fountains rattling loudly in front of the hotel. I have been visiting the sourest lawyers in the shabbiest offices. One of them spoke of the contractors whose case I am handling as "a dark and black and damnable gang." A man came into his office while I was there and described a friend's casket as "the finest casket my flashin' eyes ever laid on, the finest my flashin' eyes ever laid on." Here they spell Arthur, Arter, and so on. All this will give you some idea of the grandeurs of traveling in Tennessee. I noticed the other day that O. Henry, in one of his letters, asked, "Is it possible for anything to happen in Nashville?" Certainly not without outside help. This applies to the State as a whole. I have never been so concerned about a place. I begin to think of it as Pope thought of London: as a "dear, damned, distracting place." I slept last night, for instance, at the Colonial Hotel in Johnson City. The next room was separated by a warped wooden door that was an inch short at the top. Consequently, one could hear the least noise. Well, that room contained a baby, a small boy, a young man and his wife. They were from the country and I imagine did not know how to turn off the electricity. They snored and squalled all night with the light turned on full. What a nightmare it must have been for them! A woman with a voice like a trombone is intoning near-by. I have been listening. I wish I could jot it down. The melody is extraordinarily robust. A red-headed man has just come to use the telephone. He wants 284 Johnson City. A baby has started to cry. . . . This gives you an idea of my circumstances.

With love,
Wallace

↩

[WAS 2001 May 1, 1918 Johnson City, Tennessee]
[Stationery of the Colonial Hotel, Johnson City; envelope of the Lynwood Hotel in Elizabethton, Tennessee, to 210 Farmington-Avenue, Hartford, Conn.]

May 1, 1918

My dear Elsie:

Here is a small check for you. You may not need it all. Bear in mind that you will be able to make good use of anything you save, when you go to New-York. The heat is turned on this morning and there is a bright open fire not far from where I am sitting. This is not merely to drive the damp out of the house but because people are talking about snow. However, it takes very little to convince a Southerner that he is freezing to death. Nothing has happened since my letter to you[39] from Elizabethton except that last evening a train of negroes that had been drafted passed through Johnson City on the way to camp. The station was crowded with negroes. When the train pulled in there was a burst of yelps and

---

39. He had written "to from" and then added a very small, light "you" between those words.

yells. The negroes on the platform ran up and down shaking hands with those in the cars. The few white people who happened to be near took an indulgent attitude. They regard negroes as absurdities. They have no sympathy with them. I tried to take that point of view: to laugh at these absurd animals, in order to understand how it was <u>convenable</u> that one should feel. But the truth is that I feel thrilling emotion at these draft movements. I want to cry and yell and jump ten feet in the air; and so far as I have been able to observe, it makes no difference whether the men are black or white. The noise when the train pulled out was intoxicating.

With love,
Wallace

෴

[WAS 2002 May 4, 1918 Nashville, Tennessee]
[Stationery of the Hotel Hermitage, Nashville, to 210 Farmington-Avenue, Hartford, Conn.]

Saturday Morning

My dear Elsie:

I have been going licketty-split these last two days and have had very little time free. I arrived here this morning. It may be necessary for me to stay over Sunday. I cannot tell until later in the day. In any event I have a notion to stay here to-night just to sleep in a bed for a change. Last night I slept in an upper berth in the hottest car on earth and somehow I feel as though my eyes were red-hot this morning. I have already been down-town for several hours and expect to go down again in a moment and then, if possible, catch a train to Waverly, returning here this evening. There is just a small chance that I might be able to close up everything here to-day, but it is difficult to get hold of people on Saturday. I hope that you are keeping active, going out for walks and exercise. The last day or two have been quite stunning in this part of the world, although beastly hot at noon. I have no doubt that Spring has made great strides in Hartford. It is Summer here. Men wear straw-hats and ladies white dresses.

With love,
Wallace

෴

[WAS 2003 June 14, 1918 Albany, New York]
[Stationery of the Ten Eyck Hotel, Albany, to 210 Farmington-Avenue, Hartford, Conn.]

Friday: June 14

Dear Elsie:

I shall be back on Saturday but not for dinner. So far I have done nothing here but wait for people. I expect, however, to put things together rather quickly once I get started. It is quite lovely from my hotel[40] window and then, too, I am in New York State, so that I am more or less content. There is to be a big parade here to-day.[41] A little group of the Chasseurs Alpines have just arrived at the hotel. The great Josephus is to be present, the Marine band, and so on. It is, of course, impossible to do any work with all this going on. On the other hand, I am here to make a final disposition of the matter that brought me here and must reconcile myself to these not wholly objectionable obstacles. I went to Water-vliet this morning and finding my man still absent walked part of the way back to Albany along a canal sparkling in the fresh air. I am told that there was frost in the Adirondacks last night.

> With love,
> Wallace

Awful pen.

⤳

[WAS 2004 January 15, 1919 Palm Beach, Florida]
[Postcard: "The Little White Chapel," Palm Beach, Florida, to 210 Farmington-Avenue, Hartford, Conn.]
Dear Elsie:

It is really lovely here. I came last night and leave tonight. Expect to be in Houston, Texas, Monday and Tuesday and home toward the end of next week. Hope that everything is going well. This is the day for your music lesson.

> With love,
> Wallace

⤳

[WAS 2005 January 17, 1919 Jacksonville, Florida]
[Stationery of the Hotel Seminole, Jacksonville; no envelope.]

> Jacksonville, Fla. January 17, 1919
> Friday Afternoon

My dear:

I leave at 6.10 to-night for New-Orleans arriving there about 10.30 Saturday night. I intend to stop there over Sunday, leaving on Sunday evening for Houston, Texas, where I shall be bright and early on Monday morning. Monday and Tuesday in Houston, then Nashville, Tennessee, then home, arriving in Hartford late next week. I shall wire you as the caravan approaches.[42]

40. This word is spelled "otel" with a vertical flourish above the line for the "h."
41. This is Flag Day.
42. This is the first letter to Elsie in which Stevens puts standard paragraph indentations throughout.

To-day is the first rotten day of the trip. It is pouring. I had to see an English-man, who lives in what is known as Riverside here. He is a working-man, who owes us a substantial sum of money. After waiting on the porch an hour, he turned up and we finished in half an hour. Instead of walking, as I usually do in such circumstances, I shall have to go without knowledge of how Jacksonville looks in winter. Summer never completely fades out even in Northern Florida, but, of course, it is very much different from Southern Florida, which is four hundred miles away. To-morrow morning, I believe, I change cars in Pensacola and have several hours to spare.

Yesterday I was in Miami. After finishing I walked for several hours and in the evening, before train-time, sat in the open-air at the park listening to a brass band concert. They have strawberries and corn on the cob, etc. But really, it sounds better than it is. Who wants corn on the cob all the time? And then the wind blows incessantly. It gives a kind of fever to one's blood. True, the experience is a heavenly change; but our rich variety of four seasons, our Exquisite Spring and long Autumn give us a variety that the lotus-eaters of the South must pine for.

At Miami, on a bright, sunny day in mid-winter, the climate must be as fine as any in the world. The wind whips the water, the strange birds: pelicans and so on, fly about, there are strange trees to see. Some day, when we can afford it, we must come together.[43] But I believe that I should enjoy, just as much, walking up Fifth-Avenue, in the cold air of a late January afternoon. I always notice when the evenings at home first show signs of lengthening, as they do at the end of just such afternoons.

Now, I must hunt up a tailor and have my coat repaired.

You will find a little money enclosed.

With much love,
Wallace.

43. Though he will make this proposal here and two other times in these letters (see also WAS 2018 November 11, 1917 and WAS 2028 Jan 10, 1922), Stevens will not bring Elsie to Key West (or anywhere else in Florida) until February 1940 (and then with Holly). According to WAS 1477 April 8, 1940, Judge Powell and his wife were with Stevens "at Key West, in February" (unpublished letter in the Arthur Gray Powell Papers, Special Collections, Woodruff Library, Emory University, Atlanta, Ga.). On this trip, Elsie sent a number of cards from Florida to her mother; one that was not addressed but has a message much like those Stevens used to send to her is from WAS 4008 Feb 24–29, 1940, written on a postcard of the Casa Marina Hotel, Key West, Florida, from the air:

Key West, Florida
February 24th, 1940.
We are spending a week here and are wishing that we could stay here until New England is through with snow & cold weather.

⌇

[WAS 2006 January 20, 1919 Houston, Texas]
[Stationery of the Rice Hotel, Houston, to 210 Farmington-Avenue, Hartford, Conn.]

Monday Evening. Jan. 20.

My dear:

When this letter reaches you, I shall be almost home; for I expect to leave here to-morrow, stop at Nashville for a few hours and then start for New-York. I could leave here to-night, but I have not been in a real bed for a week and must rest. I finished at twenty minutes of five this afternoon and started at once for a walk. The dreariest fog, rolling in from the Gulf of Mexico, took the place of daylight. There is a good deal of that kind of thing in the gulf states at this season. The mist penetrates and chills and bores one to death. On the grounds at Rice Institute I noticed that the drives were bordered with beds of pansies. You will find one enclosed as evidence that such things exist outdoors in Texas in January. In a garden, there were violets—a few. With us, when violets come at all, they come in profusion. I have been a little homesick to-day. It was exciting to visit Houston two years ago but this second visit is tedious. We are losing money here and must go on doing so, for the present. I can say honestly that it would be very sweet to me to be comfortably at home to-night, with our lamps and things, and with yourself, my dear. Fortunately, just as this trip is the first I have taken for a long time, so I expect it will be the last until Spring.

With much love,
Wallace

⌇

[WAS 2007 January 22, 1919 Muskogee, Oklahoma]
[Stationery of the Hotel Severs, Muskogee, to 210 Farmington-Avenue, Hartford, Conn.]

Jan. 22 (Wednesday) 1919.

My dear:

It was frightfully gloomy on the train after leaving Dallas this morning and it remained so all day. We came through a cotton country. Last year's cotton plants are surely the rustiest things in existence. The fields were pools of water. The rain dashed against the windows.

Imagine, then, how pleasant a surprise it was, on getting out of the train here, to find it clear and cold, with the stars shining. The weather does me a world of good: the cold, particularly because last night as we left Houston, I lay bathed in perspiration—and so all night.

I am not supposed to be in Muskogee. Our train north missed its connection with the train for Tulsa, where I am going. I could still go to Tulsa to-night, arriving at 2 a.m.; but, instead, have taken a room at this hotel (which is a thousand times superior to anything of the sort in Hartford) and shall go on in the morning.

It will be necessary for me to get up early and so I must go to bed early.

> With love,
> Wallace

I had not foreseen anything like this trip when I started on it. Feel like a <u>pirate.</u>

↩

[WAS 2008 May 5, 1919 Milwaukee, Wisconsin]
[Stationery of the Hotel Wisconsin, Milwaukee; no envelope.]

> Monday Evening, May 5th

My dear Elsie:

I arrived here this evening shortly before nine o'clock after a deal of railroading. From New-York I went to Washington, where I slept Saturday night. In the morning, I left for Meyersdale, where I arrived at half-past three. It was as hot as summer there. I left Meyersdale for Cumberland at nine and at Cumberland caught the midnight for Chicago. After about two hours in Chicago where I took a short walk, for exercise, and had dinner, I came on here. The change in the weather is remarkable. There was a high wind from Lake Michigan blowing in Chicago. Here there is not so much wind but it is cold as March. They have had a deluge of rain all over this region, so that the fields are full of sheets of water. The train before ours was delayed six hours by a washout. We had no trouble, however. I was glad to see the sun coming out at sunset along the edges of dark blue clouds and hope that things are a little more cheerful in the morning. Our case is expected to commence to-morrow. So far as I am concerned, I suppose I shall be sitting in court from ten to four every day for the rest of the week. Milwaukee is a bore of a place, except in the business sense; and in that sense, of course, it is just the opposite of a bore. Well-o, I am going up-stairs to unpack, bathe and get a good night's sleep, if possible.

> With love,
> Wallace

↩

[WAS 2009 May 6, 1919 Milwaukee, Wisconsin]
[Stationery of Milwaukee Athletic Club, Milwaukee, to 210 Farmington-Avenue, Hartford, Conn.]

> Tuesday Evening

My dear:

There turned out to be a bowling alley below my window at the Hotel Wisconsin, which made a devil of a noise until midnight, so that I moved over here this evening and here I shall stay as long as I remain in Milwaukee. I have an extremely agreeable room, and, besides, there are many amenities about a club that one does not receive at the hands of a hotel. Our case was postponed this morning until to-morrow, Wednesday. The jury was on hand but the judge was in Chicago. I walked a little and spent several hours with a dentist. But I am eager to get down to business. This evening I shall read a little and work on the poems I brought along. I hope to be able to leave the poems with <u>Poetry</u>[44] when I pass through Chicago on my way home. Unfortunately the things I brought along to read were read on the train on the way out, but one or two essays will bear re-reading. We had bright, clear weather to-day, but it was colder than it has been in Hartford for a month. I noticed in some of the gardens that the forsythia is just budding, whereas, with us, it is almost gone. However, it can never really be spring-like here in the brilliant, fresh manner to which we are accustomed; for it is dingey, grimey and sootey,[45] like most places in the middle West. The middle West is ugly and never was anything else, and, perhaps, never will be.

With love,
Wallace

⌣

[WAS 2010 May 9, 1919 Milwaukee, Wis.]
[Stationery of Milwaukee Athletic Club, Milwaukee, to 210 Farmington-Avenue, Hartford, Conn.]

Friday Evening

My dear:

We are making very slow progress with our case, but still we are making progress. It is not impossible that it will take all of next week. I fully expect it to do so unless our people wake up. There have been two men out from New-

---

44. Eventually this group will be published as "Pecksniffiana," *Poetry* 15, no. 1 (October 1919), 1–11: Fabliau of Florida—Homunculus et La Belle Etoile—The Weeping Burgher—Peter Parasol—Exposition of the Contents of a Cab—Ploughing on Sunday—Banal Sojourn—The Indigo Glass in the Grass—Anecdote of the Jar—Of the Surface of Things—The Curtains in the House of the Metaphysician—The Place of the Solitaires—The Paltry Nude Starts on a Spring Voyage—Colloquy with a Polish Aunt. (See Edelstein, *Wallace Stevens*, 200–201.) In a letter to Harriet Monroe of this same period and also on stationery of the Milwaukee Athletic Club, Stevens indicates that on this stop in Chicago he will also pick up a book by Carl Sandburg and asks Monroe if Sandburg will be in town then (June 1, 1919, no. 19 of the sixty letters from Stevens to Monroe in the *Poetry* Papers at the Joseph Regenstein Library, University of Chicago). *LWS* (214) has a letter of August 16[?], 1919, to Monroe making three substitutions to the original group and adding several new poems.
45. This is Stevens's spelling for these three adjectives.

York with whom I have been talking steadily, so it seems, since my last letter to you; but they left for home to-day.

I enclose a check for '10[46] which is all I can send until after the 15th. Be sure, therefore, to keep enough of this to take care of Carrie next Thursday. My cash is very low temporarily because of a payment I made on my bonds but as you will get the bonds, be content. I have been having my teeth fixed out here in the mornings from 9 until 9.45. That leaves me just enough time to get to court by 10. But with that exception, I am leading a dull life. This afternoon, after court, I walked through the Northwestern part of the city, which consists of rows of small residences, bungalows and so on. This section is newer and more attractive than the older parts of town.

On Sunday, I expect to go down to Evanston to see Uncle Harry.[47] I have told him to have strawberry short-cake. It will be pleasant to see him again and to smoke a cigar with him.

I should be glad to have a letter from you. Send it in care of this club. If you write on Monday, it will come in plenty of time. I cannot imagine what people out here do without overcoats. They say that they often wear them on the 4th of July. The city is situated on Lake Michigan and that is what keeps it cold. From my window here I can see that Lake which looks, of course, to be as big as the ocean.

Well, I wrote an enormous report to Kearney this evening and am going to give the old ink-bottle a rest.[48]

With love,
Wallace

---

46. Stevens's symbol here for dollar (and in several other places in the letters) is an apostrophe.

47. According to Brazeau, "Harry Carle [at the time of this visit] had recently lost his wife, Anna, the youngest sister of Wallace's mother. The childless couple had been close to the Stevens children when they were growing up" (*Parts of a World*, 254). Brazeau also says that Eleanor Hatch, Uncle Carle's housekeeper at the time of Stevens's visit, was the sister of the wife of Stevens's younger brother John. See WAS 1969 April 2, 1916, for note on Anna and Harry.

48. Brazeau reports the fate of Stevens's many such reports: "Curiously, despite the hundreds of letters he wrote and the scores of files he compiled over the years, Stevens the insurance man of letters has not survived. Hartford Accident and Indemnity routinely destroyed almost all of this material to make space for new cases before any scholar thought to apprise the company of its value in re-creating this essential aspect of Stevens' life at the office" (*Parts of a World*, 39–40).

[WAS 2011 May 12, 1919 Milwaukee, Wisconsin]
[Stationery of Milwaukee Athletic Club, Milwaukee, to 210 Farmington-
Avenue, Hartford, Conn.]

Monday Evening, May 12, 1919

My dear:

It is a pleasant trip from Milwaukee to Evanston by trolley—about seventy miles through a level farming country, unlike the country at home. There is a Pullman and it is possible to have dinner on the train. I reached Evanston about noon, walked over to the Lake Front, along the grounds of North Western University (which seems to be chiefly dormitories and gymnasiums) and so on to Uncle Harry's house. He had not received my note telling him that I was coming and was surprised to find me at the door. He has been ill since my last visit, liver out of order, yet I thought he looked better. He was in good spirits. Miss Hatch, John's wife's sister,[49] who lives with him gave me more or less news. She told me that Elizabeth's husband is a man of fifty with white hair! And when I had recovered from that, she told me that Elizabeth had a daughter about a week ago.[50] She also showed me a number of photographs of John's girl and little boy. She has an old maid's fondness for photographs. I rather formed an impression that she is dull and over inclined to put her best foot forward; but she is a good person for Uncle Harry to have with him, for she is quiet and helpful. Uncle Harry has not been able to sell his house. This prevents him from making any definite plans for the future. However, he has nothing in mind anyhow and the chances are that he will be where he is now until autumn at the least. He may go down to Nantucket for a month this summer. Miss Hatch goes to Reading to visit her sister sometime next month. John's wife appears to have grown much stouter than she was, although, as to that, my recollection is so slight, since I saw her only once, that I may be wrong.[51] Uncle Harry gave rather discouraging news, perhaps I should say the usual discouraging news, about Garrett.[52] His wife has had one illness after another, including the influenza. I imagine that Garrett is holding his own, although not making much progress.

49. Stevens's younger brother John Bergen Stevens had married a Hatch. See note above to WAS 1842 May 7, 1909.

50. See WAS 1933 for note on this older sister of Stevens.

51. Stevens probably saw her at his mother's funeral, not at her wedding.

52. Stevens's older brother, Garrett Barcalow Stevens (1877–1937), was a lawyer in Cleveland at this time and until his death. Anna May Stevens, the wife of Stevens's nephew, John Bergen Stevens Jr., told this story: "Our favorite story was when he [Wallace] was in Cleveland. He saw his brother [Garrett] walking down the street. He looked fine, he looked prosperous. Wallace didn't have anything to say to him, so he crossed over [to the other side of the street] and went right on by" (Brazeau, *Parts of a World,* 280).

Well, family affairs are a bore anyhow, aren't they? It might not be so, if we were all millionaires; but not even John, who seems to be successful, is a millionaire. Uncle Harry is interested in all this sort of thing. I did not leave Evanston until about eight o'clock, reaching Milwaukee about half-past ten. The trip did not improve my cold. It is much chillier here than I had any reason to expect. Even this evening, after an uncommonly mild day, I feel and enjoy the protection of being indoors. We got under way in court to-day once more and had rather a good day of it. Our side will probably be through by the middle of next week and then the other side will open up.

I am hoping to have a letter from you while I am here.

With love,
Wallace

⌒

[WAS 2012 May 14, 1919 Milwaukee, Wisconsin]
[Stationery of Milwaukee Athletic Club, Milwaukee; no envelope.]

Wednesday Evening

My dear:

I was very glad to have your letter. To-morrow is the 15th and accordingly I send you a check for '25. If there are any bills around the house, please pay them, or such as seem proper.

I have written a note to Elizabeth.

Our case runs along from day to day. Our side is very slow and seems to be making little or no progress. Each day, after court, I take a walk, striking off in any direction that attracts me. Last evening I came across a very considerable park, Washington Park, where I indulged myself in the old fascination of looking at wild animals. A zoo interests me just as much as a botanical garden or a museum. In this particular zoo, there are numerous pheasants, particularly. They put pheasants and deer together, elk and turkeys, bison and peacocks. They have, also, two absolutely splendiferous tigers, with blazing eyes—not half-dead, somnolent beasts.

This evening I went out there again to look at some ponds and a statue. The statue is of Goethe and Schiller, in heroic size, cast in Dresden. These great creatures are quite in place here in this German city, though one wonders what they can mean to the people as a whole.

There are a number of large Catholic churches here, very ugly in appearance, and dirty in up-keep. The Catholics are extraordinarily active in all this region, although unlike the Irish Catholics of the east, they seem to confine themselves to religious and educational activity, without the very evident seeking of general political domination.

Caruso was here last night. I did not go to hear him. A thing called the Milwaukee Concertina Circle gives a concert on Saturday, which rather excites my curiosity.

With love,
Wallace

↜

[WAS 2013 May 27, 1919 Milwaukee, Wisconsin]
[Stationery of Milwaukee Athletic Club, Milwaukee, to 210 Farmington-
Avenue, Hartford, Conn.]

Tuesday Evening

Dear Elsie:

I am completely done up by the news of Catharine's death.[53] I thought of nothing else on the way out. How horrible it is to think of the poor child fatally ill in a military hospital in an out-of-the-way place in a foreign country, probably perfectly aware of her helplessness and isolation! She has been without a home, tossed from pillar to post, making her own living, always uncomplaining, sympathetic and loyal to what was good. No doubt, since her term of service was almost finished, and the winter was behind her, she was looking forward to a return home. Not that there was any home for her to return to. But she must, nevertheless, have thought of the old place, as the one thing to sustain her. In the midst of that, she was overtaken by a most dangerous and painful sickness, to which she has fallen a victim. I pity her from the bottom of my heart. It will be a cruel shock to Elizabeth, to whom I should like to write, but whose address I failed to keep. If you have her address, do, please write her at once and send her address to me, also. We made great progress in our case to-day, but as there are only two more trial days this week, it is not likely we shall finish before early next week, when I expect to come home for a long, unbroken season of work at the office. It was a great relief to me that you accepted the necessities of the present case with such good grace. I am as tired of being away from home as it is possible to be. It was agreeable to find on my arrival that the weather has grown warmer,

---

53. This is Stevens's spelling, used also in WAS 2014. His younger sister (1889–1919) (in *LWS*, 4, Holly gives her name as "Mary Katharine, also known as Catharine," and as "Catherine" on 172), who had been serving with the Red Cross in France, had suddenly died of meningitis. See Brazeau, *Parts of a World*, 255–56, for a detailed description of the events surrounding her death. At the Huntington, a letter of May 24, 1919, written by Maj. William L. Gerstle A. R. C. in Saint-Nazaire, France, tells of this event from his point of view. Another letter, from a co-worker, Constance M. Hallock, gives telling details of her life: "I remember how she used to look, with her golden head shining above the mob, for she was taller than a great many of them. Everybody liked her for who could help liking one so unassuming and kind, as well as remarkably capable and good looking?"

although to-night the air is much cooler than it will be in Hartford before autumn. I suppose that when I get home, the window boxes will be in place and that everything will be bright and fresh. I hope so.

With much love,
Wallace

⌁

[WAS 2014 May 29, 1919 Milwaukee, Wisconsin]
[Stationery of Milwaukee Athletic Club, Milwaukee, to 210 Farmington-Avenue, Hartford, Conn.]

Thursday Evening

My dear:

I expect to finish here next Tuesday or Wednesday and to be home about Thursday or Friday. I may go home by way of Reading, for I should like to see John to find out more about Catharine, if possible. But it depends on the trains. If I could reach Reading in the evening and leave in the morning I might do it. However, there is a vast amount of work piling up in Hartford that needs urgent attention and, besides, the chances are that John has merely had a brief notification without any details, for the present. What a shocking and horrible outcome of an effort on Catharine's part to do her share, unselfishly and devotedly! It is hard to think that she is in her grave. In many ways, she was extremely like my mother; so that the loss of her, ends that aspect of life. I am more like my mother than my father. The rest, I think, all resemble my father most. After court adjourned this afternoon, I walked to a suburb called Wauwatosa, about five miles away. The fruit trees are in full blossom and it was most agreeable to be in the country. To-morrow is Memorial Day. The court will not sit. I expect to take a trolley ride and walk a little. On Saturday, we shall be having a conference. So that there will be little of importance before Monday.

I shall write again shortly, sending you a little money for next week. If you are careful, you will be able to open your savings bank account with '75 on my return.

With love,
Wallace

⌁

[WAS 2015 May 31, 1919 Milwaukee, Wisconsin]
[Stationery of Milwaukee Athletic Club, Milwaukee, to 210 Farmington-Avenue, Hartford, Conn.]

Saturday Morning

My dear:

Memorial Day was a day of the most stunning weather. I went to Port Washington, a place about thirty miles north of Milwaukee, on the lake, and took a long walk on the shore. The lake was so calm that there was scarcely a sound of water to be heard. The air was clear and soft and warm. I returned to Milwaukee early in the afternoon and watched the parade, which, in my present state of mind on account of Catharine, affected me deeply. There was a group of mourners, war-mothers, each one of whom carried a gold-star flag,[54] which it was impossible to continue to look at. Fortunately, toward the end, the groups of foreigners, braced one with the less serious aspects of the demonstration. The Polish Citizens' Union contained about fifty boys, none of them over three feet high, about five or six years old, wearing long coats and high hats. The little fellows were tired out. But it was amusing to see them. There was a group of Russians in Russian dress, and another of Bulgarians. This whole region is thickly settled by emigrants from Eastern Europe. The Catholics as usual were exceedingly prominent. One saw priests every few minutes. All the great churches here are Catholic. There are, I believe, seventeen German Catholic churches alone; but as usual the congregations seem to consist largely of emigrants.

I enclose a check for [$]15. There will be the May bills to pay when I reach home so that I have to be careful. I paid the rent before I left in order to make sure that it would be taken care of promptly.

With love,
Wallace.

↬

[WAS 2016 June 1, 1919 Milwaukee, Wisconsin]
[Stationery of Milwaukee Athletic Club, Milwaukee, to 210 Farmington-Avenue, Hartford, Conn.]

Sunday Evening

My dear:

On Sunday evening, ladies come here in droves: chiefly families, to avoid dinner at home and give the Swede a chance to meet her best fellow. After dinner, they blow into this room, where one does one's writing and I swear it is a job for a man, even when he has only one good ear,[55] to think what he is doing. All kinds of people belong here. A man at my elbow has just been talking to his shirt-maker. His wife joined him and the shirt-maker is now telling her not to use starch.

---

54. This was the symbol that a family had lost a child in World War I.

55. Richardson says that this is the only reference to this impairment in all of his papers (*Wallace Stevens* 1:500). A physician's report (WAS 897 October 15, 1926, a letter from Dr. W. W. Herrick to Dr. A. D. Mittendorf of 399 Park Avenue in New York) says of Stevens, "There is a history of malaria as a boy and of a chronic discharge from the left ear."

Well, this morning I went out to Waukesha,[56] which is about twice as far from Milwaukee, as Farmington is from Hartford. The town is famous for its springs. But the springs are walled up. Then there is a cage. Then there is a pagoda over the whole thing, and around the pagoda is a fence with locked gates. But after a long search, I found one place where the gates were open and forthwith I drank all the spring water I could hold, which after several hours walking in an exceedingly hot sun, was a good deal. The water was excellent. I went out to the famous White Rock[57] spring but found it locked up tight. There is nothing in the town except the water, nevertheless I enjoyed walking around the shady streets, particularly since on Saturday I had had no exercise whatever, having spent the entire day going over my papers and in a law office.

I returned to Milwaukee about five o'clock, dropping off the car at the edge of the city and walking for an hour and a half in the newer Western streets, before I came home to get ready for dinner. It is useless to try to go on writing. There is too much chatter. I shall try to read a little. Our case reaches its climax to-morrow.

> With love,
> Wallace

⌒

[WAS 2017 July 24, 1919 Philadelphia, Pennsylvania]
[Stationery of the Hotel Adelphia, Philadelphia; no envelope.]

> Thursday Evening

My dear:

I enclose a check for [$]5. for Carrie, etc. It is not likely that I shall be home until Saturday afternoon or evening, for I shall have a good deal to do here tomorrow and have an appointment at the New-York office on Saturday. I spent yesterday at Scranton and today at Harrisburg and on the way to Philadelphia came through Reading where I stopped from 5.50 until 8.39. I made a pious visit to the cemetery, then took a Cotton Street car, coming back downtown on a Perkiomen Avenue car. I went to the Berkshire[58] where I had a piffling dinner and even walked out Fifth Street toward the station. As I passed

---

56. Stevens also mentions this walk in a letter of June 1, 1919, to Harriet Monroe (see *Poetry* papers at the University of Chicago).

57. "Seventeen miles to the west of Milwaukee is the well-known health resort, Waukesha, 'Home of White Rock,' where more water is bottled and shipped than from any other town in the country." Clifton Johnson, *What to See in America* (New York: Macmillan, 1919), 259.

58. This handsome hotel was opened at the corner of Fifth and Washington streets in Reading (within a couple of blocks of Stevens's old home on the same street) on January 1, 1915.

Hoff's house I saw Mr. Hoff[59] and stopped to talk for ten minutes. He gave me quite a batch of news about old neighbors. I saw no one else and did not even telephone John, feeling that I had too little time. On the whole, this brief survey of the holy city left on my mind a most afflicting impression. It is now quite late and I have a long memorandum to prepare and cannot, therefore, write you at more length.

With love,
Wallace

[Note: WAS 2018 November 16(?), 1917(?) is above, between WAS 1992 and WAS 1993.]

↩

[WAS 2019 April 25, 1920 Indianapolis, Indiana]
[Stationery of the Claypool Hotel, Indianapolis, to 210 Farmington-Avenue, Hartford, Conn.]

Sunday Evening

Dear Elsie:

After writing you at Youngstown last evening I received a wire which contained a further postponement of the hearing at Chicago for about a month. This changes my plans. I shall be in Indianapolis to-morrow and hope to get away in the evening for Pittsburg. I ought to be able to leave Pittsburg on Tuesday and to be home by Wednesday or Thursday, although it is quite likely that I shall have to return to Youngstown shortly thereafter for a day or two. The case there involves a great deal of money and is full of difficulties. It was a very pleasant ride down here to-day. I went up to Cleveland and caught a through train from there, riding all day through a farming region. There is still a great deal of water in the fields but here and there I saw fruit-trees in full-bloom. Everything is much further along than it was in Hartford when I left a week ago to-night. But a week makes a vast difference in this season of the year. I am terribly in need of exercise and am bored to death. It will be mighty pleasant to be home again if only for a few days.

With love,
Wallace

↩

59. John Silvis Hoff lived next door to the Stevens family (325 North Fifth Street) in 1905; he had married Elizabeth Ann Bushong and was a "Hardware Merchant, Hoff & Bro. 403 Penn St." in Reading. (See *Graduate Catalogue of the Reading High Schools: 1856–1905,* 55; Hoff was a graduate of the class of 1870.) His son, Robert Bushong Hoff, three years Stevens's junior, was a 1904 bachelor of arts graduate of Princeton University and later a law student at the office of Cyrus G. Derr in Reading.

[WAS 2020 (May 16, 1920) Erie, Pennsylvania]
[Stationery of the Lawrence Hotel, Erie, to 210 Farmington-Avenue, Hartford, Conn.]

Sunday Morning

My dear Elsie:

I have been so hard pressed by the various twists and turns of the five cases that I am juggling at once in three or four different places that I feel like a Cuban chess-player trying to beat fifty antagonists all at a time. This has made it hard to quiet myself long enough to turn away from the matter in hand to write you. Last night I was up until one o'clock getting off a report to Mr. Kearney and to-day I expect to meet Mr. Mc Aleer from Baltimore and Mr. Connolly from Pittsburg, to have a conference with our lawyer here, to go to Cleveland at 12.01 and meet two men there in the afternoon and to leave for Youngstown at 6.25. To-morrow I shall be in Youngstown, Tuesday back here and then we ought to be ready to get under way. These cases are by far the most difficult and dangerous I have ever handled for the Company and I am determined to do as nearly perfect a piece of work on them as can be done. The cursed things are never out of my mind. Well, they were out of my mind for a few minutes on Saturday morning; for when I woke up and propped myself up on my pillows to induct myself gradually into the world about me, I found that there had been a heavy frost during the night, that all the roofs were white as snow in the strong, glittering morning light. Looking at this and the great, blooming trees not far off and the blue lake beyond, at least a minor phase of immensity, I felt most agreeably inclined. I hopped into my bath and was lolling there when the telephone rang and I was under way for the day—floating on a Gulf Stream of talk with lawyers, contractors, dealers in cement, lumber and so on. I have not had a poem in my head for a month, poor Yorick. This long absence upsets our life at home abominably but it cannot be helped. I expect, however, to be home toward the end of the week and by that time to have put all this trouble behind me or substantially so. Now, the church bells are ringing and it seems very much like the Reading of long ago. But that Reading, if it ever existed anywhere except in the affections, has long since disappeared. I passed through it last Tuesday on the way from Harrisburg to New-York and walked up and down the train platform for five minutes in a drizzle. It was about as agreeable as a hardware store on a misty day. The houses looked dirty and shabby and the city looked like a dingy village. It was much like returning from the wars and finding one's best beloved remarried to a coon.[60] Erie, by comparison, in the delightful

---

60. In a letter to Ronald Lane Latimer on October 31, 1935, Stevens uses this epithet in a statement of support for Mussolini: "The Italians have as much right to take Ethiopia from the coons as the coons had to take it from the boa-constrictors" (*LWS,* 290).

sunlight of this bright day seems infinitely sweeter. I should like to go to a pleasant little Episcopalian church out far from the hotel but my Irish friends will no doubt be here in a short time and might object to my worshipping the principle of things instead of the stuff that makes the mare go round. I am glad that you finished up with Mr. Weinman[61] for I felt that he might be growing peeved. Do, please, pay Miss Stein. I enclose a check for [$]15. Speaking of money, I have been spending like a drunken sailor—but not my own.

With much love,
Wallace

⤺

[WAS 2021 May 23, 1920 Erie, Pennsylvania]
[Stationery of the Lawrence Hotel, Erie, to 210 Farmington-Avenue, Hartford, Conn.]

Sunday, May 23rd, 1920.

My dear Elsie:

Here I am in Erie once more. I got back about Wednesday and since my return I have made progress enough to make it possible to believe that I shall be able to leave here by Tuesday. But when I leave I shall have to go back to Youngstown and Lisbon for a few days. I am trying to make arrangements to have you join me and will let you know about that in a few days. It is very pleasant[62] in Erie. I enjoy particularly walks which make it possible for me to get glimpses of the lake which is, of course, large enough to give one the impression of the sea. They have extraordinarily long evenings during which I like to walk through the streets under the thick leaves, noting the lilacs and tulips and the full perfection of Spring—a rather wintry Spring when the wind happens to be blowing over the water. But it is as lovely as it can be and this is not much of an hotel. The meals are tiresome and have put my abdomen back noticeably. Then, too, the pressure and worry of my work make it hard to compose myself and when I go to bed I am usually restless for an hour or two and rather wakeful

As late as 1954, Stevens used this same epithet to refer to Gwendolyn Brooks in a photograph (Brazeau, *Parts of a World,* 196).

61. It is likely that this is a reference to the bust of Elsie, which apparently had been something of a burden for her to have done (pictured in *LWS,* plate IX, but incorrectly labeled as "circa 1913"). A letter of February 22, 1919, from Adolph Alexander Weinman to Mrs. Wallace Stevens, explains that "Sculptured portraits" such as the one he has been doing for Elsie take time and patience and that at the moment he has other projects he must finish (WAS 2495 at HEH). Thus a completion date of May 1920 seems reasonable for this project.

62. For the first time in these letters he begins to number his pages; page 2 of this three-page letter begins here.

all night. If my plans work out I shall have done an important piece of work; and this, I hope, will turn out to be the case. I am distressed to think of you alone at home and hope, as soon as my path is clear, to do something that you will like. But be as patient as you can; for the longest excursion has an end in time. Nobody would enjoy being at home just now, more than I. You will find a small check enclosed. There must be a lot of bills around the house, but they will have to wait. I have no more checks and shall have to use a makeshift. If there is anything important a wire would reach me here up to Tuesday (included.) But I take it for granted that you are all right. You can always get my address from Kearney who has a wire from me every morning.

With love,
Wallace

⌐

[WAS 2022 May 30, 1920 Cleveland, Ohio]
[Stationery of the Hotel Ohio, Youngstown, Ohio, to 210 Farmington-Avenue, Hartford, Conn.]

Sunday, May 30th, 1920

My dear Elsie:

I am sorry that you do not care to make the trip to Chicago; because I am riding a whale just now and do not expect to reach the shore of Hartford for another week or ten days. I thought that you might like to see not only a little of Chicago but something of this section of Ohio. If you change your mind and care to come wire me c/o Hotel Ohio, Youngstown, Tuesday and take Tuesday's train: the Lake Shore Limited which reaches Cleveland about 8.20 and I'll meet you there or at the Hotel Cleveland. I am going to be in Cleveland[63] on Wednesday and we could go on together from there later in the day. If you change your mind, therefore, take that train and buy your ticket to Cleveland only. I should be so glad to have you now that the worst of the jumping around is over. I have been up late and early, traveling incessantly, talking to people by the hundred it seems. In twenty minutes I start on a 60 mile automobile trip up the country to see an engineer; and then tomorrow, notwithstanding the holiday, I shall be down at Lisbon with more people to see and bother about. I am practically finished at Erie although I assume that I shall have to go out there more or less during the summer. What in the world are you doing with yourself? Do send me a letter. If you write on Tuesday I shall get a letter if sent to me in care of Hartford Accident Insurance & Indemnity Company (Mr. Thompson) Insurance Exchange Building, Chicago. But better still, come yourself. Are

---

63. The pages of this letter are also numbered; number 2 of this three-page letter begins here.

you afraid of the trip. Nothing simpler. You cannot go wrong. I am perfectly well although always in need of sleep and fresh air, neither of which do I have much time for. Yet one night last week at Lisbon I went to bed at 7.20 and slept until almost eight o'clock next morning. I slept in a four-poster bed with lace curtains and felt exactly like a man of sugar on a birthday-cake. But that was the one really good night in a month. I hope you received the money all right and that some of it will go to pay bills unless you use it for the better purpose of joining me.

With love,
Wallace

↩

[WAS 2023 June 5, 1920 Cleveland, Ohio]
[Stationery of the Hotel Cleveland, Cleveland; no envelope.]

Saturday Evening, June 5, 1920

My dear:

I have been away just a month, the longest absence from home since my trip to Tennessee several years ago. For the first several weeks of the present trip there was so much to think and worry about and so much to do that, even when I had time to write you, I was too excited to do it as I should have done it. Now, I am practically finished. If everything I have to do could be done in one place I could do it in a day. But as it is I shall have to spend Monday in Erie, Tuesday in Cleveland or Youngstown and Wednesday, then, ought to see me turning my back on this present campaign. As soon as the tension is over one feels, of course, so relieved that everything falls flat. And it has fallen flat with me. Last evening, after dinner, I was walking in the neighborhood of the hotel when I noticed an announcement of a production of Molière's "Miser" at a Little Theatre. I was there in a jiffy and spent a most agreeable evening: not that the play was well acted. After all, it was Molière. To-day, I rode about 80 miles in a machine through a cold rain, getting back at evening. Cold is the word. I had a big rug over my knees and a heavy shawl around my shoulders fastened with a safety-pin in front! Very nice. It is unbelievable how penetrating the East wind is. It comes directly over the lake. Except for the cold and the more or less bad condition of the road the ride was pleasant enough—there was so much to see as we went along, part of the time over the same route which I followed last Sunday. When I got back to the hotel I powder-puffed a little and then went down to the main dining-room where I had a veritable Saturday evening dinner. What, however, can one do about the people out here? True, people at hotels are always peculiar. Here they are most damned peculiar. Not the figures of Italian comedy or French pastorals or English promenades. They'll do, they'll do; but good souls they don't belong under crystal chandeliers or in the sound of good music. If there is anything naughtier than a Cleveland youth going down a dining-room after a damsel who looks as though she had bought her clothes by the pound, I haven't seen it recently. Well, these are the reflections with which one amuses oneself on a dismal evening in a dull place. To-day is your birth-day—thirty-seven I believe.[64] Dear me, how we are getting along! Too bad you wouldn't come out here and spend it with me. I could have spent an extra day in Chicago. I arrived there in the morning and left at night. The hotels are packed to the roof because of the Republican National Convention which is to be held there next week. I had no time at all during the day, spending the entire after-noon on the witness-stand, although it wasn't much of a stand at that. Dropped in on Miss Monroe about dinner-time and asked her to have dinner with me at a little Italian place I know. Fancy, they ask $1.60 for a spaghetti dinner now-a-days! My word! Took the lady home and then, almost frozen, I went to the depot and landed upper 1, the most odious berth in the whole galaxy of odious berths. Naturally, I dropped asleep instantly and slept like a statue until we reached the outskirts of Cleveland. But to get back to your birthday. Do believe how sorry I am to be compelled to be away and not to be able to give you the good hug you deserve. . . .[65]

⤳

[WAS 2024 June 12, 1920 Youngstown, Ohio]
[Stationery of Hotel Ohio, Youngstown, to 210 Farmington-Avenue, Hartford, Conn.]

Saturday Evening, June 12.

My dear Elsie:

You must feel like a widow. I had fully expected to be back to-day and had, in fact, arranged for a conference at the office this morning. But I have engage-ments for tomorrow, Monday and Tuesday and I now count on leaving on Tuesday evening or Wednesday morning which should bring me home by Thursday. Surely, you will have lost faith in my promises but I am handling the worst situation the Hartford ever had and I have to move carefully and slowly. A trip to one of the jobs takes a whole day and I cannot leave them until they are definitely and solidly straightened out. Take my word for it that I am bored to

64. Actually, Elsie, born June 5, 1886, was thirty-four on that date. This mistake is not included in the part of this letter printed in *LWS,* 220, and Richardson does not mention it in her treatment of this letter (*Wallace Stevens* 1:508).

65. This letter breaks off at this point, at the bottom of the page, as if there had been another page at least. After omitting these last two sentences, Holly, in a note on *LWS,* 220, says, "The last page (or pages) of this letter is missing."

death.[66] I have only my winter suit to wear and it has been like a blanket in the sun all week. Besides, this hotel, notwithstanding the lithograph of it on the other side, is as cheerless as a vault. There is an artist here, Ivan Olinsky,[67] who is painting a portrait of one of the rich men of the town, who has been good company for me. He has a little house in the hills near Lyme and is as eager to get away from Youngstown as I am. This evening we took a walk together after dinner and had a pleasant talk about artists and pictures and things in general. He has several of his things in the excellent little museum here. We went to see them and I enjoyed him greatly. He knows Mr. Weinman. The only other people I see are contractors and lawyers and similar blood-curdling people. But the trips to Lisbon are not bad. It takes the better part of two hours to go there and the trolley runs through a most unctuous country, full of real farms, fine fields and so on. And Lisbon itself is a sleepy old town like many in Berks County. The only trouble is that everything I do has such important consequences that I am kept on tip-toe to avoid mistakes. I wrote a letter of one page this afternoon which took me two hours and when I dropped it in the post-office felt as nervous as if it was a death-warrant. But as soon as it was gone, it seemed simple enough and right enough and I felt much easier about it. Well, everybody around me is here on business probably of equal importance so that I ought not to feel as if I were alone in the woods, as I have sometimes felt. Moreover, I am entirely satisfied with what I have done this past month and I hope that the office will be equally so. It all depends on how it turns out. Old man Moore[68] has been sent out to act as a watch-dog on the Erie job. He will probably be there until Thanksgiving time. He returned to Hartford yesterday to bring his wife with him. They are going to live in the country not far from Lake Erie and as he will have little to do except

---

66. This is another letter with numbered pages; this is the first word of his page numbered 2. To have more writing space, Stevens is writing on the backs of three of the four sheets, rather than the front, which has about a fourth of the space taken up by the letterhead, which is a sketch of the hotel and so forth.

67. There are numerous references to the paintings of Ivan Gregorovich Olinsky (1878–1962) in the Smithsonian catalogue.

68. This is most likely Frederick C. Moore, born in 1868, who had been in charge of the Special Risk Department of the Hartford Fire Insurance Company from 1904 until March 1920, when he was promoted to assistant secretary. In the letter WAS 2046 of February 25, 1935, Stevens will refer to John Moore again; also, in an unpublished letter at the Huntington (WAS 380 3/20/45) to Henri A. Amiot, Stevens tells the following story: "This morning we buried old John Moore, whom you may remember, who lived to be something like 85, and passed away in his sleep on Saturday afternoon, March 17th: St. Patrick's Day. He had wanted to live until St. Patrick's Day. During the afternoon he roused himself from his sleep and at that time he was told that it was St. Patrick's Day. He asked that the window be opened and as soon as it was opened he took a deep breath, fell asleep again, and was dead within ten minutes."

spend money he ought to have a good time. I have been to Erie since his arrival several times and each time he falls on my neck. His work, though light, will be important and the old horse doubtless welcomes the chance to show that he can still drag a heavy load. He will have ample space to exercise himself in. I shall miss his figure just outside of my office door. Do try to keep a little asparagus and a few strawberries for me. I haven't had fresh vegetables to eat since I left home unless potatoes are so considered. I expect to drop off in New-York to get myself a straw hat and, if it is not too expensive, a hot weather suit of light material. If there is anything you want in New-York, make a memo of it and you can let me know when I telephone you. You will find a check for [$]25. enclosed. Good-bye, dear. Don't be too put out by this long job. It will help us more than a year of work at my desk. So far it has been entirely successful.

With much love,
Wallace

⌐

[WAS 2025 June 19, 1920 Columbus, Ohio]
[Stationery of Hotel Deshler, Columbus, to 210 Farmington-Avenue, Hartford, Conn.]

June 19. 1920.

My dear:

   I sent you a wire last night to let you know that I am booked to stay here until Monday morning. The State Highway Advisory Board meets then; and as the Board has to act in a matter of importance to us, I have to wait for it to meet. I have been promised that my matter will have attention first and I hope, therefore, to get away about 11 oclock in the morning. Columbus is about six hours west of Pittsburg. I can get my train for Baltimore out of Pittsburg. It is unspeakably tiresome to hang around this way, particularly in a place where one doesn't know a soul. Yesterday (Friday) morning, when I arrived here, I found out in a very short time that I was booked to loaf around over Sunday. I started out for a walk and had been gone about an hour when a little brute of a dog bit me—left leg. Not much to look at but dog bites are dog bites. I came back to town and had a doctor fix it up. It seems all right to-night and I am going to take the bandage off in the morning. After this affair, I walked around the South End, a section of the city inhabited by German-Americans. Ach, mein Gott! The little houses, the back yards, the ornamental stone piles, the buckets and boilers of flowers! I went into a saloon (even Bryan does nowadays)[69] and had two limburger sandwiches and a

---

69. In addition to Elsie's disapproval of his drinking alcoholic beverages, Stevens faced, of course, the problem of prohibition (1920-33), which did, however, allow weak or near beer.

bottle of near-beer. You see how I worry my head off about business. Then I took a long pull around town and wound up at the hotel about dinner time. To-day I was busy until noon, arranging for Monday's meeting. This afternoon I went out to see Ohio State University—one of those <u>enormous</u> institutions that exist throughout the West without one's having ever heard of them. They have an interesting collection of local Indian remains in their exhibitions hall. —The Ohio Indians are somewhat eminent in respect to their crafts and I was interested to see what there was. The students were playing base-ball, flying air-planes, picking strawberries from an experimental patch belonging to the horticultural department—if only one had known some of them! Still, one could look on, which, certainly, was better than sitting about the hotel. I am a little in doubt what to do tomorrow. Really these two days of exercise incline me to look up a place to go swimming. If it isn't too cold! But it has been cold as the deuce. I slept under a blanket last night. Well, old dear, I'm getting away from a big job and I am intensely relieved. A day or two of loafing before I reach the office and the mountain of work that awaits me there is not unearned.

With love,
Wallace

∽

[WAS 2026 c. 1921 (Jacksonville, Florida)]⁷⁰

1. I arrived here late last night—Thursday night. The Villa Margherita at Charleston⁷¹ was closed, not to reopen until early in November, which left no

70. This communication is written on the back of five numbered postcards. No address, stamps, and no envelope. The place is derived from the cards and the text. Since one of the postcards was copyrighted in 1921 and Stevens did stay at the Villa Margherita (mentioned here as closed) in Charleston, South Carolina, on February 8, 1923, it is likely that these cards were sent some time between these dates. The numbers of the cards here correspond to the numbers in the text above:

1. "Paw-Paw Tree, Florida." Copyright 1909, H. E. Hill. Card #107382, Jax News Company, Jacksonville.
2. "Sidewalks on Fifth Street, Jacksonville, Fla." Card # R-31762, H. & W. B. Drew Company, Jacksonville, 1921.
3. "Riverside Park, Jacksonville, Fla." Card # R-31888, H. & W. B. Drew Company, Jacksonville, 1913.
4. "Travelers Tree, Florida." Looks like a cross between a palm and a banana tree; also, clouds and an ink smudge. Card #107406, Jax News Company, Jacksonville.
5. "A typical View in Beautiful Florida." Two palm trees on an island, probably in a park. Card #107362, Jax News Company.

71. He will spend the night here on February 8, 1923 (see WAS 2041). This house, now a private residence, once served as an inn catering to such guests as Henry Ford,

suitable place for me to stay in that delightful but limited place. I was really much done in when I got here and went straight to bed where I remained until nine o'clock this morning.

2. I did no work this morning but took a long walk around town in order to give my lungs a change from the dust and smoke. As it happens, while it is warm and humid, the sky has been cloudy all day and from my window, which over-looks the St. John River[,] I cannot see much except a Novemberish-looking

3. mist. To-morrow I leave for Perry, Florida, a little country town about 165 miles southeast of Jacksonville. I do not expect to be back in Jacksonville until Monday or Tuesday evening and shall not be able to start North before Wednesday or Thursday.

4. Our agent has just telephoned me that he is on his way to my room and when I have seen him my work for the day will be completed. Had a rotten cold just after leaving Hartford but my long sleep last night has completely cast it

5. out. I enjoy the mere fact of being here. Every inch of Florida is precious to me when I am in this mood to relax and take it easy. But the stiffest part of my job is still ahead of me.

> With love,
> Wallace

⌣

[WAS 2027 January 8, 1922 Miami, Florida]
[Postcard: "Bearing Cocoanut Tree, Florida," to 210 Farmington-Avenue, Hartford, Conn.]

> Sunday Morning

As it turned out, I came down here with Judge Powell,[72] although I had not, honestly, supposed it would be necessary when I left home. I hope you will not be too envious of such good fortune. It is a beautiful, clear, perfect day of summer weather.

> Wallace.

Eleanor Roosevelt, and John D. Rockefeller. It is located on South Battery Street facing White Point Gardens, the Battery, and the Ashley River as it meets Charleston harbor.

72. Judge Arthur Gray Powell (September 2, 1873–August 5, 1951), who was one Stevens's closest and most important friends until his death, was at this time a partner in a prestigious Atlanta law firm (Powell, Goldstein, Frazer, and Murphy) and someone Stevens hired to represent the Hartford Accident and Indemnity Company in surety matters in the southern region. Elected to the Georgia Court of Appeals in 1907 at age thirty-five, he had served as an appellate judge for six years before going into private practice. He played the leading role in Stevens's winter, business-vacation trips to the south of Florida for the next eighteen years, including the trip in 1940, when Stevens finally took Elsie (and Holly). Stevens is writing in pencil for the only time in this correspondence.

⌒

[WAS 2028 January 10, 1922 Long Key, Florida]
[Stationery of Florida East Coast Hotel Company Flagler System, Long Key
Fishing Camp,[73] L. P. Schutt, Manager; no envelope.]

Tuesday, January 10, 1922.

Dear Elsie:

When I reached Atlanta last Friday I found that Judge Powell had arranged a conference to be held in Miami last Sunday morning. It required absolutely no argument whatever to persuade me to make the trip with him. On Sunday, we made a satisfactory adjustment of the case, which has been the reason for each of the three trips made by me to South Florida and I believe that the matter has now been finally disposed of and that if I ever come down again I shall have to come at my own expense. The attorneys in Miami drew up the contract yesterday.[74] Powell came down here and I spent the day in Key West arriving here shortly after nine o'clock. The contract arrived here this morning, but instead of taking tonight's train for the North I am going to wait until tomorrow night's which should get me home on Friday night or Saturday morning. Powell is with a party of friends here on a fishing trip. They are going out in boats tomorrow and I am going along with them. This is one of the choicest places I have ever been to. While it in no way resembles Byrdcliffe, it is about the same size and consists of a building like the Villetta in which you get your meals and a large number of cottages distributed around a cocoanut grove. The ground is white coral broken up, as white as this paper,[75] dazzling in the sunshine. The whole place: it is an island, is no larger than the grounds on which the Hartford Fire has its building. There isn't a tree on it except large yellow-green cocoanut palms. The sea is about fifty feet from the cottage in which I slept last night. This morning I just stepped out doors in my pajamas and used them as a bathing suit, taking a surf-bath. There are no ladies here so one can do as one

---

73. This fishing camp, originally the housing put up in 1906 for Henry M. Flagler's workers building the Long Key Viaduct (the first bridge in his Florida East Coast Railroad, which arrived in Key West on January 22, 1912), catered to wealthy fishermen, one of the most famous of whom was Zane Grey. A brochure of 1917–18 provides the goals of the club: "To develop the best and finest traits of sport, to restrict the killing of fish, to educate the inexperienced angler by helping him, and to promote good fellowship." This was one of seven Flagler resorts from Saint Augustine to Key West; Casa Marina, a later favorite of Stevens and his friends, was the jewel of the seven. Everything on Long Key was obliterated on September 2, 1935, by the direct hit of one of the most powerful hurricanes ever recorded; over six hundred people were killed.

74. A year from this optimistic assessment, Stevens will still be meeting with one of McCrary's men in reference to the building of the Tamiami Trail.

75. Now yellowed. The following punctuation, with the colon, is Stevens's.

pleases.[76] The place is a paradise—midsummer weather, the sky brilliantly clear and intensely blue, the sea blue and green beyond what you have ever seen. What a fool I should be not to come down here when I can give the results already achieved in return and still have a little fun out of it. I wish you could have come—that you could see how gorgeous it is. We must come together as soon as we can and every winter afterwards. I send you a check to enable you to keep things going until I get back.

With love,
Wallace

⌒

[WAS 2031[77] January 22, 1923 Washington, D.C.]
[Stationery of the Washingtonian Hotel, Washington, D.C., to 210 Farmington-Avenue, Hartford, Conn.]

Monday Morning, January 22, 1923

Dear Elsie:

I wanted to ask you to have the tailor press my clothes while I am away: the suit I usually wear. I had a good nights sleep on the train last night. This morning it is raining hard here but there is no snow on the ground which already makes a vast improvement over things at home. I have just had my bath but have not yet had breakfast. Lots to do here to-day. The Atlanta train leaves at 3.30.

With love,
Wallace

76. This carefully high-toned account of Long Key should be contrasted with the hullabaloo spirit of the one he wrote to Ferdinand Reyher on February 2, 1922: "Now that trip to Florida would have unstrung a brass monkey. I went down there with half a dozen other people from Atlanta. I was the only damned Yankee in the bunch. I was christened a charter member of the Long Key Fishing Club of Atlanta. The christening occupied about three days, and required just two cases of Scotch. When I started home, I was not able to tell whether I was traveling on a sound or a smell. As I remember it, it was very much like a cloud full of Cuban señoritas, cocoanut palms, and waiters carrying ice-water. Since my return I have not cared much for literature. The southerners are a great people." *Hudson Review* 44, no. 3 (Autumn 1991): 398. Though there may have been no ladies present at this time, the daughter of Louis Schutt, who managed this property and later the Casa Marina, told Brazeau in one of his tapes (HM 53715 at HEH) that whole families, including women and children, came to this fishing camp.

77. Several of the following letters are out of their WAS sequence because of a mistake Stevens made in dating WAS 2029. This is the first note of this series of fourteen letters and cards that will chronicle his trip south, his time at Long Key, his quick visit to Cuba, and his long return to Hartford, punctuated by many business stops, on February 14, 1923.

↩

[WAS 2029 January 24, 1923[78] Atlanta, Georgia]
[Stationery of Georgian Terrace Hotel, Atlanta, to 210 Farmington-Avenue, Hartford, Conn.]

Wednesday, January 24, 192[3]

Dear Elsie:

That <u>Golf All The Year</u>[79] at the head of this letter is pure nonsense; for everything is coated with ice here to-day. They had a blizzard yesterday: not much of one, to be sure; yet the wind whistled loudly half the night and rain and sleet fell in sheets. Still it was not cold. However, nothing could be unpleasanter. The trees are dripping and on my way downtown this morning, my overcoat was covered with blobs of water. It has been mild until now and in the rather Siberian looking yards one catches a glimpse, here and there, of yellow forsythia in bloom: a bloom covered with ice. I suppose a warm day will clear things up here and to-morrow is to be fair. But tomorrow I shall be in Jacksonville where I shall stay a day or two before starting down the East coast. Judge Powell and a few friends are going down to Long Key for fishing shortly and I expect to see them there about Sunday. Everything is going well. I settled the case in Washington to good advantage.

With love,
Wallace

↩

[WAS 2032 January 25, 1923 Jacksonville, Florida]
[Stationery of Hotel Mason, Jacksonville, to 210 Farmington-Avenue, Hartford, Conn.]

Thursday, January 25, 1923.

Dear Elsie:

Jacksonville is a great improvement over Atlanta. True, it had a mostly wintry look when I arrived this morning. The sky was cloudy. I finished my work shortly before four o'clock and then started out for a walk. The sun came out shortly after. There are roses in bloom in the park and beds of canna and other things, of course, the names of which I do not know. The fact remains that it is chilly. One can see the breath of the horses. It is like November at home, like mid-autumn and not at all like early spring, although I saw one tree covered with bloom as it would be in the Spring with us. Then the days are decidedly

---

78. Stevens had very clearly written 1922, but a number of factors confirm that the actual date is January 24, 1923, and that this letter is a part of the whole record of this very important 1923 trip.

79. Claim made on the letterhead of the stationery.

longer. It is now shortly after six o'clock and it is still broad day light. I do not expect to start South until Saturday. That will give me all day tomorrow to get a little exercise, which I need badly. You cannot imagine what a blessing it is to get away from ones overcoat and rubbers[.] But one has to rise to it gradually. They are having the best weather of the year at Miami. Strawberries are 38 and 40 cents here and as big as dumplings although living in a hotel prevents one from taking advantage of them. There do not seem to be any vast number of tourists in town. I had no difficulty in getting a room, and a good one. The truth is that very few people stop-over in Jacksonville any more: very few compared with the vast number who pass through on the trains, for everybody knows, by this time, that in spite of a few flowers Jacksonville is not what people think of when they think of Florida in January and February. I am going to a little restaurant around the corner for dinner and after that to the movies. And then for a big sleep.

With love,
Wallace

⌐⌐

[WAS 2033 January 26, 1923 Jacksonville, Florida]
[Stationery of Hotel Mason, Jacksonville, to 210 Farmington-Avenue, Hartford, Conn.]

Friday, January 26, 1923

Dear Elsie:

I had a beautiful time to-day all about a matter of $700 which Mr. Hamilton wired me last night to try to collect from a former agent. I spent hours listening to the agents reasons why he did not owe that large sum and, getting nowhere, I then employed a firm of lawyers to bring suit and spent more hours repeating to them what the agent had said, what I said in reply and so on. That over, I took a walk through a section of the city called Riverside. It has been clear and warm all day; the chill has gone and I saw no end of summery things: children on a lawn making lemonade, tennis games, camellias in full flower and so on. It seems incredible. At our agent's office this afternoon I ran into Mr. Sisk who used to be with the Globe in New-York and is a great friend of Mr. Armstrong of the Hartford.[80] He asked me to have dinner with him tonight. I waited until 6.44 and of course, he called up at 6.45. Sorry to have missed him. Possibly he will drop into the hotel after dinner. I should be glad to see him because Constance Talmadge

---

80. This is likely Edmund G. Armstrong, superintendent of the Contract Bond Department at the Hartford Accident and Indemnity Company from 1920 until 1934, when he became an officer of the company, and then a vice president in 1939. See *Hartford Agent* 30, no. 6 (March 1939): 198.

in East is West [*sic*] is the only decent movie in town and I saw that last night. Schumann-Heink sings here to-night. However, I wouldn't give fifty cents to hear the old dame whose voice is a battered relic.[81] I did not have such a wonderful sleep last night after all. The bed was as hard as a table and the covers were short. I was awake early this morning and had some strawberries in milk. Cream is as precious, apparently, as attar of roses in this otherwise gemmy region. I leave for the South tomorrow. People here who are hundreds of miles from Southern Florida speak of it as a foreign land.

With love,
Wallace

⌐

[WAS 2034 January 29, 1923 Long Key, Florida]
[Stationery of Florida East Coast Hotel Company Flagler System, Long Key Fishing Camp, to 210 Farmington-Avenue, Hartford, Conn.]

Monday, January 29, 1923.

Dear Elsie:

I have been out at sea fishing all day with Governor Hardwick, of Georgia,[82] and a man named Pidcock from Moultrie, Georgia. These are friends of Judge Powell's. I caught four or five fish, some of them less than three feet long. I also caught a coat of tan which now burns like midsummer on my cheeks. We take our meals on a private car belonging to Pidcock's father, who is also here.[83] They

---

81. Ernestine Schumann Heink (1861-1936), born near Prague, made her American debut in *Lohengrin* in 1898; her "farewell" concert tour came only three years after this dismissive judgment by Stevens, though she continued to sing (and even appeared in a motion picture in 1935) until just before her death.

82. Governor of Georgia from 1920 to 1922, Hardwick's political orientation was complex. Though he campaigned as being against the enfranchisement of African American voters, he was voted out of office after his first term partly by the influence of the Ku Klux Klan, which he had threatened to unmask.

83. Charles Wilcox Pidcock (1866-1935), son of a prosperous peach grower and local railroad owner of New Jersey, founded the Georgia Northern Railway (from Boston, Georgia, to Albany, Georgia, a distance of some sixty-eight miles), which first reached Moultrie in 1893. C. W. Pidcock Jr. (1893-1961) followed his father as president of the Georgia Northern. See the pamphlet *Rails, Quail & Ashburn Hill*, written and published by Frank R. Pidcock III and available in the Ellen Payne Odom Genealogical Library in Moultrie, Georgia. This short-line railroad played a large role in the economic development of Moultrie and in the exploitation of the pine forests of southeastern Georgia. The private railroad car mentioned here had been built originally for Henry Flagler (1830-1913) before Charles W. Pidcock bought it; it is now in the Flagler Museum at Whiteway, Palm Beach, Florida, and a similar one is at the Ashburn Hill Plantation in Moultrie, Georgia.

have a hundred quail at the car, a large number of doves, a haunch of venison, oodles of steaks, and so on, and all this I get for my share of the cost. We sleep, not on the car, but in a large cottage here in the camp. I joined Judge Powell and his friends in Jacksonville and expect to stay here until about Thursday or Friday. The plan is to go out to the fishing grounds only every other day, so that we shall not be going out tomorrow, Tuesday. The rest of the crowd spend their time playing cards: there are seven of us in all. But as I do not play cards, I have excused myself tonight and am going to bed early. This letter is to go out on the up train from Key West and will probably not reach you before Thursday by when I shall probably be on my way again.

> With love,
> Wallace

⌒

[WAS 2030 January 30, 1923 Key West, Florida]
[Stationery of Florida East Coast Hotel Company Flagler System, Long Key Fishing Camp, to 210 Farmington-Avenue, Hartford, Conn.]

> Tuesday Evening, January 30, 1923.

My dear Elsie:[84]

This letter will not go out until morning because I am starting it just before the up train from Key West is due. I was up at seven and took a salt water shower in the open air. That, in fact, is the only way of bathing here except in the sea. The beach is not a particularly good one. It is shallow for a long way out and is covered with burrs that stick to one's feet. After breakfast on Mr. Pidcock's car Judge Powell and I sat on the veranda of our cottage while I read the Sunday Tribune and listened to stories of Georgia life. We had lunch about two o'clock, eating a baked kingfish which Mr. Banks, a member of the party, (cashier of the Citizens & Southern Bank of Atlanta) caught yesterday. After lunch Judge Powell went fishing for snappers, I took a long walk alone up the beach, not returning until after sunset, and the rest of the crowd took naps, played cards, etc. This evening we had doves on toast for dinner. Wild doves are a delicacy in the South. I can't say that they exceed anything else I ever tasted. We then sat around for several hours. The others are now playing cards. But as I do not care for cards, I dropped in here to drop you a note. In a few minutes I shall go back to the cottage, pull out a chair under the palm-trees and smoke a cigar before going to bed. It is fairly cool to-day but not too cool to sit in the moonlight in pajamas if I cared to do so. I have about decided to go to Key West on Thursday or Friday and cross to Havana on the ferry and

---

84. Stevens uses this style of indenting in this letter and in the next one, the first time he has done so since WAS 1776 Mar. 7, 1907.

spend a day or two there sight-seeing. I shall have to pay for that myself but I cannot feel that it would be a great sin to indulge myself now that I am so near. Tomorrow several of the crowd are going out in boats for the big fish but I do not intend to go along. One day is enough. Besides I got so burned by the sun on Monday that another day of it so soon might blister my skin. The beauty of this place is indescribable. This morning the sea was glittering gold and intense deep blue. When it grew cloudy later the sea turned to green and black. Later in the morning it faired off, as they say, and by noon there was not a cloud in the sky. The sky is perfectly clear and the moon full tonight. The palms are murmuring in the incessant breeze and, as Judge Powell said, we are drowned in beauty. But with all that, there are a most uncalled for number of mosquitoes. My knees and wrists are covered with bites.

With love,
Wallace

⤸

[WAS 2035 January 31, 1923 Long Key, Florida]
[Stationery of Florida East Coast Hotel Company Flagler System, Long Key Fishing Camp, to 210 Farmington-Avenue, Hartford, Conn.]

Wednesday, January 31,[85] 1923.

Dear Elsie:

I went out to the reef to-day after all. The sea was very rough. There were three in one boat: Mr. Kenzie, Pidcock & I , besides the guide. As we went along, I began to fear that I should be sea-sick. The other two were quite cheerful. However, one of them began to walk about fussily, shortly. Then the other one stopped smoking, and by one o'clock both of them were completely out of it. There was room for only one to lie down: Mr. Kenzie did that. Pidcock could scarcely hold his head up. Finally I told them that if they wanted to turn around, I was willing. I was able to eat my lunch and to keep on smoking; and although I do not boast of being a sailor I got home in ship-shape. Our boat was the Iroquois. Mr. Banks on the Seminole was also knocked out. People on the dock were expecting this and made sympathetic inquiries. But our crowd was on its feet when the boat came in and showed not the least sign of what they had gone through. We had roast venison for dinner to-night. Tomorrow is my last day here.

With love,
Wallace

⤸

85. Stevens scratched over the zero in 30 to make this 31.

[WAS 2036 January (?), 1923 (Long Key, Florida)][86]
[Postcard: Long Key, Florida (cabins and wooden walks and palms).]

They do not have postcards, other than this kind, to give an idea of the camp. But this one shows the cottages, the cocoanut palms and the immaculately white ground. Our cottage, the Bonefish, is not shown here. Each cottage is named after a fish.

[No signature.]

⤻

[WAS 2037 February 2, 1923 Long Key, Florida]
[Stationery of Florida East Coast Hotel Company Flagler System, Long Key Fishing Camp, to 210 Farmington-Avenue, Hartford, Conn.]

Friday Morning, February 2, 1923

Dear Elsie:

Judge Powell and his friends left for Miami last night and will spend the day there. I said good-bye to them because I intend to go down to Havana to-day and spend Saturday and Sunday there, seeing that celebrated city for the first time. I expect to start north on Monday stopping at one or two places in Florida and then getting back to Charleston, South Carolina next week. Very likely I shall be home about the end of next week.[87] This has been one of the most agreeable trips I have ever been on. I have been in Florida now for almost a week and during the whole of that time we have had nothing but the most gorgeous weather: flaming sun by day and flaming moon by night. It has been windy the last two days, which has served to keep the mosquitoes away. Last night I lay in bed for several hours listening to the wind: it sounded like a downpour of rain, but outside was the balmiest and clearest moonlight and when I woke this morning the palm at my door was red in the sunlight. The weather is like May or June this morning. My train to Key West, which was supposed to leave Long Key at seven o'clock this morning is <u>five</u> hours late and will, therefore, not leave until about noon. This will get me to Havana this evening about six or seven o'clock. One crosses from the United States to Cuba on a steamer which sails from Key West directly to Havana. I shall write to you on my arrival.

With love,
Wallace

86. Not mailed separately, this card is datable only as a possible part of this extended series of letters from this January 1923 visit. It is just as likely, perhaps more so, that Stevens sent this to Elsie in 1922, the visit on which he first tried to describe the place to her. This postcard is reproduced in volume 1 of Richardson, *Wallace Stevens*, near page 385.

87. Actually he will not arrive home until February 14, about a week later than he indicates here.

↜

[WAS 2038 February 3, 1923 Habana, Cuba]
[Postcard: Empedrado Street, Havana, Cuba (a street with mule-drawn wagons, pedestrians, balconies, and a Spanish-Gothic church); addressed to 210 Farmington-Avenue, Hartford, Connecticut, U.S.A.][88]

Saturday

Am going to stay here until Monday afternoon, returning by steamer to Miami. If Long Key had summer weather, this has midsummer weather. The place is foreign beyond belief. I look forward to my explorations with the greatest possible interest. This is merely to announce my safe arrival.

With love, Wallace

↜

[WAS 2039 February 4, 1923 Havana, Cuba]
[Stationery of Hotel Sevilla, Havana; no envelope.][89]

Sunday Afternoon, February 4, 1923.

My dear Elsie:

I arrived here Friday evening after a very pleasant trip from Key West on the <u>Cuba</u> of the P. & O. line.[90] The place is infinitely more Spanish than I had supposed. I went up to a nigger policeman to get my bearings and found that the poor thing could not even understand me.[91] Eventually, I wound up at the Hotel La Union where I had such an impossible bed with such remarkable pillows that on Saturday morning the first thing I did was to move over to the Sevilla. Here I am as comfortable as one would be anywhere. On Saturday afternoon I went to the races, a great institution here, and was bored to death. In the evening I went to see a game of jai alai, the Spanish national game. This morning and early this afternoon, until it grew too warm, I walked all over town. The place is enormous. I think that there are over a half-million people here. All the same, there is a dreadful sameness to it and after a half days trotting around one is glad to get back to one's room. The homes here are built around interior open air courts full of plants. The front rooms of the houses, through which you look into the courts, are full of the damnedest junk you ever saw: Statuary, eighteenth-century furniture, ornaments of all kinds. But these interior courts are the

---

88. Both sides of this card are reproduced in Joan Richardson, *Wallace Stevens: A Biography: The Later Years, 1923–1955* (New York: Morrow, 1988), opposite page 128.

89. This is Stevens's longest letter to Elsie since 1909.

90. The Peninsular and Occidental Steamship Company was a Flagler subsidiary.

91. Stevens's use of another racial epithet is mentioned in a note to the letter of May 16, 1920. The attitude that this language reveals was not an insignificant part of Stevens's personality.

coolest places in the world. Children play in them dressed in little or nothing. The sun does not enter them except at mid-day. The houses do not have wooden floors but floors of tiles. The window in my room does not have any glass in it. It consists simply of a set of blinds with inside wooden shutters. When you throw open the blinds, it is like removing a large part of the wall. The evenings are fresh but not cold and as the whole hotel is built so as to circulate the air one sleeps like the king of sleep. I take my meals in different places. Last evening I had dinner at the British Club with the representative of the Aetna. This morning I had breakfast here at the Sevilla and at noon I had luncheon at El Telegrafo, one of the best places. For luncheon I had a big glass of orangeade,[92] a Cuban lobster, banana bread, cocoanut milk ice cream and a pot of Cuban coffee. The Cubans make most excellent coffee: quite black but mild. This evening I expect Mr. Marvin, one of the representatives of the Hartford Fire, to come for me and to go to dinner with me, probably to the Casino, one of the show places of the city.[93] During my walk this morning I dropped into every big church that I passed so that I can honestly say that I went to church most assiduously. They are all Catholic, gorgeous and shabby, most of them older than the oldest buildings at home. But everything here is an object of interest: the bootblacks sit down when they shine your shoes, everybody takes off his hat when a hearse passes, colored women smoke cigars, the streets are full of Fords which carry you, usually for twenty cents, almost anywhere, the finer automobiles are as gaudy as morning-glories, the Cubans use the same kind of money that we do: silver up to a dollar. They do not have any paper money but use ours as a substitute which is a great convenience. I leave here at four o'clock tomorrow, Monday, afternoon and go by steamer directly to Miami, Florida, arriving there on Tuesday morning. From that time on I shall be at work again. I cabled a man to meet me in Miami Tuesday and I expect to leave Miami Tuesday or Wednesday[94] for Charleston where I expect to spend only a few hours. Then I go to Columbia, South Carolina, and to High Point, North Carolina, and from there to New-York and home. I find that I have no more blank checks and so I shall enclose a little money with this letter, but as I cannot get money if I run out I shall send only [$]10 and when I get back to the U. S. wire you so that I may be sure everything is all right. Of course, I feel rather sinful about running over

92. See "The Revolutionists Stop for Orangeade" (1931), which was added to the second edition of *Harmonium* (thus after this visit to Havana), for the only reference to this word in Stevens's work.

93. "Academic Discourse at Havana," with its line "Life is an old casino in a park," was published as "Discourse in a Cantina at Havana" in *Broom* 5, no. 4 (November 1923): 201–3.

94. This man will have something to do with the Tamiami Trail. See WAS 2041 February 8, 1923.

here to Havana. But it is not a very great sin and, if you really wanted me to have a vacation in my own way, I have had it; for I enjoy nothing more than seeing new places and this one is new and strange from top to bottom. But it is the last place in the world I should care to live in. There are plenty of places where English is spoken but to move about freely it is imperative to know Spanish. Even the Chinese speak it. There are a good many Chinese here. They sell cakes, fish, etc. One came up to me on the street with a big box swung over his shoulder and said "Hot Peanuts!"[95] That's the life. My window looks out over the Prado, a short boulevard running down to the Malecon or sea-wall. A Sunday afternoon procession of pedestrians and automobiles is passing. Morro Castle, the old Spanish fortress is only a few blocks away but on the other side of the harbor. I have not been over to see it because I could see all I wanted from this side. It goes without saying that good cigars are as cheap as dirt. However, I have found a good Havana cigarette made of real tobacco which I rather like and as Havana cigars are rather strong I smoke more cigarettes than cigars. I have been looking around for something to bring home to you as a souvenir but I confess that the shops are baffling: Spanish shawls that would drive you mad, etc. But I hope to find something in the morning. The lamp-lighter with his long pole is lighting the lamps on the Prado. A man on horse-back has just gone by dressed in white. The colors of the dresses in the automobiles seem chiefly to be shades of pink and orange. When I came in I put on my pajamas to cool off. But as it is now evening I shall dress again and stir about a little.

With love,
Wallace.

⌐

[WAS 2040 February 4(?), 1923 Habana, Cuba][96]
[Postcard: "Habana. Hotel Sevilla, Centro Dependientes. Sevilla Hotel, Clerk Assoc. Buildg." Addressed to:]

95. Litz, in *Introspective Voyager,* sees this event as the source of the phrase "goober khan" in "Academic Discourse at Havana" (143).

96. This card has been canceled by the post office, but most of that information is off the right edge. It has a stamp of the Republica de Cuba, and one can just read the "Ha" of "Habana" to the right of the stamp. It is dated February 4, judging by the Sunday at the top of the message. Both sides of this card are reproduced in volume 2 of Richardson, *Wallace Stevens,* after page 128. In Box 80 of the Wallace Stevens Papers at HEH, a box of ephemera, there is an envelope addressed to Elsie at 210 Farmington Avenue in Hartford in Stevens's hand; the envelope is stationery of the Hotel Sevilla in Havana, but it was mailed in Jacksonville, Florida, on February 6, 1923. There is no letter with this envelope, which was probably found with the note cards on which Elsie was making her excerpts.

Mrs. Wallace Stevens
  210 Farmington-Avenue,
    Hartford, Connecticut.
      Estados Unidos.

Sunday

This is a picture of my hotel. The building at the right hand side is the Clerks Club. On the other side of the square is the Presidential Palace.

W.S.

∽

[WAS 2041 February 8, 1923 Charleston, South Carolina]
[Stationery of Villa Margherita, Charleston, to 210 Farmington-Avenue, Hartford, Conn.]

Thursday Evening, February 8, 1923
Charleston, South Carolina

My dear Elsie:

I left Havana on Monday evening and went by steamer to Miami. This is a very poor way of returning from Havana. The steamer is small and dirty and the state-rooms stuffy. On arriving at Miami I sent you a wire and then immediately started out with one of McCrary's men to see the road in which the Hartford is interested.[97] This trip, in a Ford, lasted until nine at night. I was never so shaken up in my life and felt sore all day yesterday, Wednesday.[98] On Wednesday morning your wire arrived. I was very glad to get it. The chief trouble about being away for several weeks is the difficulty and expense of keeping in touch with things at home. On Wednesday morning I went over to Miami Beach, which is on the ocean front several miles distant from Miami, and walked around. There have been very few if any changes since I was there last. The weather was unbelievably hot. In the afternoon I left by auto-bus for Palm Beach almost seventy-five miles to the north. Most of this trip was made through a heavy downpour of rain. We arrived about seven o'clock, everything soaked with the moisture in the air. I went to the Royal Poinciana Hotel[99] and had dinner there. This is quite the sportiest thing in the way of a hotel that I have ever seen. Everybody dressed to kill but it is surely a case of all dressed up and nowhere to go; for as far as I could see people were merely standing around, looking each other over, and talking. After dinner I walked around but, of

---

97. For more on McCrary and the Hartford's involvement with the building of the Tamiami Trail, see the note to "V. Traveling for the Hartford 1916–1923" above.

98. Stevens had written the word Thursday and then crossed it out.

99. Built by Flagler in 1894, this elaborate hotel, which faced Lake Worth, operated until the 1929–30 season and was demolished in 1936.

course, it was pitch dark and cloudy and there was little to be seen. The stores along the Lake Trail made that patch of ground seem like a bit of New-York. Many of the New-York merchant have branches there which are open for only two or three months but look about as smart as anything possibly can. I got on board my sleeper about eleven o'clock and woke up this morning around Daytona. I hopped off the train at St. Augustine for a breath of air and was amazed at the sharp change in the atmosphere. I have been travelling all day, reaching Charleston at about half-past eight. Ordinarily, Charleston seems southern but to-night, by contrast, it is about as northern as the heart could desire. It is cold and damp. I am seated by a grate fire of coal. In the next room, my bed-room, an open wood-fire is flickering and there is a gas-stove burning in my bathroom. Yet twenty-four hours to the south and only one of these fires would drive one out of the house. I saw a peach-tree in full bloom in Southern Georgia this afternoon so that Spring is coming after all. I dread the plunge into the snow at home. I shall be here over night and go to Columbia, South Carolina, which will leave only one more place on my programme. I ought to be home Monday or Tuesday.[100]

> With much love,
> Wallace.

⤳

[WAS 2042 February 11, 1923 Greensboro, North Carolina]
[Stationery of the O. Henry Hotel, Greensboro, to 210 Farmington-Avenue, Hartford, Conn.]

Sunday, February 11, 1923[101]

Dear Elsie:[102] Since leaving Charleston I have been in a very poor part of the country. I went to Florence, S. C. on Friday and stopped there in a miserable hotel. From Florence I went to Conway, Saturday morning, where we have a bad case pending. By travelling a good deal on Saturday afternoon and evening I reached Fayetteville, North Carolina, and slept there last night in another unbelievably bad hotel. I travelled all afternoon to-day and reached Greensboro. The hotel here is very good and I shall stay here to-night although my business is at High Point, fifteen miles south. I shall go over to High Point in the morning by bus and return here the same way leaving for the North some time tomorrow evening. By making this my last stop I shall be able to get my clothes pressed and

---

100. The last sentence and the closing are written vertically in the left margin.
101. Stevens mistakenly wrote 1922. Because he had earlier mentioned High-Point as a part of his 1923 itinerary, this letter is surely from that long trip to Florida and back. The envelope and the match of day and date also confirm the year 1923.
102. This spacing and format appear here for the first time in this correspondence.

my laundry done before I start out for home, which I desire very much to do since, with all the knocking about I have had, I am in rather seedy shape. This hotel is named after O. Henry, the writer of short stories, who came from Greensboro. Such is fame. Fancy having your name on the soup ladle, on all the linen, shrimps O. Henry, salad O. Henry, parfait O. Henry. There's an O. Henry cigar, an O. Henry drug store and so on. Aside from this absurd hero-worship, or success-worship, the town is purely a business place: the home of Blue Bell Overalls and seems to have very little to do with worshipping anything except the dollar and the Almighty. I separate the two because in the South generally religion is still much more active than with us. In many small Florida towns, I saw tents on vacant lots with Jesus Saves as conspicuous [as] Omega Oil might be. Almost the first thing this morning I saw, "The eternal God is thy refuge and underneath the everlasting arms." The railroad stations are scrawled over with the old saw "Prepare to meet Thy God," etc. As I entered the hotel I passed a great crowd of men and afterwards walked in the direction from which they had come and found that they had been attending the Men's Meeting at the First Presbyterian Church. Apparently half of the able-bodied men in town had been there. There is a very good reason for this singular state of affairs. In the North and East the church is more or less moribund. Here, however, it takes the place of society, art, literature, etc. I can well imagine how, if I lived in one of the smaller communities a little nearer to the coast, faced constantly by the poverty around me there and feeling acutely the despair that the land and the people are bound to create, I might well depend on some such potent illusion as "The eternal God is thy refuge." One sees so many people who are physically weak and imperfect and so many others who strike one as being mentally almost as bad. I don't mean to say that I am among imbeciles: the prosperity of this town discredits all that. But at the railroad stations and on the trains one surely sees an uncommon number of people who quite obviously just eke out an existence, people brought up in dirt and ignorance with out a thing in the world to look forward to. Possibly that is a good deal truer of the rural sections of South Carolina than of North Carolina for North Carolina is making very rapid progress in every direction. She is one of the great states or will be. There is a building in this little place the equal of any in Hartford with one or two exceptions. Although I am [now][103] a long way from Havana, where I was a week ago to-day, there is still no snow. The signs of Southern spring are not so plentiful here as they were in Fayetteville where one could here [sic] the frogs chirping and could see occasional batches of daffodils and freesias. I did not tell you, I believe, that at Charleston I saw a little magnolia in full bloom, nor that I called on Hervey

103. This word is quite smudged, as if Stevens had drawn a line through it. LWS, 237, reads it as "now."

White or rather Hervey Allen,[104] the poet, before leaving and drank a cup of chocolate prepared by his August aunt. It is much warmer here than it was at Charleston. The two or three days of heavy clouds through which I have just passed made me fearful that my precious coat of tan will vanish before I reach home. I ought to be in New-York by Tuesday night. There are some things I want to get there so that I do not expect to come up until Wednesday. I wired the office to-day and unless I hear from them tomorrow I shall come straight through. No doubt it will take a lot of work to catch up again but I have had a good time and [am][105] ready to settle down to a long period of plugging. I shall try to telephone you from New-York so that if there is anything you want I can bring it along.

With love,
Wallace

I enclose [$]10. Have very little to spare.

⌐

[WAS 4034 September 7, 1923 Bethlehem, Pa.][106]
[Postcard: "Moravian Funeral of the Olden Times. Bethlehem, Pa." (drawing of a two-story house on a hill with groups of Moravians standing in solemn and formal patterns in the yard of this large house). This is the last extant communication addressed to 210 Farmington Avenue, Hartford, Conn.]

The local idea of a good time.

W. S.

---

104. William Hervey Allen (1889–1949), born and educated in Pittsburgh, taught English at the College of Charleston and at this time had just published a volume of poetry, *Carolina Chansons* (1922), with Dubose Heyward. Later he would write immensely popular historical novels such as *Anthony Adverse* (1938). The Blindman Prize for Poetry, which was given by the Poetry Society of South Carolina for five years and in competition for which Stevens's poem "The Comedian as the Letter C" took second place in 1922, was named for Allen's war poem, "The Blindman." See letter of December 21, 1921, telling Harriet Monroe that he is trying for this prize (*LWS*, 224) and letter of May 5, 1922, thanking Hervey Allen for his letter that was a "shock absorber" for Stevens's not winning. Stevens's letter concludes in the spirit that animated his southern trips: "I shall be very glad to look you up some time when I am in your neighborhood. I know from experience how desirable it is to have friends in places not altogether dry, nowadays" (*LWS*, 227).
105. This is an illegible word squeezed in after "and" and "ready" were already written.
106. Both sides of this card are reproduced in volume 2 of Richardson, *Wallace Stevens*, next to page 385.

5

Amassing Harmony
1924–1935

The five letters of this final period are not a group so much as random survivors. One of them contains an envelope with the only surviving use of the address at 735 Farmington Avenue, West Hartford, the Stevenses' address from 1924 until they moved to 118 Westerly Terrace, Hartford, in September 1932. During these eight years Stevens did not write much if any poetry. Numerous speculations have been advanced to explain the causes of this silence: the birth of his daughter Holly distracted him, disappointment at the reception of *Harmonium* led him to abandon poetry, production of his autobiographical work "The Comedian as the Letter C" had brought his career to a temporary stopping point, his work at the Hartford demanded all of his attention, he gave himself over to the pleasure of the trips to Florida each January or February of this period, and so forth. This list could be extended considerably, but the birth of Holly surely changed his life, and he surely devoted more psychic energy to his trips to Florida during this period.

Soon after the publication of *Harmonium* on September 7, 1923, Stevens and Elsie left for the longest trip of either of their lives, a two-week sea voyage from New York to San Francisco, by way of Havana and the Panama Canal. After spending four nights in New York at the Commodore Hotel, the Stevenses boarded the *Kroonland* on October 18, 1923, and did not reach California until after November 1.[1] Stevens did not return to his office at the Hartford until December 10, 1923. It is instructive to see how incorrectly Stevens would remember the relative dates of his two visits to Havana (actually nine months apart) when he recounted the experience in a letter to José Rodríguez Feo: "On my first trip, about 25 years ago I should say, I went down alone and spent the greater part of a week there. Then, about five years later, my wife and I stopped there for about a day on the way to California by way of the Canal."[2]

---

1. For Elsie's diary of this trip, see George S. Lensing, "Mrs. Wallace Stevens's *Sea Voyage* and 'Sea Surface Full of Clouds,'" *American Poetry* 3, no. 3 (Spring 1986): 76–84.
2. Letter of January 26, 1945. See Coyle and Filreis, *Secretaries of the Moon,* 39.

Stevens's series of trips to the Florida Keys in the company of Judge Arthur Gray Powell (which had begun in 1922 and was continued in 1923) was interrupted in 1924 by Elsie's pregnancy and perhaps the fact that the Stevenses had just returned from a two-month trip, but it resumed in 1925 and continued in 1926 (including a yacht trip around the tip of Florida) and 1927. The very scanty information available about 1928 and 1929 makes it impossible to say whether or not Stevens took his annual trip to Florida those years, though it is likely he did. Cards to Holly show that he went to Key West in 1930 (also in *LWS*, 258, Stevens writes a letter of February 19, 1930, from Key West to James A. Powers: "I have been down here actually for a week but it seems I had never been anywhere else and never particularly wanted to be anywhere else at least for some considerable time to come"), and the following letters here show he was there in 1931. Again, there is no evidence for 1932, though *LWS*, 266–67, shows that he and the judge had made their "annual visit to Key West" in 1933. The series continued for 1934 and 1935 (his encounter with Robert Frost) but concluded in 1936 after his fistfight with Hemingway, a real event with many fictional versions. The most reliable and least fictitious version of this fascinating event is in Hemingway's letter of February 27, 1936 to Sara Murphy:

> Hemingway had a hangover from "seeing off in southern farewell the Judge [Arthur Powell] of the Wallace Stevens evening. Remember that Judge and Mr. Stevens? Nice Mr. Stevens. This year he came again sort of pleasant like the cholera and first I knew of it my nice sister Ura [Ursula] was coming into the house crying because she had been at a cocktail party at which Mr. Stevens had made her cry by telling her forcefully what a sap I was, no man, etc. So I said, this was a week ago, 'that's the third time we've had enough of Mr. Stevens.' So headed out into the rainy past twilight and met Mr. Stevens who was just issuing from the door haveing just said, I learned later, 'By God I wish I had that Hemingway here now I'd knock him out with a single punch.' So who should show up but poor old Papa and Mr. Stevens swung that same fabled punch but fertunatly missed and I knocked all of him down several times and gave him a good beating. Only trouble was that first three times put him down I still had my glasses on. Then took them off at the insistence of the judge who wanted to see a good clean fight without glasses in it and after I took them off Mr. Stevens hit me flush on the jaw with his Sunday punch bam like that. And this is very funny. Broke his hand in two places. Didn't harm my jaw at all and so put him down again and then fixed him good so he was in his room for five days with a nurse and Dr. working on him. But you mustn't tell this to anybody. Not even Ada [MacLeish]. Because he is very worried about his respectable

insurance standing and I have promised not to tell anybody and the official story is that Mr. Stevens fell down a stairs. . . . Anyway last night Mr. Stevens comes over to make up and we are made up. But on mature reflection I don't know anybody needed to be hit worse than Mr. S. Was very pleased last night to see how large Mr. Stevens was and am sure that if I had had a good look at him before it all started would not have felt up to hitting him. But can assure you that there is no one like Mr. Stevens to go down in a spectacular fashion especially into a large puddle of water in the street in front of your old waddle street home where all took place. . . . Tell Patrick for statistics sake Mr. Stevens is 6 feet 2 weighs 225 lbs. and that when he hits the ground it is highly spectaculous. I told the Judge, the day after, to tell Mr. S. I thought he was a damned fine poet but to tell him he couldn't fight. The Judge said, 'Oh but your wrong there. He is a very good fighter. Why, I saw him hit a man once and knock him the length of this room.' And I said, 'Yes, Judge. But you didn't catch the man's name, did you?' I think it was a waiter. Nice dear good Mr. Stevens. I hope he doesn't brood about this and take up archery or machine gunnery.[3]

After 1936, the trips to Florida in the winter essentially ended. There was no trip in 1937 (see letter of December 12, 1936, to Philip May, *LWS*, 314–15: "I shall not be coming down this winter, though my heart throws off smoke every time I say so"), and in a letter of December 28, 1938, to Philip May, Stevens says, "We have had little or no trouble in Florida; certainly none at all in Jacksonville, on my side of the business" (*LWS*, 336). Stevens' final trip to Florida was to Key West in 1940 with Elsie and Holly.

⤚

[WAS 4248 Feb 14, 1925][4]

> Though Valentine brings love
> And Spring brings beauty
> They do not make me rise
> To my poetic duty

3. *Ernest Hemingway: Selected Letters 1917–1961*, ed. Carlos Baker (New York: Scribner's, 1981), 438–39. The most peculiar version of this fight is that by James McLendon in his *Papa Hemingway and Key West* (Key West, Fla.: Langley, 1972), in which Stevens, called a squirt, is presented as being half Hemingway's height, and is said to have spent three weeks in a hospital with a wired jaw.

4. This holograph poem is in Stevens's hand and dated in Elsie's hand. Its date indicates that it may have been sent from Florida.

But Elsie and Holly do
And do it daily—
Much more than Valentine or Spring
And very much more gaily.

W.S.
Valentine's Day. Feb 14—1925

⌒

[WAS 2047 February 28–March 1, 1931 Miami, Florida][5]
[Stationery of the Columbus, Miami, Florida; no envelope.]

Saturday

Dear Elsie & Holly:

Judge Powell and I left Atlanta yesterday morning and rode all day and all night and here we are. Occasionally, we saw groups of peach-trees pink with buds—not orchards, but small groups around the cottages of negroes—and taller and statelier groups of pear-trees, white from top to bottom. In the door-yards jonquils were yellow. There were a few japonica bushes. Yet this had none of the thrill that the same thing will have later at home, because there is none of the feeling of Spring that ought to go along. Spring is an end of darkness and of ugliness and, much more, it is a feeling of new life or of the old activity of life returned, immense and fecund. In South Georgia, however, there never was much of the activity of powerful vitality and certainly there never was anything immense and fecund; for that stiff and tough soil never gave birth to much more than a sense of melancholy and was never much more than a field where courageous people could make the most of a bad lot. It is not a scene in which the visitor steeps his imagination. At Jacksonville as we strolled around the Terminal between trains, we ran into Jim Powers[6] who went down to Miami with us on

5. There is no envelope for this letter; the date was determined by Holly Stevens. See *LWS,* 261. However, there is reason to believe that the letter could be from 1926. On one of Elsie's three-by-five-inch cards in Box 80, Folder 18, HEH, there is a passage from this letter: "Spring is an end of darkness and of ugliness" though it "is not a scene in which the visitor steeps his imagination." This card is identified as from "Packet No. 28. April 4th, 1926." It is possible that Elsie's dating is accurate and that Stevens's statement that "this has not been a good year for the town" refers to the collapse in the real estate boom that hit Miami in 1926. The most important evidence against 1926 is the reference Stevens makes to having met James A. Powers "some years ago," an event that Holly dates as having happened in 1926. See next note.

6. Payroll records at the Hartford for James Arthur Powers indicate employment date of April 1, 1927, as an attorney in the Surety Bond Department. Termination date is listed as March 31, 1929. Holly Stevens gives a helpful note on Powers: "When Powers and Stevens first met at Miami in 1926, Powers was acting as personal attorney for J. C.

the same train. He was looking very smart and pleased with himself. He told me that he had "a car that runs," a nurse, etc. Well, if I had not met him here some years ago and taken him away he would have none of those things. He would, I suppose, have staid here in association with Richardson Saunders, he would have prospered as Saunders prospered, he would have had a finger in Penny's affairs here and have been in the banks with Saunders and then when the banks closed he would have been in the same position that Saunders is in to-day: out of a job. Actually, however, while Saunders is out of a job and although not to blame is blamed, Powers is here in possession of everything that Saunders has lost. I have not had an opportunity as yet to see the baby.

Sunday

Harry Kearney of our New York office is at a hotel around the corner. I expect to have lunch with him to-day. Judge Powell sleeps late on Sundays— usually until noon, so that I am having an hour of quiet. Your telegram came a little while ago. It gave me pleasure as always to hear from you when I am away. We expect to loaf to-day. Tomorrow, we expect to go to West Palm Beach and to carry out the settlement in the bank case. Tuesday we expect to be here all day working on the power company case. We hope to finish our work on Tuesday and then to run down to Key West for a few days where there is no reason for us to go except to enjoy ourselves in the sun, which is a good reason I think. Miami does not look attractive to me this time although I have not been around it much. The old Royal Palm Park is now merely a parking space for the world's greatest collection of second-hand automobiles. This has not been a good year for the town. Even the weather has been depressed.

With love for both of you,
Wallace

Penney in a transaction in which Stevens was acting as attorney for the Hartford Accident and Indemnity Company. Stevens was so impressed by the young lawyer that he persuaded him to come to Hartford as his assistant for two years, after which time he returned to private practice in New York and, ultimately, in Portland, Ore." (*LWS*, 258). Powers, one of Stevens's young protégés at the Hartford, and Stevens maintained relatively close contact with one another for the rest of Stevens's life. See *LWS*, 301, for Stevens's identifying Powers and his wife as the two named characters in his 1934 poem "A Fish-Scale Sunrise," which is a souvenir of "not so much the bat we went on in New York as of the distorted state in which that bat left me." See Brazeau for more on this episode and for Margaret Powers's account of her and especially her husband's relations with Stevens: "He felt that Jim was his boy. He used to say it several times: 'How's my boy?'" (Brazeau, *Parts of a World*, 89).

[WAS 2043 March 5, 1931 Key West, Florida][7]
[Stationery of Casa Marina Key West, Florida, addressed to Mrs. Wallace
Stevens, 735 Farmington Avenue, West Hartford, Connecticut.][8]

Thursday Morning
March 5, 1931.

Dear Elsie:

We were up at six o'clock this morning and got an early start at Miami to
come down here for a few days. We are not quite finished at Miami but no
person ever is quite finished at Miami where they can put more things off for a
longer time and with less reason than one expects even of such confirmed
lotus-eaters. We have been sitting around with almost one hundred and fifty
thousand dollars in our hands for them and they have agreed to take it but, as
yet, have not got to the point of saying <u>Now</u>! It is cold here. A log fire is burning in the grate. Yesterday at Miami they had a log fire burning at Fred Cason's
house.[9] The wind is growling. This is all part, I suppose, of the storm in New

7. In *LWS* (242), Holly accurately points out that "there are no letters to his wife
between 1923 and 1931." However, there is a revealing telegram from Elsie in Hartford
to Wallace at the Hotel Pennsylvania in West Palm Beach, Florida:

> 1927 May 8 AM 12 23
> Glad for your wire it must be very pleasant there all well but able to have
> woman for house cleaning only a half day all week Holly misses you this time
> and at supper tonight she chose a cookie for you couldn't understand why
> you do not come home. Love E. V.

The original telegram is at the University of Massachusetts–Amherst with this note:
"Originally laid in a copy of his Transport to Summer, New York, Knopf, 1947." The
text of this telegram is in Richardson, *Wallace Stevens* 2:47–48.

8. On this envelope for the first time, Stevens has used what is now the common
block form of address, and this is the first letter to this address, though Stevens and
Elsie, with their new baby Holly, had been living here since the latter part of 1924.

9. Brazeau identifies Cason as a Miami lawyer who, with his wife, "had been occasional guests at Long Key Fishing Camp in the 1920s" (*Parts of a World,* 98). Brazeau
interviewed Mrs. Frederick Cason to get her account of Stevens's account in 1936 of
the fight he had just had with Ernest Hemingway in Key West: "Judge Powell was
there and Mrs. Powell; Mr. Stevens, Mr. Cason and myself. . . . Stevens and Judge
Powell had been down there, and Hemingway was there at the same time. They dis-
agreed on certain things and had quite a fight. They were both pretty well lit. He said
he was a fool to get that drunk. He was laughing. Stevens himself was telling it" (*Parts of
a World,* 98). There are numerous versions of how this fight started, where it took
place, and what it did to Stevens. In all of them, Stevens lost, and it is likely that he
apologized to Hemingway the next day. In Polk's *Miami City Directory* for 1931, Cason
is listed as Fred W. Cason, attorney-at-law, his wife as Bess, and his law firm's name as
Hudson and Cason. This business information remains the same until 1948, after which
time he does not appear in the directory.

England which this morning's paper is so full of. It is to be warmer tomorrow. As yet we have not had a day of full and mellow sunshine. We expect to stay here until Saturday or Sunday and, unless it becomes necessary to stop off at Miami, we shall go straight back to Atlanta.[10] We then expect to go to Birmingham, although I may not personally do that. In any case, I expect to be home about a week from to-day. Have I told you that I saw Powers' little boy the other day? Powers is as proud as a peacock and seemed to be ready to fight, when, having asked Judge Powell what he thought of the baby, Judge Powell said merely that all babies look alike to him. Judge Powell has five grandchildren, loves them all and cannot be expected to do much more. Mrs. Powers looks as if she could do nicely with a long rest. I am sending Holly[11] several post-cards of the hotel although I imagine she has had the same ones before. I have the same room that I had last year and with nothing to do for three or four days I ought to be able to get something out of life—at least if I don't freeze to death.

With much love to both of you,
Wallace

↩

[WAS 2044 February 23, 1934 Key West, Florida]
[Stationery of the Key West Colonial Hotel, Key West; no envelope.][12]

February 23rd 1934.[13]

Dear Elsie:

We expect to leave here Monday evening. This will put us in Jacksonville Tuesday morning and will put me in New-York on Wednesday morning. If everything goes as planned I shall be home for dinner Wednesday evening and back in the office on the following day: March 1.

10. "Miami" has been crossed out.
11. This is the first mention of Stevens's daughter Holly (1924–1992) in this correspondence; throughout much of the thirties (1930–36), Stevens wrote postcards to Holly while on his trips, primarily to Florida (but also to Duke University, New Orleans, Washington, D.C., and Baltimore), and they were clearly intended to be for both her and Elsie.
12. Though there is no envelope, this letter was likely sent to the address at which the Stevenses would live for the rest of Wallace's life: 118 Westerly Terrace, Hartford, Connecticut.
13. Stevens drew a box around this year, perhaps after the fact, since he was made a vice president of the Hartford Accident and Indemnity Company on February 15, 1934, as a result of an office coup that made his friend and mentor, James L. D. Kearney, president (see Brazeau, *Parts of a World,* 59–60).

We changed our plans at Tampa and instead of going from there to Jacksonville and then down the east coast we started in an automobile driven by one of
[the] company's men and between 4.15 and 10.30 made the whole distance from
Tampa to Miami. At Miami we merely stayed until morning, starting by train at
7.20 for Key West and arriving at noon.

Yesterday was our first real day here. I left Judge Powell after strolling about
with him for an hour and walked up the ocean boulevard to the Martello tower
shown on several of the enclosed post-cards[14] and walked back to the little beach
at Fort Taylor, where he waited for me. I was soaked with perspiration by the
time I got back, which did me a world of good; and what is more I seem to have
picked up a good coat of tan, at least I am as red as a boiled lobster. After lunch
we took naps; and in the evening walked again. It is so extremely hot here at
noon and up until three and even four that a nap is much the best thing one can
think of.

This morning we walked down to what is called Porter's dock and looked off
over the water of the Gulf which has what must be a Mediterranean beauty. The
air was crystal. We could see the whiteness of occasional sails at immense distances in the morning sun. Afterward we went over to the railroad dock. The
boat for Havana was tied up there waiting for the arrival of the train and I poked
around all over here. But Judge Powell, who was hot and tired, found a sofa and
listened to the radio. He is having a great deal of trouble with his throat and
sinuses and the truth is that, when we were back up town, he suggested that we
come in so that he might lie down a little before lunch. He knows a good many
people here and loves to sit around, talk and smoke, which cannot do his throat
any good.

Owing to the disturbed conditions in Cuba there have been warships in port
here for a good many months. At the moment, the <u>Wyoming</u> is lying at anchor
out near the Casa Marina.[15] The men from this great vessel and from others that
are in the basin at the Navy Yard come on shore in large numbers and from
about four o'clock until all hours of the night they are walking up and down the
streets. In Florida they have prohibition under the state laws. The result is that
these men flock to ice-cream shops and drug-stores and in general look like a lot
of holiday-makers without any definite ideas of how to amuse themselves. Key
West is extremely old-fashioned and primitive. The movie theatres are little bits

14. Not extant.

15. Relying for justification on the Platt amendment to the Cuban constitution
(1901), the United States was threatening once again to intervene in Cuban politics,
this time to make sure Batista chose an appropriate president. See James Longenbach,
Wallace Stevens, 156–57, for a discussion of how this episode may have influenced "The
Idea of Order at Key West."

of things. Well, last night it seemed as if the whole navy stood in the streets under our windows laughing and talking; and that, too, may be a reason why Judge Powell is taking a nap.

Tell Holly that I arranged with Fred Cason of Miami[16] to send her a palmetto frond, some young cocoanuts and some dates in a cluster. Olives do not grow in Florida; and while there are date palms, the dates do not mature. Fred will do the best he can. The fan-like[17] leaves of the palmetto are probably what Holly is thinking of when she thinks of a palm. Next to the royal palms, the most striking one seems to be the cocoanut palm. However, the branches of this are from ten to twenty feet long. In Key West, there are many strange trees and flowers and particularly vines. The soil and climate are favorable to roses and everywhere and all year round roses grow. I don't know of a single beautiful garden. This may be because the town is too poor for gardens. It is, in reality, a place without rich people, a village, sleepy, colonial in aspect, individual.

By the way, if you wonder about my handwriting, let me say that I was unable to find a pen in either Judge Powell's room or my own and borrowed his fountain pen.

I sincerely hope that by the time I reach home, the worst effects of your blizzard will have worn off. The papers here always make much of bad weather up north and certainly they had imposing headlines the other day: New York buried under snow. I know that you are all right.

With much love to both of you,
Always, Wallace

⌒⊃

[WAS 2045 February 18, 1935 Key West, Florida]
[Stationery of Casa Marina Key West, Florida; no envelope.]

Monday, February 18, 1935[18]

Dear Elsie:

They are having a Norther here to-day and everyone is sitting close to the log-fires. The palms are tossing noisily outside my window and the sky is not blue but of the color of lead. . . . Well, I arrived about three hours late. Judge Powell met me at the station. One could see at once that Key West had been cleaned up. The Government has found employment for crowds of men not only in town but in the everglades and on the keys and everything looks a bit better. This very beautiful hotel is precisely as it was in 1932, the last year when

---

16. He is identified in a note to WAS 2043 above.

17. The word "fan" has been written over another word beginning with an *f*.

18. Stevens has been a vice president in the Hartford Accident and Indemnity Company for a year.

it was open. The delightful porches full of palms on which you take your meals are just as good as they ever were. But I have not really had a good look yet. We came straight to the hotel, had lunch and Judge Powell, who is next door to me, then went to take a nap, while I took a good bath and got my bags unpacked. Apparently, I have put on a bit of weight, for when I put on my summer clothes at Jacksonville yesterday they almost suffocated me: they were so tight. We spent most of Sunday riding around. Phil May[19] took me down to Summer Haven for lunch on the sea-shore. Afterwards we crossed Shands Bridge at Green Cove Springs and visited Fleming Island which is thickly grown with holly-trees some of them a century old.[20] They are heavy with live moss and many of them were overgrown with yellow jasmine, a fragrant, musky vine which blooms in the early spring and, like the red-bird, is one of the first things to respond to the changes in the season. They have had a cold winter here. In Miami the palms looked like shocks of corn in October at home. But here they never have frost and nothing has been touched. Please tell Holly that I asked Mr. May to send her a young alligator or two. It is, of course, utterly impossible to keep them alive in the North. But if Holly wants to show them at school, it would be doing the best she could to take them to the green house in Elizabeth Park afterwards. It is now after four o'clock and not having walked a step for three days I am going to try to interest Judge Powell in making an excursion

19. A Jacksonville attorney, a partner in Crawford and May, May worked for the Hartford on various cases and had known Stevens since at least 1930; he would become an important Stevens correspondent, often sending him and his family fruit from Florida. A local-history student, May often played a role in Stevens's trips as he passed through Jacksonville on his way to or from south Florida. In a letter of January 27, 1936, on company letterhead, Stevens tells May that because he is on a diet, as he had told May in a letter of January 20, 1936, "any form of hell raising is simply out. . . . The trouble is, Phil, that every time I go down to Florida with Judge Powell, while I never do anything particularly devilish, nevertheless I invariably do a good many things that I ought not to do. The result is that I always return feeling pretty much like a flagellant. I want to go down to get the sea and the sun and to loaf, and that is really all I want to do. Puritanism has nothing to do with it; I simply want to be myself as much in Florida as anywhere else. I don't, of course, object to the Ribaut Club but the idea of knocking round the country with a couple of girls doesn't click a bit." *LWS* (307) has all of this letter, with the exception of the final sentence here, which comes from Richardson, *Wallace Stevens* 2:122, with the correct spelling of Ribaut (also spelled Ribault) from the original at the Houghton Library Harvard.

20. This was a considerable outing, going below St. Augustine and returning by way of the long bridge over the St. Johns River south of Jacksonville.

down town. He has been ill but says that he has slept well here and feels much better. He has been here for three or four days.

> Always with love for
> both of you,
> Wallace.

∽

[WAS 2046 February 25, 1935[21] Key West, Florida]
[Casa Marina stationery; no envelope.]

Monday

Dear Elsie:

This is the hottest day we have had. This morning we walked up the boulevard, returning about eleven. From then until lunch time, one o'clock, I loafed on the dock and the beach, sunning myself. In Hartford, with the Spring snow ahead,[22] it is hard to believe that the sun does much except give light. But here it gives much more than light. There has hardly been a cloud in the sky for week. We are now in the last few days of our holiday. On Wednesday evening (5.40) we leave for Miami where we arrive about 10. At Miami, I separate from Judge Powell who will continue on to Atlanta. On Wednesday night, I expect to be at the Dallas Park Hotel in Miami, where I shall meet John Moore of Hartford and John Steele of our Tampa office. Early on Thursday morning the three of us will start by automobile to drive from Miami to Tampa over the Tamiami Trail, across the Everglades, and up the Gulf Coast.[23] I have been planning to leave Tampa for New-York Thursday night, which would put me in New York Saturday morning. But I have a wire from John Moore[24] which indicates that he expects me to stay in Tampa until Friday night. If I stay I shall not get home until Sunday. But I really want to leave Tampa Thursday, because eager as one is to get away from one's routine, just so eager one is to get back to it. Robert Frost[25] was on the beach this morning and is coming to dinner this evening. We are having what is called conk chowder, a thing in which he is interested. I took over to

21. With no envelope, the date is determined by adding a week to the letter above, written at the beginning of this year's holiday. Other cues indicate that this letter is from the same year as the letter above.

22. The words "of you" have been scratched out.

23. On February 28, 1935, Stevens sent Holly a postcard from the Hotel Charlotte Harbor, Punta Gorda, Florida, and reported that he had stopped there for lunch as he and his party were "Driving from Miami to Tampa" (WAS 2235 at HEH).

24. See note for WAS 2024 for identification of this man and Stevens's story of his death in 1945.

25. There is a photograph of Stevens and Frost together in Key West near this time (see plate XV in *LWS*).

him a bag of sapadillas (or sapotes),[26] some of which I once brought home. The windows are open and through them I can hear the rustling of the cocoanut palms and the washing of the sea. Nothing could be lovelier. With much love to the both of you,

Wallace

26. In a letter of October 25, 1948, to José Rodríguez Feo, Stevens is still calling on his memory of such exotic fruit: "When I go into a fruit store nowadays and find there nothing but the fruits du jour: apples, pears, oranges, I feel like throwing them at the Greek. I expect, and you expect, sapodillas and South Shore bananas and pineapples a foot high with spines fit to stick in the helmet of a wild chieftain" (*LWS*, 622).

Afterword

After 1935, there are no more extant letters from Stevens to Elsie, though they had another twenty-one years of life together, years in which their daughter grew up, attended Vassar (the institution of Stevens's choice) for a little more than a year, dropped out of college, married a man of whom Stevens did not approve, had his only grandchild, got divorced, and returned to the family circle. During these twenty-one years, Stevens wrote thousands of other letters to other correspondents, most of them still unpublished, many of them giving glimpses, carefully controlled ones, into Stevens's life with his family. It seems that during the 1940s, the marriage reached its greatest accord, as both Stevens and Elsie worked on their genealogies and took such vacations as the 1940 family trip to Key West Holly described in "Holiday in Reality" and the 1946 trip to Hershey, Pennsylvania, that Stevens described in a letter to José Rodríguez Feo as "one of the happiest times of our lives" (*LWS*, 534–35).

Another glimpse, in February 1950, also reveals a moment of happiness. After a fall on the ice had laid Stevens up for a several weeks, he reports to Barbara Church, "It takes a squalid interval like this to realize the opportunities of low spirits and the ravages they make on one's pride and ambition. Fortunately, I was not alone. Mrs. Stevens was a true angel and from the point of view of being at home with her it was a happy time" (*LWS*, 663). We know from a letter written a week before their marriage that he had thought of Elsie as a potential nurse who would take care of him (WAS 1901 September 19, 1909).

One thing that would have brought Stevens and Elsie together is the publication of these letters, to which they would have both strongly objected. Publishing these letters is a serious intrusion into the lives of two very private people, both of whom ensured that most of their letters did not survive, and yet they are the ones that preserved the letters presented here. Thanks to their daughter, we have what survived, and one takes comfort from the extraordinary role she had in their preservation and dissemination.

Stevens and Elsie possessed a language and a world we will never fully understand, and that is as it should be. From our outside reading of these letters, in conjunction with the many negative lines of poetry he wrote about a troubled relationship, we are tempted to conclude that this marriage was a failure. Certainly no one else would have felt comfortable inside that small world of two, not even their daughter, and it is clear that Stevens himself, and presumably

Elsie, did not feel complete happiness in it. He was at times stunned at the unhappiness he experienced with Elsie, someone he had thought of as his "second self." Just as he found Havana in 1923 "foreign beyond belief," so he found his own home at times to be a "wild country of the soul" (*CP*, 240). He had to learn, had to help create, its language and its customs, its mythology, and he had to find what would suffice. He finally achieved what he had originally sought in his relationship with Elsie: a home, even if the imaginary element was more important than in many marriages. Perhaps the foreign element was stronger than he had anticipated as a young man in his twenties, but it was a home, large and with an element of luxury.

Their continued life together was not an accident. It was an essential revelation of the character of the man whose poems so openly and so obliquely reveal him. The letters and poems Stevens wrote are parts of a whole, a world of personal revelation. His letters to Elsie reveal him in ways nothing else can do, and thus they offer us help in reading his poems in direct and indirect ways. On the other hand, without insight from a reading of his poems, we would not be able to determine what these cautious and censored letters meant to him. Knowing that these letters to Elsie, the most important person in his life, were written by the author of "Sunday Morning" and "Final Soliloquy of the Interior Paramour" (among dozens of other works that have contributed expressions to the English language) enhances their significance and enables us to see in their simple lines intimations of the complex "world of words" that Stevens created to the end of his life. Poems and letters mutually inform one another.

Index